The Origins of
Chinese Literary Hermeneutics

SUNY series in Chinese Philosophy and Culture

Roger T. Ames, editor

The Origins of Chinese Literary Hermeneutics

A Study of the *Shijing* and the Mao School of Confucian Exegesis

MARTIN SVENSSON EKSTRÖM

Publication of this book was partially funded by the Gunvor and
Josef Anér Foundation

Published by State University of New York Press, Albany

© 2024 State University of New York

All rights reserved

Printed in the United States of America

No part of this book may be used or reproduced in any manner whatsoever
without written permission. No part of this book may be stored in a retrieval system
or transmitted in any form or by any means including electronic, electrostatic,
magnetic tape, mechanical, photocopying, recording, or otherwise
without the prior permission in writing of the publisher.

For information, contact State University of New York Press, Albany, NY
www.sunypress.edu

Library of Congress Cataloging-in-Publication Data

Name: Ekström, Martin Svensson, author.
Title: The origins of Chinese literary hermeneutics / Martin Svensson Ekström.
Description: Albany, NY : State University of New York Press, [2024] |
   Series: SUNY series in Chinese philosophy and culture | Includes
   bibliographical references and index.
Identifiers: LCCN 2023009086 | ISBN 9781438495392 (hardcover : alk. paper) |
   ISBN 9781438495408 (ebook) | ISBN 9781438495415 (pbk. : alk. paper)
Subjects: LCSH: Mao, Heng, active 2nd century B.C. Mao shi zhuan jian. |
   Shi jing. | Chinese literature—History and criticism—Theory, etc. |
   LCGFT: Literary criticism.
Classification: LCC PL2466.Z6 M36378 2023 | DDC 895.109—dc23/eng/20230802
LC record available at https://lccn.loc.gov/2023009086

10 9 8 7 6 5 4 3 2 1

For Laura and Alexander
天保定爾

Contents

Abbreviations		ix
Introduction: The Shepherd Dreams—The Great Man Divines		1

Part One
Metaphor's Other: The Discourse on "Imagery" in Modern *Shijing* Scholarship and Sinography

1	The Concept and Conceptuality of Xing	17
2	Intertextuality and Orality in C. H. Wang's *The Bell and the Drum*	23
3	Chen Shih-hsiang and the Primal Scene	37
4	The Totemic Xing	43
5	Rhyme without Reason	45
6	Xing and the Art of Quoting the *Odes*	51
7	Marcel Granet and the Poetics of the Primeval Scene	55
8	Nature Is Metaphorical, Poetry Literal	61
9	Discipline and Comfort: The *comparatisme de la différence*	79
10	Dichotomy Reenforced	85
11	Uncomfortable Sinology: Confucian Exegesis as a Performative Mode of Reading	87

| 12 | Primary Metapoetics, Authorial Intent, and Textual Integrity in the *Odes* | 93 |

Part Two
Xing and the Origins of Chinese Literary Hermeneutics

13	The Metaphor: A Return to Richards	109
14	The *Commentary* versus the *Minor Preface*	119
15	The *Great Preface*, a Rereading	123
16	The *Minor Prefaces*	143
17	In Service to Two Masters	151
18	Mao's "Canonical" Xing	155
19	Analogy and Instrumentality: The "Analogical Xing"	215
20	Xing, Ironically	241
21	Mao's Pragmatic Hermeneutics	267
22	Intertextuality and Repetition	297
23	Crisis—Causality	341
24	Reorientation and Conclusion	361

Appendix A. The Xing: Supporting Evidence — 367
Appendix B. Inconclusive Commentaries — 384
Appendix C. Inconclusive Odes about Confucian Hierarchy — 398
Afterword and Acknowledgments — 403
Notes — 405
Bibliography — 471
Index I — 485
Index II — 489

Abbreviations

BMFEA *The Bulletin of the Museum of Far Eastern Antiquities*
SSJYJS *Shi sanjia yi ji shu* 詩三家義集疏
SSJZS   *Shisanjing zhushu* 十三經注疏

Introduction

The Shepherd Dreams—The Great Man Divines

In early China, was poetic language conceived of as a continuation of nature, a metonymy of the extralinguistic world? Was *shi* 詩 ("poetry") thereby a symmetric opposite of what allegedly characterizes the poetic tradition in the West: re-presentation, abstraction, and figurality? Or should one perhaps suspect that this way of equating "China" with the "anti-West"—a cultural, philosophical, and literary antipode promising a *lux ex oriente* for the reader weary of a Western mimesis thrice removed from reality—is rather a cunning trick from a branch of comparative literature seeking to justify its own discipline?

The object under scrutiny is the *xing* 興, an intricate little concept that first surfaced in the Han dynasty *Mao Commentary* on the *Book of Odes*, acknowledging the existence of what very provisionally may be called "indirect language," and marking the start of a systematic rhetorical analysis in China. As food for thought for the journey on which we are about to embark, consider the fourth stanza of the 190th ode, "No Sheep" ("Wu yang" 無羊).[1] The "imagery" under consideration is not labeled xing by Mao Heng, the eponymous author of the *Commentary*; indeed, it is prevented from being a xing by not appearing in the xing's privileged position, the first two lines of a given poem.[2] Nonetheless, the stanza may serve as an introduction both to the ancient *Odes* and to Mao school exegesis, in that it thematizes cosmology, the Confucian distinction between Superior Man (*junzi* 君子) and commoner, and, not least important, the devious ways of language and the constant need for interpretation.

> The shepherd then dreams:
> many are the fish

there are tortoise-and-snake banners and falcon banners
The great man divines it:
"Many are the fish"
the harvest will indeed be great
"There are tortoise-and-snake banners and falcon banners"
the house and clan will be multitudinous[3]

牧人乃夢
眾維魚矣
旐維旟矣
大人占之
眾維魚矣
實維豐年
旐維旟矣
室家溱溱

The previous stanza speaks of "your shepherd," indicating that the dream is not interpreted for the simple herdsman himself but for a man of high status and power.[4] It is not a coincidence that the preceding ode, "Si Gan" 斯干, describes a similar scenario, in which a lordling (*junzi*) has dreams of bears and serpents that are divined by a "great man." Nor is it by chance that the figure of the "great man" appears several times also in the divinatory, and possibly contemporary, *Book of Changes*.

Dreams appear spontaneously, and outside the control of the person in which they occur. Here, the uncanny independence and serendipity of dreams are underscored by the fact that they occur not in the person they concern but in a simple commoner. The shepherd's unconscious is thus conceived of as a writing pad on whose surface the signs of the cosmological forces are inscribed, not unlike the sky with its constellations, cyclic occurrences, and extraordinary phenomena.

Mao Heng—here the interpreter of an interpreter—comments that "When yin and yang are in harmony, fish are multitudinous. *Zhenzhen* means 'multitudinous'" 陰陽和則魚眾多矣. 溱溱, 眾也.[5] The oneiric fish are thus signs that point both backward and forward. On the one hand, they are a symptom (and thereby the final link in a causal chain) of the harmonious state of the cosmological yin and yang forces. On the other hand, as mantic signs they refer to the plentiful harvest that the future will bring. Mao's comment thus points to a chain of interrelated phenomena; when "harmonious," the yin and yang forces generate a multitude (*zhong*

眾) of fish that, in its turn and according to the laws of the language of dreams, indicates a plentiful harvest in the future.

Several important observations may be made at this point. First, while "fish" is a symptomatic sign of the harmonious balance of yin and yang, this order of causality is broken in the following stage of semiosis, as the multitude of fish is a sign, but obviously not the cause, of a plentiful harvest.[6] The shepherd's dream, and whatever causes it, must make a detour around the message it wants to convey, and instead of dreaming of a great harvest the shepherd therefore dreams of fish. The second stage—"fish" signifying "harvest"—thus escapes cosmological causality and enters into the order and logic of rhetoric, in that it takes one sign (fish) to stand for another (harvest). Why substitute harvest for fish? Mao Heng implies that the transference from fish to harvest is metonymic, and banks on their shared origin, namely the harmony of yin and yang. Fish and harvest, therefore, exist at the same level in the cause-effect hierarchy that underlies this example of oneiric semiosis, and are interchangeable because of their proximity.

If "fish" and "harvest" can be exchanged metonymically on account of their common origin, how about the appearance of banners in the shepherd's dream? The poem itself says that the "great man" interprets the banners as an omen of a clan rich in offspring, and Mao explains the logic of that interpretation: "Tortoise-and-snake banners and falcon banners are what is used to gather a crowd" 旐旟所以聚眾也.[7] We note in passing that Mao uses the character *zhong* 眾 (which translates as "many," "crowd," "plenitude," or "multitude") three times in his comment on this stanza. This is a subtle trick often employed by the *Commentary* to create a sense of continuity. By using the character *zhong* so abundantly, Mao—almost on a subliminal level—makes the idea of plenitude the hermeneutic center of the poem. Mao's ideological exegesis strives, among other things, for textual coherence, and *zhong* is the word that unites "banner," "fish," and "clan" and makes the text consistent. More importantly, the cosmological forces of yin and yang are irrelevant to the generation of meaning here. Yin and yang, and their interaction, are not the origin of those banners, at least not in the same direct way that they are the cause of the many fish and the plentiful harvest, and can therefore not explain why the two phenomena are linked.

Metonymy is nonetheless what allows "banner" to stand for "multitude." Banners, Mao explains, are instruments used to gather people in groups. In the subconscious of the shepherd, instrument or cause (banner) is therefore mistaken for product or effect (the crowd thus gathered). Yet this instrument-for-product metonymy does not derive from the mundane knowledge of what banners are used for. Realizing the detour in the shepherd's dream language, the dream-diviner interprets the (imaginary) crowd gathered together under the (imaginary) banners as referring to the many people of the aristocrat's "house and clan." Compared to the fish-harvest metonymy, the transfer from "banner" to "clan" is more abstract and relies on a common denominator ("multitude") that can only be deduced by the hermeneut who knows the devious ways of the language of dreams—and that "banners" refers to the aristocrat's clan.

In both cases, one image or motif appears as the substitute of another, based on a perceived proximity. I later discuss the theory that early Chinese poetics describes poetic language as straightforward, hypermimetic, even antirhetorical, and that what may seem like tropes (say, metonymies or metaphors) are in fact literal representations of cosmological correspondences in the text-external world. That idea will be put to the test over the next three hundred or so pages.

What the fourth stanza of "Wu yang" demonstrates beyond doubt is the need for and the task of a hermeneut or, at this particular historical stage, a diviner. This is how the shepherd's dream was experienced and processed: an ordinary "reader" of the language of dreams senses that the oneiric imagery of "fish" or "banners" might have another meaning (or, lapsing into semiotic terminology, other *signata*) than its conventional one. A "great man" familiar with the devious ways of language is called upon to supply extratextual information, and "fish" is thereby interpreted as "plentiful harvest," "banner" as "crowd," and, thence, as "many offspring." The diviner, the divinatory hermeneut, is called for because language is not transparent. There is no simple, immediate correspondence between oneiric, linguistic, or pictorial representation and its supposed meaning—or, in more technical terms, between *signans* and *signatum*. We observe lastly that the interpretation banks on, or introduces, a distinction between primary (or "literal" or "original") and secondary meaning; that is, between the shepherd's dreams and the secondary meanings that the "great man" is able to extract therefrom.[8]

In his *Commentary*, Mao Heng is effectively assuming the position, function, and indeed the techniques of a textual diviner. There is thus a direct historical connection between the "great man" described in ode 190 and the early Han dynasty exegete whose commentary we shall read in some detail. In the middle of speaking, dreaming, and writing, there was—even to the Chinese of ancient times—a crisis of the sign and a demand for interpretation and reinterpretation.

Methodology and Scope

In this study of the *Book of Odes* (詩經 *Shijing*), the *Mao Commentary* and the exegetical tradition from which the 305 odes became inseparable in the early Han Dynasty (the second century BCE), I read the *Commentary* in isolation, despite its often terse and ambiguous wording. In spite of the references to the Western tradition of hermeneutics sprinkled here and there, it has been my ambition to allow the early Chinese texts to inform us of how the *Odes* were produced and read without forcing them to speak the language of Western literary theory. This study is therefore one that aspires to be text-centered in the most concrete sense of the term. Although this mode of operation necessarily leaves some of Mao's comments unexplained, it would be futile and plainly illogical to consult later commentators whenever Mao is unclear. Even Zheng Xuan 鄭玄 (d. 200 CE)—often held to be Mao's most faithful follower—deviates considerably from his predecessor.[9] In short, I try to use internal evidence only.

Naturally, those comments of Mao Heng's that are clear pose no problem. Other comments can be explained through a close comparison with the poems they annotate. Here, Mao's paraphrases or puns ("subliminal," as I sometimes call them) reveal how he understood the text in question. A third category of comments can be made clear by way of intertextual comparisons, that is, by comparing Mao's interpretation of one poem with that of another. In the instances when Mao is too obscure to allow any of these options, I have acknowledged my defeat by placing those comments in "Appendix B" below.

The dating and origins of the 305 odes are highly uncertain. From the extensive historical chronicle *Master Zuo's Commentary* (*Zuozhuan* 左傳), it may be surmised that the compilation was still not completed in 621 BCE, whereas striking similarities between certain odes and certain passages in the *Zhouyi* 周易 and certain Zhou Dynasty bronze inscriptions, respectively, point to a *terminus post quem* somewhere in the ninth century BCE.[10]

I underscore the great difficulty we have in ascertaining, for instance, if the word written approximately 詩 in early manuscripts and pronounced *shi* in modern Mandarin referred to a collection of poetry, or to "poetry" or "songs" in general. Indeed, it is also uncertain to what degree the body of odes mentioned in the *Zuozhuan*, and in other pre-Han texts and manuscripts, is identical to the received *Shijing*. On the one hand, the presentation or recitation (*fu* 賦) of "Ye you si jun" 野有死麕 ("The Wilderness Holds a

Dead Doe") described in the *Zuozhuan* narration of the First year of Duke Zhao (541 BCE) suggests that the poem known to the reciter—a certain Zipi 子皮 who died in 529 BCE—corresponded to the three stanzas of the received version.¹¹ On the other hand, the 285th ode in the Mao recension, "Wu" 武, is markedly different from the poem of that title quoted in *Master Zuo's Commentary*, and there attributed to King Wu of Zhou.¹²

Similarly, "Qi ye" 耆夜, a recently discovered manuscript dated to circa 300 BCE, contains a description of King Wu's brother, the much lauded Duke of Zhou, quoting, composing or extemporizing (*zuo* 作) a song (*ge* 歌) called "Xishuai" 蟋蟀 ("The Cricket"), which is only partially similar to the poem of that name in the received *Shijing*.¹³ These two examples seem to suggest that an ode did not necessarily have set lyrics or a fixed number of stanzas but that both content and form could be adapted to fit the particular situation in which the ode was quoted, performed or improvised. Differently put, a certain title (such as "The Cricket") may have been loosely associated with a limited number of motifs and themes, which could have been combined extemporaneously into a poem at ritual gatherings such as that described in "Qi ye"; perhaps this kind of modular, improvised composing of poetry resembled what C. H. Wang describes in *The Bell and the Drum*, as discussed below.

Yet this hypothesis is contradicted by a passage in the *Zuozhuan* in which Zichan 子產, a dignitary from the state of Zheng 鄭, quotes (*fu*) the ode "Gao xiu" 羔裘 ("The Lambskin Furcoat").¹⁴ It is specified that the ode Zichan quotes is "'The Lambskin Furcoat' from Zheng" (*Zheng zhi 'Gaoxiu'* 鄭之羔裘), probably to distinguish that poem from two other poems bearing the same title in the received *Book of Odes*.¹⁵ The hypothesis is also contradicted by the passage in which the ruler of Qi tries to "make the Grand Master [of music] sing the last stanza of 'Artful Words'" (ode 198 in the Mao version) 使大師歌巧言之卒章.¹⁶ When the Grand Master declines to do so, one of his colleagues named Cao instead performs the task, knowing full well that the message imparted by the poem's last stanza is likely to make the two visitors present at the court of Qi attack the ruler, against whom Master Cao bears a grudge. The same version of the "last stanza of 'Artful Words'" must therefore have been known by the two Music Masters and the ruler, and probably also by the two visitors to the Qi court.

These examples, again, would suggest that the *Odes* as a corpus of poems was fairly stable at the time of the *Zuozhuan*, and that a particular title (such as "The Wilderness Holds a Dead Doe," "The Lambskin Furcoat," "Artful Words," or "The Cricket") did refer to a specific poem and was not merely a tag for a poem containing a particular set of motifs and themes.¹⁷ The two are of course not mutually exclusive; the practice of quoting (*fu*) from a corpus of poems already in existence may well have existed alongside the practice of "making" or "extemporizing" (*zuo*) poems from a set of traditional themes and motifs also derived from that corpus. Although my main objective is to explain the logic of Mao Heng's Han dynasty *Commentary*, I make a brief return to the questions of authorship, authorial intent, and the "integrity" of the *Odes* in chapter 12 below.

During the Spring and Autumn (770–476 BCE) and the Warring States (476–221 BCE) periods, the *Odes* were pivotal for the champions of traditional learning and rituality called—somewhat frivolously and anachronistically—*Ru* 儒, "Classicists" or "Confucians."¹⁸ Confucius, as quoted in the *Lunyu* 論語, considers the *Odes* an absolute necessity for the person who wishes to learn not merely how to "speak" or "converse" (*yan* 言) but also how the world functions in general. He says that through the *Odes* one learns the "names of birds, beasts, plants and trees" 鳥獸草木之名 and, conversely, that not knowing the "Zhou Nan" and "Shao Nan" sections of the *Odes* is like "standing facing a wall" 牆面而立.¹⁹ Thinkers as different as Mozi 墨子, Mencius 孟子, and Xunzi 荀子 all use quotations from the *Odes* to amplify and exemplify their arguments, and many manuscripts excavated during the past decades also display this characteristic.²⁰ *Master Zuo's Commentary*, as described above, records multiple instances of high dignitaries reciting or quoting (*fu*) from the *Odes* as a roundabout and courteous way of communication (which, perhaps, is what Confucius's remark about the *Odes* as a "means to discourse" 以言 refers to).²¹

Let us linger a moment at this particular form of quotation because it may very well shine a light on the question of the xing, the exegetical tool at the center of this study. The "Qiu ren" 求人 chapter of *Master Lü's Chronicle* (*Lüshi chunqiu*) 呂氏春秋 describes how "Qian shang" 褰裳 (ode 87) was recited at a diplomatic meeting between representatives from the states of Jin 晉 and Zheng 鄭, one of whom was the above-mentioned Zichan:

"The men of Jin wanted to attack Zheng and so sent the envoy Shuxiang 叔向 to make an official visit and inspect their capacity. [The Zheng minister] Zichan made a recitation of an ode for him:

> If you love and desire me
> I shall hitch up my underskirt and wade the Wei river
> If you do not desire me
> how could there not be other gentlemen?

Shuxiang returned home and reported: 'There are [able] men in Zheng, Zichan is among them. Zheng cannot be attacked. [The states of] Qin and Chu are nearby. His poem had another meaning [or: "his poem had a rebellious intent"]. Zheng cannot be attacked.' The people of Jin thereupon discontinued their attack on Zheng." 晉人欲攻鄭, 令叔嚮聘焉, 視其有人與無人. 子產為之詩曰子惠思我, 褰裳涉洧. 子不我思, 豈無他士. 叔嚮歸曰鄭有人, 子產在焉. 不可攻也. 秦、荊近. 其詩有異心. 不可攻也. 晉人乃輟攻鄭.[22]

The situation in which the poem is quoted may appear slightly comical but is in fact coolly hostile. That Zichan assumes the persona of a young woman who promises to lift her skirt and wade the river clearly suggests that if Jin will not offer its protection Zheng will find other and more caring allies, as indeed becomes obvious to Shuxiang when the poem is decoded and properly reinterpreted, hence his report that "Zheng cannot be attacked for Qin and Chu are nearby." The female role, furthermore, indicates that Zheng is not itself strong but derives strength from the alliances that it may form with other states.

For my present purposes I draw two conclusions. Zichan's quotation of this ode depends on an analogy, and hence a perceived similarity, between the states of Jin and Zheng on the one hand, and the poem's narratrix and her prospective beau on the other. Zichan's act of quoting thus depends on, and produces, a tension between what provisionally may be called a primary and a secondary meaning. This, in turn, introduces a need for hermeneutics, understood as an act of interpretation and contextualization. In this regard, Shuxiang appears as a direct precursor of Mao Heng, and a successor of the "great man" who divined the shepherd's dream in ode 190. If Shuxiang had not contextualized ode 87 but regarded Zichan simply as a lover of erotic poetry, or his quotation a way of showing off his command of the *Odes*, Zichan's message (as distinguished from the poem's primary meaning) would not have been communicated. The potential for language, and the *Odes* in particular, to become decontextualized and invested with secondary meaning was thus not only realized in the Warring States tradition of poetry quotation; it is also what caused Mao Heng to coin the concept of xing.

In the early Han dynasty there were already several recensions, or manuscript traditions, of the *Odes* that incorporated commentaries explaining both the general meaning of the poems and their often arcane language, among which the so-called Lu 魯, Qi 齊 and Han 韓 schools seem to have been the most long-lived and famous.[23] Then, probably in the first half of the second century BCE, Mao Heng 毛亨 composed a systematic annotation on the *Odes* commonly known as the *Maozhuan* 毛傳, the *Mao Tradition*, or (as in the following) the *Mao Commentary*.²⁴ The *Commentary* consists partly of linguistic glosses explaining the obscure vocabulary of the ancient *Odes*, and in this respect probably represents an endeavor to recapture a Zhou dynasty tradition to a large extent arcane in early Han times. The Mao recension gained in influence and the *Commentary* was subsequently recognized as the canonical and authoritative exegetical companion to the *Shijing*, whereas the other three schools fell into oblivion.²⁵

Apart from the *Odes* and the *Commentary*, the *Mao Recension of the Odes* consists of two texts. The first of these is the *Great Preface*, a short but not unambiguous exposition on the origins, nature, and function of *shi* 詩 (of which "poetry" is an approximation).²⁶ The other is the so-called *Minor Preface* (or *Prefaces*), which consists of brief comments on each individual *Shijing* poem. In contrast to Mao's *Commentary*, they do not analyze the poetic and stylistic traits of the *Odes* but inscribe them in a historic and dogmatic context.²⁷ The *Commentary* is thus not as blatantly ideological as the *Minor Prefaces*; yet it is clear from his comments on poems such as "Guanju" (ode 1), "Er zi cheng zhou" 二子乘舟 (ode 44) and "Xiao pan" (*sic*) 小弁 (ode 197) that Mao partook in the allegorizing tradition, at least to some extent. Moreover, the brevity of Mao's comments, and his casual references to two predecessors called Meng Zhongzi 孟仲子 and Master Zhongliang 仲梁子, lead one to speculate that they were written as detailed annotations to a more general commentarial tradition that contextualized the poems.²⁸ Perhaps this hypothetical earlier commentary was the so-called *Older Prefaces*, or the "upper" part of the *Minor Prefaces*; perhaps it was the "Commentary" or "Tradition" (*chuan* 傳) cited in the "Da lüe" 大略 chapter of the *Xunzi* ("Regarding the sensuous lust expressed in the 'Guofeng' section a commentary says 'it is desire filled to the brim but it stops at the right point'" 國風之好色也, 傳曰盈其欲而不愆其止); perhaps it was the exegetical tradition found in the excavated manuscript called *Kongzi Shilun* 孔子詩論 (Confucian discourses on the *Odes*), according to which the first ode "'Guanju' [analogically] explains ritual principles by [describing] sensuous desire" 關雎以色喻於禮.²⁹

Why did the *Mao Commentary* survive and the Three Schools decline? I suggest that by introducing the concept called xing, which marks the start of a formal rhetorical analysis in the Chinese exegetical tradition, Mao had an advantage over his predecessors and colleagues in the project of transforming the *Odes* into Confucian dogma.³⁰ What, then, is Mao's "xing"? The term is complex, and has been defined, redefined, and distorted so many times over the centuries that an answer can only be tentative at this stage: Mao's xing is a marker of nonliteral, figurative meaning; or—much bolder—a way of describing one entity in terms of another; or (from another perspective) a semantic expansion of a given word according to principles that we can provisionally call metaphorical.[31] For example, when the first poem speaks of *jujiu* birds ("ospreys"), Mao calls that statement a xing because it refers to the young couple later described in the text, and it does so by way of an analogy: the young couple is "virtuous" and the osprey a "virtuous" bird. The method of the xing, it seems, is to describe human traits or action in terms of natural objects or events, such as animals, plants, and climatic phenomena.

Reader's Guide

While also serving, indirectly, as an introduction to some of the key themes of the *Shijing* and to Mao Heng's *Commentary*, the book's first part revolves around one question: How have the *Odes* and early Confucian exegesis been described in the twentieth and twenty-first centuries? Western and Chinese scholars have been surprisingly unanimous in their efforts to present Chinese poetry and hermeneutics as radically different from the literary tradition of the West. According to the Sinological consensus, early Chinese poetics described *shi* 詩 ("poetry, song, ode") as unpremeditated and nonmetaphorical. Permutations of this idea are omnipresent in the modern works on ancient China treated here, and their goal, one sometimes suspects, is to make the early Chinese literary tradition the absolute opposite of its Occidental counterpart.

This tendency is perhaps most explicit in the works—doubtless insightful but also intriguingly problematic—of Pauline Yu, François Jullien, and more recently Cecile Chu-chin Sun. The typical Western reader, Yu claims, is on the lookout for a "deeper" or "secondary" meaning of a text, whereas the reader in the Chinese tradition tends to take the text at face value and as the product of a particular context; he or she expects no extended or allegorical meaning transcending the given personal, historical context, or, indeed, the " 'literal meaning' of the songs."[32] The Western literary tradition can thus be described as abstract, metaphorical, and metaphysical in contrast to its Chinese counterpart, which is concrete, literal, and cosmological.

This is also how the concept of xing is typically contextualized. The first part of the book thus begins with a lengthy discussion about C. H. Wang's reconstruction of *Shijing* poetics and then demonstrates how Wang's project developed out of the theories of his mentor, the great Sinologist and comparatist Chen Shih-hsiang 陳世驤 (1912–1971). For both scholars, the xing is a marker of nonmetaphoricity, literalism and rootedness in a particular historical context. Chen holds that xing was originally a "heave-ho" exclaimed by the people of yore united in work—a claim repeated almost verbatim in 2011 by Cecile Sun.[33] Wang, banking on the works on oral poetry by Milman Parry and Albert B. Lord, understands the xing as a way of composing songs by putting together ready-made phrases. I suggest that what these theories describe were never xing in early China and has little to do with the concept coined or advanced by Mao Heng. I then attempt to demonstrate how variants of these notions of literalism and nonmetaphoricity appear in most important modern works on the *Odes*.

The essay that constitutes the first part thus takes as its prime object the tendency among modern scholars to denounce the traditional allegorizing readings of the *Odes*. One has attempted to reach beyond Confucian allegoresis in order to find the "authentic" and "original" meaning of these poems. This tendency occurs with some variation, depending on the interpretational preferences of the respective scholar. One common denominator, however, is a strong suspicion of figurative language. Allegorical and metaphorical literary language, it seems, did not exist until the revolutionizing advent of Confucian exegesis, when Mao Heng et al. introduced the analytical instrument known as "xing" to usurp the literal truth expressed by the *Odes* and distort it into figurative, fictitious language characterized by abstraction.

Toward the end of the essay there occurs a slight change in subject. Whereas the first five studies (chapters 2 to 6) deal with different aspects of the xing, the following four (respectively devoted to the works of Marcel Granet, Pauline Yu, François Jullien, and Cecile Chu-Chin Sun) consider the "reading of imagery in the Chinese poetic tradition" from a comparative perspective. We see the formation of a dichotomy of China and the West, based on what the Sinologist Frederick Mote once called the "cosmological gulf" between the two traditions.[34] Indeed, Chinese literature, philosophy, *and* hermeneutics are described in terms of literalism, concretion, and correlative cosmology, as opposed to their Occidental counterparts, which allegedly are characterized by metaphoricity, abstraction, and metaphysics.

By way of conclusion, I consider the notion of Confucian exegesis as a "performative" mode of reading that "works upon" and refines the textual raw material, in keeping with the Xunzian theory of the lauded Confucian Rituals as a *wei* 偽—which relevantly translates both as "falsification" and "refinement" or "working over"—of primitive human instincts. Ultimately, however, my analysis of the Mao *Commentary* also gainsays the description of Mao's hermeneutics as purely performative since it is obvious that Mao's "xingish" readings, at their best, succeed in explaining the mechanisms of poetic language in the *Odes*. In chapter 12, which the book's first part closes with, I briefly develop the comments made above on the authorship, authorial intent, and integrity of the *Odes* in an attempt to show how these three concepts relate to each other and to the notions of orality and an early Chinese "performance culture."

The theory of metaphor outlined in chapter 13 is sketchy and *ad hoc* rather than systematic. It is offered here as a heuristic device to explain the heterogeneity of Mao Heng's xing, as explained momentarily. In chapters 14 and 16, I briefly explore the relationship between the *Minor Prefaces* and the *Mao Commentary*, and how the *Prefaces* describe the origins, function, and formal characteristics of *shi* ("poetry"). Chapter 15—in effect a bridge between the first and the second part—is probably the most contentious portion of the book: a short, exploratory essay on the *Great Preface*. "[According to the *Great Preface*] poetic expression is involuntary," claims one modern-day exegete.[35] The famous opening lines of the *Preface* undoubtedly speak of a spontaneous, unbridled expression of emotions in speech, sighing, song and dance; yet that statement is contradicted, or at least modified, by the latter part of the text. My reading of the *Preface* through Xunzi and the *Minor Prefaces* rather proposes that poetry is *made* by the superior man in order to convey a carefully deliberated message by means of allegory and metaphoricity. The "commoner," on the other hand, cannot help being moved by the external world. He sings and hollers, wields his arms and stomps his feet, and produces mere "sound" since he is incapable of deliberation. Poetry, to the author of the *Preface*, is the product of intent, whereas "sound" is the outcome of the common man's spontaneous feelings. The notion of spontaneity, moreover, feeds directly into the lore of the literalness of the Chinese poetic tradition. Because if poetry is wholly unmediated—so the tacit argument goes—it cannot be metaphorical since the metaphor is a trope and so presupposes deliberation.

If I were to make a programmatic statement it is this: any hypostatization or reification of xing must be rejected. Instead of assuming that "the xing" is actually and essentially a part of the *Odes*, and that an all-embracing definition thereof may be found if only the scholar tries hard enough, I suggest that the xing is a tool for literary analysis used by many classical authors, among whom Mao Heng was the first. Therefore, a diachronic study of the different versions that have appeared through the ages in order to find the "true" xing would be futile. One ought instead to study the internal organization of the *Mao Commentary* to expose its rules and contradictions. In 116 (or roughly 38 percent) of the 305 *Odes* Mao identify a xing element.[36] I categorize them according to the kind of relationship Mao establishes between the natural descriptions and the descriptions of human activity in the poem under analysis. In other words, the project aims at establishing a typology of early Han dynasty literary semiotics.

The remainder of the second part is thus divided into seven chapters. The first (18–20) focus on the formal aspect of the xing, in the hope of discerning the rules that govern Mao's use of it. I conclude that most xings are based on a perceived similarity between natural phenomena and human action but on an increasingly complex scale, going from what I call simple metaphor (as in the first ode) to analogy and irony. Chapters 21 and 22, on the other hand, argue that the xing is predominantly "pragmatic," and that Mao uses it as a tool to transform the *Odes* into idealized representations of Confucian ritual behavior. This claim is sustained in two ways, first by a short discussion about Confucian (or, more exactly, Xunzian) dogma as it appeared in the second century BCE, and by showing how Mao, by way of the allegory and metaphoricity invested in the xing, can find or insert Confucian topics in the *Odes*. Conversely, I explain how a number of *Shijing*-motifs are metaphorized and allegorized into Confucian dogma. I argue that Mao's xing is pragmatic—rather than law-bound and systematic—by discussing several poems where a certain natural description, whose meaning has already been established by Mao, is repeated in a similar context but with a different interpretation.

Chapter 23 aspires to be pivotal in the scholarship devoted to the xing. If in the preceding chapters I defined Mao's xing as the habit of interpreting natural imagery as metaphorical statements about human situations, then by juxtaposing this alleged norm to deviating instances one must rather conclude that the xing, in its earliest incarnation, obviously lacks the coherence that later scholars have presupposed in their attempts to find an all-comprising definition. While a perceived similarity between nature and the human realm certainly is the most common trait of the xing, there is a subgroup of poems labeled xing where the xing trope is based on a causal link between the descriptions of natural phenomena and man. Perhaps this causal xing, as opposed to the "normal" and normative metaphorical xing, was a residue from the divinatory hermeneutics of the *Zhouyi*; perhaps Mao, living in an age where Confucian "rationality" and textuality were slowly replacing "superstition" and divination, took up the fallen mantle of the oracular interpreters and became a textual diviner—a hermeneut of the literary text.

Part One

Metaphor's Other

The Discourse on "Imagery" in Modern *Shijing* Scholarship and Sinography

1

The Concept and Conceptuality of Xing

The xing has remained a prestigious enigma in Chinese literary history and poetics. Indeed, it could be claimed that through the many ingenious definitions and interpretations the Chinese tradition and Western Sinology have both fondly nursed the notion of the xing as a gateway to a uniquely Chinese form of poetic expression and aesthetics. Part of the reason is obvious in my own words where I speak of *the* xing as though it were a substantial object, a clearly defined entity in a clearly defined context laid bare in front of the objective eyes of the scholar.

This is not the case. What this study calls "xing" is a concept—and as such context-bound and historical—with vastly different functions, sometimes seemingly defining the emotional and psychological role of *shi* 詩 ("poetry") as in Confucius's statement that "poetry can xing [uplift? enthuse? inspire?]" 詩可以興.[1] Sometimes it is conceived as a tool for textual interpretation, as in Mao Heng's *Commentary*; sometimes it refers to the mental associations, unspoken suggestions, or mystical experiences beyond words that poetic language in felicitous instances may produce, as in Zhong Rong's (鍾嶸 469–518) definition of xing as the "unarticulated implications that remain when the text of the poem has formally ended" 文已盡而意有餘, 興也; sometimes xing is a technique used to compose poetry, as in Liu Xie's (劉勰 ca. 465–523) treatment of the triad *fu, bi* and xing in the *Wenxin Diaolong*.[2]

This is by no means a revolutionizing statement, yet the historicity of the concept—its very conceptuality—often seems to be enclosed in brackets by scholars seeking to solve the mystery of the xing once and for all. With some modern scholars it thus defines the communicative function of poetry, as in Donald Holzman's interpretation of xing as the act of quoting the

Odes among the ruling classes of the Warring States period; with others xing denotes a mode of poetic creation, as in C. H. Wang's or Zhao Peilin's reconstructions of the origins of the *Odes*;[3] or, again, the very essence of Chinese lyric poetry, as in Chen Shi-hsiang's interpretation of the character xing: a depiction of four hands (a synecdoche for the two men to whom they are attached) lifting an object while screaming out a "heave-ho" in unison.[4] For Chen, a key figure in *Shijing* scholarship, the xing *bodies forth* poetry. It is the birth of poetry out of the primitive exclamations of prehistoric men unified in the double mission of toiling the earth and conquering Nature. Cecile Sun, greatly in debt to her predecessors, quotes with approval Chen's interpretation and further pinpoints the xing as the most salient feature of the Chinese literary tradition, fundamentally different from mimesis and metaphor, which she sees as the hallmarks of Western poetry and poetics. (Indeed, Sun even holds that mimesis and xing constitute "two modes of viewing reality.")[5]

The tendency to view "the xing" as essential to (and an essence of) primeval Chinese culture is not, as one might be led to think, limited to Anglophone or Francophone studies presenting the *Odes* to a non-Sinologist audience. In his 2004 study, Inoi Makoto's 家井眞 expressly sets out to investigate the "original meaning of the *Shijing*"—and not Mao Heng's Han dynasty interpretations thereof—and while he acknowledges that the religious aspect of the primeval, sacrificial "incantations" (*zhouyu* 咒語) with which he equates "the xing" eventually thinned out, he nonetheless claims that the "shamanistic" (*wushu* 巫術) mindset determines the "meaning and content of [this] poetry."[6] Similarly, Ye Shuxian's 葉舒憲 and Peng Feng's 彭鋒 studies, from 1994 and 2003 respectively, are exceptionally erudite in their contextualizations of the *Odes* and "xing" as integral parts of a pre-Confucian cultural pattern.[7] Yet from the perspective presently assumed—that of a systematic, text-centered investigation of Mao Heng's xing—they appear as methodologically flawed, operating from assumptions that lead the reader into an orbit of ever larger circles away from the texts and tropes under scrutiny.

For instance, Peng Feng acknowledges that Mao's ideological use of the word "xing" differs greatly from earlier times (when "xing," according to Peng and his predecessor Chow Tse-tsung 周策縱, referred to a particular ritual), but assumes that Mao Heng's usage of "xing" in the sense of *piyu* 譬喻 (which may tentatively be translated as "simile") is not only a distortion of the original sense but also leads to an equally skewed understanding of the imagistic organization of the *Odes* themselves.[8]

In the following, I simply argue to the contrary that despite their strong ideological undertones, Mao Heng's xingish readings go a long way toward accurately, or at least persuasively, describing the rhetoric and "imagistic organization" of the *Odes*. Elsewhere, however, I propose that Mao's xing should be understood as part of the discourse on misleading appearances that not only occurs in historiographic and philosophical texts from the fifth century BCE onward but is also integral to the *Odes* themselves.[9] I similarly argue against the sharp East-West dichotomization that Peng and Ye share with many Western Sinologists—Peng speaks for instance of the typically Chinese "poetic intelligence" as distinct from the Western "philosophical intelligence"—and that presupposes an opposition between the Chinese and Western traditions that is not so much false as oversimplifying.[10]

The above is a small but representative sample of how "xing" has been defined in the Chinese and Sinological discourse on the *Odes*. In exegetical works on the *Odes* after Mao Heng, the xing is typically seen as the magic wand that in one stroke can resolve the tangle of natural imagery, voices, and plots that make up the canonical corpus of the *Shijing* and turn it into pure, translucent meaning. As a first conclusion, then, one may say that "xing" constitutes a variety of concepts or exegetical tools performing different tasks in different contexts. It would be possible to make a historical, diachronic study of these usages; however, this is not my intention. Rather, I expand my critique of the prevailing view of the xing—that elusive entity allegedly endowed with the double faculty of structuring the poetic text and providing the key to the *Odes*—and begin by discussing some modern studies of ancient Chinese poetry and hermeneutics in general and of the xing in particular.

Mao's Double Gesture

In the Western tradition of biblical exegesis, the words *hermeneia* and *hermeneutica*—"interpretation, explanation" and "practice or rules for interpretation," respectively—are associated with collections of glossaries and commentaries aimed at parsing and elucidating opaque passages of a text. Hermeneutics is thereby a word that connotes understanding and illumination, the very concepts that we have come to connect with this term. But is not something lost in the process of textual illumination? If we contrast the hermeneutic impulse with the *hermetic* one, we are in a better position to appreciate the complexities of textual understanding. If, as I suppose, the poetic text is often multilayered and polysemic, then a definition of a word or a phrase is precisely a "de-finit-ion," a delimitation that precludes a fuller understanding of the text by narrowing it down to one layer of meaning. In one single stroke, this tracing of textual boundaries opens up the text and closes it again. The present work describes literary exegesis as a double gesture that simultaneously illuminates and renders obscure; the moment of interpretation is therefore both hermeneutic and hermetic. The Mao school of *Shijing* exegesis both exemplifies this double-faced mode of reading and offers a more comprehensive model for the understanding of a poetic text.

The Matter of Comparison

What the majority of scholars to whom the following sections are devoted have in common is that they deem it necessary to investigate the moment of creation of a given poem (or *shi*)—the intertwinement of psychology, rhetoric, and tradition that constituted that moment—to reach a true definition of "xing."

I offer a more detailed discussion of "Sino-methodologies" elsewhere, but any discussion of the xing in a Western language presupposes and necessitates a discussion of comparative method and terminology: could the xing be described in Western terms (e.g., imagery, trope, allegory) and, if so, under which provisions? The matter of comparison is thus innate in Sinology, as indeed it is in any hermeneutic endeavor aimed at a tradition with linguistic and intellectual habits far removed from the observer. The character *shi* 石 may be translated by the English words "stone" or "rock" without any serious loss of information, but if we turn to more complex linguistic, textual, or cultural units we must be more cautious. To take a well-rehearsed example, if we translate *shi* 詩 as "poetry" we should take into consideration the differences that obtain between Greco-Roman and Chinese conceptions of rhymed or metrically bound or ritualized language—what one instinctively would call "poetry"—and compare what the ancient sources say about the origin, function, and formal qualities of *shi* and *poiêsis*, respectively. And like Chow Tse-tsung and Jesper Svenbro, to mention but two eminent scholars, we may explore the etymologies of *shi* 詩 and *poiêsis* ("fabrication, creation, production") for further clues to what those words were used to conceptualize.[11]

The matter of comparison is thus a matter of method. I suggest elsewhere that the inclination to draw a demarcation line between the intellectual traditions of ancient Greece and early China and determine a series of essential themes that allegedly characterize the respective traditions and separate them from each other, has made even the finest of contemporary Sinologists blind to certain important strains of thought in early texts. I furthermore argue that perhaps there is need for a methodological shift away from grand comparative enterprises on a macro level toward lateral, micro-level readings that explore not only the contradictions and discontinuities inherent in the two traditions but also the overlaps between them.

That a reading of China and the West with the pronounced aim of finding essential differences may lead to a partial understanding of the two traditions, and of their internal relations, seems likely. But how about the opposite approach, which also may be deemed a macro-level project but banks on the presupposition that East and West may be compared largely without caveats? To what extent does it lead to blind spots and distortions?

2

Intertextuality and Orality in
C. H. Wang's *The Bell and the Drum*

C. H. Wang's *The Bell and the Drum* remains one of the most influential, stimulating, and seminal books in modern scholarship devoted to the *Odes*.¹ Wang imported to the study of the earliest Chinese poetry a theoretical model developed in and for the analysis of poems from a very different tradition. It is thereby a book that practices comparative literature in the raw, without pretense, on the assumption that literary phenomena from different cultures obey the same laws and may be studied with the same conceptual tools. Wang's book interests me, in other words, not only for its contributions to our understanding of the *Shijing* and the commentarial tradition but also for putting the cardinal rules of comparative literature to the test, hence the somewhat detailed analysis of *The Bell and the Drum* that I now begin.

Toward the end of the book, Wang makes a far-reaching claim that, if correct, would revolutionize our understanding not only of early Chinese poetry but also of the origins of Chinese literary exegesis. Wang claims that what in the course of his argument he has variously called "theme," "type-scene," or "motif" are "identifiable with the *hsing* [xing] element in the Chinese aesthetics of the short lyric,"² and "the key to the ancient Chinese art of *Shih Ching*."³ Let me contextualize these statements.

The concept of xing, as we know, appears in the canonical *Mao Commentary* as a tool for analyzing the meaning and function of natural imagery—descriptions of landscapes or of natural activities and phenomena—in the *Shijing*. The concept of xing is thereby the first critical tool in the Chinese tradition designed exclusively to analyze the *Odes* in their capacity as *shi* 詩, that is, as a discursive genre governed by a particular set of rules, just as Wang intimates in the quote above. But what does Wang mean when he equates xing with "theme" and "motif," and what are the consequences for his analysis of the *Odes*?

What is a "Formula"?

Wang's study rests on a sound, conventional hermeneutical assumption: namely that for a proper understanding of the *Odes* we must return to the time and situation in which they were created. But what were those origins? Based on the theories of oral poetry by, most notably, Milman Parry and Albert B. Lord, Wang puts forward the hypothesis that the *Odes* were derived from a tradition of oral composing, just like the Homeric epics or "The Seafarer."[4] To a large extent the *Odes* were created out of a corpus of formulas that were commonplaces—*loci communes*—of the early Zhou period. These formulas were ready-made phrases that a singer would put together *ad hoc* in different constellations in order to provoke certain reactions (or associations) from his or her audience. Wang's own definition of the formula runs as follows: "A formula is a group of not less than three words forming an articulate semantic unit which repeats, either in a particular poem or several, under similar metrical conditions, to express a given essential idea."[5]

The goal is thus to describe the ancient bards, their technique, and the process of creation that, allegedly, resulted in the *Odes*. However, to comprehend how this affects the understanding and interpretation of the *Odes* (as opposed to the way in which they were created), we must grasp the two implicit presumptions on which the argument rests. First, the individual formula has the same meaning regardless of context. Not only is this valid for the "literal" meaning of the formula but also for its rhetorical one; if, for example, a formula is ironical in one context it will be ironical in another. Second, the logic according to which the formulas were organized was not primarily semantic but musical or metrical, since the bard was more concerned about the lyrics fitting the music (or the rhyme scheme) than the internal semantic coherence of the formulas thus put together.[6] Consequently, we cannot expect full congruence at the semantic level. The imagery is bound to be incohesive, unrealistic, or in the author's own words, "excessive, wild."[7]

In other words, when the reader happens upon a passage that is not immediately understandable, it is either because the word or phrase in question is a fragment derived from another context—find that other context and you will grasp what initially was incomprehensible. Or because the passage in question is not really understandable or relevant at all since the author, or singer, threw in whatever formula or fragment that was at hand to make the words fit the music or provoke a desired association from the audience. As a reader of the *Odes*, Wang is thus more interested in the tracing the intertexts than in exploring the internal dynamics—the interaction of the formulas—in the given poem.

This is exemplified by Wang's analysis of a "formula" occurring once in "Da dong" 大東 (ode 203) and once in "Ge ju" 葛屨 (ode 107), and which Wang translates as "Fibre shoes tightly woven / Are good for walking upon the frost" 糾糾葛屨, 可以履霜.[8] On both occasions the formula is ironical, Wang alleges, since "the shoes of fibre are coarse and thin and not 'good for walking upon the frost'."[9] Therefore, this formula is the poet's way of suggesting—by way of irony—the hardships of a man traveling on a wintry road.

In poem 107 the formula occurs as a part of the first stanza that reads (in my slightly modified translation):

> Tightly woven fibre shoes
> could be used to walk on frost.
> Delicate, the woman's hands
> with them she could sew a shirt.
> [she] makes a waist and a collar for it,
> the good man wears it.[10]

> 糾糾葛屨
> 可以履霜
> 摻摻女手
> 可以縫裳
> 要之襋之
> 好人服之

A quick glance at the Confucian tradition, which obviously but paradoxically has colored Wang's interpretation, would seem to corroborate the ironic reading. As demonstrated by the meticulous Chen Huan 陳奐 (1786–1863), the Confucian scholars of the Han seem to have read "Ge ju" in light of a passage from the "Shi guan li" 士冠禮 chapter of the *Yili* 儀禮, whose prescription for the proper shoes to wear in summer and winter, respectively, is echoed by Mao's *Commentary*.[11] Mao says that "in summer one wears fibre shoes and in winter leather shoes. Fibre shoes are not used to walk on frost" 夏葛屨, 冬皮屨. 葛屨非所以履霜.[12] In Mao's view, wearing fiber shoes in winter violates ritual decorum and is, furthermore, a symptom of a perverse government (which is also suggested by the *Minor Preface*). Zheng Xuan annotates thus: "Fibre shoes are cheap, those of leather expensive. According to the customs of Wei, even in winter 'fibre shoes could be worn on frost.' This is turning poverty into an advantage [i.e., the people of Wei are frugal]" 葛屨賤, 皮屨貴. 魏俗至冬猶謂葛屨可以履霜. 利其賤也.[13]

But does the information (however canonical) that fiber shoes were worn in summer and those of leather in winter justify Wang's claim that the rhetorical mode of these four lines be called ironic? If we stick to the conventional definition of irony as "saying one thing but meaning another" that claim is improbable. It is equally likely—or more so—that the lines about wearing fiber shoes on frost represent bad times and an evil government (the commoners have to wear fiber shoes in winter), or prudence (the commoners are frugal enough to make do with these simple shoes rather than demand those made of leather), or craftsmanship (the tightly woven shoes are so skillfully made that one may walk upon the frost, despite their being made of fiber).

We may certainly hypothesize that the formula originated as an ironic description of the hardships of traveling and that this description was "formualized" and made part of the *loci communes* of the ancient bards. But even if this were the case, the ironical meaning of the formula would still be no more than a faint trace hardly recognizable in this new context (the topic of which is not arduous journeys). The assertion that in both poems that contain this formula, the poet aims at "suggesting the hardships of a wayfarer in times between autumn and winter" is, I claim, contradicted by the parallelism that structures the first stanza.[14] The reduplicated phrase *jiujiu* 糾糾 ("tightly") corresponds formally with the phrase *shanshan* 摻摻 ("delicate"), and *ke yi* 可以 is likewise repeated symmetrically. If the description of the woman's delicate hands is made the hermeneutic center of this poem, another interpretation becomes possible in which the lines about the shoes are part of a description of a skillful female weaver who produces shoes woven so tightly that they can be used to walk on the frost even though they are made of fiber. The formula has thus been organically integrated in the text.

Difficulties abound as one tries to understand the *Odes*. We know too little of the denotations and connotations of the *Shijing* vocabulary. Our comprehension of the language used in these poems is in many cases limited to conjectures, especially knowing the early exegetes' urge to transform the *Odes* into Confucian dogma. Our relation to these annotators is therefore somewhat strained as we can neither fully trust them nor escape their influence, and this tension is also obvious in Wang's book. *The Bell and the Drum* is, ultimately, an offshoot of the great modernist project from the early days of the People's Republic—instigated by the group of scholars and intellectuals who branded themselves the Doubters of Antiquity (*yigu xuepai*) 疑古學派—to make a clear break with the allegorizing modes of reading that emerged in the early Han dynasty and transformed (what Wang sees as) fragmented and paradoxical song texts marked by a "lack of realism" into poems characterized by narrative logic and metaphorical sophistication.

Let us have a final look at the "formula" and Wang's translation of it:

Fibre shoes tightly woven
Are good for walking upon the frost

糾糾葛屨
可以履霜

The poem does not say that the shoes are "good for" walking upon the frost, only that they "may be used to" (*ke yi* 可以) do so, which significantly weakens the argument for an ironical reading. The same argument can be put forward with regard to poem 203.

My reading of "Ge ju" thus stands in obvious opposition to the idea that a "formula" or "motif" can only be understood as an isolated fragment tied inextricably to the moment and situation in which it was uttered, and whose meaning is repeatable and transferable from one text to another without any semantic alteration. Instead, "Ge ju" suggests that a fragment conforms to the context in which it is put.

A few additional remarks should be made regarding Wang's relation to the so-called allegorical tradition. Wang claims that to the great Confucian scholar and exegete Zheng Xuan, the *Odes* were "esoteric and cryptic, with great messages underneath the surface," and that "the literal meaning does not count for an allegorist." "To restore the *Shih Ching* poem to the pre-Cheng [Zheng Xuan] tradition . . . will increase our chance of grasping the real aesthetics of the poem."[15]

When the Confucian allegorists—and not least Confucius himself—used the *Odes* for "the purpose of moral cultivation," they distorted their original meaning. Wang's goal, therefore, is to understand the *Odes* "as they must have originally been apprehended."[16] The focus on "literal" meaning as opposed to allegorical meaning may seem sympathetic enough at first glance, but consider how Wang moves from one extreme to another: if the *Odes* are not allegories it seems they must be everything that allegory is not, namely literal, haphazard, and sometimes "wildly" metaphorical. Second, although Wang speaks in favor of "literal meaning" he paradoxically employs a mode of reading that violates the integrity of the individual ode. Retaining Wang's main hypothesis but turned on its head, I suggest that the shift of focus from the musical to the semantic (or oratorical) aspect instigated an interest in the content and thematics of the *Odes* and that the allegorical tradition so brilliantly represented by Zheng Xuan introduced a sophisticated hermeneutics of *Shijing* "imagery" in some, if not all, of its complexity.

What Is a "Theme"?

Although equated with the xing, it is not entirely clear what defines a theme in Wang's model. At first, Wang agrees with Lord's definition formulated (by Wang) as "that group of ideas which, in the process of oral-formulaic composition, serves as *a guideline to the plot*, the larger structure, of the tale."[17] The theme, consequently, is opposed to the plot, which is conceived of as the actual and primary event dealt with by the poem. This would indeed be an accurate description of what Mao Heng calls xing, which typically interprets natural images in analogy with the primary event (or the "plot") described by the poem. But already on the following page, "plot" is paradoxically defined as an "articulate sequence" of themes.[18] Such a definition no longer maintains the distinction between tenor and vehicle so crucial in Mao's xingish readings.[19] Since Wang, as we know, will later equate the "theme" and the "xing," this statement merits a closer look.

To Wang, a *Shijing* poem is typically "structured in imagistic analogy with some stock themes."[20] A certain "image," in other words, is related to a certain plot and serves as an invocation to it. However, although Wang regards the poet as the poem's Creator whose intentions should guide our understanding of the poem, the act of creation itself is, paradoxically enough, beyond the poet's full control. Not only has he to resort to a rather limited reservoir of formulas but also, on the semantic level, to a fixed interaction between theme and plot. A prime example is "Gu feng 谷風" (ode 35):

> Gently blows the valley wind:
> Bring darkness, bring rain.

Try, let us try to be of one mind,
And have no anger in between.[21]

習習谷風
以陰以雨
黽勉同心
不宜有怒

Here, what Wang calls "the general kinetics of a distressed wife's complaint" demands "a definite motif [or theme], the valley" that corresponds to the plot, namely the wife's complaint.[22] We may thus reconstruct the situation of the poet/singer, and the origin of the thirty-fifth ode, in the following manner. The poet decides to sing about a maltreated and complaining woman. Due to the literary conventions of his time, he "must" start the poem with the two lines describing a valley, and because of the conventionalized association between the valley-motif and the plot, these lines make the listener immediately realize that the poem will describe a "complaining wife." Conversely, the fixed interplay between certain motifs and plots facilitates the process of composing songs for the singer.

However, the origin and nature of the interaction of "valley" and "wife's complaint" is a question largely bypassed by Wang. In general, the oral-formulaic poem is described as semantically haphazard and characterized by "wild" and "excessive" metaphoricity.[23] If the meaning and function of the ironical fiber-shoes motif in the example above was explained with recourse to the "real" and extratextual hardships a person experiences when traveling on a wintry road in thin shoes, then "the valley motif [or theme] *probably arose* from an *early* metaphorization of the wife."[24] Wang sums up the traditional explanation of the "valley-wind motif" as "when *yin* and *yang* are in harmony, the wind is generated in the valley."[25] Zheng Xuan, otherwise portrayed as an allegorizer and obfuscator of the worst kind, is quoted as saying that in a similar fashion matrimonial harmony depends on the union of husband and wife. The conclusion (which Wang does not draw) must be that the occurrence of the valley motif in this context is a consequence of a perfectly logical correspondence between the "theme" and the "plot," since Zheng's interpretation of the motif of the harmonious valley wind is predetermined by the subsequent description of a harmonious couple. By approving of this intricate (albeit traditional) explanation, Wang implicitly argues against his own description of the "wild and excessive" imagery of oral poetry. (Within parentheses it may be noted that the thematic emphasis in poems 35 and 201 does not really lie on "valley" but on "wind.")

The "probable" process of metaphorization is, moreover, described as "early," which is an attempt to maintain what Wang considers to be the dominant feature of oral poetry: its lack of order. This oral-formulaic poem, to Wang's mind, was pieced together by a poet not fully aware of what he was doing or why he was doing it. In other words, the metaphor was created so long ago that the poet does not know why he associates "valley" with "wife." Hence, the poet can be described as both "careless" and as the person whose intentions should be normative for a proper understanding of the text.[26] Against the background of Wang's self-proclaimed goal to find the "original" meaning of the *Odes*, it is noteworthy that he approves of Zheng's traditional explanation ("esoteric" and "cryptic" as it is called in the introduction to the book) of the motif's metaphorical origin. However, this "original" origin is immediately denounced in favor of a "later" origin, sprung out of the milieu of the careless bards where music—and not semantics—was the organizing principle. The paradox of the two origins of the valley/wife trope is a giveaway for the kernel in Wang's argument, namely the idealized Moment of Creation, in which the true meaning and the "true aesthetics" of the *Shijing* were created and manifested. The poet carried away by the music, the formulas, the interdependence and tension between the singer and his audience are all prerequisites for Wang's speculations about a mythological origin of the *Odes*. This idealized moment—and the struggle to reach it by scrubbing away the filth of the "allegorists"—is implicit throughout Wang's book.

A thematic element such as "valley" is, furthermore, not necessarily linked to the subject of wifely complaint but rather functions as part of the binary structure so typical of the *Odes* (which is precisely what Wang's interpretation of the valley theme quoted above suggests). For example, "Fa mu" 伐木 (ode 165) does not describe a complaining wife in spite of carrying the valley motif:

> Chopping wood *treng, treng*[27]
> the bird's crying *eng, eng*
> it leaves the dark valley;
> moves up a high tree
> *Eng* goes its cry
> seeking a friend's voice
> Look at that bird
> if it seeks a friend's voice

Then how could this man
refrain from seeking a friend?
If the spirits listen to them
peace and harmony will follow.²⁸

伐木丁丁
鳥鳴嚶嚶
出自幽谷
遷于喬木
嚶其鳴矣
求其友聲
相彼鳥矣
猶求友聲
矧伊人矣
不求友生
神之聽之
終和且平

In this poem, of which I here only present a reading that differs from a "formulaic" one, the function of the phrase "deep valley" is not to elicit a fixed response from the audience in the form of an association with a "complaining wife." (To be on the safe side, one should perhaps say not its *primary* function.) Instead, "deep valley" corresponds to the phrase "high tree," and its meaning is generated "intratextually" out of this dualistic relationship. It should be made clear that poem 165 is not treated by C. H. Wang as an example of a highly formulaic poem; yet the tendency to downplay the significance of the formulaic poem due to its alleged origin in semantic and logical disorder would no doubt end in a similar negligence of the binary structure.²⁹

"Fa mu" provides a textbook case of the rhetorical construction that dominates the *Odes*. Threatened by the axes and forced to leave the deep valley for the high tree, the bird corresponds to the man (or woman) portrayed; it is man's nature to engage in social intercourse, and humankind should therefore exert itself to make it perfect (as is described in the following stanzas). Consequently, we find two sets of binary oppositions at work in the poem. The first, which is rhetorically subordinated to the second, puts in opposition the low-lying, secluded valley where the bird hides and the high tree to which it must flee. Again, the words "deep valley" do not function as a link of association to a certain "plot" but are rather a counterpart to the description of the tree. Second, and more importantly, there is the all-pervading complementary opposition of nature and man. Unlike most other poems of this character, in "Fa mu" the analogy between the two realms is explicit. If a bird must seek a friend or mate, the poet asks, then how could a human being not feel the same necessity?

Wang argues that a theme, both in lyrical and in epic poetry, serves to "unify the singer and his audience by evocative memory of common '*argumentorum sedes*' ['storehouses of trains of thought']."[30] We are, of course, familiar with this argument since it is similar to Wang's description of how the so-called formula functions. But does a fragment also have this function when it appears in a short lyrical poem, where the interaction between the different fragments is inevitably more intense than in a long, narrative epic poem, and where the imagery suggests an analogy between nature and man? Furthermore, is it possible that an image—to keep to this vague and problematic term—is limited to a singular function in any given text? Does the "early metaphorization," in which "valley" was in some way considered analogous to "female" or "wife," morph imperceptibly into the second stage, when among the ancient bards it becomes a *locus communis*, and when neither audience nor singer knows why they associate one with the other? At this stage "valley" functions as a sign that arouses a certain response from the audience ("this song is about a deserted woman"), according to Wang. But is this stage final? Will the fragment, the formula, the theme or the motif forever stay semantically and rhetorically intact? Would it not be more accurate to say that at this point the nostalgic longing for a stable and constant origin must yield to a hermeneutics of the literary text itself? For Wang, however, the authentic *Odes* are forever tied to the moment of *ad hoc* composing by the bards. The idealization of this moment forces Wang to disclaim not only the earlier stage of "metaphorization" but also the change of meaning that must have been the result of later emendations.

Mine is a primitive, speculative, and perhaps laughable delineation of the semantic transformations of a concept or an "image," but it brings to the fore a methodological problem. To give a plausible account for the genesis of a literary text or tradition is one thing; to make that account a model for the *total* understanding of this text or tradition is quite another. If we leave the text and its internal structure we are no longer dealing with literature but with the history of literature.

C. H. Wang's Answer to the Question, What Is Mao Heng's Xing?

As this chapter is drawing to a close, I feel compelled to reiterate my claim that there is in *Shijing* scholarship an inclination to provide a final, all-encompassing definition of "xing." "Until recently," Wang writes, the "*hsing* was treated as arcane or mysterious," thereby implying that his identification of xing with the oral-formulaic theme or motif, has finally ended this mystery. I have already indicated that Wang's terminology ("theme," "formula," "myth," "plot") is at times imprecise, and at the beginning of the book he claims that "opening formulas" such as that of "Gu feng" ("gently blowing is the valley wind") are identical to what Mao calls a "xing," and that a "theme" or a "motif" is an idea used by the poet as he develops the plot.[31] But how is the theme—or motif or "opening formula"—and the plot related? In my tentative definition, xing is Mao's name for a passage (typically two lines, or eight characters) of natural descriptions—flying birds, flourishing bushes, trees with branches placed high, etc.—interpreted as statements about human beings or certain phenomena pertaining to the human realm. We may then further specify this tentative definition: the xing is the vehicle in a trope in which the tenor is man and his actions.

But is Mao's xing, thus defined, identical with the "motif," as Wang sees it? Ode 188, "Wo xing qi ye" 我行其野, contains the "plant-plucking motif":

> I walk into the fields;
> I pluck the pokeweed.
> It was as bride and wife,
> That I came to live with you;
> Now as you will not keep me,
> I walk, back to where I came from.[32]

> 我行其野
> 言采其蓫
> 昏姻之故
> 言就爾宿
> 爾不我畜
> 言歸斯復

Plant-picking is indeed a frequent "motif" in the *Odes*, but is it a xing as Mao understood the term? According to Wang, the plant-picking motif is used by the poet to allow the listener, in a cognitive process better described as metonymic or synecdochic than metaphoric, make an association with "women in distress," and—as was the case with the valley motif above—this association had been established long before this poem was actually composed. Yet Mao's xing, as I argue in the second part, does not usually work by means of association but banks on a perceived similitude between vehicle and tenor; it is therefore metaphorical or analogical and for that reason more "abstract." Furthermore, "Wo xing qi ye" is not labeled "xing" by Mao, apparently because he read the "motif"—the act of picking plants—as pertaining to the human realm, the description of which cannot readily be used as a xingish vehicle.[33] Any blurring of the distinction between tenor and vehicle, and between human action and natural scenery, must be considered a failed description of Mao's xing.[34]

Second, when Wang states that in "the traditional art of composition by themes, the singer's selection of specific images or motifs is sometimes crucial to the poetic meaning he intends, and sometimes hardly at all," he clearly speaks of his perception of the creation of *shi*, whereas for Mao the xing is foremost an exegete's device to make the *Odes* conform to Confucian dogma; therefore, there can be no superfluous meaning.[35] Indeed, the aim of Mao's literary-ideological hermeneutics is to make *every* part of the poem meaningful for a didactic purpose. Whenever Mao defines a natural description (or "motif") as a xing he endows it with significance; it is therefore *always* crucial to "the poetic meaning he intends."

Sino-methodology and Comparative Literature

In a sense I am willfully misreading *The Bell and the Drum*. What C. H. Wang—himself a major poet—offers is a hypothesis of how the *Odes* were composed, not of how they were interpreted in the early Han dynasty by an unduly dogmatic Confucian named Mao Heng. Wang's categorical claim that the formula, motif, or theme is "identifiable with the *hsing* [xing] element in the Chinese aesthetics of the lyric," and "the key to the ancient Chinese art of *Shih Ching*" is, from the perspective assumed here, nonetheless slightly peculiar since no attempt is made to contextualize, or trace the provenance of, the *concept* of xing. As a description of Mao Heng's xing it is simply erroneous. Although the xingish organization of certain *Odes*—the correlation of accounts of human action with sceneries drawn from the natural world—may have had its origins in the employment of "themes" or "motifs" in Wang's sense, even the quickest glance at Mao's commentary will refute the idea of a fixed response between the "xing-element" and the human act with which it appears in the given poem.³⁶

The intertextual model of interpretation that Wang advances for the *Shijing* as supposedly oral lyrics is interesting as a hypothesis—indeed one that, given the undoubtedly formulaic character of some odes, had to be put to the test—but it not only yields interpretations whose validity is hard to substantiate; in the larger context it also typifies the Sinological tendency to associate early Chinese poetry (or *shi*) with a concrete *scene* of creation to which the poem must always be returned, with spontaneity (as opposed to a calculated rhetoric), and with nonmetaphoricity. Somewhat ironically, despite the absurdity of many allegorical interpretations of the *Odes*, it is Mao Heng's and Zheng Xuan's xingish readings that provide the more convincing analyses of the *Odes* in their capacity as poetic texts.

Thus, the macro-level assumption that early Chinese lyric poetry developed under more or less the same circumstances as Greek lyric poetry leads C. H. Wang to describe the *Odes* not as *poiêsis* but as products of an intense, intimate, and spontaneous interaction between an inspired bard and his audience, just as Parry, Lord, and (among others) Jesper Svenbro have described the origins of Greek and Balkan epic poetry. The *Shijing* is indeed "demonstrably formulaic," as Wang puts it. But what does that mean in the early Chinese context? Lois Fusek, in her review of *The Bell and the Drum*, hypothesizes that the *Shijing* is a "composite of both oral and written features," and that the real task lies in describing how the oral and the written interact.³⁷ One may add that neither "the written" nor "the oral" is a single, homogeneous practice but that there are different kinds of orality and writing. And we may tentatively exemplify Fusek's thesis by pointing in the direction of the Zhou dynasty bronze inscriptions, which sometimes bear a strong resemblance not only to the *Odes* and the *Book of Documents* but also to the *Zhouyi* 周易. These inscriptions are highly formulaic but also eminently "written," or inscribed, and thus seem to indicate a particular early Chinese amalgam of the oral and the written.³⁸ They are a peculiar crossbreed and a point of resistance against attempts at an all-comprising, cross-cultural theory of the poetical, scriptural, and ritual.³⁹ A resistance that is challenging but also liberating.

3

Chen Shih-hsiang and the Primal Scene

In a classic essay called "The *Shih Ching:* Its Generic Significance in Chinese Literary History and Poetics," C. H. Wang's mentor Chen Shih-hsiang proposes an interpretational model of the *Odes* that was not only to be echoed in the magnum opus of his disciple but also invoked by Cecile Chu-Chin Sun in *The Poetics of Repetition in English and Chinese Lyric Poetry* (2011).[1] The importance of Chen's short study for contemporary Sinology and its theories of early poetry and poetics is thereby manifest. As with C. H. Wang, xing is regarded as the "crucial key concept" for a true understanding of the *Odes* and Zheng Xuan as an usurper of their original meaning.[2] Chen's vision of the pristine moment and scene of poetic creation surpasses Wang's in sublimity, however, as he speaks of poetry emerging at the dawn of civilization when the world was "fresh" and "innocent," and when "to speak was to be a poet, to name objects an inspiration."[3]

We find traces of this antediluvian poesy in the graphs xing 興 and *shi* 詩 ("poetry"). According to Chen, the character *shi* consists of the main element "foot" 足, which originally referred to the tapping of a foot against the ground, and the "radical" 言 *yan*, "speech."[4] In the early days of an "innocent" world, Chen states, poetry, music, and dance were fused together, as suggested by the notion of a foot "beating rhythm" on the ground.[5] When the songs were written down and read instead of listened to, the original character was augmented by the element denoting "speech," marking the transition from an oral culture (in thrall to rhythm and dance while relatively indifferent to semantics) to a textual one.[6] The character "xing" originated in a similar context. The character xing 興 is a pictogram of four hands holding an object—perhaps a tray—combined with a "mouth"

□ in the middle.⁷ The original meaning of this character is therefore to be understood as the unified exclamation, a *heave-ho* as it were, emerging from a group of people unified in labor. This "heave-ho" was "ejected in joy and high spirits with a feeling of emotional and physical *uplift* [Chen's translation of "xing"; my italics] by a group turning around a central object, which joined their hand together in a dancing circle . . . herein lies the primeval organization of the *Songs* [i.e., the *Odes*] as *shih,* which was to be the name of all later Chinese poetry."⁸

Chen's presentation of the emergence of an individual poetic expression, of the poet's voice rising over the murmur of the mass, is similarly sublime. If the *heave-ho* emerged as a "collective impulse," during this "inarticulate cry" a poetic genius "grasped the meaning of the occasion" and was "inspired by immediate objects or contingent events symbolic of the feeling of the whole occasion, and became articulate with more words."⁹ The poet would then "trace the theme" and utter "inspired rhythmic and expressive phrases which would form 'motifs' to 'start' the song. . . . Such was the *hsing* in the ancient Chinese case."¹⁰

From the two graphs xing and *shi* have thus been salvaged and reconstructed an entire poetics of prehistoric China from which we learn that xing was originally a mode of creation born in and out of a specific occasion whose true meaning was understood by an individual poet and reflected by his usage of corresponding imagery. To say that the poem was "born" out of a certain occasion is indeed accurate because the process of poetic creation is described in terms analogous to childbearing—the poet who breaks away from the group is inspired and becomes articulate with words and utters phrases that reflect the situation and the objects around him. To make the metaphor more accurate, one should perhaps not speak of the immaculate conception of poetry but rather of a poetic impulse that ravishes the poet, planting the seed of poetry in an act of force from which he or she cannot escape. The poet is unable to control or color the product for which he or she is a mere medium.

Chen's description of poetic creation—a description that necessarily denies primeval poetry any deliberate rhetorical features—is, as I suggested above, typical of the modern Sinological view of ancient Chinese poetry (*shi*) and poetics. As will be demonstrated in chapter 15, the view of the poet as a passive medium has dominated nearly all contemporary interpretations of the most central text on poetics from the Han dynasty: the *Great Preface*. According to mainstream Sinology, classical Chinese poetics never considered *shi* an artifact deliberately produced by a skillful poet but rather the unmediated result of sensory stimulation, which feeds into the claims about the *Odes* (at least the xingish ones) as haphazardly thrown together, "wild" and "excessive." My own, somewhat polemical reading of the *Preface* notwithstanding, this is not the fundamental theoretical assumption behind Mao Heng's *Commentary*; the very introduction of xing as an instrument for the analysis of the rhetorical modality of a poem instead suggests that its meaning is not immediate or objectively given but has to be interpreted. This is certainly a central question for all hermeneutic enterprises (literary commentary, anthropology, linguistics, psychoanalysis, etc.): was the meaning of a gesture, a facial expression, a poetic "formula," a ritual, a psychosomatic symptom ever translucent, stable, or self-identical, even at its (imagined) origin?

Second, and of equal importance, Chen's concept of xing bifurcates into "motif" and "theme" (the distinction of which, however, is clearer than Wang's). Quite correctly, in my view, Chen separates the descriptions of inanimate objects and of animal life—the motifs—from the descriptions of human activity that constitute the "themes." Speaking of the motif of "crying cicadas" in ode 168, Chen suggests that one of the functions of the "image" of the cicadas is to represent men engaged in warfare endlessly marching; he thus touches upon the metaphorical relationship between motif and theme and, thereby, also upon the kernel of what I will later call Mao's "canonical" xing.[11]

The similarities, however, are only apparent. First, Chen's model—like Wang's—presupposes two origins, the first stemming from the "fresh world," where the simple act of speaking was also an act of poetic creation, and where xing as a mode of creation also included song and dance. The second origin can be traced to a time when the motifs and themes were still extant but had freed themselves from their paradisiacal origins and become stereotypes used by the bards in their songs. For instance, what Chen calls the "prominence of women's position" in the *Odes* is not due to women actually being privileged during the Zhou but a residue from an earlier epoch when women played a leading part in rituals and amorous dances.[12] We must therefore pass with blinkers backward through the Zhou period to gain a better appreciation of the *Odes*, and here the contradiction in Chen's reasoning becomes obvious. On the one hand, the motifs and themes are alienated from the primeval situation in which they once originated as spontaneous reflections of the external world; on the other, these motifs must be traced back to the original *scene*—the expression is Chen's—where song, music, and dance were fused together. Instead of presuming, reasonably, that the motifs and themes underwent several semantic and rhetorical transmutations, forming a new poetic practice during the Zhou, Chen holds that we must return to the scene to grasp the "real" meaning of the word and practice "xing." The xingish ode, as Chen understands it, is therefore unable to deviate from the semantic realm of its creator, and from this tenet emerges a fundamental paradox: the author is the organizing principle of the text, yet incapable of anything but mere reflection.

Second, I would argue that Chen Shih-hsiang hypostatizes "xing" by assuming that the variant of the character found on ancient bronze artifacts (from which his hypothesis of the origin of Chinese poetry derives) is in fact identical in meaning and function to the analytical tool used by Mao in his Han dynasty *Commentary*. Chen indeed claims that the "distinct identity" of the xing survives in the *Commentary* and generates "subtle poetics and literary theories."[13] Mao, therefore, does use the "original meaning" of the "xing" but fails, in Chen's eyes, whenever his comments deviate from Chen's own definition of the concept.[14] I will return to this evidently circular argument in a moment and instead briefly indicate how Chen's theorizing, unsurprisingly, also involves an aversion to the metaphorical.

The xing-elements, according to Chen, "carry with them . . . the ancient integrity, the oneness or the unity of the musical speech and the rhythm of the spontaneous and simultaneous primeval 'uplifting dance'. Their appeal is therefore instantaneous, even kinesthetic as well as imagistic."[15]

They furthermore generate "a host of alliterations as well as rhymes or pararhymes."[16] That Chen's xing is "kinesthetic" means that it is noncerebral and affects the body and senses directly, without any detour through the intellect, a claim that in turn banks on the presumption that the *Odes* are foremost musical and characterized by "instantaneous" imagery (the latter by default nonmetaphorical, since metaphor is deliberated and presupposes at least a modicum of intellectual activity); music and imagery also determine the "mood and atmosphere" of the *Shijing*. While "poetic language" in a general sense may be said to be musical and suggestive, it is hard to see why—if not for being in thrall to a comparative literature that thrives on opposing a metaphysical Occident to the immediacy and concretion of the Orient—Chen attempts to trace a notion of xing that is consistent throughout history and why he sets up a dichotomy between a true and a false version of the xing and puts the Mao tradition in the latter category. The reasoning is manifestly circular.

The methodological fallacy is conspicuous in Chen's analysis of the xing-element in "Guanju" 關雎 ("The Krooing Osprey"), the first piece in the *Shijing* corpus and one of the most annotated poems in the history of literature; it is an ode to which I will return intermittently. Here, Chen speaks with great vigor and insight about the "mood," "atmosphere," "spiritual or emotional 'sensation'" that the opening lines (the so-called xing) provoke in the listener or reader:

> *Guan guan* the *jujiu* bird calls
> On the islet of the river
> The beautiful and good young lady
> Is a fine mate for the lord [*junzi*][17]

According to Chen (and the whole tradition of Confucian exegesis) it is the first two lines about the screaming *jujiu* bird (or birds) that constitute the xing-element in "Guanju": what they arouse in the listener is a "meaning beyond words," a "feeling" that is "genuinely felt."[18] From the point of view assumed here, and because he claims that the "distinct identity" of the "original xing" survives in the *Commentary*, it is remarkable that Chen never consults Mao's interpretation of this poem, clear and explicit as it is, and in which the birds represent the loving couple who are the poem's protagonists.[19] Despite the occasional overlap, what Chen calls xing is strikingly different from Mao's version. Chen's xing organizes the poem by providing the atmosphere, rhythm, and timbre that color the poem through "incremental" repetitions; it structures the "whole sound, sense and imagistic relationship."[20] With Mao Heng, the xing plays a similarly crucial role but is used to take instant command of the text so as to make it fit Mao's ideological program. More importantly, Mao's xing (that is, the descriptions of natural sceneries or inanimate objects that typically open the *Shijing* poem) never dominates the text but represents the human activity subsequently described.

Despite Chen Shih-hsiang's great sensitivity as a reader of the *Odes*, the enthusiastic idea that xing—either as a technique for the composition of *shi* or for the interpretation thereof—could remain itself for centuries, retaining an essence of "spontaneity" and "immediacy" also in Mao's systematic commentaries, is questionable. To be able to criticize Mao's inconsistent use of "xing," Chen must, strictly speaking, present evidence to the effect that "xing" referred to the rhetorical organization of poetic discourse (*shi*) prior to Mao Heng's *Commentary* in the second century BCE. No such evidence can be found.

4

The Totemic Xing

Although inscribed in a different theoretical context—that of Claude Lévi-Strauss's polemical 1962 book on "totemism today"—the interpretational strategies regarding the *Odes* in Zhao Peilin's 趙沛霖 study *Xing di yuanqi* 興的源起 (The origin of Xing) are nearly identical to those of Wang and Chen.[1] In Zhao's account, the practice of xing, and the xingish representations of animals in particular, emerged in a prehistoric China permeated by the ideology and practice of totemism, when certain animals were considered the founders of the tribes into which society was organized. Consequently, when "Yanyan" 燕燕 (ode 28) speaks of "swallows" (*yan* 燕) it refers ultimately to a totemic forefather; although the original meaning of this "xing" was lost long before the composition of the *Odes*, once the associative connection had been established it was unconsciously used by the bards to invoke associations of deceased forefathers or of faraway relatives.[2]

I have in principle no objection to Zhao's hypothesis that the swallow was once a totem and, in prehistorical China, connoted a longing for one's forefathers or absent relatives; to disprove it would not only be impossible but also irrelevant to the present investigation into the rhetoric of the *Odes* and the anatomy of Mao Heng's *Commentary*. However, we note that, just as in Wang's and Chen's studies, the meaning or connotations of the totemic xing element have been set before it enters the poem and are unaffected by their immediate context. I simply suggest that, on the contrary, the supposed original meaning of a concept or motif is compromised the moment it is integrated into a larger setting, in particular that of a short and dense poem. Consider the opening lines of ode 28:

44 | The Origins of Chinese Literary Hermeneutics

> Swallows in flight
> uneven their wings
> This bride travels to wed
> [we] follow her far into the wilds
> When [our] gazes no longer reach her
> tears fall like rain[3]
>
> 燕燕于飛
> 差池其羽
> 之子于歸
> 遠送于野
> 瞻望弗及
> 泣涕如雨

Zhao's totemistic reading, according to which the description of the swallows immediately informs the listener that the poem thematizes separation and longing, bars—in a shift from the hermeneutic to the hermetic—several other possible interpretations. The mass of birds driven to migrate by their instincts and the natural order may for example be understood as analogous to the girl and her entourage, while the wedding journey is a corresponding, season-bound event in the human realm. The girl's feelings—ambivalent at the very least—toward the idea of getting married and performing her female duties at a distant location is certainly evoked by the word "wilderness" (*ye* 野), with its undertones of psychological bewilderment, and in the scene of a tearful goodbye. Conversely, the birds represent the notion of escape or freedom by their ability to fly (a reading attested in the *Commentary*). Alternatively, the poet is here simply juxtaposing the migrating birds and the similarly traveling bride and her escorts, etc. The description of the swallows may engender all of these somewhat extemporary readings simultaneously in an instance of harmonious ambiguity.

Although possibly historically accurate, Zhao's notion of a totemic *xing* is therefore an unfortunate starting point for, in a qualified sense, a reading of a poetic text; an ode might be composed of a miscellany of intertextual fragments, but the primary task of the reader is nonetheless to study the new constellation, not to trace the intertexts. More specifically, the function of Mao Heng's *xing* is to hem this ambiguity in and provide a canonical reading; Mao's concept thus bears little resemblance to Zhao's totemic, symbolic *xing*, which is underscored by the fact that Mao does not define the opening lines of ode 28 as a *xing*.[4]

5

Rhyme without Reason

"Shan you fusu" 山有扶蘇 (ode 84) is a typical *Shijing* poem in that it commences with two lines that describe an event in nature as a preamble to the following two lines that describe human action.

> On the mountain there are mulberry trees
> In the swamps, lotus flowers
> I do not see Zi Du
> I see a mad man[1]

> 山有扶蘇
> 隰有荷華
> 不見子都
> 乃見狂且

How do the mountain, the mulberry tree, the swamps, and the lotus flowers relate to the narrator who expects to see a certain Zi Du but, to his or her surprise, only sees a lunatic? Formally, the natural and human realms are coupled through rhyme, since *su* 蘇, *hua* 華, *du* 都 and *qie* 且 all belong to the same rhyme group. Does this mean that there exists a deeper, more meaningful relationship between these things and events? Not necessarily. With reference to semantics, rhyme is a notoriously unreliable matchmaker. "Roses are red / Violets are blue / Sugar is sweet / And so are you" goes the old doggerel. That the "dog-poet" speaks of violets has less to do with a deep-seated correspondence between the blue flowers and the person whom he woos than with the simple fact that the word "blue" rhymes with "you."

Is poem 84 of the *Shijing*—the Canon of Poetry celebrated already in the *Zuozhuan* as a "storehouse of righteousness" (*yi zhi fu* 義之府)—perhaps no more than an early Chinese doggerel?[2]

Gu Jiegang 顧頡剛 (1893–1980) belonged to a group of immensely influential scholars who, in the early days of the Republic, branded themselves the Doubters of Antiquity (*yigu xuepai* 疑古學派), and took it upon themselves to salvage the ancient texts—not least the *Odes*—from the dogmatic Confucian interpretations that for over two thousand years had distorted them. In a diminutive but influential article called "Qi xing" 起興, dating from the 1920s, Gu proposes a mode of reading of the *Odes* that must be considered extreme even among the vehemently antiallegorico-metaphorical tenets put forward in the iconoclastic *Disputes on Ancient History* (*Gushi bian* 古史辨).

Gu was an avid collector of folk songs from his native Suzhou and saw in them modern-day vestiges of the *Odes*, particularly with regard to the function of natural imagery, as in the following lines:

> On Mount Yang stands a small flower basket
> The newly wed girl has many troubles.[3]

陽山頭上花小籃
新做媳婦多許難

In Gu's view, this is a strictly formal juxtaposition of nature and man. The poet wanted to tell the story about a troubled young bride but, like the author of the doggerel verse above, felt he should start the poem with an image drawn from nature in order to avoid introducing his subject matter too abruptly. But why choose the image of the flower basket on Mount Yang? It is at this point that Gu's analysis evolves into an interesting and revealing fantasy. The appearance of this image, Gu claims, is overdetermined, linguistically as well as by the concrete circumstances of the poet. *Lan* 籃 ("basket") rhymes with *nan* 難 ("troubles"), which explains the occurrence of the flower basket in the poem. Mount Yang enters the picture for another even simpler and more scandalous reason. It is, Gu explains, the highest mountain in the Suzhou region, and when the poet began composing his poem his gaze happened upon Mount Yang, the image of which he "spontaneously" (*suikou* 隨口) and without premeditation incorporated into the poem.

Gu's phantasmatic, fanciful reconstruction of the *scene* of poetic creation interests us not only because he holds that this is exactly how *Shijing* poems like "Shan you fusu" came into being, or for the immense influence it has exerted on twentieth-century Sinology; it interests us also because Gu describes the poet's gaze as perfectly passive and gullible. The landscape in which the poet finds himself is automatically reflected in the poem without the imagery being in any way processed, as if the poet had composed the poem in a semitrance. In other words, nature and man coincide in the poem by sheer accident. No similitude, no extra-linguistic correspondence obtains between man and nature. Nor are the "images" of mountains, flower baskets, mulberry trees, marshes, and lotus flowers descriptions of the landscape in which the human activities take place but rather—and this is an altogether different matter—of the landscape in which the *poet* found himself when he composed the poem. The poet's eye and imagination cannot but automatically reflect the landscape in which he finds himself.

Thus far, Gu Jiegang's analysis of a latter-day Suzhou folk song. In "Guanju," as we already know, we find a similar scenario: the first two lines describe an event in nature and the following lines an event in the human realm.

> Kroo kroo the *jujiu* cries
> on the islet in the river
> The beautiful and good girl
> a fine mate for the lord.[4]

> 關關雎鳩
> 在河之洲
> 窈窕淑女
> 君子好逑

As in the preceding cases, nature and man are joined by rhyme (洲 *zhou* and 逑 *qiu* belong to the *you* 幽 rhyme group) but are the *jujiu*, the girl, and the lord connected also at a level other than the linguistic, as indeed is claimed in the many intricate Confucian interpretations of "Guanju" against which the Doubters of Antiquity raged?[5] Gu Jiegang unsurprisingly answers in the negative; "Guanju" is essentially a folk song, and the natural imagery simply a randomly chosen prelude initiating the poem (hence the name of Mao Heng's concept, since xing means "to start, to rise, to raise").[6] Like the Suzhou poem, "Guanju" is the product of a primitive poet, whose innocent gaze met the crying bird on the islet, and who spontaneously incorporated that scenery into the poem he was improvising.

Is Gu's comparison of the Suzhou poem with "Guanju" fair? That is, is the juxtaposition of the flower basket on Mount Yang and the troubled newlywed similar, in any relevant way, to the juxtaposition of the screaming osprey and the "beautiful and good girl" in "Guanju"? Although the descriptions of nature and man in the first four lines are joined by rhyme, the absence of copulas calls for further contextualization.

The poem continues thus:

Uneven are the water plants,
Left and right [he?] catches them.
The beautiful and good girl
Awake and asleep he seeks her,
Seeks her, but does not get her.
Awake and asleep, pining,
Longing, longing,
Tossing, turning; rolling from
side to side.[7]

參差荇菜
左右流之
窈窕淑女
寤寐求之
求之不得
寤寐思服
悠哉悠哉
輾轉反側

The protagonist is consumed with lust for the young woman described as "beautiful and good" and a "fine mate." She disturbs his sleep and enters his dreams, but in contrast to the water plants—both the girl and the plants are often referred to by the pronoun *zhi* 之—which he is able to catch, the girl is unreachable. If, in light of this information, we reread the opening lines, it is obvious that the screaming bird who sits isolated on the islet in the river appears in perfect parallel with the unreachable young lady; this parallelism is much more striking, and more rigorously executed, than the juxtaposition of man and nature in the Suzhou poem.

Even a highly cautious interpreter could therefore be persuaded that the *jujiu* appears in "Guanju" as a correlate of the girl—the object of the protagonist's lust and reverie, described as unattainable, circumscribed by masses of water but seductively calling out to the young man—and that a strict parallelism sometimes implies a similarity between nature and man in the *Odes*. The suggestion that the *jujiu* serves as a representation of the girl (in other words, that the natural imagery is subordinated to the description of human action) is further supported by the fact that the poem unambiguously thematizes the male protagonist's desire.

Although Gu's originality as a thinker is unquestionable, the comparison with the Suzhou song is methodologically flawed. It is not only unlikely that a modern folk song could impart any relevant information about the rhetorical organization of the much older "Guanju," Gu's choice of comparandum is itself strangely *far-fetched*, since the flower pot does not lend itself to a comparison with a young bride as readily as the screaming bird, as indeed is demonstrated in Mao's comments (wildly allegorizing yet simultaneously soberly analyzing) to which we turn below.[8] And like Wang and Chen, Gu's analysis rests on the assumption that "the xing" is a poetic composition technique that has remained consistent from the conception of the *Odes* down to the Suzhou folk songs of the early twentieth century and that, for instance, Mao Heng's and Zhu Xi's "xing" also refers to this self-same concept, albeit in a deviating and arcane way.

6

Xing and the Art of Quoting the *Odes*

Not until Cao Pi's (曹丕 187–226 CE) "Essay on Literature" (*Lun wen* 論文) did the Chinese tradition get a theory describing "literature" as anything but an ideological instrument, according to Donald Holzman.[1] Therefore, Confucius's statement (*Lunyu*, Yang Huo 陽貨 17.9) that "poetry can xing" 詩可以興 does not refer to poetry's psychological or emotional effects, as suggested by the usual rendering of this passage as "poetry can *uplift*"; the sage was more likely thinking of the custom among dignitaries during the Warring States period of quoting lines from the *Odes* as a courteous and oblique mode of communication, exemplified by Zichan's recitation of "Qian shang" (ode 87) above.[2] This practice uses the poem's primary meaning as, let us say, an extended metaphor of the situation in which it was quoted. In a similar situation in 546 BCE, Zitaishu 子大叔, a high minister from Zheng, recited (*fu*) ode 94, "Ye you wan cao," to a potentate from Jin.[3] The second stanza runs as follows:

> In the wilds there is grass spreading vastly
> the falling dew is plentiful
> There is a beautiful person
> beautiful are the eyes and forehead
> We meet by chance
> with you I will be happy[4]

> 野有蔓草
> 零露瀼瀼
> 有美一人

婉如清揚
邂逅相遇
與子偕臧

To Holzman, what Zitaishu did was precisely to "xing" the poem—that is, use it as a "metaphorical allusion" to the states of Zheng and Jin and as a weaker state's plea to a stronger one for protection: "With you I will be happy." The poem has thereby been metaphorized in the etymological sense of having been "transferred" from one (semantic or referential) realm to another, and Holzman further suggests that this is also the meaning and function of "xing" in Mao's *Commentary*: "The term *hsing* . . . is very ancient in reference to poetry and with a related meaning of 'analogy' or 'allusion'. It seems dangerous . . . to ignore this technical meaning of the term and to translate [xing] as 'incite people's emotions' (Waley)."[5]

Holzman thus seems to include Mao's xing in the "technical" category along with Confucius's "metaphoric allusion." Let us therefore briefly consult Zhu Ziqing's 朱自清 (1898–1948) pioneering 1945 study *Shi yan zhi bian* 詩言志辨, as it provides a hypothetical bridge between Zitaishu and Mao Heng.[6] The xing as it appears in the *Mao Commentary* has two main traits, Zhu explains; it starts off the poem in question, and it is a *piyu* 譬喻 (a simile or metaphor).[7] Unlike Holzman, Zhu does not equate Mao's xing with the practice of quoting the *Odes*; the Warring States dignitaries did not "xing" the *Odes* but "present" (*fu* 賦) them.

Zhu's argument may nonetheless elucidate Holzman's. When the ancient Warring States dignitaries quoted the *Odes*, which they in all likelihood knew by heart, they were perfectly aware of the difference between the message they wanted to convey and the original and literal meaning of the poem. Several centuries later, Mao Heng inherited and adopted the practice of transposing the "proper" meaning of an ode into a different context, but whereas the dignitaries had immediate access to the new context (and thereby to the "new" or "secondary" meaning of the ode recited), it had been lost by the time of the *Commentary*, hence the uncanny feeling instilled in later readers that Mao created meaning "out of nothing."[8]

Yet the suggestion of a continuity between Holzman's xing (and, possibly, Confucius's) and that of the early Chinese exegetical tradition in general and Mao's *Commentary* in particular must be treated with some caution. What Zitaishu did when he quoted "Ye you wan cao" was to adapt the poem to a new situation by changing its personage. The "metaphoric allusion" that Holzman speaks of builds on the similarity that obtains between the man and woman described in the text and between Zheng and Jin in the text-external, historical context; it is therefore conditioned by a movement from text to historical context, or from text to "extratext." In stark contrast to the "extratextuality" of the *Minor Prefaces* and of Holzman's xing, Mao's concept concerns the relationship between nature and human action described by the *Odes*; xing therefore denotes a semantic or tropological movement *within* the text. What consequence does this have for our understanding of early *Shijing* exegesis? Most importantly, it shows that already with the *Maozhuan* in the second century BCE, the formal aspect of poetry was studied, not just its potential use for Confucian didacticism. We may even say that with Mao's *Commentary* a first, albeit hesitant, step toward a formal analysis of literature was taken, and it is to the great credit of Zhu and Holzman to have discerned this, the "origins of Chinese literary hermeneutics."[9]

Although seemingly counterintuitive, Holzman's definition of xing as a "metaphorical allusion" may be regarded an eccentric example of the animosity against figurative meaning so conspicuous among modern-day scholars of Confucian hermeneutics and early Chinese poetics since the possibility of metaphoricity appears only when the notion of a *scene*—staged by a speaker and his addressee interacting in a concrete situation—has been introduced. The presence of both speaker and addressee vouches for semantic concretion and stability, and the risk of misunderstanding or misinterpretation, which might have been the result of metaphorical language without a readily identifiable origin, has thus been eliminated. Indeed, it could be held that the practice of quoting the *Odes* as described by Donald Holzman and Zhu Ziqing results not in "metaphoric allusions" but its very opposite, as the fictive love song is transposed into a concrete situation and provided with an interpretation anchored in text-external reality.

7

Marcel Granet and the Poetics of the Primeval Scene

I have thus far tried to reveal the key assumptions that underlie and determine the treatment of the concept of xing in contemporary Sinology and now turn to the phantasmagorical "primeval scene" elaborated in Marcel Granet's *Fêtes et chansons anciennes de la Chine*.[1] Although harshly criticized by some scholars, this 1919 study (together with a number of other works on Chinese intellectual history by the same author) has exerted a noticeable influence on Western scholarship on ancient China.[2] Granet, being foremost an anthropologist in the Durkheimian tradition, never saw the xing as a privileged problem. For him, the *Odes* were not primarily "literature" in the sense of a highly rhetorical discourse typified by tropes, repetition, alliteration, rhymes, and the like: but rather a source of information about the origins of Chinese culture and thinking, and his reconstruction of the genesis of the *Odes* inaugurates the tendency in modern Sinology to dismiss the metaphorico-allegorical Confucian mode of reading.

Granet set out to reveal not only the true, original meaning of the *Odes* but also the fundamental conceptualizations—the "thought patterns"—that later were to generate the peculiarities of Chinese philosophy as a whole. Not surprisingly for a proto-structuralist, Granet described ancient Chinese society as neatly organized in binary oppositions: the most conspicuous of which was that of gender.[3] The categories of men and women formed "two corporations" based on their respective work (men labor in the sunny fields and women in the secluded chambers of their homes).[4] The difference between the sexes also related to the changes of the seasons, as the share of labor distributed to men was carried out in the "active" season (*la bonne saison*) whereas women worked during the season that is "the least intense" (*la morte-saison*).⁵ The men and women, moreover, gathered together in "local groups," and these groups, albeit bound together by a mutual sense of sympathy or "community," had no contact other than during the important feasts, traditional and ritualized in nature, that marked the seasonal changes in spring and autumn.⁶ Granet attaches the highest importance to the vernal feasts. These feasts were principally for the young people: the most conspicuous rite therein was a game consisting of dances and songs, a rhythmic tournament (*tournois rythmique*) generating love between the people whom the traditional rules of the community had predestined as spouses.⁷

The vernal rituals, dramatically described by Granet as "sexual orgies," and whose task it was to regulate the sexual activities of the community, were occasions when the inactivity and routine of the "dead season" were changed into extreme tension. This moment of tension was "terrible" for the community, their future being at stake, and "dramatic" for the individuals—a moment in which love awakens and poetry is born.⁸

Of even greater importance was the staging of the spring rites, the primal scene of Chinese civilization: a group of young men standing in the sunny part of a sacred valley (*vallon sacré*) facing a group of young women standing in the valley's shady part. The men and women formed two choirs that alternated in singing the love songs later incorporated into the *Guofeng* section of the *Shijing*.⁹ This *scene* (and the word should indeed be italicized, underlined, and put in bold type) gave birth to the primary dualistic thought-figure that was to determine the Chinese mode of thinking and the Chinese conception of time and space, namely the yin-and-yang.

Thus originating in the distribution of work in prehistoric China, yin and yang signified the location of the two groups. The men were standing in the sunny part of the valley simply because they worked in the sunny fields during the "good season." The women, correspondingly, occupied the shady spot due to their work in the dark interiors of their houses in winter. The meaning of yin (north of a hill, south of a river) and yang (south of a hill, north of a river) were thus derived from the *concrete* placement of the two groups of people during the vernal feast.¹⁰ Slowly, the concepts of yin and yang were "expanded" into an all-embracing thought pattern, encompassing other notions of the same origin: yin—darkness, humidity, passivity, the underworld, femininity, and yang—clarity, dryness, activity, the world of the living, masculinity.

Consequently, the concept of space, to the ancient Chinese, was not conceived of as an expanse in which a variety of elements were assembled in a jumble but, rather, as a container of entities put in binary opposition (*genres contraires*). Similarly, the proto-Chinese concept of time originated in what Granet describes as "the representation of a succession of periods, linked together and defined by the alternate singing of the male and female voices."[11] Time, to the Chinese of antiquity, was thus not a linear succession of moments similar in quality but a succession in which the two opposing forces of yin and yang succeeded each other rhythmically—a "history" that can only repeat itself.

The most conspicuous feature of Marcel Granet's theory is the radical attempt to, in one fell swoop, reduce all complexity, abstraction, and figurality of Chinese poetry and philosophy to a primeval situation, a scene, where obscure ("wild" and "excessive," with C. H. Wang) metaphoricity is dissolved as text—the *Odes*, the concepts of yin and yang, the notions of time and space—meets with context. Granet holds that the process of ever-increasing metaphoric complexity and abstraction—going from the concrete allotment of work (males in the sunny fields and females in the secluded homes) via the vernal rites (in which the very location of the two groups reflected the distribution of labor) to the philosophic and metaphorical notions of yin and yang—must be reversed if we are to understand truly the Chinese mode of thinking. The idea that the (alleged) process of abstraction can be reversed and an original philosophical truth be recovered suggests that figurative interpretations are erroneous and fallacious distortions instigated by the loss of an original context. These assumptions lead us again to the core problem of the xing: how are natural imagery and descriptions of human actions related in the earliest of Chinese poetry?

In the section on "rustic topics" (*themes champêtre*) in the *Odes*, Granet translates the concepts of xing and *bi* 比 as, respectively, "comparison" and "allegory."[12] "When Chinese authors [i.e., the Confucian commentators] speak of comparisons and allegories, pay attention," warns Granet, because more often than not their interpretations are not "artistic" but moralizing. Natural imagery no longer expresses the beauty that the poet found in nature but the Confucian exegete's desire to conform the poems to the "order of nature" (*dao* 道).[13] For the Confucian commentator, therefore, while a poem describing two birds flying in tandem builds upon a perceived similarity between birds and humans it is ultimately an "exhortation" to fidelity between humans.[14] The word "exhortation" is significant because Granet sees in it the characteristic traits of Confucian poetics; neither does the Confucian reader take pleasure in the sensuous beauty of nature nor use it as embellishment in the form of (Western) metaphor. In the Confucian act of reading the natural descriptions are *made abstract* and understood as models of virtue.

But does the allegorizing, moralizing program of which Mao Heng's xing is undoubtedly a part disqualify it from serving what one might anachronistically call an aesthetic or formalistic purpose? The answer must be in the negative. It is a central tenet of the present work that the *literary* hermeneutics found in Mao Heng's very Confucian *Commentary* was the first successful attempt in the Chinese tradition to analyze *shi* 詩 in its capacity as *shi*—defined precisely as a "highly rhetorical discourse typified by tropes, repetition, alliteration, rhymes, et cetera"—Mao's moralizing intentions notwithstanding. One could claim, opposing Granet, that in analyzing the Confucian mode of reading it is not only possible but also necessary to separate the tools used for text-analysis (*bi*, xing, metaphor, allegory, etc.) from the ideological motives that partially govern them.

"Seasonal Sayings" and the Syntax of Pure Poetry

Granet claims, moreover, that the Confucian interpreter regarded the natural imagery of the *Odes* as "seasonal sayings" (*dictons de calendrier*), a concept that, says Granet, easily lends itself to a moralizing mode of reading. A *dicton de calendrier* indicates the season in which the poem is set, and Granet draws an example from "Ye you wan cao" (野有蔓草, ode 94), the first stanza of which he translates as follows:

> In the fields there is bindweed / full of dew
> [She:] He is a beautiful person / with lovely eyes
> [He:] I have met with her / she is my only desire[15]

In Granet's view, the poem is a charming, uncomplicated love song in the form of a dialogue between a girl and a boy, whereas the Confucian, allegorizing reading is that a meeting taking place when dew covers the plants is illicit, since the time of courtship should be over when spring has advanced so far. In the Confucian version, the poem as a whole is thus understood as a symptom of the ruler's failure to make the populace act according to the rites.

As an antidote, Granet suggests we read the *Odes* with a particular intertext, namely the traditional farmer's almanacs, where descriptions of nature and human activity, Granet alleges, correlate in much the same manner as in the *Odes*. In the *Minor Calendar of Xia* 夏小正, the year is divided into months, and the advent of each month marked by a particular natural phenomenon.[16] For instance, one month "there is singing from the oriole" 有鳴倉庚 that serves as an indication of that time of year.[17] It is precisely here, Granet claims, that we find poetry at work, not only because this particular phrase also occurs in "Qi yue" 七月 (ode 154) but foremost because of its extraordinary syntax.[18] Normal prose (as in the corresponding section of a contemporary calendar, "Yueling") would simply have it as "the oriole sings" 倉庚鳴.[19] The *Minor Calendar of Xia*, on the other hand, is "completely poetic."[20] Granet's notion of poetical syntax is noteworthy. In prose we find words distributed according to a linguistic order: "the oriole sings" (subject—predicate or noun—verb); the representation of an extra-linguistic, natural event has been filtered through the grid of language and imprinted with the pattern of culture.

By contrast, in poetic diction the sequence of phenomena is represented as it appears in nature. First you hear singing, then you see the bird—there is thus singing from the oriole.[21] Despite its seemingly unconventional, contorted syntax, poetry (or *shi*) is thus more natural, concrete, and primeval than prose. Granet's hyper-mimetic poesy here exceeds even the wildest dreams of scholars such as Gu Jiegang, Xu Fuguan, Chen Shih-hsiang—or indeed Ernest Fenollosa and Ezra Pound. Not only is external reality represented without a hint of figurative language, the linguistic representation of natural phenomena is also arranged as they spontaneously appear to man. To Granet, original and "true" poetry is concrete, literal, and natural whereas the perverted interpretations engendered by Confucian hermeneutics are abstract, metaphoric, and cultured (that is, manipulated and worked on).

Extraordinary, "poetical" syntax is thus a hint that poetry and "seasonal sayings" stem from a common source, hence Granet interest in "Qi yue." Every stanza of this long piece, says Granet, is a "seasonal saying" marking a specific time of year; it is in fact a *versified almanac* written in a style typical for the "Chinese annals" (*fastes chinois*). These annals or chronicles were not a poetical "game" (*jeu poétique*) but possessed unity and sense; and as these songs were sung at the harvest-feast that marked the end of the agricultural year, may we not, Granet asks, assume that all poems containing "calendar sayings" did indeed originate in the seasonal feasts?[22]

But Granet's "seasonal sayings" could be contextualized quite differently. Perhaps they should be seen as springing from a deeply human quest to make the exterior world understandable, either by compiling and taxonomizing facts about natural phenomena or by interpreting the omens of the world, as in the *Zhouyi*. Similarly, the view of the primeval Chinese poet that has emerged from studies of texts such as the *Great Preface*, *Xunzi* and *Yueji* should be revised. To the notion of an inspired bard who produces poetry spontaneously and out of inner necessity could be added another one: that of an organizer or synthesizer who reshapes the data that nature gives him or her into an intelligible structure.

Given the tenor of the present work, I have focused only on what I believe are flaws in Granet's analyses of the *Odes*, now more than a century old. The insights of *Fêtes et chansons* are of course both very real and plentiful; one is that Granet brings to light the paradoxical nature of the Confucian terminology in which a concept such as xing is used to designate a whole range of different hermeneutical operations. As we will see in the next chapter, there is an innate tension in Confucian hermeneutics between "figurative" readings and a contextualization striving to link the poem to a specific time and situation. Similarly, Granet's description of Confucian exegesis as a manipulation of a "pure" and original text may, somewhat paradoxically, introduce to us the hypothesis that Confucian interpretation is—or saw itself as—a conscious *refining* of the poetic text.

8

Nature Is Metaphorical, Poetry Literal

Granet's theories about the literalism of the *Odes* and the origins of Chinese thought in the concrete spatial organization of men and women in the ancient vernal rites reverberate in Pauline Yu's 1987 study of the *Shijing* and its early reception.[1] In *The Reading of Imagery in the Chinese Poetic Tradition*, Yu poses two questions of fundamental importance for the present work and, indeed, for comparative poetics overall. To what extent are the *Odes* allegories in the strictly traditional, and markedly Western, sense of the term? Conversely, but from the same comparative perspective, is it accurate to call early Confucian *Shijing*-exegesis an interpretation in an allegorizing mode, an allegoresis? We may add a third question that certainly is implicit throughout Yu's study and explicit in many of François Jullien's works. "Figurative meaning," says Jullien, "cannot be conceived of independently from a certain view of the world."[2] Is this hypothesis correct—that, for instance, Aristotle's concept of *metaphora* is inextricably linked to a typically "metaphysical" distinction between the everyday world we experience through our senses and the abstract and eternally "selfsame" forms—or may concepts such as xing and *metaphora* emerge and be elaborated "independently" of the larger contemporary assumptions of how reality is constituted?

What determines and shapes Yu's argument is the concept (as Yu sees it, a quintessentially Western one) of metaphor, and in particular one facet thereof. Aristotle's formal definition of metaphor as "the application of a word belonging to something else" (*onomatos allotriou epiphora*) is less interesting to Yu than that in the *Poetics* Aristotle stresses, or seems to stress, the *creation* involved in the making of a metaphor: "The greatest thing by far is to be a master of metaphor . . . it is also a sign of genius, since a good metaphor implies an intuitive perception of the similarity in dissimilars."[3] Yu remarks that the "metaphor-maker looks and thinks in a fundamentally new way," and approvingly quotes Paul Ricoeur's words about metaphor being a redescription of reality.[4] The metaphor is thus not only a rhetorical transference of a "word" from one realm of experience (or linguistic category) to another; it is also a route to new information or "a mode of cognition."[5] With the quote from Aristotle begins an argument that ends in a description of the Western literary tradition as essentially metaphorico-metaphysical. In her discussion of Occidental theories of tropes and figurative language, Yu construes metaphor as an unnatural artifact (made by a poetical genius) and defines mimesis—the concept that embodies and structures Western poetics—as "the notion of the poet as maker and of the poem as something made, existing in relation to reality . . . yet *ontologically distinct from it.*"[6] Literature, in the traditional Western sense, is thus fictitious, yet Yu is not tautologically claiming that in the Western tradition external reality is considered "real" and the literary representation of that reality unreal. What concerns Yu is rather the *abstraction* of Western literary language and that it has "access to universals beneath the surface of daily events"; "the view of poetry as a representation removed from the level of concrete reality has prevailed."[7]

Let me reformulate. Western literature equals mimesis, and metaphor is its preferred trope, the human animal's means of conceptualizing—and thus constructing and construing—the world. Metaphor, furthermore, does not merely designate the transference of a word from one category to another but also a philosophical stance vis-à-vis that which is outside the subject—reality. Western metaphor rewrites reality: reality is given, and literature made. Moreover, metaphor is characterized by a movement from concretion to abstraction.[8] Indeed, if Marcel Granet posits the festive scene as the origin of Chinese culture and intellectual life, Yu in a similar gesture points to the metaphor as the process typifying Western culture. By quoting Jacques Derrida's quotation of Martin Heidegger's *Der Satz vom Grund*, Yu links the use of metaphor to Western metaphysics: "Metaphor rests on the distinction . . . between the physical and the non-physical, [it] is a basic feature of what is called 'metaphysics' . . . The metaphorical exists only within the boundaries of metaphysics."[9]

The picture Yu is painting is slowly emerging: Western culture and literature are imbued with metaphor, abstraction, and metaphysics whereas the Chinese counterparts are distinguished by literalism, concretion, and correlative cosmology. Aristotle's description—arguably a formal and linguistic one—of the "transference" (*metaphora*) of a word from one context to another is here exchanged for a philosophical understanding of metaphor as fundamentally underpinned by metaphysics. Methodologically speaking, is this separation of East and West and the concomitant distinction between rhetorical and philosophical metaphor accurate? May metaphor and "figurative meaning" not "be conceived of independently from a certain view of the world"?

Allegory—to Yu an unequivocally Western concept—is an "extended metaphor," the meaning (or interpretation) of which cannot be substantiated by reading the text in question literally or naively.[10] Allegory thus differs from metaphor formally in that it lacks the interaction between the literal and figurative senses of a word, phrase, or concept; the figurative meaning is instead added to the text in the allegorizing act of reading. On the transcendental implications of allegory Yu writes, in a Heideggerian mode, that "Western allegory creates a hierarchal literary universe of two levels, each of which maintains its own coherence, but only one of which has ultimate primacy."[11] Western allegory thus banks upon a distinction between what is seen (the world of the senses, the text) and what is unseen (the abstract forms, the allegorical meaning). And here one suspects that the Heideggerian maxim that "the metaphorical obtains only within Metaphysics" has a special purpose for Yu since it suggests that a tradition freed from the plague of metaphysics—namely, the Chinese tradition, as the Other of Metaphysics—also lacks metaphor and allegory.

This short summary cannot do justice to the erudition and elegance with which Pauline Yu treats her subject, but it may serve as a point of reference for a discussion of Chinese allegory and metaphoricity that eventually runs counter to hers. I would foremost question Yu's exclusive focus on the supposed philosophical underpinnings of Western theories of the metaphor. Chinese, like all languages, abounds with what in common parlance is called "metaphor." As the simplest of examples, consider the graph or word 口 *kou*, whose earliest meaning in all likelihood was "mouth." When this word was used to denote an "opening" in a building or on a vessel it was a transference (*metaphora*) of a word or concept from the human realm (the human mouth) to the, let us say, architectural realm (that of houses). Furthermore, this transference was based on resemblance and analogy, a mouth being an opening of the human body and a door an opening of a house—or a spout the opening of a vessel.[12]

A defendant of Yu's theory would claim that naming a door "mouth," or vice versa, is not necessarily a metaphor in an Aristotelian sense, since the human mouth and the "mouth" of a building, despite being discrete objects, were always already considered to be of the same "kind" (*lei* 類) to the early Chinese; therefore, the Chinese "metaphorizer" did not invent the likeness (*to homoion*) between "this" and "that," but merely reported on it. This is a perfectly legitimate argument, although I argue against it both here and elsewhere. The central issue in this context, however, is not the two manifestations of a cosmological "mouthness" or "cavity" but the *act* of putting them together in speech, in writing, or in the mind under the same name or using the same sound. The act of linguistic transference is, in Aristotelian terms and *pace* Jullien's claim to the contrary, "metaphorical," the underlying philosophical ideas notwithstanding.[13] In other words, although it could be argued that this word use banks on a perceived preexisting correlation between mouth and door, I claim that the shift itself—口 *kou* "mouth" becoming 口 *kou* "door" or "spout"—is irrevocably linguistic and metaphorical in nature.

The assumption on which my claim rests, and the corollary following from it, is that this very basic kind of metaphor is a universal linguistic and cognitive process, and that Aristotle's notion of a transference based on the perceived "likeness" or "similarity" (*to homoion*) between "this" and "that" is an adequate delineation thereof. Vice versa, although the early Chinese tradition did not formulate a concept as densely charismatic as Aristotle's *metaphora*, we certainly find scattered therein a highly sophisticated theorizing on the linguistic and cognitive processes that create basic metaphors. The metaphorical does not obtain only "within Metaphysics."

The discussion above has been restricted to metaphor in what may tentatively be called everyday language. To distinguish (as is my wont) between this and "literary," "rhetorical," or "poetic" metaphor requires a detailed elaboration that cannot be afforded within the scope of the present study; instead I simply suggest, somewhat tautologically and inevitably simplifying, that poetic metaphor differs from everyday pragmatic metaphor by delaying, or even being an obstacle to, the conveying of a message.[14]

The Evocative and the Metaphorical

In the theoretical section leading up to her reading of "Guanju," Pauline Yu observes that "there is a difference between an *evocative image* . . . and the often more grammatically distinctive metaphor proper," and that this distinction is "especially important when we examine the Chinese poetic tradition."[15] I shall briefly pursue this assertion, which is strongly reminiscent of Chen Shih-hsiang's statement (also made with reference to the first ode) that the xing-elements in the *Odes* generate a "meaning beyond words," and a "feeling" that is "genuinely felt."

Due to its prominent position as the first poem of the *Shijing*, "Guanju" sets the tone for the entire collection, and it was therefore of utmost importance for the Confucian exegetes to take immediate control over and transform what is—or at least seems to be—an ardent love song into a piece that propagates Confucian dogma. With reference to the great length and detailedness of Mao Heng's exegesis of "Guanju," to which we turn in due time, it would be no exaggeration to say that it constitutes a paradigm of Confucian literary hermeneutics.

"Guanju," as we know, juxtaposes descriptions of nature (the *jujiu* bird and the water plants) and of humans (the young lady and the "lord" or "young master") without any explicit indication of how they relate. Can "Guanju" be called an allegory? Or does the juxtaposition of "images" allow for a reading that in some general way may be called metaphorical? No, Yu answers, there are no "implicit comparisons that are being developed in the poem."[16] That the *jujiu* birds could be a metaphor for the young couple described in the poem is ruled out since "most modern commentators reject this idea."[17] Nor is the act of plant picking a metaphor for mate-searching since even "traditional scholars" disagree.[18] Moreover, the descriptions of the *jujiu*, the young couple and the plant-picking all lack the "normal relation of concretion to abstraction" which Yu sees as a significant feature of "Western metaphor"; the images in "Guanju" are all "drawn from the same *concrete* realm."[19]

Let me offer some objections at this juncture. That "modern commentators" reject that the birds function as a metaphor for the young couple is a curiously flippant argument, especially considering the aversion to metaphor and celebration of literalism and concretion in modern *Shijing* scholarship. Interestingly, however, as an early example of a "concrete" and nonmetaphorical reading of "Guanju," Yu refers us to the Song dynasty literatus Su Zhe 蘇轍 (1039–1112), according to whom the poet fortuitously happened upon a flock of birds perched on an island and incorporated that image into the poem.[20] Su Zhe's theory of *shi* as a spontaneous reflection of whatever caught the poet's eyes at the scene of creation certainly forebodes, for example, Gu Jiegang's and Chen Shih-hsiang's speculations about primeval

Chinese poetry—"when to speak was to be a poet"—but it also deviates markedly from Mao Heng's analysis of *Shijing* "imagery," as well as from the internal evidence provided by the *Odes* themselves.

Yu quotes, again with the greatest approval, Christine Brooke-Rose's distinction between the poetic technique ("dangerously lazy" in Brooke-Rose's elegant phrasing) of juxtaposing natural descriptions with human action, and "proper" metaphor: if there is no formal link, there is no real metaphor.[21] We note that Yu, in the quote above, slightly but significantly revises Brooke-Rose's statement by opposing "the often more grammatically distinct metaphor," not to "juxtaposition" but to the "evocative image."[22] We may here consider a poem that certainly belonged to Brooke-Rose's frame of reference, namely Ezra Pound's "In a Station of the Metro," written in 1912 or 1913. The famous Imagist poem, which consists of only two lines (in addition to its title), is indeed interesting to the student of the *Shijing* since it juxtaposes *images* drawn from the human and the natural realms:

In a Station of the Metro

The apparition of these faces in the crowd;
Petals on a wet, black bough.[23]

Here, juxtaposition (or parataxis) appears as a limited interaction between two "images," in this case, the respective descriptions of the human faces and the petals. Pauline Yu's notion of an "evocative image," on the other hand, suggests that an image—or, with Wang and Chen, a "motif"—evokes emotions in its own right, regardless of the context it is put into.[24] But in the cited passage Brook-Rose is in fact not referring to "evocative" imagery but to Pound's careful juxtaposition of "*contrasting* and *similar* facts, building up his ideograms, each passage, each Canto and each group of Cantos juxtaposing one an(other)."[25] Likewise, any work devoted to the "reading of imagery in the Chinese poetic tradition" must study the *interaction* of the two imagistic strata or elements thus juxtaposed in the typical *Shijing* ode.

Would it be inaccurate to interpret the petals as a figuration—a phantasmatic re-presentation—of the faces that appear in the metro station? While it may not necessarily be the only possible reading or even the best one, it suggests itself through the interaction of the two lines, and of the poem's title.[26] A mere juxtaposition of "images" is thus, under certain circumstances, enough to suggest a "likeness" (*homoion*) between them. If we consider "Guanju," with its strict parallelism and rhyme scheme, the reasons for a similar interpretation are even more pronounced, as I attempted to demonstrate in my previous discussion of Gu Jiegang's "Qi xing."

An Antimetaphorical Theory of "Metaphor"

Is "Guanju" an allegory? It is a strange and frustrating question that cannot be answered straightforwardly. An allegory is by definition a narrative with two layers or sets of meaning, one literal, concrete, and transitory, the other figurative and final. Since the figurative meaning is absent from the allegorical text (or only hinted at), there is always the possibility that any text may yield an allegorical interpretation, and there are therefore only two ways to answer the question posed by Yu. Either we know the authorial intention or we draw a tentative conclusion about the text's rhetorical status from an investigation of the poem itself. Since in this case we know next to nothing about the author or of the early tradition of which he or she was a part, the fate of this frustrating question lies in the study of the text itself. The answer to our question can only be tentative: "Guanju" does not *require* an allegorical reading to be fully understood, much less to be of literary value.

As for the second question—is Confucian exegesis an allegorizing mode of reading? Let us consult the *Mao Commentary*. Mao's terse comments on the first two lines of "Guanju" were to leave an everlasting imprint on Chinese literary hermeneutics. Mao explains that male and female *jujiu* birds live separated from each other and that *kroo kroo* are "harmonious sounds" (*he sheng* 和聲) uttered by the birds.[27] Furthermore, Mao claims that the "beautiful and good girl" and the "lord" refer to the founder of the Zhou dynasty, the sagely King Wen of Zhou (who died around 1047 BCE) and his queen consort.[28] The queen rejoiced in the moral behavior of the king, and their relationship was characterized by harmony, prudence, and sexual moderation, just like the *jujiu* birds that live in separation.[29]

Pauline Yu accurately describes Mao's reading of "Guanju" as a process in two steps. The initial analysis of the imagery employed by the poet (what Mao calls a xing) is followed by a contextualization in which the poem is linked to a historical period and personage: in other words, to a *scene*.[30] However, Yu considers the former merely an auxiliary to the latter, which concerns "the poem as a whole."[31] Therefore, there is in Mao's reading of "Guanju" no movement from "concretion to abstraction," which Yu contends is the hallmark of Western metaphor.

To augment her theory, Yu then makes a statement that is the epicenter of what may be called the poetics of correlative cosmology and, by the same token, the most translucent but also most seductive and insidious formulation of a nonmetaphysical poetics and an antimetaphorical theory of "metaphor." Even if, according to Yu, Mao did perceive a likeness between the *jujiu* and the royal couple, he believed that they belonged to the "same class of events."³² As suggested above, Yu holds that this sameness between the human and the natural realms was not believed by Mao and his colleagues to have been *created* to serve as a rhetorical figure but was considered a cosmological correspondence between nature and human action that existed a priori and independently of any text, speech act, or conceptualization.

In other words, when Mao interprets the *jujiu* as a description of the royal couple he is merely stating a literal and concrete fact about the interrelation between man and nature; he is not indulging a fictitious, hypothetical, and abstract metaphor. (Granet makes the same point with regard to the *Odes* themselves.) As a consequence, Yu concludes, representations of man and nature are granted the same importance by the Chinese exegete. Neither of them is seen as "the fulfillment of the other," whereas in Western metaphor and allegory the vehicle is subordinated to the tenor.³³ Yu thus purifies and takes to its logical extreme Chen Shih-hsiang's idea of plain speech as a poetical activity, and the conclusion is a full inversion of what is commonly considered the order of poetic imagery. Figures or tropes are in fact not rhetorical, linguistic or conceptual; the early Chinese bards merely presented the cosmological correlations of which the world consists. The world is "metaphorical"—poetry, and language in general, is literal.³⁴

At first glance, Yu's ingenious, insidious theory appears impossible to refute without explicit statements to the contrary by Mao and his contemporaries, yet it builds on assumptions that, at closer inspection, are open for reinterpretation. When Aristotle says that only a person with a particular aptness (*euphuia*) can "observe the likeness" (*to homoion theorein*) between two apparently different entities, he is indeed suggesting that the likeness or similarity (*to homoion*) between the two things is not immediately or tautologically obvious. Aristotle's *homoion* is not the similarity between monozygotic twins; it does not jump out and hit you on the nose.³⁵ But is it invented? Is it a fictitious, cerebral, and abstract conceptualization in contrast to Yu's *lei* ("similar because of the same class"), which is wholly concrete and in existence prior to and independent of language and cognition? We would search in vain, I hold, for a statement from Aristotle to the effect that the "likeness" between "this" and "that" is untrue or unreal.

Nor is Yu's Chinese likeness (*lei*) immediately obvious, as proven by the pains taken by Mao to explain that what the *jujiu* and the royal couple have in common is "virtue." Nor does Western metaphor necessarily build on by a shift from the concrete to the abstract; both tenor and vehicle in a textbook metaphor such as "the bow is a stringless lyre" (Aristotle, *Rhetoric* 1413a) are drawn from the same "concrete realm."

Second, as I hinted above, although the Chinese tradition never produced a concept as beguiling and triumphant as *metaphora*, there is certainly a highly sophisticated *thinking* about "the metaphorical" scattered in early Chinese philosophical and commentarial texts. *Master Lü's Annals* and *Shuo yuan* 說苑 both contain models of "the metaphor," which in their precision and ingeniousness rival Aristotle's definitions in the *Poetics* and the *Rhetoric*, as I argue at length elsewhere.[36] And Mao's suggestion that the author of "Zheng yue" 正月 (ode 192) purposefully misnames a struggle of shrubby bushes a "forest" as a figuration of deceitful appearances and governmental chaos is a "reading of imagery" that completely contradicts the standard narrative of *shi* as spontaneous and unreflected.

Third, with reference to Jullien's assertion that a theory of the metaphor could not have been "conceived of independently from a certain view of the world," I repeat my claim that the cart has here been put behind the metaphorical horse. The notion of cosmological correspondences is less important than the discernible motive behind Mao's mode of reading, which manifests itself in the interpretation of the "image" of the *jujiu* birds as a *description* of the virtuous "lord" and "girl"—and not as a statement to the effect that the behavior of birds and the humans are two manifestations of virtue (*de*). "Guanju," as Mao construes it, is thus not a statement about cosmological correspondences but a poem about a "lord" and his virtuous queen consort. And if phenomena from the animal realm are used to conceptualize events in the human realm, then this arguably constitutes a *metaphora*, a linguistic or rhetorical transference.

Let me briefly draw an example from the Western canon. When the narrator of Baudelaire's "Une Charogne" addresses his lady as "soleil de ma nature," he describes their relationship in terms of a natural phenomenon (although *nature* may also denote the mental disposition of the speaker).[37] Are we to understand this line as a metaphor ("you, my dear, are the life-giving object around which my very existence revolves") or as a statement about the Swedenborgian "cosmological" correspondences in which we know the French poet took such a keen interest? Fortunately, we do not have to make this choice; the two readings can exist simultaneously. Yet—and this

70 | The Origins of Chinese Literary Hermeneutics

is equally valid for Yu's rendition of Mao's hermeneutics—a reading that acknowledges only the "cosmological" aspect mistakes the message of the poem for its philosophical presuppositions (and vice versa), making a poem "of flesh and blood" into little more than dull, versified philosophy.

Contextualization and a Counter example: *Zhouyi* and "Zhen lu" 振鷺 (ode 278)

The *Zhouyi* constitutes the earliest stratum of the *Book of Changes* (*Yijing* 易經) and has been described as a "divination manual" that either predates or is contemporaneous with the *Odes*. In the present context, the *Zhouyi* interests me foremost because of the striking resemblances between certain segments of the two texts, as in the correlations of natural phenomena with human action in the examples below.[38]

The *Zhouyi*, as we know, is organized around 64 hexagrams, each of which is typically followed by a general hexagram statement and six so-called line statements that explain the significance of each of the six lines of the hexagram. In the first line statement to hexagram 36, we find the following stanza:

> The *mingyi*-bird in flight
> droops its left wing
> The lordling on a journey
> for three days does not eat[39]

> 明夷于飛
> 垂其左翼
> 君子于行
> 三日不食

Similarly, in the line statements to the first hexagram, there appears a "dragon" (or *long* 龍):

> Flying dragon in the sky—
> beneficial to see the great man[40]

> 飛龍在天
> 利見大人

Nature Is Metaphorical, Poetry Literal | 71

We recognize in both examples the parallelistic arrangement from the ode "Guanju" but what logic governs the juxtaposition of Nature and Man in the *Zhouyi*? An exhaustive answer is not altogether easy to give. Although we know a great deal about the usage of the *Zhouyi* in the late Western Zhou dynasty, our knowledge of its composition and original meaning is limited.⁴¹ We know that the divinations by the *Zhouyi* recorded in the *Zuozhuan* were not, in the words of Edward Shaughnessy, "prompted by the fantastic appearance of a dragon in the sky or any other natural omen."⁴² Divination was rather conducted in the following manner: a topic was formulated (e.g., "should the King's elder son be made ruler?"), after which followed a complex process of manipulating a set of milfoil stalks, through which a specific hexagram was obtained. The hexagram was subsequently explained in accordance with the *Zhouyi* tradition by a diviner who either knew the hexagram explanations by heart or consulted a written version thereof. Given their abstruseness ("Flying dragon in the sky"), these explanations were frequently further interpreted either by the diviner himself, or by the person for whom the divination was made.⁴³

As represented in Zuo's *Commentary*, the *Zhouyi* text—the collection of general explanations to, and individual line statements for, each of the 64 hexagrams—thus seems to have functioned as a manual for the interpretation of divinations by stalk casting. But, again, the origins of the text are not revealed by these accounts in the *Zuozhuan*. There seems to be a distinct discontinuity between the original *Zhouyi* tradition and the uses it was later put to: what was the original meaning of the two examples above? In Edward Shaughnessy's 1983 study of the *Zhouyi*, the natural phenomena that the "associative intellect of ancient China" correlated with human events are described in terms of "portents" or "omens."⁴⁴ Thus, with regard to the first example, Shaughnessy speculates that originally the sight of the *mingyi* was itself considered an "inauspicious portent" which "portended imminent danger."⁴⁵ This is a plausible hypothesis, and not unrelated to Gu Jiegang's theory of how the poet's vision was immediately reflected in the text, or to the "great man's" interpretation of the shepherd's dream in ode 190. A more authentic interpretation of the above lines would thus be as follows.

> *Whenever* a *mingyi*-bird in flight
> droops its left wing,
> the lordling on a journey
> for three days *will* not eat.⁴⁶

72 | The Origins of Chinese Literary Hermeneutics

In this context, the word *mingyi* does not refer to anything beyond itself. That the bird droops its left wing is presented plainly, as a law-bound natural phenomenon that foretokens an event in the human realm. The second example is more intricate but obeys the same logic. "Dragon" does not refer literally to a "fantastic" celestial creature. But nor is it, as among others Wen Yiduo 聞一多, David Pankenier and Edward Shaughnessy have convincingly argued, a metaphor for a sage, a deity or the Emperor, or any such imposing figures towering, or "flying," above the people.[47] Although such metaphorical interpretations did emerge at a later stage, at around 800 BCE (when the composition of the *Zhouyi* seems to have begun) "dragon" most likely referred to a dragon-shaped assembly of stars—a constellation—seen in the firmament from spring to autumn.[48] Other occurrences in the same hexagram text of the "headless" or "submerged" Dragon describe, according to this interpretation, the appearance of the constellation during its different phases, and thereby declare the progression of the seasons. Consequently, the *mingyi* and the Dragon fill the same purpose in that they, as omens, indicate to man what action to take at the time of their respective appearance. We may reread the second example in accordance with this insight as

> *At the time* when the Dragon flies in the sky
> it is beneficial to see the great man[49]

These correlations are not fictional or—as in "Guanju," or in the yoking together of "dirty clothes" and "sorrows" in ode 26—made for the purpose of illustration, but causal (although cause and effect here work in mysterious ways) and thus very real.[50] The "author" of the *Zhouyi* incorporates the external landscape into the text but with substantial differences from Gu Jiegang's model. Most importantly, the natural imagery is not detached from the human action which it precedes, nor attached to it randomly, and we must therefore understand these extracts from the *Zhouyi* not as descriptions of natural phenomena and human action *created* by a writer and artfully joined together by him or her but rather as careful quasi-scientific observations of how Nature and Man interact. To wit, as a record of experiences drawn from the natural realm with the intention of guiding man in his daily life. In this respect, Yu provides a precise definition of the worldview manifested in the *Zhouyi*: "the connections between subject and object or among objects, which the West has by and large credited to the creative ingenuity of the poet, are viewed in the Chinese tradition as already pre-established."[51]

This is an elegant formulation of what is commonly known as correlative cosmology, and Yu here tacitly refers to the Aristotelian claim that only a person with ingenuity (*euphuia*) can "perceive the similarity" between things that are or appear to be different.[52] At this juncture, we may simply conclude that the inevitable consequence of a worldview according to which all things of the same category spontaneously connect with each other is that a *law-bound, positive connection* always obtains between a natural phenomenon (or the image thereof) and human action. Cosmos, let us say, knows of no irony.

Let us return to the *Odes*. The claim that a concept like Aristotle's *metaphora* could not be conceived "outside metaphysics," since early Chinese thinking did not separate lived experience from abstract truths (which here refers to the hidden "likeness" that unites the two apparently dissimilar things) is perhaps the cleverest and most elaborate attempt to do away with the notion of a Chinese practice and theory of metaphor. Consider, however, the first stanza of "Zhen lu" (振鷺 ode 278):

In flocks, the *lu* birds in flight
in those western swamps
Our guests arrive
also having this appearance

振鷺于飛
于彼西雝
我客戾止
亦有斯容

This poem is not organized paratactically since the imagery of the *lu* birds explicitly and unambiguously functions as a description of the arriving guests. The imagistic arrangement may, of course, still be partly rooted in a notion of cosmological correspondences between natural and human phenomena (the guests congregate for a certain ritual or banquet in a timely fashion, at the time of year when the birds gather on the marshes). Yet the poem explicitly stresses the notion of appearance (*rong* 容), not a deeply rooted cosmological kinship between man and bird.

The guests "also" have this appearance—just as the "corrupt words of the people," according to "Zheng yue" (ode 192), are "also" greatly exaggerated. The inconspicuous little word *yi* ("also") has brought the comparative element in the imagery of the *Odes* to the fore. Therefore, on the textual level, the only verifiable role that the imagery of the *lu* bird plays is that of a description of the guests—the poet did indeed *to homoion theorein*, "perceive the likeness (between apparently different things or events)."[53] We are here dealing with a rhetorical and linguistic transference and not with a literal statement about the cosmological similarity between birds and man.

To Yu, as we have seen, early Chinese exegesis assumes a process in which literal representations of two discrete cosmological phenomena are put side by side to show a certain correspondence between them. But did the notions of cosmological correspondences, literalism, and concretion pervade every aspect of Confucian hermeneutics? Could a literary hermeneutics not have developed independently of correlative cosmology and focused primarily on textual phenomena? Let us reconsider Mao's analysis of "Guanju." The birds are not simply a representation of the royal couple. The link between the birds and the couple is, rather, made possible, not through a philosophy of cosmological correlations but through a process of abstraction that Yu chooses to bypass. Just as Yu claims, Mao's hermeneutics here rests on two operations: one contextual (or metonymical) and one metaphorical. In the former Mao identifies the young couple described in the poem as the queen consort and her "lord." In the latter he speaks of the harmony and prudence that characterize their relationship which, in its turn, explicitly *resembles* (*ruo* 若) the separation of males and females among the *jujiu*. The birds not only represent the royal couple but also introduce an abstract concept: (conjugal or sexual) *virtue*.

Let us attempt to reconstruct the tropological movement: the male and female ospreys (concretion) live in separation from each other; therefore they are virtuous (abstraction) which, in turn, makes them a perfect image of the virtuous king and his queen. With a slightly different twist, we may say that the abstract notion of virtue is the *tertium comparationis* that unites ospreys and men and makes this metaphor possible. Therefore, even if Mao did subscribe to the theories of ying and yang, the five phases (*wu xing*), stimulus-and-response (*gan ying*), cosmological categories (*lei*)—that is, what is commonly referred to as "correlative cosmology"—his ideological transformation of the text into Confucian dogma still depends on a process of abstraction.[54] Since "Guanju" is a poem about lust and sexuality it was necessary for Mao the arch-Confucian to read it as precisely the opposite. A simple juxtaposition of bird and man is in fact a reading that must be avoided at all costs. Through the process of metaphorization (called "xing"), Mao can extract from the natural imagery exactly the statement demanded by Confucian philosophy. Mao must make "Guanju" a poem about moral behavior and therefore invents the fantasy about the birds' (now in plural) behavior in order to reach the concept of virtue.[55]

If compared to my insipid but nonetheless sound interpretation of Pound's paratactic "In a Station of the Metro," Mao's tendency toward abstraction becomes even clearer. Pound uses the wet petals on the bough to "re-present" (the appearance of) the faces in the metro station. Mao, at his end, is neither interested in describing the superficial appearance of the royal couple nor in simply identifying "the general category to which both [the birds and the human couple] belong."[56] From the concrete depiction of the birds and the lovers he must abstract their common denominator, virtue. By contrast, my "basic" reading of "Guanju"—the crying *jujiu* represents the elusive and alluring girl for whom the protagonist pines—is far less abstract and thereby less refined than Mao's.

Yu's contention that the metaphorical operation is subordinated to the contextual one, which concerns "the poem as a whole," must therefore be questioned. Without the metaphorical process leading to the notion of virtue, "Guanju" would be utterly worthless, or even dangerous, to Mao, since it would produce an iconoclastic, forbidden, and sexual reading. The xing is a method of taking instant command of the text, of explaining or, indeed, obscuring its organization. In Mao's transformative reading of "Guanju," the metaphorizing and contextualizing processes play an equally important part; in the *Commentary* as a whole, the xing method prevails.

Second, Yu claims that the Confucian hermeneuts conceived of *Shijing* imagery as drawn from the two concrete realms of nature and man, neither of which was considered "the fulfillment of the other."[57] However, the xing in Mao's *Commentary* is a mode of reading that constantly uses nature tropologically, as a statement about human actions and situations. Therefore, on a rhetorical (or textual) level there is a distinction between the realm of nature and the realm of man; the former is never taken for granted, it is always present in the text for another purpose than pure representation or duplicity. Perhaps Mao conceived of the two realms as simultaneous; perhaps he even saw them as ontologically equal, as Yu suggests, but there can be no doubt that the representation of natural elements was, to Mao, a way of expressing additional information about the human action described in the *Odes*.[58] Hence, the images drawn from the natural realm are always subordinated to the human realm in the Mao School of poetic rhetoric. And this subordination of vehicle (nature) to tenor (humans) constitutes a linguistic transference, a *metaphora*.

Chinese Allegoresis

Would it be accurate to call the Confucian exegesis of the *Book of Odes* an allegorical mode of interpretation? Yes, to the extent that we can use Western concepts to describe non-Western literary phenomena. There are several reasons for my postponed answer to be in the affirmative. The first concerns the view of allegoresis as a method to willfully distort a text. Yu holds that Maureen Quilligan's definition of allegoresis as the "manipulations that a reader can make with a text" would not be a fitting description of Confucian exegesis.[59] Contrary to the Western allegorist, the Confucian exegete never felt that he deviated from the literal sense of the text. Although King Wen and the queen consort are not mentioned in "Guanju" they are nonetheless *literal*, since they emerge from the process of historical contextualization; that is, the anchoring of the poem in a specific time and place. Yet Quintilian's canonical description of allegory in *Institutio Oratoria* as "presenting one thing in words and another—sometimes the very opposite of those words—in meaning" allows for a more generous application of the term; Western allegory does not exclusively aim for a metaphysical, Platonic truth enigmatically concealed in the text.[60]

Indeed, even the time-honored allegorical interpretations of *The Song of Songs* as an allegory about the marriage between Christ and the Church share a fundamental exegetical mechanism with the Mao school hermeneutics.[61] When the groom and bride of the biblical love song are identified as, respectively, Christ and the members of the Church, the figurative organization of the poem is maintained, albeit with a different personage. In Mao's reading of "Guanju" we recognize the same strategy of allegorical identification, enabling the Confucian reader to "manipulate" the text.

As a final example, consider Quintilian's analysis of a passage from the beginning of the ninth song of Virgil's *Bucolics*—or the *Eclogues*—and its description of one of its main characters, the shepherd and poet Menalcas, who has been forced to leave his farm.[62] Quintilian understands the lines about Menalcas metapoetically, as an allegorical self-portrait of Virgil himself; it is a subspecies of allegory *sine translatione*, "without metaphor."[63] Here, Quintilian's interpretation differs from Mao's reading of "Guanju," but not through a transfer from the concrete to the abstract (since neither Menalcas nor Virgil are abstract or metaphysical entities).[64] The difference rather lies in how the two hermeneuts manipulate their respective poem, which in turn simply reflects the difference in rhetorical or imagistic organization therein, not an ontological divide between East and West. Song nine of the *Bucolics* speaks only of the shepherd, and Quintilian's identification of him as Virgil is consequently purely an extratextual addition. Mao's reading of "Guanju" banks on the supposition that the *jujiu* birds metaphorically represent the young couple, and also on the allegorical (and "extratextual") identification of the young lovers with the royal couple. Mao's allegoresis is overall identical to Quintilian's, as both recognize the text's literal meaning but give it a new significance through what could be called an allegorical identification. Both exegetical procedures on which Mao's reading rests—one insisting that there is a "likeness" (indicated by the copula *ruo*) between animal and man in that both exemplify virtue; one allegorical and metonymical, referring outside the text—are necessary for Mao in his transformation of "Guanju" from erotic song to Confucian dogma.

9

Discipline and Comfort

The *comparatisme de la différence*

François Jullien's *La valeur allusive*, according to a review that appeared in *Harvard Journal of Asiatic Studies* in 1994, is "both a useful supplement to, and a confirmation of, the directions Chinese poetry scholars in America have been taking."[1] The reviewer, who is here referring to Yu's *The Reading of Imagery* and Stephen Owen's 1985 *Traditional Chinese Poetry and Poetics*, takes "comfort in realizing that these three scholars, working more or less independently, have come to very much the same conclusions on the aesthetic and metaphysical roots of the Chinese reading tradition." Owen, Yu, and Jullien have laid down and elaborated the "theoretical basis" for the "hitherto unexpressed assumptions" in "the field of Chinese poetry studies."[2]

The choice of word ("comfort") is noteworthy, as is the timeline. Twenty-five years separate Jullien's, Yu's, and Owen's books from Cecile Sun's study, published by the prestigious Chicago University Press in 2011, but the "theoretical basis" remains unshaken.

Again, a more detailed discussion of "sino-methodologies" takes place elsewhere, but François Jullien's candid exposition of his methodological and theoretical assumptions helps us understand not only how mainstream Sinology functions (and comforts its practitioners) but also how easy it would be to depart from near-identical assumptions and arrive at very different conclusions. *La valeur allusive*—Jullien's important 1985 study of early Chinese poetics in general and the concept of xing in particular—is formulated as a critique of and corrective to Sinology, and Sinology's habit of describing (and unconsciously distorting) the early Chinese literary

79

tradition by uncritically using a Western terminology sprung from very different cultural, historical, and philosophical circumstances. Adhering to Western schemes of thought, Jullien argues, severely limits the Sinologist's perspective, and by posing the questions he or she has inherited from the Western tradition, the Sinologist can only turn Chinese literary criticism into a "pale reflection" of its Western counterpart.[3] The Sinologist should not turn to the Chinese tradition for answers to questions habitually posed by the Western tradition but rather "discover other questions and, furthermore, discover that some questions that he has always asked himself—since they could not not have been asked—have never been asked outside of his own cultural context, being unable to be asked outside of it."[4] The reviewer is thus slightly off the mark when he suggests that Jullien merely expresses "hitherto unexpressed assumptions." Jullien is rather fine-tuning the Sinological analytical machinery by locating a flaw in its design.

Jullien illustrates the Sinologist's predicament with a reference to James Liu's classic *Chinese Theories of Literature*. Liu, Jullien says, accepts M. H. Abrams's Western conception of the author of a literary work without considering that early Chinese poetics conceived of the process leading to a literary work, or text, in a radically different manner. The Western notion of the author

> is based on a conception of the subject brought out very early on by our linguistic categories, one which our entire history of philosophy has endeavored to take charge of. However, nothing allows us to suppose that such a category was so decisive in the representation that the Chinese have developed regarding the emergence of literature: according to the "original" conception that is theirs, the order of the literary is naturally linked to the order of the World, of which the created work represents both a deployment and an accomplishment (of which our "author" appears only—rather—as the channel).[5]

Jullien here makes two gestures that I would call arch-Sinological. He opposes the Western author (who consciously crafts a literary artifact) to the Chinese "author" (who channels the world and whose emotive response results in an "artistic" expression), and claims that the Chinese and Western traditions of thought are determined by the respective linguistic idiom in which they are formulated. What is the consequence for Sinological methodology? Jullien's answer—the gist of which, in my opinion, is correct—is that Sinology is always and everywhere a comparative enterprise. The Sinologist, who strives to understand the Chinese tradition from the outside, must "preserve within any comparative thinking that which constitutes the original perspective of both cultures, the internal and intimate relationship on which a particular field of representations builds, this primitive and unique gesture through which each of these conceptions came about."[6]

Again, Jullien's claim is quite correct if one takes this to mean that the Sinologist's "réflextion comparatiste" should not be a quest for Chinese near-equivalents to Western topics, tropes, and categories ("metaphor," "epic," "aesthetics," "philosophy") but rather involve a heightened sensitivity—the direct result of an intimate knowledge of the Western tradition—for the particular configurations of the Chinese discourses. Qian Zhongshu 錢鍾書 (1910–1998), for all his erudition and ingenuity, produces catalogues of near-identical formulations from the Chinese, Indian, and Western traditions but often fails, in Jullien's opinion, to account for what makes a certain topic or trope significant within its own traditional context.[7]

Jullien makes two further, and interconnected, comments on Sinology as a comparative enterprise. Since the Western and the Chinese traditions developed independently, "The comparative enterprise cannot take root in any concrete location . . . and thus necessarily has an 'utopic' (or, rather, 'atopic') character." And furthermore,

> the position assumed here is therefore deliberately that of an essentially fictitious comparison, but one enhanced by its heuristic capacity since it cannot remain without effect vis-à-vis the representations concerned: from this external point of view assumed by the comparatist, certain essential "choices" can more easily be brought to light, certain initial orientations that characterize a particular civilization but are so deeply anchored in it that it itself no longer perceives them, no longer pays them any attention, and conveys them only in the form of platitudes and banalities.[8]

Let us contextualize. One may object to Jullien defining his comparative project in opposition to what is a rather dated methodology hailing from the comparative linguistics of the nineteenth century, as if comparative literature, poetics, or philosophy were usually equated with establishing genealogies of schools of thought and of themes and styles with a shared, if distant, origin. Such a critique, however, would be anachronistic. For

Jullien, writing in the early 1980s, the implicit reference is rather to Austin Warren and René Wellek's vision of, and prescription for, the discipline of comparative literature in *Theory of Literature* (the influence of which is also manifested in the title of James Liu's work). Warren and Wellek write that "one must recognize a close unity which includes all Europe, Russia, the United States, and the Latin American literatures."[9] That the comparatist "must recognize" the "unity" of European-Western-Russian-Latin literature means that the work that Jullien strives to do—and that we also try to accomplish—is a comparison in the second degree: one "must" realize that Western literatures spring from the same origin and, conversely, that early Chinese literature can be "compared" to its Western counterpart only with difficulty and in a roundabout manner.

This is, admittedly, a myopic reading of a short passage in Wellek and Warren's great book, but I suggest that it is precisely this heritage that Jullien reacts against yet cannot help being determined by. Equally important is Jullien's remark about the comparatist approach as being "essentially fictional," which cannot be underestimated as an explanation of his particular brand of sinology—both in *La valeur allusive* and his later works—especially when read in conjunction with the following statement:

> the comparatist sinologist will therefore have no other resource than to operate in a strategical manner by focusing first and foremost on the punctual: working from individual representations that seem to him or her particularly representative of a certain cultural context as a whole, so as to be able to confront them with the external cultural field of the other civilization.[10]

The ambition to unravel, in the Chinese tradition, "certain essential 'choices'" and "certain initial orientations" that are too obvious for the native Chinese reader is methodologically important—but only, I suggest, as a first step. Jullien should be praised for elaborating a methodology for "comparative sinology." But a comparative reading that aims at punctual analyses of "initial orientations" runs the obvious risk of producing caricatures, rather than in-depth studies, of the Chinese and Western traditions.

This slightly long-winded discussion of Sino-methodologies is necessary to explain the peculiarity of Jullien's treatment of the xing in the *Mao Commentary*; it is shrewd but neither extensive nor deeply probing, precisely for the reasons I enumerate above. Let us distinguish between the formalism and the historization in Jullien's study. Jullien's *formal* analysis of

Mao's xing—influenced (like mine) by Zhu Ziqing's all-important study—is perceptive and respects the integrity and idiosyncrasies of the *Commentary* without either anachronistically reading it through earlier or later texts or conflating Mao's exegetical and ideological tool with other cognate but different uses of the term "xing." Jullien says at first that for Mao, "who assigns a primary importance to it, the notion of xing is generally used to designate the particular manner in which, in many poems of the *Book of Odes*, the first line(s) serve(s) to evoke a natural and concrete motif before the human theme, carrying a psychological or moral sense, is developed."[11]

Later he adds that "through all the examples furnished by the *Mao-zhuan*, the only constant trait of the xing is that it introduces the [natural] motif (at the beginning of the stanza)" and that Mao's xingish reading of the second ode is metonymic rather than metaphoric—three formal observations that are inconspicuous but precise and important.[12] Let me now formulate my objections. Jullien, as we know, champions a "fictive comparison" in order to reach what is "intrinsically original" in the Chinese tradition and to reach beyond facile similarities between the Western and Chinese traditions. In other words, Jullien believes (again, quite correctly) that it is insufficient to define a Chinese concept such as xing according to Western categories, as being, for example, "analogical," "metaphorical," or "metonymical." The Sinologist must instead contextualize the Chinese concept by situating it within the Chinese tradition, and perhaps has an advantage over the Chinese scholar in that he or she may perceive new connections in material to which the "native" scholar has become all too accustomed: such is Jullien's case for a comparative approach.

But the most crucial methodological question remains unanswered: How does the Sinologist find the point of entrance that will correctly contextualize a Chinese concept? In the passage quoted above, Jullien criticizes James Liu for uncritically using Western concepts in his analyses of early Chinese literature, Liu thereby tacitly assuming that the two traditions are principally similar. It may be said, however, that the mainstream Sinological assumption—that of Jullien, Owen, and Yu, in the reviewer's list—is indeed an exact but inverted replica of that attributed to Liu. If Liu holds that the Western concept of author is by and large compatible with the Chinese one, then Owen holds that the Western concept of *poiesis* ("poetry, creation") is fundamentally incompatible with the Chinese notion of *shi*, since *shi* is not a product of a conscious act of creation but the result of a process in which external impressions force themselves upon the bard, compelling him to express himself spontaneously.[13] Yu, as we know, holds that the Western concept of allegory is fundamentally alien to the Confucian exegesis of the *Odes*, although it may *seem* allegorical at first glance. And Jullien, having concluded (correctly) that the only constant characteristic of Mao's xing is that it introduces the theme of the poem that it starts off, continues by stating that "its originality derives from its capacity to incite [*la valeur d'incitation*]: aroused by contact with the World (the order of *wu* 物), poetic consciousness expresses itself spontaneously through the natural elements that constitute its landscape, and this motif itself serves as an invitation to a more organized discursive development directly related to the affective or psychological situation of the subject."[14] The gap between a formal analysis and what Jullien calls "une comparaison essentiellement *fictive*" is nowhere more exposed than here. To the dry, matter-of-fact account of Mao's xing is added a contextualization that aims at placing xing in its proper Chinese and non-Western historical place. Like Gu Jiegang, Jullien associates xing with the cosmological and emotional processes that force man to express himself in song and dance and, further, with the notions of spontaneity, external influence, and *shi* as anti*poiesis*. This conclusion, as we shall see (and as I discuss in greater detail elsewhere), is determined not only by a disproportionate emphasis on the *Great Preface* but also, in particular, by a certain time-honored interpretation of the *Preface* that should be called into question.

The present study focuses in the main on, in the reviewer's ambiguous phrase, "Chinese poetry scholars" who describe the early Chinese tradition by problematizing intercultural translation, but the tendency among more traditional Chinese and Japanese *Shijing* scholars of the twentieth and twenty-first centuries is also to combine a formal analysis of the concept of xing with speculations about how the *Odes* emerged in and from a moment of overwhelming emotional excitement; Jullien's occidental sideways glance at the Chinese tradition does not, in this case, reveal anything extraordinary.[15] But—regardless of the cultural, ethnic, or ideological background of the person posing the question—is this the *correct* contextualization? It is undoubtedly a tempting one since it enables the discipline of comparative literature, and Sinology as Jullien conceives it, to describe *systematically* the Chinese tradition as eccentric and as an exotic alternative to the Western one. In this respect, Jullien's long-spanning project has faithfully obeyed the Warren-Wellek exhortation to "recognize a close unity which includes all Europe, Russia, the United States, and the Latin American literatures."

10

Dichotomy Reenforced

Cecile Sun's 2011 study, *The Poetics of Repetition in English and Chinese Lyric Poetry*, reads like a synthesis of the conclusions drawn by Chen Shih-hsiang, Pauline Yu, François Jullien et al. It is thereby a prime example of a grand Sinological narrative that postulates a sharp, neat, and symmetrical division between the Western and Chinese respective traditions.

Sun's readings are illuminated by an extraordinary sensibility for the complex fabric of imagery, rhymes, assonances, allusions, and puns that make up the poems in question.[1] The theoretical and methodological assumptions are wobblier, often expressed in general terms and in slightly convoluted language. Early Chinese poetry and poetics are said to be rooted in "the primordial resonance between man and nature universally embraced in Chinese culture," and the "crucial distinction" between the Western and the Chinese traditions lies in the fact that "both lyrical relationships intersect at the point of expressing inner reality through correlation with outer reality."[2] In the Western tradition inner reality is expressed through an "explicit transference (in the case of metaphor)," in contradistinction to the Chinese tradition and its "implicit rapport (in the case of the 'scene-feeling'-relationship)."[3] Furthermore, "the interaction [between tenor and vehicle] is directed by an anthropomorphic dominance, demonstrating . . . a metaphorical thinking typical of the Western tradition." And, finally, "the most significant and radical distinction between English and Chinese poetry . . . is the dominance of *mimesis* in one tradition and that of 興 *xing* in the other."[4] Like with Jullien, Sun's will to elevate "xing" to the status of the main artery in the body of Chinese culture is neither original nor an insight resulting from the privileged vantage point of a Sinologist with a command of both the

Western and Chinese traditions but wholly in line with what Chinese and Japanese scholars such as Zhao Peilin, Peng Feng, Li Zehou, and Shirakwa Shizuka have been claiming since at least the 1980s and, before them, C. H. Wang and Chen Shih-hsiang. What concerns me is the drive to dichotomize.

The East-West dichotomy that Sun proposes is, Sinologically speaking, quite conventional and may be paraphrased as follows. Metaphor, the arch-trope of the Western metaphysical tradition, banks on a distinction between the sensible vehicle and the abstract tenor. The Chinese poetic tradition (embodied in what Sun calls "xing") merely correlates and juxtaposes but does not establish a hierarchy. The *jujiu* and the young couple in "Guanju" coincide in the poem on an equal ontological footing, whereas in a metaphor the vehicle is by necessity subordinated to the tenor. For example, when Arthur Rimbaud writes "Ainsi, j'ai aimé un porc," *porc* does not refer to the ungraceful animal that rolls around in filth and eats swill but to a man with swinelike qualities: the primary, *natural* referent of *porc*—sus scrofa domestica—has been bypassed—suppressed—in exchange for a more abstract, anthropomorphic meaning.[5] Sun links, moreover, this Chinese and supposedly xingish lack of metaphoric hierarchy and subjugation to what she perceives as a typically Chinese mode of poetic creation. Consider the following quote, which is a condensation of the ideas and the vocabularies of C. H. Wang, Xu Fuguan, Chen Shih-hsiang, and Pauline Yu: "In Chinese poetry, the predominant thrust lies in the implicit and spontaneous correlation between 'feeling' and 'scene,' evoked in the poetic medium as an ideal expression of what might have taken place during the creative process, namely, the dynamic resonance between poet and what is encountered in nature."[6]

I analyze the larger thought pattern of which these ideas are a part elsewhere and will in this context only indicate that, if taken as a study of the xing as it appears in Mao Heng's *Commentary*, Sun's analysis is wrongheaded. As I hope to prove in the course of this study, Mao's xing is an exegetical tool precisely for establishing or underscoring a hierarchy between (representations of) nature and human action, subjugating the former to the latter. Indeed, in Sun's terminology, the vast majority of Mao's xing are metaphorical.

11

Uncomfortable Sinology

Confucian Exegesis as a Performative Mode of Reading

What constitutes the Western tradition of mimesis and metaphoricity? What are this tradition's most distinctive features? The inventiveness, the creative instinct, the "reshaping of reality," according to Pauline Yu. But if so, to what extent? And to what extent do these extraordinary traits differ from the ways of Confucian exegesis? Expanding on and systematizing Isocrates's notion of a linguistic "tranferefence" (*metaphora*), Aristotle did not simply hold that to "metaphorize well" (*eu metaphorein*) was an imposing art; he also emphasized that the mastery of metaphor necessarily entails a well-developed sense of proportion and propriety.[1] More specifically, to "metaphorize well" is to "perceive the likeness" (*to homoion theorein*) between disparate objects or actions. A functioning *metaphora* must therefore, one assumes, be drawn from objects or actions linked by an a priori likeness or correspondence, a likeness that may not be obvious but that nonetheless cannot be created *ex nihilo*. A good metaphor can bring to light hitherto unseen affinities but never convincingly establish affinities not condoned by reality. It cannot in fact reshape reality; nor is this implied by Aristotle's statement that metaphorizing and the "perception of the similar cannot be learnt from others."

The notion of "metaphorizing well," then, should not be confused with catachresis—abuser of language and bastard son of metaphor proper. Indeed, the unorthodox and insane interbreeding of logical categories performed by the catachresis is more akin to Yu's conception of Western metaphor than is Aristotle's mildly innovative version.[2] Let us elaborate. Metaphor, to the Chinese tradition as interpreted by Pauline Yu, is a perverter of reality. For the Chinese *bard* (the word "poet," as we know, derives from the Greek *poiein* and an Occidental conception of artistic creation) there is no intermediate stage of artistic deliberation between inspiration and poetic articulation; when overwhelmed with emotions he spontaneously bursts out in a poesy that more resembles a natural object than an artifact. The Chinese bard *responds* to external stimuli but does not create.[3] One obvious consequence of such a poetics is that it stresses the psychology of the moment of inspiration to the point that it precludes any discussions on poetic method or technique. Method equals deliberation, which is an equation that does not tally well with the notion of poetry as a spontaneous response to cosmological processes. But is this reading of the *Great Preface* an adequate contextualization of Mao's *Commentary*? As this introductory part is drawing to a close we must conclude that this is not the case. With the *Maozhuan* came a revolution, synthesizing what we may call "phenomenological poetics" and "rhetorical analysis."

It has been my intention, in this part, to show that the view of poetry as the spontaneous response to cosmological phenomena yields a skewed description of the Chinese poetic text as literal and nonfigurative (and of the early Chinese hermeneutical tradition as espousing only those characteristics). Furthermore, I have suggested (and intend to further demonstrate) that the highly rhetorical mode of exegesis that revolved around the concept xing in Mao's *Commentary* strongly argues against the common Sinological analysis. As a bridge between the first and second parts, let us try to indicate the nature of and historical background to Mao Heng's xingish readings of the *Odes*. For this purpose we will consider some observations in Haun Saussy's 1993 study *The Problem of a Chinese Aesthetic*.[4] The first is a note in passing on the term *fuhui* 附會, a derogatory word frequently used by modern scholars about less convincing allegorical readings.[5] The phrase, which nowadays can be located somewhere on a semantic scale ranging from "impertinent" and "farfetched" to "absurd," originally (and literally) meant "'addition [of meaning] from outside.'"[6] As Saussy observes, the etymological meaning gives us a hint about the kernel of Confucian hermeneutical methodology, namely its extratextuality. But the addition of external meaning to a text never posed a problem to readers in antiquity. On the contrary, the hallmark of a good reader was the refinement he or she could perform on the text. It is symptomatic of the problematic relationship between ancient and modern *Shijing* scholarship that the trait once celebrated now serves as an invective.

We recall Marcel Granet's tenet that the Confucian exegetes willfully distorted a poetic text that originally was characterized by literalism, concretion, and authorial presence. With the same point of departure, but without

Granet's assumptions about textual concretion and Confucian hermeneutics, Saussy paints a very different picture. He locates the arch metaphor of Confucian exegesis in and around the ninth ode, "Han guang" 漢廣:

> In the south there are tall trees; one cannot rest under them.
> On the Han there are frolicking girls; one cannot ask for them.
> The Han is so broad, you cannot wade it;
> the Chiang is so long, you cannot cross it by raft.
>
> The thick firewood grows tall; I cut thorn from among it.
> Here a bride is setting out to be married; I feed her pony.
> [. . .]
>
> The thick firewood grows high; I cut the stalks of the *lü* plant.
> Here a bride is setting out to be married; I feed her colt.
> [. . .]⁷

We instantly recognize the themes of passionate lust and longing. Even the mysterious, elusive and seductive girls who "frolic" on the Han River, and whom the author of "Guanju" correlates with the image of the screaming *jujiu*, are present in this ode. Not surprisingly, the Confucian tradition comes up with a cunning scheme to convert the lustful poem into a moralizing piece. The *Preface* says that it "shows the vast spread of virtue."

"Han guang" is thus construed as an account of how the virtuous influence of King Wen transformed (*hua* 化) every part of the southern states. Moving into the particulars, Saussy describes how later exegetes performed a thoroughly metaphorical reading to make the poem fit the pattern laid down by the *Preface*.⁸ The poet's description of the high trees (identified as the xing-component) was further defined as "trees with high branches"—which consequently give no shade and are useless for resting under. The comparison between the xing-element and the "wandering girls" on the Han amounts to saying that the girls are so virtuous, as a result of the spread of King Wen's virtue, that they cannot be approached without the proper rituals, just as it is impossible to rest under the highly branched trees. To the Confucian exegetes, the ninth ode is thus a moralizing piece about the importance of proper nuptial rites. For Zheng Xuan, the protagonist who cuts thorns and stalks and feeds the girl's horses is a rite-abiding bridegroom.⁹ In Zheng's reading, the poem builds on an analogy; cutting the thorn—the tallest among the firewood—means that the narrator wants the purest and most virtuous of all the girls wandering by the River Han. By feeding the bride's horses, the bridegroom indicates (without explicitly saying so) that the bride is meant for him: "By carrying out the ritual, I let my wishes be known."[10]

"Whenever the poem speaks of menial labor the commentators allegorize it," Saussy observes and quotes Chen Huan (1786–1863): "Man and woman need ritual to become complete, just as firewood needs human labor . . . to be bound up into bundles."[11] Saussy concludes that the enterprise of interpreting "Han guang" evolves from a founding metaphor that describes ritual in terms of work and vice versa. In a complex pattern this two-way metaphor (work equals ritual which equals work) folds and unfolds, expands, and recedes, until it permeates the entire hermeneutical practice of the Confucian tradition—and itself becomes *the* metaphor for the exegesis of the *Odes*.

At this point in Zheng Xuan's interpretation the narrator is no longer simply a bridegroom posing as a woodcutter and horse-feeder (work that the gentry would likely be loath to perform) to show off his adherence to rituals. He now represents the ideal ritual worker, who in a true Confucian spirit creates virtue from a refractory raw material (just as, one may add, the Xunzian Superior Man both falsifies and refines base human nature). At one level in the series of oscillations between literalism and metaphoricity and between "work" and "ritual" that make up the Confucian reading of "Han guang," the bridegroom/woodcutter is he who trims the southern trees so that they will not encourage people to idly repose in their shade; yet at another level, he does so in order that they may serve as a metaphor for the virtuous river girls. The Confucian worker of rites is like—if a blasphemous simile may be allowed—a hoodlum in reverse who steals into town, does his business, and leaves nothing but virtue and pure hearts behind.

Saussy argues that the work-rite metaphor bodies forth the hermeneutical project of the Confucian exegete. Just like the woodcutting bridegroom in the poem, the Confucian reader had to conduct an interpretation beyond philological annotations and mere paraphrases of the text's content; he was supposed to *perfect* the textual raw material that the text in question presented. We may illustrate Saussy's thesis with Xunzi's description of how the Confucian Superior Man (*junzi*) "bends and unbends as the occasion demands" 與時屈伸, a description equally applicable to the ideal hermeneut, "flexible . . . like rushes and reeds" 柔從若蒲葦, who "bends and unbends" the text to make it decorous.[12] Even more pertinent in this context, as suggested just now, is Xunzi's insistence on the need for a "falsification," or "re-working" (*wei* 偽), of man's evil nature.[13] We may in Xunzi's concept of *wei* see a parallel between the painstaking refashioning of man's imperfections by way of Confucian rituals and the true hermeneut's attitude toward the poetic text. The reader has to be a "strong" reader and must *work* on the text, perfecting it in accordance with Confucian ritual thinking. Saussy calls this a performative mode of reading.[14] And we may tentatively confirm Saussy's thesis by locating a passage where a decree to a Confucian "ritual" reading is implied, if not explicitly pronounced. When the *Zuo Commentary*—on which Mao often builds his readings—calls the *Odes* (and the *Documents*) a "storehouse of righteousness" (*yi zhi fu* 義之府), it is a fact that Mao and his colleagues must a priori accept and adjust to.[15] Consequently, when Mao sits down to comment on the text he already knows that the *Odes* contain exemplary expressions of righteousness—all he has to do is find them. It is, therefore, partly as a tool for a ritualized reading that we should regard Mao's xing, although the word "partly" should be emphasized, since Mao's xingish readings of the *Odes* are not merely performative in the above sense but also constitute an embryonic but systematic literary hermeneutics.

As we shall see in the second part, the practice of xing is ambivalent and illogical only if considered a tool for formal analysis. The xing serves the two contradictory purposes of alternately revealing *and* obscuring the poetic text, in an act of interpretation determined a priori by the demand that the *Odes* make Confucian sense.

12

Primary Metapoetics, Authorial Intent, and Textual Integrity in the *Odes*

Although my main concern is early Han dynasty interpretations of the *Odes*, by claiming that the xing, as an interpretational tool, not only enables Mao to make the *Odes* "speak Confucianism" but also (at least every now and then) adequately reveal how they are constructed rhetorically, I implicitly make a statement about the poems themselves. With reference to "Guanju," I thus argue that although Mao's identification of the poem's female protagonist—the "beautiful and good lady"—as a *houfei* 后妃 is unwarranted as the text itself neither mentions a "queen consort" nor needs this supplementation to be fully comprehensible, meaningful, or aesthetically pleasing, his metaphorical, xingish identification of the "beautiful and good lady" with the screaming osprey is supported by the poem itself, as I explain below.

To push the inquiry one step further, I pose the following question: Is the phrase "supported by the poem itself" not a faint-hearted way of speaking about authorial intent and of saying, for instance, that the person or persons who "authored" the first ode "intended" the description of the ospreys to function as a statement about the protagonists? Although our knowledge of the origins of the *Odes* is severely limited, do they not sometimes impart at least a minimal knowledge of the authors, their intentions, and rhetorical techniques? I would answer in the affirmative and take this opportunity to expand briefly on the questions of authorship, intention, and textual integrity in the *Odes*.

Consider, as a first step, the heterogeneity of the *Odes*. An ode such as "Yu li" 魚麗 (no. 170) seems to be more formulaic—in C. H. Wang's sense, with motifs, themes, and topics joined together somewhat randomly—than for instance ode 23, in whose three stanzas the topic and the imagery are introduced, developed, and brought to a conclusion.

The first of the six stanzas of "Yu li" goes as follows:

> The fish pass into the trap
> it is *chang* and *sha* [fish]
> Our lord has spirits
> exquisite and in abundance[1]

魚麗于罶
鱨鯊
君子有酒
旨且多

From the fourth stanza of "Wu yang" (ode 190), we know that the motif of fish was associated with agricultural abundance or fertility. In this ode—perhaps to be performed in a sacrificial setting—"fish" may have been used by the poet to make the listener associate to a state of abundance; or the fish, together with the "exquisite" spirits, may have suggested a sumptuous festive meal or sacrifice.[2] "Yu li" in any event appears to be a typical *Shijing* ode, with a description of a natural phenomenon as a preamble to an event in the human realm; the traditional, almost clichéd character of the poem is underlined by the simple, songlike rhyme scheme in which the last word of the first line ("trap" 罶) rhymes with the last word of the third line ("spirits" 酒), and the second word in line two (*sha* 鯊) with the last word of the stanza ("abundant" 多).

We observe further that the second and third stanzas are variants of the first, with the names of the fish changed, or with the word order changed, or with one word changed to a synonym, but with lines one and three, and also the rhyme scheme, remaining the same:

> The fish pass into the trap
> it is *fang* and *li* [fish]
> Our lord has spirits
> abundant and exquisite
>
> The fish pass into the trap
> it is *yan* and carp
> Our lord has spirits
> exquisite and plentiful

魚麗於罶
魴鱧
君子有酒
多且旨
魚麗於罶
鰋鯉
君子有酒
旨且有

At this point—after the first three stanzas and before the last three—I shall comment briefly and tangentially on a recent debate concerning the composition and origins of *Shi* (understood broadly as the *Odes* or poems in that tradition).[3] Although the interpretation of "Yi li" presents few problems linguistically, the questions of the "authorial intent" behind this ode, and of how it came to be included in the canonical *Book of Odes* in this particular format, are more complex. I suggested above that it might have been performed on sacrificial or festive occasions, but it is also possible that it was construed as such by the compilers who may have wanted to create the *Shijing* as a monument to proto-Confucian customs, in which case the notion of an ode titled "Yu li" and originally performed in a ritual setting was part of the message that this *Shijing* poem wished to convey.

In other words, the origin—the moment when the poem supposedly was performed in its proper, organic context and fully understandable to poet and listener alike—may itself be imaginary, inscribed into "Yu li" as an implicit layer of meaning. This prompts the question, again, of the supposed authors of the *Odes*, and of how an understanding of the *Odes* is colored by the assumptions that the reader makes regarding their creators and their intentions. Is "Yu li," in its capacity as poem 170 of the *Shijing*, the product of a poet who authored the six stanzas with the intention of having them performed in a ritual setting? Did he or she therefore match the theme of an abundance of food items with the fish motif because that connection was preestablished and sanctioned by tradition, as C. H. Wang would have argued, with theme and motif chosen from a limited but time-honored and culturally prestigious repertoire? If so, is this particular poetic product in its expression "wild" and "excessive," since the laws of the genre forced the poet to pair topic and motif with less precision than that granted to a poet outside a strong tradition? In other words, did tradition override the authorial intent?

In an attempt to answer these questions, I turn to what is perhaps the most conspicuously germane statement of the aforementioned debate: "The individual poem, if such a concept is even appropriate, was not generated by some original authorial intent but, to the contrary, arose in ever new form under specific circumstances."⁴

The crucial word is "intent," which seems to contradict the notion of a poem arising "under specific circumstances." How could a poem "arise" "under specific circumstances" without there being an "intent" of some kind behind it? I admittedly quote the author unfairly and out of context; what Martin Kern is arguing is that the "Qi ye" 耆夜 manuscript—dated to the third century BCE, championed by Qinghua University, and discussed at the beginning of this book—imparts important information about the "the textual identity of a poem in early China," and of its "authorship."⁵ Kern's slightly ambiguous phrase "some original authorial intent" must be read with an emphasis on "original"; when, as described in the "Qi ye," the Duke of Zhou recites (*zuo* 作) a song (*ge* 歌) titled "Xishuai" it is futile to ask if the duke's poem was older than, or derived from, the poem of the same name in the received *Book of Odes* (that is, to ask which poem is the original), since a poem or a song in the early tradition of the *Odes*—predating Mao's *Commentary* and perhaps also the *Zuozhuan*—was drawn from "sets of topics and phrases that could be compiled in modular ways, yielding ever new poems that were always similar but never the same."⁶ The poem called "Xishuai" in the "Qi ye" manuscript is, according to this theory, thus not a variation on the "Xishuai" of the received *Book of Odes* (or vice versa); rather, both poems are permutations of a traditional repertoire in which a certain theme was paired with certain generic formulae.⁷

Moreover, this early Chinese "performance culture" in which "existing repertoires of earlier performances and texts could be selectively reenacted" was "how ritual and cultural memory worked in premodern societies . . . where defining moments of a society's past were . . . continuously reimagined, reperformed, communicated, and perpetuated."⁸ This is probably entirely correct, but I should like to question the statement—integral to the theory of a typically early Chinese performance culture—that in "early China, there were arguments over ideas, but there was never an argument over texts."⁹ Consider here the chapter of the *Lüshi chunqiu* called "On the Necessity of Scrutinizing That Which Has Been Transmitted" ("Cha chuan" 察傳) and that describes Confucius's disciple Zixia 子夏 traveling to the state of Jin.¹⁰ Passing through the neighboring state of Wei, "someone read aloud (*du* 讀) from historical documents" 有讀史記者 and presented Zixia with the following account (or "tradition" [*chuan/zhuan* 傳]): "The Jin army and three pigs crossed the river" 晉師三豕涉河.

Reacting to the absurdity of this entry—why would the army have crossed the river in the company of three pigs and, if true, why would it have been recorded for posterity?—Zixia comments laconically: "This is incorrect. It should read 'on the *sihai* day,' for [the graphs] *si* and *san* are close [in form], and *zhu* and *hai* are similar" 非也, 是己亥也. 夫己與三相近, 豕與亥相似. The episode concludes with Zixia corroborating his suspicion upon his arrival in Jin: "He asked about this matter, and [someone in Jin] said 'The Jin army crossed the river on the *sihai* day'" 至於晉而問之則曰晉師己亥涉河也.

Although this early example of Chinese dry-wit humor is almost certainly a fictional account, it does inform us of the status and function of writing (or at least the conception thereof) before 239 BCE, when the *Lüshi chunqiu* was submitted to the court of Qin. Zixia, who is not a mere scribe but a prestigious disciple of Confucius, is being read an entry from a manuscript and immediately deducts that one of the scribes who had copied, and thus "transmitted," this passage had misread the graph 己 (*si*) for 三 ("three"), and the graph 亥 (*hai*) for 豕 ("pig"). Differently put, Zixia hears two specific sound-units and realizes that the scribe is seeing and pronouncing the graphs 三 and 豕, and that these are erroneous representations of graphs that are similar in form but carry totally different meanings and pronunciations.

I can but conclude that learned men such as Zixia were used to (or were conceived of as being used to) reading—and perhaps writing—manuscripts and had a profound knowledge both of the orthographic conventions of their age and of the stylistic features of such "historical documents." One may also conclude that some scribes, at least in the imagination of some thinkers in the third century BCE, were either incapable of detecting obvious mistakes in a transmitted text or too overwhelmed by the prestige of the document to dare to make an emendation.

More to the point, although a fine illustration of an oral "performance" of a "cultural memory," in this narrative the acts of writing, storing, transmitting (the *chuan* or *zhuan* 傳 of the chapter's title), controlling and correcting the manuscript are of central importance. Furthermore, while the original writer of the entry in the Annals of Jin is anonymous, it is not impossible that the figure of the scribe or "historian" (supposed to guarantee the veracity and integrity of the text) filled a function similar to that of an "author" and that also the person who read the passage out loud was identified as part of that community and carried the same authority with reference to the document or "record" (*ji* 記) thus read.

This passage from the *Lüshi chunqiu* offers no definitive or sustained evidence of what may be called a "culture of the text" in pre-Han China. Again, the humorous narrative of Zixia as a textual critic is most likely fictive, and it may be held that the notion of textual integrity expressed therein derives from what Kern describes as a "new textual culture in need of a stable historical past complete with genealogies of discrete texts, intellectual lineages, and individual authors" that emerged in "the late third century BCE."[11] It nonetheless suggests that the claim that in "early China, there were arguments over ideas, but there was never an argument over texts" is a tad too categorical.[12] Perhaps the reason there are few recorded arguments "over texts" is that they were ubiquitous to the point of being banal.[13]

Similarly, although the question of an *original* "authorial intent" may be moot, according to the logic of the narrative of the "Qi ye" manuscript, the poem titled "Xishuai" certainly represents, and was a product of, the intent of its composer; it represents—perhaps imperfectly, as do all linguistic utterances—the message the duke wanted to communicate through his poem at the drinking party in celebration of the victory over the state of Qi.

The Duke of Zhou is the author of this poem, and his intent, and the context in which it is articulated, is the guide to a proper understanding thereof—and this according to a text dated to 300 BCE.

Primary Metapoetics

A few odes contain what I, using a makeshift term, call a primary metapoetics in that they explicitly comment upon their own mode of production, performance, or interpretation, whereas metapoetics otherwise is typically implicit.[14] "Wu yang" (ode 190) is a prominent example, and I reiterate that the "great man's" seemingly bizarre interpretation of the imagery emerging in the shepherd's dreams prefigures methodologically the sometimes outlandish and ostensibly illogical interpretations that Mao Heng performs on the *Odes* (and to some extent also Freud's concept of displacement, *Verschiebung*, in his *Traumdeutung*).[15] Thus, although the *Commentary* is foremost governed by an ambition to transform the *Odes* into Confucian dogma, technically speaking Mao's readings have a direct antecedent in the *Odes* themselves and probably also in the mantic traditions of the oracle bones and the *Zhouyi*.

Meaningless Repetition—Thematic Development

I return to the question, which Kern shares with C. H. Wang and the tradition of *Shijing* interpretation of which Wang was a part, of whether the authorial intent—and by extension the text's "integrity"—is less pronounced in poems "compiled in modular ways." Wang's claim about the "wild" and "excessive" metaphoricity of formulaic, or modular, composition suggests that the bard had to be less precise than he or she may have intended so as to keep within the traditional repertoire of topics, themes, and motifs. Kern makes a similar claim with regard to the repetitiveness of certain pieces in the *Shijing*, and writes about ode 152, "Shijiu" 鳲鳩 ("The *Shijiu* Bird"), that while "the four stanzas differ in some of the details, they are nothing more than variations on one another. If there were another three stanzas, they would do just the same; if a stanza went missing, nothing would be lost."[16]

The "textual integrity" of a poem from which one stanza could be removed, or to which three could be added, without any significant change in meaning (which is how I interpret the proposition that under such circumstances "nothing would be lost") is seriously compromised. What I tentatively call "textual integrity" should not be conflated with the notion of "authorial intent," but they are, at least in some cases, related. In a perceptive article, Hung Kuo-liang 洪國樑 (b. 1949) has challenged the opinion that many odes originally consisted of one stanza that was subsequently repeated with minimal variation by the people who performed them in a ritual setting, and who wanted the lyrics to be longer in order to fit the tune.[17] Hung instead claims that in such stanzaic repetitions the poem's theme is often developed in subtle ways, which would indicate that the ode in question contains an intentional narrative progression that would be disturbed if one or more stanzas were removed.[18]

Yet to pit one theory again the other would, I opine, create a false opposition. Kern's claim (". . . nothing would be lost") is valid with reference to "Yi li," to which I now belatedly return. Its second and third stanzas are simply variations on the first, and although there is a noticeable metric change, the last two stanzas repeat rather than develop the fourth:

The abundance of the[se] objects
and their excellence!
The exquisiteness of the[se] objects
and their orderliness!

The plentifulness of the[se] objects
and their timeliness!

物其多矣
維其嘉矣
物其旨矣
維其偕矣
物其有矣
維其時矣

But while one or two stanzas could arguably be added to or subtracted from "Yi li" without any substantial change in meaning, an ode like "Ye you si jun" 野有死麕 (The wilderness holds a dead deer) is quite different. As discussed previously, according to a passage in the *Zuozhuan* a high official named Zipi "recited" or "presented" (*fu*) the "final stanza" of ode 23 at a meeting in the state of Zheng.[19] That the *Zuozhuan* entry suggests that this particular poem was indeed fixed in 541 BCE (or was considered fixed at that time when the *Zuozhuan* was composed) is interesting in its own right; my objective in this context, however, is to demonstrate that the cohesion, and thus the integrity, of the poem as it appears in the Mao edition is much greater than that of "Yi li."[20]

The motif of the dead deer and the topic of a young woman with nascent lustful "spring feelings" in the first stanza of ode 23 are not repeated with minimal (and meaningless) variation in the second stanza; instead, and in keeping with Hung Kuo-liang's theory, they are developed and intensified.

The wilderness holds a dead deer
white grass wraps it
There is a girl with spring feelings
an auspicious gentleman leads her astray

In the woods there are sticks and shrubs
The wilderness holds a dead doe
white grass binds and entangles it
There is a girl like jade[21]

野有死麕
白茅包之

有女懷春
吉士誘之
林有樸樕
野有死鹿
白茅純束
有女如玉

Thus, if we read—ironically enough against the grain of Mao Heng's moralizing interpretation—the dead deer as a xingish representation of the young woman, the situation is growing more intense and threatening in the second stanza.[22] The grass no longer simply "wraps" the dead deer but "binds" and "entangles" the carcass; to wit, the girl is increasingly ensnared by the simultaneous feelings of lust and confusion and by the "auspicious gentleman" who "leads her astray."

With the third and final stanza, which consists of three exclamations from the girl and thereby effects a change in rhetorical mode from distanced representation to intimate vocal expression, there occurs a noticeable change in rhyme and meter, and the poem thus ends with a coda instead of a fade-out.

> Be gentle and slow
> Do not disturb my sash
> Do not make the dog . . . bark[23]

舒而脫脫兮
無感我帨兮
無使尨也吠

Thematically, the succinct final stanza further compounds the ambivalence between lust and fear, and between seduction and threat, that the previous two stanzas have presented. We also note that with their undertone of violence, the lines about the "ragged dog" (*mang* 尨) and touching the girl's sash—the "auspicious man" now threatens to invade the woman's most intimate space—activate the more morbid aspects of the main motif.[24] In light of the final stanza, the dead doe is thus belatedly revealed as a representation of a young girl overpowered by the force of an "auspicious man" and her own sexuality, and with "death" suggesting sexual climax, or rape and murder.

Although sketchy, my reading means to suggest that the textual or formal integrity of "The Wilderness Holds a Dead Doe" is far greater than that of "Yi li" in that every segment of the poem functions to move the narrative forward, and in that the implications of the final stanza are realized only after the first stanza is reread in view thereof (in other words, in that the poem is circular in its composition). While it cannot be ruled out that an *ur*-version of ode 23 consisted of what is now the first stanza or, conversely, that at some point additional stanzas were tacked on to the three stanzas to form an alternative version, I hold that in this particular case it would be incorrect to claim that "if a stanza went missing, nothing would be lost" and, as a consequence, indeed appropriate to speak of an "individual poem."

Supposing now that ode 23 is an "individual poem" characterized by a high degree of textual cohesion, does it inform us how and to what extent authorial intent and textual integrity relate? More precisely, do textual integrity and cohesion signal that a particular poem is the product of one author, who produced poetry (or *shi*) freed from the fetters of convention, and unambiguously expressed his or her intent, which could be decoded and reconstructed by a reader? The answers to this faux-naïve question can only be in the negative. Ode 23 could well have been produced by several authors and over a period of time, but it is likely that these authors worked within a tradition where motifs drawn from nature were typically used to represent situations in the human realm, as, for instance, in the first ode.

This remark may in turn seem wholly self-evident, but not only does the insight into the formal conventions and constrains of the *Odes* contradict Mao Heng's nonmetaphorical interpretation of ode 23, according to which the male protagonist presents a dead doe wrapped in white grass to the female protagonist as a primitive but nonetheless ritualized gift of betrothal; the formal conventions and constrains also indicate what the "authorial intent" was.[25] I add in passing that even if the compositional technique behind ode 23 was "modular" or "formulaic" it does not cancel out the question of authorial intent; nor does it follow that the poems thus composed could not be cohesive and intensely sophisticated in form. I emphasize that neither Kern not Wang make these claims explicitly; yet both Wang's description of formulaic poetry (whose metaphoricity is "wild") and Kern's similar statement to the effect that modular composing tends to produce poems in which "if a stanza went missing, nothing would be lost" seem to lead to those conclusions.

To ask of the *original* authorial intention would indeed be futile not only because we lack reliable information about the authorship and composition of what is now ode 23 but also—and from the exact opposite perspective—precisely because the poem does not have the open or unfinished quality of "Yi li." To a much higher degree than "Yi li," ode 23 creates its own context and, therefore, from the point of view of a history of Chinese literature, it seems likely that the intent of the author(s) of ode 23 was to produce a poem that should be read more or less as outlined above.[26]

An important caveat to this claim is the possibility that the poem may have been composed to be quoted out of its immediate context (designed, let us say, for a situation in which a representative for a small and weak state finds himself cajoled into a relationship that is intensely appealing but may lead to ruin), and that the seemingly primary erotic reading was only the prerequisite for the final realization of the poem as an allegory in and of a particular historical setting, but this objection is unrelated to the question of "unfinished" poems such as "Yi li" (where "if a stanza went missing, nothing would be lost"), and to the question of authorial intent of the kind discussed above.

Irony, Metapoetics, and Authorial Intent

As a final musing on textual integrity and authorial intent, consider what at least is a trace of irony and metapoetics in the *Odes*. Although we know nothing of the biography of the author of the two stanzas that constitute ode 184 ("Crane Calls"), and even though the second stanza is a close variation on the first, I argue that the poet's intent was at least partly to playfully overturn the convention of using natural descriptions as statements of human situations.

The two lines with which the poem opens do describe an event in nature ("The crane calls out in the Nine marshes / its voice is heard in the wilds") but they are not—as would the laws of the genre prescribe—followed by a description of human action but, surprisingly enough, by another natural motif ("the fish plunge in the deep / or lie by the islet"), and then by yet another ("Happy is that garden / There is a *Tan* tree / and thereunder withered leaves"). By so doing, the author refuses to put the motif of the calling crane to use as what Mao would later call a xing and, by the same token, refuses to endow the natural motif with ideological meaning. The last two lines of the stanza ("Stones of other mountains / can be used as whetstones") explicitly speak of a refusal to be used for a particular purpose.

That this is not an accidental deviation from the standard model of composing *shi* is demonstrated by the perfect overlap between form and content that this poem bodies forth—a convergence that testifies to its unity and cohesion. The celebration of uselessness that ode 184 takes at its theme is manifested and driven home by the author's ironic negation of the standard format; that is, the author's obviously intentional refusal to use a natural motif as a metaphorical statement for human action. Thus, on a metapoetic level, the poem—and perhaps the phenomenon of *shi* itself—is celebrated as a "useless" and nonutilitarian object or activity, analogous with the neglected but "joyous" garden and with the stones of "this" mountain that are not transformed into tools.

However objectionable or irrelevant one may find the concept of authorial intentionality in literary studies, my brief formalistic-thematic reading of "Crane Calls" is inevitably in part a reconstruction of an "original authorial intent." And although ironical odes such as "He ming" and "Da dong" (and also the nonironical "Ye you si jun") are not tied to an author, there lies precisely an *intention* in the playful deviation from a set scheme—in this instance, the xingshi correspondence of natural and human activity so prominent in the *Shijing* corpus—and I suggest that such intertextual referencing constitutes a form of authorial intention.

I return, finally, to the crucial word "original." With Kern, we remember, the phrase "original authorial intention" occurs as part of an argument leveled against the endeavor to find which of the two poems titled "Xishuai" (one in the received *Odes* and one found in the newly excavated "Qi Ye" manuscript) is the older and to establish a stemma of the *ur*-version of the poem and its subsequent variations. This undertaking, Kern holds, builds on a fallacy and forfeits the more pertinent and historically accurate understanding of how the early odes were improvised *ad hoc*, coupling certain (in C. H. Wang's terminology) themes and motifs in response to a certain historical situation and to elicit a certain response from their audience.

The school of *Shijing* interpretation to which Kern and C. H. Wang belong *categorically* describes authorial intent as flimsier than in my estimation: the ancient poets invariably composed odes by putting together stock phrases into units that only with great hesitancy could be called "individual poem[s]." My readings of "Yi li," "Ye you si jun," and "Crane Calls" have tried to refute—or at least complicate—that hypothesis. The notion of the author, and of his or her intentions, has proven surprisingly tenacious and persists also despite my own attempt to shift the emphasis to the more formal notion of "textual integrity."

Part Two

Xing and the Origins of Chinese Literary Hermeneutics

13

The Metaphor

A Return to Richards

While a more ambitious investigation of the overlaps and disjunctions between the Greek concept of *metaphora* and early Chinese poetics and language philosophy has been attempted elsewhere, I shall propose a working definition of "metaphor" suitable for the present investigation of Mao's *Commentary*, and of the xing as (let us say) a marker of a semantic change in a word or phrase.[1] As an alternative or complement to the all-pervasive conceptual metaphor theory (CMT), which I suggest is unable to explain fully the mechanisms and effects of rhetorical or literary metaphor, we shall briefly consider a theory formulated long before George Lakoff and Mark Johnson rode their tractor onto the field of metaphor studies, and that has made a partial comeback through the so-called deliberate metaphor theory (DMT) advanced by Gerard Steen.[2]

In a 2016 review of a book on Pindar and the "emergence of literature," the reviewer noted with surprise that the author "positions his [second] chapter within the early twentieth-century tenor-vehicle frame of metaphor developed by I. A. Richards and within analogous frames of other late nineteenth- and early twentieth-century intellectuals."[3] The reviewer explained, or justified, his feelings of misgiving by claiming that "specialists on metaphor theory have now moved away from using traditional metaphor theory in favor of using conceptual metaphor theory (developed by G. Lakoff and M. Johnson in their 1980 book *Metaphors We Live By*)," and he concluded that "given that conceptual metaphor theory has now been *empirically verified by cognitive scientists* (see, e.g., R. Gibbs, "Psycholinguistic studies on the conceptual basis of idiomaticity,"[. . .]) and that it is *widely employed by literary scholars*, it seems to me that, at this point in time, one would have to argue for why one is 'reverting' to studying metaphor within the frame of traditional metaphor theory rather than studying metaphor within the frame of conceptual metaphor theory."[4]

The first argument (if not necessarily the second, since popularity does not equal truth) entails a series of questions that indeed should be addressed by literary scholars, cognitive linguists, and rhetoricians alike. First, what exactly have "cognitive scientists" "empirically verified" with regard to "metaphor theory" (or to metaphor itself)? More to the point for our study of Mao Heng's xing: Do the "tenor-vehicle frame of metaphor" and "conceptual metaphor theory" automatically exclude each other, the latter having supposedly replaced the former in the paradigm that now determines, or should determine, the way we study "literature"? And on which assumptions is such a statement based? Is there an objective—reified, hypostasized—"metaphor" that we as literary scholars have access to and that could be studied scientifically?

The efficiency and elegance of the conceptual metaphor theory are obvious and may be illustrated by elaborating a cherished example. We tend, Lakoff and Johnson observed in their famous book, to understand and conceptualize time in terms of money: the metaphorical concept "time is money" thus underlies, structures, and generates common expressions such as "a *waste* of time."[5] We may add that the metaphorical expression "time is money" itself—but at a more complex and interesting level—likewise depends on an intricate *interaction* between some of the different conceptualizations through which we understand "time" and "money."

For instance, we conceive of time as consisting of *units* (such as days and hours) that can be *filled* with value-generating activities, the products of which can be exchanged (proportionate to the amount of time "invested") for *units* of coins or bills that symbolize and represent value. The claim that "time is money" banks on a perceived similarity (*to homoion* in Aristotle's parlance) between the two components—both are valuable—is therefore correct but oversimplified, since this perceived shared quality obviously in its turn depends on a more intricate series of conceptualizations, and their interlocking.[6] Raymond Gibbs—a chief proponent of CMT and a critic of Gerard Steen's DMT—thus describes the metaphoric process (according to what he calls the "view of metaphor as conceptual structure") as "the mental act of putting together" the "metaphorical mapping of two disparate domains" into a "unit."[7]

To this very hasty analysis one may first add that conceptual metaphors always build on experience, and that the expression "time is money" therefore is more valid in certain situations than in others. Time is more likely to "be money" to a Hong Kong stockbroker than to an octogenarian living off a pension in a remote village. Similarly, one may certainly use the linguistic formula of metaphor ("X is [like] Y") and say, for instance, "man is a lamppost" but any (novel) meaning that we may extract from such a figure must appeal to a thought pattern that we are already familiar with.

Secondly, only some conceptualizations of time are realized in a conceptual metaphor. For instance, a conceptualization of time like the expression *tempus fugit*, which suggests that time is a *criminal* that *flees* the confinements in which we wish it to remain, and in the process of escaping *deprives* us of our most precious belongings (health, youthful vigor, friends, life itself) plays only a minor role, if indeed any, in the "time is money" trope.

Thirdly, we should acknowledge that the central insight of Lakoff and Johnson's book—that many ostensibly literal expressions, such as "a waste of time," build on metaphorical conceptualizations—had been formulated elsewhere, for example in Umberto Eco's masterful 1980 entry on "metafora" in volume nine ("Mente-Operazioni") of *Enciclopedia*, where he speaks, quoting the Belgian scholar Albert Henry (1910–2002), of such seemingly "literal" expressions as "secondary phenomen[a]" resulting from "preliminary metaphor[s]."[8]

The Tenor and the Vehicle

To indicate instead some of the limitations—at least for "literary scholars"—of the conceptual metaphor theory and to question the tacit assumption that it and the "tenor-vehicle frame of metaphor" are mutually exclusive, or that it explains "the metaphor" better than the latter, I will discuss some observations regarding the metaphor in I.A. Richards's 1936 *The Philosophy of Rhetoric* and in the important 1992 article by Raymond Gibbs referenced above. In "When is Metaphor?," Gibbs proposes that many of the contesting theories of metaphors focus on different aspects (or intervals) of the production and interpretations of metaphors and are thus in fact not incompatible. While some theorists try to describe how a metaphor is *immediately* "comprehended" by the listener or reader, others focus on how it is *later* "appreciated": "The conscious recognition of a metaphor, or of a metaphor's having multiple readings through the free play of signifiers, occurs at a later point than that of immediate comprehension and *requires a different kind of theory to account for such psychological and/or literary judgments*."[9] Although I am uncertain if (as Gibbs claims) the analysis of conceptual metaphors alone can sufficiently explain "why people find such great beauty and power in poetry and literary prose," the distinction between the "psychological and/or literary judgments" and the "immediate comprehension" of metaphor is valuable and a precursor of Steen's deliberate metaphor theory, and it reminds us that *metaphora* ("transference") is itself a conceptualization, itself indeed a metaphor, and not an object awaiting its scientific explanation by a taxonomist in a sterile laboratory.[10]

If Gibbs through this meta-theory tried to bring order to a range of seemingly conflicting theories of the metaphor, the impetus behind I. A. Richards's terms "vehicle" and "tenor," which he introduced in his Mary Flexner Lectures at Bryn Mawr during the academic year 1935–36, rather came from a frustration with earlier (and contemporary) explanations of the workings of the metaphor that he felt were substandard and underdeveloped. In *The Philosophy of Rhetoric*, which came out of those lectures, Richards is acutely aware of the conceptuality and historicity of "metaphor," saying that the "traditional theory noticed only a few of the modes of metaphor; and limited its application of the term *metaphor* to a few of them only."[11]

Richards is equally aware that the metaphor is what we—in agreement with Gibbs and the proponents of CMT—would call a conceptual rather than a "verbal matter" or an "embellishment," saying that "*thought* is metaphoric, and proceeds by comparison, and the metaphors of language derive therefrom," and that "metaphor is the omnipresent principle of language. . . . we cannot get through three sentences of ordinary fluid discourse without it."[12] Interestingly enough, Richards also argues against the notion (associated with Quintilian, the authors of the *Progymnasmata* and, as we soon shall see, Christine Brooke-Rose) that the expert speaker or writer puts the subject matter of his or her discourse "before the eyes" (*pro ommaton*) of the audience: "Rhetoricians think that a figure of speech, an images or imaginative comparison, must have something to do with the presence of images . . . in the mind's eye or the mind's ear. But, of course, it need not. No images of this sort need come in at any point."[13]

It is, furthermore, expressly only as a "first step" toward a better understanding of metaphor "at its simplest"—referencing Samuel Johnson's statement that a "metaphorical expression . . . gives you two ideas for one"—that Richards proposes we call the "two members of a metaphor" vehicle and tenor, respectively.[14] Rather than relegate Richards's two terms to the dustheap of the history of ideas and literary studies, I suggest (not unlike Gibbs) that the "conceptual metaphor theory" and "the early twentieth-century tenor-vehicle frame of metaphor developed by I. A. Richards" target different aspects of the metaphor, and that Richards's foremost aim is to explain the rhetorical impact—what Gibbs in 1992 would have called the "appreciation"—of "metaphor." In the following, I direct my attention only to some passages in Richards's famous book that are glaringly at odds with the conceptual metaphor theory.

In Richards's reading of John Denham's (1615–1669) poem "The Thames," the descriptions of the river ("deep, yet clear," "gentle, yet not dull," etc.) constitute the vehicle in that they make a statement about the narrator and, according to Richards, the "flow" of his "mind," which thus constitute the tenor.

> O could I flow like thee, and make thy stream
> My great exemplar as it is my theme!
> Though deep, yet clear; though gentle, yet not dull;
> Strong without rage, without o'er flowing, full.[15]

What interests Richards is how the metaphor in this passage seems simply to bank on, and express, a perceived similarity between the mighty river and the "flow of the [narrator's] mind," but in fact does not: "the vehicle, the river, come to seem an excuse for saying about the mind something which *could not be said about the river*."[16] Richards develops this idea thus:

> Take *deep*. Its main implications as regards a river are, "not easily crossed, dangerous, navigable, and suitable for swimming, perhaps." As applied to a mind, it suggests "mysterious, a lot going on, rich in knowledge and power, not easily accounted for, acting from serious and important reasons." *What the lines say of the mind is something that does not come from the river.* But the river is not a mere excuse, or a decoration only, a gilding of the moral pill. The vehicle is still controlling the mode in which the tenor forms.[17]

While one may disagree with Richards's interpretation of the word "deep" here, by describing the insidious and subtle dissonance between that word as a description of the river (the "vehicle") and as part of a statement about the mind (the "tenor"), Richards's approach is arguably more effective in identifying the complex rhetorical strategy of Denham's poem than is the conceptual metaphor theory. To claim that the poem builds on the conceptual metaphor "the mind is a river," or "thoughts are currents," would be factually correct but of less relevance for the student of poetry and rhetoric than Richards's analysis of how Denham's "metaphor" works in this instance—which, I would add, is also how many of Mao Heng's xingish readings of the *Odes* function.

I insert here Gibbs's remark, drawn from "When Is Metaphor?," that "poetic verse embellishes more mundane ways of thinking about our worldly experiences."[18] Given the sophistication of Gibbs's larger argument, the claim is somewhat surprising: Is the primary assumption of the literary scholar interested in the workings of conceptual metaphor that a poem rests on its author's ability to "embellish" poetically certain root metaphors, such as "thoughts are currents"? Would that in turn not risk turning the reading of poetry into a near-mechanical exercise in detecting and decoding conceptual metaphors? Does Gibbs's observation that "poetic verse" *embellishes* "more mundane ways of thinking about our worldly experiences" not entail a reduction of the dynamics of Denham's poem (or Dave Smith's "Messenger," which is Gibbs's own example and whose "beauty and power" he explores through the conceptual metaphor theory)?[19] And does Gibbs's notion of a poetic "embellishment" not expose a danger inherent in this theory, namely its somewhat paradoxical tendency to regard literary metaphors as embellishments in a manner that people like I.A. Richards rebelled against (with the obvious but not essential difference that what poetic metaphors "embellish" is the "more mundane" metaphors we "live by," rather than "literal language")? I submit that all these questions must be answered in the affirmative.

In an earlier passage in *The Philosophy of Rhetoric*, Richards says that "the tenor may become almost a mere excuse for the introduction of the vehicle, and so no longer be 'the principal subject.'"[20] Although Richards is somewhat unclear at this point, and does not provide an example, the notion of a "free-floating" vehicle may be taken as a recognition of how in certain texts, perhaps most often in so-called poetic texts, what may seem as the vehicle of a tenor (or occupy formally the position of a vehicle) cannot be definitively pinned down as such, or when the vehicle—for example in ode 185 where a solider says "I am the King's *teeth and claws*"—is so striking or bizarre that it, at least momentarily, overshadows the tenor, lingering on the retina of the mind like the imprint of a bolt of sharp light.

Richards, furthermore, argues that a "word may be *simultaneously* both literal and metaphoric," which, if taken in its radical sense (that is, if the passage *hinges upon* the word's or expression's simultaneous literalness and metaphoricity), refers to a rhetorical scheme that obviously is out of reach of the conceptual metaphor theory, and more akin not only to Gerard Steen's concept of "deliberate metaphors"—"those metaphors that draw attention to their source domain as a separate detail for attention in working memory"—but also to what Gibbs himself writes toward the end of the article cited as proof that the "conceptual metaphor theory has now been empirically verified by cognitive scientists."[21] He says: "Although many idioms are transparent and can readily be seen as corresponding to certain conceptual metaphors (for example, *blow your stack*), other idioms have *opaque metaphorical or poetic origins* [italics added] (for example, *trip the light fantastic*). People are *less likely to recognize why these idioms mean what they do* [italics added]."[22]

Gibbs is here—importantly and insightfully—both suggesting that some "idioms" or metaphors ("trip the light fantastic") are attractive and effective precisely because they are not immediately decodable and acknowledging that conceptual metaphor theory may run into problems explaining "opaque" or "poetic" expressions.[23] Regarding the review of the book on Pindar with which I began, it is rather the "literary scholar" who studies the function of "metaphor" in texts of great rhetorical complexity and literary density with CMT as the primary analytical tool who would be expected to "argue" for his or her choice of method.

With reference to Mao Heng, the natural imagery in the *Odes* was (or could be read as) descriptions of the human acts that these poems related. In the semiotic practice presented in the *Commentary* under the name of xing, images of nature play the role of vehicle to the human actions that Mao reads as the xing-poem's tenor. But, as Richards has reminded us, poetic metaphor tend to differ from that of everyday language. In the poetic text the vehicle is *given* and never fully coincides with tenor; we may call this the *materiality* of poetic metaphor, with a nod of respect to Paul Gordon's seminal study *The Critical Double*.[24] In this respect, the vehicle retains a rest that defies the demands for total translatability. One may even say that poetry reverses the usual metaphorical movement that runs from vehicle to tenor, and, instead, makes the reader conscious of the sensuous character of the image or word, as well as its role as a vehicle. Indeed, poetic metaphor ends up a perpetual oscillation between vehicle and tenor, between materiality and extended meaning. In the paratactically structured *Odes*, the nature element—what Mao called a *xing*—is bestowed with the two functions of sensuous image and abstract vehicle; the absence of the copulae *as* or *be* in the xing poem renders the consummated marriage between vehicle and tenor impossible. The xing structure forces the reader to an everlasting movement to-and-fro the metaphorical.[25]

Outside, Inside, and Between the Texts

At this point I shall introduce three basic and roughly hewn interpretational tools that have surfaced now and then in the first part and which will occur more frequently in the following analysis of Mao's *Commentary*. The terms "intratextuality," "extratextuality," and "intertextuality" denote three interpretational techniques in Mao's reading of the *Odes*. Intratextuality refers to the play of meaning within the given text. Extratextuality, on the other hand, describes all instances in which the meaning of a word is established outside (or before) the interactions of the whole text. When Mao claims that the *jujiu* birds refer to the "lord" and the "girl" mentioned in the first ode, the metaphor is intratextual since both tenor (the "lord" and the girl) and vehicle (the birds) are named in the text. But when Mao identifies the couple as a certain king and his queen consort, he banks on information that can only be found outside the text.

Let us, furthermore, draw a line of demarcation between metaphor and symbol. The metaphor is the intratextual trope par excellence since it results, in my particular usage of the term, from the interaction of words found in the text. Formally speaking, I distinguish between two versions of the xing. In the first kind—exemplified by Mao's reading of "Guanju"—both vehicle and tenor are explicitly given by the text. The other kind supplies only the imagery (the vehicle), the meaning thereof (that is, the tenor) being determined by the interaction of all the components that make up the text. In ode 155, "Chixiao" 鴟鴞, the narrator presents him- or herself as a bird begging the aggressive *chixiao*-owl for mercy. In the first stanza, a series of nouns wavering between the literal and the figurative is introduced: "You have already taken my *child* [*zi* 子], do not destroy my *house* [*shi* 室]."[26] In the anthropomorphic utterance attributed to the bird, the function of the words or graphs "child," "house" and, in the third stanza, "hand" (*shou* 手) is ambiguous, and their status as vehicles or tenors cannot be readily determined. Are we to understand them as *nestling, nest,* and *claw,* that is, as words belonging to the world of animals rather than to that of man?

Or is "Chixiao" an allegory criticizing a violent and powerful person? Such an interpretation is plausible, not only because a bird is given the human faculty of speech but also because the bird-persona, in the second stanza, addresses "you lowly people," thereby explicitly crossing the line between bird and man, and between literalness and metaphor. What concerns me at this stage, however, is the simple fact that the bird-man metaphor can be located *in the text*, even though the tenors (that is, the attacked speaker and the person depicted as the violent *chixiao*) are not mentioned explicitly.

The symbol, correspondingly, may be regarded as the arch trope of extratextuality. The symbol, in the sense I use the term here, consists of only the vehicle. The tenor—the "meaning" of the word—cannot be deduced from the text but is supplied from outside. For instance, Wen Yiduo claims that the character for "fish" 魚 *yu*, in ancient times, also referred to the male member.[27] If, with regard to ode 171, "Nan you jia yu" 南有嘉魚, we accept Wen's claim, the link "fish—genitals" is purely symbolic and based on information not given by the poem itself.[28] Here, my definition of symbol borders on the concept of a dead metaphor, in that what probably originated as a metaphor has become a conventional sign.[29] Another example may further elucidate the distinction that we wish to make between the word functioning as a sign, as a metaphor, or as a symbol. What may tentatively be called the primary meaning of *jujiu* 雎鳩—Karlgren's "osprey" and Arthur Waley's "fish-hawk"—is a certain kind of waterfowl. It is characteristic of a word's primary meaning that it can be translated into another language without any serious obstacles or loss of meaning. When the description of the *jujiu* interacts with its context, Mao interprets it as a token of the ideal marriage between the people he identifies as the queen consort and the king. Here, a secondary meaning of *jujiu* is activated by way of the intratextual interaction previously discussed; the *jujiu* has become a metaphor. Once this word has been firmly established as a metaphor for conjugal harmony (which certainly was the case with the first ode), *jujiu* can in its own right appear in other texts with connotations of conjugal harmony. The original metaphorical movement has come to a stand-still and the word has become, in my sense, a symbol.

Intertextuality, finally, is here a term closer to C. H. Wang's mode of reading than to Julia Kristeva's original (and more general) version.[30] Intertextuality denotes the relationship between the given poem and the other 304 poems that make up the *Shijing*.

The notions of intra-, inter- and extratextuality also describe the phenomenon of textual violence. By moving from hermeneutical center to hermeneutical periphery, by bringing in meaning from the outside (since there is indeed an outside of the text), the reader must subject the text to an increasing amount of violence.[31] This is not a derogatory judgment passed on a degenerated hermeneutical methodology but a description of textual interpretation that suggests itself as we abuse the text with external facts to make it serve our own purposes. In short, textual violator is a role necessarily played by all readers, even the most ardent of formalists. Moreover, the distinction between intratextuality and extratextuality is not called for by a naive and dogmatic idealist dreaming of the "pure" text, hermetic and unaffected by the world. As suggested in my discussion on metaphor, the experience of "the world" obviously precedes the identification of a particular (turn of) phrase as a metaphor, therefore extratextuality pervades our understanding of the text. My crude distinction between intra- and extratextuality rather aims at elucidating the relationship between the word (or the phrase) and its meaning. When Mao, in a comment we are now familiar with, interprets the *jujiu* bird as a metaphor for the "gentleman" and the "girl," tenor and vehicle are found in the text.[32] When he proceeds to identify the "girl" as a royal concubine, Mao turns to matters beyond the (intra-)text. No such identification is warranted by the text per se: this is extratextuality in the sense of interpretational violence.

As my metaphorical detour draws to an end, and the terms have been set, we may return to the real object under investigation: Mao's *Commentary*. My discussions will move within an area defined by two landmarks, the *Shijing* as the primary text, the navel around which everything orbits, and Mao's *Commentary*, which is by definition a derivative text, a meta-text. To these are added my own interpretations of the *Odes* and of the *Commentary*. The former naturally belongs to the category of meta-texts whereas the latter could be called, tongue in cheek, a "meta-meta-text," or an interpretation of an interpretation. I urge the reader to distinguish between statements about the *Shijing* and those that concern Mao's *Commentary*.

14

The *Commentary* versus the *Minor Preface*

Apart from the *Odes* themselves, three texts make up the recension known as the *Maoshi*, namely the *Great Preface* 大序, the *Minor Preface* or *Prefaces* 小序, and the *Mao Commentary*. The authorship and date of composition of these texts are uncertain and the earliest sources contradictory. As a case in point, the *Hanshu* 漢書 (composed mainly in the second half of the first century CE) claims that Master Mao 毛公 was a man from the state of Zhao 趙, whose teachings, which he claimed stemmed from Confucius's disciple Zi Xia, was appreciated by Liu De 劉德, prince Xian 獻 of Hejian 河間, but not "established."[1] Elsewhere in the same work, however, it is said that Mao was indeed appointed *boshi* 博士 ("erudite" or classics specialist) at the court of prince Xian.[2] A third passage in the *Hanshu* is more specific, claiming that Hejian was a center for scholarly activities where prince Xian, among other things, "established *boshi* in the study of Mao's recension of the *Odes* and Zuo's recension of the *Chunqiu*" 立毛氏詩左氏春秋博士 in the mid-second century BCE.[3] The latter passage thus suggests, not that Mao himself was made a *boshi* but that his exegesis of the *Odes* was so "appreciated"—on par with the *Zuozhuan*—that prince Xian appointed scholars to carry on his legacy.

Zheng Xuan's (d. 200 CE) *Shi pu* 詩譜 tells of an Elder Master Mao 大毛公 and a Younger Master Mao 小毛公, of which the former was the author of a *guxunzhuan* 詁訓傳 on the *Odes*.[4] Mao the Elder composed this work in his home state Lu 魯, and it was handed down via prince Xian in Hejian to Mao the Younger who was made a *boshi*. Another fragmentary text attributed to Zheng Xuan, *Liuyi lun* 六藝論, suggests instead that Mao was a *boshi* at prince Xian's court and "was expert at explaining the *Odes*"

善說詩, for which reason the prince "called it the 'Mao *Odes*.'"[5] A later commentator, Lu Ji 陸璣 (third century CE), informs us that whereas Mao the Elder came from the state of Lu and bore the personal name of Heng 亨, Mao the Younger came from Zhao and was called Chang 萇.[6] That the information gets increasingly detailed over time may reflect an increase in knowledge about the provenance of the *Commentary* but may also indicate that a largely unsubstantiated lore had built up around the figure of Mao the commentator. However, all the early sources agree on one point, namely that the *Commentary* was composed during a relatively limited amount of time and by one person. Although these early testimonies do not constitute absolute proof, and although our knowledge about "textual production" in early China is too scant, it allows us, as I have suggested above, to read Mao's exegesis systematically, as a commentarial text permeated and united by a certain logic.

More important than the exact identity of Mao is the relationship between the *Commentary* and the *Minor Preface*. In addition to the gaps in our knowledge of their origins, the lapidary style of both texts, as well as the corruptions that may have occurred when the manuscripts were copied, mean that all conclusions regarding dates and authorship must be tentative. As argued above, the issue here is not whether the *Commentary* or the *Preface* is the earlier text but rather the realization that the two meta-texts are incompatible. No one has successfully proven one text older than the other, but it can be surmised that they were not written by the same person.[7] As an example, let us consider poem 18, "Gao yang" 羔羊:

> Furs of lamb
> white silk in five strands
> They withdraw from court to eat
> slowly and dignified

> 羔羊之皮
> 素絲五紽
> 退食自公
> 委蛇委蛇[8]

Mao's *Commentary* simply explains that furs made of lamb were worn by high ministers in ancient times.[9] "Furs of lamb," therefore, does not refer to anything but the furs themselves and, metonymically, to those who wear them, namely the ministers. The *Minor Preface* interprets the first line quite differently: "The states to the south of [Duke] Shao conformed to the [ideal] government of King Wen. [Those] in power were all rite-abiding and frugal, correct and forthright, [they were] virtuous as lambs" 召南之國化文王之政, 在位皆節儉正直, 德如羔羊也.¹⁰

To the author of the *Preface*, "lamb" contains a split reference since it refers both to the material of the coats and to the notion of "virtue," which is attributed to the men wearing the coats. Ironically, Mao, whose readings often abound with metaphoricity, builds his reading on the "literal" meaning of "lamb," whereas the *Preface* depends on a turn of phrase rather similar to what Mao calls a xing. The contradiction between the *Commentary* and the *Preface* bears witness to the danger of taking the two texts *en bloc* or of using the latter to illuminate obscure passages in the former. The *Commentary* and the *Preface* certainly belong to the same tradition, but to maintain rigor and stringency in our investigation of Mao's xing I cannot but treat them as separate entities. Finally, however systematic and groundbreaking, the use of xing as an interpretational tool does not, of course, make Mao into a formalist in any modern sense of the word. Such a notion would undoubtedly be a flagrant mistake since Mao's "xing" is always a means to a Confucio-ideological end, no matter how terse and seemingly formal his annotations might be.

15

The *Great Preface*, a Rereading

Although united by their paramount influence on later poetics, the *Commentary* and the *Great Preface* are texts of two very different orders. Mao turns his attention away from the main concern of the *Great Preface*—the origin of the poem in the poet—toward poetry's formal characteristics. Below, I shall go against the usual creeds of modern Sinological scholarship and argue that Mao's xing is not antimetaphorical but metaphorical, that it is not concrete and spontaneous but abstract and premeditated, and that it is not nature but culture. In other words, "xing" does not designate natural imagery carelessly thrown into the text due to the poet's spatial proximity to nature but, in fact, carefully construed metaphorical statements about the human activity described by the poem.

Can anything be found in the discourse on poetry in the early Han dynasty that would corroborate such an unorthodox hypothesis? First, let us distinguish a canonized, ideological poetics such as that of the *Great Preface* from the hermeneutical practice of the *Commentary*. It is hardly surprising that the close-reading *Commentary* is characterized by an interest in formal aspects, whereas a poetics incorporating the poetic text into a holistic philosophy of the world yields a different picture. Modern scholars claim that ancient "cosmological" poetics describes *shi*, which I conventionally translate as "poetry," as a spontaneous and automatic reaction to external phenomena. But do the *Great Preface* and the *Commentary* really offer fundamentally different theories of *shi*? And is it correct that the *Preface* depicts poetic creation in terms akin to Chen Shih-hsiang's vision of the spontaneous bard? In opposition to this customary pattern of thought I argue that in the *Great Preface* there *is* a distinction—obvious to the point of being obscure—between the idea of *shi* as a man-made artifact and the cosmological pattern that is simply printed in the soul of primitive man.

Contemporary Chinese and Western scholars have been surprisingly univocal in their interpretations of the *Great Preface*. To Li Zehou and Liu Gangji, perhaps the two most authoritative scholars on early Chinese aesthetics in the 1990s, the *Preface* represents a significant change in ancient poetics. The two authors see therein the notion of poetry as a fusion of intent and feeling: "Not only does the first paragraph of Mao's *Great Preface* point out the unity of poetry ["speech"], song and dance but, more importantly, it also stresses that poetry, song and dance all emerge from the expression of human feelings."[1]

"[According to the *Great Preface*] poetic expression is involuntary," claims Stephen Owen, echoing Steven Van Zoeren's more specific assertion that "[the *Great Preface* holds that] the expression of a *zhi* ["intention"] in an Ode is spontaneous and unmediated by artistry or calculation."[2] Variations on same idea are expressed by François Juillien, as well as by Paula Versano, Alexander Beecroft, and in the canonical *Cambridge History of Chinese Literature*, Martin Kern.[3] These claims by meticulous scholars tally badly with descriptions of *shi* as an oblique, ritualistic, and deliberated form of communication. Although I venture a more detailed and daring analysis elsewhere, for the sake of the present argument I shall here below indicate how this pivotal but multilayered and ambiguous text allows for a reading that radically modifies the standard Sinological interpretation.

Analysis

The *Great Preface* starts off by stating that

> *Shi* is the place to which intent goes
> Resting in the heart it is intent
> when articulated in words, it is *shi*.[4]

詩者志之所之也
在心為志
發言為詩

And it continues seemingly by making much the same claim albeit in a slightly different wording:

Emotions stir inside and take shape in words

情動於中而形於言

These two statements, the first concerning intent and the second emotions, are usually—and understandably—interpreted as describing two consecutive stages in a movement of inspiration and involuntary expression, a supposition strengthened by similar passages and trains of thought in *Yueji* and *Kongzi shilun*. The *Preface* immediately continues by describing how emotions may exhaust the possibility of language to express them and how they instead are conveyed in sighing, singing, and finally in the "unconscious" dancing movements of the hands and the stamping of the feet:

> when words do not suffice, one then sighs them
> when sighing does not suffice, one then prolongs and sings them
> when sighing is not enough, then unwittingly the hands express
>   them in dancing movement,
> and the feet in stamping on the ground

言之不足故嗟嘆之
嗟嘆之不足故永歌之
永歌之不足不知手之舞之
足之蹈之也.

Thus far the *Preface* indeed seems to characterize *shi* as part of a process in which emotions are expressed with increasing urgency and decreasing deliberation or consciousness. According to the canonical Sinological interpretation of this passage, the *Preface* holds that *shi* is not poetry in the Greek or Western sense of *poiêsis*—a premeditated, craftlike "fabrication" of a literary artifact—but the result of someone's spontaneous reaction to a given historical situation.[5] *Shi*, moreover, is "generated by the fundamental participation of the human mind in the workings of the cosmos."[6] The person through whom *shi* spurts forth is thus, not unlike a shaman, "fundamentally" part of a complex interaction between all agents, events, and objects in the universe—what in Sinological parlance is called "correlative cosmology," which, in turn, is an umbrella term for the early Chinese concepts of yin and yang, stimulus-and-response (*gan-ying*), the Five Processes (*wu xing*), and cosmological correspondence (*lei*).[7] The opening passage of the *Preface*, read in this fashion as describing *shi* as the spontaneous expression of emotions and the Chinese antipoet as receiving and answering to cosmological forces, has exerted an enormous influence and become the founding block of the canonical Sinological narrative on early Chinese poetics.[8]

But let me complicate matters. First, it should be noted—in passing but with some emphasis—that the *Preface* does not say that *shi* is unconscious, only that the movements of hands and feet, which occur when the emotions aroused exceed the possibility of language to express them, are. Second, we turn to the complex question of narrative structure—"structure" understood in the dual sense of "building" and "organizing principle."[9] The *Preface* is possibly a multilayered, multiauthored text, with bits and pieces transferred from other contexts, and with later comments interspersed among earlier segments. If this is correct it may be futile to look for a narrative that logically progresses from one point to the next without serious contradictions. Instead, we may be dealing with a textual collage assembled on the basis of a superficial thematic similarity that, in fact, conceals fundamental differences in terminology and "philosophical" assumptions (*zhi* versus *qing*, tones versus *shi*).

I will not try to analyze the provenance of the strata that (according to this hypothesis) make up the *Preface* or propose to answer definitely if this assembly of textual borrowings forms into a new and coherent context or remains a collage of possibly contradictory fragments. Instead, I shall merely suggest that toward the end of the *Preface* there appear two statements that complicate the canonical Sinological reading.

Next, it is said that

> Emotions turn into sounds
> Sounds formed in patterns are called tones
> The tones of an ordered state are peaceful and joyous
> its government harmonious
> The tones of a disordered world are sad and angered
> its government wayward
> The tones of a ruined state are grieving and pensive
> its populace troubled

情發於聲
聲成文謂之音
治世之音安以樂
其政和
亂世之音怨以怒

其政乖
亡國之音哀以思
其民困

The argument made here—"tones" stem from "emotions" and reflect the situation from which they emerge—is fairly uncomplicated and squares well with the arch-Sinological claims that the *Preface* describes a "spontaneous" poetic expression "generated by the fundamental participation of the human mind in the workings of the cosmos." What interests me is its connection with the following paragraph, which begins with the conjunction *gu* 故. *Gu* often translates as "therefore" or "thus," indicating either a causal relationship between two clauses or that the second clause expresses the conclusion of an argument made in the first clause. But *gu* may also mean, in a weaker sense, "then," "moreover," or "similarly." I leave it, for the time being, untranslated.

> *Gu*
> to even out gains and losses
> move heaven and earth
> rouse ghosts and spirits
> nothing comes close to *shi*

故
正得失
動天地
感鬼神
莫近於詩

This is no small claim. *Shi* may, demonically, move heaven, earth, ghosts, and spirits—and even out irregularities in the cosmic or moral balance sheet. *Shi* is thus not only the most elevated form of discourse; it also outstrips in effectiveness and intensity all other forms of ritual activity. On a casual reading, these two paragraphs seem to validate the standard interpretation of the *Preface* as espousing a typically Chinese "affective-expressive" poetics, according to which the poet both spontaneously mirrors the world and, thereby, in a circular movement, effectuates a similar change in the world.

This reading rests, however, on one fundamental supposition, namely that both paragraphs take *shi* as their object and that "tones" (defined by the *Preface* as originating in "emotions" and "sounds") equal *shi* (defined as originating in "ambition"). And here I return to the question of the conjunction *gu*. If taken in the sense of "therefore" the *Preface* indeed seems to argue that *shi* is both the spontaneous response to the world (a poet in an ordered state automatically emits tones—the building blocks of *shi*—that are tranquil and joyous) and affects the world in a similar manner.

If taken in the sense of "moreover," the interpretation becomes more complicated. I noted above that the *Preface* does not claim that *shi* is produced "unconsciously." Similarly, the *Preface* does not say, in the two paragraphs above, that *shi* automatically reflects the state of the world. On the contrary, it explicitly claims that *shi* has the extraordinary faculty of effecting a change in the world (and the extramundane realm), whereas "tones" can merely passively reflect it. Save for the ambiguous particle *gu*, there is thus no explicit link between *shi* and "tones," nor between *shi* and the spontaneous expression of emotion and the fervent hand-waving and foot stomping. This opens up several possibilities regarding the interpretation of the *Preface* and our understanding of how it is organized. *Gu* may be understood here as a compositional device used by the author or compiler to link two arguments, derived perhaps from different sources or traditions, that are similar but not identical and that may be either complementary and logical in that the sublime *shi* is contrasted with the lowly "tones" or paradoxical in that the two argumentative strands (*shi* and "tones") are merely lumped together without regard to their internal incompatibility.[10] I return to these alternatives momentarily.

> With this the former kings used to
> regulate man and wife
> perfect filial piety and reverence
> solidify human relations
> improve education and social change
> change customs and mores
>
> 先王以是
> 經夫婦
> 成孝敬
> 厚人倫
> 美教化
> 移風俗

The context does not allow us to determine conclusively if the word *shi* 是 ("this") in the first line refers to poetry alone, or to poetry and "tones" as complementary parts: one actively affecting the world, the other passively reflecting it. But since "this" is unequivocally described here as an active agent in, and indispensable ingredient of, sagely statecraft, the passage connects directly to the preceding paragraph and thus primarily to poetry (詩 *shi*), not "tones."

Then follows a passage whose terminological complexity we need not, in this context, explore in detail. It concerns the six *yi* 義, a word that here very roughly approximates "rhetorical modes" and "genres" and, again, it begins with the conjunction *gu*.

> There are, then, six [modes of] meaning in *shi*
> The first is called *feng*, the second *fu*, the third *bi*
> the fourth xing, the fifth *ya*, the sixth *song*

> 故詩有六義焉
> 一曰風二曰賦三曰比
> 四曰興五曰雅六曰頌

This enumeration of the six "modes" of *shi* is cognate with, or perhaps even directly modified from, a segment of the "Chun guan" 春官 chapter in the *Zhou li*, which it is formally similar to but set in a different context.[11] Again, I am not attempting an analysis of how the *Preface* relates thematically to other texts but simply suggest that the conspicuous similarities in wording between the *Preface* and, for example, the *Yueji* and the *Zhouli* strengthen the two hypotheses proposed above, namely that the author-compiler decontextualized and incorporated bits and pieces of other texts and traditions into the *Preface* and that the particle *gu* serves to glue those textual patches together without signaling that the propositions made in one segment strictly follow from those made in the preceding one.

Feng, *Ya*, and *Song* refer here, of course, to the three major sections of the *Book of Odes* and to their respective origins and functions, whereas *fu*, *bi*, and xing designate, one supposes, the rhetorical modalities used in the *Odes*: the straightforward and literal narration of *fu*, as contrasted with the oblique and nonliteral *bi* and xing. Then follows an explanation of *feng*, *ya*, and *song* (but not of *fu*, *bi*, or xing), of which the first is the longest. The *Preface* begins by claiming that *feng* facilitates communication between men of different rank:

> Those above use *feng* to move those below
> those below use *feng* to criticize those above.

If one remonstrates craftily and, in doing so, emphasizes form
then he who says it has no guilt
and he who hears it [understands] enough to take heed
Thus we call it *feng*

上以風化下
下以風刺上
主文而譎諫
言之者無罪
聞之者足以戒
故曰風

Feng means "wind" but also, in an extended usage, "air" (in the sense of "song"), and "to recite," "discuss," and "criticize."[12] The final line above is in all likelihood a paronomastic and quasi-tautological definition: "We call this section of the *Odes feng* ("Airs") because it is used to *feng* ('criticize')."

Hitherto, the *Preface* has described how *feng* functions in ideal circumstances. But now an exception, in the form of the so-called altered Airs and *ya*, is introduced. At first the historical factors that led to this shift are explained.

When the decline of the Kingly Way came to pass
Rites and Morality degenerated, governance and teachings became deficient
the principles of governance differed from state to state, and customs from household to household
and the altered Airs and *Ya* emerged

至于王道衰
禮義廢政教失
國異政家殊俗
而變風變雅作矣

Then the agents and their motives are specified.

The state historians could discern the traces of gains and losses,
were distressed by the changes in human interaction,
worried by the severity in punishments and government

> They expressed in chanting their inner emotions to criticize their superiors
> because, having realized the change in affairs, they longed for the customs of old

國史明乎得失之跡
傷人倫之變
哀刑政之苛
吟詠性情以風其上
達於事變而懷其舊俗者也

This passage, like much of the *Preface*, generates more questions than it answers. Were the state historians the authors of the "altered Airs," or did they merely "chant" odes that were already in existence? And if the first question is answered in the affirmative, does it imply that all Airs were authored by state historians? For our present purposes, however, the most pertinent question is a slightly different one: what distinguishes the so-called altered Airs from the "regular Airs," which occurred in times of harmony, order, and high morality? Are there thematic or formal or functional differences?

The answer to this question depends, I contend, on how one relates the segment in question to the rest of the *Preface*. The account of how the state historians composed the altered Airs resonates with the opening lines about "emotions stirring inside and taking shape in words" and to the subsequent description of how the "tones of a disordered world are sad and angered, and its government wayward." Since the historians reacted to their environment and "chanted" their inner emotions, it may be argued that the altered Airs were a (cosmo-)logical consequence of the alteration of the Kingly Way. And this seems to corroborate the time-honored Sinological claim (which harks back at least to Kong Yingda) that the *Preface* describes *shi* as "generated by the fundamental participation of the human mind in the workings of the cosmos." This, I suggest, is too neat an interpretation, which obfuscates not only the text's internal contradictions and tensions but also the question of what distinguishes the "regular" Airs from the altered ones.

Let me reread. Having stated above that *feng* is ordinarily used as a means of communication between superiors and inferiors, the *Preface* adds that "to remonstrate craftily and with an emphasis on form [*zhu wen*]" 主文而譎諫 ensures that admonitions and critiques may be exchanged without "guilt" or violation of decorum.[13] The word *jue* 譎—which translates as "crafty," "deceitful," or "weird"—is important for our understanding of the difference between "regular" and altered Airs. What does it mean for communication to be "crafty" or "weird"? The classic interpretation represented by Zheng Xuan and Kong Yingda is that the *Preface* here refers to "indirect and circuitous remonstrations" 依違不直諫 by way of *piyu* 譬喻 ("exemplifications through analogy"), the kind of which we find in the *fu*-quotations of the *Odes*, and in Mao's xingish readings.[14]

Although this interpretation is most likely correct, it is noteworthy that the *Preface* never defines *shi* in technical, rhetorical terms but always in terms of psychosocial origin and function. With the usual provisions—the *Preface* is multilayered, contradictory, and allows for different interpretations—it is entirely possible to read this segment as saying that the difference between the two kinds of Airs lies in that the "regular *feng*" are used in a bilateral communication that is circuitous and "crafty," whereas the altered Airs are unilateral—uttered by the state historians, the inferiors, to vent their "natural emotions" (*xingqing* 性情). Thus, what defines the altered Airs in their capacity as signs of degeneration is that they were *not* intended as ritualized, coded messages to righteous superiors but were expressions of raw emotion discharged with no addressee to receive and decode them. This simultaneous celebration of linguistic craftiness and denigration of expressions of emotion stand in diametrical opposition to the standard Sinological interpretation of the *Preface*.

The three lines that follow are, again, crucial for a full understanding of the *Preface*; they explain, modify, and develop the above argument. At first, it is stated that "the altered Airs, then, emerge out of emotions but stop within Rites and Righteousness" 故變風發乎情, 止乎禮義.

We recognize the theme and terminology from Xunzi's "Li lun" 禮論 chapter, and the passage that stresses the necessity to strike a balance between raw emotion and ritualistic formality, and between human instincts (*xing* 性) and ritual "artifice" (*wei* 偽).[15] But more importantly, this statement further underscores that unbridled expressions of emotions are uncouth and that Rituality and the expression of emotions—although complementary rather than mutually exclusive—are located at opposite ends of the spectrum of human behavior.

The author or editor of the *Preface* then adds two lines that do three interconnected things: reconnect to the notion of the Kingly Way, introduce the term *min* 民 (approximately "people, populace"), and stress the distance between emotions and Rituality—almost to the point of dichotomizing them.

> Emerging from emotions: this is the nature of *min*
> Stopping within Rites and Righteousness: this is the benevolence of the Former Kings

> 發乎情，民之性也
> 止乎禮義，先王之澤也

Again, a full analysis will not be attempted here. My present aim is simply to review the standard Sinological reading of the *Preface*. The passage above claims that to *fa hu* 發乎—"emerge from," "begin in," or "express oneself in"—emotions is the nature of *min* 民, and (conversely) that "stopping within Ritualism and Righteousness" is the result of the "gracious influence" (*ze* 澤) of the sagely Former Kings. The argument is thereby organized into a set of opposites, which ranges from the popular, the raw and unrefined to the kingly, the ritualized, and moralized. At the one end we thus find emotion, *min*, human nature and *fa* 發 (beginnings, emergence, spontaneous expression), and at the other Rites-and-Righteousness, the Former Kings and their benevolent influence, and restraint ("stopping within . . .").

The point I wish to make is simple. This pericope very clearly describes restraint and rituality either as an ideal against what is raw and unrefined or, at the very least, as a necessary corrective and counterbalance to the raw and unrefined. This, in turn, expressly contradicts the standard reading of the *Preface* as saying that *shi*—Chinese anti*poiesis*—is the "involuntary" result of a burst of emotions that starts "inside," gains momentum, and ends in foot stamping and hand waving.

The Ritual and the Plebeian

The pericope warrants two further comments, the first short and the second more detailed and meandering.

1. "Stopping within Ritualism and Righteousness." It may be objected that the rites serve to integrate human action into, and as a harmonious part of, a larger cosmological whole and that the notion of *li* (rites, ritual principles) is thus part and parcel of what is called "correlative cosmology." On this reading, then, *shi* may begin as emotions, be restrained by rituals, and still be considered to have been "generated by the fundamental participation of the human mind in the workings of the cosmos." I do not deny

the possibility of such an interpretation but dispute a one-sided definition of *li* as the mere prolonging or embodiment of the "workings of the cosmos." There are numerous counterexamples, both in the *Preface* and in traditions related to it, that may project my interpretation in a direction different from that of standard Sinology. For instance, although the connection between the concept of Airs and the concept of *li* cannot be established with full certainty, the *Preface* certainly implies that a discourse carried out in conformity with ritual principles is *jue* 譎—crafty and circuitous. In a similar vein, Xunzi's aforementioned "Li lun" chapter, by which the *Preface* was conceivably influenced in one way or another, contains an analysis of the "phantasmatic" logic of the ancient burial and mourning rituals in which ritual communication is described precisely as circuitous and ironical.[16] These examples argue against a theory of *shi*—at least in its incarnation as Airs—as "generated," "spontaneous" and "involuntary," and in favor of one that describes *shi* as deliberately constructed, reflective, and artful.

2. "The nature of *min*." Mine is a defective translation. By rendering the first sentence above as "emerging from emotions: this is the nature of *min*," I avoid its most problematic and interesting component, namely the term *min* 民. A more honest rendition, drawn from an authoritative translation and analysis of the *Preface*, is "that they should emerge from the affections is human nature."[17] But does *min zhi xing* 民之性 mean "human nature" here? Was the meaning of *min* in the early Han dynasty unambiguously "man" in this nonspecific—even abstract—sense? And is the common assumption that *min* refers not to mankind in general but to a certain stratum of society with a specific set of characteristics thus incorrect?

The scope of the current project does not allow for a comprehensive investigation into these questions, and the following overview of the concept of *min* simply aims at supporting my unorthodox interpretation. I begin and end with Xunzi and as a point of departure take the observation that *min* originally seems to have referred to the lowest social stratum—"slaves," "serfs" or "the masses"—and that the graph in its oldest form appears to depict an eye penetrated and supposedly blinded by a sharp object, which in turn seems to have inspired later speculations as to why "diseased eye" or "eyes shut" was originally chosen as a designation for the masses: "By 'eyes shut' the sages were saying that [the *min*], if not guided and led straight, would descend into disheveled madness" 以瞑者言弗扶將則顛陷猖狂.[18]

Be it as it may with the early history of the concept *min*, in the "Jundao" 君道 chapter of the *Xunzi*, it is said that

The ruler is the sundial, *min* its shadow
If the sundial is straight then the shadow is straight
The ruler is the bowl, *min* the water
If the bowl is round then the water is round
The ruler is the basin
If the basin is square then the water is square[19]

君者儀也民者景也
儀正而景正
君者槃也民者水也
槃圓而水圓
君者盂也
盂方而水方

And, in the same chapter

The ruler is the *min's* wellspring
If the wellspring is clear then the stream is clear
If the wellspring is muddy then the stream is muddy[20]

君者民之原也
原清則流清
原濁則流濁

The *min* are described as passive, malleable, without a will of their own, and easily swayed by external forces. In a similar spirit, Confucius is quoted in the *Lunyu* as saying, "If the superiors love the Rites, then the *min* are easily employed" 上好禮則民易使也.[21] In other words, *min* are those who are governed, employed, and used by their superiors.

Yet in these passages *min* does not seem to be a demographic term in a socioeconomic sense and does not necessarily refer to "the masses" as the lowest segment of the population. Indeed, *min* often refer to people close to the court. In the first example above, Xunzi, as a response to a question on "state craft" (*wei guo* 為國), speaks of *min* sheepishly imitating their ruler, and adds:

If the ruler is the shooter, then the minister (*chen* 臣) is the thumb-hook on which the bow's string is suspended.

> King Zhuang of Chu liked slim waists, and consequently the court was full of people (*ren* 人) starving themselves[22]

君射則臣決
楚莊王好細腰故朝有餓人

Although this further validates the observation that the concept of *min* connotes passivity and malleability, the shift in terminology—in the same passage and context—from ruler versus *min* to ruler versus "minister," and the subsequent anecdote about the self-effacing and emaciated members of King Zhuang's court, indicates that the word *min* is not restricted to "the masses." Similarly, the "Zi Zhang" 子張 chapter of the *Lunyu* says:

> If the ruler has proven himself trustworthy he may make his
>   *min* toil hard
> If not, then [the *min*] will think they are being abused
> If [the *min*] have proven themselves trustworthy then they may
>   remonstrate with the ruler
> If not, then he will think he is being slandered[23]

君子信而後勞其民
未信則以為厲己也
信而後諫
未信則以為謗己也

Although the third sentence lacks an explicit subject, what Confucius has in mind here seems to be the interaction between ruler and *min*, and since it is unlikely that the lowest stratum of society would "remonstrate" with their ruler—*jian* 諫 suggests adherence to ritual protocol—*min* could not refer to "the masses." Furthermore, with reference to a text that predates the *Analects*, when the narrator of "Zheng yue" 正月 (ode 192) complains that "the distorted words of the *min* / are also greatly exaggerated" 民之訛言, 亦孔之將, *min* must be figures of some importance because the narrator is an official and would in all likelihood not consider the gossip, however malicious, of serfs or peasants. From the above examples we discern a set of connotations that gravitates around the term *min*: they are plastic, passive, herdlike, and slanderous. However, when Bo Yi 伯夷 and Shu Qi 叔齊—early Confucian paragons of virtue—are described as "fugitive *min*" (*yi min* 逸民) the word *min* refers neither to people who are lower class nor to those easily swayed by external forces, but rather to well-born men of outstanding moral integrity.[24]

The precise nuance of the word *min* thus depends on the context, and I suggest that a strong case can be made that the phrase *min zhi xing* 民之性 in the *Great Preface* does not mean "human nature" in an unqualified sense but that *min* carries with it the negative connotations that we have previously seen.

If we now return to the *Xunzi* and the "Ru xiao" 儒效 and "Li lun" chapters, we find in the former the following statement:

> To consider it a good thing to follow the vulgar flow
> To consider consumer goods and material possessions the most supreme treasure
> To consider upholding and nourishing the bare life one's highest calling
> This is the virtue of the *min*

> 以從俗為善
> 以貨財為寶
> 以養生為己至道
> 是民德也

This is all Xunzian irony.[25] The so-called virtue of the *min* is a complete reversal of the virtuous characteristics that Xunzi attributes to the Superior Man. The *min* are associated with vulgarity, greed, egoism, and short-sighted opportunism; and, rather than being a demographic category, the word connotes immoral, "plebeian" conduct in general.

In the "Li lun" chapter, the word or concept *min* appears toward the end of a long exposition on the function and principles of the rites.

> The rites
> use precious and plain objects as instruments
> use noble and base as ornaments
> use more and less as means of distinction
> use abundance and dearth as a principle rule[26]

> 禮者
> 以財物為用
> 以貴賤為文

以多少為異
以隆殺為要

My skeletal rendition attempts to retain something of the Xunzian jargon and style, and despite the difficulties they present it is obvious that Xunzi here holds that the accoutrements (clothing, jewelry, funeral goods, etc.) used in the rituals are chosen, and manipulated, with regard to quality and quantity in order to express class distinctions.[27]

Xunzi next distinguishes between excess and lack in rituals; that is, between a ritual expression in which form dominates over content, and vice versa.

> Patterns and embellishments abound whilst emotion and function are diminished: this is ritual abundance
> Patterns and embellishments are diminished whilst emotion and function abound: this is ritual dearth
> Pattern, embellishment, emotion and function existing together as lines of demarcation between inner and outer, and proceeding in tandem and integrating: this constitutes the middle current of the rites.
> The Superior Man, therefore, is utmost lavish toward superiors, utterly meagre toward the lowly, and posits himself in the middle for the middle category[28]
> Not even in running, galloping, or dashing forth does he go beyond this.
> This is the Superior Man's "altar, eaves, house, and courtyard."[29]

> 文理繁，情用省，是禮之隆也
> 文理省，情用繁，是禮之殺也
> 文理情用相為內外表裏並行而雜
> 故君子上致其隆，下盡其殺而中處其中
> 步驟馳騁厲騖不外是矣
> 是君子之壇宇宮廷也

Elsewhere in the same chapter, Xunzi says that the rites serve to moderate sentiments of joy and sorrow; to "shorten the lengthy and prolong the curtailed; to diminish what is excessive and increase what is deficient" 斷長續短，損有餘，益不足.[30] Thus, the rites ensure that joy and grief do not escalate into wantonness or "destructive fear," respectively. This crucial balancing of extreme sentiments, Xunzi continues, constitutes the "middle current of the rites" 禮之中流.[31] Here the same expression ("the middle current") refers to a related but slightly different matter; namely the balance struck between the plain and the embellished in ritual expression, as distinguished from moderation in human emotions. This balance or mean (*zhong* 中) is not a goal in itself, as line four makes clear, but instead one of three modalities which the superior man uses to procure a ritual expression appropriate for a given situation. Adherence to this principle constitutes the framework or homestead—"the altar, eaves, house, and courtyard"—within which the Superior Man exists and acts.

These are important ingredients of Xunzi's discourse on the rites. For our immediate purposes, however, the most salient part is the statement that follows next, where the category of *min* appears as diametrically opposed to the category of *shi junzi* 士君子, which I translate as "the scholar and the Superior Man."

> Among men, those who remain within these [boundaries] are
>   the scholar and the Superior Man
> those outside are the *min*

人有是, 士君子也
外是, 民也

To exist and act, like the *min* do, "outside" the limits defined by the rites entails that one disregards class distinctions, compromises one's integrity and comportment when under pressure, and—if this statement is read as part of the larger argument of the "Li lun" chapter—that one is incapable of restraining one's emotions.

As my meandering commentary on the concept of *min* is drawing to a close, I return to the *Great Preface* and the pericope that claims that to "emerge from," "begin in" or "express oneself in" (*fa hu* 發乎) emotions is the "nature of *min* 民," and that "stopping within Rites and Righteousness" is a consequence of the "gracious influence" of the Former Kings. As a first step we should observe that the opposition of the Former Kings to the *min* is not unlike Xunzi's opposition of *min* and Superior Man. The translation of *min zhi xing* 民之性 as "human nature" may thus be slightly off the mark. From a Xunzian perspective, *min* may indeed translate as "man" or "human being" but only as a reference to human nature in its base, unrefined form—in opposition to the ritualized and refined Superior Man (*junzi*).

Second, the association in the *Preface* of "emotions" with *min* tallies with Xunzi's description of *min* as passive, malleable, and unable or unwilling to restrain their emotions. I have emphasized the textual openness of the *Preface*—that it affords different contextualizations and interpretations—and a "Xunzian" reading of the relevant paragraph could thus be paraphrased as "that the state historians, in times of terrible moral decline, reacted with feelings of unadulterated disgust is wholly consistent with man's most primitive instincts, but that they stopped within the boundaries of the Rites and Righteousness was due to their having absorbed and preserved the benevolent influence of the Former Kings."

What consequences does the reading proposed above have for our understanding of the *Preface*? More specifically, how does the passage analyzed and paraphrased just now relate to the opening description of emotions that emerge "from within" and eventually are manifested in hand-waving and foot stamping? I have suggested elsewhere that the *Preface* may be interpreted as entirely coherent, held together from start to finish by a unique discursive logic; that it is organized into a series of opposites—spontaneous emotions, "tones," and *min* on the one hand, and calculated ambition (*zhi*), poetry (*shi*) and state historians on the other—and that it argues that *shi* is *not* spontaneous and born out of overwhelming emotions but ritualized, deliberated, and "circuitous."[32] My aim in this context has been more modest: to indicate how the cherished Sinological theory of a "cosmological poetics" (*shi* is spontaneous, emotional, unpremeditated, rhetorically naive), which arguably derives from an overemphasis on an extraordinary passage of the *Preface*, may be contradicted by the text itself, in a reading that explores its antecedents in ritual theory such as that developed in the *Xunzi*.[33]

This is, in the literal sense of the word, an exceptional reading. It eradicates the Sinological notion of *shi* as a spontaneous fusion of song and dance and replaces it with an account of Confucian rituality. As suggested in the first part, and as I hope to prove beyond reasonable doubt in the following pages, Mao's *Commentary* is characterized not only by a division between nature and man on the rhetorical level but also by an analogous demarcation line drawn between the populace (*min*) and the lofty "gentleman." It is clear that the *Preface* maintains and reflects this "aristocratic" contempt and fear for the common man's feelings and uninhibited behavior. Indeed, a reading that blurs the dualism of populace and Superior Man ends up an anomaly, describing poetry (the educated man's privileged means of communication) as a soulless reflection of external matters that "proceeds from feelings" (which is "the nature of the populace").

Moreover, the conception of *shi* as an unmeditated reaction to external matters connects directly to Chen Shih-hsiang's "bard" and the general idea of Chinese poetry as fundamentally nonmetaphorical. Because if the act of poetic creation is automatic and takes place in a foot-stomping, hand-waving man overwhelmed by his feelings, then there is no room left for the metaphor which, by definition, is a deliberated trope and a rhetorical artifact. A strictly intratextual reading of the *Great Preface* thus reveals an all-pervading stratification that separates the common man, his feelings, and the "sound" and "tones" he utters from the intentions and the poetry so meticulously crafted by the Superior Man, here *in his capacity as* poet. Poetry, in outright contrast to the primitive man's grunting and wailing, expresses intention, not feelings. When poetry, under extreme circumstances, does originate in feelings it results in a perversion of the sublime poetic form. However, even when perverted by its low origin, the poetry of the educated man—the historian—keeps within the boundaries of the rites.

16

The *Minor Prefaces*

The distinction between populace and superior man—insisted upon with such intensity by Xunzi—is not contradicted by the *Minor Preface*. It is the task of the *Minor Preface* to identify the author and describe the political background of the poem under scrutiny. Often the "people" of a certain state are said to have composed a poem to voice their complaints about bad government, which at first glance would seem to support the standard Sinological hypothesis that *shi* is not *poiêsis* but a spontaneous reaction to a given situation. However, the words that often have been translated simply as "people" are *guo ren* 國人, "men of the state," an expression that lacks the derogatory character of "populace," or *min*. For instance, the *Preface* to "Zai qu" (ode 105, 載驅) says:

> [This is a poem in which] the men of Qi 齊人 criticize 刺 the Duke of Huan. [The duke] completely lacked [the sense of] rites and righteousness. Extravagant were his carriages and clothes. In high speed he drove his carriage in the public streets of the capital. He engaged in licentious behavior with Wen Jiang, and spread [his] evil to the myriads of the populace.

> 齊人刺襄公也. 無禮義, 故盛其車服. 疾驅於通道大都. 與文姜淫, 播其惡於萬民焉.

Here "populace" and the composers of poetry stand in complete opposition. There is a world of difference between the righteous "Men of Qi" who, disgusted with the immoral conduct of Duke Huan, express their resentment

144 | The Origins of Chinese Literary Hermeneutics

in a poem and the populace who cannot help but automatically copy the duke's behavior.

Another candid example is the *Minor Preface* to "Ju xia" 車舝 ("The Carriage's Linchpins," ode 218).

> "Ju xia" [is a poem in which] high officials criticize [the notoriously corrupt] King You [with whom Zhou rule effectively ended in 771 BCE]. [You's consort] Bao Si was jealous and envious. She had risen through the ranks along with immoral officials. Slander and intrigues were ruining the state, and no virtuous grace was bestowed on the populace (*min*). The men of Zhou considered getting a virtuous and able woman to be the lord's mate, and therefore made this poem.
>
> 車舝, 大夫刺幽也. 褒姒嫉妒, 無道並進, 讒巧敗國, 德澤不加於民. 周人思得賢女以配君子, 故作是詩也.[1]

Two conclusions may be drawn immediately. It is quite clear that the authors—the men of Zhou—did not belong to the populace; they were explicitly "high officers." The *min* and the "men of the state" are here put in diametrical opposition. High officers and makers of poetry are men of action whereas the populace consists of those who have action directed at them. Moreover, the poem is indeed made in response to a certain situation but with a special purpose, namely to criticize the king. It is not an immediate and unmeditated response to a political situation but, rather, holds the potential to change that situation. It is a poem created (*zuo*) by men who knew how to canalize their resentment into poetry and who would never have resorted to the hand-waving and the foot stomping associated with the *min*.

If "Ju xia" was composed with the sole purpose of expressing the view that the king should get a new spouse, how was this done in terms of rhetoric and form? These are the five stanzas that the "high officers" of Zhou, according to the preface, made for their king. It is impossible to know whether the pronoun *wo* 我 should be understood, in the original, as representing the first person singular or plural, and I maintain that ambiguity below.

> Inserting the carriage's linchpins
> a fine, reverent girl is coming here

There is neither hunger nor thirst
the virtuous tones are what brings us together[2]
Though there are no good friends
[We] feast and rejoice

Dense is yonder forest on the plain
flocked together are the pheasants
Timely is that imposing girl
she comes to teach virtue
[We] feast and are content
loving thee limitlessly

Though there are no fine spirits
we shall nonetheless drink
Though there is no fine meat
we shall nonetheless eat
Though there is no gift for thee
We shall sing and dance

Ascending that high ridge
splitting that firewood of oak
Splitting that firewood of oak
its leaves are moist
Happily, I see thee
my heart is relieved.

Gazing toward the high mountain
traveling on the big road
The four stallions rush on
the six reins look like a *qin*-lute
Seeing thee, new bride
sets the heart at rest[3]

間關車之牽兮
思孌季女逝兮
匪飢匪渴
德音來括
雖無好友
式燕且喜

依彼平林
有集維鷮
辰彼碩女
令德來教
式燕且譽
好爾無射
雖無旨酒
式飲庶幾
雖無嘉殽
式食庶幾
雖無德與女
式歌且舞
陟彼高岡
析其柞薪
析其柞薪
其葉湑兮
鮮我覯爾
我心寫兮
高山仰止
景行行止
四牡騑騑
六轡如琴
覯爾新婚
以慰我心

The five stanzas of "Ju xia" deserve to be quoted in full since they illustrate the mechanisms of poetic expression described by the *Minor Preface*. The *Great Preface* has told us that poetry, or *feng*, is ideal for criticizing those of superior rank without offending them, a description suggesting that poetry is a roundabout, ritualized mode of discourse. And the high officials' appeals to their king have indeed yielded a long poem that celebrates the arrival of a bride. We recognize the "thou" and "thee" as the archetypal addressee of love songs: a female figure, young and refined. But who is speaking? Who is the "I" who raises his voice to speak of love, longing, and the bliss of togetherness? "The bridegroom," a reader unfamiliar with the story related by Confucian exegetes might answer. And it is possible to interpret the poem as words put in the king's mouth, directed to his bride to be. According to such a reading, "Ju xia" remains the straightforward love song it appears to be on the surface except, of course, for the fact that it tells of love on a royal level.

If this interpretation is paired with the preface above, then the officers of Zhou made a poem that was thoroughly rhetorical, ritualized, and crafty (譎 *jue*), as the poem's narrator is not one who spontaneously bursts out in poesy but a persona, a poet speaking in a borrowed voice. And if the "I" of a poem is no longer identical to the subject defined as the author, then the poetic text cannot be dismissed as naive and transparent. It cannot be the product of Chen Shih-hsiang's primeval and primitive bard.

Zheng Xuan finds "Ju xia" governed by a slightly different rhetorical order.[4] According to Zheng, the voice filled with amorous tenderness does not belong to the king *qua* bridegroom but to the high officials on the lookout for a virtuous bride for their king. The first lines of the stanza describe the officers preparing their carriages for a journey on which they hope to obtain a beautiful young girl with a strong sense of virtue. Having set out on that arduous trip, the officers are hungry and thirsty, yet so engrossed in their important mission that they do not feel it.

"The trees in the forest on the plains are luxuriant so fine birds gather together there" 平林之木茂則耿介之鳥往集焉, Zheng says of the second stanza.[5] Analogically, this imparts (*yu* 喻) that if the king's virtue is luxuriant, then a worthy girl will come to join him and through "mutual instructions" 與相訓告 further "revise his virtue" 改修德教.[6] Having thus explained the analogy between the natural world and the state of Zhou, Zheng goes on to say that the officers, delighting in the arrival of this "fine bird," instigate a drinking party in her honor. And in the last line of the stanza, the officers exclaim—to the king, in Zheng's view—that "we shall love you without ever growing tired."[7]

The fourth stanza describes the lowly task of splitting firewood. "When someone climbs a high ridge," Zheng says, "he will need to cut its trees into firewood, and doing so entails covering the height of the ridge with the lush leaves of the tree" 登高崗者, 必析其木以為薪. 析其木以為薪者, 為其葉茂盛, 蔽岡之高也.[8] After elaborating on the literal sense, Zheng Xuan explains the "allegorical" meaning of these lines, saying that "this means [*yu* 喻] that when the virtuous girl has reached the [high] position of being the queen, she will inevitably expulse the envious and jealous woman, as she too is obscuring the ruler's splendor" 此喻賢女得在王后之位則必辟除嫉妒之女, 亦為其蔽君之明.[9] At this point, the Men of Zhou's anxiety clears away when they realize that the girl indeed meets their expectations.

In his comments on the fifth and final stanza, Zheng reads the high mountain as a metaphor for (high) virtue and makes a pun on the character *xing* (or *hang* 行), "road," "conduct," and "rank": "The ministers assumed that when the sagely girl had entered [the court], the king would move closer to the [conduct of the sagely] ancients, holding those of lofty virtue in high esteem, and employing those whose conduct were illustrious" 諸大夫以為賢女既進則王亦庶幾古人, 有高德者則慕仰之, 有明行者則而行之.[10]

Zheng then compares the art of kingship to that of a horseman.

[And that] when managing [御 *yu* lit. "driving a carriage"] the many subjects he would make them adhere to ritual principles,[11] like [a horseman] driving a carriage with four horses unceasingly, maintaining his instructions, making them [the horses or the subjects] run harmoniously and even, again like [a horseman] adjusting his grip on the six reins in accordance with the speed of the individual horse, thereby maintaining their harmony. When we [the men of Zhou] see your new bride [acting] like this, the anxiety harbored in our hearts vanishes.

其御群臣, 使之有禮, 如御四馬騑騑然. 持其教令, 使之調均, 亦如六轡緩急有和也. 我得見女之新昏如是則以慰除我心之憂也.[12]

Zheng Xuan's reading may for good reasons be regarded with suspicion. Zheng is a voracious, omnivorous hermeneut for whom no part of a poem is superfluous. Everything can and must be digested in the hermeneutical metabolic process. Each line occupies a part of the totality of the poem, either literally or metaphorically. Zheng's forte, on the other hand, is that he pinpoints the metaphorical undertones of the piece—why talk of pheasants, dense trees, and moist leaves when you want your king to take a new and beautiful wife?[13] Furthermore, the narrative structure of Zheng's reading is simpler than the interpretation contemplated a moment ago. Zheng follows the *Minor Preface* meticulously and identifies the "I" of the poem (the *voice* of the lover) as the high officers of Zhou. The modern reader marvels at the seemingly bizarre logic: you want the king to take a new wife but you also do not want to offend him by telling him so to his face; so you write a love song in which you yourself play the part of the lover and (at least prima facie) tell your king's future wife that you shall love her forever. Such a mode of communication demands, in modern terms, that addresser and addressee be in total agreement about the code of the communication—and yet we recognize in the *Odes* themselves, namely the fourth stanza of "Wu yang," the assumption that communication of the highest order may take place in a language that is tortuous beyond normal comprehension.

I leave all possible interpretations and misinterpretations here. The point to be made, with regard to "Ju xia," is that the preface describes a form of poetry that was not only aesthetically appealing but, moreover, crafted with the utmost precision. A crude message ("your wife is ruining the country, get a divorce") has been diplomatically transformed into the five beautiful stanzas of a love song. Artistry and abstraction were certainly the hallmarks of the poetry composed by the "men of the state."

The *Minor Prefaces* and *Poiêsis Sinensis*

As suggested previously, I submit that in the *Minor Prefaces zuo* 作 typically means to "create" a poem, rather than to "invoke," "recite," or "perform" a preexisting one. As further evidence, consider the preface to "Huang niao" (ode 131), according to which that poem "Laments three worthies. The men of the state criticized Duke Mu for having [living] men accompanying him in death, and therefore *zuo*-ed this poem" 哀三良也. 國人刺穆公以人從死而作是詩也. Since ode 131 names the three "worthies" interred alive with the duke, according to the preface it must have been composed (or "made" or "created") as a response to this particular occasion. While this in turn does not absolutely exclude the possibility that *zuo* here refers to a remonstrative "performance" of "Huang niao" by the indignant "men of the state" (who in that case may or may not have authored it), it strongly suggests that *zuo* indeed refers to the "making" of the ode in question by those men.

If *zuo* in the *Minor Prefaces* meant "recite" or "perform," it would presuppose, first, that the author(s) of the *Prefaces* was (were) interested only in explaining the situation in which the ode in question was quoted, and was (were) indifferent to the origins of those songs; second, that there existed a corpus of songs that could be recited—or reorganized and patched together ad hoc—as detailed responses to a wide variety of very different situations. (One may add that even if this hypothesis were true it would still be incompatible with the reading of the *Great Preface* as describing *shi* as the result of a wholly spontaneous reaction to a particular situation or sensory impression. The *intention* of the person making the recitation—or the edition, or the "patching together" of preexisting formulae—would still be the key to the understanding of the poem, according to the *Minor Prefaces*.)

I find no hard evidence either to prove or disprove the assumptions above, but the circumstantial evidence argues in favor of the hypothesis submitted in this book. Ode 39 "Quan shui" 泉水 is attributed by the preface to a "female of Wei who longed to return home" 衛女思歸. Unable to do so, she "consequently *zuo*-ed this ode in order to make herself [i.e., her longing] visible" 故作是詩以自見也.[14] Considering the many details (such as toponyms and names of clans) specified in the poem's four stanzas, it seems improbable that the author(s) of the preface supposed that there had already existed a song with the contents of "Quan shui," which the lady of Wei merely recited.

17

In Service to Two Masters

In the poetics of the *Minor Prefaces*, the author is indeed regarded as the center and origin of the poem. But it is a poet that creates deliberately and with a purpose; therefore the Sinological assumption of the spontaneous poet, and the accompanying aversion to metaphoricity, must be questioned. The working hypothesis for the present project is thus that the concept of xing, as it appears in Mao's *Commentary*, designates a maneuver that is metaphorical in the Aristotelian sense and should be regarded as an artifact not unlike the fabricated Western metaphor. Similarly, but on a larger scale, the Chinese poetic text—or the interpretation thereof—is the result of an intellectual process. It is an entity created rather than spontaneously generated.

The rhetorical operation that Mao calls "xing" is—this was the assumption underlying the first part of the present work—a concept with a history. Mao's xing is related to, but not identical with, the practice of quoting the *Odes* while making a speech in a diplomatic context or as part of a philosophical argument, to what has variously been called "extracting meaning from broken stanzas" (*duanzhang quyi* 斷章取義—that is, quoting lines from the *Odes* out of context), "pointing out similar cases and relating to instances of the same category" (*yinpi lianlei* 引譬連類) or "reciting poetry to express one's intent" (*fushi yanzhi* 賦詩言志). In *The Problem of a Chinese Aesthetic*, Haun Saussy identified the early Chinese utilitarian approach to literary exegesis by describing the Confucian reader as a worker whose task it was to transform a potentially immoral text into a message of morality.[1] Simultaneously, one may add that the xing was never a consistent hermeneutic technique or a part of an all-embracing interpretational program but rather a tool used arbitrarily whenever the Confucian reader had to "work" on the text. This entails the sheer impossibility of arriving at a formal definition that would cover all examples.

I also argue that Mao's xing is much more complex and paradoxical than is usually acknowledged and that it was a heterogeneous concept even in its first incarnation as an analytical tool in the *Mao Commentary*. Two insights follow from this line of reasoning. First, speaking of "Mao's xing" is itself a risky undertaking, at least when done only from the point of view of a literary aesthetics (and excluding the role played by Confucian ideology). Second, and as a corollary to the above, I must modify the arguments put forward in the first part. To be able to show that the xing was not an entity with a constant and stable meaning in the history of Chinese literary exegesis, I had to succumb to an oversimplification, namely to speak of "Mao's xing" precisely as if it were a standardized, constantly self-identical interpretational method. Only then could the definition of xing proposed by the various scholars discussed there be presented as different from Mao's concept.

In following chapters I go one step further. I retain the idea of a "standard" xing and then proceed to those instances where Mao deviates from this "prototype." Naturally, Mao saw no contradiction in giving the same name ("xing") to what today may seem like widely different rhetorical models. Instead, this opposition between a standard and a deviating xing should be seen as a convenient way of organizing the argument about the heterogeneity of Mao's concept, a heterogeneity that evolved from its role as servant to two masters: Confucian ideology and a budding literary aesthetics.

The Sign

To describe the function of the xing I borrow from the terminology of semiotics its most central concept and define the xing as a *sign*, made up of a *signans* and a *signatum*. The signans is the spoken or written, nonsemantic component of what we call a "word," and the signatum the meaning bestowed on the signans in the act of enunciation or interpretation. The meaning of a sign is determined by the position it occupies in a certain context, from which follows that the signatum depends on the context in which its signans is put; meaning is not the outcome of a direct correspondence between a word-body (signans) and a preordained meaning (signatum). Philosophers and theorists of literature are quick to point out the obliqueness implied by this split: there is no immediate presence that will sponsor or validate the unanimity of the signans and the signatum. In short, the meaning of a sign is unstable and not deducible from a study of a signans in isolation.

As suggested above, the "xing-sign"—the calling *jujiu*, the yellow bird, the fish lurking in the deep water, the highly branched tree, the sunny slope or the murky swamp—is a signans with an ambiguous signatum. Apart from the split between signans and signatum that characterizes any ordinary word or sign, the xing-sign obtains its effect precisely from a play between a primary signatum and secondary one.

The xing element in the first poem, the *jujiu*, has a primary and conventional signatum, namely a kind of bird that may be referred to in English as "osprey" or "fish-hawk." The second signatum (the virtuous girl and the "lord") bases itself on a perceived likeness, a shared characteristic (virtue) between the ospreys and the two people. Mao's xing would indeed be impossible without this play between a primary and secondary meaning. Consequently, the "calling *jujiu*" may be described in conventional terms as a metaphorical sign since its signans is linked to its signatum by way of a perceived likeness, or *tertium comparationis*. But is this true of all of Mao's xings? By investigating the relationship between the signans and signatum of the xing-sign I shall establish a typology of Mao Heng's interpretation of poetic language. This is my aim and methodology at this initial stage, and as a first step I shall try to establish a general definition of xing as it appears in Mao's *Commentary*.

18

Mao's "Canonical" Xing

"Guanju" 關雎 (ode 1)

Mao's concept xing, the great scholar Zhu Ziqing says in an essay from 1945, "has two meanings: One is 'start' [of a stanza], the other is 'simile' [*piyu* 譬喻]. Only when these two criteria coincide do we have a 'xing.'"[1] The xing is thus described as having one strictly formal trait (it refers to the "image" with which the first stanza of an ode opens) and one rhetorical (it implies that some kind of likeness obtains between the xing image and its "referent," and that the poet chose to describe one object or phenomenon in terms of another). "Earlier scholars," Zhu continues, "did not notice these two features [of the xing], hence the never-ending confusion" in the attempts to reach an understanding of the xing's true nature.[2] Zhu's essay is pathbreaking in that it seems to focus only on Mao's xing and consider all later users thereof as usurpers, or as secondary emendators, of an original concept. Zhu thereby realizes that the xing is a meta-textual *concept* and not an inherent feature of the *Odes*. Nonetheless, Zhu is traditional in that he claims that the xing actually exists as a self-identical, nonparadoxical concept, and that he has found the two principles that govern it.

Let us take Zhu's observations one or two steps further. It is correct that with Mao Heng "xing" most often refers to an image (or natural description) with which a poem opens up: But why does it occupy that privileged position, and what logic governs the two or three exceptions to that rule? Zhu's second principle must also be scrutinized, not merely because it purports to reveal the fundamental principle of Mao's semiotics but also because the claim that xing builds on *piyu* ("likeness" or "similitude") seems to imply that Mao's xingish readings obey a logic of an aesthetic or linguistic kind, which might be an anachronistic fallacy. Lastly, are Zhu's (or Mao's) two principles interrelated and, if so, how?

Let us return to the first ode. Our obsession with this poem is justified because it is arguably the most significant piece of the *Shijing* corpus, the interpretation of which immediately establishes a methodology for the correct understanding of poetry (*shi*). As suggested previously, one may also assume that Mao was particularly eager to demonstrate how "Guanju" should be read, so as to avoid deviant readings of the following odes. This assumption is sustained by the fact that Mao's comments on the poems in the first part of the book are generally longer and more detailed than those toward the end. Another testament to the importance of this ode is that a substantial number of scholars have made Mao's comments on "Guanju" the starting point of their attempts to understand what "the xing" is—a practice that, as we shall see momentarily, tends to diminish the complexity of Mao's hermeneutics since it neglects the contradictory testimony presented by the other "xing" poems.

To the first lines of "Guanju" ("*Kroo kroo* cry the ospreys / On the islet of the river") Mao provides the following commentary:

> This is a xing. *Kroo kroo* are harmonious calls. Although the *jujiu* . . . is a passionate bird, the male and the female maintain separation. The queen consort rejoices in the virtue of her lord; nothing is unharmonious and there is no discord, nor [does she] overindulge [her] sensuality. [She] carefully guards [her] deep seclusion [in the palace], like the *jujiu's* living separated from each other. The situation having become thus, it may be used to influence and change the world. If man and woman maintain separation, father and son will bond closely; if father and son bond closely, ruler and subject will respect each other; if ruler and subject respect each other, the proceedings of the royal court will be ordered; if the royal court is ordered, the kingly transformation will be perfected.
>
> 興也. 關關和聲也. 雎鳩 . . . 鳥摯而有別 . . . 后妃說樂君子之德, 無不和諧又不淫其色. 慎固幽深若雎鳩之有別. 然後可以風化天下. 夫婦有別則父子親, 父子親則君臣敬, 君臣敬則朝廷正, 朝廷正則王化成.³

Here, in Mao's comment on the first two lines of the *Shijing*, we find the keywords that will appear and reappear in different combinations all through the *Commentary*: regulation, hierarchic rigor, and harmony are the concepts that underlie Mao's interpretation. The negativity of Mao's idiom ("nothing is unharmonious"; "there is no discord") presents disharmony, fornication, and chaos as the *prima materia* that must be fought and negated. By describing harmony in terms of negated disharmony and "correct" sexuality in terms of negated sexual misconduct, Mao underlines the fragility of a state in which "the kingly transformation" has been perfected and discloses the Confucian fear of sexuality, excess, licentiousness, and hierarchic chaos. Sex and sexuality, we observe, are the very pivots of human society. Thus, if man and woman only regulate their sexual behavior the primary condition for a paradisiacal society is fulfilled. Conversely, if sexuality is allowed to flourish in a chaotic state the world will go awry, the two parallel hierarchies—that of the family and that of the government—will break down and anarchy will ensue.

Technically speaking, the order of the benevolent influence (*feng hua* 風化) must always go from high to low; the lower "classes" can never themselves instigate a change in the moral (to wit: sexual) behavior of mankind. Like the bard allegedly described in the *Great Preface*, the common man cannot but mirror his immediate surroundings, and if the king and his consort fornicate, the commoner automatically fornicates. The language of negation is paradoxical in that it simultaneously confirms the existence of that which it wishes to condemn, just as the xing—as we shall see in a moment—sometimes paves the way for the deviant readings it sets out to abolish.

Turning our attention to the tropological organization of the piece, we find that the *jujiu* bird—the "osprey" or "fish-hawk"—does not merely refer to a bird that Mao describes as passionate yet chaste. *Jujiu* has a secondary and more important *signatum*, namely the royal couple that Mao celebrates for their regulated sex life. The bird and the two people are linked to each other on a textual level by means of similitude since both that avian animal and these human animals share the characteristic of having a well-ordered sex life. This link is explicitly manifested in the *Commentary* by Mao's usage of the copula *ruo* 若 ("like" or "resembling").

It is precisely at this point that we should return to the cosmologists previously discussed. To this group of scholars Chinese poetry and Confucian hermeneutics are fundamentally concrete and antimetaphorical. Whatever imagery appears in a poetic text is to be taken literally or, with C. H. Wang, as the accidental outcome of the peculiarities of oral song composing. Pauline Yu took the notion of literalness to its extreme—indeed, to its logical extreme—with her claim that in *shi* in ancient China we find not "metaphors" but only literal descriptions of the correspondences of the world. But even a quick glance at Mao's comment on "Guanju" refutes these notions. As concluded earlier, the fallacy of "correlative poetics" results, at least partly from a failure to appreciate the motive behind Mao Heng's metaphorical equation of bird and man. Mao may very well have conceived of the world as full of correspondences between things of the same category (*lei*) and thus between ospreys and lovers (with a healthy but restrained libido). If we focus on the textual level, however, these speculations lose their relevance since the poem is obviously not *about* cosmological correspondences in the text-external world. On the contrary, the *jujiu* are present in the text as a description of—or predication about—the king and the queen consort, and this description (or predication) is made possible through the presence of a *tertium comparationis*, namely the well-regulated sex life that both birds and the royal couple allegedly display. In sum, the xing consists of a transfer of meaning from the natural realm to the human world. This transference is performed strictly on a textual or linguistic level and does not, hypermimetically, mirror a situation in the text-external world. The xing, as Mao conceives it, is therefore a *trope*.

Hitherto we have only read Mao's comment on the first two lines of "Guanju." A "direct," "naïve," and non-Confucian reading would probably understand the first ode as a charming song about passionate love, as in the following stanzas when the "lord" or "young master" is described as "seeking" his young lady while tossing and turning in his sleep. The enormous tension between what the poem is saying prima facie and the Confucian message that Mao must find therein explains the copiousness of Mao's comments, as well as his "negative" idiom. Since the poem itself speaks of passionate love Mao must make a direct and violent counterattack to make the poem speak of nonpassion and of sexual regulation, hence the allegoresis, the metaphoricity, and the mass of words whose function it is to add force to his comments (sometimes, one suspects, by overwhelming the reader). Hence, also, there is the hermeneutical strategy of negation. Mao realizes that the poem is explicitly speaking of passion and that this fact cannot easily be swept under the rug. But by making the ospreys (and thus the two people) creatures of sexual moderation Mao is able to negate, on a metatextual level, the theme of sexual passion. Consequently, the "lord's" feverish longing for the girl now becomes the Superior Man's longing for a chaste mate and for a relationship characterized by noncloseness (that is, distance), nonfornication, and nondisharmony, as in the third and fourth lines:

The retreating, good girl—
a fine mate for the lord

窈窕淑女
君子好逑

Mao comments that "*Yaotiao* means 'dark and secluded' . . . bespeaking that the queen consort has the virtue [*de* 德] of the *jujiu* bird. This dark [i.e., concealed] and secluded, chaste and loyal good woman is fit to be the lord's good mate" 窈窕幽閒也 . . . 言后妃有關雎之德。是幽閒貞專之善女宜為君子好匹。[4]

"Dark and secluded" refers, at least with Zheng Xuan, to the dark interiors of the palace to which the chaste queen consort is confined.[5] We are beginning to grasp the rhetorical structure of the poem. The bird, screaming on an isolated islet in the river, is taken as a description of and metaphorical statement about the queen in her seclusion, a chaste "girl" determined to keep her (sexual) integrity intact. More importantly, we can now distinguish between the two kinds of figurality at work in the poem, which I call allegory and metaphoricity. On the one hand there is Mao's allegorical identification of the poem's personae as the king and the queen.[6] Such an act of identification is not warranted by the text itself but builds on extratextual information given by Mao, the hermeneutic *auctoritas*, in an act of interpretational violence that corrupts the text's integrity. On the other hand, Mao establishes a link within the text, in that the ospreys function as metaphors of the lord (*junzi* 君子) and the girl 女. We have already concluded that the characteristic shared by the birds and the young couple is sexual moderation. Now Mao narrows the *tertium comparationis* down to a single concept, virtue (*de* 德); virtuous is the osprey and virtuous are the girl queen and her lord. The link between the ospreys and the "lord" and the girl is, in my tentative terminology, intratextual, since both tenor (lord/girl) and vehicle (osprey) are present in the text.[7] The xing, therefore, is a hermeneutical tool that enables Mao to establish a metaphorical link between nature and humans or, rather, the descriptions thereof. As proposed above, the parallelistic structure of

"Guanju" itself suggests a metaphorical relation between the *jujiu* and the personage of the poem.⁸

It could therefore be said that Mao's xing actually reveals the imagistic structure of the first ode in a nonviolent act of interpretation. But to reveal the imagistic structure and to interpret it are two different things. The irony is that the very concept that Mao invented as a means of transforming a nonideological text into Confucian dogma can easily end up a weapon directed against Mao's own project. Once we have grasped the parallelistic and metaphorical structure revealed by Mao's xing we cannot but identify the islet confined and screaming osprey with the "girl," thereby opening the text for a "deviant" and forbidden reading that understands the girl as the unreachable object of the "lord's" feverish dreams or, equally probable, as a young girl alienated, in a most physical manner on her islet, by her lust. The schizophrenia between what the poem explicitly says and what Mao *wants* it to say—between the approved, Confucian reading that the xing aims at and the perverse, sexual, and excessive reading that the xing inevitably suggests—is always a possibility in Mao's exegetics, as Ulrike Middendorf has demonstrated.⁹ On this level, the xing is characterized by a painful tension between Mao's pragmatism (the xing is used to transform the text) and the purely rhetorical scheme that the xing reveals (the *jujiu* being a metaphor for the amorous couple).

The fifth and sixth lines of the poem describe plant picking.

> Varied in length are the *xing* plants
> Left and right she gathers them.

參差荇菜
左右流之

Mao comments that "since the queen consort has the virtue of the *jujiu* she can supply the *xing* plant and prepare the many objects, and therewith [procure] the service in the ancestral temple 后妃有關雎之德乃能共荇菜備庶物以事宗廟也.¹⁰ Mao's main task as an exegete, apart from making the *Odes* acceptable for the Confucian reader, is to make the text univocal. Here, Mao repeats the hermeneutical keyword that simultaneously binds osprey and man together in a metaphor and makes the poem thematically acceptable: virtue. Furthermore, in the description of the virtuous queen who picks and prepares the herbs for the temple rituals we encounter the very first instance of the work-rite metaphor discussed previously in conjunction with

Saussy's thesis about the "performative" nature of Confucian hermeneutics. In the process leading to hermeneutic integrity and wholesomeness, Mao must avoid devious or superfluous meaning. Indeed, every fragment of the poem must be significant and fit harmoniously into the wholeness that Mao wants to present.

Consequently, Mao faces three interrelated difficulties when explaining these lines: the plant used as a xingish vehicle cannot be just any plant, the picking of the plant cannot merely be the everyday *vulgar* picking of plants, and finally a queen cannot be imagined carrying out the lowly work of the *vulgus*. The solution to these problems comes with the explanation of plant picking as a preparation for rituals. The *xing* plant is bestowed with significance since it is used in rituals, which is what distinguishes man from nonman and aristocrat from commoner in the Confucian, or *Ru*-ist, doctrine.[11] The queen's plant picking is simultaneously rescued from the fate of misunderstanding (why would a lady of the royal family pick plants?), as work is understood as ritual.

The pattern of the first four lines thus reoccurs in that the poem itself speaks of passion, youthful lust, and menial work, whereas Mao, presenting an interpretation digestible by the Confucian metabolic system, claims that the poem speaks of nonpassion, of a king's search for a chaste queen, and of rituals. Mao, as a paragon of Confucian hermeneutics, does indeed work on the poem: he trims and cuts it, removing all traces of these lowly, embarrassing themes, and the end product of this hermeneutical refinery is a poem that smells faintly of flowers and tells of ladies and gentlemen and their well-bred love. The poem goes on to describe how the lord "waking and sleeping" seeks the "chaste and good young girl"; however, for Mao the job is done, as the poem has been domesticated and can no longer be taken for a simple love poem.

Let us instead return to the xing. In this trope, "images" taken from nature are used to describe certain situations, acts, or phenomena pertaining to the human realm. Mao's xing entails, therefore, a split between nature and culture—between the plants and animals and the man who has risen above them. On the textual level, nature is ontologically inferior to the descriptions of humans; in other words, statements about nature in themselves carry little weight and can only be interpreted as statements about mankind. In this manner, Mao's hermeneutics always stresses the superiority of the animate over the inanimate, the conscious over the nonconscious, and the being over the not-quite-being. Our understanding of this hierarchic structure is of paramount importance since it is related to the distinction made in the *Great Preface* between the aristocratic Superior Man and the uncouth commoner. The rhetorical inferiority of nature in Confucian exegesis is thus a part of a more general suspicion directed against the natural, the unrefined, and the unintentional; it is precisely this thought pattern that produced Mao's xing. And as a corollary, Confucian hermeneutics understands the unsophisticated commoner not as a subject or rational individual but as a piece of nature.[12] All this derives from the same founding metaphor; raw material—be it a poem, a natural image, or a human being—must be worked on and brought under the influence of culture. The figurality and indirectness of Mao's xing belong to the same area as rites and rituals in that they, as refined artifacts, can be used to distinguish culture from nature and the Superior Man from the common person. The natural poet—as Chen Shih-hsiang's or C. H. Wang's spontaneous bard—cannot express himself in a cultured way and must be ostracized from Mao's Confucian republic.

Returning now to our principle task of defining the xing, we have concluded that Mao's *Commentary* identifies two different processes of figurality in "Guanju," one extratextual (the "girl" refers to a certain queen consort) and the other intratextual (*jujiu* refers to the virtuous couple). Having identified, using a tentative and approximate terminology, the movement from bird to man as metaphorical we ask ourselves if the "allegorical" identification of the poem's personae as historical characters should also be included in Mao's xingish strategy of reading. That this question is anachronistic (and perhaps also somewhat misguided) is quite clear because Mao aimed at neither a formal categorization of tropes nor a description of the poetic text as a purely aesthetic or linguistic object. Nonetheless, it is a question that may incite a discussion that will shed some further light on the xing.

"Zhen lu" 振鷺 (ode 278)

Let us repeat. In Mao's canonical, xingish reading of "Guanju" vehicle is linked to tenor by means of a shared characteristic (virtue) expressed and underlined by the copula *ruo* 若, which is not found in the text itself but added by Mao in his comment. The text itself "merely" juxtaposes the two lines about the ospreys with the lines about the amorous couple. Was Mao's metaphorical reading simply a violent hermeneutic innovation unheard of and unthinkable in earlier times? Or did he, as I suggest, in fact reveal a mode of reading and writing metaphorically that must have existed, at least as a possibility, in the cultural environment in which the *Odes* were generated?

"Zhen lu," which has been briefly discussed, appears in the *Song* 頌 section of the *Odes* together with poems that celebrate the early kings of Zhou or their officials—or they describe performances of sacrifices and rituals. The poem is structured according to the binary logic with which we are familiar.

> In flocks, the *lu* birds in flight
> in those western swamps
> Our guests arrive
> also having this appearance[13]

> 振鷺于飛
> 于彼西雝
> 我客戾止
> 亦有斯容

Mao comments: "A xing . . . The egret is a white bird . . . The 'guests' are descendants of the two kings [of the Xia and Shang dynasties]" 興也 . . . 鷺白鳥也 . . . 客二王之後.[14]

"Zhen lu" is a textbook example of Mao's canonical xing. That "egrets" functions as a description of the arriving guests is explicitly stated by the text itself and underscored by the copula *yi* 亦, "also," which connects natural and human activity. Furthermore, what links fowls to man is not a deep-seated cosmological correspondence but their shared appearance, possibly the most superficial of all traits. Mao's reading of "Zhen lu" thus supports the assumption that xing is a trope based on likeness in which human situations are described through natural sceneries and, conversely, that such a reading—or technique of reading—was not simply a trick invented by Mao *qua* Confucian ideologue but an inherent possibility of the text.

As to the question of whether the xing trope also includes an extra-textual, allegorical maneuver, Mao's comment on "Zhen lu" provides no definitive answer. Mao clearly takes part of the allegorical tradition of the Lu school (and, possibly, the *Minor Preface*) by identifying the "guests" as the descendants of Xia and Shang, which seems to indicate that Mao's xing also includes the allegorico-historical identification of the poem's protagonists, in addition to the metaphorical relationship between egret and guests.[15]

Let us at this point consult an intertext that points in another direction, namely "You bi" 有駜 (ode 298). In this poem, the "image" of the flock of egrets occurs in the middle of a stanza; that is, in a position that normally is not that of a xing:

> Sturdily, sturdily
> sturdy are those teams of bays[16]

有駜有駜
駜彼乘黃

Mao comments that "'Sturdy' [refers to] the appearance of a well-fed and strong horse. If a horse is well-fed and strong he can ascend heights and travel far. If a minister is strong and forceful he can pacify the state" 駜, 馬肥彊貌. 馬肥彊則能升高進遠. 臣彊力則能安國.[17]

> Morning and evening in the palace
> in the palace [they are] very bright
> Flock-wise, the egrets [fly]
> the egrets go alight
> the drums sound *yan, yan*
> Drunkenly we dance
> together we rejoice!

夙夜在公
在公明明
振振鷺
鷺于下
鼓咽咽
醉言舞
于胥樂兮

Mao comments: "The egret is a white bird. [This imagery] is used as a xing [lit. "to *xing*"] for the pure and white official" 鷺白鳥也. 以興絜白之士.[18]

The comment on "You bi" is one of only three instances where Mao identifies a xing in the middle—and not at the beginning—of a poem. One may speculate that the unorthodox verbal usage of "xing" (以興 "so as to xing") reflects Mao's uneasiness about breaking his habit, although "xing" does appear as a noun in the other two cases, Mao's comment on ode 126,

"Ju lin" and on ode 171, "Nan you jia yu."[19] Of more urgent interest is that Mao, in his xingish reading, clearly and unambiguously identifies the relationship that obtains between the natural and the human realms as one based on a supposed likeness; however, he does not engage in a historico-allegorical interpretation of the poem's personage as this or that king, vassal, or queen consort. Mao explicitly says that the image of the white egret is used "to *xing*" the white pureness of the official. The *tertium comparationis* that links the two strata is thus "whiteness." Mao's comment on "You bi" firmly contradicts the claims about the concretion and literalism of early Chinese poetry and hermeneutics.

In my previous reading of "Guanju," I remarked that the *jujiu* could function as a description of the virtuous "gentleman" and the "beautiful and good girl" because they too were virtuous (or so Mao claimed), and I argued that Mao's xing was an exegetical instrument used to confer an abstract, extratextual meaning (the concept of *de* 德) upon the plain imagery of screaming ospreys or fish-haws on an islet. Xing thus depends on, and entails, a movement from concretion toward abstraction.

Here, in Mao's reading of "You bi," bird and man are linked through a very similar—yet manifestly more abstract—process. The egret is a white bird, and the official (or the "guests" described in poem 278) is "white"; that is, pure and unsoiled. The egret's whiteness is concrete and literal whereas the official's "whiteness" must be taken in an abstract sense, unless we understand Mao's words *jie bai* 絜白 to mean that the official has been washed clean and actually painted white. The *meta-phora*, or "transfer," from *bai* 白 "white" as a color—or lack thereof—to "whiteness" in the sense of immaculateness and absence of vices is precisely an abstraction and, of course, a conceptualization that occurs in many cultures and historical periods. Consequently, when Mao says that the white egret "xings" the pure, virtuous official, that statement already involves abstraction. Mao's xing is thereby able to connect the natural and human strata through a pun on the double meaning of *bai*, "white," "unsullied."

Moreover, what decisively speaks against the school of hyperrealism is that Mao's xing trope involves a transference between two different categories since the egret's whiteness refers to the bird's appearance whereas the official's "whiteness" refers to behavior. If, as a hyperrealist would claim, there were an extratextual correspondence between egret and man, it would have to take place at the same existential, phenomenological or cosmological level; that is, the official must actually be white (by color of skin, by his clothes or by paint), or the egret must be "white" in the sense that it is without moral blemish, which is not what Mao is saying in the *Commentary*.[20] Nor is this what is said in what is arguably the *locus classicus* of correlative cosmology, namely the canonical definition of correlative or cosmological categories (*lei* 類) in *Master Lü's Annals*: "[Things] of the same category attract each other, [things] of the same *qi* ether spontaneously congregate, sounds that are essentially comparable spontaneously respond to each other. Thus, if you strike a *gong* note, another *gong* will resound; strike a *jue* and another *jue* will vibrate" 類同相召, 氣同則合, 聲比則應. 故鼓宮而宮應, 鼓角而角動.[21]

Mao's implicit theory of how the ancient poets used the technique of xing argues expressly against what I have called the poetics of correlative cosmology. Pauline Yu's metaphor and mimesis are the core of Western poetics—in fashioning a metaphor the likeness between "this" and "that" is *invented*—whereas, to Pauline Yu, the early Chinese theoreticians of *shi* assumed that "analogies already exist, to be *discovered* by the poet, not manufactured." Again, despite the assertion that a "good metaphorizer" must possess a particular aptness (*euphuia*), Aristotle nowhere claims that *to homoion* is fabricated, fictional, or unreal.

Conversely, with reference to Mao's notion of how the poet composed the ode "You bi," if we assume that xing builds on a likeness (as expressed by the word *ruo* in Mao's comment on the first ode), then is the "likeness" between the white bird and the morally pure official an "analogy to be *discovered*" in Yu's sense of the word? Is it the tautological sameness between a *gong* note played on a string instrument and a *gong* note struck on a drum, as described in *Master Lü's Annals*? I am inclined to answer both questions in the negative. To claim that the actual and concrete whiteness of the egret stands in a cosmological "analogy" with (or correlates to) the purity and the immaculateness of the official contradicts the rhetoricity, metaphoricity, and abstraction that Mao obviously associated with the act of describing the white bird in order to "xing" the purity of the official.

Mao's xingish poet cannot be said to have simply juxtaposed egret and man (with Brooke-Rose) "lazily" and paratactically; instead, Mao's xingish *act* is here much closer to Holzman's Spring and Autumn period diplomat who, by quoting ode 87 obliquely, rhetorically, and metaphorically refers to himself and his stronger opponent in terms of a young woman and her suitor. The Aristotelian metaphoricity of the tradition of quoting the *Odes* which Holzman (in my view perhaps a little too hastily) identifies with the xing is nowhere clearer than in the instances in which the hidden message of a quoted poem is misunderstood, or simply overlooked, by the listener—"to perceive the likeness" indeed demands a certain "aptness," also on part of the receiver.

"Lu ming" 鹿鳴 (ode 161)

"Lu ming" is the first ode in the second section of the *Shijing*, "Xiaoya" 小雅, and therefore occupies a position similar in importance to that of "Guanju," which opens the first part. In both cases it is important that the reading of the poem be regulated and does not stray into forbidden areas. The word "deer" (*lu* 鹿) appears in "Ye you si jun" 野有死麕 (ode 23) as a highly sensual correlate of the young woman who is the poem's protagonist. In his reading of ode 23, Mao narrowly escapes an immoral reading by denying the xingish mode of reading that he elsewhere puts so much effort into explaining and enforcing. The present case calls for a different strategy.

> *Youyou* the deer call out
> Eating the *ping* plant in the wilderness[22]

呦呦鹿鳴
食野之苹

Mao comments: "A xing . . . When deer find *ping* plants they call out to each other, going *youyou*. [This] sincerity and honesty [*ken cheng*] emerge from inside. [This] is used to xing [the fact] that the fine and happy guest should have sincerity and honesty and summon each other in order to perfect the rites" 興也 . . . 鹿得萍呦呦然鳴而相呼. 懇誠發乎中. 以興嘉樂賓客當有懇誠相招呼以成禮也.[23]

The first stanza continues thus:

> I have fine guests
> [I have my servants] play the lute [and] blow the *sheng*-flute
> [they] blow the *sheng*-flute [and] vibrate its membrane
> The *kuang*-baskets presented, them [I/We?] take
> Someone loves me
> [and] shows me the perfected way[24]

我有嘉賓
鼓琴吹笙
吹笙鼓簧
承筐是將
人之好我
示我周行

168 | The Origins of Chinese Literary Hermeneutics

For our purposes, this is an informative poem. First, as to the link between nature and man, the poem tells us that the benevolent deer express loyalty and honesty by inviting their "friends" to eat the newly found *ping* plant. When loyalty and honesty, correspondingly, appear at a higher level they serve as the raw material, or instrument, for the rites that are to be perfected by the fine guests. Second, the xing is here, just as in the two preceding cases, structured as a simple metaphor since "sincerity" and "honesty" (*ken cheng* 懇誠) are explicitly named as the traits shared by the deer and the guests and thereby the point into which the two strata converge.

However—granted there is a metaphorical link between man and deer—the poem does not say that the traits shared are sincerity and honesty. Indeed, the sensual connotations of the words "deer" and "wilderness," together with the fact that the poem thematizes togetherness and orality (the blowing of flutes and flute membrane), fill the poem with erotic rather than political overtones. Third, scrutinizing Mao's wording, the manner in which he uses the word "xing" as a verb ("to xing" 以興) clearly suggests that to *xing* is not simply the act of juxtaposing nature and man but a predication. In other words, the image of the sincere and honest deer sharing the *ping* plants with their friends "xings"—indicates by way of xingish metaphoricity—that man should also act thus if he wishes to perfect the rites.

Finally, in this case the xing does not involve allegory. Mao (or the *Minor Preface*) does not explicitly identify the "guests" mentioned by the poem as any historical figures, a fact that seems to indicate, again, that the concept of xing primarily refers to the metaphoric transference from the natural to the human realm—not the allegorical component. However, we must not forget that all contemporary Confucian commentaries on the *Odes* partake in a greater allegorizing scheme determined by the central *mythos* of the paradisiacal reign of King Wen. This becomes obvious in the Lu comment on this poem. This school understands "Lu ming" as a remonstration mouthed by a grand official of Zhou against his king who, failing to promote worthies and take proper care of business, indulged in feasts and in the pleasures provided by concubines.[25] As the xing is foremost a pragmatic interpretational tool for converting a naïve, nonideological poem to Confucianism, Mao allegorizes whenever he sees fit. However, "You bi" and "Lu ming" provide solid and explicit evidence that the central characteristic of Mao's xing is the intratextual, metaphorical transference from nature to man, and this will henceforth be the primary object of this study.

Thus far we have walked along the path staked out by Zhu Ziqing and his thesis about the xing as a *piyu*. I have concluded that the metaphoricity that Zhu speaks of rests on the assumption of (the educated) man's superiority to nature, and that representations of nature and man coincide in a single point, a *tertium comparationis* ("virtue," the "appearance" of flying egrets, "sincerity" and "honesty"), thereby forming a what I call a simple metaphor. As a consequence, the metaphorical movement always goes from nature to man or, in other words, nature always plays the role of vehicle to the personae that are the xing's tenor. Let us also note in passing that there is, in these examples, no logical opposition between what the xing predicates and what the rest of the poem predicates. There is no *irony*.

Counter example: "Dong men zhi fen" 東門之枌 (ode 137)

Ode 137 begins with a natural description that, at first glance, seems identical in kind to those of the poems above.

> The elms of the eastern gate
> the oaks on the piled-up hill[26]

> 東門之枌
> 宛丘之栩

Mao's comment on these lines is, however, wholly devoid of xingish undertones, and he explains the elms and the oaks in purely literal, topographical terms: "*Fen* refers to the white elm, and *yu* to oak. They were the gathering places for men and women during the meetings between the various states" 枌, 白榆也. 栩, 杼也. 國之交會, 男女之所聚.[27]

The poem continues, like the others, with an introduction of the human activity that it takes as its main subject.

> Zi Zhong's child
> dances thereunder[28]

> 子仲之子
> 婆娑其下

What interests us in this context is not the sociohistorical background to ode 137—the identity of "Zi Zhong's child" and if dancing (*poso*) was a sign of loose morals—but that the natural description, according to Mao, is to be understood literally, as denoting the location in which human activity takes place rather than as a metaphorical predication about it. One may well imagine a Confucian moralizing reading ("Elms and Oaks grow in their natural places, just like men and women dance the ritual *poso* in locations proper for that activity") but the text itself supports, or rather determines, Mao's literal reading by defining the elms and the oaks as the place under which the human activity takes place.

"Mao Qiu" 旄丘 (ode 37)

The kudzus of the sloping hill
How widely-spread [are] their joints²⁹

旄丘之葛兮
何誕之節兮

Mao comments: "A xing . . . The vassals are mutually linked and related through their states. When sorrows and perils occur they reach out to each other, like the kudzus' spreading far and wide whilst being mutually united. *Dan* 誕 means 'wide'" 興也 . . . 諸侯以國相連屬. 憂患相及, 如葛之蔓延相連及也. 誕, 闊也. ³⁰

This poem, traditionally held to have been written by an official of Li 黎 blaming the state of Wei 衛 for not helping its ally against the *Di* people 狄, uses the kudzu as its metaphorical vehicle.³¹ The kudzu is a highly proliferating plant whose ability to spread over great areas is, as we will see, often likened to family relations in two ways, either as an early version of the "generic tree" metaphor (branches of a family originating from the same trunk or stem) or, more ambiguously, connoting simultaneous distance (the kudzus spreading over a vast area) and continuity (the plants forming an unbroken line). Technically speaking, this is a simple xing in which a natural description is used as a statement about humans, and Mao expresses this perceived similarity through the copula *ru* 如.

We also note Mao's "subliminal" maneuvers, aimed at sanctioning his interpretation by assimilating the language of the poem into the language of his *Commentary*, and vice versa. Mao explains that the vassal lords are "mutually united" (*xiang lian* 相連) and that they, in times of calamity, "come together" or "reach out to each other" (*xiang ji* 相及). As he proceeds to comment on the kudzu trope he combines the two expressions and says that the kudzus spread while being "mutually united" (*xiang lian ji* 相連及), highlighting the fact that the kudzus are both "united" by their shared origin and "mobile" (they move just as the vassals do in perilous times).[32] He defines the character *dan* 誕 as "wide" *kuo* 闊 but uses the cognate character *yan* 延 ("spread") in his paraphrase, probably because the latter character is etymologically closer to that used by the primary text.

Counter example: "Po fu" 破斧 (ode 157)

We have broken our axes
and splintered our hatches[33]

既破我斧
又缺我斨

Mao comments: "Axes and hatchets are used by commoners. Rites and righteousness are used by a state" 斧斨民之用也。禮義國之用也。[34] The poem goes on:

The Duke of Zhou marches eastward
the four states, them he corrects[35]

周公東征
四國是皇

This is clearly a version of the rites-are-work metaphor as the poem's description of the instruments designed for everyday work is understood as a metaphor for "work" at a higher level, namely the lofty task of governing a state by means of rites and rituals. The logic behind Mao's dogmatic rendering is that the poem fuses two incompatible levels: that of the populace and that of the ruling class—and such heterogeneity cannot be accepted. The distinction made between the two social strata in the text-external world must be maintained on a rhetorical level by the text. Hence Mao's analogical reading that understands descriptions of the *vulgus* only as metaphors for a "higher," upper-class reality. "Work" and "populace," consequently, have a rhetorical function similar to that of nature, which follows logically from the idea that the *vulgus* indeed is nature (or, at best, semicultivated).

In an alternative reading of the poem, the first two lines may be construed as actually uttered by a group of commoners—or soldiers of humble origins—acting as a "chorus" narrating the tale of the Duke of Zhou. But this hypothetical interpretation inevitably overlooks the parallelism of the text since it is a priori assumed that the populace cannot express itself metaphorically, that is, in a manner pertaining to the rites. A nonmetaphorical reading, then, would necessarily understand "axe" and "hatchet" as belonging to the men following (and narrating the adventures of) the Duke of Zhou and, in turn, suggest that the duke did not "correct" the four states by means of rites and righteousness but with the sheer force of which the "axes" and "hatchets" are metonymies.[36]

Mao interprets this poem metaphorically to maintain the myth of the Duke of Zhou as a paragon of virtue—although, ironically, if the logic of the metaphor is followed rigorously, the broken axes and hatchets rather suggest that the duke's rites and righteousness are defective. The analogy between work and rites is, nonetheless, not labeled a xing. Comparing "Po fu" and the three previous examples we understand why, as the metaphor or analogy consists of a transfer from the realm of (common) man to the realm of (aristocratic) man—not from nature to man.

Counter example: "Fa ke" 伐柯 (ode 158)

Mao's interpretation of this poem banks on a logic identical to that of the previous example since the perceived similarity between commoner and ritual man does not involve a xingish transfer from the natural to the human realm. What interests us here, however, is that "Fa ke" clearly shows how Mao "adds meaning from outside" (*fuhui* 附會) in a complex hermeneutical operation.

> How does one hew an axe handle?
> Without an axe it cannot be done
> How does one take a wife?
> Without a go-between one does not get her[37]

> 伐柯如何
> 匪斧不克
> 取妻如何
> 匪媒不得

Mao comments: "A *ke* is an axe handle. Rituality and Righteousness, too, are axe handles of the business of governing a state. A go-between is that with which the rituals are employed. In the ruling of a state, if the rituals cannot be used the state is unsettled" 柯斧柄也. 禮義者亦治國之柄. 媒所以用禮也. 治國不能用禮則不安.[38]

Mao's reading of ode 158 builds on an explicit analogy, as the art of taking a wife is likened to the hewing of an axe handle and Mao, as often do the authors of *Master Lü's Annals*, condenses the analogy into a metaphor by stating that Rituality and Righteousness are the metaphorical "axe handles" of governing a state.[39] The poem itself uses the "lowly" work of hewing as merely a vehicle for ritual activities, the concept uniting vehicle and tenor being *instrumentality* (how to hew an axe handle and how to take a wife). Although the poem distinguishes between low and high social positions, and between menial work and ritual, Mao is not content with a poem that simply speaks of the frivolous business of wife taking. The poems preceding and following ode 158 are parts of a cycle of poems celebrating the ideal rulership of the Duke of Zhou. The context, therefore, forces Mao to find a "higher" and more suitable content—namely the noble art of statesmanship—in a poem that speaks only of marriage.

Claiming, correctly, that the poem itself thematizes the instrumentality and purpose of rites (禮 *li*), Mao adds a third layer of figurality, making the poem say that (1) the way of axe hewing is like (2) the way of wife taking, which in turn is like (3) the way of ruling a state. Thus the first layer, the description of hewing an axe handle, is also understood as a metaphor for rulership but very indirectly since it is the handle—the object and product of lowly work—that is metaphorized. Instead of saying, as a more straightforward logic would have it, that *axes* are the instruments that must be used to hew a handle (and, metaphorically, to rule a state), Mao says that rites and righteousness are the "axe handles" of rulership. Whence this asymmetric interpretation? As in the previous example, Mao must avoid connotations of brutality since the instrument of virtuous statesmanship cannot be metaphorically represented by an instrument of crude violence. Consequently, Mao cannot equate the axe itself with rites on the rhetorical level.

Finally, we observe the circularity and the paradoxality of the hewing analogy: you need an axe to hew an axe handle. But with what was that first handle hewed? And who was that "first hewer"? The corresponding Xunzian questions "Whence come the rites?" and "Who was the initiator of the rites?" fall outside of the scope of this study.

"Lin zhi zhi" 麟之趾 (ode 11)

The feet of the *lin*
Trustworthy and considerate are the lords' sons
Oh! The *lin*!⁴⁰

麟之趾
振振公子
于嗟麟兮

Mao comments: "A xing. *Zhi* 趾 means *zu* 足 [foot]. It refers to the fact that the [auspicious fabled animal] *lin* is trustworthy and acts in correspondence with the ritual rules, using its feet to reach [moral perfection]. *Zhenzhen* means trustworthy and considerate" 興也. 趾足也. 麟信而應禮, 以足至者也. 振振信厚也.⁴¹

"Lin zhi zhi" offers little resistance to our attempts to understand and taxonomize Mao's xingish readings of the *Odes*. Mao here identifies a set of characteristics that he perceives are common to nature and man. The *lin* 麟—a mythological animal so benevolent that its feet never touched the grass over which it moved—is said to be trustworthy and rite abiding, just like the "lords' sons." Let us instead close in on a detail that testifies to Mao's voracious hermeneutical appetite and his impulse to incorporate all parts of the poem into a coherent ideological narrative. Mao's analogy between the "trustworthy" *lin* and the morally upright sons of lords does obey a certain logic; but why does the poem celebrate the feet of the animal?

Mao's answer comes in the form of a pun; he says that the *lin* "uses its feet to go forward" (*yi zu zhi*) 以足至.⁴² The word translated here as "to go," *zhi* 至, referred in the Confucian jargon of the Han dynasty to the perfection of, for example, virtue (as in the phrase *zhi de* 至德, "having reached the perfection of moral fortitude"). In Mao's rendering, the feet of the *lin* are thus celebrated as the objects with which this auspicious animal (and, on a metaphorical level, the lords' sons) reaches virtue. Likewise, when in the third stanza the horns of the *lin* are celebrated, Mao says they are "that with which it displays its virtue" 所以表其德也, with Zheng Xuan adding that "the tips of the *lin's* horns are fleshy, which indicates that it has weapons but does not use them" 麟角之末有肉, 示有武而不用.

The observant reader detects a deviation here. How can an animal be trustworthy, abide by the rites, and—using its famous feet—be on its way to moral perfection? How can it be a semiotic creature, using its flesh-clad horns to "communicate" its virtue? Does this not blur the distinction between nature and culture that so clearly determines Mao's readings? Mao's exegesis does display a near-hysterical fear of the nonhuman, of that which pertains to the natural realm and an earlier and lower stage of human life. The *lin*, however, is a legendary, fabulous animal long since extinct. As such, it is no longer a part of what we refer to as "nature" but has entered mythology as symbol of virtue. The *lin*, appearing as a sign in the poetic text, has put a distance between itself and its lowly origin. Therefore it appears in the *Commentary*, only seemingly disturbing its fundamental categorical order.

"Zhong feng" 終風 (ode 30)

The whole day a fierce wind has blown
[You] look at me and laugh[43]

終風且暴
顧我則笑

Mao comments: "A xing . . . *Bao* means fierce. 'Laugh' [means that the person described by the narratrix] humiliates her [the narratrix]" 興也 . . . 暴疾也. 笑侮之也.[44]

Ridiculing me [you] laugh arrogantly
In [my] heart I mourn this

謔浪笑敖
中心是悼

Mao comments: "This bespeaks ridicule and lack of respect" 言戲謔不敬.[45] Mao's comment on "Zhong feng" is, at first glance, less than informative but we may infer that the "fierce" wind to Mao represents the cruelty with which the narratrix is treated or, alternatively, the male culprit himself, or the desperation of the whole situation.

The thematic link between the two strata is inconspicuous and indicated only by the etymology of the word *xue* 謔, paraphrased by Mao by the compound word *xixue* 戲謔, to "joke" or "ridicule." *Xue* is related to the word *nüe* 虐 ("fierce," "harmful" or "violent"), whereas *xue* basically means to "crack a joke" but has an undertone of violence easily understandable given its etymological origin. The close thematic and grammatological relationship between the two words is, furthermore, exposed by two intertexts, odes 55 ("Qi yu" 淇奧) and 254 ("Ban" 板). In the former poem, the last two lines of the last stanza run: "You like to joke around 善戲謔兮 / [but] don't be cruel 不為虐兮."[46] To go from *xue* to *nüe*, from joke to ridicule to cruelty, seems but a small step.

We may thus infer that the description of a natural phenomenon (the "fierce" wind) again functions as a xingish statement about a human situation, more specifically, the cruel joker who ridicules the female protagonist.

Three Counter examples

"Hu ye" 瓠葉 (ode 231)

> Waving about are the gourd leaves
> [we/they] pick [and] cook them
> The lord has wine
> [He/we] fill[s] the cup and taste[s] it[47]

> 幡幡瓠葉
> 采之亨之
> 君子有酒
> 酌言嘗之

Mao comments: "[The gourd] is a plant used by the masses" 庶人之菜也.[48]

The phrase "gourd leaves," is thus understood literally, as referring to objects that can be picked and cooked, and not as a metaphor for any human activity. Hence, it is not labeled xing.

"Nan shan" 南山 (ode 101)

> The southern mountain, high and big
> The male foxes go seeking their mates[49]

> 南山崔崔
> 雄狐綏綏

Mao comments: "A xing. 'South mountain' refers to the South Mountain of [the state] of Qi. *Cuicui* means 'high and big.' The state's ruler is awe inspiring and stern, like the South Mountain. The male foxes follow each other indiscriminately, having lost their [proper] mates according to [the law of] yin and yang" 興也. 南山齊南山也. 崔崔高大也. 國君尊嚴如南山然. 雄狐相隨無別, 失陰陽之匹.[50]

The poem continues:

The road to Lu is smooth and easy
The daughter of Qi travelled thereon to get married
It is said that she is already married
Why still yearn for her?[51]

魯道有蕩
齊子由歸
既曰歸止
曷又懷止

Mao comments: "The 'Daughter of Qi' is Wen Jiang" 齊子文姜也.[52]

In their comments on "Nan shan," the Confucian commentators return to their favorite subjects: sexual perversion and excess. According to the *Minor Preface* this ode speaks of Duke Xiang 襄公 who indulged in the "behavior of beasts" and in incestuous fornication (*yin* 淫) with his younger half-sister Wen Jiang who had married into the house of Lu, a neighboring state.[53] The poem, the *Preface* continues, was written by the great officials of Qi as a reaction to this "evil" situation. The *Preface's* reading is thus thematically consistent with Mao's, although the latter holds that the foxes have lost their sense of proper natural order, whereas the *Preface* presupposes that beasts are by nature incestuous and promiscuous.

The xing is conventionally metaphorical, albeit split into two images that both refer to the lustful Duke Xiang. On the one hand he is awe inspiring like (*ru* 如) the mountain; on the other, he is perverted as the foxes.

"You hu" 有狐 (ode 63)

There is a fox looking for a mate
On the breakwater of the Qi river[54]

有狐綏綏
在彼淇梁

Mao comments: 興也. 綏綏匹行也. "A xing. *Suisui* means 'walk in pairs'."⁵⁵

The sorrows of the heart
This (wo)man has no upper garment

心之憂矣
之子無裳

Mao comments: "'This (wo)man' is a person with no house or clan" 之子無室家者.⁵⁶ And on the third stanza: "This says that to have no home or clan is like [*ruo* 若] a person having no clothes" 言無室家若人無衣服.⁵⁷

With "Nan shan" as intertext, "You hu" is a suggestive poem in which the slightly surreal description of the half-naked (wo)man corresponds to the image of the perverted fox. As in the former poem, the xing-element functions as a simple metaphor in that the motif of the fox seeking a mate thematizes togetherness and human mating. Neither the poem nor the *Commentary*, however, elaborates on the question as to whom "fox" refers. "This (wo)man" (之子 *zhi zi*) can thus be interpreted as the "fox" on the lookout for a mate, as well as the object of the beast's pursuit. The expression is familiar to the student of the *Odes* as it occurs in the common phrase *zhi zi yu gui* 之子于歸, "this woman is on her way to be married"; here, we find the phrase cut in half, the two first words making the reader expect a story about marriage and the two subsequent ones surprising him or her by substituting obscene nudity (*wu yi* 無裳) for the bridal trip (*gui* 歸).⁵⁸

The theme of bridal journeys inevitably connotes sexuality; the bride's sexual innocence and fearful anticipation of meeting her husband and in-laws are expressed by the suggestive descriptions of the "wilderness" (*ye* 野) through which she travels to reach her new home. To keep "You hu" from collapsing into a merely sexual poem lacking the "righteousness" that the xing ought to discover, Mao adds another trope by interpreting "clothes" as a metaphor for "house and clan," banking on the idea that without a home and clan one is as unprotected as if one had no clothes. Thus, the poem no longer speaks of nudity—a dangerous subject in conjunction with the fox imagery—but of vulnerability. By making the absence of clothing a figure of defenselessness, Mao is able to desexualize the poem and make the image of the fox *qua* libertine a more neutral image of a presumed bride or bridegroom. Nonetheless, Mao's interpretation of this poem bears witness to the great risk that follows in the wake of Mao's xingish readings. If the present poem and its fox imagery were read in the light of "Nan shan," then "fox," "nudity," and "mating" would provoke a decidedly sexual, non-Confucian reading.

Counter example and First Hint of a Different Order: "Xishuai" 蟋蟀 (ode 114)

The cricket is in the hall,
The year draws to a close;[59]

蟋蟀在堂
歲聿其莫

Mao comments: "The cricket . . . In the ninth month it is in the hall" 蟋蟀 . . . 九月在堂.[60]

if we do not now enjoy ourselves,
the days and month will be passing by[61]

今我不樂
日月其除

This is a counter example to which special attention should be paid. In the definition that was my starting point, Zhu Ziqing stated that a xing is a trope founded on *piyu*, or similitude. Following Zhu—and thus far I have found no reason not to—we immediately understand why the first two lines of "Xishuai" are not labeled a xing. The poem starts with an image suggesting temporal flux; the cricket in the hall signals that autumn, the time of decline and death, has arrived. Then the message of these lines—the passing of time and, eventually, death—is superimposed on the following lines, which also speak of dying and vanity: this time on the level of the human animal. At a first glance, we find that the rhetorical order of the xing is maintained: the description of the cricket, and the natural realm of which it is a synecdoche, is merely a statement about human existence ("the autumn of our lives will eventually come").

However, while it is certainly true that the poem "is about" people and not crickets, the image of the cricket is never *rhetorically* subordinated to the "you-and-I" that the poem takes as its primary personage. In other words, the cricket does not serve as the vehicle of a metaphor in which "you-and-I" would be the tenor. What role, then, does the natural descriptions play here? "In the ninth month," says Mao, "the cricket is in the hall"; according to the rules of nature—of yin and of yang and the Five Phases—crickets will find themselves in the hall at the beginning of autumn. Outside any text, the cricket is therefore itself a sign in which the link between signans (蟋蟀 "cricket") and signatum ("autumn") is automatic, nonarbitrary, and mirrors the order of nature. The cricket is thus a symptom, indicator, or synecdoche of the time of year referred to as "autumn" (since "autumn" and "cricket" is analogous to the order of cause and effect).[62] When "cricket" is made a textual sign and put into the (con-)text of "Xishuai" it does not, as previously concluded, assume a place in a tenor-vehicle hierarchy but is a statement ("the cricket is in the hall") somehow consistent with the rest of the text ("the year is drawing to a close" and "the days and months will pass us by"). Mao, whose task it is to make the text congruent, must therefore explain that "cricket" does not have a metaphorical meaning and is not a xing. However, it cannot be interpreted literally either since that would make the line about the cricket in the hall superfluous and confusing ("What have crickets to do with *carpe diem*?"). With Mao's reading of "cricket" as a symptom of "autumn"—the season of decline and impending death—all threatening ambiguity is abolished.

With reference to Zhu Ziqing's model, similitude is not at play in this ode but rather causality. Mao's interpretation of the cricket image is governed by a rhetorical order different from that of the xing. The semiotic play of signans and signatum is extratextual and not the outcome of the interaction between the descriptions of nature and man. The "crickets in the hall" is not understood as, in an Aristotelian sense, a metaphoric statement about the poem's personage, and does therefore not constitute a xing.

First Excursion:
Similitude and Causality in the Sun-and-Moon Trope

The dualism of similitude and causality brought to light by the previous example involves also the dualism of abstraction and concretion, which brings us back to the "hyperrealists" discussed in the first part and to the idea of cosmology. The central idea behind Pauline Yu's denunciation of metaphoricity in Confucian hermeneutics is that the resemblances between nature and man indicated by Mao's xing were not abstract and rhetorical but literal representations of concrete, extratextual correspondences that preceded the text. I argue, however, that this attempt to make the Chinese tradition concrete, nonmetaphorical and non-Occidental is—the acuteness of Yu's argumentation notwithstanding—a fallacy (which is not equal to stating dogmatically that the idea of cosmology and cosmological correspondences was absent from Confucian hermeneutics, only that it did not cancel out a notion of metaphoricity).

Indeed, there are cases in which the two orders exist side by side without any apparent contradiction, and I shall preface my investigation of the sun-and-moon motif with a reading of the sixth poem, "Tao yao" 桃夭, whose first stanza opens thus:

> The youth and vigor of the peach-tree
> Flourishing [are] its flowers

> 桃之夭夭
> 灼灼其華

Mao comments: "A xing. When the flowers of the peach tree are flourishing, *yaoyao*-like are their youth and vigor" 興也. 桃有華之盛者, 夭夭其少壯也.[63]

How does Mao interpret the description of the flourishing peach tree, technically speaking? The information supplied by the *Commentary* is too scanty to provide an answer; on the one hand, Mao's xing signals similarity; on the other, the example of "Xishuai" has alerted us to the possibility of interpreting natural descriptions as markers, indicators, or symptoms; that is, to a mode of reading in which the xingish opposition between nature and man is operative but in a fundamentally different way from what I have called the "metaphorical xing."

The poem continues:

> This bride is on her way to her new home
> appropriate she is towards her [new] house and clan

> 之子于歸
> 宜其室家

Mao comments: "'Appropriate' refers to not being late in the matter of [marrying into a new] house and clan" 宜, 以有室家無踰時者.[64]

The bride, according to Mao, is "on time"; that is, she is going to her new home when spring has arrived and the peach trees are in bloom, just as the Confucian rituals prescribe.⁶⁵ Such ritualistic timeliness is itself a sign of the moral status of a state or, on a smaller scale, a clan or a person; conversely, when morals run low rites are neglected. What interests me here, however, is not the minutiae of Confucian political sign interpretation but the apparent deviation in Mao's xing since the imagery that is normally subjected to a metaphorizing reading is here understood metonymically, as a temporal indicator. In technical terms, the signatum of the signans ("peach tree flower") is "spring" on the extratextual level and "the correct time for marriage" on the rhetorical, textual level. But is this really an instance of xing that would undermine Zhu Ziqing's definition ("xing is *piyu*")? The next stanzas, and Mao's comment thereon, demonstrate that the xingish order of metaphoricity is still intact:

> The youth and vigor of the peach-tree
> fruit-like its fruits [sic]
> This bride is on her way to her new home
> Appropriate, her house and clan
>
> 桃之夭夭
> 有蕡其實
> 之子于歸
> 宜其家室

Mao comments: "Not only has she the [beautiful] looks of a flower but also the moral fortitude of a [good] wife" 非但有華色又有婦德.⁶⁶

Here, Mao combines the order of causality with that of similitude. By assigning the most superficial characteristic of the peach tree flowers—their sensuous appearance (*se* 色)—to the bride, Mao adheres to the metaphorical order proposed by Zhu Ziqing: the bride is beautiful *like* the flowers of the peach tree.⁶⁷ This uxorian "virtue," however, is not represented in the same manner as the virtue of the ospreys in the first poem. There, "virtue" was the *tertium comparationis* that linked vehicle (*jujiu*) to tenor (the king and his queen consort). Here, virtue is a trait whose presence in the poem can only be deduced from the knowledge that the signata of the peach tree flower is "spring" and thus "correct time for marriage"; the bride is virtuous since the blossoming flowers indicate that she abides by the rites. Consequently, the imagery of the peach tree is *simultaneously* at work on the rhetorical level (as a metaphorical representation of the bride) and on a quasi-literal level (as a temporal indicator).

The third stanza follows the same pattern:

The youth and vigour of the peach tree
In full bloom [are] its leaves
This bride is on her way to her new home
Appropriate ["are"; "to"?] her family

桃之夭夭
其葉蓁蓁
之子于歸
宜其家人

Mao comments: "*Zhenzhen* refers to the appearance [of the leaves] in full bloom. She has beauty and inner virtue; her form is in full bloom" 蓁蓁, 至盛貌. 有色有德, 形體至盛也.[68]

I quote the *Commentary* here, not because it can add any further information about how Mao perceives the rhetorical structure of the piece but because it shows what a wholesome and harmonious end product "Tao yao" has become after passing through Mao's hermeneutic refinery. Very cleverly, Mao brings out the temporal aspect inherent in the near-identical imagery of the three stanzas. The flowers of the first stanza are "young and vigorous." Then, with regard to the second stanza, Mao says that the "fruits are fruit-like," or plentiful. In the third stanza, the leaves of the peach tree are "in full bloom," suggesting an enhancement of the ripeness, the tone of the poem becoming increasingly intense and feverish.

Mao's comment on the third stanza is also a logical conclusion of his previous notes. The two rhetorical orders formerly separated now merge by way of another of Mao's "subliminal" tricks; by stating that *zhenzhen* means "in full bloom" he makes the flourishing leaves a metaphor for the bride whose—and this is the vital point—looks *and* virtue are "in full bloom." The poem, as Mao understands it, has always used the flowers, fruits, and leaves of the peach tree as metaphors of the beauty of the bride. Now the bride's virtue, which formerly we knew about only through a process of rather roundabout nonmetaphorical semiosis, is incorporated into the metaphorical xing structure: her virtue, just like the leaves, is in full bloom.

Quite inconspicuously, Mao has made the xing element speak both the language of cosmology (and, thus, causality) and of similitude. This enables us, Mao's present-day students and interpreters, to draw an important conclusion: Mao did indeed interpret the flourishing peach tree as a temporal marker. Putting ourselves in Mao's position, the easiest way to make the poem "speak Confucianism" would have been to interpret the peach tree directly as a metaphor for the bride's flourishing virtue. That strategy, however, would simply have relied on Mao's *auctoritas* to convince the reader that flourishing peach tree flowers equal bridal virtue—"because I say so." The strategy that Mao finally chooses is consistent with the first principle of hermeneutical economy, which tells Mao to make every part, and every level, of the text coherent as so as to shield the poem from alternative, perverse readings. Mao performs a reading that cunningly uses the xing as an indicator (and thus nominally a nonxing) *and* a metaphor. He seduces his reader masterfully, first by making the reader think that the text, after all, means exactly what it says on the surface. Then, once the reader is off guard, the flowers, fruits, and leaves of the peach tree are subliminally made into metaphors of what was previously nonmetaphorical, namely the bride's alleged virtue.

Let me at this point make a short detour. In an article titled "Metaphor and *Bi*: Western and Chinese Poetics," Michelle Yeh performs a reading of "Tao yao" that is similar to mine but whose conclusions about Chinese poetics are radically different.[69] What Yeh calls the *bi* metaphor 比 differs from the "Western" metaphor in that it is a paratactic trope that presents "a pair of images that are paradigmatic of the ontological correspondence . . . between things in the organic universe."[70] Yeh then makes a crucially important remark. For the Western metaphor, not only similitude but also "the difference between tenor and vehicle is . . . essential."[71] What separates the two traditions is therefore that "[in the Chinese *bi* metaphor] there is no presupposition of radical difference between the two [i.e., the categories of nature and man]. Quite on the contrary, they arise from the same empirical and conceptual context."[72]

Similarly, she contends that "there is no difference" because "both [peach and bride] are part of the larger context of Spring."[73] Although Yeh implicitly distinguishes between the creation and interpretation of poetry, her *bi* is structurally identical to Mao's xing since she finds that the image of the peach tree is both a metaphor for the bride and an indicator of spring.[74] As Yeh moves between theories of creation and theories of interpretation, between the "dangerously lazy method" of parataxis and the idea of explicit metaphoricity, her argument builds tension. A poem, I submit, may certainly be paratactically structured, but as soon as we interpret a peach tree flower as a metaphor for a bride we automatically enter into a rhetorical hierarchy that depends on a difference (as well as the necessary similitude) between vehicle and tenor. Such difference is, of course, not a cultural bias of the Occident but a universal trait of language that makes possible the *metaphora*, the *translatio*, the *Übertragung*, and also the xing. Yeh, however, claims that there is "no contrast, conceptual or imagistic, concomitant with the comparison."[75] But if there were no difference—if the tradition of Confucian hermeneutics that Yeh so obviously builds on did not draw a distinct line of separation between man and nature and nature and culture—how could the poem describe the bride's beauty as a peach tree flower? The reading of the blossoming peach as a symptom of spring works precisely because "peach" and "spring" are linked under a nonmetaphorical order.

If this order were to be carried over to the metaphor there would be no metaphor—or a "metaphor" the tenor and vehicle of which would be identical, in other words, a "trope" without a "turning" and a trope that inevitably ends up a tautology, saying that the peach is like a peach, and the bride is like a bride. To hold that, in the peach tree flower-as-bride metaphor, both peach and bride belong to the greater context of "Spring" is, I would claim, a fallacy because it fails to recognize the all-pervasive nature-man dualism at work in the Confucian tradition. "Beauty" is the *tertium comparationis* of "Tao yao," with "nature" and "man" as its two conceptual categories, and their mutual border is what is transgressed in the metaphorical movement.

Although causality was found alongside similitude in the xing element of "Tao yao," similitude or likeness finally gained the upper hand in Mao's comment on the last stanza. The order of the xing remains, as yet, intact. As our investigation of cosmology continues we will see what rhetorical roles "sun" and "moon" play in the *Commentary*. It is reasonable to assume that the two major celestial bodies occupied a special place in the conception of the early Chinese, given the idea about the rulership of "Heaven," or the later idea of yin and yang as the two alternating and intertwining actors in the process and progress of cosmos.

In ode 29, for our purposes aptly called "Ri yue" 日月 ("Sun and Moon"), the two heavenly bodies are found in the firmament, as opposed to the narratrix and her "man":

Sun! Moon!
brilliant [you] look down on the earth below
As for this man
he does not come to the old place.[76]

日居月諸
照臨下土
乃如之人兮
逝不古處

Mao does not define "sun" and "moon" (or "days" and "months") as parts of a xing but merely offers a paraphrase.[77] The absence of the xing tag thus suggests that for Mao the sun and the moon represent the passing of time through their successive and alternate appearance in the sky, and that things have changed since the days associated with the "old place."[78] As rule-bound celestial bodies that appear and reappear every day and every month, the two also represent constancy, in contrast to the flow of unpredictable events of which the change that has taken place "on the earth below" is an example. One may add a third commonsensical reading, similarly founded on a notion of a difference between heaven and man: the sun and the moon, in explicit contrast to "this man," reach everywhere—including "the old place." In classical rhetorical parlance, these interpretations build on *comparatio* rather than *similitudo* and, consequently, do not rely on a metaphorical assimilation between man and "moon" or "sun"; nothing is ever described in terms of something else. The comparison is explicit, as the text first talks of the radiant sun and moon and then relates that description to the human world through the words *nai ru zhi ren* 乃如之人, "and as for this person."

When the sun and the moon reappear in ode 99 ("Dong fang zhi ri" 東方之日), they do so in a context that forces Mao to come up with a more complex hermeneutical strategy to make the text fit the Confucian paradigm:

> The sun is in the east!
> That newlywed girl
> [She] is in my chamber!
> In my chamber!
> Stepping [carefully] to me she comes
>
> The moon is in the east!
> That newlywed girl
> [She] is inside my door!
> Stepping [carefully] to me she comes[79]

東方之日兮
彼姝者子

在我室兮
在我室兮
履我即兮
東方之月兮
彼姝者子
在我闥兮
在我闥兮
履我即發

The consternation that the Confucian commentators must have felt when confronted with this piece is easy to imagine. Why would Confucius canonize a poem that, on the face of it, is intimate and sensuous? The narrator speaks of a newlywed girl in "my" chamber and behind "my" door. Such a "you-and-I" dualism, paired with the intimacy of the chamber in which the two lovers are enclosed, makes it a conventional love poem. If, furthermore, the sun and the moon represent the passing of time—a reading that suggests itself through the parallelism of the two stanzas—the erotic theme is further enforced and the poem even more awkward for Mao, since it suggests that the bride has spent the whole day and the whole night in the room of her groom. Such excess would certainly disturb the Confucian ideal of sexual moderation.

Mao, however, comments:

> A xing. The sun emerges from the east; this refers to the ruler, who is bright and splendid, there is nothing not shined upon and illuminated [for scrutiny]. *Li* 履 ["to step"] means *li* 禮 '[to proceed in accordance with] rituality'. That the moon is strong in the east refers to the ruler's being bright above, like the sun, and the subject [or "minister"] being illuminated below, like the moon 興也. 日出東方, 人君明盛, 無不照察也. 履禮也. 月盛於東方, 君明於上, 若日也. 臣察於下, 若月也.[80]

The xing tag indicates that this ode carries a metaphor for which the sun and the moon are the vehicles. Although "sun" and "moon" no longer function as temporal markers indicating the time spent together by the two lovers, a metaphorical reading of "sun" and "moon" might be equally dangerous and lead the text away from an interpretation consistent with Confucian dogma: and for this reason they must not be identified with the two protagonists of the poem. "The poet says that he rejoices in the strength and beauty of [her] appearance, which resembles the sun in the east" 詩人言所說者顏色

盛美，如東方之日, the Han School claims.⁸¹ This is exactly the reading that Mao wishes to avoid, and for the amorous dualisms of day-and-night and man-and-woman he consequently substitutes the Confucian dualisms of high-and-low and ruler-and-ruled. Mao validates his reading by simultaneously clinging to and deviating from the dualistic pattern of the text and uses the xing to bypass the love theme and make the poem speak of Confucian hierarchy. The sun and the moon are uncommonly suited for this purpose since they already pertain to a string of celestial and earthly phenomena that easily take on metaphorical values: day/night, enlightenment/darkness, warmth/cold, big light/smaller light, and so on.

The sun is now a metaphor for a ruler occupying an exalted position, and the moon is a metaphor for he who is ruled and passively illuminated from above. Although we have already obtained the information we sought in our investigation of the sun and moon imagery, we notice with interest that Mao goes on to state that *li* (or, approximately, *lier* 履), "to step," is a loan character for the homophonous word *lier* 禮, "rites," thus making the text say that "following the rites she has come to me" and "following the rites she has travelled to me," respectively.⁸² What calls for our attention is the fact that Mao's interpretation stops here, almost as in panic, leaving the text in a jumble quite uncharacteristic of a xing. Mao's figurative reading of the sun and moon as representations of Confucian hierarchy may have been a reply to the Han School's more frivolous interpretation. The Han version made the poem wholesome and rhetorically economical ("the new-lywed is as beautiful as the sun, and she has come to my chamber"), tenor and vehicle corresponding without any loose ends. Mao, by contrast, is in such a hurry to refute the Han reading that his figurative reading makes the ruler and his minister stand side by side with the virtuous lover and his bride without any apparent reason. The hermeneutical work, it seems, has been left half done.

In Mao's reading of ode 99 the sun and the moon are clearly metaphors for the relationship that obtains between ruler and ruled. The sun and moon resemble (*ruo* 若) the ruler and his minister on a textual, metaphorical and "fictitious" level. In ode 193, "Shi yue zhi jiao" 十月之交, the idea that "sun" relates to ruler as "moon" does to subject resurfaces but under different rhetorical presuppositions:

> At the conjunction in the tenth month
> on the first day of the moon, the day *xin mao*
> The sun was eclipsed [lit. "eaten"]

it was found ugly
That moon got weaker
this sun got weaker
Now the people below
also greatly laments it

The sun and the moon announce disaster
[they] do not follow their paths
The four states are without government
[they] do not use their good [officials]
When the moon there is eclipsed
it is just normal
When the sun here is eclipsed
what evil lies therein?

Flashing is the lightning of the thunder
things are not peaceful, not good
The hundred streams come out and rise
the mountain tops break and collapse
High banks become valleys
deep valleys become mountain hills
Alas for the men of these times
why has no one put an end to [these wrong-doings]?[83]

十月之交
朔月辛卯
日有食之
亦孔之醜
彼月而微
此日而微
今此下民
亦孔之哀
日月告凶
不用其行
四國無政
不用其良
彼月而食
則維其常
此日而食

于何不藏
爗爗震電
不寧不令
佰川沸騰
山冢崒崩
高岸為谷
深谷為陵
哀今之人
胡憯莫懲

The *Minor Preface* simply says that in this ode the "great officers [of Zhou] criticize King You" 大夫刺幽王也, a claim that very well may be historically true, considering the catalogue of various ministers in the fourth stanza.[84] Apart from the historical setting, the poem is largely self-explanatory. Indeed, the first stanza reads almost like a lapidary entry in a chronicle, starting dramatically *in medias res* with the account of the solar eclipse on the *xin mao* day (of what year we are not told). The sun being "eaten" by the moon is considered "ugly" and, as a sign of a future disaster, a cause for lament. The second stanza confirms this reading, saying that the sun and the moon "announce" (*gao* 告) disaster because they deviate from their "paths" (*xing* [sic] 行).[85] This situation mirrors, or is mirrored by, the degenerated "four states," which deviate from the path of good statesmanship by not using their "benevolence" (or, with Karlgren, their "good men"). The idea of deviation or malevolent change immediately reappears as lunar eclipses are described as "just normal," whereas the more unusual event of a solar eclipse signals a catastrophe.

We recognize the suspicion toward change and deviation, and the concern with stability, from the poetics of *bian* 變 ("changed" or "perverse" poetry) and *zheng* 正 ("straight" or "upright" poetry), a dualism that nostalgically points back to a lost, paradisiacal order.[86] We also note the deictics—"that" moon and "this" sun—which serve to distance the narrator from the evil of the moon, "that" ominous object. The third (and increasingly apocalyptic) stanza describes in an almost biblical terms how mountains are leveled and transform into valleys—and valleys into hills. The word *beng* 崩—"collapse, be destroyed"—connotes disaster and the destruction of a dynasty or the death of a ruler.

To Mao, "Shi yue zhi jiao" does not build on a xing trope; there is no figurative language at play in the poem. The reader may at first be puzzled by Mao's comment about the first stanza: "The moon [is] the minister's *dao*.

The sun [is] the lord's *dao*" 月臣道。日君道.⁸⁷ *Dao* 道 is here used both as a synonym for the *xing* 行 of the second stanza, describing how the sun and moon deviate from their celestial "paths," and in the more abstract sense of "principle," alluding perhaps to Xunzi's two chapters on the "principles" of the lord and the minister ("Jundao" and "Chendao"). Not only is the solar eclipse a bad omen because it is unusual (and therefore deviant) but also because the "eating" of the sun by the moon is an omen of the perverse situation in which a lesser "body" consumes a bigger one. The celestial signs thus "announce" usurpation in the state. But why are the lines about the sun and the moon not defined as a xing when, effectively, they bank on a perceived correspondence between the heavenly bodies and the lord and his minister?

The problem gets less problematic if the poem is compared to "Dong fang zhi ri." There, the sun and moon also correspond to the power structure of lord and minister but in a fundamentally metaphorical manner. The sun resembles the lord because the sun shines stronger than the moon, and because the former is associated with daytime and light and the latter with nighttime and darkness. In the first stanza of the present poem, by contrast, the sun and the moon never enter into a metaphorical relationship with "ruler" and "minister." Instead, the relationship between the celestial bodies and the men of power is established pretextually and extratextually; it is there before, outside, and independently of the poem.

Here, at last, the notion of cosmological correlations enters the equation and benefits the explanation of the *Commentary*, since—just as Pauline Yu claimed is generally the case with Mao's xings—what at first sight appears to be a figure of speech is the poet's (and Mao's) repetition of perceived correspondences that lie outside the text. Hence the representation of the solar eclipse in "Shi yue zhi jiao," like the appearance of the cricket in the hall, does not constitute a xing.

In his comment on the third stanza, however, Mao says that "the two sentences starting with 'high banks' bespeak a change of positions" 高岸二 句, 言易位也.⁸⁸ We should first note the shift from a cosmological order to a poetic and linguistic one, as Mao turns his attention from the sun and moon, which make extralinguistic "announcements," to the sentences or lines (*ju* 句) of the stanza, which instead "bespeak" an upturning of the proper societal hierarchy. In rhetorical terms, Mao's comment here signals a change from plain representation to figuration, or from nonxing to xing, as textual signs (the lines describing the leveling of banks and the transformation of valleys into hills) are substituted for the cosmological, extratextual, and ominous sign of the solar eclipse. Mao thus reads the lines about the rise of valleys and the leveling of hills as a metaphorical—indeed xingshi—representation of how high and low change positions.[89] The eclipse described in the poem and the "changing of places" both refer to the usurpation of the lord's throne by his minister; but whereas the first accompanies or heralds this usurping, the other figures it.

"Bespeaking"

On a side note, to "bespeak" (言 *yan*) is Mao's most inconspicuous and neutral term for an expression that imparts a message beyond its immediate or conventional meaning; it occurs already in his comment on "Guanju," where he argues that the phrase "dark and secluded" "bespeaks"—is in fact referring to—"that the queen consort has the virtue of the *jujiu* bird."

Although Mao does not say so explicitly, the eclipse of the sun and the minister's changing positions with his ruler, as described in ode 193, are both instances of the imbalance of yin and yang. I make this claim since the dualism of yin and yang is used in several other Mao comments as a means to an ideologico-hermeneutic transformation of the *Odes*. For instance, in the third stanza of ode 197, "Xiao pan" (sic) 小弁, the poem says "I am not attached to [the garment's] hairy side; I am not attached to the [garment's] lining" 不屬于毛, 不罹于裏.[90] In what is seemingly one of his more outlandish annotations, Mao says that a garment's hairy, furry, or downy exterior—which is exposed to the sun—belongs to the yang sphere, wherefore it here "bespeaks 'father.'"[91] The lining, correspondingly, is yin since it is found on the dark inside of one's clothes and, therefore, "bespeaks 'mother'" (陰以言母). Hence the "ultimate" meaning of these lines according to Mao: "I am not attached to my father or to my mother."

Mao's reading is metonymic, or synecdochic, in that the exterior of a garment is naturally exposed to the sun, and the name of such a place is yang, which in cosmological theory is also the masculine realm of existence. Yin is similarly both the name of a dark, secluded place (such as that of the garment's lining) and of the female realm in cosmological theory. "Hair" and "father," "lining" and "mother" are continuous because they belong to yang or to yin, respectively; thus the exterior of a garment may "bespeak" the narrator's father.[92]

This explanation of the logic of Mao's interpretation of "Xiao pan" warrants two further comments. First, although Mao's reading depends on the yin-yang dichotomy so fundamental for correlative cosmology, these lines do not simply reproduce a literal, extratextual correspondence. The poet, at least according to Mao, tells of garments in order to *yan* 言—"bespeak," or make a statement about—the protagonist's solitude. This shift of meaning is arguably itself a turn of phrase or a figure of speech.

Second, while Mao's metonymic interpretation may appear exceedingly circuitous, and although I frequently speak of his "ideological transformation" of the *Shijing*, the hermeneutical logic is here identical to that of the "great man" who "divines" the shepherd's dream in "Wu yang" 無羊 (ode 190), and who finds that "fish" and "banners" stand for—"bespeak" with Mao Heng—harvest and offspring, respectively. Mao's outlandish interpretation of "Xiao pan" is therefore, at least methodologically, sanctioned by the *Odes* themselves.

"Shijiu" 鳲鳩 (ode 152)

The *shijiu*-bird is in the mulberry tree
Its children are seven[93]

鳲鳩在桑
其子七兮

Mao comments: "A xing. When the *shijiu* feeds its children it starts with the oldest in the morning and with the youngest in the evening. This [manner of feeding] is just, everyone being treated equally 興也 . . . 鳲鳩之養其子朝從上下, 莫從下上. 平均如一.[94]

The poem continues:

The good man, our lord
his deportment is invariable
His deportment being invariable
[my] heart is as if tied up [=unwobbling][95]

淑人君子
其儀一兮
其儀一兮
心如結兮

Mao comments that "this means that if one acts righteously and consistently, one's efforts will be firm" 言執義一則用心固.[96]

Since a righteous lord is likened to a righteous bird, Mao's xing is a "simple metaphor" rather than an analogy.[97] Just as in "Guanju," Mao here depends on information (namely, the manner in which the *shijiu* feeds its children) assumed not to be directly available to all readers and by which he is able to unify the two strata and make the poem convey one message.

"Hong yan" 鴻雁 (ode 181)

The wild-geese go flying
su su go their wings
These men go on an expedition
toiling and suffering in the wilderness[98]

鴻雁于飛
肅肅其羽
之子于征
劬勞于野

After the second line Mao comments: "This is a xing ... 'These men' refer to the noblemen and dignitaries [engaged in the war expedition]" 興也 ... 之子, 侯伯卿士也.

Because of their colorfulness, their singing and their being, from a human point of view, topographically unrestrained and able to become airborne, birds are excellent metaphor material. Here, Mao's xing tag signals that the description of the wild geese is metaphorical, but it is not until the third stanza and Mao's comment thereupon that the reader understands what the xing actually means: "The wild-geese go flying / grieved they call *ao ao*" 鴻雁于飛, 哀鳴嗷嗷. Mao comments: "Not having found a safe place to gather at, they go *ao ao*" 未得所安集則嗷嗷然, which means that the concept that combines the two strata, the *tertium comparationis*, is "unsettledness" or "vulnerability."[99] The xing of poem 181 is thus a simple metaphor.

"Jie Nan shan" 節南山 (ode 191)

High and steep is that southern mountain
The stones are piled up

節彼南山
維石巖巖

Mao comments: "A xing. . . . *jie* means [a] 'high and steep' [mountain]; *yanyan* means 'in the manner of piled-up stones'" 興也 . . . 節高峻也. 巖巖積石貌.

Splendid and vigorous [is] Master Yin
The populace all look at you

赫赫師尹
民具爾瞻

Mao comments: "*Hehe* means 'splendid and vigorous' in appearance" 赫赫顯盛貌.

As in "Nan shan," the high and steep mountain is used to describe the splendor of the "high" lord, Master Yin. This is thus a simple metaphor.

"Sang hu" 桑扈 (ode 215)

Small are the *sanghu*-birds
oriole-like their wings

交交桑扈
有鶯其羽

Mao comments: "A xing. 'Oriole-like' [means] patterned" 興也. 鶯然, 有文章.

The lords are all happy
they receive the blessing of heaven[100]

君子樂胥
受天之祜

Due to the brevity of Mao's comment we must rely on circumstantial evidence to reach at least a provisional understanding of the xing element. Zheng Xuan defines *jiaojiao* 交交 as "flying back and forth" and understands the *sanghu* as, in my terminology, a simple metaphor for the noble men who "rise and descend" in the palace.¹⁰¹ This is probably inconsistent with the *Commentary*. Mao does not gloss *jiaojiao* here, but he has already defined it as meaning "small" in his comments on odes 131, "Huang niao" 黃鳥, and 196, "Xiao yuan" 小宛.¹⁰² On both occasions, Mao claims, the poems in question describe "small" birds. In all likelihood the *tertium comparationis* in Mao's xingish reading should be sought elsewhere.

Mao's comment on ode 298 ("You bi" 有駜) offers an alternative explanation. There, as we know, Mao understands the white bird as a metaphor for a "white"—to wit, morally impeccable—official. Analogously, Mao's definitions of *yingran* ("oriole-like") as "being patterned" (*you wenzhang* 有文章) suggest a similar shift from concretion to abstraction, from the concrete pattern observable on the birds' wings to the more abstract notion of *wenzhang* in the sense of "cultural order" that we encounter in, for example, Confucius's celebration of Emperor Yao 堯: "How radiant, his having *wenzhang*" 煥乎, 其有文章.¹⁰³ The *sanghu* is therefore both a bird whose wings are patterned and a bird imprinted with culture. It is the latter interpretation that makes possible a reading of the *sanghu* as a simple metaphor for the felicitous lords who receive Heaven's "blessings."

"Qing ying" 青蠅 (ode 219)

> The green bugs, back and forth [they go]
> stopping by the fence

青蠅營營
止于樊

Mao comments: "A xing. *Yingying* is the appearance of going back and forth" 興也. 營營, 來往貌.

> Happy and carefree lord
> Do not believe slanderous words¹⁰⁴

豈弟君子
無信讒言

If Mao's comments get increasingly sparse toward the latter part of the collection it is most likely because he felt he had already sufficiently explained the xingish workings of the poems and thus prevented the poems in question from being misunderstood. Zheng Xuan, whose comment is more elaborated than Mao's, claims that the green bugs, which "defile what is white into being black, and what is black into being white" 汙白使黑, 汙黑使白, refer to the slanderous sycophants at the court who "bring into confusion what is good and what is bad" 變亂善惡.[105] Mao himself stresses the fact that *yingying* means coming and going and that *fan* 樊 means "fence," the former word connoting instability while the latter is synonymous with "border." In order to reach a broader, more comprehensive understanding of the xing figure we must consider "Qing ying" as a whole. The second and third stanzas go on to say that the "slandering of other people has no limits" 讒人罔極.[106] This "limitlessness" belongs in the same semantic area as "fence" and "border," suggesting that the to-and-fro movements of the green flies is used, in the xing trope, as a "simple metaphor" for the slanderers who through their lack of limits defy rites and decorum.

"Tiao zhi hua" 苕之華 (ode 233)

> The flowers of the *tiao* plant
> flourishing is their yellowness

> 苕之華
> 芸其黃矣

Mao comments: "A xing. When [the flowers of the *tiao* are] about to fall they turn yellow" 興也. 將落則黃.

> The sorrows of the heart
> are painful indeed[107]

> 心之憂矣
> 維其傷矣

Mao's reading is explainable in simple Lakoff-Johnsonian terms: it is determined by the concept of *falling*, which, in turn, involves the deictics of "up" and "down" or "high" and "low." As we shall see in subsequent chapters, "high," in Mao's conceptual world, signifies a position of power and magnificence and "low," correspondingly, a subordinated standing. This is unsurprising, but how do the yellow *tiao* flowers connect with the representation of human activity here? The third stanza describe how ominous signs appear in the state:

> The ewes have big heads
> the Three Stars are in the Fish-trap
> Even if people can find food
> few can eat themselves full[108]

牂羊墳首
三星在罶
人可以食
鮮可以飽

Mao comments: "*Luo* refers to a widow's fish-trap. 'The ewes have big heads' bespeaks that there is no such order. 'The Three Stars are in the fishnet' bespeaks that it cannot last for long. The days of order are few and the days of chaos many 罶, 寡婦之筍也. 牂羊墳首, 言無是道也. 三星在罶, 言不可久也. 治日少而亂日多."[109]

These words are heavy with doom and the insight of decline. Big-headed ewes are, according to Mao, an anomaly, a symptom of a lost order and an omen of a coming disaster. To the hermeneut of suspicion, big-headed ewes might not seem abnormal—size is after all relative—but Mao the Confucian hermeneut must at all costs avoid redundant or deviant meaning. In this context, Mao's understanding of the big-headed ewes is determined by the lines about suffering (the "sorrows of the heart" and the famine), which forces him to give a negative twist to his interpretation, thereby making the description of the ewes a harmonious part of the whole poem. Semiotically, this "image" does not pertain to the logic of the xing—the ewes are not used as a metaphor for anything else. Just as the cricket in "Xishuai," the big-headed ewes point both backward and forward. They are simultaneously symptoms of the disharmony of yin and yang and omens pointing to the future decline of the state of Zhou, destroyed by barbarian tribes.[110]

In semiotic terminology, "big-headed ewes" is here a mantic sign the interpretation of which aims at deciphering the logic of a higher supernatural force—a hermeneutic practice not unlike the "great man's" deciphering of the shepherd's dreams in "Wu yang." I bring up the difference between a semiosis built on similitude (which is how we have come to define Mao's xing) and mantic semiosis, which depends on cause-and-effect because recognizing this opposition yields important insights about the nature and origin of Mao's xing. The causality of Mao's interpretation of "big-headed ewes" and of the cricket in the hall (ode 114) is, it seems, a residue of a time-honored divinatory hermeneutics.

Then follows one of the most cryptic lines in the *Odes*. "The Three stars are in the (widow's) fish-trap" imparts, according to the *Commentary*, that the demise of the Zhou is near. Zheng Xuan, in an elaboration of Mao's comment that perhaps expresses Mao's intentions, says that only for a very short time is the constellation known as the Three Stars reflected in the small area of water demarcated by the fish trap.[111] What, with reference to a poetics pertaining to the thought pattern of correlative cosmology, is the logic underlying Mao's and Zheng's readings here? Few passages are, in fact, better suited to illustrate the imagistic complexity of certain *Odes* and the figurality and all-pervading metaphoricity of Mao's poetic exegesis. Mao's and Zheng's interpretation of this line does not bank on a perceived correspondence between cosmic processes and human action but on an extended and opaque simile: the remaining time of the Zhou is as short as the time the Three Stars are reflected in the widow's fish trap. That the Three Stars are sighted not in the high heavens but in the water is, furthermore, a poignant image of a topsy-turvy world where the habitual points of reference have been inverted and "up" has become "down."

"When the flowers of the *tiao* are about to fall, they turn yellow . . . and their leaves turn green" 將落則黃 . . . 葉青青然 says Mao.[112] This yellowness and greenness is the last intense glow of a once magnificent state now on the brink of destruction, a state where "the days of order are few and those of chaos many."[113] The *tiao* plant is thus a "simple" metaphor for the moribund state of Zhou, and the *tertium comparationis* is the concept of falling.

Second Excursion: Rats, an Owl, and Three Yellow Birds

I have, in passing, described Confucian hermeneutics as pragmatic rather than aesthetic, which is to say that the primary aim of Mao's interpretation of the *Odes* was not to explain the structure or function of the poetic text, or what the sagely Russian formalists named *literaturnost*. Instead, armed with the xing as a weapon against an unruly textual corpus, Mao sought to bring out the didactic qualities of the *Shijing*, transforming the sometimes opaque and sometimes explicitly amorous *Odes* into a manual for Confucian statesmanship. I deal with the question of hermeneutical pragmatism in a more detailed fashion below but will touch upon that subject briefly as we try to understand why a poem about rats is not labeled xing when a poem about a yellow bird—seemingly built on the same rhetorical principle—is.

Ode 187 bears the title of "Huang niao" 黃鳥 ("Yellow bird") and the first stanza begins as follows:

> Yellow birds, yellow birds
> Do not gather in the millet
> Do not eat my growing grain[114]

> 黃鳥黃鳥
> 無集于穀
> 無啄我粟

Mao comments: "A xing . . . It is proper that the yellow birds settle in trees and eat grain" 興也 . . . 黃鳥宜集木啄粟者.[115] The ode continues:

> The people of this state
> are unwilling to like me
> I return, I go home
> back to my state and clan[116]

> 此邦之人
> 不我肯穀
> 言旋言歸
> 復我邦族

In a comment on the last four lines that reads remarkably like one of the *Minor Prefaces*, Mao explains the historical background and that the poem was written during the last days of King Xuan's 宣 (d. 782 BCE) reign. The aristocratic houses and clans were in decay and "consorts and their mates separated from each other. There were those that did not adhere to the rites" 妃匹相去, 有不以禮者.[117] Of greater interest is the logic behind Mao's usage of the xing here. Against the background of our earlier findings in this chapter, this poem poses no problems since the malevolent yellow bird destroying the narrator's crops is obviously a metaphor for the "people of the state" that force him or her to return home. Problems arise only when we juxtapose poem 187 to ode 113, "Shi shu" 碩鼠, which has an identical imagistic structure:

> Big rat, big rat
> Do not eat my millet
> For three years [I] have served you
> Never have you looked after me[118]

碩鼠碩鼠
無食我黍
三歲貫女
莫我肯顧

Mao comments: 貫, 事也. "*Guan* means 'to serve'."[119] The poem continues:

> It has gone so far that I will leave you
> [and] go to that happy land
> Happy land! Happy land!
> There I will find my place[120]

逝將去女
適彼樂土
樂土樂土
爰得我所

The first two lines connect with the two following ones through apostrophe, parallelism and the use of pronouns. The rat is addressed directly and urged not to eat *my* millet. In the third and fourth lines the narrator complains that although "I" have served "you" for three years "you" have never looked after "me." The I-and-you dualism of the first line is mirrored directly by the next lines but explicitly on a human level (since you cannot serve a rodent). Apparently, this is also the reading condoned in silence by Mao. Mao is, in fact, so certain that the reader will understand that "rat" does not refer to a "long-tailed rodent" (but is a representation of a despotic lord) that he supplies nothing but the gloss on *guan* 貫. But where does this sudden trust in the reader come from? And why is the xing tag necessary in the comment on ode 187? In both poems, the natural descriptions could well be understood literally. In the former case, Mao perceives this danger, steps in, and declares that the yellow bird is indeed a *xingish* metaphor. Why is there no danger of deviousness and superfluous meaning in "Shi shu"?

A corollary of my tenet about the pragmatic nature of the *xing* is that Mao does not need to bring in this hermeneutic weaponry if he considers the meaning and structure of a poem to be obvious. Let us, in pursuit of the meaning of "rat" (*shu* 鼠) for the Han dynasty reader, consider a few pertinent intertexts, beginning with ode 52, "Xiang shu" 相鼠:

> Look at the rat, it has [its] skin
> A man [and yet] without manners
> A man without manners,
> Why is he not dead?

相鼠有皮
人而無儀
人而無儀
不死何為

Mao comments: "The conduct of a person without rites or manners is shady even when he is in a venerated position" 無禮儀者雖居尊位猶為闇昧之行.[121]

The second and third stanzas of "Xiang shu" are slight variations of the first:

> Look at the rat, it has teeth
> A man [and yet] without limits
> A man without limits
> Is he not dead? What does he wait for?
> Look at the rat, it has limbs
> A man [and yet] without rites
> A man without rites
> Why does he not meet with death?[122]

相鼠有齒
人而無止
人而無止
不死何俟
相鼠有體
人而無禮
人而無禮
胡不遄死

"Xiang shu" provides its reader with important insights about the poetics of the *Odes* and about Confucian hermeneutics. It is thoroughly structured according to the dualism of the natural and the human: the rat, belonging to the natural realm, is said to have skin (皮 *pi*), teeth (齒 *chi*) and limbs (體 *ti*), corporeal and concrete objects that are juxtaposed to the more refined and abstract traits that a Superior Man should possess but which this particular man lacks, namely manners (儀 *yi*), limits (止 *zhi*) and rituals (禮 *li*). The link between the strata is further fortified by the rhymes between the key words.[123] But how do nature and man interact rhetorically in this poem?

Strictly speaking, there is no metaphoricity involved. Nowhere has the word "rat" another *signatum* than "long-tailed rodent"; nowhere is "rat" used to describe the man without manners, limits, or rites. Indeed, it is the task of the poem to reinforce the distance between crude nature and refined humanity by stating that rat and man *should not* share any characteristics. Consequently, there is no *tertium comparationis* that combines the two strata and Mao does not call it a xing. What we have here, then, is a case of the classic opposition between *similitudo* and *comparatio*. While the former concept demands that tenor and vehicle share a certain characteristic, the latter denotes the mere act of comparison, of putting two objects side by side. At this point in my investigation, "Xiang shu" demonstrates that the description of man in terms of nature is at the very center of the trope that Mao calls a xing and that it is not a simplistic comparison of *this* and *that* but a figure built on similitude.

Let us return to the main question. How does "Xiang shu" explain why Mao considered the imagistic element of "Huang niao" a xing but not that of "Xiang shu"? We shall consult an intertext, this time the *Zuozhuan* which, as Chen Huan and Bernhard Karlgren have convincingly demonstrated, is a text that Mao makes constant references to and that he used to validate his interpretations of the *Shijing*.[124] The opening passage of the chronicle of the twenty-seventh year of Duke Xiang (546 BCE) describes how Qing Feng 慶封, a high dignitary from the state of Qi 齊, came to visit the state of Lu 魯. An aristocrat by the name of Meng Xiaobo 孟孝伯 admired the carriage driven by Qing Feng and made a casual remark about the beauty of the car to his friend Shusun Bao 叔孫豹. The latter responded thus: "I have heard this: if beautiful attire does not find a match [in beautiful actions] the result is bound to be ugly. What can a beautiful carriage do?" 豹聞之, 服美不稱, 必以惡終. 美車何為.[125] Shusun Bao then had dinner with the visiting dignitary, whose demeanor and deportment were "not respectful," and presented (賦 *fu*) "Xiang shu." Qing Feng, however, failed to grasp the drift of Shusun Bao's presentation.

This is a story that Mao certainly was aware of when he, in his comment, stated that a person without rites is immoral even is he happens to be the ruler of a state. Like Mao, Shusun Bao knew that fancy clothes, a beautiful carriage, and a high position do not necessarily entail the good character that Confucianism demanded from a Superior Man (*junzi*). It is in this context that "Xiang shu" is recited. The "rat" in the poem represents the antithesis of everything considered proper by Confucian ethics. A rat is an animal and, as such, has the animal's basic characteristics, namely skin, teeth, and limbs. The clever and very effective logic of the poem—a logic underlined by the *Zuozhuan* narrative—is that man is supposed to be a Superior Man and have manners, limits and, rites. If not, if he has been stripped of these noble characteristics then he has returned to nature and is no more than skin, teeth and limbs—he is but a rat. This is what the poem says, and it says this skillfully, using the absence of a metaphorical convergence to stress the separation of nature and man.

We return, finally, to "Shi shu." I have made this long detour to demonstrate that "rat" is a word or concept that is already impregnated with negative associations when it appears in "Shi shu." It is a word that has been used, in "Xiang shu" and by Mao's fellow hermeneut Shusun Bo, in a comparison of man to something utterly subhuman. Furthermore, apart from "Xiang shu," "rat" has only bad connotations in the *Odes* and the *Commentary*: the rat is an intruder to one's house (odes 17 and 189) and, similarly, a vermin that has to be smoked out of the house (ode 154, stanza five). Consequently, when the "big rat" is begged not to eat "my" grain, Mao knows that the reader is familiar with the tradition of rat imagery of the *Odes* and the *Zuozhuan* and understands it as an image of an "animalistic" ruler deviating from the Confucian, humanizing path. Consequently, the xing tag is obsolete.

If "rat" is a word whose figurative meaning remains constant throughout the *Odes*, "yellow bird" (*huang niao* 黃鳥) is quite different. This phrase appears three times in the *Shijing*, each time with a different metaphorical value. In ode 187 the yellow bird is described as a threat to the narrator ("don't eat my grain") and serves as a metaphor for the malevolent "people of the state." This negativity is not carried over to ode 131, also called "Huang niao." Here Mao interprets the first lines ("Small is the yellow bird / It settles in the jujube tree") as an analogy: "A xing . . . the yellow bird finds its dwelling place in accordance with the seasons. Man, too, finds his ground in accordance with the lifespan [naturally allotted to him]" 興也 . . . 黃鳥以時得其所，人以壽命終亦得其所.[126]

In ode 230, "Mian man" 緜蠻, the yellow bird has a similar function, and the xingish lines "Small is the yellow bird / It settles on the slope of the hill" 緜蠻黃鳥, 止于丘阿 are also part of an analogy, according to Mao: "Birds settle on hills and men settle on [take as their ground rule] benevolence" 鳥止於阿, 人止於仁.[127] In both ode 131 and ode 230, the bird acts according to its own lowly nature. And just as the rule of the xing prescribes, these animal and avian acts are subsequently refined by the Confucian commentator and understood as representations of human behavior.

This provides an answer to the initial question. Contrariwise to the semantic stability of the rat, the topos of the yellow bird is used paradoxically, once representing an immediate threat to the narrator and twice representing virtuous (or at any rate normal) behavior. Therefore a certain feeling of bewilderment threatens the reader as he or she encounters a description of the yellow bird in a *Shijing* poem: does it signal violence or benevolence? In this moment of suspense, Mao the hermeneutic *auctoritas* lays down the law and dispels the ambiguity through the xing tag.

I round off this excursion into the metaphoric landscape of the *Odes* by contemplating the "owl" that appears in ode 155, "Chixiao" 鴟鴞:

Owl, owl
You have already taken my children
[but] you will not crush my house

鴟鴞鴟鴞
既取我子
無毀我室

Mao comments: "A xing. *Chixiao* refers to the *ningjue* bird. 'You cannot crush my house' because it is well built and strong. You have destroyed two sons but you cannot crush my house of Zhou entirely" 興也. 鴟鴞, 鸋鴂也. 無能毀我室者攻堅之故也. 寧亡二子, 不可以毀我周室.[128]

The first stanza ends with the following two lines:

Love! Toil!
Alas, the young one, for him I worry

恩斯勒斯
鬻子之閔斯

Mao comments: "'The young one' refers to King Cheng" 鬻子, 成王也.¹²⁹ The second stanza comprises the following five lines:

> When heaven had not yet become dark with rain
> I peeled those bamboo roots
> twined them into window and door
> Now you low populace
> who dare ridicule me?¹³⁰

迨天之未陰雨
徹彼桑土
綢繆牖戶
今女下民
或敢侮予

Traditional exegetes hold that "Chixiao" refers to the famous story about the Duke of Zhou's (benevolent) usurpation of his nephew's, King Cheng, throne after the death of the duke's brother, King Wu of Zhou.¹³¹ This allegorico-historical interpretation aside, the rhetorical organization of "Chixiao" is interesting against the background of "Huang niao" and "Shi shu." The violent *chixiao* may be a metaphor for the slanderous people of "the low populace," where "low" (*xia* 下) is a pun referring both to social inferiority—the *vulgus*—and, consistent with the bird metaphor, to the idea of the speaker as a bird that has sought refuge in a *high* tree. In contrast to the poems about rats and yellow birds, the narrator of "Chixiao" transgresses the nature/man dualism and presents *himself* as a bird, referring in the last stanza to his "torn feathers and tail."¹³² Yet the poem can never become fully allegorical due to a subtle rhetorical movement in which the metaphorical categories are mixed, where vehicle is confused with tenor and the avian realm with that of humans: although you have killed my sons, the "bird" says, you will not destroy my house; my hands grasped the *tu* plant and my *mouth* is sick.¹³³

If we suppose that the narrator is in fact a bird, then "house" (instead of "nest"), "sons" (instead of "nestlings"), "hands" (instead of "claws"), and "mouth" (instead of "beak") are figures of speech that depend on a transfer from *man to nature*: an inversion of the rule of the xing. Naturally, such an idea is empirically and logically impossible. A bird cannot compose a poem (let alone effect a xing) or manufacture windows or doors from the peels of the bamboo root. However, this to-and-fro movement between nature and man demonstrates that "Chixiao" is structurally more complex than the average xing poem, whose clear dividing line between nature and human activity it lacks. Facing this rhetorical jumble, Mao must immediately take control of the poem and stake out the metaphorical territory with his xing tag. When "house" has been identified as the robust house of Zhou and "the young one" as King Cheng, the danger of complete misinterpretation is gone and order (temporarily) established. Despite the confusing oscillations between the natural and the human, "Chixiao" follows the logic of "Huang niao" and "Shi shu" in that the owl is understood as an aggressor threatening the speaker.

This interpretation is, admittedly, not necessarily identical in all parts with the one Mao had in mind. Rather, it is a tentative reading reconstructed from Mao's anorexic comments and made in light of Mao's and Zheng's xingish readings of the poems already discussed. My assumption that Mao identified the narrator as a small bird under attack is supported by his comment on the third stanza. Here, Mao says that by using his "hands" and "mouth" until they are "sick," the narrator is able to avoid the attacks from "the big bird."[134]

Having thus reached a temporary understanding of "Chixiao," I suggest an alternative reading. Before anything else, however, we must ask ourselves if the *chixiao* bird itself has not been subjected to slander by modern-day translators. All four schools (including Mao) defines "chixiao" as the *ningjue*-bird.[135] In a comment that certainly may represent the view of all four schools, the Han school says that the *chixiao* (or *ningjue*) "loves" and "nourishes" its offspring, and that it takes great pains to do so.[136] This description of the *chixiao* as a virtuous, loving bird stands in remarkable opposition to the fierce bird of prey in my initial translation. We will keep this paradoxical definition in mind as we discuss Mao's interpretation in greater detail.

The main problem lies in identifying the allegorico-historical superstructure that Mao builds on and, in particular, which version of the story about the Duke of Zhou he refers to. Two pieces of information must be correlated and made parts of a bigger whole: who are the "two sons" (or "two men," *er zi* 二子) about whom Mao speaks, and how do they correspond to Mao's identification of "the young one" as King Cheng? Supposing that the narrator is rhetorically assuming the voice of a bird that takes every measure to defend King Cheng ("the young one") against the evil "owl," then the two "sons" already killed must belong to the same "nest," or to the same *phalanx* in the struggle for the throne of Zhou. The "Jin teng" version in the *Shujing* describes how, in the power struggle following the death of King Wu, some of the Duke of Zhou's brothers spread rumors about his intentions to do the young king harm, and how the duke instead turned to two other members of the royal house who were aware of his good intentions and who, supposedly, assisted him in his resolve to stop the slanderers.[137] Opposed to the Duke of Zhou and his two allies were thus the duke's malevolent older brother Guanshu Xian and a group of unnamed "younger brothers."[138] If the two benevolent men—or, indeed, any two people allied with the Duke of Zhou—are who Mao refers to as the "two sons," then my reading is valid. In that case, the "owl" must be understood as the duke's slanderous and evil brothers, and the duke himself as the narrator posing as the bird who defends his "nest" (the house of Zhou) against violent intruders.

Presuming, on the other hand, that Mao depended on an account of the struggle more akin to the Lu school version than to that of the received *Shujing*, then this interpretation must be reconsidered. The Lu version does not mention the duke's benevolent allies but simply says that on King Cheng's command the Duke of Zhou organized a punitory expedition to the East, executed Guanshu Xian, exiled his younger brother Caishu Du, and also killed Wu Geng, the leader of the vanquished Shang.[139] Thereupon he returned to the capital and wrote "Chixiao," which he presented to the king. Considering this information, the interpretation of the poem and its rhetorical mode must be radically different. Since the Duke of Zhou, in this version, is both the narrator and the destroyer of two "sons" (that is, Guanshu Xian and Caishu Du) the difference in identity between the "owl" and the bird under attack can no longer be upheld. The duke is the murderous bird—*he* is the *chixiao*—and, as Kong Yingda observed, the poem must be paraphrased thus:

> I am the *chixiao*
> I have destroyed two gentlemen
> The house of Zhou cannot be crushed
> I have loved and toiled
> For you, young one, I have worried[140]

The poem (and its putative author) excels in self-glorification and self-pity, describing how the Duke of Zhou, like the *chixiao*, has defended his "nest" and how he made windows and doors for it and fortified it with the *tu* plant until his "hands" bled and his "mouth" was sick. The poem must now be read as the duke's allegorical defense for having executed one of his brothers and exiled another. Such an iconoclastic reading is confirmed by the Lu school's comment on the second stanza in which the *chixiao*, "this small bird," is explicitly defined as an image of a virtuous ruler (and not as a vicious usurper). Just like the *chixiao*, who knows how to build and fortify its nest, the good ruler knows how to govern his country: "who," asks the Lu school, "dares ridicule him?"[141]

Returning to the *Commentary*, we find that Mao's xingish reading of the first three lines can be interpreted in two radically different ways. On one reading, the *chixiao* is a violent, murderous owl who has slain the narrator's "sons," a description that, on the textual level, functions as a metaphor for the evil men who want to usurp the throne and destroy the house of Zhou. According to the other reading—more difficult to square with the poem itself, but equally justifiable as shown by the contemporary intertexts—the *chixiao* is a virtuous small bird who only murders reluctantly, defending himself and his "nest" (the house of Zhou) from the maltreatment of a violent aggressor who, significantly, is not identified or even mentioned by the text itself.

The two readings of "Chixiao" discussed here differ in rhetorical structure. The first follows the pattern of "Huang niao" and "Shi shu," rhetorically as well as thematically. According to this matrix, an animal (a rat or a bird) is used as a metaphor for a violent intruder. What argues for this interpretation of "Chixiao," apart from the obvious similarity in structure, is that Mao would probably have stated that "owl" referred to the Duke of Zhou, had that been his interpretation. However, even if the latter reading would turn out to be the correct one (corroborated by, let us say, a newly excavated version of the *Mao Commentary*), the juxtaposition of "Chixiao" with the rat-and-bird odes would not have been made in vain because it demonstrates how easily Mao breaks the rules he himself has established. Finally, my two contradictory readings of "Chixiao" offer a foretaste of the coming discussion about Mao's pragmatism—because they so clearly demonstrate that to Mao's identification of a "xing" must be added a detailed guide to its meaning. If not, the puzzled reader might attempt at his or her own xingish reading and arrive at an interpretation that goes against Mao's intentions, describing the Duke of Zhou as a bird that murders to maintain order and keep out usurpation, instead of a defenseless bird whose offspring have been murdered by the violent and ruthless owl.

"Qi yu" 淇奧 (ode 55)

Look at that cove of the Qi river
The royal fodder and the creeper are beautiful and luxuriant[142]

瞻彼淇奧
綠竹猗猗

Mao comments: "A *xing* . . . *Yiyi* means beautiful and luxuriant in appearance. Duke Wu's character was beautiful and his virtue luxuriant" 興也 . . . 猗猗, 美盛貌. 武公質美德盛.

The poem goes on:

Cultured is the gentleman
he is as if cut, as if filed
as if chiselled, as if polished

有匪君子
如切如磋
如琢如磨

"Qi yu"—which, according to both the *Minor Preface* and *Mao Heng*, celebrates the virtue of Duke Wu—is built on a "simple" metaphor as the beauty and luxuriousness of the plants refer to the beautiful character and virtue of the duke.[143]

"Mian shui" 沔水 (ode 183)

Abundant is that flowing water
it goes to pay [spring and summer] court to the sea[144]

沔彼流水
朝宗于海

Mao comments: "A *xing*. *Mian* refers to flowing and abundant [river-]water. It is as if the water had someone to pay court to" 興也. 沔, 水流漫也. 水猶有所朝宗.[145]

Swift is that flying hawk
it flies up and settles down
Oh! Brothers of mine
All friends of the state
No one can [bear to] think of the chaos
Who does not have a father and mother?[146]

鴥彼飛隼
載飛載止
嗟我兄弟
邦人諸友
莫肯念亂
誰無父母

The *Commentary* says that by "friends of the state" the poet addresses the vassals (*zhuhou*), and that "Brothers of mine" refers to the ministers of the same family as the speaker.[147]

The second stanza also opens with a xingish image:

Abundant is that flowing water
it flows without restraint[148]

沔彼流水
其流湯湯

Mao comments: "This imparts [that the water has] no restraint and no place to enter [into its proper path]" 言放縱無所入也.[149] The stanza continues:

Swift is that flying hawk
it flies up and soars[150]

鴥彼飛隼
載飛載揚

Mao comments: "This imparts that [the hawk] has no fixed place to settle at" 言無所定止也.[151]

[I] think of those unvirtuous men
they rise, they go

The sorrows of the heart
they cannot be stopped or forgotten[152]

念彼不蹟
載起載行
心之憂矣
不可弭忘

The third stanza wraps up the poem with a caveat:

Swift is that flying hawk
it goes along that middle hill
The slander of the populace
[why does] nobody stop them?
Friends of mine, be prudent
slanderous words are rising.[153]

鴥彼飛隼
率彼中陵
民之訛言
寧莫之懲
我友敬矣
讒言其興

Mao comments: "The distressed king cannot investigate the slander" 疾王不能察讒也.[154]

The first—and perhaps most important—thing that we notice is that the xing element itself constitutes a complete metaphor. Typically, nature is used to describe man, but here that order is inverted as nature is obviously anthropomorphic: the flood rushes to the sea like a vassal on his way to the court. What does this metaphor tell us? It is, on the one hand, a conceptualization of the power structure of the Warring States period where the vassals (*zhuhou*) were regarded as part of a greater whole toward which they move quite naturally and ceaselessly. The vaguely Kafkaesque description of the sea as a big, distant, and not-quite-graspable power center is, as we shall see momentarily, merely one of several metaphors of Confucian hierarchy. On the other hand, it is a version of the "family tree" metaphor, describing how the vassals—who were almost invariably related to each other—spring from the same origin.

However, one does not yet see how the xing connects to the main theme. Mao's comment on the following lines speaks of "ministers of the same family" and of "mother and father," which would seem to fit what the xing has to say about family relations. It is only with the comment on the "xing-element" of the second stanza that the meaning of the metaphor become obvious: Mao's comment tells of how the flow of abundant water has lost its order; it has nowhere to go (to "enter") and can no longer reach its "court." The image of abundant and unruly water can now be carried over to the human realm, which speaks of chaos, sorrow, and the deeds of men who do not follow the Path (*dao*). The theme of chaos and unsettledness is further illustrated by the image of the birds who fly up and down without finding a safe place to settle down at.

Just as we have come to expect from the xing, it unifies the text through Mao's description of the rhetorical organization of the poem, his prowess as an ideological reader, and his sense of hermeneutical economy. Primarily, the overflowing and "promiscuous" water is a representation of the dangerous situation in which the state finds itself, with its lawless men and slanderers. But the ever-so-economical Mao does not, and cannot, waste the metaphoricity that the xing is founded on. When the first stanza describes the water as clogged up with nowhere to go, this obstruction of the water path connects directly to the initial metaphor of water "going to court" and the notion of vassals as parts of a feudal clan, inferior to the king. Now the flooding is no longer merely a metaphor for danger in general but the more specific danger of hierarchic chaos.

This flood metaphor can thus be interpreted in two ways. It can either be a description of how the power channel is blocked—the intercourse between ruler and ruled is obstructed since the "water" (that is, the vassals) has nowhere to go. Or one can interpret this metaphor as a description of how something inferior (the water and the vassal) that should be just part of a greater context swells out of proportion and threatens that which by nature should be bigger and superior (the sea or ruler). The xing initially seemed to build on a deviant metaphorical movement from man to nature and describe the water in terms usually restricted to the human realm. The flow of the water-goes-to-court metaphor, which ran backward in the first line, has now reverted back to describing man in terms of nature, enabling Mao to let the metaphor run through the whole piece, merging the three themes of flooding, Confucian hierarchy, and governmental chaos.

Why is the insight into this multilayered rhetorical structure so important? Because not only is it a telling example of Mao's complex and sophisticated analysis of the poetic text but also a nail in the coffin of cosmological, hypermimetic poetics. For argument's sake, let us construct a "cosmological" reading of "Mian shui." The central idea of cosmological poetics is the absence of metaphoricity; what appears to be a metaphor is, in fact, only the literal representation of extratextual correspondences between nature and man. In this case it would be possible to claim that floods and governmental chaos and usurpation are cosmically and metonymically connected since both the natural and the human phenomenon are, allegedly, the effects of a disharmony between yin and yang.[155] Yet such an interpretation fails to recognize the fact—which is also the nucleus of the Aristotelian *metaphora*—that *this* is brought into the text to say *that*. In other words, the xing does not primarily speak of floods and usurpation—it speaks of floods as a *description* of disaster on the human level of the government. This transference from nature to man, as I have argued several times, is itself profoundly rhetorical and fabricated.

Furthermore, as soon as we acknowledge the initial metaphor of the xing, then the cosmological reading becomes untenable. To say that the water "goes to pay court to the sea" is, whatever philosophical ideas may lie behind it, a metaphor. The text is not paratactic; it does not simply juxtapose images of nature with descriptions of human situations. Nor is it parallelistic; it does not present natural images and human situations in a way that is syntactically, grammatically, or metrically corresponding. Instead, "water" (tenor), "to pay court" (vehicle), and "sea" (tenor) are all given in the same clause. The metaphor results from the interaction between these words and their logical incompatibility. To Mao, "water" and "sea" must be understood in their literal sense, whereas the expression "to pay court to" cannot be interpreted this way. The tenor and the vehicle are, furthermore, not drawn from the same realm of existence.[156] The poem describes a natural phenomenon, the flowing of a river, in terms that belong to a human situation that most emphatically is not natural but ritualistic and cultural. To say, with the "cosmologists," that the xing of "Mian shui" is literal and not metaphorical would be a misunderstanding of the literariness of the *Odes*. The way that the xing element functions here is excellent proof of the rhetoric and metaphoricity of the *Commentary* and also of the *Odes* themselves. This double metaphor, flowing backward and forward to permeate the whole text breaks conclusively with the poetics of correlative cosmology.

19

Analogy and Instrumentality

The "Analogical Xing"

In the preceding chapter I hope to have demonstrated the metaphorical character the xing as it appears in Mao's *Commentary* and, at the same time, to a large extent refute what I have called a "cosmological poetics." I have discussed a trope, the xing, whose structure was that of a simple, straightforward metaphor in which the tenor and the vehicle shared a common feature, a *tertium comparationis* (virtue, loyalty, honesty, trustworthiness, etc.), which served as a point into which the two parts of the metaphor coincided. Now I proceed to an instance of the xing that appears to lack that point of convergence, a variant that seems to be—just as the theory of cosmology contends—a mere juxtaposition of natural and human phenomena. If the *tertium comparationis* was the main characteristic of the "simple" xing, the rhetorical structure of what I will call the analogical xing is more complex. It consists of two chains of events put side by side: one pertaining to nature and the second pertaining to man. This putting side by side of nature and man, however, is not aimlessly paratactic but metaphorical; just as was the case with the simple xing, natural descriptions are here used as predications about the human realm (which, of course, is what defines a "xing" in the first place). We therefore still move within the boundaries defined by Zhu Ziqing's model.

Since in Mao's analogical xing nature parallels man, it is understandable that earlier scholars have been led to claim that the poem (in Mao's interpretation) is a literal statement about analogies that exist outside and predating the text. But it may be argued, again, that this idea builds on a misunderstanding, not only of the relation between Mao's *Commentary* and the *Odes* but also of what a metaphor is. Confronted with Mao's analogical interpretation of an image, one must not mistake the *Commentary* for the primary text. In the *Odes* only the natural description is given. Mao provides the metaphorical analogy so as not to waste poetic imagery or, worse, make it the prey for perverse hermeneutical poachers. Through the analogy, there indeed occurs a transfer of meaning, based on similitude, from the realm of nature to the realm of humans. I consequently argue that despite the difference in structure the analogical *xing* maintains the two most dominant characteristic of the "primitive" version, namely the simultaneous similitude and difference between nature and humans (difference on a conceptual, ideological and extratextual level and similarity on the rhetorical level), and the shift from literal concretion to metaphorical abstraction. Finally, I try to demonstrate how Mao's analogical *xing* banks on the persuasive authority of the simple *xing* but, at the same time, distorts and transforms this "simplistic" structure of similitude into something quite different.

"Jiu yu" 九罭 (ode 159)

As an illustration of the difference between simple metaphor and analogy, I contrast Zheng Xuan's reading of "Jiu yu" to that of Mao's and to Mao's interpretation as rendered by Kong Yingda. "Jiu yu" shares its historical background, Mao, Zheng, and Kong all agree, with "Chixiao" (ode 155). Written by a high official somewhat earlier than the latter, it celebrates the heroic Duke of Zhou exiled in a small, eastern state having been wrongly accused of trying to usurp King Cheng's position. The poem should also be regarded as a critique of King Cheng's lack of respect and concern for his uncle (or, with Zheng in Kong's interpretation, as criticism of the ignorant members of the royal court). The first two lines of the poem are as follows: "The fishes in the fine-meshed net / [are] rudd and bream" 九罭之魚, 鱒魴.[1] Zheng comments: "To set up a fine-meshed fish-net and then, afterwards, catch rudd and bream bespeaks that the acquiring of objects all have their own instruments. The *xing* conveys [*yu* 喻] that if the king wishes to meet the Duke of Zhou upon his arrival, he [the king] should abide by the rites [proper to that occasion]" 設九罭之罟乃後得鱒魴之魚. 言取物各有器也. 興者喻王欲迎周公之來當有其禮.[2]

As he so often does, Zheng puts the stress on method, instrumentality, and *activity*: you need a net to catch fish and ritual behavior to "catch" the virtuous Duke of Zhou. The xing trope is structured according to the classical definition of analogy: net (A) relates to fishing (B) as rites (C) relate to statesmanship (D). The text itself gives only A and B, with C and D being added extratextually by the Confucian commentator.³ We note, moreover, that in Zheng's reading (in which fishing is compared to ritual performance) the metaphorical *point of convergence* is that both activities are governed by specific rules. Kong Yingda's extrapolation of Mao's comment that rudd and bream are big fishes in a net designed for small fish is also founded on an analogical reading: "Rudd and bream are big fish. To set up a smallish, fine-meshed net is inappropriate. This is a xing [saying that to have] the Duke of Zhou—this sage—live in a small hamlet in the [barbaric] east is also inappropriate. How come the king did not reach out to him earlier?" 鱒魴是大魚. 處九罭之小網非其宜, 以興周公是聖人, 處東方之小邑, 亦非其宜. 王何以不早迎之乎.⁴

Kong, giving Zheng's reading a slightly different spin, stresses the anomaly of the xing (the attempt to catch big fish with a small net) and interprets the xing as saying that the duke is a big "fish" in a small and barbaric state. The condensed version of Kong's metaphor notwithstanding, it is clear that the trope depends on the idea that rudd and bream stand in the same relation to the small net as the duke does to the small state and, more importantly, that the xing ultimately criticizes the fallacy involved in the treatment of the fish and the duke.

Mao himself comments laconically: "A xing. The fine-meshed net is a net for small fish. Rudd and bream are big fish" 興也. 九罭緵罟小魚之網也. 鱒魴大魚也.⁵ Mao's comment involves no analogy, nor any mention of instrumentality (of how to catch big fish or how to "catch" the duke of Zhou). If the first lines constitute a xing referring to the Duke of Zhou (of whom the following lines speak, according to Mao), then we must conclude that Mao understands the xing as a simple metaphor, saying precisely that the duke is a "big fish" in a small net. With Mao, the *tertium comparationis* that unites the lowly fish and the aristocratic duke on the rhetorical level could be paraphrased as "misplacedness." Mao's xing is a description of the duke and not a statement about method. Yet Kong's reading should not be mistaken for a malign distortion. Instead, it demonstrates how easily most "simple" metaphors can be understood or misunderstood as elliptic analogies.

More important for our understanding of Confucian literary hermeneutics is that this example clearly demonstrates that the effectiveness of the analogical xing lies precisely in the juxtaposition of natural and human *chains of events*. In contrast to the more static and passive "simple" xing, which just describes single traits, such as the royal couple's "virtue" or the duke of Zhou's "misplaced-ness," the analogical xing focuses on action, procedures, and events, such as the setting up of the fish net to catch fish. On the one hand, the descriptions of these lowly activities are troublesome for the Confucian hermeneut since they threaten to maculate the sacred text with ignoble meaning, speaking of the populace instead of the Superior Man. On the other hand, they provide excellent allegorico-metaphorical material, enabling the Confucian reader to reinstall ideological order by substituting figurative and spiritual meaning for the *sensus literalis*.

The concepts of proper behavior, rites, and rituals were crucial to Han dynasty Confucianism and hermeneutics; consequently, the *Shijing* text must be made to speak its language. The problems of how to run a state, how to run a clan or a family, and how to be a perfected *junzi* all revolve around the concept of instrumentality. If a fish net is the proper instrument for plebeian work, then the rituals are the proper, and indeed universally applicable, instrument of the Superior Man. Zheng and Kong, in an interpretational move we will soon be familiar with, expand Mao's original simple metaphor into an analogy that describes the practice of rites in terms of fishing.

That the so-called analogical xing builds on a metaphorical transfer from nature to man is thus obvious. But from a technical point of view, what characterizes the hermeneutic procedure that transforms the poem's seemingly literal description of mundane objects such as rudd, bream, and fish traps into a statement about rites and righteousness? What interpretational technique enables the Confucian hermeneut to substitute a dynamic analogy for static similitude—and action for passive description? A reconstruction of this transformation from simple, literal meaning to higher metaphorical *significance* reveals an interpretational model that in fact distorts the flow of lowly, literal meaning from nature to man and usurps the name of "xing," replacing it with a trope that formally and nominally banks on the distinction between nature and man but, in fact, exchanges it for the two levels of populace and aristocrat. The discovery of an analogical xing is of interest not only for reasons of hermeneutics and literary criticism but also because it so obviously shows the Confucian "aristocratic" aloofness from the commoner: the latter replaces, in the rhetorical scheme of the xing, nature's role as merely a vehicle for higher meaning. This idea is echoed in the *Great Preface* and the three fundamental dichotomies of commoner and Superior Man, "tones" and "music," and "emotions" and "intent" that it banks on.

A sketchy reconstruction of the analogical xing thus comprises three phases. There is, at first, the text itself and its literal account of the rudd and the bream in the net. In the second phase, the commentator emphasizes *action*: the fish are no longer the focus of attention—that is, the object of Mao's drive to metaphorize; now it is the act of catching them that serves as the focus. This involves the question of how fish are caught and thereby the theme of instrumentality. Third, with the shift of attention from the fish to the popular activity of fish catching there occurs a change of vehicles, as for the nature-man dualism of the simple xing has been replaced a commoner–Superior Man dualism.

In the "simple" xing, the literal descriptions of nature were interpreted as metaphors of certain phenomena on the human level. In the analogical xing that function has been allotted to a group of quasi-natural creatures—the commoners. In the third phase one popular, lowly, and literal activity (the catching of fish) is thus interpreted as a metaphor for another aristocratic, noble activity, namely the art of statesmanship as represented by the king's attracting a sage. Nonetheless, the xingish transfer of meaning from nature to man remains (since the letter speaks of nature and the spirit of rituals), but it is a rhetorical procedure more complicated and "violent" than Mao's simple xing and entails a rhetorical structure that nearly obliterates the central characteristic—the nature/man dualism—of the primitive version. In Zhu Ziqing's terms, it is a *piyu*—but not the *piyu* found in "Guanju."

"Yuan you tao" 園有桃 (ode 109)

> The garden has a peach tree,
> Its fruits, them [one takes as] meat

園有桃
其實之殽

Mao comments: "A xing. The garden has a peach tree, its fruits one eats. The state has the populace, and uses its strength" 興也. 園有桃, 其實之食. 國有民, 得其力.[6]

> The sorrows of the heart
> I sing and chant

心之憂矣
我歌且謠

Mao comments: "Lyrics and music put together is called *ge*. To sing without music is called *yao*" 曲合樂曰歌. 徒歌曰謠.

> Those who do not know me
> say that I am an arrogant man
> That person is right!
> She says: "what do you want"?
> The sorrows of the heart
> Who knows it?
> Who knows it
> Indeed they give it no thought[7]

> 不知我者
> 謂我士也驕
> 彼人是哉
> 子曰何其
> 心之憂矣
> 其誰知之
> 其誰知之
> 蓋亦勿思

These are the troubled words of a *shi* 士, an "official" or "gentleman" (Mao never defines this word) who complains about being misunderstood as arrogant by people who see that he sings and chants but, in Zheng Xuan's words, "do not know the meaning of the chants and songs I make" 不知我所為歌謠之意.[8] Stylistically, the poem opens with wonderful force. The first, third, and fifth word of the xing hammer their way into the mind of the reader, moving from big to small, zooming in on the object that seduces the senses and the palate: garden—peach—*fruit*. The quietude and blossom of that garden, the beauty of that peach tree (which we know also connotes the beauty and fertility of a young bride) and the tastiness of that peach—all serve as a most striking contrast to the anxiety expressed by the rest of the text. It is as if the angst-ridden speaker sought mental refuge in that restful and sensuous imagery that Mao calls a xing.

Mao, however, will not stand such sentimental and lustful indulgence. He is a hermeneutical worker with the intention of cutting, reshaping, and polishing that piece of raw material we call a text. In the reading attempted a second ago, the static image of the peach on the tree in the garden was never transformed into a metaphor of any sort. Rather, it works by connotation (causing "summer," "beauty," and the taste of a peach to arise in the reader's mind) and by contrasting peace, beauty, and sensuous pleasure to the anxiety and alienation described by the ensuing lines. With Mao the ode is metaphorized and the static image made into a dynamic analogy, implying that the peach is to the garden as the populace is to the state. The dynamics of the analogy, however, comes into motion only as Mao, arbitrarily and self-willed, adds that *eating* the fruit is a metaphor for *using* the populace. Here enters the theme of proper conduct. On a lowly, literal level we have the peaches in the garden, eaten by the commoners; on a lofty, more sublime and metaphorical level there is the populace, used by the wise lord. Both are objects that must be subjected to appropriate measures in order to avoid governmental harm and waste (just as Mao, the economical hermeneut, must not waste the xing to a literalism that can harm the text's loftiness through deviant interpretations).

Mao does not understand the populace as the fruits of the state, as he would have had this been a "simple xing." Such a positive description of the lowly people would not tally with the Confucian idea of the *vulgus* as a creature occupying a space between nature and the Superior Man. The Confucian view of the *vulgus* is much crasser, namely that the commoners have crude physical strength (*li* 力)—as contrasted to the Superior Man's intellectual and virtuous "ability" (*neng* 能)—that should be used and, mixing the rhetorical levels, devoured.

Mao's comment on "Yuan you tao" thus exemplifies most of the traits that I argue pertain to the analogical xing, namely the quasi-metaphorical transfer from nature to man on which the de facto metaphor (the Superior Man as a sublimated commoner) relies, the lack of a *tertium comparationis* and a metaphoric copula; the "dynamic" focus on action ("eating," "using") in contrast to "static" natural descriptions, and finally the themes of proper conduct and instrumentality. What further distinguishes Mao's analogical xing from its "simpler" version is the absence of intratextuality. In for example "Guanju," the reading of the *jujiu* bird as a metaphorical description of the young couple is justified by the parallelistic structure of that poem. "Yuan you tao," by contrast, is not metaphorical in the same obvious manner. The poem indeed speaks of statesmanship but never of the populace as a vehicle for it. The analogical xing thus seems to be more blatantly ideological than the simple xing since Mao's Confucian exploitation of this poem lacks the persuasive rationality that at least partly characterizes his comment on the first ode.

While certainly banking on the persuasive force of that canonical comment, the analogical xing is more obviously designed to exercise hermeneutical power, with "xing" being the official seal of a correct, authorized interpretation. Anticipating an argument that will be put forward momentarily, one may explain this lack of interest in the text itself as a symptom of Mao's pragmatic stance—the text must be made to "speak Confucianism," and the xing is a tool (just as the fine-meshed fish net) to achieve that goal with.

"Chou mou" 綢繆 (ode 118)

Tied round [is] the bundled firewood
The Three Stars are in the heavens

綢繆束薪
三星在天

Mao comments: "A xing . . . 'In the heavens' means that [The Three Stars] have begun to appear in the east. Man and woman depend on the rites for their [matrimonial] fulfillment just like firewood and hay depend upon man's work to be rolled up in a bundle. When The Three Stars appear in the heavens the time is right for men and women to get married" 興也 . . . 在天謂始見東方也。男女待禮而成, 若薪芻待人事而後束也。三星在天, 可以嫁娶矣.

The poem continues thus:

What evening is this?
I see these fine persons
Young ladies, young ladies . . .
What shall I say of these fine persons?

Tied round is that bundled hay
The Three Stars are in the corner
What evening is this?
I see these happy ones
Young ladies, young ladies . . .
what shall I say of these happy ones?

Tied round is that thornwood
The Three Stars are in the door
What evening is this?
I see these beauties

Young ladies, young ladies . . .
what shall I say of these beauties?⁹

今夕何夕
見此良人
子兮子兮
如此良人何
綢繆束芻
三星在隅
今夕何夕
見此邂逅
子兮子兮
如此邂逅何
綢繆束楚
三星在戶
今夕何夕
見此粲者
子兮子兮
如此粲者何

"Chou mou" is a love poem that in Mao's interpretation describes the marriage of a high official.¹⁰ The appearance of the constellation called the Three Stars signals that the time is right for marriage. The xing element, as understood at this stage, is the analogical relationship between bundled firewood and ritually executed marriage. The focus of Mao's attention is of course not the bundled firewood and hay (which appears in the second stanza) but the *act* of bundling firewood, a lowly work carried out by the populace. From the examples above, we know that popular action can never be the actual, final meaning of a poem. The *significance* of this piece of canonical poetry must be sought on a higher, more aristocratic level. Therefore, the Confucian hermeneut performs his textual work by making the bundling of firewood a metaphor for the "bundling" together of man and wife. The analogical reading (itself a ritual of sorts) is thereby perfected: the human labor that put together firewood and hay into roundly tied bundles is a metaphor for the rituals with which man and wife are united in matrimony. For the concretion of firewood and firewood bundling has been substituted the abstraction of rites and marriage. The transformation in three stages so characteristic of the analogical xing is obviously at work here, as the static natural description is transformed into dynamic, albeit plebeian, action that is then transformed into ritual action on the aristocratic and rhetorical level.

In the case of "Chou mou," Mao is rather successful in incorporating all the poem's components into a harmonious whole. The poem itself speaks of the amorous dualism of you-and-I, which makes the marriage theme not too far-fetched. The function of the constellation of the Three Stars is not only to signal that the time of marriage is here; it also corresponds to the line in the third stanza that (with Mao) speaks about the beauty of "three ladies," thus making the three heavenly bodies refer to three earthly bodies.[11] The interpretation of firewood bundling as a metaphor for marriage, finally, is also compelling, given that both thematize unification. Yet at one juncture Mao's reading nearly collapses. The second stanza says, "I see those happy ones," with reference to the three ladies. However, in his comment on ode 94, "Ye you wan cao," Mao glosses *xiehou* 邂逅 not as "happy" but as "to meet without having planned so" (*bu qi er hui* 不期而會).[12] And since a meeting between a man and a woman that happens by chance clearly suggests extra-ritual and licentious behavior—which is quite incompatible with the rest of the ode—Mao must abandon his earlier definition and gloss *xiehou* as "relaxed and happy" (*xie yue* 解說). Later commentators understood *xiehou* in accordance with Mao's original definition and, consequently, interpreted "Chou mou" as a "depraved" poem, describing the chaos (*luan*) and the negligence of rites and virtue in the state of Jin.[13]

"Jingjing zhe e" 菁菁者莪 (ode 176)

Flourishing is that *e* plant
in the middle of that slope

菁菁者莪
在彼中阿

Mao comments: "A *xing* . . . The gentleman-ruler [*junzi* 君子] is able to grow and foster talents [lit. "man-material"] like the slope grows the flourishing *e* plant" 興也 . . . 君子能長育人材, 如阿之長莪菁菁然.

When I have seen my gentleman
I am happy and courteous[14]

既見君子
樂且有儀

"When I have seen my lord," the second and fourth stanzas say, "my heart rejoices," "my heart is at rest."[15] The line "I have seen my lord" (*ji jian junzi* 既見君子) is normally part of a stock expression that runs (with some variation) "When I have not seen my gentleman / I am distressed / When I have seen my gentleman / I am relieved."[16] More often than not, it is transformed by the Confucian commentators into the passionate idiom of a minister (or subject) describing his feelings for his master. *Junzi* 君子 translates both as "(virtuous) ruler" and "lover," thus paving the way for another metaphor that runs through the *Odes* and the *Commentary*, namely the description of the relationship that obtains between a ruler and his minister in terms of an amorous relationship between a man and his woman. This is not illogical since in the cosmological thought pattern of the Han dynasty the structure of a family corresponded to that of the state. The ruler of the state and the man of the house (or clan) both belonged to the active yang sphere of the universe; the minister and the wife belonged to the passive yin sphere that was subordinated (but complementary) to the yang. However, for an age that so stressed normality, regularity and the importance of a harmonious, well-proportioned and complementary interaction between yin and yang, to equate ruler and minister with husband and wife is a slightly surprising move, not least given the active-passive dichotomy at play therein. Yet the overriding imperative for Mao—a reshaper and polisher of texts—is to find a way to transform amorous odes into poems about hierarchy and ritual behavior.

The ode opens with the xing element—the flourishing *e* plant on the slope—and then says that the protagonist is happy now that she has seen her gentleman. It would be possible to read the xing as a temporal indicator signaling that the time is right for marriage, as a literal description of a flourishing landscape that connotes the intensity and the passion of love, as a Freudian phallic symbol (the *protruding* hill) or as a metaphor for the beauty of the girl. The plausibility of these readings (except, of course, for the Freudian interpretation) is verified by Mao Heng's comments on similar passages. But Mao chooses an analogical reading founded on the idea that the slope stands in the same relation to the flowering *e* plant as (*ru* 如) the virtuous ruler does to the talented ministers and advisors of his state. And, in keeping with my hypothesis, the analogy focuses not on the slope and the minister but on the *action* of growing (*zhang* 長). Again, the stress is on instrumentality and method ("how does a virtuous ruler govern his state?"); again, a static image of nature has been transformed into a description of action—and again, a lowly activity has been metaphorized into the noble activity of statesmanship.

We further note that, in contrast to the preceding examples, the metaphorical transfer in ode 176 again goes from nature to man. This is not due to a change in Mao's hermeneutical scheme but an effect of the pragmatism with which he operates the xing and the fact that nature and populace are interchangeable as metaphor material. The subordination of nature to man is visible in an inconspicuous deviation in the wording of the analogy: the slope grows plants, and the gentleman-ruler "has the ability" (*neng* 能) to grow and "foster" talents. The little word *neng* opens up an abyss between nature and culture. Just as the seminatural, quasi-human commoner who, incapable of mediation and deliberation, shakes his arms and hollers when affected by external matters, nature spontaneously grows the *e* plant. Nature and the populace cannot be changed or cultured—except on the rhetorical level.

"Yuanyang" 鴛鴦 (ode 216)

The *yuanyang* ducks in flight
We catch them with handnets and spreadnets

鴛鴦于飛
畢之羅之

Mao comments (after the second line): "A xing. The *yuanyang* duck is a bird that [mates for life and] lives in pairs. In times of peace and stability, their [the ancient wise rulers?] intercourse with the ten thousand objects of the world was in tune with Tao. Catching them [the birds] requires timeliness. When they are in flight one catches them with handnets and spreadnets" 興也. 鴛鴦匹鳥. 太平之時, 交於萬物有道. 取之以時. 於其飛乃畢掩而羅之.

The poem continues thus:

May the lord have ten thousand years
May felicity and blessing come to him as his right due[17]

君子萬年
福祿宜之

The *yuanyang*, Mao points out, is a bird that mates for life and, as such, excellent metaphor material for a Confucian hermeneut who wants to make the text speak of virtue and sexual restraint. Another option, which Mao seemingly takes advantage of, is to interpret the bird as an auspicious omen; in times of peace, the sagely ruler interacts harmoniously with the ten thousand things. Formally speaking, the parallelism of this piece and the rhymes (羅 *luo* and 宜 *yi*) links the *yuanyang* to the lord but does not, of course, specify how bird and man relate.[18] The relation could easily be explained as causal (the bird is to be presented as food or as a gift to the ruler), symbolic (the *yuanyang* symbolizes happiness and fortune, which is exactly what the poet wishes the lord) or metaphorical (echoing "Guanju," the *yuanyang* could be a metaphor for the ruler and his queen and concubines). This is, however, an analogical xing with Mao putting all hermeneutic stress on action, instrumentality, and method. As Mao sees it, the poem asks about when and how one catches a *yuanyang*.

With this insight in mind, we can read Mao's words about the Way in a slightly different light. *Dao* 道 not only refers to the Way in a moral sense but also to the *logic*, the "path" that things follow according to their own proper category (*lei* 類). Therefore, if you want to catch the *yuanyang* you have to know their habits in order to figure out the right measure; you must be on time (*yishi* 以時) and, in their flight, catch them with handnets and spreadnets. Against the background of the previous examples, we clearly perceive that "yuanyang" is not used as a simple metaphor, providing a *tertium comparationis* that can be used as a description of this or that person. Instead, the lowly work of bird catching functions as an analogy for the timeliness and perfection with which the superior ruler governs his state.

We leave Mao's *Commentary* here and for a brief moment indulge in the *Minor Preface* and the Qing dynasty scholar Mao Ruichen's 馬瑞辰 (1782—1853) comments on "Yuanyang." For methodological reasons I have hitherto mostly refrained from consulting the *Minor Preface*. As we see with reference to this poem, the *Preface* operates under a rather different set of rules than does the *Commentary*. In its capacity as a canonical preface, it is the task of the *Minor Preface* to imprint the poem with its mark of authenticity by informing the reader of the particular historical moment in which the poem was written (or, possibly, quoted). As it stands in the received *Shijing*, "Yuanyang" is preceded by eight poems criticizing (*ci* 刺) the notoriously hapless and incompetent King You (幽王, r. 781–771 BCE) and followed by two poems directed against the same unfortunate king. Thus, the *Preface* finds itself in the precarious position of having to follow Mao's interpretation of "Yuanyang" as a eulogy of an ideal ruler while, at the same time, maintaining the critique of King You.

The solution is as simple as it is cunning. In the time-honored tradition of "displaying the past to criticize the present" (*chen gu ci jin* 陳古刺今), the *Preface* simply contends that the narrator speaks of the virtuous kings of old times as an oblique critique of today's ruler King You. In this particular historical setting, the poem is wholly ironic, and its description of the virtuous and timely ruler is, literally speaking, a lie. Ma Ruichen offers an interpretation of the poem's imagery that wholly differs from my reconstruction of Mao's comment. Ma argues against the thesis (proposed by Kong Yingda and also by me) that the *dao* of the Superior Man is embodied in the knowledge of how and when to catch the *yuanyang* bird. Instead, Ma claims that the poem "displays" the ideal past by invoking the gentlemanly behavior of not shooting at a sitting bird. Indeed, Ma continues, the gentlemen of yore did not even shoot at a flying bird but caught it with nets.[19] Ma's thoroughly literal reading challenges my interpretation, not only by insisting that *dao* actually means "way" or "virtue," rather than "logic," but also because he equates the lowly work of bird catching, of which the poem itself indeed does speak, with the aristocratic ritual of archery. From my point of view, he fails to recognize the analogical element at play in Mao's reading.

"Cai ge" 采葛 (ode 72)

There I pick the kudzu
If I do not see [him] for one whole day
it is like three months

彼采葛兮
一日不見
如三月兮

Mao comments: "A *xing*. Kudzu is used to make fine and coarse cloth. Although one's task is petty, if a day goes by when one does not appear before the ruler one fears slander[ers]" 興也. 葛所以為絺綌也. 事雖小一日不見於君, 憂懼於讒也.

The poem continues:

There I pick the *xiao* plant
If I do not see [him] for one whole day
it is like three autumns

彼采蕭兮
一日不見
如三秋兮

Mao comments that "the *xiao* plant is used as offerings in sacrifices" 蕭, 所以供祭祀.

There I pick the *ai* plant
If I do not see [him] for one whole day
it is like three years

彼采艾兮
一日不見
如三歲兮

Mao says that "the *ai* plant is used to heal ailments" 艾, 所以療疾.[20]

Mao's interpretation of what appears to be a simple love song is, ironically enough, the most difficult one to categorize thus far. The temporal structure of the ode is as simple as it is effective—as time passes the sense of longing increases, and what initially felt like three months now feels like three years. But for Mao, an ode must speak of more elevated topics than female sentiments and plant picking, and just like "Po fu" above, this poem itself thematizes the act of picking, thereby presenting Mao with the possibility of reading it as a metaphor for aristocratic "work." Is this why Mao defines it as a xing?

If, on the other hand, one assumes that it is the presence of the kudzu, the *xiao*, and the *ai* that constitutes the xing one is equally puzzled as the functions of these plants are clearly defined by Mao. Since the plants are picked for specific purposes they are to be understood literally and not as metaphors for anything else. It is precisely this contradiction between metaphoricity and literalism, and the simultaneous focus on the action of picking and the plants themselves, that is bewildering. However, on closer examination we see that Mao does perform a quasi-metaphorical reading. "Cai ge," says Mao, is a poem whose narrator complains about being slandered, with the objective of making himself stand out as a paragon of virtue among immoral men. According to Mao, the poet achieves this objective by saying that although he loyally performs his humble duties, the protagonist still must fear those slanderers. Following my "analogical paradigm" we notice how the kudzu is described as a material out of which cheap clothing is made ("nobler" clothes were of course made of silk). This information is then put side by side with the seemingly analogous discussion about petty work. At this point, the problem could be solved by claiming that the plebeian kudzu picking is a metaphor for "work"—however small—on a higher, official level and that Mao uses "kudzu" as that piece of nature that legitimizes the xing label. But that interpretation is flatly contradicted by Mao's insistence that the *xiao* and the *ai* are plants with specific ritual and medical functions, which again puts the focus on the plants. If we turn to the only alternative left—to identify the speaker as an actual picker of plants "made aristocratic" by their ritual and medical functions—we obliterate the metaphoricity and, again, force the poem into a straightforward, nonfigurative mode.

For the time being, I leave "Cai ge" here, in this dilapidated and contradictory state, as an irritating indication that Mao's xing cannot be fully explained by the analytical tools hitherto presented. With reference to what I call the analogical xing, there is nonetheless enough evidence to consider "Cai ge" an instance, albeit somewhat paradoxical, of the species of xing that downplays nature (here represented by the kudzu) in favor of action (the work of picking plants), and subsequently makes plebeian work a metaphor of work on a more elevated level (the "petty" work performed by the narrator). I return to "Cai ge" in the next chapter, arguing that the theme of plant picking falls between, or outside, the two categories of nature and man and very nearly forms a thematic subcategory with its own rhetorical laws.

"Jian jia" 蒹葭 (ode 129)

"Jian jia" has in style, content, and ambience more in common with the mystical sensuality of certain poems in the *Chuci*, such as "Yunzhong jun" 雲中君 or "He bo" 河伯, than with the dry Confucian discourse on ideal rulership that the *Ru* exegete must extract from it. But it is precisely because of the conflict between the sensuality of the poem and the dullness of the

Confucian ideology that Mao's comment makes for interesting reading. What strategy does he choose to make the text speak Confucianism?

The poem begins with a typically xingish natural description.

> The reeds and rushes are flourishing
> the white dew turns into frost

> 蒹葭蒼蒼
> 白露為霜

Mao comments: "A xing . . . The white dew freezes and turns into frost; thereupon the work of the agricultural year is completed. The state and the clans depend on rites; thereupon they prosper" 興也 . . . 白露凝戾為霜, 然後歲事成. 國家待禮, 然後興.

The poem continues thus:

> He whom I call "that man"
> is at one end of the river
> I follow him against the stream
> the road [dao 道] is blocked and long

> 所謂伊人
> 在水一方
> 遡洄從之
> 道阻且長

Mao comments: "At one end [of the river]: this place is hard to reach. To go up against the stream is called *suhui*. Going against the rites, no one can reach perfection" 一方, 難至矣. 逆流而上曰遡洄. 逆禮則莫能以至也.

The first stanza ends with the following lines:

> I follow him along the stream
> [elusively] he is in the middle of the water

> 遡游從之
> 宛在水中央

Mao comments that "to follow the stream and cross [the river] is called *suyou*. Following the rites to seek a ford [or 'perfection'], the Way will itself come and greet you" 順流而涉曰遡游. 順禮求濟, 道來迎之.[21]

The narratrix (or narrator) of the poem is stubbornly pursuing someone who constantly eludes her and appears in the middle of the river. The dreamlike imagery suggests amorous rather than political passion. The xing element, moreover, introduces the idea of decay, violence, or death as the dew turns into frost, hurting the flourishing reeds and rushes. But with Mao the oneiric poem turns allegorical and ideological; nothing in the text should be understood literally, as the ultimate meaning of the poem must be sought at a higher level. Due to its negative tinge (the frost damaging the plants), Mao cannot use the xing element as what I call a simple metaphor. Instead, he makes the xing focus on the "action" of dew turning into frost, which then can be metaphorized according to the rules of the analogical xing and to a perceived analogy between husbandry and statecraft saying that only when the state and the clans have been subjected to the rites can they prosper, just as the "work of the agricultural year" is completed only when the plants have withered.

With regard to the poem itself, the description of the reeds and rushes may be understood simply as a description of the landscape in which the amorous quest takes place, or as a temporal indicator signaling for instance that autumn has arrived—"White Dew" 白露 is, of course, the fifteenth solar term in the traditional calendar. Let me at this juncture briefly return to the question of early Chinese poetics and correlative cosmology and their interconnections. By arguing against the standard reading of the *Great Preface*, I deny neither the existence nor the deep impact of the thought pattern for which the Sinological shorthand is "correlative cosmology." I do suggest, however, that Mao's xing cannot be satisfactorily explained within those parameters. Although the rites by all accounts should be timely and "correlated" with the seasons, it does not follow that they were conceived of as spontaneous expressions of raw emotions or as literal and nonmetaphorical. On the contrary, there is strong evidence that ritual communication, at least in Xunzian theory, is closely connected with the topic of optical illusion, duplicity, and what I elsewhere call "si-militude."[22] In his comment on "Jian jia," Mao typically enough does not read the description of reeds and rushes as a temporal indicator but chooses the significantly more farfetched analogical reading.

"Jian jia" similarly exposes the inherent opposition between Mao's hermeneutic program and the actual interpretations that such a program (that is, the xing) generates. Mao's comment clearly illustrates the ambiguous and double stance that Mao sometimes takes with regard to representations of nature and the nature that is out there—that elusive extratext. For the Mao

School exegete, nature (or representations of nature) is always semantically suspect and seldom itself in possession of a meaning that is significant or "final." In interpreting such representations, Mao's xingish comments suggest, one must always suspect that they hide a deeper meaning in which nature merely constitutes metaphor fodder. Consequently, the xing element is not interpreted as a literal representation of the reeds and rushes in the external world but function instead as material for a "higher" and more aristocratic discourse about statesmanship.

But in the third to eighth lines of this poem, success is granted only to the person who follows nature; if you go against the natural direction of the stream, the *dao* will be long and full of obstacles, and "no one can reach their goal thus" 莫能以至. If, instead, you go with the natural flow you will find what you seek. But this rule, as I have repeatedly suggested, does not apply on the rhetorical and metapoetic level where nature stands in opposition to culture. A *Ru* hermeneut in the Xunzian tradition must be "unnatural" and should not "go with the flow" and interpret naturally and literally. Instead, the *Ru*-ist and Xunzian hermeneutic *dao* must be difficult and full of obstacles—one must work and rework the unpolished text; only then can the object sought for (namely, the *significance* of the ode) be found.

The paradox becomes more pronounced as Mao transforms the lines about going with and against the stream into a metaphor for following and violating the rites, thus implying that rites equal nature or at least that rites and nature function according to the same logic. The very conception on which Mao's rhetorical concept xing is founded—nature is anticulture and antiritual—here stands in sharp opposition to the underlying assumption that naturalness in fact equals *dao* and, thereby, also the rites. The clash between Mao's hermeneutic, ideological program and his actual reading of "Jian jia" suggests that nature is simultaneously an ideal model and the principle (or mode of being) from which the Confucian Superior Man (*junzi*) must take his leave. Differently put, Mao's interpretation implies that the gentlemanly activity of rituals indeed maintains the basic principles of nature but elevates them to a higher level.

Finally, it is important for the subsequent analyses that we note how the subthemes of transportability and alienation run through ode 129 and Mao's comment thereon. *Dao* 道, as we know, means "way" in the basic sense of "path" or "road," but it may also refer to the "way" of the perfected Superior Man, or to the Tao—the order, or logic, of the cosmos. In the figurative and punning language of the Han dynasty Confucians, *dao* often takes on all these meanings simultaneously. Since "Jian jia" itself thematizes pursuit, saying that the road (*dao*) is full of obstacles, Mao transfers this theme to a metaphorical level, making the text speak of the perfection of rites in terms of transportation: you reach perfection not by going against the rites but by following them.²³ Mao makes another pun when he says that one should "follow the rites to find a fording place" 順禮求濟, as *ji* 濟 means both "ford" and "to accomplish." To accomplish the rites and make the state prosperous, therefore, is tantamount to crossing the troubled waters and overcoming the hardships of the *dao*. Water, consequently, is that which separates and alienates man and woman from their pursuits, both on a literal level (exemplified by the man in the "middle of the river") and on a metaphorical, aristocratic level (exemplified by the "ford" one has to cross to reach prosperity).

To contextualize and conclude, while "Jian jia" is a text governed by the logic of the analogical *xing*, it maintains and banks on the metaphorical transfer from nature to man.

"Jue gong" 角弓 (ode 223)

The well-adjusted horn-bow
has warped and become askew

騂騂角弓
翩其反矣

Mao comments: "A *xing* . . . If not kept in good order on the bow-frame and skillfully handled, [the exquisite bow] will warp and become askew" 興也 . . . 不善緌檠巧用則翩然而反.²⁴

brothers and relatives
should not be kept distant²⁵

兄弟昏姻
無胥遠矣

At first glance, one may think that the warped bow (which is not part of nature but an inanimate and manmade object) functions as a metaphor for the dysfunctional family that this poem describes, thereby making "Jue gong" an instance of the simple *xing*. But the focus of Mao's *xing* is not the bow itself but the actions of keeping it in order and using (*yong* 用) it. For a bow to function well one must keep it in order and be able to use it correctly, just as the leader of a clan must not keep a distance (*yuan* 遠) between himself and his relatives; in other words, he should treat them in a manner that pertains to the rites. The poem thus analogously positions the notions of abusing and distancing.

"Pao you ku ye" 匏有苦葉 (ode 34)

The gourds have bitter leaves
The ford has a deep crossing[26]

匏有苦葉
濟有深涉

Mao comments: "A *xing*. Gourds [. . . their] leaves are bitter and inedible. *Ji* means 'to ford'. Wading across waters higher than one's knees is called *she*" 興也. 匏 . . . 葉苦不可食. 濟, 渡也. 由膝以上為涉.[27]

Where the waters are deep, one wears one's clothes over the waist
Where the waters are shallow, one holds up one's clothes and wades across

深則厲
淺則揭

Mao comments:

To wade across a river fully clothed, i.e., with the water rising above your waist, is called *li*. To maintain what is appropriate behavior in, on and for different occasions is like happening upon a river. If it is deep one wets one's clothes; if it is shallow, one can hold up one's lower garments and wade across. As for the intercourse between man and woman, how could ritual propriety not be used? [Without ritual propriety] one would lack the means with which to perfect oneself. 以衣涉水為厲, 謂由帶以上也. 揭, 褰衣也. 遭時制宜如遇水. 深則厲淺則揭矣. 男女之際安可以無禮義. 將無以自濟也.[28]

Just like "Jian jia" above, "Pao you ku ye" speaks of passion, distance, and amorous pursuit in terms of water and transportability. As the thematic richness of the river motif will be explored elsewhere, I here concentrate on the *xing* element. Zheng Xuan understands the bitter gourd leaves and the overflowing river described in the first line as temporal markers indicating that the eighth month has come, the time when yin and yang intersect and interbreed, and when marriages can be consummated.²⁹ Zheng's interpretation, which places human affairs within a greater cosmological context, is symptomatic or causal (the bitterness of the leaves and the flood are both symptoms of the current state of the yin and yang forces) which deviates from the hypothesis that I have followed thus far and that stipulates that a *xing* is based on a perceived similarity between nature and human activity.

"The gourds have bitter leaves / the ford has a deep crossing" seems, at first glance, to constitute a typical *xing* in the form of a natural description that functions as a predicate about an event in the human realm, but Mao interprets neither the bitter leaves nor the flood as metaphors but concentrates on the word *she* 涉, "a ford," making it into a verb, "to ford." The *xing* element thus consists of an analogy between fording and marrying. In both activities one must be timely and know the proper execution—the "instrument" of correct fording is the knowledge of how to wear one's clothes when crossing the river, just as the instruments of correct behavior are rites and righteousness, or "ritual propriety." Mao has thus completed his interpretational "way"—*dao*—and transformed a static natural image (the ford) into a common and lowly activity (river crossing), which then is turned into a description of proper ritual behavior (marriage).

Note also how the water motif entails, on two levels, the seemingly antithetical themes of separation and continuity. *Ji* 際 is a pivotal word for the understanding of how the motifs of water, streams, and rivers are used in the *Odes* and the *Commentary*. My translation ("intercourse [between man and woman]") above is tentative and does not bring out the complexity of the concept. Like a Freudian *Urwort*, the connotations of *ji* ranges from "distance" and "separation" to "border" and, eventually, to "continuity" and "meeting." This is precisely how the bodies-of-water motif functions in the *Odes* and in the *Commentary*. A river or stream is simultaneously that which separates people—that is, a border—and a means of continuity. We saw, in the first ode, how the female *jujiu* is separated from her mate on the islet in the river, and we see in the present poem how the river (as a marriage metaphor) is a border that must be crossed in accordance with ritual propriety. Likewise, we saw in "Mian shui" how water was used to describe the continuity and interrelationship of a family.

"Huang niao" 黃鳥 (ode 131)

Small, small is the yellow bird
it settles in the jujube tree

交交黃鳥
止于棘

Mao comments: "A xing . . . The yellow bird arrives and departs and finds its dwelling in accordance with the seasons. As for man, he finds his place in accordance with life and death [i.e., the time-span allotted to the human animal]" 興也 . . . 黃鳥以時往來得所. 人以壽命終亦得其所.[30]

In Mao's analogical reading, the human lifespan relates to human beings like the seasons relate to the yellow bird; more precisely, the instrument with which ritual man navigates his existence in the world is timeliness, just as the instrumentality of the bird lies in its inherent knowledge of the seasons. Here, the metaphoric transfer goes from nature to man. This xing should be classified as "ironic," since the murdered men do not find their place in accordance with the natural lifespan.

"Fu tian" 甫田 (ode 102)

Do not till the big field
the weed will be too high
Do not long for someone faraway
the heart will be too grieved[31]

無田甫田
維莠驕驕
無思遠人
勞心忉忉

The analogy in the first and second stanzas suggests that, just like tilling an oversized field, longing for a loved one who is far away is an overwhelming undertaking and that both enterprises will not come to fruition. Read as a "metaphor"—taking plowing a big field as a predication about amorous longing and sorrow—the stanzas poignantly describe the sorrows of the heart as an uncultivated field with weed growing uncontrollably.

Whereas the second stanza is largely a repetition of the first, the third stanza advances the agricultural imagery. The protagonist is told that she will soon see her beau wearing the official cap that signifies manhood; correspondingly, the uncontrollable weed is substituted with young grain neatly collected:

> Delicate, beautiful
> tufts of hair collected in horns
> When soon you will see him
> suddenly he will be wearing a grown man's hat[32]

婉兮孌兮
總角丱兮
未幾見兮
突而弁兮

Mao comments after the second line of the first stanza: "A xing. *Fu* means 'large'. A field that is *fu* is excessively large and, thus, if there is no human effort [put into cultivating it], eventually one will be not able to reap anything" 興也. 甫, 大也. 大田過度而無人功, 終不能獲.[33]

The ode is entirely literal since the comparison between tilling and longing is fully developed in the text itself. Mao's comment is little more than a paraphrase that seems equally simplistic. Why, then, does Mao feel the need for the xing tag? His brief comment does not allow for any definite conclusions to be drawn, but a clue lies in the very simplicity of the poem; it is clearly a love poem. By labeling "Fu tian" a xing, Mao signals that there is a deeper meaning behind the textual surface and, with the aid of our knowledge of the analogical xing, we may reconstruct Mao's reading in the following manner. The theme is again instrumentality and proper conduct. A good ruler, like a good tiller, should know not to take on tasks that they cannot handle since in the end nothing good will come of it. The yeoman's knowledge of proper behavior is thus potentially an analogy for the aristocrat's knowledge of how to rule the state according to the rites and the Way. A more far-fetched and less convincing reading would be to understand "the big field" as a simple metaphor for a bad ruler who—excessive (*guo* 過) and without measures—is of no use to his state. Regardless of which interpretation the reader chooses, Mao has succeeded in neutralizing the poem, making it lopsided by drawing all hermeneutic attention to the first two lines.

20

Xing, Ironically

I set out on my investigation of Mao Heng's xing by discussing the theories of earlier, highly gifted scholars who had dedicated much effort to the question of early Confucian hermeneutics. The hyperrealism of Pauline Yu and Chen Shih-hsiang was opposed by Zhu Ziqing's more reasonable, less "comparative" and less ideological theory about the xing as a trope founded mainly on similitude. For reasons of clarity, I postulated a model of a "simple" and "canonical" xing and, for obvious reasons, chose Mao's comment on the first ode to represent it. With compelling logic and hermeneutic brilliance, Mao here appeals to the reader's sense of rationality by carefully explaining how "Guanju" is organized rhetorically and how the different elements interact and take their places in a hierarchy that subordinates nature to man. In this the simplest model of a xingish "metaphor," the description of the virtuous osprey functions as a statement about an equally virtuous couple; vehicle thus corresponds positively with tenor. Indeed, the poems analyzed in the first chapter all have this characteristic.

In chapter 19 I argued that the so-called analogical xing depends on a semiotic process that is more complex and oblique, with Mao *finding* themes such as timeliness and instrumentality that could provide metaphor material for a discourse, befitting the Confucian agenda, on ritualism, statesmanship and ritual behavior. Moreover, the arbitrariness of Mao's xing became increasingly clear as we found that the analogical xing often depends on an extratextual analogy not warranted by the text. In many cases, it seemed as though Mao was more interested in diverting the reader's attention away from the poem and its organization as a whole and toward a rather forced analogy that would "speak Confucianism" rather than of passionate emotions. Although the xing was still a *piyu* depending on similitude, the clarity and the persuasive force of Mao's "Guanju" were long gone. Indeed, at this stage one could question the soundness of my methodology: Could a hermeneutical program whose main trope is described as arbitrary and accused of helping the hermeneut to "find" meaning "added from outside" really be the subject of a *formal* analysis? It would seem that something beyond a set of formal, rhetorical rules is governing Mao's xing. I entertain this suspicion in next chapter.

In this chapter I bring attention to a variant of the first xing model, a mutation that is distinctively intratextual and founded on similitude but also a mocking negation of the carefree positiveness of "Guanju." This is not without consequences for our understanding of early Chinese poetics. Correlative cosmology—the thought pattern that the hyperrealists assume underlies and informs the *Mao Commentary*—holds that cosmos (or "the world") is made up of correspondences that tie all earthly and celestial phenomena together into a web of mutual interaction and dependence. A necessary corollary of that notion is that only *positive relations* can exist: cosmos (or nature) can accommodate no negative correspondences. Let us, for argument's sake, assume that Mao saw the *jujiu* as a virtuous bird but that the description of the bird in "Guanju" functioned in contrast to an evil and nonvirtuous ruler. It would then have been impossible to claim that the poem is a literal representation of extratextual phenomena since a virtuous bird cannot, in the text-external world, correspond to something that is its complete opposite, namely an unvirtuous ruler. Admittedly, this is not how Mao interprets the first poem; but if one were able to put a wedge between the two strata and identify a negative or somehow distorted relationship between the natural xing image and the human situation it metaphorically represents, then the cosmological, hyperrealistic theory would crumble. In other words, the correlation between the xing element and the tenor would not be literal and cosmological but artificial and rhetorical—as well as ironic.[1]

Such an ironic xingish moment appears, I contend, in "Wanlan" 芄蘭 (ode 60), which begins with the following natural description:

The offshoots of the *wanlan* plant

芄蘭之支

Mao comments: "A xing . . . A gentleman-ruler's virtue [or "power"] should be soft and [moist=] generous, warm and benevolent" 興也 . . . 君子之德, 當柔潤溫良.[2]

This seems to be a classic case of, in my terminology, a simple xing where a static natural description is used to characterize a person. The *tertium comparationis* that the xing indicates are the softness and "moisture" of the plant, and we note in passing that the word *run* 潤 takes on the double meaning of "moist" and "refined" (or "generous"). Here, Mao does not attempt to transform the static image into action by bringing in an extratextual analogy (by claiming for example that the *wanlan* is able to nurture its offshoots so well that they become soft and moist, just as the virtuous ruler takes care of his talented ministers and makes them "moist" and refined). Instead, the image of the "Wanlan" is used by the poet as a straightforward description of the true lord's virtue. However, this metaphorical description of an ideal ruler is negated by the following lines:

> A young boy with a knot-horn pendant
> although [he wears] a knot-horn pendant
> [he] cannot [say] 'I have knowledge'[3]

> 童子佩觿
> 雖則佩觿
> 能不我知

Mao comments: "A knot-horn . . . is a pendant worn by the grown-up [or 'perfected'] man. A ruler governs the affairs of grown-up [or 'perfected'] men. Although [the ruler] is but a boy he nonetheless wears a knot-horn [signifying that] he perfected his virtue very early. He does not say 'I have no knowledge,' thereby being [conceived of as] haughty" 觿 . . . 成人之佩也. 人君治成人之事. 雖童子猶佩觿, 早成其德. 不自謂無知, 以驕慢人也.[4]

Three striking deviations take place here. The first two involves the knot horn which, according to Mao, is a pendant worn by a *chengren* 成人, meaning both "adult" and "(morally) perfected man." That a boy is wearing a knot horn is an important deviation because it signals that the ruler (to whom "boy" refers) is precocious and has become a *chengren* already as a child. Such a ruler should by Confucian standards possess a virtue "soft and moist" like the *wanlan*. From now on, the two signs—the knot-horn and the *wanlan*—are united by their reference (a young virtuous lord, "soft," and fit to wear a knot horn) and the ironic turn they are about to undergo. The *wanlan* and the knot-horn pendant are, furthermore, signs of two different semiotic orders. The pendant is an extratextual and mundane nonrhetorical sign; it signifies "manhood" in a cultural context and is, as such, part of a semiotic process independent of the poetic text. The *wanlan*, by contrast, is a wholly rhetorical sign since it acquires a secondary meaning only by means of a metaphorical, textual process.

What happens next is a simultaneous negation of the cultural and the rhetorical sign. In the idyllic first lines of this poem, the pendant is a symbol of maturity and virtue and is the emblem of the true Superior Man whom the first line describes by way of the image of the *wanlan*. Here, however, the young ruler usurps and belies the signatum of the pendant sign by his arrogant behavior—he is no longer a ruler so virtuous that he, still only a boy, can be regarded a *chengren*.[5] This negation of signata is repeated on the textual and rhetorical level as the signatum of the xing lines ("softness and moisture, warmth and benevolence") is contradicted by the description of the arrogant *junzi*. Put in the language of the metaphor, the tenor of the *wanlan* metaphor (a virtuous lord) exists only as a negative, inverted tenor—as an antixing.

We have returned, after the increasingly extratextual analogical xing, to intratextuality. But it is an intratextual xing that is a mocking parody of the original and simple version. There, the xing element actually corresponds to the description of human activity that follows it. Here, that privileged relationship is broken since the activity described is the very opposite of everything the xing promised it would be. I will in the following note that this dialectics of promise and disappointment invariably goes from good to bad. The xing sets up an ideal that the poem (and the poet) subsequently and intentionally frustrates.

"Shan you fusu" 山有扶蘇 (ode 84)

> On the mountain there are *fusu* trees
> In the swamps there are lotus flowers

> 山有扶蘇
> 隰有荷華

Mao comments: "A xing . . . saying that high and low, big and small all obtain what is appropriate [for them]" 興也 . . . 言高下大小各得其宜.

> I do not see Zi Du
> I only see a mad man!

不見子都
乃見狂且

Mao comments: "Zi Du [lit. "the urbane, elegant man"] was a beautiful person of that age" 子都世之美好者也.⁶

"Shan you fusu" reads like a love song opposing the masculine, protruding, *yang* mountain to the feminine, moist, *yin* marsh. Not surprisingly, Mao is quick to transform it into a metaphorical piece about Confucian hierarchy. The mountain/marsh dichotomy is commonly used by the *Commentary* as a metaphor for "high" (ruler) and "low" (minister, subject) positions in the Confucian power structure. Here, the xing element describes the ideal manifestation thereof, in that on the high mountain there are trees and on the low marsh (the smaller) lotus flowers. The next lines introduce the inversion of this scene as the good and beautiful Zi Du is not to be seen (on the throne), only a mad man. The first lines promise order, the following lines deliver only disorder. The relationship between the xing and the human stratum is thus ironical.⁷

"Xiong zhi" 雄雉 (ode 33)

The male pheasant goes flying
Yi yi go his wings

雄雉于飛
泄泄其羽

Mao comments: "A xing. When the male pheasant sees the female pheasant, he flies up and beats his wings *yi yi*-style [with a whooshing sound?]" 興也. 雄雉見雌雉飛而鼓其翼泄泄然.⁸

Oh, my beloved one
you have yourself given me this trouble [first stanza]

I look at that sun and moon
longing, longing are my thoughts
The road being so long
when can you come? [third stanza]⁹

我之懷亦
自貽伊阻

瞻彼日月
悠悠我思
道之云遠
曷云能來

The description of the pheasant in "Xiong zhi" echoes the first ode and its use of the *jujiu* as a metaphor for an amorous but, in Mao's view, virtuous couple. That the xingish pheasant corresponds to the amorous you-and-I dualism of this poem is obvious, as Mao explicitly acknowledges the love theme by explaining that the male bird flies to his mate as soon as he sees her. But since the image of the pheasant reoccurs in "Pao you ku ye" (ode 34) as a metaphor for an excessively passionate couple we should not be too quick to ascribe the connotations of the *jujiu* (virtue and sexual moderation) to the pheasant. For my present purposes it suffices simply to note that Mao explains the xing by saying that the male bird approaches his mate since hereby the xing describes the unification of male and female.

As the harmony described by the first lines reacts with the harsh reality of the human realm irony shows its mocking face. In the third stanza the narratrix inverts the positive xing image when she (rhetorically) asks her *absent* man when he will be able to come home. Again, the relationship between the two strata is ironic since the xing element promises unification whereas following lines supply only estrangement and separation.

By way of the negative relation between the xing and the human stratum, "Xiong zhi" becomes an important test case for the denouncement of cosmological poetics. If the avian imagery of "Xiong zhi" is compared to that of "Guanju" we see that in the latter ode the xingish description of the birds corresponds positively with the nonfigurative description of human activity; the "gentleman" and the "girl" are indeed as harmonious and virtuous as the *jujiu*. In the former poem, by contrast, the birds are unified, but the two people are separated. In Mao's view, the poet intentionally begins "Xiong zhi" by speaking of unification as a mocking contrast to the separation that is its proper theme. The poem can thus no longer be the spontaneous pairing of two realms (the natural and the human) linked together simply because they spring from the same "order of existence," as Pauline Yu, Michelle Yeh, and other contemporary commentators on the *Great Preface* would claim. It is instead a carefully deliberated and rhetorical piece that not only speaks of humans in terms of birds but also transforms the similarity on which such a transference of meaning is based into dissimilarity. The imagery therefore is not natural and concrete and unaffected by premeditation, but ironical, artificial, and rhetorical. With reference to Zhu Ziqing's model, "Xiong zhi" indeed builds on a perceived similarity between bird and man, but it is a homology that has lost its innocence.

"Chen feng" 晨風 (ode 132)

Swift is that morning wind
dense is that North Forest

鴥彼晨風
鬱彼北林

Mao comments: "A xing . . . 'Morning wind' refers to falcons . . . The rulers of former times attracted worthies and the worthies came to them riding hurriedly, like falcons flying into the North Forest" 興也 . . . 晨風鸇也 . . . 先君招賢人, 賢人往之駛疾, 如晨風之飛入北林.
The poem continues:

When I have not yet seen my lord
my grieved heart is full of thoughts and longing
How is it? How is it?
He [forgets:] neglects me truly too much

未見君子
憂心欽欽
如何如何
忘我實多

Mao comments: "Today they [the rulers] have come to neglect them [the worthies]" 今則忘之矣.[10]

Pre-Qin philosophers and poets typically criticize the shortcomings of their lords by painting a vivid and nostalgic picture of virtuous former rulers, presenting them as sages and paragons of virtue and then proceeding to discuss the situation at hand. In a similar manner, Mao's xing promises a ruler who so excites the worthies of the world that they rush to him swiftly as falcons. The lines describing human activity negates, as we have come to expect, this ideal situation and disappoints the reader by describing how the ruler of today "has forgotten" about the fine tradition of attracting good ministers to his state.[11] The xing element thus stands in an ironical relation to the rest of the poem. What on the surface is a simple love song has been transformed, by way of Mao's xingish interpretation of the amorous man-and-woman dualism as a description of the relation between ruler and minister, into a more appropriate and loftier poem.

"Gu feng" (ode 35)

> Harmonious and peaceful is the eastern wind
> it brings clouds and rain

> 習習谷風
> 以陰以雨

Mao comments: "A xing. *Xixi* [means] harmonious and peaceful in appearance. The eastern wind is called valley wind. When yin and yang are in harmony the eastern wind arrives. If man and wife are in harmony, then the family will be perfected, and heirs will be born" 興也. 習習, 和舒貌. 東風謂之谷風. 陰陽和谷風至. 夫婦和則室家成而繼嗣生.

The poem continues:

> I strive to be of the same heart as you
> It is not appropriate to be angry

> 黽勉同心
> 不宜有怒

Mao comments: "This imparts that she who 'strives' longs to be of the same heart as her lord" 言黽勉者思與君子同心也.[12] The third and fourth lines of the third stanza completely negate the promise of conjugal union and harmony that the xing has given us:

> You feast your new wife
> and will not associate with me[13]

宴爾新昏
不我屑以

Mao's comment on ode 35 comprises all of the elements discussed thus far. On the one hand, the xing could be said to be "simple," in that the *tertium comparationis* that unites the natural and the human strata is "harmony," *he* 和. On the other hand, it would be more appropriate to classify "Gu feng" as an analogical xing, since what Mao stresses through his xing trope is not a static description of harmonious birds or people but the *result* of conjugal harmony, namely the many descendants that will ensure that the families and clans never die. The offspring thus stands in the same relation to the harmony between man and wife as the eastern wind does to the harmony of yin and yang. We also observe how Mao, by way of this analogical xing, presents a reading that gets increasingly extratextual and, in the literal sense of the word, far-fetched, in that the poet speaks of conjugal harmony but never of such harmony as a means to many offspring.

Let me return briefly to the question of correlative cosmology. Mao's juxtaposition of the cosmological dualism of yin and yang with the amorous dichotomy of man (yang) and woman (yin) would seem to argue in favor of Pauline Yu's and Michelle Yeh's "cosmological poetics." But such a cosmologically inclined interpretation must be met with two counterarguments. First with my reoccurring, principal objection to the cosmologists, namely that the xing speaks of the harmonious eastern wind in order to express the idea of spousal harmony and, consequently, a plethora of descendants. The transference of meaning from the "eastern wind," which the letter speaks of, to the flourishing aristocratic houses and clans that is the letter's spirit (or, more prosaically, the poem's "message") is by definition rhetorical and metaphorical, Mao's stance toward correlative cosmology notwithstanding.

Second, since the Maoist analogies invariably thematizes instrumentality and ritual behavior ("*how* do you make the clans and houses prosper?") I argue that the idea of a cosmological correspondence between the eastern wind and—via the concepts of yin and yang—matrimonial harmony is irrelevant since the process, or instrument, by which the latter can occur is the rituals. Still, there is indeed an element of cosmology at work in Mao's comment, namely the interpretation of the arrival of the eastern wind as a symptom of cosmological harmony. Moreover, Mao's analogy is the ideological hermeneut's way of making a text which itself speaks of wind, clouds, rain and amorous relations speak of ritual behavior and the ruling elite. The xing here performs its cardinal task in that it sublimates the popular text.

With reference to the current discussion, Mao's analogical reading of "Gu feng" is set in the ironical mode since the marital harmony promised by the xing is vehemently contradicted by the rest of the poem.

"Gu feng" 谷風 (ode 201)

Harmonious and peaceful is the eastern wind
There is wind and rain

習習谷風
維風及雨

Mao comments: "A xing. Wind and rain affect each other. Friends and companions rely on each other" 興也. 風雨相感. 朋友相須.

When fear and dread awaits
there are [only] I and you
When peace and joy awaits
you cast me off

將恐將懼
維予與女
將安將樂
女轉棄予

Mao comments: "This says that the friends are greedy and opportunistic, and that their friendship depends on the circumstances of failure or success" 言朋友趨利, 窮達相棄. In the first lines of the second stanza, the xing element is slightly altered:

Harmonious and peaceful is the eastern wind
There is wind and the tornado

習習谷風
維風及頹

Mao comments: "The *tui* is an unruly, whirling wind. [It is made up of] two weak winds that rely on each other to ascend. This is like friends and companions relying on each other to reach perfection" 頹, 風之焚輪者也. 風薄相扶而上. 喻朋友相須而成.¹⁴

Mao's interpretations of the two odes called "Gu feng" and their almost identical xing imagery are markedly different. What is stressed here, in ode 201, is the interaction of the wind and the rain and, in the second stanza, the wind and the tornado. In his comment on ode 35, by contrast, Mao disregards the "wind" and "rain" and focuses all attention on the "eastern wind," which he understands as a symptom of cosmic harmony and from which his analogical interpretation of the xing element is derived. Both readings are nonetheless analogical, as wind and rain (or wind and tornado) stand in the same relationship to each other as do two friends. In Mao's opinion, ode 201 is ironical because the harmony promised by the xing is ultimately contradicted by the rest of the poem which describes how the two friends split up.

"Yuan you tao" 園有桃 (ode 109)

The garden has a peach tree,
Its fruits, them [one takes as] meat
The sorrows of the heart—
I sing and chant

園有桃
其實之殽
心之憂矣
我歌且謠

"Yuan you tao," interpreted as an analogical xing above, is simultaneously an instance of the ironical xing. The ideal governmental situation described in the garden-state metaphor which makes up Mao's xing is negated by the account of intrigues and slander presented in the poem.

"Kui bian" 頍弁 (ode 217)

Thematically, "Kui bian" belongs to the *carpe diem* category of *Odes*, and the last stanza consequently says "Death and ruin strike without warning / and then there is no time to meet / let us merrily drink tonight" 死喪無日, 無幾相見, 樂酒今夕.[15] Throughout the ode, its addressee is exhorted to use his "fine wine and perfect meat dishes" to feast his closest relatives at a banquet.

What interests me primarily in this context are the first two lines and the interpretation thereof by the commentarial tradition. Mao's comment—which, like the first lines of the poem, is fraught with editorial and linguistic uncertainty—on the first line is tautological. He says: "This is a xing. *Kui* means 'in appearance like a *bian*-cap'. A *bian*-cap is a leather cap" 興也. 頍, 弁貌. 弁, 皮弁也. (Karlgren, frustrated, complains that "this tells us nothing.")[16] The first line thus translates, with Mao, as "Cap-like is the *bian*-cap" 有頍者弁. The second line, whose meaning is similarly difficult to fully grasp, and which for two millennia has been translated and paraphrased quite differently, inquires either about the function and nature of the cap ("What is it?") or about its wearer ("Who is it?"): 實維伊何.

I hazard a guess that most commentators, beginning no later than with Kong Yingda, have misunderstood Mao's intentions, and that Mao's "this is a xing" in fact refers to the xingish imagery of the seventh and eighth lines of this first stanza—"the mistletoe and the dodder / spread themselves over the pine" 蔦與女蘿, 施于松柏—in which case this is a "simple," nonironic xing.[17] But since Mao's comment as it stands in the *Shisanjing zhushu* recension is too brief to sustain this hypothesis or, indeed, explain the xingish logic of the first lines, I briefly and speculatively explore Zheng Xuan's significantly later subcommentary, although this example is thereby stripped of any real scientific value.

Zheng's comment is strongly reminiscent of Mao's interpretation of the motif of the knot-horn pendant in "Wanlan" but with two obvious differences. When Zheng wrote his subcommentary to the *Maozhuan* he relied more obviously than his predecessor not only on historicizing, allegorical readings of the *Odes* such as the *Minor Prefaces* but also on nostalgic reconstructions of Zhou ritual rules and regulations such as the *Liji* 禮記, the *Zhouli* 周禮 and the *Yili* 儀禮, three texts for which Zheng also provided canonical commentaries.[18]

According to the *Minor Prefaces*, in "Kui bian" the "noblemen of Zhou criticize King You. Violent and cruel and with no sentiments for his relatives, he would not feast the members of his family nor cultivate the relationship with distant cousins. Thus isolated they [he?] risked going under. For this reason, they made this poem" 諸公刺幽王也. 暴戾無親, 不能宴樂同姓, 親睦九族, 孤危將亡. 故作是詩也.[19]

Zheng similarly identifies the addressee as the incompetent King You and claims that the first lines "are saying that King You is wearing this leather cap kind of headgear, and [then they inquire] what it is for" 言幽王服是皮弁之冠, 是維何為乎. The translation of the first lines should thus read:

Cap-like is the *bian*-cap
What is it for?

有頍者弁
實維伊何

The first stanza, as we know, describes how "your spirits and meat dishes are perfect and fine" and admonishes the addressee to feast his closest relatives and no others. For Zheng Xuan, however, the central message of the poem hinges upon the question in the second line about the function of the ceremonial cap. Zheng holds that the poem imparts that "it is appropriate [for King You] to use it at a feast but that this is not done. According to ritual rules, the Son of Heaven and his vassals don court robes at banquets" 言其宜以宴而弗為也. 禮, 天子諸侯朝服以宴. He adds, apparently quoting the "Yu Zao" 玉藻 chapter of the *Liji*, that "At the court of the Son of Heaven, leather caps are used at daytime court sessions" 天子之朝, 皮弁以日視朝.[20]

With reference to the following lines about the fine wines and meat dishes, Zheng says that "this imparts that he knows how to execute the ritual practices for this particular event but does not do it" 言其知具其禮而弗為也.[21]

Just like the knot horn in "Wanlan," and the *gu*-goblet 觚 of which Confucius speaks in *Analects* 6.25, the cap is an object invested with ritual significance but misused. Hence also the significance of Mao's tautological comment, as Mao's argument is that the *bian* cap indeed has the authentic appearance of a leather cap worn at rituals. By posing this question and then describing the banquet scene, "Kui bian" demonstrates how a morally decrepit ruler usurps the true meaning of the ritual leather cap by his deviant, antiritual usage thereof. In other words, the xingish description of the cap promises a feast with all the proper ritual accoutrements for the king's closest relatives, while the rest of the poem frustrates the reader's expectations by describing an imaginary banquet.

"Xiao yuan" 小宛 (ode 196)

Small is that screaming *jiu* bird
it flies up high and reaches heaven

宛彼鳴鳩
翰飛戾天

Mao comments: "A *xing* . . . Those who walk the petty man's path in pursuit of high and illustrious merits will, in the end, not achieve them" 興也 . . . 行小人之道責高明之功, 終不可得.

My heart is grieved and pained
I think of the people of yore[22]

我心憂傷
念昔先人

In his comment on "Xiao yuan," Mao depends on "subliminal" linguistic ruses to join the *xing* element with the ensuing lines. The result, I suggest, is far from convincing. In all other examples of the ironical *xing* nature is used as the model from which the human action described by the poem goes astray, but here that movement is reversed. The keywords in Mao's comment are "small" (*xiao* 小) and "high" (*gao* 高). As in most cultures and languages, the dichotomies of "big" and "small" and "high" and "low" are metaphorized in classical Chinese. And as always, "high" has positive connotations—referring here to high position and lofty ideals—whereas *xiao* can best be rendered as "petty." To make the *xing* element fit the poet's critique of a bad ruler (King You again, according to the *Preface*) Mao highlights the words *yuan* 宛 and *tian* 天, the former being a synonym of *xiao*, "small," and the latter meaning, of course, "heaven"—that which by definition is "high." Simultaneously, the small bird that reaches high heaven is understood as a *xing*ish representation of the petty man who cannot reach the achievements of the lofty gentleman ruler. Mao has succeeded in connecting the strata, but it is a Pyrrhic victory since he makes the bird that actually reaches a high position a metaphor for the petty man who cannot. This is the bizarre message of the *xing*: you reach lofty and noble ideals by walking down the wrong path. Unwittingly, the *xing* is saying exactly the opposite of what Mao, apparently, wanted it to say. The *xing* and the rest of the poem contradict each other, but it is *nature* that is "in the wrong" by suggesting that a small bird (to wit, a petty man) can reach heaven. By making nature—that which is subordinated to man yet supposedly perfect in its organization—argue in favor of the "petty man," Mao perverts the tacit ideological system that underlies the *Commentary* and, indeed, demonstrates the pragmatic character of his xing.

Aprosdoketon sinense: "Da dong" (ode 203) and "Zheng yue" (ode 192)

"Da dong" 大東 and "Zheng yue" 正月 are not only supreme examples of irony in Mao's *Commentary*; a careful examination of these odes and Mao's comments upon them reveals the presence of a theme, or topic or "thought pattern" inherited by—and, in the case of Mao Heng, from—the philosophical discourse of the third century BCE, a theme that runs counter to what I have called correlative cosmology. I explore the coincidences of early Chinese philosophy, the Confucian commentarial tradition and *Shijing* metapoetics elsewhere, and below merely explain how these two poems demonstrate the illusory and thoroughly rhetorical character of the xing.[23]

"Da dong" begins thus:

Full to the brim of cooked grain is the *gui*-vessel
long are the thornwood *bi*-ladles

有饛簋飧
有球棘匕

Mao comments: "A xing. *Meng* 饛 refers to the appearance of a full *gui*-vessel . . . one uses a *bi*-ladle to fill up a *ding*-vessel" 興也. 饛滿簋貌 . . . 匕所以載鼎實.[24]

The first stanza continues:

The way of Zhou is [smooth] as a whetstone
its straightness like an arrow
[This is the way that] the gentleman-ruler treads on
[and] that which the petty man only looks at
Turning my head, I regard it [him]
flowingly I shed tears[25]

周道如砥
其直如矢
君子所履
小人所視
睠言顧之
潸焉出涕

Just like "Zheng yue," this poem is a lamentation of governmental chaos and the loss of an ideal order that used to be. The reader of the *Odes* is familiar with the rhetoric in which such a critique is put and recognizes the punning usage of *dao* 道, meaning both "way" in the sense of "path" as well as "Way" or Tao in the sense of "order" or "principle." "The Way of Zhou," so smooth and so straight, thus represents the lost order of former times. The trope of the *dao* is then developed in two ways by the shrewd—rather than "naïve," "spontaneous," "wild," or "excessive"—poet who thereby unites the first stanza and makes the text wholesome and harmonious. The fifth line mixes the literal with the figurative saying that the gentleman ruler "treads" (*li* 履) on the way of Zhou, meaning, of course, that a true king follows the rules laid down by the virtuous early Zhou rules. The last line describes the protagonist's flowing tears. He is crying mainly because the rulers of today know nothing about the way of Zhou. Rhetorically, however, the poem is still banking on the literal meaning of *dao* since "path" (or "way" or "road") connotes parting and distance.

When the fifth line says that the gentleman ruler treads on the way of Zhou the implied reader understands it as a metaphor saying that good ruler follows the order of virtue. Here, in the last two lines, the metaphorical flow reverts, making "way" and "tread" regain their original, literal meaning. The way of Zhou is thus both the abstract order that is now gone and commemorated by the poem and the concrete way ("the road") that the true Superior Man treads on, moving away from the speaker who sheds his tears in despair. This double sense of parting (from the Way or Tao and from someone actually leaving) is underlined by the penultimate line that speaks the language of separation, with the narrator saying that he turns his head to regard "it" (*zhi* 之, referring both to the way and the departing gentleman). We recognize the motif of tearful parting and the sorrowful gazing toward a person disappearing into the distance from wedding poems such as "Yan yan" (ode 28).

If the first stanza is unified by the poet's pun on the double meaning of *dao*, then what about the xing element with which it starts? How the apparently literal description of the *gui*-vessel filled with grain and the long thornwood ladle functions as a xing is intriguingly difficult to explain. What do they represent apart from themselves? Or what, to Mao's mind, do they resemble? Obviously, the xing element conjures up an image of abundance. Mao's explicit definition of a *bi* ladle as "what is used to fill up a *ding*-tripod" 所以載鼎實 contributes to the positive connotations and the impression of wealth. With our newly acquired insights into the Maoist mode of irony we may put forward the hypothesis that the xing element evokes the abundance of food that is a natural effect of a well-governed state such as the Zhou in its early stages and thus functions as a contrast to the poverty and misgovernment of the present day, as described in the following stanzas. This tallies both with the ironic pattern of presenting a glorious past to set off the degenerated present and the focus on instrumentality—how should a state ideally be governed?—that I have suggested is at work in the analogical xing.

The fourth stanza goes on to describe how a correct hierarchic pattern is compromised:

> The sons of the men from the East
> toil without encouragement
> The sons of the men from the West
> bright and splendid are their clothes
> The sons of boatmen
> of black bear and brown-and-white-bear are their furs
> The sons of servants
> in the hundred offices they are used[26]

> 東人之子
> 職勞不來
> 西人之子
> 粲粲衣服
> 舟人之子
> 熊羆是裘
> 私人之子
> 佰僚是試

Mao comments: "'Boatmen' refers to rowers of boats. 'Furs of black bear and brown-and-white-bear' bespeaks wealth" 舟人, 舟楫之人. 熊羆是裘, 言富也.[27] The last four stanzas announce a perverse deviation from the hierarchic pattern that both on a factual and rhetorical level underlies Mao's *Commentary*, namely the elitist separation of the populace from the gentleman. The text hereby follows the pattern of promise and surprise since one line tells of sons of simple boatmen and the next surprises the reader by linking these lowly people to bear-furs, a (metonymic or synecdochic) sign of wealth. One line tells of sons of servants and the next line shocks the reader by placing these uncouth commoners in governmental offices. Things no longer have their appropriate place; the unwashed masses have appropriated and usurped the true, aristocratic significance of bear furs and governmental offices.

The imagery of the last stanza connects, in a circular movement, directly with the enigmatic xing image that started the poem, which provides a vital clue to its meaning and rhetorical mode:

In the south there is the Winnowing Basket
but you cannot winnow with it
In the north there is the Ladle
but you cannot ladle wine or congee with it[28]

維南有箕
不可以簸揚
維北有斗
不可以挹酒漿

The description of the two celestial constellations, the Winnowing Basket and the Ladle, is the poet's final utterance of despair and distinctly imprinted with the rhetoric pattern of "what seems to be but is not" (*si er fei*). The first line promises a winnowing basket and the second line mockingly produces a winnowing basket that cannot winnow; the third line introduces a ladle, and the fourth line presents us with a nonladling ladle—in other words, an antiladle. This dualism of promise and disappointment is present already in the initial xing image that, as noted, also depicts domestic utensils. It is clear that in the light of those ill-named star-images, my initial hypothesis about the function of the xing must be modified, but how?

It is thus correct but, again, not enough to say that the abundance described by the xing element relates ironically to the rest of the poem. To appreciate the importance and radicalness of Mao's comment on "Da dong," I return to and pursue the most fundamental question, namely why

Mao tags the opening lines as a xing. Is there, as a follower of Zhu Ziqing would expect, a component of similarity or comparison herein? I postpone that question briefly and instead observe that the poem itself, and what Mao defines as a xing, are marked by a movement of negativity and crossing out. Just as the seventh stanza displays a winnowing basket and a ladle just to reveal immediately their illusory character and nonexistence in the following lines, so the xing speaks of food and food containers so that the rest of the poem can negate this abundance. Using Mao's own terminology, the xing is that which "seems to be but is not"; there seem to be vessels full of food but, in reality, there are none. Read in juxtaposition, the deceptive imagery of the last stanza—full of the resentment and nihilism of a declining aristocrat—thus brings to the fore the rhetorical, manipulative, and contrived character of the ironical xing: the *gui* vessel full of grain is as illusory and whimsical as the Willowing Basket in the heavens; they are mere images.

Consequently, the reason that Mao defines the two nonmetaphorical opening lines as a xing is not simply to make the reader attentive to likenesses between the xing element and whatever the poem goes on to describe; he does so to mark their illusory character. Although literal and nonmetaphorical, the xing element is anything but a mimetic description of a situation that is at hand. In Mao's comment on "Da dong," the xing is thus revealed as a hyperrhetorical figure that mocks the reader hungry for real and truthful accounts of the world, just as the image of the full vessels mocks the hungry nobleman who sees the Way of Zhou being trodden on by the Western barbarians.

The manipulative rhetoric of "Da dong" is irreconcilable with the claims of the literal, concrete, spontaneous, and cosmological nature of the *Odes* and Mao's *Commentary* but, at least hypothetically, cognate with the rhetorical "craftiness" (*jue* 譎) which the *Great Preface* identifies as a hallmark of *shi*, and with the metapoetics of "Crane Calls" (ode 184) and the injunction there to let "other stones serve as whetstones."[29] But let me return to the question of similarity and comparison. In an alternative or complementary interpretation of Mao's comment, one may argue that the xing element does contain an instance of similarity—the *tertium comparationis* of which is the concept of illusoriness—in that the xing element corresponds to the descriptions of plebeians decked out in expensive clothing and to constellations that look like, but are not, food utensils. But on what presuppositions does such a reading rest, and what are its consequences? First, the rhetoric and temporality of the poem is highly intricate. The illusoriness of the first lines is realized only after the poem has been read in full, whereas on a first reading they appear descriptive and literal. Woven into the flesh of the poem is thus an injunction to reread.

Second, what the poem (on this alternative reading) is comparing is the manipulation and thus the illusoriness of certain speech acts, acts of naming and signs (fur coats as signifiers of nobility). The first lines seem to describe vessels, ladles, and food but do not, just as the names of constellations possess only the names but not the reality of ladles and winnowing baskets. Read for the second time, after one has grasped belatedly how the themes of illusoriness and negation and the circularity of the poem presuppose each other, the xing element becomes a meta-comment on the use of language and of the possibility of using it falsely. Like in "Zheng yue" below, the poet *lies*. When he describes the vessels, ladles, and food he pretends that these words are used to refer to things in the text-external world, and it is this instance of rhetoric and linguistic trickery to which Mao's "this is a xing" brings attention.

"What seems to be but is not"

Mao's comment on "Zheng yue" 正月 (ode 192) provides us with a formula for what may be called the "tropological movement" that Mao finds operative in "Da dong."

The ironic xing model rests upon a moment of deviation as the ironic poem disappoints and surprises the reader by negating the ideal set up by the xing, which is used in contrast to the aberrant and often chaotic situation described by the rest of the poem. This poetics of contrast, surprise, and disappointment occupied a central position in Han dynasty Confucian rhetoric and derived, ultimately, from the nostalgic and paradisiacal vision of a former Golden Age in which sages ruled the world with perfect virtue, as described in Mao's comment on "Chen feng." The notion of a former *paradeisos* (we have already met the garden/state metaphor in "Yuan you tao") of perfected statesmanship was of great practical value for the post-Maoist commentators of the *Odes*, as it provided them with a technique that could resolve many frustrating paradoxes that occurred when a poem refused to fit into the allegorical paradigm. When the author of the *Minor Prefaces* had to make "Yuanyang" 鴛鴦—unambiguously a eulogy to a virtuous lord—into a "critique" (*ci* 刺) of King You he simply contended that the whole poem was written by a poet who criticized the inadequate King You by "thinking of the illustrious kings of the past" 思古明王.

When this opposition between eulogy and critique occurs in ode 73 ("Da ju" 大車), the *Preface* says that the poem "displays the past in order to criticize the present" 陳古以刺今.[30] Thus, if the hermeneut was unable to reconcile a poem—or part of a poem—with the greater context, he could simply argue that the discrepancy was caused by the temporal hiatus evoked by the poem: namely, the difference between the glorious past (*gu* 古) and the degenerated and perverted present (*jin* 今). Indeed, the past/present dualism is omnipresent in the philosophical works of the late Zhou and Han dynasties as a conventional part of the author's criticism of present-day degeneration. It is uncertain, however, if or to what extent Master Mao followed an authoritative commentator (such as the *Old Preface* or the Three Schools) who would identify the historical situation in which a certain poem was made.[31]

"Zheng yue" is a long-drawn lamentation about governmental chaos. The *Minor Preface* and, according to Wang Xianqian, the Three Schools take it as a straightforward critique of the wicked King You articulated by the great officials (*dafu*).[32] Be it as it may with the exact temporal and geographic location of this chaotic state, the timbre of sorrow and desperation is undoubtedly present in the poem. Although the *Commentary* does not define it as a xing, "Zheng yue" persistently employs a highly rhetorical and ironical figure of speech that permeates the whole text. The ode starts by describing a disturbing anomaly:

> It is the *zheng* month, ample is the frost
> my heart is grieved and hurt
> The false words of the populace
> are heavily exaggerated[33]

> 正月繁霜
> 我心憂傷
> 民之訛言
> 亦孔之將

The *zheng* month, Mao points out, refers to the fourth month of the *Xia* calendar and, thus, to a time of year that normally does not see any frost.[34] We could read these lines literally and conjure that the speaker is shocked and distressed at nature's untimeliness, a deviation that, furthermore, could be interpreted as a disastrous omen. We could also understand the image of frost in the fourth month as a rhetorical trope used by the skillful (and not at all "naive" or "spontaneous") poet to set the tone for a poem that will describe a *saeculum* out of joint and deviating from the path of true virtue. In any case, the poem's description of ample hoar frost shows us a nature that does not really behave as nature should. Ironically, there is deviation within nature *itself* which breaks the narrator's (and our) expectations of the stable and cyclic path of the seasons.

The dialectics of norm and deviation, and promise and disappointment, run through the whole poem. The second stanza evokes "mother and father":

> Father and mother you bore us
> Why do you make us suffer?

> 父母生我
> 胡俾我瘉

Mao comments: "'Father and mother' refers to [the Zhou kings] Wen and Wu" 父母, 謂文武也.[35] The shocking accusation directed against "father and mother" (or, with Mao, Wen and Wu) for inflicting agony on the world again sets up a norm only to immediately violate it: parents (either of the blood or of the culture) are supposed to be benign and caring. It is unnatural and abnormal for parents to make their children suffer. In the fifth stanza, the issue of linguistic perversion is addressed. The usurpers of power that have caused the present-day havoc have also usurped language:

> They say "the mountain is low"
> [but] there are ridges and cliffs
> The false words of the populace
> why has no one put a stop to them?

> 謂山蓋卑
> 為岡為陵
> 民之訛言
> 寧莫之懲

Mao comments: "On the throne is not a gentleman-ruler but a petty man" 在位非君子乃小人也.[36] Rhetorically, this is effective stuff since only a regime led by a petty, perverse ruler can claim that up is down and that a mountain—that which per definition is high—is low. The deviation from a correct pattern thematized in the first two stanzas is here carried over to the poet's description of men in high positions. The narrator puts the usurper's perversion on display by quoting his "false" and absurd speech. Yet the absurdity of the statement "the mountain is low" carries a certain logic in this context since on a metaphorical level it says precisely that the "high" ruler (often represented by the word "mountain" in the *Odes* and in Mao's semiotics) is in fact small and petty. We have seen that, in the *Commentary*, "mountain" (山 *shan*) is a word that appears frequently as a metaphor for a ruler (often correlated with "marsh" as a metaphor for the lowly minister).

In the topsy-turvy world described by "Zheng yue," the usurper is not the "stern" and "imposing" ruler that "Nan shan" (ode 101) described in its mountain-ruler metaphor but a "petty man." Thus, the perverted speech act (where that which is high is called "low") becomes, in another ironic turn, metaphorically a truthful description of the depraved ruler himself: although occupying a high position he is base and "low." The seventh stanza tells of how grain stands ripe and flourishing on a distant field on a slope with "heaven" beating down on it.[37] With Mao and Zheng Xuan, this image says that there are no good men at court but that they—metaphorically represented by the flourishing grain—are forced to live in seclusion.[38]

The eleventh stanza again repeats the theme of deviation:

> The fish is in the pond
> yet he cannot rejoice
> Although by diving down it can hide on the bottom
> yet the [light] greatly illuminates him
> The grieved heart is in pain,
> thinking of the cruelty carried out by the state[39]

魚在于沼
亦匪克樂
潛雖伏矣
亦孔之炤
憂心慘慘
念國之為虐

If in the first line everything seems to be in perfect order, as the fish is found in its proper and natural environment, the second line disappoints us, destroying the naturalness that the first line has just promised. The third and fourth lines alludes intertextually to "He ming" (ode 184) and Mao's comment about how fine fish (as opposed to small, petty fish) hide in the dark, just as a good ruler is "hidden yet obvious."[40] Here, in the present description of a state in turmoil, the fish attempts to hide on the bottom but is prevented from being a "fine" fish by the light—the *Lichtzwang*, to speak with Paul Celan—which threatens its existence.

It is in his comment on the fourth stanza, however, that Mao is moved to pinpoint this frustrating pattern of naturalness and deviation, this ironic pattern of promise and disappointment. The first lines of the fourth stanza go:

I look at the middle of that forest,
[there is] only firewood and brushwood

瞻彼中林
侯薪候蒸

Mao comments: "'Firewood and brushwood' imparts that it looks like [a forest] but is [in fact] not" 候蒸, 言似而非.[41]

In the world gone awry that the poem describes, this is yet another sign of disappointment and deviation. In a first, naive reading, the forest/firewood irony seems to have two functions. On the one hand, it pertains to poem's general pattern of things and events that turn out to be different from one's expectations. On the other hand, the ironic imagery opposes genuineness and solidity (trees, forest) with lightness and inferiority (firewood as an inferior "version" of trees). With reference to the situation of the state, the poem says that what may look imposing from the outside is, on a closer look, mere rubbish.

I contend that Mao's words about what *seems to be but is not* (*si er fei* 似而非) also describe the rhetorical organization of this ode. The first line describes how the eyes of the narrator catch the sight—the appearance—of a forest. That image is then contradicted by the actual, extratextual fact that the "forest" consists merely of firewood and brushwood. The reader is thus made to realize that the "forest" was merely an illusion and the very word "forest" (*lin* 林) a misnomer. A forest is, by definition, an assembly of trees, and a "forest" lacking trees, strictly speaking, cannot be a forest. But here, in the fourth stanza of "Zheng yue," it is not nature that lets us down by deviating from its own presumed naturalness, as was the case when nature sent down frost in the fourth month. Here—just as in the statement that "mountains are low" and in the description of vessels, ladles and carriages in "Da dong"—the deviation takes place at the level of language and rhetoric. The reader is disappointed mostly because the signans "forest" does not possess the signatum he or she had expected, not because the "forest" turned out to be only firewood. It could indeed be held that the narrator is at fault for misnaming the firewood as a forest on purpose. Unless one believes that this stanza is ultimately about a person mistaking firewood for a forest, relating that experience moment by moment, one cannot doubt that the two first lines are part of the rhetorical pattern of promise and disappointment. Now we can point our fingers at the bard and accuse him of the very same crime that he has spent thirteen carefully embroidered stanzas denouncing: usurpation. To be able to say that, today, things are not what they seem, the poet purposely calls the firewood and brushwood a "forest." In other words, he uses the rhetorical model of "that which seems to be but is not" in that he sets up a model (forest) and then disappoints us by deviating from it. Now we understand the true colors of a poet who indulges in irony: he is a "misnamer," or a disturber of the holy alliance of signans and signatum. In the parlance of the *Great Preface*, he is "crafty."

This false and wholly rhetorical attribution of characteristics to inappropriate objects and personae is what constitutes the ironical xing, making forest into firewood for the rhetorical effect of linguistic disappointment. In the fourth stanza of "Zheng yue," the mockery of irony appears in full effect in the form of what possibly is a graphic pun. The character translated as "forest"—*lin* 林—is a depiction of two trees. The concretion (and here that word is finally appropriate) of that character contrasts noticeably and comically with the factual misapprehension since, just as the poet wished, the reader actually *sees* the trees of the forest and can hardly believe his or her eyes when, in the next line, they come upon only firewood and brushwood.

The ironical technique of "that which seems to be but is not" mocks likeness and the relationship between a word (or *ming* 名) and its meaning. The ironic xing promises to present similarity (*si* 似) but fails to deliver anything but dissimilarity, or negation (*fei* 非). This, then, is my argument: if Mao has instinctively described the ironic xing with the formula of *si er fei* he has, by the same token, asserted the fictionality and the illusory character of the xing and, consequently, the rhetorico-manipulative character of his whole hermeneutical enterprise. For a xing to qualify as a xing, it must present the reader with an image whose ultimate meaning cannot be deduced from its face value. It must present an image that *seems to be but is not*. The hyperrealistic, "cosmological" idea of the xing as a literal description of external, actual correspondences is, indeed, incorrect.

21

Mao's Pragmatic Hermeneutics

Thus far my treatment of the "simple," the analogical, and the ironical xing has moved within the confines of Zhu Ziqing's *formal* definition according to which the xing is a *piyu* and thus founded on similitude. However, by contrasting the simplicity of the simple xing (a *tertium comparationis* combining the two strata) with my reconstruction of the more complex and extratextual—the analogy often being added from the outside—analogical xing, and with the mocking negativity of the ironic xing, there is a nagging suspicion that a strictly formal definition of Mao's concept might be inadequate. To the naked and coldly analytical eye, the imagistic structures and rhetorical arrangements of the poems that Mao interprets as either "simple" or analogical xings all look the same.

Wherein, then, lies that which makes Mao find an extratextual analogy? In the text, in Mao's imagination or in the fact that Mao must make the text "speak Confucianism"? Why is the description of the screaming osprey in "Guanju" interpreted as a simple metaphor (virtuous bird equals virtuous couple) and not as an analogical xing (the virtuous ruler seeks virtuous ministers just as passionately as the virtuous osprey seeks its virtuous mate)? Is Mao's interpretation warranted by the text itself? And why is the image of the *e* plant 莪 in ode 176 not read as a metaphor for a beautiful young bride or as an seasonal indicator but as a part of an analogy? Is there something—some hidden feature—in that poem that univocally points to an interpretation such as Mao's and, at the same time, discourages a different reading?

I have argued that it is to Mao's great credit to have, by virtue of the xing, directed attention to the question of rhetoric and figurality in the

268 | The Origins of Chinese Literary Hermeneutics

poetic text. Similarly, there is no doubt that the figures, metaphors, and metonymies of the *Odes* ought to be interpreted in a way that grants them more importance than C. H. Wang's dismissal of *Shijing* metaphoricity as "wild" and "excessive." But how, exactly, should such an interpretation be performed? From the comparative point of view that I have been assuming sporadically, the question is the following: Did Mao address the problem of figures, tropes, and metaphors with the same presuppositions as in the West? Jacques Derrida's categorical assertion that any definition of "metaphor" implicates a whole "conceptual network in which philosophy as such has been constituted" notwithstanding, one can at least register the observation that the "Western tradition" (as represented by Aristotle and Quintilian) tends to exemplify "metaphor" with tropes whose meaning *we already know*.[1] We know that "the evening of life" refers to old age and that "the *cup* of Ares" refers to a shield; what the rhetorician does is explain the processes through which the signans reach its signatum.

By contrast, the objects of Mao's xing are not obvious rhetorical figures such as "the river goes to pay tribute to the sea" (ode 183), "he is a whirlwind" (ode 199, stanza five), "my heart is not a stone" (ode 26) or the description in ode 185 of ministers as "the king's claws and teeth." These metaphors are less interesting to Mao than the looser and, in Brooke-Rose's felicitous phrase, "dangerously lazy" figurative structure of the so-called xing since the paratactic or parallelistic imagistic structures allow Mao much more freedom to make the text carry the message he wants. In light of the insight (discussed in chapter 11) that the Confucian commentator saw the hermeneutic activity as work rather than as an explanation in formal terms of what the reader already knew, the enterprise, bold and noble that it may be, of trying to reach a definition of the "xing" through an investigation of different metaphorical models must be questioned.

The essential difference between early Western rhetoric such as that of Aristotle and Quintilian and Mao Heng's Han dynasty hermeneutics is not that the latter is cosmological, concrete, and literal and the former metaphysical, abstract, and metaphorical but that rhetorical analysis (that is, the xing) in Confucian hermeneutics was the first step in the work of making the text house trained. Rhetorical analysis was, in the first place, not a device for textual understanding as such but a way of making the text understandable on what was conceived as a higher, more "aristocratic" and significant level. The xing does not merely indicate a rhetorical figure but also the hermeneutic center of the poem; it *sums up* what the commentator sees as the message of the poem. Since it stands in the middle of the Confucian enterprise of endowing the *Odes* (so often evasive and hard to grasp) with higher meaning, it is quite natural that the xing plays a different and more important role than the Western concepts to which it is sometimes compared. The xing was in itself a tool of hermeneutical power with which Mao could lay down the law. This is why we find so much inconsistency in the usage of the xing—it is, first and foremost, not a concept for the formal analysis of the text as an aesthetic object but a device in service of Confucianism.

The *Commentary* and the xing are thus characterized by a tension between the will to "Confucianize" the text and the more "aesthetical," hermeneutical stance that would emerge later and take the text *qua* literature (to use a highly Occidental concept) as its primary subject. Put more succinctly, the Confucian tradition of hermeneutics of which Mao is a part is pragmatic rather than formalistic. And nowhere is the pragmatic character of Mao's hermeneutics more clearly visible than in his allegorical (or, with Pauline Yu, "contextual") readings: nothing in "Guanju" itself supports or verifies Mao's claim that the poem celebrates the virtue of a king and his queen consort. But contrary to the reader's first impression, the rules that govern Mao's usage of the "simple" or analogical or ironically mocking trope called xing are not complex or mysterious. I have already concluded that we are not dealing with a text-oriented, intricate tropology that aims at establishing a manual of text production, or with a manual for the formal interpretation of a poetic text. The *Commentary* instead uses the *Shijing* as an authority that—by dint of its status as a text canonized by the sage himself—will exemplify and fortify the Confucian conception of the world. The notion of the *Odes* as "a storehouse of righteousness" 義之府 is explicit in the authoritative *Zuozhuan* and determines Mao's interpretation: he *must find* the righteousness hidden in the text.²

It is therefore my hypothesis that Mao's mode of reading is determined by a dogmatic, almost dull Confucian repertory that manifests itself in the *Commentary* as a cluster of keywords such as ruler (*jun* 君), minister/subject (*chen* 臣), Superior Man (*junzi* 君子), rites (*li* 禮), righteousness (*yi* 義), virtue (*de* 德), and—referring to a world gone awry—sex (*se* 色), promiscuity (*yin* 淫), excess (*wu du* 無度), and perversion (*bian* 變). In the *Zuozhuan*, the *Odes* are, of course, already inscribed in a political context through the tradition of poetry recitation (*fu* 賦) as a means of ritualized and lofty communication. But it is most likely in the *Xunzi* that we find the Confucian program that most directly governs Mao's *Commentary*. Here, rites and rituality are instrumental in the construction of a person's civilized character and are analogously described as the instruments "with which the state is rectified" 禮 . . . 所以正國也.³ To adhere to the rites furthermore means to assume one's proper place in a strictly defined dualistic hierarchy where—on the macro level—the minister is subordinated to his ruler and the official of lesser rank to the official of higher rank. This hierarchic power structure is mirrored on the micro level where the wife is subordinated to her husband, the son to his father, the younger brother to his elder brother, the concubine to the first wife, the student to his teacher, and so on. It is the duty of the person in power (the ruler, husband, elder brother, etc.) to be magnanimous and protective toward his underling who, in turn, is supposed to be loyal and obedient.⁴ A virtuous man who abides by the rites is called a "Superior Man" (*junzi*).⁵ A Superior Man is everything that the "populace" (*min* 民) is not: someone who engages in *xue* 學 (he studies moral precedents and emulates superior role models) and who deliberates before taking action in accordance with ritual principles. Whereas the *min* just go with the flow, the Superior Man seeks knowledge in order to cultivate and rectify himself. He is, furthermore, an analyst capable of inferring analogies (*tui lei* 推類) in order to see that each matter is dealt with according to its particular characteristics.

The opposition of "Superior Man" and "populace" thus constitutes a dualism that runs all through the doctrine of the *Xunzi* as well as that of the *Commentary*—and, I argue, the *Great Preface*. Finally, since the *Odes* in so many cases are (or seem to be) love songs, it is of vital importance to understand the emphasis that the Confucians put on rites that would correct, restrain, and render harmless human sexuality. Without ritual principles regulating the union of man and woman, Xunzi says, people would face a "disastrous competition for sensual pleasures" 爭色之禍.⁶ The best evidence of this *Ru* hostility toward licentiousness is, of course, Mao's comment on "Guanju," which contends that *only* if the sexual relationship between man and wife is well regulated, and does not go to extremes, can the state flourish. Sex—or rather the absence thereof—is the very foundation that the state is built on.

Mao thus reads the *Odes* as a manual in which the ruler as well as the minister can find the parameters of true statesmanship. This is the key to Mao's mode of reading and to the pragmatic nature of the xing. As previously suggested, the reason the Mao recension of the *Odes* was canonized and the competing Han, Qi, and Lu schools fell in gradual disuse was most likely that Mao, in a stroke of genius, came up with a reader's tool that in one elegant movement would reveal the structure—and thus the meaning—of the text *or*, if need be, transform a potentially "deviant" text into *Ru* dogma. For Mao, then, being a good reader of poetry automatically meant being a Confucian reader. Although no opposition existed between literary hermeneutics and ideology, there is a palpable tension between pragmatics and formalism in the *Commentary*. On the one hand, Mao must conform the poem to Confucian standards (in the case of "Guanju," to make the image of the calling birds a metaphor for the virtue of the queen consort and her lord). On the other hand, the poem is manifestly *there*, with a variety of possible interpretations and with a structure of its own. Mao's xing describes the rhetorical structure of the poem; that is, it makes a normative statement about how to interpret the text correctly and how to distinguish between literal meaning and figurative meaning.

Not only is the xing Mao's way of taking charge of the text—of pinpointing its hermeneutic center so as to avoid misinterpretations—it is also his way of avoiding textual superfluity; through the xing Mao can transform potential nonmeaning into meaning and significance. The xing is simultaneously a tool of interpretational power and a symptom of a hermeneutical *horror vacui*.[7] Let me exemplify this tension with reference to "Guanju." By revealing the rhetorical structure—the metaphorical link between ospreys and man—Mao also exposes himself to an enormous risk since through this revelation he also opens up the poem for a possible "erroneous" immoral reading. The revealed link between screaming bird(s) and man may *logically* generate a reading in which the calling expresses sexual passion and the bird on the islet, surrounded by water, is a metaphor for the girl desperately sought by the man who tosses and turns in his sleep. Such a reading must never stand a chance, and Mao is therefore quick to impose an appropriate meaning on the metaphorical relationship between nature and man thus exposed by the xing figure. The xing, in other words, combines a formal analysis of the text's figurality with an interpretation that befits the Confucian agenda. In this manner Mao gives and immediately takes back. He opens up the text and then closes it, being simultaneously a hermeneutic and a hermetic reader.

Five Versions of Confucian Hierarchy

I shall entertain the suspicion that the hermeneutical apparatus in the *Commentary* is not as complicated as first imagined; that Mao's usage of the xing is entirely logical but of a different logic than I have hitherto assumed. It is,

I assume, the combination of an ambiguous, sometimes hermetic primary text and the ideological injunction to "Confucianize" the *Odes* that makes Mao's mode of reading seem chaotic and arbitrary. Early *Ru* texts champion the ideals of rigorous hierarchy and of sagely statesmanship, and I start by showing how Mao *finds* these themes in the *Odes*. I observe, furthermore, how the xing is used as a practical and powerful tool to make many different textual configurations speak of Confucian power structures and hierarchic order. In other words, the order of ruler and subject, and their correct and harmonious relationship, is a theme that is made to occur throughout the *Shijing* corpus, manifested in a variety of metaphors. Before proceeding to the poems themselves it should be noted again that the metaphoricity developed in Mao's xingish interpretations of the *Odes* predates the *Commentary*, not only through the metaphorical readings performed by the Three Schools but also by Xunzi and the *Zuozhuan*. Not surprisingly, Xunzi produces many versions of the ruler-ruled metaphor, saying once that the ruler (*jun*) is a boat and his many subjects (*shuren* 庶人) the water that can both sustain and capsize the boat.⁸ On another occasion, the philosopher compares the ruler (*jun*) to a sundial and the populace (*min*) to the shadow that it casts: "If the sundial is straight, then the shadow will be straight" 儀正而景正.⁹

In the same passage, Xunzi also compares the ruler to a bowl (*pan* 槃) and a wellspring (*yuan* 原) and the populace to, respectively, the water that fills the bowl and the water that springs from the well.¹⁰ In all metaphors, the ruler is described as one that molds the populace who, in turn, are seen as a mindless herd lacking a will of its own and thus reacting spontaneously to any external influence. Similarly, the *Zuozhuan* speaks of the hierarchy of ruler and ministers in terms of "high" and "low": ruler and subject do not remain in their respective positions forever. "From ancient times this has been so. Therefore, an ode [*Shijing* 193] says: 'high banks become valleys, deep valleys become mountain hills.' The descendants of the three dynasties of antiquity belong to the multitude today—as you well know" 君臣無常位. 自古以然. 故詩曰高岸為谷, 深谷為陵. 三后之姓于今為庶. 主所知也.¹¹

Commenting on these lines from ode 193, Mao says 言易位也 "It tells of changing positions."¹² The tradition of interpreting natural imagery as metaphoric representations of situations or actions in the human realm was thus obviously firmly established prior to Mao's *Commentary*, as was the reading of high and low natural objects (such as "ridge" and "valley") as metaphoric representations of high and low positions.

Let us at last proceed to the metaphors of Confucian hierarchy that Mao finds in such abundance in the *Odes*.

First Metaphor: "Shan you fusu" 山有扶蘇 (ode 84)

On the mountain there are *fusu* trees
in the swamps lotus flowers
I do not see Zi Du
I only see a mad man!

On the mountain there is the high pine tree
in the swamps the floating dragon plant
I do not see Zi Chong
I only see this crafty youth![13]

山有扶蘇
隰有荷華
不見子都
乃見狂且
山有橋松
隰有游龍
不見子充
乃見狡童

How was this ode understood before it fell into Mao's ideologico-hermeneutical hands? One cannot know if there ever existed a "private" and nonideological reading or if "Shan you fusu" was indeed originally written and understood as a metaphorical piece about Confucian hierarchy; however, one can contrast the letter with its Confucian spirit. The first lines record a meeting that is disappointing or, at least, surprising since the narratrix expects to meet (or "see") a man by the name of Zi Du—who according to Mao is a "beautiful and good person"—but comes upon only a "mad man."[14] It is clear that the text thus suggests togetherness ("I" and Zi Du) and that the narratrix in vain expected a pleasant encounter. But of what kind is this togetherness? What kind of "pleasant encounter" did the protagonist expect? And what evidence can be produced in support of my implicit claim that the speaker is really a woman who expected to see her beautiful lover but, in fact, only met with a lunatic. What does the natural imagery mean? It is possible, as Mi Wenkai and Pei Puxian contend, that the first two lines are merely a literal description of the place where the lovers had agreed to meet.[15]

A more exciting but equally reasonable reading understands the mountain and the marsh as a metaphor for man and woman. A mountain belongs to the masculine yang realm. It is protruding, hard, and stands in the air and the sun. A marsh, by contrast, is typically yin. It is harder to reach for the sun's rays than the mountain; it is wet and soft and, thus, feminine. Moreover, the protruding trees on the mountain and the soft, beautiful flower in the marsh further add to the male-female dualism inherent in the xing element. Such an intratextual reading—suggested already in my analysis of this ironical poem in the previous chapter—fortifies the amorous and sensual theme ascribed to the poem through the assumption that it speaks of a failed meeting between two lovers. Intratextual or not, this reading would doubtless have been highly objectionable to Mao, as it fails to transform the lowly love poem into an elevated, aristocratic text.

Instead, Mao Confucianizes "Shan you fusu" in one, elegant stroke. He comments after the first two lines that "This is a xing . . . saying that high and low, big and small all obtain what is appropriate [for them]" 興也 . . . 言高下大小各得其宜. After the fourth line Mao says: "Zi Du was a beautiful person of that age" 子都世之美好者也, referring to the last line, that: " 'This crafty youth' refers to Duke Zhao" 狡童, 昭公也.[16]

It is the inconspicuous word "appropriate" (*yi* 宜) that is the connection between the xingish imagery and Confucian dogma. What is deemed appropriate here is the fact that big trees grow on the high mountain, whereas small flowers grow in the low marsh. That Mao reads ode 84 as a political piece is obvious, not only because the high/low dichotomy was conventional in Mao's day (as proven by the previous quotation of the *Zuo Commentary* and Mao's comment on ode 193) but also because Mao understands "this crafty youth" to be Duke Zhao, certainly a political—not amorous—figure. The xing speaks of "high" and "low" in the Confucian power structure to indicate that it is appropriate for the greater man to occupy a high position and for the lesser man to be in a lowly position.

Thus we have found the first ruler/ruled metaphor, which is the *high* mountain and the *low* marsh. Through which hermeneutical method has Mao reached this ideologically correct and antisexual interpretation? One could, on the one hand, claim that Mao's chaste interpretation keeps within the confinements of the contemporary yin and yang theory, since "ruler" and "subject" were indeed categorized as, respectively, yang (the superior, masculine, and active agent) and yin (the inferior, feminine, and passive agent). On the other hand, it is clear that Mao's interpretation neither speaks of cosmological correspondence between the masculine and feminine realms, nor of an "amorous" landscape such as that suggested by Mi Wenkai and Pei Puxian. Indeed, what Mao finds useful in the mountain/marsh motif is not the alleged correspondences between the realms of yin and yang but the fact that a high mountain can be made to represent a high position. Thus, Mao's xing depends rather on a sociolinguistic pun than the "concrete," extratextual analogies of yang (mountain/ruler) and yin (marsh/subject) that would put ruler and subject in opposition. Differently put, trees befit the high mountain, not because mountain and trees are both yang but because high and big go together in Mao's semiotics. Such a reading must disregard the poem's sensuous descriptions of the mountain, the tree, the marsh, and the flower and, instead, reduce them into the abstract dualisms of "high and low" and "big and small."

Mao's transformation of the male/female dualism into the ruler/subject dualism, and his transformation of the themes of love and sexuality into the themes of politics and power, involves two different procedures. The first being, of course, the metaphorical reading conducted under the name of xing. By closely examining Mao's reading and by comparing it to our attempt at a nonideological, "aesthetical" reading, we perceive how pragmatism and formalism combine into one, wholly integrated hermeneutical tool. By his "this is a xing," Mao indicates that the description of the mountain and the marsh is not to be understood literally but as a rhetorical figure; this pertains to the formal analysis. At this initial stage, however, the reader does not know exactly what the xing refers to—he or she may very well understand it as a metaphor for man and woman, as previously suggested.

There occurs therefore a short moment of suspense, a hiatus of hermeneutic anarchy, before Mao follows his formalistic description of the poem's rhetorical structure by supplying the information that "mountain" and "marsh" are metaphors for ruler and subject, an interpretation without which the poem would collapse into deviousness or nonmeaning. At last, the reader realizes both that the opening lines are metaphorical and that they refer to the dualistic Confucian power structure: not to man and woman as sexual beings. As we can see, to the formalistic analysis must be added information that makes the reader link the vehicle to the correct tenor. It is precisely here that Mao's xing turns pragmatic and arbitrary since nothing in "Shan you fusu" itself suggests univocally that it deals with Confucian hierarchy. Indeed, my deviant, sexual reading could be equally justified, and it is precisely this possibility that elicits Mao's authoritative comment. Mao's xing, consequently, is not only an exposition of the text's metaphorical structure but also a way of circumscribing the text and of shutting out perverse interpretations; the xing is thus simultaneously an exposure and a closure.

While the interpretation of the poem's metaphorical organization appeals to the reader's rationality for the simple reason that it is a rational way of explaining the function of the poem's natural imagery, the more arbitrary interpretation of "mountain" and "marsh" as metaphors for ruler and subject must depend on Mao's authority only. This insight constitutes in fact a major threat to the very foundation of the present project in the form in which it has hitherto appeared. Because if the formalistic analysis in Mao's xing is subordinated to the need to "Confucianize" the text, my categories (simple, analogical, and ironical xings) are valuable only as a convenient way of arguing against the idea of a cosmological poetics by showing how the Maoist trope indeed involves metaphoricity on an increasingly complex scale. But these categories, I must admit, lead us nowhere in our search for the rules that govern the xing since those rules are not only formalistic but also equally pragmatic.

The second method used by Mao to politicize the text is the allegorical and wholly extratextual identification of "that crafty youth" as Duke Zhao. Again, nothing whatsoever in the text calls for such a reading. By way of the pragmatism of xing metaphoricity and allegory, Mao is able to steer the poem away from its erotic undertones and make it speak of righteousness and Confucian order.

Second and Third Metaphor: "Tuo xi" 蘀兮 (ode 85)

Oh! Withered leaves. Oh! Withered leaves
the wind blows you about
Oh big brother! Oh little brother!
sing first and I will [harmoniously] join in with you[17]

蘀兮蘀兮
風其吹女
叔兮伯兮
倡予和女

"Tuo xi" frustrates the reader by being simultaneously linguistically clear and hermeneutically opaque due to our ignorance of the context in which the poem should be understood; we know what the text says but not what it means. Formally, "Tuo xi" is a strictly parallelistic poem where the first and third lines are identically structured and where the second and the fourth line both end with the pronoun "you" (*ru* 女) in the object position. Thematically, we note that "air" is a common denominator of the two strata since the natural stratum speaks of "blowing" and the ensuing lines—the human stratum—of "singing." We also note that there occurs a hierarchic inversion in the second half of the stanza. Whereas the first lines describe how the addressee ("you" or *ru*), the *passive* leaves, are helplessly blown about by the *active* and vigorous wind, the third and fourth lines make "you" (*ru*) the lead singer whom "I," the narrator, must follow. This inversion (or irregularity) has puzzled the Confucian commentators for more than two millennia and made them come up with increasingly farfetched interpretations to save the text from a devastating paradox while at the same time retaining the parallelism.

Mao does little to clarify the situation. He comments after the second line that "this is a xing . . . the ministers [should] wait for the ruler to initiate [the song] and then join in" 興也 . . . 人臣待君倡而後和.[18] After the fourth line he says: "'Big brother' [and] 'little brother' refers to the older and younger [among the mass of] ministers. This [line] describes how the ruler intones and the ministers join in" 叔伯, 言群臣長幼也. 君倡臣和也.[19] Mao knows that although the text does speak of hierarchies it is far from certain what hierarchies it refers to. "Big brother" (*shu* 叔) and "little brother" (*bo* 伯) could, of course, refer to the members of a family. Here, however, Mao follows the *Zuozhuan* by defining *shu* and *bo* as the courteous forms of address between younger and older ministers.[20] By transforming "brothers" into "ministers" Mao elevates the text to a higher level and at this stage it seems as if the poem speaks of the hierarchy of ministers and of how the lower (or younger) ministers harmoniously subordinate themselves to their superiors (or elders), just as the chorus follows its lead singer.[21]

We observe that such an interpretation would be quite sound because it moves within the limits defined by an intratextual reading; nothing is "added from outside." But Mao is not yet satisfied. "Initiate" (*chang* 倡) and "joining in" (*he* 和) are words that very clearly distinguish between a leader (the "initiator") and his followers (the chorus), and while there certainly exists a hierarchy among the "mass of ministers," no one among them can be a "leader" in the absolute sense that Mao demands (unless that leader is an usurper). Therefore, Mao must go *extra textum* and add the "ruler" (*jun*) to the interpretation. Thus, by virtue of this violent and completely extratextual addition, the text now speaks of harmony between ruler and ruled. We have thereby found the second version of the ruler/subject metaphor: the lead singer and the secondary singers.

The *pragmatic* nature of Mao's exegesis is obvious since the text he claims speaks of the harmonious relationship between a virtuous ruler and his loyal subjects does not, in fact, mention the word "ruler." Furthermore, by defining the opening lines as a xing, he fashions another ruler/subject metaphor—the third in our investigation—namely the withered leaves that are helplessly blown about by the forceful wind. As observed above, the xing element divides into passive (the leaves) and active (the wind), a dualism easily to reconcile with the theme of the ruler and the ruled and with the motif of the lead singer and the chorus. But, as I also intimated, if one follows the strict and explicit parallelism that organizes the text, Mao's xingish reading cannot escape the paradox of the hierarchic inversion. The fourth line says that "If you initiate the song, I [we] will follow," which means that "you" refers to the "initiator"; that is, the *ruler*. But in the first lines, the person addressed as "you" is the passive agent, the withered leaves subjected to the caprice of the wind.²² In order to make "Tuo xi" a eulogy of hierarchic harmony Mao must ignore the paradoxical parallelism, ignore the negativity inherent in the description of the *withered* leaves, and ignore the fact that the poem never mentions a "ruler." Although Mao's xingish reading certainly exposes the metaphoricity of this poem it also closes the text for a deeper understanding of its rhetorical mode.

It is again evident that Mao's metaphorical reading is not a formal analysis meticulously following the primary text but, rather, a pragmatic mode of reading that does not hesitate to step outside the textual boundaries to *find* the meaning stipulated a priori by *Ru* dogmatics. The xing element here is doubtless metaphorical, and one may proceed to categorize it in order to show the rhetoric modalities of the *Mao Commentary*. But since it is a rhetoric that followed in the wake of a pragmatic and ideological hermeneutics, a typology of Mao's xing is a typology of the various figures that Mao discovered or *invented* as he "worked" on the text. It is by no means always a typology of the rhetorical configurations of the *Odes* themselves.

Fourth Metaphor: "Dong fang zhi ri" 東方之日 (ode 99)

The sun is in the east!
That newly-wed girl
[She] is in my chamber!
In my chamber!
Stepping [carefully] she had come to me

The moon is in the east!
That newly-wed girl
[She] is inside my door!
Inside my door!
Stepping [carefully] she has come to me[23]

東方之日兮
彼姝者子
在我室兮
在我室兮
履我即兮
東方之月兮
彼姝者子
在我闥兮
在我闥兮
履我即發

"Dong fang zhi ri" is, as noted above, an explicit love poem in which the narrator praises his newlywed wife. There are, furthermore, no indications that this poem engages any metaphoricity. "Sun" and "moon" may be understood literally, as temporal markers indicating that the groom and his bride are in his chambers all day and all night. Or, just as probable, we may take them as representations of woman and man, as belonging, respectively, to the spheres of yin and yang. Either interpretation would mean that ode 99 speaks of togetherness and of an amorous meeting in the seclusion of the narrator's chamber that lasts all day and all night. It would therefore be a text that transgresses the boundaries of marital decorum and speaks of sexual passion. To Mao the reading thus suggested would not merely be plebeian and meaningless but also ideologically dangerous. "Dong fang zhi ri," in his opinion, is a text that needs hermeneutic polishing and therefore he comments (after the third line of the first stanza): "A xing. The sun emerges from the east: this refers to the ruler who is bright and ample, there is nothing that is not shone upon and investigated. *Shu* refers to the appearance of a newly-wed. *Li* 履 ['to step'] means *li* 禮 'rites.' The moon is ample in the east. The ruler is bright above just like the sun. The subject [or 'minister'] is shining [illuminated] below, just like the moon" 興也。日出東方，人君明盛，無不照察也。姝者初昏之貌。履，禮也。月盛於東方，君明於上，若日也。臣察於下，若月也。[24]

With Mao's claim that "sun" and "moon" are to be taken figuratively we have reached the fourth version of the ruler/subject metaphor. "Sun" and "moon" form a dualism that easily lends itself to a figuration of leader and follower by its representing the oppositions of day and night, warmth and cold, enlightenment and darkness, and illuminator and illuminated. Yet as natural description meets with human action there occurs a disturbing problem: *why* would the text speak of love on a literal level and Confucian hierarchy on a figurative level? The love theme—explicitly acknowledged by Mao through his gloss on *shu* 姝: "appearance of a newly-wed"—and the ruler/subject metaphor are never reconciled but left in the text standing side by side.

Is this not an indication that Mao panics when confronted with this blatant and outright love song? And does this not suggest that Mao performs an utterly unconvincing reading just to make the text seem domesticated, just to make the text speak of Confucianism at least to a very small degree, just to find the "righteousness" that *Master Zuo's Commentary* and Confucius has promised him lies hidden therein? Is this, moreover, not evidence that Mao's xing is not, let us say, an "aesthetical" or formalistic tool for a scientific analysis of a poetic text but a pragmatic tool designed to reshape and polish a text that does not spontaneously speak of righteousness and Confucian order but of passionate love—in other words, an unperfected text? Does this, furthermore, not indicate that although the xing can be categorized according to the process through which the vehicle reaches its tenor, a definition in purely formal terms can never reveal its true nature? These rhetorical questions could be countered by a "cosmological" and "correlative" reading saying that when the ruler is like the sun and his subject like the moon, then man and wife will abide by the rites. But such a reading would still be marred by the inability to incorporate figurality and literalness into a hermeneutic whole. It would still be a neurotic, schizophrenic poem torn apart by an acute crisis of meaning. Perhaps, in this case, "neurosis" and "schizophrenia" characterize, not the poem, but a hermeneutics that cracks under the pressure of serving the two lords of Confucian ideology and the Text.

Fifth Metaphor: "Jingjing zhe e" 菁菁者莪 (ode 176)

> Flourishing is that *e* plant
> in the middle of that slope
> When I have seen my gentleman
> I am happy and courteous[25]

菁菁者莪
在彼中阿
既見君子
樂且有儀

I suggested in the chapter on the analogical xing that this ode could be read as a love poem and that "gentleman" refers to the lover of the narratrix rather than to a gentlemanly ruler. Not only does the poem tell of togetherness and the happiness of coming together, but the description of flourishing plants could, as in "Tao yao" (ode 6), be understood both as an indication that the time of marriage has come and as a metaphor for the beautiful bride. Neither interpretation would, of course, satisfy Mao who, after the second line, comments that "this is a xing . . . The gentleman-ruler [*junzi* 君子] is able to grow and foster talents just as the slope grows the *e* plant so that it flourishes" 興也 . . . 君子能長育人材, 如阿之長莪菁菁然.[26]

The ruler-as-slope and subject-as-*e*-plant figure is the fifth version of the ruler/ruled metaphor. I hope to have already sufficiently explained the mechanism of the "analogical xing" and Mao's transformation of static natural descriptions into descriptions of dynamic processes. Here it suffices to repeat that the poem itself never speaks of "growing"—that is an extratextual addition by Mao. However, it is important to note that Mao's xingish reading is not analogical by accident since by virtue of the "slope" described by the opening lines it can fall back on the high/low pattern that we saw at work in odes 194 and 84. A slope is a protrusion altitude-wise and the concept of altitude thus associated with the description of the slope enables Mao to identify it as a metaphor for the ruler and, consequently, the *e* plant that grows thereupon as an image of the talented subject nurtured and cultivated by his virtuous lord. By turning the reader's attention to the issue of statesmanship, Mao's xingish reading simultaneously exposes the text's metaphoricity and closes the text, thus making it inaccessible for deviant readings. One may for good reasons call it a hermeneutic-hermetic mode of reading.

Hermeneutic Violence

In the preceding analyses I argued that Mao's hermeneutics is dictated by a preexisting and dogmatic demand to find in the *Shijing* certain Confucian themes. I argued, furthermore, that Mao uses the xing both as a formalistic tool exposing the metaphoricity that slumbers in the text and as a highly pragmatic tool manipulating the text into speaking Confucianism. On several occasions, I indicated Mao's inability to account for the text in its entirety, as in "Shan you fusu" (ode 84), where the fact that the leaves blown about so helplessly were withered, thereby indicating exhaustion or death, was left unexplained, or as in "Tuo xi" (ode 85), where the inversion of the power structure was left unexplained. In this fashion, and with the aid of the xing, Mao can highlight the part of the poem that he wishes to stand out and, correspondingly, downplay any textual segment that may disorder his Confucio-hermeneutical program. With reference to the analogical xing, one could say that Mao manipulates the poem's hermeneutic center by luring the reader's attention away from what is actually said of human activity and toward an extratextually given analogy.

I now proceed to two poems, incidentally two more versions of the celebrated theme of the virtuous ruler, where Mao obviously suppresses the meaning of the actual text.

"Fa mu" 伐木 (ode 165)

> Chopping wood *treng, treng*
> bird's crying *eng, eng*
> it leaves the [tree in the] dark valley
> moves up in a high tree
> *Eng* goes its cry
> seeking a friend's voice
> Look at that bird
> if it seeks a friend's voice
> Then how could this man
> refrain from seeking a friend?
> If the spirits listen to them
> peace and harmony will follow[27]

伐木丁丁
鳥鳴嚶嚶
出自幽谷
遷于喬木
嚶其鳴矣
求其友聲
相彼鳥矣
猶求友聲

矧伊人矣
不求友生
神之聽之
終和且平

"Fa mu" tells of a bird who, facing the destruction of its abode by the cruel axes, must flee the dark valley to the high tree where it rests in exile. The image describing violence and terror—*eng, eng* are "[cries of] alarm and fear" 驚懼, says Mao—is then explicitly linked to the human stratum by way of the conjunction *shen* (矧 "increasingly so, *a fortiori*"), which makes "Fa mu" one of the rare odes in which the use of a natural description as a statement—here in the form of a simile rather than a metaphor—about the human realm is spelled out. But although Mao admits that the xing element, or the first two lines, contains an element of violence and fear, he cannot tolerate a poem that merely speaks of birds and lonely people. He argues instead that this is an ode about the harmonious relationship between a high-positioned gentleman (or ruler) and his subjects: "Even if a Superior Man moves to a high position he cannot for that reason forget his friends" 君子雖遷於高位不可以忘其朋友.[28]

To reach this "lofty" interpretation, Mao thus downplays both the fear expressed by the bird (and, on a metaphorical level, the Superior Man) and the cutting down of the tree, as well as the bird's (or the Superior Man's) flight into exile. Mao instead transforms the opening lines—which conform harmoniously with the rest of the ode as a description of a lonely, scared individual seeking the warmth of friendly company—into another example of the high/low dualism so often used in metaphors of Confucian hierarchy: namely the interpretation of the bird's flight to the high tree as a metaphor for the "Superior Man's" advancement to a high position.

Mao highlights the words "move" and "up" while downplaying words with negative connotations such as "cut down," "fear," "scream," and "flee," hence the reduction of an ode characterized by intensity and rhetorical brevity to a dull, perfunctory inventory of Confucian themes. More importantly, by equating "bird" with the Superior Man, Mao himself paves the way for a deviant, perverse reading. The interpretation of "Fa mu" is a clumsy attempt at disrupting the meaning of an ode that is more integral than Mao may have imagined. Any attentive reader not blinded by Confucian dogma or dumbstruck by the *auctoritas* with which Mao lays down the poem's canonical meaning must ask *why* the ruler *qua* bird moves to a "high place." Precisely by identifying metaphorically the terrified bird as a ruler, Mao runs the risk of depicting the ruler as one threatened by a coup d'état, not least since the chopping down of trees in "Mu men" (ode 141) is used as a xingish metaphor for a revolution:

> At the gate of the graveyard there are jujube trees
> with axes one hews them
> The [assistants=] ministers are not good
> the people of the state know it
> Knowing it without putting a stop to it
> who can act like that for long?²⁹

> 墓門有棘
> 斧以斯之
> 夫也不良
> 國人知之
> 知而不已
> 誰昔然矣

The second stanza of that poem ends as follows:

> The ministers are not good
> With my song I admonish them
> Although I thus admonish them
> they pays no attention
> [but] when overturned, they will think of me³⁰

> 夫也不良
> 歌以訊之
> 訊予不顧
> 顛倒思我

"Mu men" describes incompetent ministers and how the "citizens of the state" 國人 are about to "overturn" (*diandao* 顛倒) the ruler they hold responsible for the mismanagement of the state. We see how the parallelism of the text links the jujube to the ministers as the second and the fourth lines both end with the pronoun *zhi* 之, which first refers to the tree that is cut down and then to the useless ministers. Mao indicates that the splitting of the jujube tree is used as a metaphor for revolution by calling the first two lines a xing, saying that the jujube tree grows in a secluded area and that one needs an axe to be able to access its firewood.³¹ An intertextual reading of "Mu men" thus discloses a thematic link between tree cutting and revolution, and thereby produces an interpretation of "Fa mu" that flies in the face of Mao's intentions: the ruler is a bad ruler (which justifies the usurpation of power by truly virtuous subjects), or the subjects are themselves bad and cut down the virtuous ruler. In either case, the meaning of the actual text is irreconcilable with Mao's optimistic reading.

That "Fa mu" is self-explanatory (the human animal is forlorn without her friends) and its theme much too plebeian forces Mao to Confucianize the text through a xingish reading that adequately exposes the rhetorical structure of the text but also hampers a true understanding thereof. The crux is that the reading of the bird image as a metaphor for a good ruler must not tell of violence directed against him, which means that Mao's xing metaphor in "Fa mu" contains its own antithesis. In the comment on ode 165, Mao's pragmatism is clearly visible as he alternately highlights and downplays then exposes and closes the poetic text. Although Mao always aims at making the text intact and wholesome, his xingish interpretations are, as in this case, often marred by the inability to incorporate all textual elements into a hermeneutic whole, thereby leaving the rest undigested.

APROSDOKETON: "HE MING" 鶴鳴 (ODE 184)

> The crane calls out in the Nine marshes
> its voice is heard in the wilds
> The fish plunge in the deep
> or lie by the islet
> Happy is that garden
> There is a *Tan* tree
> thereunder are withered leaves
> Stones of other mountains
> can be used as whetstones
>
> The crane calls out in the nine marshes
> its voice is heard in the heavens
> the fish lie by the islet
> or plunge into the deep
> Happy is that garden
> There is a *Tan* tree
> thereunder are *gu*-bushes

Stones of other mountains
can be used to work the jade[32]

鶴鳴于九皋
聲聞于野
魚潛在淵
或在于渚
樂彼之園
爰有樹檀
其下維蘀
他山之石
可以為錯
鶴鳴于九皋
聲聞于天
魚在于渚
或潛在淵
樂彼之園
爰有樹檀
其下維穀
他山之石
可以攻玉

I return to "Crane Calls," which is an exquisite example of the figure of *aprosdoketon* and of the poetics of surprise according to which odes such as "Shan you fusu" 山有扶蘇 (84) "Chen feng" 晨風 (132), the fourth stanza of "Zheng yue" (ode 192) and, perhaps most magnificently, "Da dong" are organized.[33] "Crane Calls" both offers and thematizes a quiet resistance in that it celebrates indolence, happiness, and nonaction; precisely for that reason it is in dire need of the Confucian hermeneut's "work," and demands a metapoetic reading. The opening lines describe how the crane's cries punctuate space, being carried length-wise into the wilderness.[34] The reader is then shaken by a mild shock as the first two lines are not followed, as one would expect, by a description of human activity but by yet another natural image: that of fish roaming carelessly in the water. Is "He ming" a poem that deliberately mocks the hermeneut's will to a metaphoric reading? Then follows the description of the "happy garden." "What joy is there in going to see that garden?" 何樂於彼園之觀乎 asks Mao in his comment, and the poem answers by describing the *tan* tree and the fallen fruits that lie under it, uneaten and useless.[35] The garden—the most cultivated and sophisticated of all landscapes—is depicted as neglected and dilapidated.

The first stanza ends with an antisocial *non serviam* by way of the exhortation to the stones of "other mountains" to serve as whetstones. This structure is repeated in the second stanza with the small but stylistically important difference that the crane's cries are carried altitude-wise into the heavens. This, then, is a poem that celebrates pleasure and the right to depend on other people's work. It not only frustrates the Confucian hermeneut's attempts at a metaphorical reading but also mocks the very foundation of Confucian philosophy—the sense of responsibility toward the state and the world. Mao senses the danger, hastens to his interpretational work, and says (after the second line): "This says that although the body is hidden the reputation [*ming* 名] is bright" 言身隱而名著也.[36] Mao's reading probably derives from Xunzi's quotation (and interpretation) of this poem in his "Ru xiao" 儒效 chapter: "The Superior Man is hidden yet obvious, faint yet bright, yielding yet conquering" 君子隱而顯, 微而明, 辭讓而勝.[37] The crane thus constitutes yet another metaphor for a Superior Man who occupies a high position and rules with subtle means and without an ostentatious display of power. With regard to the third and fourth lines, Mao explains—with no support from the text itself—that good fish hide in the dark whereas small (or petty) fish swim in the shallow water surrounding the islet, to be seen by everyone.[38]

After the first stanza, Mao comments that "if you promote worthies and uses what is discarded you can properly rule a state" 舉賢用滯則可以治國.[39] Mao's xingish reading connects to several rhetorical configurations familiar to the *Shijing* student, and we recognize the state-as-a-garden metaphor from "Yuan you tao" (ode 109), the theme of attracting scholars from other states from "Chen feng" (ode 132), and the image of the true Superior Man as a fish hidden in deep water from eleventh stanza of "Zheng yue" (ode 192). According to Mao, the poem now speaks of instrumentality—to govern a state you must be able to attract worthies from other states ("the stones of other mountains"), and you must not waste what falls from the trees.

This is an astonishing reading, since of the poem that praises passivity and carelessness has been made a manual for Confucian statesmanship. But the bird's state is in fact a garden where the fruit is left on the ground; it is a garden that has given up its former cultivation and succumbed to antisocial nonaction and whose inhabitants are more than happy to turn the task of "polishing jade" over to others.[40] It is, in fact, a garden more Taoist than Confucian, more akin to the intellectual landscape of Laozi and Zhuangzi than Mao Heng's. If "He ming," as Mao purports, is a poem about a Superior Man or a ruler, it must be an utterly worthless and careless leader or, perhaps, a former officer turned recluse, disappointed and broken by the world. "He ming" once again demonstrates how Mao—this time with the help of Xunzi—can only transform the self-willed poetic text into dogma by way of a metaphor that, in the final analysis, contradicts its own purpose.

Repetition

I have tried to demonstrate that Mao's exegetic project is not governed by a will to a formal analysis of the text and that it is not an interpretational model that carefully tries to unravel the text's meaning and its rhetorical structure by rigorously keeping within the text itself. On the contrary, it is a hermeneutics dictated by the pretextual demand for Confucian meaning and therefore a mode of interpretation that must succumb to violence whenever it comes upon a self-willed and integral text.

As a consequence thereof, the xing, which stands at the center of Mao's project, is a pragmatic concept rather than a formalistic one, and I have tried to demonstrate how it enabled Mao to *find* five versions of the ruler/subject metaphor in texts that, at least on the surface, seem to say nothing about Confucian hierarchies. Similarly, I tried to show that Mao's interpretations of "Fa mu" (ode 165) and "He ming" (ode 184) depended on figurative readings that, in the end, contradicted his own intentions. Of course, to argue that the *Commentary* and the tradition of Confucian hermeneutics of which it is a vital part are "far-fetched" and unfaithful to the "real" meaning of a poem is far from original in the field of modern *Shijing* study. Indeed, few claims could be more conventional. But I have conducted my argument with a specific aim in mind, namely to describe how the xing, in its first incarnation, was a tool for the simultaneous exploration and closure of the poetic text and its figurality: and also how this tension between formalism and ideology produced a pragmatic concept that—almost by accident—became the foundation of a Chinese literary hermeneutics.

I have thus far tried to demonstrate how the xing enables Mao to find certain Confucian themes in the *Odes*. But how does Mao react when a certain *Shijing* trope whose meaning has already been established is repeated in a similar context? Repetition and intertextuality, we note, are subjects that must be treated with utmost caution. For hermeneutics, the main question vis-à-vis theories of intertextuality is this: How is the meaning of a word, image, or line affected when that particular line, image, or word is used in a different context? Of course, there can be no instance of *perfect* repetition simply because the context in which a semantic unit (a "word" or "concept") is repeated necessarily differs from that first, original context. I am aware that this statement borders on the ridiculous, but it raises an important question: how far can Mao go in transforming the poems of the *Shijing*? To what extent are Mao's interpretations restrained by what the texts say on an nonallegorical, non-Confucian level, and how are they determined by the intertexts (that is, the other *Odes*) and internal parallels? To conclude simply that Mao interprets a given image differently in different contexts leads nowhere since the uniqueness of each text is always taken for granted. Instead, to prove convincingly the pragmatic and arbitrary character of Mao's xing technique it is necessary to show how Mao in his capacity as hermeneutical *auctoritas* first establishes the meaning of a certain a xing image only to deviate, paradoxically, from this "primary" meaning.

"Shan you ou" 山有樞 (ode 115)

As Zhu Xi, among others, has observed, "Shan you ou" continues and enhances the *carpe diem* theme introduced by the preceding poem, "Xishuai" (poem 114).[41]

> The mountain has thorn-elms
> the marsh white-elms
> You have robes and shirts
> but do not wear them
> You have carriages and horses
> but do not gallop them or drive them on
> When you are lifeless and dead
> other men will take pleasure in them
>
> On the mountain there are *kao* trees
> in the marsh *niu* trees
> You have your courtyard and chambers
> but do not sprinkle and sweep them
> You have your bells and drums

but do not play and strike them
When you are lifeless and dead
other men will keep them

On the mountain there are lacquer trees
in the marsh chestnut trees
You have your wine and food
why do you not daily play your lutes?
With them you should make merry
and prolong the day
When you are lifeless and dead
other men will enter your chamber[42]

山有樞
隰有榆
子有衣裳
弗曳弗婁
子有車馬
弗馳弗驅
宛其死矣
他人是愉
山有栲
隰有杻
子有廷內
弗灑弗埽
子有鍾鼓
弗鼓弗考
宛其死矣
他人是保
山有漆
隰有栗
子有酒食
何不日鼓瑟
且以喜樂
且以永日
宛其死矣
他人入室

In "Xishuai," the appearance of the cricket in the hall moved the speaker to reflect upon the passing of time. Here, the tone is more intense, almost desperate, with the narrator speaking incessantly of the transience and vanity of life and the certainty of death. No matter how fine your food and clothes are, they cannot be enjoyed in the afterlife. No matter how many bells and drums you possess, their reverberations will not be heard in the great beyond. The catalogue of clothes, carriages, horses, wine, food, lutes, bells, and drums puts these riches on display only to show their impermanence. And just like life, all three stanzas end with death and the loss of one's earthly possessions. What do the lines about the elms on the mountain and in the marsh mean? The text's parallelism ("the mountain *has* thorn-elms"; "you *have* robes and shirts") certainly suggests a relationship between natural descriptions and human action—but of what kind? One option is to understand the description of an "eternal" (or, at least, longer-lasting) landscape with trees, mountains, and marshes as a contrast to man's ephemeral existence.

From the horizon of Confucianism, "Shan you ou" is problematic in that it speaks not of moderation but of the necessity of excesses—and of enjoying life to the fullest. It is a critique of the *lack* of sensuous pleasure, a critique that originates in narrator's knowledge of human finitude. Pleasure, death, and the meaninglessness of life are certainly themes not readily approved of by Mao. He must find the righteousness hidden under the vulgar surface and therefore comments (after the first two lines): "A xing . . . A ruler who has [riches=] talents and commodities yet is unable to use them, is like the mountain and the swamp which cannot themselves use their riches [i.e., their trees—they have to be exploited by a person with knowledge]" 興也。國君有財貨而不能用, 如山隰不能自用其財。[43]

Mao downplays the themes of death and existential anxiety, transforming the desperate poem into a didactic text about statesmanship. We discern the three steps that characterize Mao's analogical xing. The static image of the elms on the mountain and in the swamp is in itself relatively unimportant. What Mao seeks are not nouns but a verb: the mountain and the swamp cannot exploit their tress just as—on an aristocratic level—the incapable lord cannot properly (that is, in accordance with the Tao of a gentleman-ruler) *exploit* his talented ministers or the commodities of his state. The mountain and the swamp thus stand in the same relation to their "riches" (their trees) as the bad lord does to the "riches" of his state. As always, the analogical xing is Mao's most cherished way of making a "profane" text speak of ritual behavior by way of arbitrary and extratextual additions. Here, Mao puts all stress on the idea of *instrumentality* since neither nature nor man is in possession of the instruments it takes to exploits their riches.

Before proceeding to the real subject under discussion, I shall make two passing remarks on Mao's analogical reading. First, nothing in the text indicates that the person spoken about is a ruler. Second, we note how the text only speaks of *material* riches (*huo* 貨), which makes Mao add that the ruler also has *cai* 財, which, as in "Jingjing zhe e" (ode 176) refers to *human* riches, referring to the worthies that could be used to make the state good.[44] Thus, by way of the little word *cai*, Mao can make "Shan you ou" speak of how the ruler does not properly use the human resources as he should, according to the rules of ritual statesmanship.

Let us return to the phenomenon of repetition in the *Odes*. We recognize the mountain/marsh figure from ode 84, "Shan you fusu." Juxtaposing the two texts, we observe how Mao's xing behaves under the pressure of, on the one hand, textual overdetermination and, on the other, the demand for Confucian meaning. In his comment on ode 84, Mao made mountain (*shan* 山) and marsh (*xi* 隰) metaphors of ruler and subject since the former word connotes height and the latter word lowness. In ode 84, the xing described a world in perfect order, where big trees grow on the high mountain and small flowers in the marsh—and where a great man occupies a high position and the smaller man a low position.

In my analysis of "Shan you fusu," I took pains to demonstrate that nothing in the text actually endorses Mao's metaphorical reading. Instead, the mountain/marsh dichotomy may be read as a literal description of the landscape where two lovers have decided to meet, or as a yin-yang metaphor for man and woman. Mao's ideological reading supported, I argued, my description of the xing as a pragmatic concept. When the mountain/marsh configuration reappears in "Shan you ou," Mao's earlier interpretational model must be discarded lest it produce an aberrant reading. Because if "mountain" and "marsh" were to be understood as metaphors of high and low positions in ode 115, the xing would describe a situation where the hierarchic equilibrium has been upset, where trees grow *both* on the mountain and in the marsh, and where *both* high and the low ranks are occupied by great men.

Mao could have used this reading to say that in good times both the ruler and his ministers are excellent men or, with a negative twist to the metaphor, that the ruler's unique power has been usurped. But such an interpretation would not have been reconcilable with the text as a whole, and Mao's alteration of the xing structure is thus overdetermined by the context. By discarding the earlier model of what I have called simple metaphor (as in ode 84) and by bringing in the extratextual analogy of the incapable ruler, Mao actually succeeds in making his reading aristocratic and wholesome, if not exactly convincing. He is able to explain how the elms in the marsh and on the mountain rhetorically connect with the ruler and his unused resources and, at the same time, distract the reader's attention from the awkward "seize the day" theme and the poem's praise of excess. But Mao pays a great price for his deviation since he produces an anomaly by making both the high mountain and the low marsh metaphors for the ruler—that unique figure who by definition is "high."

What would happen if this alteration instead is reversed; that is, if the analogical xing model employed by Mao's comment on ode 115 is applied to ode 84? The result would be a surprisingly harmonious interpretation. If the xing element of poem 84 imparts that the lord of the state cannot use his "riches," just as the mountain and the marsh are incapable of using theirs (the *fusu* tree and the lotus flowers), then lines three and four could be understood as saying that the lord is incapable of using the good man Zi Du and, instead, uses a "mad-man" as minister. In ode 84, both xing models work equally well as means of transformation of "low" meaning into "high," aristocratic and Confucian meaning.

What this intertextual reading of "Shan you ou" and "Shan you fusu" once again demonstrates is that the xing is not a formalistic tool for literary analysis. It is not enough simply to state that a poem contains a xing metaphor; Mao must go on and explicitly specify what the xing means. If not, the metaphorical relationship indicated by Mao's "this is a xing" can lead the reader to a nonsensical, devious interpretation. If Mao had not given the exact meaning of the xing element in "Shan you ou," the reader might have interpreted it according to the ruler/subject model prescribed for "Shan you fusu," and thus paired a positive description (ruler and subject are both good men) with an exhortation to pleasure—a meaningless or even obscene reading in Mao's view. Similarly, there is no formal method of deducing what a xing figure in the *Shijing* actually means, or if it is "simple" or analogical. The xing elements look identical in both poems, and at least the analogical reading can make good sense in both places.

I will round off our discussion about hermeneutical pragmatics, intertextuality and repetition with a reading of ode 126, "Ju lin" 車鄰.

> There is a carriage going *linlin*
> there is a horse with a white forehead
> while I have not yet seen my lord [gentleman]
> I give orders to the servant

> On the slope there are lacquer trees
> in the marsh there are chestnut trees
> When I have seen my lord
> we sit side by side, playing the lute
> If we do not enjoy ourselves now
> then, as time passes, we will grow old
>
> On the slope there are mulberry trees
> in the marsh there are poplars
> When I have seen my lord
> we sit side by side, playing the flute
> If we do not enjoy ourselves now
> then, as time passes, we will be dead[45]

> 有車鄰鄰
> 有馬白顛
> 未見君子
> 寺人之令
> 阪有漆
> 隰有栗
> 既見君子
> 并坐鼓琶
> 今者不樂
> 逝者其耋
> 阪有桑
> 隰有楊
> 既見君子
> 并坐鼓簧
> 今者不樂
> 逝者其亡

"Ju lin" may be read as a synthesis of "Shan you fusu" and "Shan you ou." We immediately identify the *carpe diem* theme from odes 114 ("Xishuai") and 115: this too is a poem that speaks of pleasure, togetherness, and the brevity of life. We further note how the narration of the poem follows a strictly linear temporal sequence, starting with the description of the bride's journey to see her "lord," how she gives orders to the servant in the palace and then, finally, sits down side by side with her lover. The sense of simultaneous intimacy and desperation is enhanced in the second and third stanzas as the poem proceeds from describing the manual act of playing the lute to the oral act of flute playing, and proceeds from naming "old age" (*shi* 耋, lit. "octogenarian") to naming "death" as the inevitable end of the human animal's lifecycle.

Mao, for his part, is remarkably brief, obviously understanding "Ju lin" as a description of the harmonious relationship between a lord (*junzi*) and his subject.[46] Mao indicates a xing metaphor, not after the first two lines but after the second line of the second stanza.[47] There are two reasons for this deviation from the rule that says that the xing should appear in the poem's very first line. First, horses are never used as xings in the *Commentary*—they can only refer to humans by way of metonymy and synecdoche (the first line imparts that the bride is coming because her horse is an "extension" of herself). Second, the slope/marsh dichotomy falls back on the mountain/marsh dichotomy that we know from odes 84 and 115, and the xing is here governed by intertextual overdetermination.[48] However, Mao neither explains exactly what the xing means nor indicates whether the correct interpretational method is that of a "simple" xing (as in ode 84) or that of an analogical xing (as in 115). Does this lack of hermeneutical precision stem from negligence on Mao's part or from the fact that *both* models are applicable here? At a quick glance, the latter answer seems to be correct. The simple xing of "Shan you fusu," describing ruler and subject in terms of "mountain" and "marsh" (and "great" and "small") befits "Ju lin" and its depiction of hierarchic harmony excellently.

Similarly, the analogical xing of "Shan you ou," which describes the mountain and the marsh and their "riches" while juxtaposing them to the complains about a ruler's inability to properly use his "commodities and talents," also handsomely becomes the *vanitas vanitatum* theme of "Ju lin." With reference to ode 115 and Mao's claim that the mountain (or slope) and the marsh refer metaphorically to an incapable ruler (*junzi*), the second and third stanzas of "Ju lin" invert this negativity by describing a lord that indeed does sit down to play the lute and the flute with the worthies of his state. We can, therefore, understand the *carpe diem* odes 115 and 126 as being engaged in an intertextual dialogue, with "Ju lin" responding to the negativity of "Shan you ou" with a positive image of a good lord.

However, as the analogical model is carried over from ode 115 to ode 126 we reach a bizarre result: only the metaphorical structure can be retained, not the interpretation of the xing itself. In other words, the slope and the marsh described in "Ju lin" can no longer be understood as being "unable to use their riches" but, absurdly enough, *capable* of using those valuables. Thus, if we want to use the analogical model of ode 115 we must reformulate Mao's comment as "the lord of the state is able to use his riches just as the slope and the marsh can themselves use theirs." Nature, it seems, has suddenly become able to exploit its own resources. Conversely, a reading of ode 126 that remains completely faithful to negativity of "Shan you ou" inevitably ends up as a paradox, describing the good lord who does know how to feast his subjects as a bad lord without the knowledge of how to use his riches.

My preposterous rendition of the Maoist xing in "Ju lin" once again brings to the fore the bewilderment experienced by the reader when Mao merely indicates the xing trope without supplying a guide to its exact meaning. Again, there is no certain way of formally determining if the xing should be understood as a simple metaphor, as an analogy or, indeed, according to another model. And again, C. H. Wang's suggestion that the xing element is semantically stable and possible to repeat without a change in meaning has been proven wrong—certainly so in the case of Mao Heng's xing. In deciphering a xing, intertextual comparisons and plain Occidental logic are obviously insufficient.

22

Intertextuality and Repetition

The intertextual readings of "Shan you fusu" (ode 84), "Shan you ou" (ode 115) and "Ju lin" (ode 126) that concluded the preceding chapter revealed both the pragmatism and the arbitrariness at work in Mao's xing. The xing is first and foremost a tool for endowing the high-low, yin-yang dichotomies employed by some odes with proper Confucian meaning. With its apparent focus on rhetorical analysis, the xing may resemble a formalistic instrument, but it is an instrument *with a purpose*, always on the lookout for the *yi* 義 (the moral message or guide to proper behavior) concealed by the text's vulgar, deviant and sometimes perverse surface. The arbitrary and pragmatic character of Mao's arch concept had already become increasingly clear in the preceding chapters as it was discovered that "xing" is not the name of a single and perfectly consistent interpretational model. Though fundamentally metaphorical, the "simple" and the analogical xing yield different readings. In other words, the two models can be used to make the text convey totally different messages, depending on the hermeneut's whims. What was both fascinating and frustrating in regard to the three poems analyzed above was that a study of the text itself could not determine which interpretational modus ("simple," analogical) befitted it. On the surface, the xing element in all three poems looked identical. The decision as to the text's rhetorical status, I argued, must have been made dictatorially by Mao in his role as a Confucio-ideological hermeneut. Moreover, "Ju lin" showed how Mao's "this is a xing" does little more than confuse the reader if not accompanied by a detailed manual of usage that informs him or her if the trope should be understood as a "simple" or analogical xing. The pragmatism of the xing thus revealed, the investigation of the Maoist trope can, strictly speaking, only be unidirectional—one may study and categorize the xing according to formal criteria, but one can neither study the primary text itself and determine if it contains a "xing," nor (conversely) from Mao's xing definition deduce exactly what message the trope is supposed to convey.

Another intriguing fact suggested by "Ju lin" is that Mao tends to set up rules for the correct interpretation of certain *Shijing* motifs (such as the descriptions of mountains and swamps, trees, and flowers) only to deviate from them whenever they contradict his agenda. Admittedly, these deviations are sometimes determined by the texts themselves but just as often arbitrary and determined by Mao's compulsion to Confucianize the *Odes*. This pattern of lawmaking and deviation is truly a symptom, not only of the arbitrary and pragmatic nature of Mao's xing but also of the neurotic hermeneutics that follows in the wake of the clash between an "immoral" text and a moralizing, didactical mode of interpretation.

In the present chapter I demonstrate the pragmatism, the arbitrariness, and the neurosis at the very core of Mao's xing. I do so in the simplest possible way, by selecting five prominent *Shijing* motifs and tracing their manifestations in different contexts while observing Mao's behavior and stratagems as he struggles to make motif and text cohere.

The Whirlwind

Thus runs the first stanza of ode 252, "Quan [Juan] e" 卷阿:

> There is a curving slope
> the whirlwind comes from the south
> The joyous and pleasant gentleman
> diverts himself and sings
> in order to let forth his airs[1]

> 有卷者阿
> 飄風自南
> 豈弟君子
> 來遊來歌
> 以矢其音

It is unclear exactly how Mao Heng understood the narration of "Quan e." Against Zheng Xuan (and Bernhard Karlgren), I argue that the "gentleman" (*junzi*) who sings "in order to let forth his air" in the first stanza must be identical to the man who, in the tenth and final stanza, is described as "letting forth many [sic] poems / to have them sung [by the court musicians]" 矢詩不多，維以遂歌. Mao says in his comment on the tenth stanza that "an enlightened king makes his dukes and ministers present poems to let forth their intent" 明王使公卿獻詩以陳其志.[2] We can hereby infer that, to Mao's mind, the *junzi* described by the first and last stanzas of the poem is a vassal at court.[3]

The second stanza continues with a direct address to a "you" (*er* 爾):

Great and refined is your diversion
pleasant and easy is your rest
Joyous and happy gentleman
[?] fulfill your natural years
continue [the work of] the former princes and achieve it[4]

伴奐爾游矣
優游爾休矣
豈弟君子
俾爾彌爾性
似先公酋矣

To whom is the second stanza addressed? It would seem that the penultimate line holds the answer to this question. The character *bei* 俾 is represented in my translation with a question mark. *Bei* is glossed as *shi* 使, "to make, effectuate" in Mao's comment on "Lü yi" (ode 27).[5] Thus, the line in question could be translated as "[the joyous and happy lord] will make you fulfil your natural years." In this reading, the person addressed cannot be the vassal but rather his superior, the king. The poem would then have to be understood as a eulogy to a virtuous vassal but directed to the *king*, urging him to appoint "worthies" that can fulfill his ideals.[6] Yet the two stanzas are connected by the word *you* 游, "diversion" or "pleasure," which, in the first stanza clearly refers to the vassal. It would seem logical, then to assume that the person whose diversion is described as "great and refined" in the second stanza is identical to the vassal described the moment before. If so, we would have to assume Karlgren's translation of the penultimate line as "may [*bei* 俾] you [end=] fulfil your natural years" and understand the "you" being addressed throughout the poem as the vassal himself.[7] Although "logic"—in the modern, Occidental sense—is not the most striking feature of Mao's hermeneutics, I nonetheless keep to my argument and, henceforth, read "Quan e" as a eulogy to a virtuous vassal. Consequently, the first and last stanzas both describe the *junzi's* appearance before his king. The ninth stanza describes the male and the female phoenixes, earlier defined by Mao as "humane and auspicious" (*ren rui* 仁瑞)[8], and the *wutong* tree 梧桐 as symptoms of a harmonious world:

> The male and the female phoenix call
> on that high ridge
> The *wutong* tree grows
> on that east-facing slope
> [it is] dense and luxuriant
> [the birds sing] harmoniously and in unison[9]

> 鳳皇鳴矣
> 于彼高岡
> 梧桐生矣
> 于彼朝陽
> 菶菶萋萋
> 雝雝喈喈

Mao comments: "The *wutong* . . . grows in peaceful times on the east-facing slope. When subjects exert themselves then the earth transforms itself to the utmost. When the world is harmonious and unified, the male and female phoenixes are happy and virtuous" 梧桐 . . . 太平而後生朝陽. 臣竭其力則地極其化. 天下和洽則鳳皇樂德.[10]

The harmony brought on by a good subject, or the "gentleman" in question, is thus spontaneously mirrored in nature, not only by the male and female phoenixes but also by the *wutong* tree (the "earth") which grows on the slope, facing the sun. The tenth and final stanza describes the carriages and horses that the vassal has received as ritual gifts from his king. The subject reciprocates by "presenting poems":

> The carriages of the gentleman
> [are] many and numerous
> The horses of the gentleman
> [are] well trained and swift
> He lets forth many [sic] poems
> to have them sung [by the court musicians][11]

君子之車
既庶且多
君子之馬
既閑且馳
矢詩不多
維以歌矣

Mao comments that "the superior [i.e., the king] is able to present [the gentleman] with carriages and horses . . . The enlightened king makes his dukes and ministers present poems to let forth their intent, after which he has the court musicians sing them to him 上能賜以車馬 . . . 明王使公卿獻詩以陳其志, 遂為工師之歌焉."[12]

My somewhat preliminary understanding of Mao's comment notwithstanding, it is quite clear that "Quan e" is read by Mao as a celebration of a virtuous gentleman (*junzi*). If we now return to the first stanza and the opening lines we should pose the following question: What is the relation between the whirlwind and lines three to five? By studying the poem itself we detect how "whirlwind" and "gentleman" are paralleled, as the wind comes "from the south" 自南 and the *junzi* "comes to divert" (*lai you* 來遊) himself. Since both the wind and the gentleman are described as *arriving* it would seem natural to read the former as a simple metaphor for the latter. The force and vigor of the whirlwind could be interpreted as representing the energetic gentleman who can make the state peaceful and harmonious. Yet Mao does not choose such a simple and convincing solution. In fact, he cannot do so—he must avoid at all costs a direct metaphorical connection between "whirlwind" and "gentleman." After the second line he comments: "This is a xing . . . Evil men are dispersed by the virtuous transformation, just as the whirlwind enters the curved slope" 興也. 惡人被德化而消, 猶飄風之入曲阿也.[13]

This is, first of all, an analogical xing, as the whirlwind stands in the same relation to the curved slope as the virtuous transformation does to evil men. The text never says that the whirlwind actually enters (*ru* 入) the curved slope; this is an extratextual addition that enables Mao to talk about ritual activity, namely the "virtuous transformation" (*de hua* 德化). We also observe that Mao's analogical xing depends to a certain degree on a "subliminal" trick: he is able fortify the link between "wind" (*feng* 風) and "transformation" (*hua* 化) by inconspicuously activating the secondary meaning of *feng*, "influence," and use it as a synonym for "transformation," both words thereby designating the beneficial influence on the populace exerted by a virtuous ruler. However, from the strictly literary and text-oriented position I have adopted, this is an exceptionally unconvincing xing. We understand that Mao aims at describing moral transformation as a "whirlwind" that sweeps away all evil, but the analogy becomes disturbingly disproportional since the wind does not *disperse* the slope in the same radical manner as the virtuous transformation allegedly does.[14]

But what interests us in this context is not the details of Mao's interpretational method but the reason he chooses to read the opening lines of "Quan e" as an analogy and not as a simple xing. An intertextual reading will reveal how Mao's *neurotic* interpretation in fact aims at steering the reader's attention away from the text, toward something—anything—beyond the text at hand. The whirlwind appears for the first time in Mao's comment on "Fei feng" 匪風 (ode 149). This ode starts with an image curiously not labeled a xing by Mao:

> The whirlwind blows
> the unruly carriage speeds
> [I] look at the Way of Zhou
> [My] heart is grieved[15]

> 匪風發兮
> 匪車偈兮
> 顧瞻周道
> 中心怛兮

Mine is, as always, a translation that follows Mao's idiosyncratic glosses. *Fei feng* 匪風 means literally "it is not the wind." Here, however, Mao interprets the phrase as an ellipsis of 非有道之風 "it is not a wind in possession of [a/the] way" or, more smoothly, "wayward wind."[16] He then paraphrases the opening line as "Rushing, rushing is the whirlwind" 發發飄風.[17] The phrase opening the second line *fei ju* 匪車—literally "it is not the carriage"—is also elliptic, this time of "carriage without way," "wayward carriage" 非有道之車, and the whole line is paraphrased as "the wayward carriage speeds and rushes" 偈偈疾驅.[18] The narrator, Mao suggests, is grieved because the small state he comes from "is in chaos, due to the decay of the Zhou Dynasty" 下國之亂, 周道滅也.[19] As so often, Mao cleverly fuses the textual elements together by way of a subliminal pun, here on the double meaning of *dao* 道, "way" or "road" and "(moral) Way" or "principle." Through this pun, the wind and the carriage described as having lost their "ways" turn into an description of the degenerated Zhou, as a dynasty that has also lost its Way.

Dao is the pivotal word in Mao's reading. Indeed, we can claim that the inconspicuous word *dao* governs Mao's transformation of the text's "it is not the wind" into the expanded ellipsis "wayward wind," since had he taken the first two lines at face value ("it is not the wind/carriage") the whole metaphorical correspondence between wind, carriage, and the Zhou dynasty would have been lost. We also observe how the theme of derailment, deviation, and loss of control is linked to the image of the unruly wind and, more obviously, to the image of the carriage that has lost its way and rushes toward its annihilation. As suggested in "Appendix A," the idea of a lost order and the despair that follows in its wake is also manifested in a similar motif, that of the drifting boat.

With reference to "Quan e" and to Mao's interpretation of its opening lines, it is highly intriguing that Mao so clearly defines "whirlwind" in negative terms, as a wind that does not move straight ahead but precisely whirls—it is a wind without the Way and, as such, it can be metaphorically correlated to a grieving heart and to the loss of an enlightened government. In short, "whirlwind" is an image with bad connotations, an image of despair and cruelty.[20] The reader of the *Odes* finds this cruel, devious, perverse wind in three other poems. In the fourth stanza of "He ren si" 何人斯 (ode 199), the narratrix (or narrator, depending on whether we take it as a political allegory or not) exclaims:

> What kind of man is that?
> He is a whirlwind [. . .]
> Why come to my fish-dam?
> only to make chaos in my heart[21]

> 彼何人斯
> 其為飄風 [. . .]
> 胡逝我梁
> 祇攪我心

Read in isolation, this ode speaks the language of love. The he-and-I dualism, the fishpond ("fish" connoting fertility, sexuality and wife-taking) and the girl's chaotic sentiments are testifying to passion. The narratrix remains passive: *that* man is coming *here*, to my pond, to wreak havoc in my heart.

In this fashion, "He ren si" speaks of love but also of violence. Mao comments that "the whirlwind is a wind that rises violently" 飄風暴起之風, and that *jiao* 攪 means *luan* 亂, "chaos."[22] The whirlwind, to return to my proper subject, is thus used as a metaphor for a cruel intruder, someone who stirs that which should be left un-stirred. It is a metaphor that banks on the same notion of an anarchic wind, a wind "without way," that we saw at work in "Fei feng," and here it is evident that this loss of order also involves a violent element.

In "Lu e" 蓼莪 (ode 202) the narrator laments his bad fate. In the fifth stanza the whirlwind rises again:

> The southern mountain is very difficult
> the whirlwind rushes and rushes
> Among the people there is no one who is not happy
> why am I alone harmed?[23]

南山烈烈
飄風發發
民莫不穀
我獨何害

Here, "whirlwind" is not used as a metaphor for a certain person but rather as more general, connotative image of the hardships spoken of in lines three and four. It is, however, perfectly clear that the whirlwind is associated with difficulties and suffering and thus cognate with the anarchic and violent wind in odes 149 and 199. An almost identical instance of this trope occurs in the third stanza of "Si yue" 四月 (ode 204): "The winter days are very difficult / the whirlwind rushes and rushes / Among the people there is no one who is not happy / why am I alone harmed?" 冬日烈烈, 飄風發發, 民莫不穀, 我獨何害.[24]

Informed by these intertextual readings, we return to ode 252. We now understand the bewilderment and hermeneutic despair that Mao must have experienced as he came upon "Quan e." Here is a poem that, apart from the first eight words, praises and almost obsessively celebrates a virtuous vassal, commending his good rapport with the lower officials, and lauding the harmony between vassal and king. But as can be seen in the four poems analyzed above, "whirlwind" is a trope or "image" with an exceptionally bad track record. In the comment on "Fei feng," Mao himself (driven, admittedly, by the necessity to find a "way" to metaphorize the first lines) explicitly defined it as a "wind without *dao*," a definition whose negativity was further proven by Mao's subsequent usage of it as a metaphor for the lost "way" of the "destroyed" (*mie* 滅) Zhou. In other words, commenting upon ode 149, Mao himself univocally establishes a rule for the interpretation of "whirlwind" by defining it as a "bad," destructive wind. In "He ren si," the negativity of "whirlwind" seems to be determined by the text itself.

Yet ode 199 is a love song, describing the narratrix's somewhat ambivalent stance toward her lover, the "whirlwind." In that instance, "whirlwind" could indeed have been understood in a slightly more nuanced way: as an image of a ravishing lover who arouses the simultaneous pleasure and disturbance of amorous desire. But, again, Mao's comment focuses only on the negativity of the image, speaking of "violence" and "chaos." In odes 202 and 204, the image of the whirlwind appears in juxtaposition with steep mountains, chilly winter days, despair, and suffering; that is, in a context that overdetermines our interpretation of the whirlwind as a climatic phenomenon that, on a textual level, connotes hardship. We observe that all examples speak quite clearly, explicitly and unambiguously about the negativity that Mao associates with the whirlwind. Therefore, when the whirlwind reappears in the *eulogistic* ode "Quan e," Mao cannot, indeed must not, follow his own rules and establish a metaphorical link between the wind and the vassal (*junzi*). If he had, as I suggested above, interpreted the opening imagery as a simple xing—thus equating the arriving *junzi* with the arriving whirlwind—the vassal would have been described with a metaphor that had transformed him into everything that Mao claims he is not: a chaos maker, a violent anarchist, a *man without Way*.

In such a reading, the negativity of the xing element would clash with the eulogy of the human stratum. The two strata would thus stand in ironical opposition, but it would be a deviant, nonxingish irony since it would invert the typical promise/disappointment dialectic of the ironical xing, making *nature* paint a negative, gloomy picture as a contrast to the actual harmony and joy described in the rest of the poem. Similarly, an analogical reading following the interpretational rules that we have become familiar with would also produce an aberrant reading. That is, if we equate the *high* "slope" with the "ruler" it so often represents and, furthermore, approve of the negativity inherent in the whirlwind motif we arrive at an analogy that describes a ruler being attacked, invaded, or at least threatened by a revolutionizing movement from the south, just as the slope, in Mao's own words, is "entered" by the violent and chaotic southern whirlwind. Therefore, if the simple xing would describe the "joyous and happy" gentleman as a potential revolutionary, the analogical xing would suggest that the ruler (a vassal or, perhaps, the king) himself is threatened. And this is my conclusion: the mere fact that Mao tells us that the first eight words constitute a "xing" does not in any way help the reader understand *what* that trope means. Both interpretational models would fit the natural imagery given in the opening line, and both models would yield different interpretations. It must, moreover, be emphasized that these are *not* far-fetched interpretations but logical and rational readings that simply bank on the information provided by earlier instances in the *Commentary*.

Let us, finally, return to Mao and his predicament. Through my lengthy and rather intricate intertextual explorations I have traced the whirlwind motif and demonstrated the negativity bestowed upon it, both by the texts themselves and by Mao's metatextual comments. When the motif finally occurs in ode 252 it is with an assembly of bad connotations ("lacking *dao*," "violent," "chaotic," etc.) that Mao must downplay lest they interfere with the eulogy that he considers "Quan e" to be. How does he go about it? He cannot let the description of the whirlwind stand unanswered and unmetaphorized since its "bad track record" would be enough to disturb the eulogy. Nor can he make the motif into a simple xing (for obvious reasons) or use "slope" as a metaphor for a "ruler." He has no alternative but to go *extra textum* to create an analogy that actually attempts to dupe the reader and steer the reader's attention from the text. I said earlier that Mao's analogical interpretation of this xing was "exceedingly unconvincing," yet it is fully logical in its own right. Knowing that the whirlwind is considered a "bad" wind, Mao uses one of his subliminal tricks and *retains* the "badness" inherent in the xing motif but *transfers* it to the "evil men" 惡人 allegedly "dispersed" by the virtuous transformation.

Mao has now "satisfied" the naive reader who came upon the whirlwind motif and expected violence, chaos or plain evil to follow in its wake. Still, the power with which Mao's xing is invested cannot hide the fact that this xing trope is unfortunate and unconvincing since it still describes the "virtuous transformation" as a whirlwind; that is, as a "bad," anarchic, and decisively unvirtuous wind.

One important question remains that concerns the interrelated subjects of intertextual and intratextual overdetermination: is the analogical reading performed by Mao determined by the text itself? Differently put, does Mao deviate from the intertextual rule ("whirlwind equals negativity") because the eulogy-theme is "stronger" than the negativity suggested by the xing motif? These questions are probably both meaningless and inadequate since they presume that Mao's hermeneutics is not arbitrarily extratextual but indeed follows the text or intertexts rigorously when deciding on a poem's theme. We may demonstrate the arbitrariness of Mao's interpretation simply by suggesting an alternative reading of the xing element that would follow Mao's own rules. It would, I hypothesize, be possible to retain both the negativity implied by the opening lines *and* the eulogy by claiming that "Quan e" praises a virtuous "lord" (or vassal) who, unknowingly, joyous, and happy, faces a threat from the south.

Another, more stimulating, option would be to understand the xing-element as the actual message that the virtuous vassal "lets forth" in poetry to his king—a metaphorical warning about revolutionaries in the south ready to invade the country and usurp the throne. Both interpretations would be analogical xings and take "slope" as a metaphor for the vassal/king and "whirlwind" as a metaphor for "stirring" men—revolutionaries—or as a metaphor for "chaos" in general. The readings may be far-fetched but certainly not more so than Mao's own.

What has this study of "Quan e" and its intertexts proven, with regard to the pragmatism and arbitrariness that I have claimed are dominant features of Mao's Confucian hermeneutics? First, we have learnt that there is no absolute continuity in Mao's reading of imagery. "Whirlwind" is fully and clearly defined in negative terms, as a violent, chaotic, and disruptive natural phenomenon; yet Mao ends up using it as a metaphor for what by definition is benevolent and establishes order—the virtuous transformation. This semantic instability stands in blatant opposition to C. H. Wang's implicit idea of *Shijing* imagery as repeatable without a change of meaning or rhetorical mode and also to the constancy with which Mao treats the "drifting boat" motif.[25] Commenting on "Quan e," Mao uses the xing to deviate from the seemingly law-bound metaphoricity of the whirlwind motif. This further proves that Mao's xing is a pragmatic tool that enables the hermeneut to capriciously highlight and downplay whatever parts of the text he wants to stand out or be forgotten. It allows him to transform the text's elements until he can present a poem that fits his purposes. Second, we have again been able to conclude that a mere indication of the rhetorical structure of a given ode ("this is a xing") does no more than suggest the presence of a trope or figure that can be interpreted in an almost endless variety of ways.

If by "xing" Mao indicates that a certain layer of the text is figurative rather than literal, it is also *he* who, arbitrarily and dictatorially, chooses which kind of figure ("simple," analogical) is at work in the text, and it is he who endows this figure with meaning. The reader can neither deduce if

308 | The Origins of Chinese Literary Hermeneutics

the xing is to be understood as "simple" or analogical, nor what it actually means simply by studying the text and its figuration. The interpretation of the trope must come from a hermeneutic *auctoritas*, in this case Mao Heng. From this authoritarian hermeneutics stems the semantic instability that I have demonstrated above—the reader must not be allowed to draw his or her own conclusions, not even by following Mao's own intertextually given instructions, because that could lead to a deviant understanding of a text conceived of as a "storehouse of righteousness." To reach this textual wisdom, to make the *Odes* into a manual for ritual behavior and statesmanship, Mao must constantly and arbitrarily deviate from the laws he himself had laid down.

The Sun and the Moon

We have come upon evidence of Mao's hermeneutic capriciousness several times before. Why, I asked previously, are the sun and the moon understood as metaphors of ruler and subject in "Dong fang zhi ri" (ode 99) but not in "Ri yue" (ode 29)?[26] As we have already analyzed the intertextual relationship between these two poems and the motives for Mao's deviation it will here suffice with a short recapitulation. First and foremost, Mao's deviation from the previous model ("sun" and "moon" understood nonmetaphorically as concrete objects) cannot be warranted by the text. "Dong fang zhi ri" is an obvious love song, explicitly speaking of the girl who "is in my chamber" and keeping quiet about Confucian power structures.[27] There is therefore no formal justification for Mao's metaphorical reading, which consequently means that Mao has arbitrarily and dictatorially decided that "sun" and "moon" are to be interpreted as a ruler/subject metaphor. That Mao's reading is "arbitrary" with regard to the "literal meaning" of the text does not, of course, mean that it lacks a logic of its own. Quite the contrary: by way of this figurative reading Mao is able in one fell swoop to obliterate the love-theme by metaphorizing "sun" and "moon" (temporal markers signifying the length of time passed in the amorous "chamber") and in its stead Confucianize the text by making the celestial bodies metaphors of the ruler and his subject.

In this double and admittedly elegant act of downplaying the theme of love while highlighting the theme of an ideal Confucian order, Mao's pragmatic, arbitrary, and dictatorial hermeneutics is easily discernible. It is evidence of a model of interpretation that must *find* its stipulated themes at the cost of disturbing the integrity of the text. It is, in other words, a profoundly ideological and violent mode of interpretation.

The Rooster's Crowing

In Mao's comment on "Xishuai" (ode 114), the cricket's appearance in the hall is interpreted as a sign of the arrival of autumn. In this context, "cricket" is a signans with double signata, as on the one hand it signifies an insect and, on the other hand, a time of year. The cricket's appearance in the hall is, furthermore, a natural, automatic, and nonarbitrary sign; in other words, it is an *extratextual* sign that outside and before any text signals the beginning of autumn. To the same category of signs belongs the rooster. Its crowing signifies—automatically and nonarbitrarily—the arrival of morning and a new day; it is a natural and spontaneous sign and not a culturally determined, conventional one. In the *Shijing*, the rooster crows in three odes, namely "Nü yue ji ming" 女曰雞鳴 (ode 82), "Ji ming" 雞鳴 (ode 96) and "Feng yu" 風雨 (ode 90). Indeed, commenting upon the former two poems, Mao interprets the crowing rooster as a sign of "morning" but deviates from such a model in his reading of "Feng yu." Interestingly, all three odes can be read as love songs; but whereas odes 82 and 96 can be made to speak of, respectively, the feasting of fine guests and a zealous couple, the much shorter "Feng yu" is unambiguously a love song:

> The wind and rain are cold
> the rooster crows *jiejie*
> When I have seen [my] gentleman
> how can [I] not be happy[28]

> 風雨淒淒
> 雞鳴喈喈
> 既見君子
> 云胡不夷

Nothing in this stanza (or in the two very similar ones that follow it) seems to call for a figurative interpretation. Lines three and four are suggestive yet quite clear, speaking of the happiness that comes from the meeting with a "gentleman." We recognize the third line's "When I have seen my gentleman" 既見君子 as part of a stock phrase ("when I have not seen my gentleman . . . when I have seen my gentleman") that speaks of the anticipation, tension, and relief that accompany love and passion. The ode, furthermore, opposes the "happiness" that emerges from the amorous intimacy with the chilling rain and wind that rage outside. The rooster's crowing, finally, signals that morning has come, thereby subtly suggesting that the narratrix and her beau have spent the night together. We also note that *jiejie* 喈喈 is glossed, in Mao's comment on "Ge tan" (葛覃, ode 2), as a bird's "long-spreading" and "harmonious" calls, a definition that certainly speaks in favor of an "amorous" reading.[29] At the same time, we know that such a lowly reading would be nonsensical and deviant according to the hermeneutic rules that Mao obeys and establishes. Consequently, Mao comments after the second line: "This is a xing. Although the wind and rain are cold the rooster keeps the time, crowing *jiejie*-like" 興也. 風且雨淒淒然, 雞猶守時而鳴喈喈然.[30] Now the poem speaks not of love but of the more easily digestible themes of duty and timeliness. Simultaneously, the rooster is no longer a temporal indicator—conveying the awkward suggestion that the narratrix and the gentleman have spent the night together—but a metaphorical paragon of duty. And although Mao does not link the rooster vehicle to a specific tenor (satisfied, perhaps, with steering the reader's attention away from the theme of love), the *Minor Preface*, Zheng Xuan and Kong Yingda are certainly right in taking the time-keeping fowl as a metaphor for the *junzi* who "does not alter his measures" 不變改其節度 in "chaotic times" 亂世.[31] The fact that Mao's metaphorical interpretation is uncalled for by the text, and that Mao, precisely by way of the xing trope, arrives at a reading that is so obviously Confucian in character (downplaying love and highlighting virtue) again illustrates that the xing is a pragmatic tool for text-transformation rather than a tool for a formal analysis of the text.

Mao's arbitrary interpretation of the rooster motif becomes even clearer if we compare "Feng yu" with "Ji ming" (ode 96):

> The rooster has already crowed
> the courtyard is already full [of officials]
> But it was not the rooster that crowed
> It was the sound of blue flies[32]

雞既鳴矣
朝既盈矣

非雞則鳴
蒼蠅之聲

That this is predominantly a love song is verified by the third stanza's "it is sweet to lie dreaming with you" 甘與子同夢: this expression of intimacy, amorous contemplation, and reverie cannot be metaphorized into a dialogue between ruler and subject.[33] The first stanza is a variant of the "that which seems to be but is not" (*si er fei*) figure that occurs so frequently in the *Odes* and in the *Commentary*. That it was not the rooster that crowed but only the sound of blue flies means, of course, that morning is not yet here and that "we" can go on "dreaming." Mao, however, pretends not to notice the sensuous undertones but simply comments: "When the rooster crows the wife arises; when the court-yard is full the lord arises" 雞鳴而夫人作，朝盈而君作.[34] This is not a xing since, according to Mao, there is no figurality at work in "Ji ming"; yet he has transformed a text that itself speaks of lust, pleasure, and sweet dreaming into a description of virtuous behavior. It is easy to see that the metaphorical model used in "Feng yu" would be of little use here since it risks turning the poem that Mao has decided is a description of virtue into a critique of untimeliness and degeneration.

The Qi school puts a different spin on the poem by claiming that it describes a rooster that has lost its timeliness (*shi shi* 失時) and entrusted the task of signifying "morning" to the blue flies.[35] Using the rhetorical model of "Feng yu," the untimely rooster can now be understood as a metaphor for the similarly untimely "gentleman" who turns his back to the world in order to go on dreaming with his partner. This is not Mao's reading, but it is perfectly conceivable and fits both the poem itself, Mao's simple xing model and the Confucian agenda (as proven by the Qi-school reading). It is a reading that, in fact, tallies better with the actual poem than Mao's strained interpretation.

Why, then, does Mao metaphorize "Feng yu" and not "Ji ming"? Since both models would yield a reading compatible with the Confucian program, this is a question that lies beyond both my reach and the scope of the present project. It suffices to have demonstrated that Mao used the xing model to appropriate ode 90 for Confucian ends and that ode 96 (which is not a xing) could very well have been subject to a critical, xingish reading. What is thereby proven is that Mao uses the xing arbitrarily. He uses it pragmatically to make the text Confucian, and in a way that cannot be deduced or predicted from a study of the text in isolation.

The Solitary Pear Tree

The phrase "There is a solitary pear tree" 有杕之杜 occurs in three odes (119, 123 and 169) that all thematize loneliness and longing, and by stressing different elements in this "cluster" Mao provides three variant interpretations.

> There is a solitary pear tree
> its leaves and branches not joining [sic]
> Alone I walk, and forlorn
> are there no other people?
> Still, they do not equal my siblings
> Oh, you travelers
> why do you not join company with me?
> A person who has no brothers –
> why do you not help me?
>
> There is a solitary pear tree
> its leaves are flourishing
> Alone I walk and without anyone to rely on
> are there no other people?
> But they are not equal to kinsmen
> Oh, you travelers
> why do you not join company with me?
> A person who has no brothers –
> why do you not help [me]?[36]

有杕之杜
其葉湑湑
踽踽獨行
豈無他人
不如我同父
嗟行之人
胡不比焉
人無兄弟
胡不佽焉
有杕之杜
其葉菁菁
獨行睘睘
豈無他人

不如我同姓
嗟行之人
胡不比焉
人無兄弟
胡不佽焉

The imagery of "Di du" (ode 119) offers, it seems, its reader no particular resistance. The image, or "motif," of the solitary pear tree corresponds metaphorically to the lonesome wanderer, the *tertium comparationis* of this simple metaphor being "loneliness." We observe, furthermore, how the text opposes the stationary tree to the ambulatory wanderer, and that the flourishing leaves, as in "Tao yao" (ode 6), may connote "bride" or "bridal journey" as a metaphor for a beautiful, "flourishing" bride or a temporal marker indicating that the time for mating has come.

Mao's terse comment suggests a reading akin to ours since he comments after the second line: "This is a xing. *Di* 杕 means solitary-looking . . . *Xuxu* means that the leaves and the branches are not joining. *Juju* means that one has no relatives. *Jingjing*-like the leaves flourish" 興也. 杕特貌 . . . 湑湑, 枝葉不相比也. 踽踽, 無所親也. 菁菁葉盛.³⁷

We immediately notice how skilfully Mao coordinates the natural and human strata of the poem by glossing *xuxu* 湑湑 as "leaves and branches not joining," thereby making both xing lines speak of loneliness and alienation. Indeed, Mao's very words "not mutually *joining*" 不相比 echo and allude to the poem's "why do you not *join* me" 胡不比焉. It would seem, then, as if Mao took *xu* 湑 as a loan word for *shu* 疏, "sparse" or "scattered."³⁸ However, as Bernhard Karlgren has most emphatically pointed out, *xu* is glossed as *sheng* 盛 ("flourish") in Mao's comment on "Shangshang zhe hua" (ode 214) which makes Karlgren contend that the text has been corrupted, and that a *bu* 不 ("not") has erroneously been added.³⁹ The original, uncorrupted version of Mao's comment on this poem should thus read "*xuxu* means that the leaves and branches are joining"—meaning that the tree is *dense*—a gloss that would correspond better to the "flourishing" leaves described in the second stanza. Yet knowing the irregularities of the *Commentary* and the "subliminal" interpretations employed therein, it is most likely that Mao did understand *xuxu* as a description of a tree with its leaves and branches far apart, thus strengthening the already existing metaphor of the lonesome narrator as a "solitary pear tree."

Conversely, it is unlikely that he would have given such an extensive gloss on *xuxu* if it simply meant *sheng*, "flourishing." Lastly—and I applaud the reader who has followed me in exploring these intricacies—that the leaves and the branches are "far apart" does not, of course, in any way exclude the possibility that the leaves themselves are flourishing. It is, therefore, advisable to dismiss Karlgren's modern, linguistic, and logical attempt to make the text integral and hermeneutically wholesome as the kind of error so easily made if one does not recognize the arbitrariness of the *Commentary*. The deviation from *xu* ("flourish") to *xuxu* ("far apart") should instead be regarded as a telling example of the semantic instability that is the result of Mao's pragmatic hermeneutics.

With a high degree of certainty Mao's interpretation of "Di du" may thus be reconstructed as a simple xing, taking the *solitary* tree as a metaphor for the *lonely* traveler, and the distance between the leaves and the branches as yet another metaphor for the wanderer who finds herself (or himself) at a distance from her family, the latter metaphor banking on the idea that a family stems from a common "root." It is, moreover, important that we note that the loneliness inflicted on the narratrix (or narrator) is not of an amorous kind—the people separated are not lovers but members of a family.

However, when the "solitary pear tree" reappears in "You di zhi du" 有杕之杜 (ode 123), the narratrix of that ode is longing for a lover:

> There is a solitary pear tree
> it grows to the left of the road
> That gentleman!
> Approaching, he is willing to visit me
> In the core of my heart I love him
> what shall I give him to drink and eat?
>
> There is a solitary pear tree
> it grows at the twist of the road
> That gentleman!
> Approaching, he is willing to come and play
> In the core of my heart I love him
> what shall I give him to drink and eat?[40]

有杕之杜
生在道左
彼君子兮
噬肯適我
中心好之

曷飲食之
有杕之杜
生在道周
彼君子兮
噬肯來遊
中心好之
曷飲食之

Ode 123 unambiguously uses the terminology reserved for amorous discourse in the *Odes*. The I-and-he dualism and the "love" felt "in the core of my heart" are sufficient evidence that this is a poem expressing a woman's desire for her "gentleman." The eating and drinking mentioned in the last lines of both stanzas also connote sensuous joy and, possibly, also pleasures of a sexual kind (since fish eating corresponds metaphorically to wife taking in ode 138). That pleasure is the main incentive for the gentleman's journey becomes clear as we compare the fourth line of both stanzas: the former says that "approaching, he is willing to visit me" 噬肯適我 whereas the latter line presents the reason for his visit by substituting "me" (*wo* 我) with "play" (*you* 遊): "Approaching, he is willing to come and play" 噬肯來遊. On a rhetorical level, then, the narratrix and pleasure (or "play," *you*) are equated and interchangeable. Like "Di du" (119), this is a poem about longing for someone who is absent and must undertake a journey to get here.

However, in opposition to the former poem, the man wished for is not a relative but a lover. The spatial difference between narratrix and lover is emphasized by the deictics: *that* gentleman is *coming* to me. If we return to the image of the solitary pear tree that opens the poem it would be logical to understand it too as a simple metaphor for the solitary girl who narrates the poem. Yet such a simple and straightforward reading would only enhance the obviously un-Confucian theme of passionate, amorous longing. Mao comments enigmatically after the second line: "This is a xing. The sunny left side of the road is an appropriate place to rest" 興也. 道左之陽, 人所宜休息也.[41] Mao's comment is obscure—as is my attempt at a translation—and has produced many intricate explanations from the Confucian commentators after him. The minutiae of this tradition notwithstanding, what interests us here is that Mao uses the xing as a turning away—indeed a *tropos*—from the metaphorical model we saw at work in his earlier comment.[42] "This is a xing" indicates that the pear tree is to be understood figuratively and in line with its earlier use as a simple metaphor. Yet by claiming that the left side of the road—the place of the pear tree—is an "appropriate" place for a rest, Mao underlines the concretion of the pear tree motif and downplays its metaphoricity: it is a literal tree, and it is to be found in a "literal," geographically definable place. If the xing element had been left without a comment then the reader would have had no choice but to read "You di zhi du" as the love poem it seems to be on the surface. By way of the xing Mao tricks the reader, steering his or her attention away from the text and the simple xing that he *himself* has prescribed intertextually.

What, then, does the second line about the "left side of the road" really mean? Perhaps it has no deeper meaning; perhaps it should be allowed to remain a rest or leftover, undigested by the ravenous hermeneut. Or perhaps Mao's emphasis on "appropriateness" (*yi* 宜) is neurotic and reveals an anxiety that the poem is really about inappropriateness. We know that Mao is wont to pun on the double meaning of *dao* 道 ("road" or "[moral] Way"). If one takes into consideration the explicit love theme and the possibility that "pear tree" connotes longing, then the image of the pear tree "by the side of the *dao*" and "where the *dao* twists" could be interpreted as a metaphor for the longing, passionate girl who has strayed from the true Way, from the correct *dao*, leading an unsavory life beside the norm, where normal behavior "twists."

When the pear tree motif resurfaces again in ode 169 ("Di du"), it bears a striking resemblance to the xing of ode 119 ("Di du"), but yields a very different interpretation by Mao:

> There is a solitary pear tree
> fruit-like its fruits [sic]
> The king's service must not be defective
> following one upon the other are our days
> The time of the year is the tenth month
> the women's hearts are pained
> but the soldiers will have leisure[43]

有杕之杜
有睆其實
王事靡盬
繼嗣我日
日月陽止
女心傷止
征夫遑止

"Di du" tells of the difficulties of warfare, not an uncommon theme in the *Odes*.⁴⁴ Just as ode 119, this poem starts off with an instance of the "solitary pear tree" motif, and proceeds to tell of longing, sorrow, and of separation from one's family. As so often, it is hard to distinguish the voices that narrate the story, but the poem seems to relate the hardships of warfare from both the women's and the soldiers' perspectives. The first stanza's "following one upon the other are our days" could be uttered by both parties. However, the second stanza's "*Our* hearts are grieved" and the subsequent "the *women's* hearts are grieved" must either mean that the soldiers narrate the stanza or that some parts of the poem are narrated by a third person: an anonymous voice or chorus. In the third stanza, however, the picking of the *ji* plants suggests that the textual voice now belongs to the longing women, since plant picking is normally conceived of as a female task.⁴⁵ The fourth stanza, finally, should be understood as describing the anxiety of the waiting women: when their men do not return on time they consult the various oracles ("The tortoise-shell oracle and the milfoil oracle are in accord / the assembled men say that they are near / the soldiers are close at hand" 卜筮偕止, 會言近止, 征夫邇止).⁴⁶ It would seem, then, as if "Di du" is narrated by a conglomerate of voices, a fact that does not seem to bother Mao in the least. With reference to ode 119, the image of the stationary and solitary pear tree that abounds with fruits and luxurious leaves reads as a poignant metaphor for the soldiers' wives alone at home. Yet it is here, in comparison with ode 119, that Mao's technique of highlighting and downplaying resurfaces.

In contrast to the simple xing of ode 119, Mao here hints at an analogical and ironical trope: "This is a xing . . . the solitary pear tree gets to flourish and bear fruit on time. The soldiers toil and suffer bitterness [and] do not [get to] fullfil their heavenly [given] nature" 興也 . . . 杕杜猶得其時蕃滋. 役夫勞苦不得盡其天性.⁴⁷ In this analogical reading, fruit bearing and flourishing stand in the same relation to the pear tree as does the "fulfillment of one's heavenly nature" to the soldier. It is an ironical xing, of course, since the timeliness displayed and promised by the first lines is denied and inverted by lines three and four. Mao's analogical xing model, as we know, is characterized by his emphasizing human activity rather than static natural imagery, which is evident in "Di du" (ode 169) since the blossoming and fruit-bearing pear tree is, in itself, of minor importance. What Mao's analogical reading aims at is the idea that, under ideal circumstances, nature and man "obtain" (*de* 得), respectively, their fruit-bearing capacity and "heavenly nature," and this idea connects, moreover, logically to the theme of timeliness. Thus, for the flourishing pear tree could be substituted virtually any other flourishing plant, tree or vegetable. Similarly, the solitude of the "solitary pear tree"—the *tertium comparationis* in Mao's reading of ode 119—is also a completely irrelevant piece of information. The flourishing pear tree has one task and that is to signify "timeliness" as a contrast to the unlucky and untimely soldiers who are forced to transgress, or cut short, their stipulated time.

But what precisely has generated Mao's analogical xing? Where did Mao find the text's hermeneutic center? If the lonesome act of walking was what made Mao read the "solitary pear tree" as a simple metaphor in ode 119, and if the distance between the narratrix and her relatives was what made him come up with the "deviant" reading of *xu* 湑 ("flourish") as *shu* 疏, "sparse," then Mao's analogical reading of ode 169 emanates from the third line of the fourth stanza: "The stipulated time is past and they [the soldiers] have not come" 期逝不至, describing untimeliness and the soldiers' unfortunate incapability to live out their heavenly given destiny. As soon as Mao has decided that this is the text's dominant theme, he deviates from the previous, "simple" xing model that would understand the solitary tree as a representation of the lonely soldier's wife. Instead, he *finds* the analogy between pear tree and soldier that makes the xing speak directly about what Mao conceives as the poem's message. By the same token, the shift from simple xing to analogical xing, from the theme of loneliness to the theme of (un)timeliness, also depersonalizes "Di du" (169), turning the grief and frustration of the soldier and his wife into a more abstract and ideologically correct discussion about timeliness and statesmanship.

We have, thus, one example of a "simple" xing (ode 119), one example (ode 123) where the xing is obviously used to downplay the metaphoricity that might lead the reader to a meaningless or "perverse" reading and one example of an analogical xing (ode 169). But how about the crucial question of overdetermination? My demonstration has failed if I am unable to prove the arbitrariness of Mao's readings. In other words, if the Maoist reading is *univocally* warranted by the text then I can no longer accuse him of being arbitrary. I have demonstrated that the opening lines of all three poems can be read as simple xings. With regard to ode 169, one could criticize Mao's analogical reading for being far-fetched, extratextual, and unduly ideological, yet it does tally with the theme of untimeliness. There is thus no violent, head-on contradiction of the kind found in Mao's treatment of the whirlwind motif.

Nonetheless, by comparing ode 119 with ode 169 I suggest that we clearly perceive the arbitrariness at work in Mao's xingish readings. Ode 169 can be read according to the "simple" xing model, but could Mao have read ode 119 as an analogical xing? It is, I argue, entirely possible to understand ode 119 as a poem narrated by an "untimely" traveler, perhaps a soldier, who does not get to fulfill his heavenly ordained destiny, as a contrast to the timely tree that blossoms in the right season.[48] The arbitrariness and pragmatism, then, lies in the fact that both models can be applied to both poems, proving that there is no certainty in Mao's xing and that it is Mao Heng who ultimately chooses which interpretational model fits which poem. One model yields a poem about loneliness and the other a poem about (un)timeliness. It is true that both themes befit both poems, but the difference is nonetheless there, both with regard to interpretational methodology and textual content.

The Perturbed Waters

Mao Heng's interpretation of the phrase "perturbed waters" (*yang zhi shui* 揚之水), which appears in and lends it name to three *Shijing* poems, reveals his arbitrary hermeneutics but not the motifs behind his deviations. It occurs for the first time in ode 68:

> Perturbed waters
> do not float away bundled firewood
> That person there
> is not with me defending Shen
> Yearning . . . yearning . . .
> what month shall I return home?[49]

揚之水
不流束薪
彼其之子
不與我戍申
懷哉懷哉
曷月予還歸哉

Mao labels the first two lines a xing but remains silent about the meaning of the trope.[50] Even if we cannot know its exact meaning, it obviously describes a state of weakness and inability, perhaps a state of frustration and fatigue. It is a suggestive image, cast as a "that which seems to be but is not" trope, and intimates that the fretful water appears powerful and vigorous but is, in fact, so weak that it cannot even float away firewood or, as in the following stanzas, thornwood (*chu* 楚) or willows (*pu* 蒲). We also observe that the negativity of the xing ("cannot float away") is mirrored by the negativity of line four ("is not with me"). It is, thus, reasonably clear that the xing element in ode 68 builds on similitude and is used as a metaphor for weakness and inability.[51] However, what interests us is that this phrase is repeated in ode 92 as—or so Mao claims—a rhetorical question:

> Perturbed waters
> do not float away bundled thornwood
> Few are we brothers
> there are just you and me
> Do not believe people's words
> people are truly deceiving you[52]

> 揚之水
> 不流束楚
> 終鮮兄弟
> 維予與女
> 無信人之言
> 人實誑女

With regard to the first two lines, Mao comments: "Stirred waters, could you [really] say that it could not wash away bundled thornwood?" 激揚之水, 可謂不能流漂束楚乎.[53] What was formerly a statement about the weakness of fretful waters has now become—in identical phrasing—a rhetorical question that asserts the forcefulness of the perturbed waters. The phrase must now be understood as an absurd statement, as a joke at the expense of a fool, namely the brother addressed in the poem: do not believe what people tell you about fretful waters not being able to float away a bundle of thornwood, they are merely tricking you. The heart of the matter is, of course, that the motif of the stirred waters makes a general statement about nature, and if stirred water cannot wash away firewood in one poem then how could it do so in another? Nature has, it appears, taken a sudden leap. In Mao's defense, the interpretation of ode 92—as expounded here—makes good sense, and there are no apparent ideological motives behind his contradictory interpretations of the two poems. Yet the paradox remains. It would have been possible, as Kong Yingda has suggested, for Mao to read the xing element in ode 68 as a rhetorical question, saying that "of course stirred waters can carry a bundle of firewood, and of course the king's regime should be able to provide grace and beneficence for the populace," but nothing in the *Commentary* suggests that Mao took the opening lines of ode 68 as a rhetorical question.[54] Indeed, the difference in rhetorical structure is explicitly indicated by the fact that Mao defined the opening lines of ode 68—but not those of ode 92—as a xing.

What we have here, then, are two manifestations of the same motif—bundled firewood/thornwood in perturbed waters—and two fundamentally different interpretations thereof. Since the motif make a normative statement about nature, which should *logically* be true in all contexts, it is hard to explain this paradox as anything else but the outcome of the sheer and heedless pragmatism that governs Mao's interpretational program. Yet considering the insufficient information provided by the *Commentary* we should perhaps in this case give Mao the benefit of the doubt and see his readings here as a symptom: not so much of an ideologically determined arbitrariness but of carelessness and the lack of a systematized hermeneutics.

When the motifs recurs in ode 116 only the first half of the phrase remains:

> [In] the perturbed waters
> white stones bright and shining
> The dress is white with red embroidery
> I follow you to Wu
> When I have seen my lord
> how could I not be happy![55]

> 揚之水
> 白石鑿鑿
> 素衣朱襮
> 從子于沃
> 既見君子
> 云何不樂

After the second line of the first stanza, Mao comments: "This is a xing. *Zuozuo* means 'bright and shining'" 興也. 鑿鑿然鮮明貌.[56] The opening lines are then slightly varied in the second and third stanzas, describing the "clean white" and "limpid (sic)" stones.[57] After the third line Mao says that the clothes referred to were worn by the vassals (*zhuhou*).[58] Consequently, we must understand the xing, and its description of the pure white stones in the stirred-up waters, as a metaphor for the white clothes (or as a metonymy for the person who wore them). It is a straightforward xing in which the white and shining stones are used as a simple metaphor. The "perturbed waters" from which the poem takes its title plays only a minor role in the metaphorical process and has, therefore, nothing to do with Mao's rhetorical interpretations of odes 68 and 92.

I have argued that the logic governing Mao's exegesis of the *Odes* in general, and his usage of the xing in particular, is not that of a formalist literary analysis. Notwithstanding the lack of what we, gradually and for specific historical reasons, have come to understand as the "logic" of an aesthetic literary analysis, it has become increasingly clear that Mao's readings of the *Odes* are indeed law-bound and "logical" when regarded as ideological interpretations that were made in order to *find* the "righteousness" that Mao knows resides under the text's surface. Therefore, the words that I have used so abundantly in this chapter—"arbitrary," "pragmatic," "contradictory"—are not meant to accuse Mao of an "illogical" mode of interpretation; they merely illustrate the gap between my text-centered and formalist analysis and Mao's Confucio-ideological hermeneutics.

What my observation of this gap and of Mao's "pragmatism" calls attention to is, in fact, the contradiction inherent in the present project, as it is not possible to give a full account of Mao's Confucian, ideological, and pragmatic hermeneutics simply by way of a formal analysis. The attempt to categorize Mao's xing has been successful only insofar as it has revealed the fundamental and quite different rhetorical models employed under that famous name. Nonetheless, such a formal categorization could never reveal the motives and rules that lie behind Mao's elusive xing and, consequently, it is only in light of my own text-centered analysis that Mao's pragmatic hermeneutics seems "arbitrary."

In this chapter, I have argued that Mao's pragmatism and antiformalism are displayed in two ways. First, by the well-demonstrated fact that the reader can neither deduce whether a text contains a xingish trope from a simple study of the text itself nor, conversely, deduce the *meaning* of such a figure (as indicated by Mao) by looking at the text. In both cases, a hermeneutical *auctoritas* has to step in as arbiter. In fact, since the "xing" comprises at least two different metaphorical models, we can hardly call it a "formalist" concept at all. When it occurs in the *Commentary* it does not point to a specific figuration—to a "simple" analogical or ironical *xing*—but merely indicates that the expression be taken in some sort of nonliteral sense.

Furthermore, the permutations of the five prominent *Shijing* motifs we have studied and Mao's behavior as he struggles to make text coherent with *Ru* decorum, further proved Mao's pragmatism. In his treatment of the whirlwind, the sun and the moon, the rooster's crowing, the solitary pear tree and the stirred waters, Mao set up definitive rules for the interpretation of a given motif only to break those rules when the image reappeared in a context that, from a "formalist" point of view, did not call for a deviation. In most cases Mao's neurotic and "illogical" reading could be convincingly explained as symptoms of the compulsion to Confucianize an obviously non-Confucian text. In some cases, where both the "simple" and analogical *xing* models would have aligned with the text, Mao's deviations simply did not seem law-bound at all.

The Kudzu and the Picking of Plants

I have claimed repeatedly that pragmatism must be the key word in any description of Mao's project, and since the hermeneutic arbitrariness concomitant with such pragmatism is all-pervading this portion of my investigation may stop here. It would be beyond the point, and beyond the taxonomic impulse, to produce a list of Mao's arbitrary twists and turns. I will instead round off my discussion about Maoist pragmatism by showing the complexity of Mao's *Commentary*, how Mao's "this is a xing" often involves an intricate net of interrelated metaphors, and how problematic—not to say impossible—it is for the reader to discern all these layers of figurality. At the center of my attention stand two themes that occur frequently in the *Odes* and that occupy a position between xing and nonxing: the kudzu and plant picking.

THE KUDZU (GE 葛)

The kudzu, as we know, is a highly prolific plant and in the *Odes* its fibers are sometimes described as a material used to make items such as simple clothes and shoes. Its botanical name (named for Linnaeus's disciple Carl Peter Thunberg) is *Pueraria thunbergiana*, and it is sometimes translated as "dolichos creeper." In "Ge sheng" 葛生 (ode 124), the kudzu appears in the opening lines:

324 | The Origins of Chinese Literary Hermeneutics

> The kudzu grows and covers the thorn
> the *lian* creeper spread to the wilderness
> My beautiful one is not here
> with whom can I associate?—Alone I dwell
> The horn-pillow is beautiful
> the brocade coverlet is bright
> My beautiful one is not here
> with whom can I associate?—Alone I have my mornings.[59]

> 葛生蒙楚
> 蘞蔓于野
> 予美亡此
> 誰與獨處
> 角枕粲兮
> 錦衾爛兮
> 予美亡此
> 誰與獨旦

How does nature connect to human activity here? Perhaps the description of the prolific plants should be understood as a symptom of distress and depression: when "my beautiful one" is gone (or, with certain annotators, "dead") the protagonist dwells alone in "our" house, heartbroken and apathetic. The garden is neglected and dilapidated and the weed spreads unhampered—a description that mirrors the protaganist's dilapidated state of mind. Given this interpretation of the natural image as a double exposure of inner (or mental) and outer landscape, the depiction of the *lian* spreading to the wilderness (*ye* 野) may be taken not only as an intensified description of the weeds' stretching out in time and space but also as a description of the speaker's despair imparting that her mind has turned into a mental wilderness.

Mao Heng comments after the second line: "A xing. The kudzu grows, extends and covers the thorn. The *lian* grows and spreads to the wilderness. It signifies that the wife matures in another home" 興也. 葛生延而蒙, 蘞生蔓於野. 喻婦人外成於他家.[60] Mao's use of *yu* 喻 ("compare," "explain") suggests that the xing element builds on similitude, but is it a simple or analogical xing and, more importantly, what does it mean? The third stanza describes, according to Mao, how the narratrix abides by the rites and takes care of her husband's horn pillow and coverlet in his absence, which demonstrates that she is a virtuous wife who does not neglect the rites even when her husband is away.⁶¹ Cleverly, almost imperceptibly, Mao steers away from the themes of passionate longing, desperation, and despair. The prolific spreading of the plants is now a metaphor for perfection, and the narratrix's nostalgic contemplation of the pillow and bed cover (artifacts that connote sexuality and, as in ode 96, "sweet dreaming") and her complaint about spending her mornings alone now signify ritual behavior.

Mao thus presents an antithesis of my initial reading. What I understood as dilapidation and lack of control is now understood as prosperity and order; what I took as the protagonist's despair is now taken as her calm acceptance of her fate. Scrutinizing Mao's wording, it would seem as if his xing is here "analogical" since the kudzu and the *lian* stand in the same relation to the thorn and the wilderness as does the wife to the "other" home. Both the plants and the wife originally appear in one place but mature and reach their perfection in another. The focus of Mao's attention is, as always with the analogical xing, action: the plants "spread and cover" 延而蒙 and the wife, analogically, reaches perfection (*cheng* 成), which implies virtue.

In "Ge tan" 葛覃 (ode 2) we come upon a different use of the kudzu motif:

The spreading of the kudzu—
it reaches to the middle of the valley
The leaves are flourishing⁶²

葛之覃兮
施于中谷
維葉淒淒

The Lu school interprets the flourishing kudzu as a seasonal indicator signaling that the time for marriage has come.⁶³ The whole poem, moreover, is understood as the expression of a bride-to-be of her worries that her wedding might be untimely (*kong qi shi shi* 恐其失時) and, thereby, deviate from ritual principles. Mao's explanation is altogether different, he comments: "A xing. The kudzu is what fine and coarse cloths are made of. Among the tasks carried out by women it is bothersome and lowly" 興也. 葛所以為絺綌. 女功之事煩辱者.⁶⁴ This is puzzling, since it seems as if the xing element is wholly literal. Next stanza, however, offers a clue to the figurality that we have come to expect from a xing:

The spreading of the kudzu
it reaches to the middle of the valley
The leaves are in perfect bloom
them [I] cut, them [I] boil
[and therefrom] make fine cloth, make coarse cloth
[He] will wear them without growing tired[65]

葛之覃兮
施于中谷
維葉莫莫
是刈是濩
為絺為綌
服之無斁

Mao comments that *momo* 莫莫 means "the appearance of perfection" 成就之貌, referring, one assumes, to the kudzu leaves that are in full bloom.[66] More important for our present purposes is that this stanza suggests that what is subjected to a nonliteral interpretation, what is "xinged," is not the kudzu's visual or tactile appearance but the *usage* it can be put to, namely clothmaking. After the second stanza, Mao goes on to give a lengthy explanation of how, in ancient times, the queen consort, the wives of the prince, the ministers, the great officials, and the knights, as well as the wives of the commoners, all manufactured clothes for their men that befitted their respective positions.[67] In this context, then, kudzu picking and clothmaking are regarded as ritual action, and the performance thereof as a sign of virtue and abidance by the rites. An intertext, "Cai ge" 采葛 (ode 72), confirms that interpretation. There Mao comments that the picking of kudzu is a "petty task" (*xiao shi* 小事) which, nonetheless, must be carried out carefully lest the person picking the plant be slandered.[68]

The situation calls for precision. The xing element in "Ge tan" consists of a description of nature that speaks of ritual action, yet it is not an analogical xing since nothing in Mao's comments suggests that the plant picking described in this ode is to be understood figuratively. When the xing element of "Ge tan" speaks of the flourishing kudzu in order to evoke the narratrix's virtue it does so not through a perceived likeness between nature and woman but rather by way of synecdoche; that is, by way of a causal chain of events that successively links kudzu to clothmaking, and clothmaking to ritual activity. This is, consequently, a kind of xing hitherto unknown and for which I have not yet constructed a category. Let us nonetheless return to "Ge sheng" (ode 124) and juxtapose its xing with that of the second poem. In ode 124, as we remember, the xing also spoke of the spreading kudzu, but Mao interpreted it as an analogy—taking "spreading" as a metaphor for the lonely wife's "reach of perfection"—as a contrast to the *causal* trope employed by "Ge tan."

Causality and metaphoricity thus standing in opposition, can the xing element in the two poems be reconciled in any way? There are indeed two points of convergence between "Ge tan" and "Ge sheng." First, both poems describe how a woman reaches perfection in another home; this is the core meaning of Mao's analogical xing in ode 124 and of the description of the virtuous and zealous bride-to-be in the second poem. When Mao glosses *momo* 莫莫 as the "appearance of perfection" 成就之貌 it definitely anticipates a connection to "Ge sheng" and Mao's metaphorical equation of "spreading" and "reaching perfection." It is therefore possible to read the description of the kudzu in "Ge tan" simultaneously as a "causal" (or metonymic) xing and as a metaphor (founded on similitude) for how the narratrix reaches "perfection" just like the kudzu leaves reach their *chengjiu* 成就. Both readings combine in the opening trope.

In order to reach the second point of convergence we must link the third and final stanza of "Ge tan" to yet another intertext. This stanza tells of ties of blood:

> I tell the matron
> I tell her I am getting married
> I wash my private clothes and my garments
> which shall I wash, which not?
> I will return to wish peace to my father and mother[69]

言告師氏
言告言歸
薄汙我私
薄澣我衣
害澣害否
歸寧父母

Mao comments that *gui* 歸 means "to marry" (of a woman), and that a "matron" was a female teacher who taught young women "wifely virtue," "wifely discourse," "wifely beauty," and "wifely skills."[70] This stanza relates how the narratrix prepares to leave her parents and her native home, and how she, as a virtuous woman, will return home in due time to pay respect to her parents (*guining* 歸寧) in accordance with the rites. It is a description of uprooting and of a bridal journey that will take the bride-to-be from her home, through the suburbs (*jiao* 郊) and into the wilderness (*ye* 野) until she reaches her destination and her fate a long way from her family. Does this scene of nostalgia and tearful *adieus* in any way connect to the opening lines and the spreading kudzu depicted therein? Mao's interpretation of ode 71, "Ge lei" 葛藟, gives us a hint:

> Long-drawn-out are the kudzu and the *lei*
> on the banks of the river
>
> 緜緜葛藟
> 在河之滸

Mao comments that this is "a xing, *mianmian* describes the appearance of [the kudzu's being] long and never-ending" 興也. 緜緜, 長不絕之貌.[71]

The first stanza continues:

> Already far away from my brothers
> I call another man "father"
> Calling another man "father"
> yet he does not look at me[72]
>
> 終遠兄弟
> 謂他人父
> 謂他人父
> 亦莫我顧

Mao comments that "the paths of the brothers have long since parted" 兄弟之道已相遠矣.[73]

Presented here is a third permutation of the kudzu motif and, although departing from the same idea of the kudzu as an object drawn-out, spreading, and never-ending, it is markedly different from the two preceding instances. This is neither an analogical xing (as in "Ge sheng") nor a "causal" xing (as in "Ge tan") but a simple xing that correlates the *length* (*chang* 長) of the plants to the *distance* (*yuan* 遠) between the siblings. It is a paradoxical yet wholly logical metaphor where the drawn-out kudzu simultaneously represents the distance between the brothers and the continuity between them. In other words, the kudzu describes both the length that separates and the link that binds the brothers together. It is thus a metaphor both for separation and for blood ties. With reference to the third stanza of "Ge tan" (ode 2), with its themes of separation, distance, and blood ties, it is quite possible to add this third interpretational model to Mao's ambiguously defined concept of xing.

We have now nearly exhausted the meaning that "kudzu" takes on in the *Mao Commentary* and created a group of cognate metaphors. Banking on the prolific growth and drawn-out spreading inherent in its very nature, "kudzu" connotes primarily—and like the two sides of a coin—"distance" and "continuity." It then takes on the derivative and more far-fetched meaning of "perfection" (as in the "perfect bloom" in ode 2 and the "spreading and covering" in ode 124).[74] "Kudzu" then changes its trajectory, first becoming a metonymic representation of the usage that it can be put to (clothmaking) and then, in a second rhetorical movement, a metonymy for the ritual behavior that such work signifies. The xing element in "Ge tan" comprises all these meanings and models, describing the narratrix as a virtuous woman because she dutifully performs her "humiliating and troublesome" tasks, describing her "perfection" in a "another house" (with "Ge sheng" as intertext) and describing, in the final stanza, the simultaneous distance and continuity between the bride-to-be and her parents through a simple metaphor (with "Ge lei" as intertext). But what does my reading of this metaphor grouping demonstrate? Most importantly it proves that Mao's aim is not to present a neat, well-ordered, and well-defined analytical reading, describing the rhetoric of the text in a detailed and unambiguous manner. Rather, by allowing simple metaphor, analogy, and metonymy to coexist he performs a hermeneutical overkill, in that he does everything in his power to Confucianize the text and make it speak of virtue and dutifulness. Such an unholy and, from a Western standpoint, "paradoxical" mode of exegesis necessarily results in an overload of meaning. This acceptance of polysemy and (harmonious) ambiguity makes Mao's an interpretational program that flies in the face of Western hermeneutics in general until Empson's book on ambiguity in the 1930s.[75] Although an acceptance of the idiosyncrasies of the multilayered poetic text should not be hastily dismissed as "illogical" but indeed be taken as a model for a more truthful and comprehensive analysis of the semantic and semiotic play of poetry, one must not forget that the poetic "openness" and "indeterminacy" thus suggested sprang from the quest for the righteousness hidden in the text. The acceptance of poetic ambiguity and polyvalence that may startle and fascinate a modern reader is, in fact, a by-product of a pragmatic mode of reading.

The basic sense of "spreading" is activated when "kudzu" subsequently appears in "Mao qiu" (ode 37) as a metaphor both of the vassals' even spread over the country and their interrelation by kinship, and in "Jiu mu" (ode 4) as an image of how the subjects spread and thrive under the benevolent government of a wise ruler.[76]

Plant Picking

The picking of plants is a common motif that occurs in more than twenty odes. It interests us because it transgresses the borderline drawn between nature and human activity by describing both—the picking and the plants—in one instance. As such, it oscillates between xing and nonxing. I will discuss some ten poems in which the plant-picking motif occurs, while paying close attention to Mao's interpretational movements as he strives to transform these descriptions of menial labor into statements about Confucian rituality and morality. My brief investigation is naturally divided into two groups, the first of which deals with poems where Mao does not metaphorize the plant picking but connects it to ritual behavior by way of a metonymic reading. The second group consists of poems where Mao indeed interprets plant picking as a vehicle for more mundane activities. We came upon the first category already in our reading of "Ge tan" (ode 2). There, Mao interpreted the opening description of the spreading kudzu as referring to the picking of kudzu and the subsequent ritualized making of cloth. As noted in chapter 18, a similar link between plant picking and ritual activity also appears in the second stanza of the most influential ode, "Guanju":

> Varied in length are the *xing* plants;
> left and right, gathering them.
> The good and chaste girl
> waking and sleeping he sought her[77]

> 參差荇菜
> 左右流之
> 窈窕淑女
> 寤寐求之

In my numerous previous discussions of "Guanju" I pointed out that the first stanza uses the osprey as a *xing* metaphor for the young couple and, in particular, for the girl described as a "good mate" for the lord. Through rhyme and parallelism the second stanza goes on to correlate the picking (*liu* 流) of plants to the lord's feverish search (*qiu* 求) for the girl who appears in his dreams and daytime fantasies.[78] Read in isolation, the text is self-explanatory and warrants no extratextual intervention. We can either understand the stanza as juxtaposing the desired girl's plant picking with her admirer's "search" for her or, much bolder, as a representation of the dreamlike bewilderment brought on by amorous desire, with the "dreamer" mixing the categories by depicting the object of his lust as a plant that shall be "plucked." Naturally, Mao must downplay the theme of desire and does so by focusing all his interpretational attention on the plants and the act of plucking them.

He comments: "Since the queen consort has the virtue of the osprey she can supply the *xing* plant and prepare the many objects and therewith [procure] the service in the clan temple" 后妃有關雎之德乃能共荇菜, 備庶物以事宗廟也.[79] Here plant picking is, as in "Ge tan," understood as metonymically related to the ritual activity that will take place in the ancestral temple. The longing expressed so explicitly by the poem has now been completely obliterated; now the poem speaks exclusively of virtue and ritual behavior, and if the lord yearns for the queen consort it is now a virtuous and desexualized longing for a virtuous mate. This is undoubtedly a violent, albeit unconvincing, attempt to Confucianize an obvious love song (proven not least by the fact that the text never identifies the "chaste" girl as the queen consort), but this is not as far-fetched as one might think. There are two poems that themselves explicitly establish a causal link between the picking of plants and the execution of rituals, namely "Cai fan" 采蘩 (ode 13) and "Cai pin" 采蘋 (ode 15):

> [She] goes to pick the *fan* plant
> by the pond, on the islet
> [She] goes to use them
> in the prince's offerings[80]

> 于以采蘩
> 于沼于沚
> 于以用之
> 公侯之事

Mao explains that the prince's wife gathers the *fan* plant in order to "assist the offerings" 助祭.⁸¹ In this instance Mao cannot be accused of ideologico-hermeneutical abuse since the text itself states that the *fan* is picked for a ritual purpose. Similarly, "Cai pin" (ode 15) is a literal narration of the picking and the preparation of the *pin* plant that, explains Mao, was used to feed the fish subsequently sacrificed in a prewedding ritual.⁸² It is clear from these examples that the plant-picking motif always carries with it a connotation of virtue and ritual activity, a connotation to some extent warranted by the *Odes* themselves. Moreover, "Cai shu" 采菽 (ode 222) opens with a xing that, just like "Ge tan," banks on a causal (or metonymic) link between plant picking and rites.

Things get more intriguing as Mao deviates from this pattern of causality and metonymy to metaphorize the act of plant picking. "Cai ge" (ode 72) was treated earlier as an instance of the analogical xing:

> There [I] pick the kudzu
> If [I] do not see him for one whole day
> it is like three months
> There [I] pick the *xiao* plant
> If [I] do not see him for one whole day
> it is like three autumns
> There [I] pick the *ai* plant
> If [I] do not see him for one whole day
> it is like three years⁸³

> 彼采葛兮
> 一日不見
> 如三月兮
> 彼采蕭兮
> 一日不見
> 如三秋兮
> 彼采艾兮
> 一日不見
> 如三歲兮

As previously argued, "Cai ge" could be understood as a straightforward, almost simplistic love song in which a plant-picking girl expresses her longing for her lover. However, given the knowledge we have gathered about the motifs of plant picking and "kudzu" it would be easy to Confucianize this poem and make it speak of the chaste, desexualized longing for a virtuous mate. Commenting on "Ge tan" (ode 2), Mao explains the image of the spreading kudzu as a metonymy for the lowly "task" of picking and preparing this plant, a ritualized work carried out by a woman in order to make "fine and coarse cloth" for her husband. Consequently, when the motif of kudzu picking appears in "Cai ge" it already connotes female virtue and ritual behavior and, following Mao's own instructions, this poem should be understood as describing a virtuous young woman picking the kudzu that she will later use to make clothes for her husband.

The kudzu is here not only a metonymy for ritual work, and thus female virtue, from the girl's perspective; "kudzu" is also a metonymy for the man who subsequently will wear the clothes. "Kudzu" is what makes the girl's thoughts stray to her beau, serving as a link of association: kudzu—clothes—husband. It must be emphasized that this nonmetaphorical, metonymic reading is perfectly justifiable since it follows the rules that Mao himself has laid down. That Mao actually deviates from his own tacit interpretation and the work/ritual trope cannot be regarded as anything but a symptom of a pragmatic and arbitrary hermeneutics. The interpretation that Mao now introduces is clearly metaphorical in nature: ""A xing. Kudzu is used to make fine and coarse cloth. Although one's task is petty, if a day goes by when one does not appear before the ruler one fears slander[ers]. The *xiao* plant is used as offerings in sacrifices, the *ai* plant to heal ailments" 興也. 葛, 所以為絺綌也. 事雖小一日不見於君, 憂懼於讒也. 蕭, 所以供祭祀. 艾, 所以療疾.[84]

In my previous nervous and self-conscious interpretation of this poem, "Cai ge" was puzzling because it could not be made to fit snugly into the paradigm of the analogical xing. One problem was that the poem itself spoke of action (plant picking), thereby differing from the static imagery of the simple and analogical xings. Another problem was its confusing mixture of literalism and metaphoricity. Mao, it seems, understands the plant picking as a metaphor for a "humble task" carried out by a minor official, yet he goes on to explain the actual, concrete functions of the plants. But with an insight into the arbitrariness and the polysemy of Mao's xing we can return to this poem with more confidence.

Postulating a relationship between ode 72 and the analogical xing was certainly not incorrect but at this point we understand that "Cai ge" belongs to a subgroup, that of plant picking, that must be interpreted in its own right. In his comment on ode 72, Mao deviates from the model established in connection with "Ge tan" by indicating that the description of kudzu picking should not be understood at face value but on a "higher," figurative level. The picking of the kudzu, as just noted, is by definition a female task that connotes ritual behavior, but it is not one that is inspected by the ruler (*jun* 君).[85] In other words, the "humble task" that Mao claims is performed is not kudzu picking itself but some lowly official task. The literal description of female, menial work has turned into a metaphor for "higher" (albeit "petty") work on an aristocratic level. At the same time, the theme of amorous longing has been downplayed; for instance, *jian* 見 no longer means "to see" but the more far-fetched "to appear [before the ruler]." Similarly, the subtle intensification in yearning ("one day without seeing you is like three days . . . three month[s] . . . three years") is unacceptable here, and Mao, consequently, bypasses the last line in each stanza and substitutes it with his wholly extratextual fantasy about the anxiety of defamation: "one day without the lord's inspection and I fear slander." The passion of love has turned into petty fearfulness.

The metaphorization of action and the heterogeneous mixture of figurative and literal meaning made in the name of xing have ceased to bewilder. There is enough evidence to prove my initial hypothesis that Mao's *Shijing* exegesis is pragmatic rather than formalistic, that it is crude and violent hermeneutical *work* that aims at finding the righteousness that the poem, obliquely and mysteriously speaks of. A reader who comes to Mao's *Commentary* expecting to find a minute and careful examination of the text will be disappointed and frustrated. I hope, moreover, to have demonstrated the arbitrariness and the pattern of lawmaking and law-breaking that follows such a program. Lastly, in my interpretation of "Ge tan" (ode 2), I demonstrated how Mao tries to make every part of the poem significant by allowing several, contradictory interpretational models to coexist. Consequently, we should not be surprised that Mao metaphorizes action since without the reading of kudzu picking as a metaphor for official work he would have been unable to avoid the theme of longing. Nor should we be surprised that he mixes the picking-work metaphor with detailed and quite literal descriptions of the plant's functions because Mao executes his "work" properly by reading "plant-picking" as a metaphor *and* by emphasizing the connotations of ritual activity invested in the words "kudzu," "*xiao* plant," and "*ai* plant." The seemingly chaotic overload of meaning results from Mao's conviction that the text's "righteousness" can be found on several rhetorical levels at the same time. It is the consequence of a hermeneutical economy that hates textual superfluity.

Mao's xingish interpretation of "Cai ling" 采苓 (ode 125) further increases this complexity:

> Picking the *ling* plant, picking the *ling* plant
> on the top of the Shou Yang-mountain
> People's fabricated tales
> should really not be believed
> Put them aside, put them aside
> [they] really are not true
> People's fabricated tales
> what can be found therein?[86]

> 采苓采苓
> 首陽之巔
> 人之為言
> 苟亦無信
> 舍旃舍旃
> 苟亦無然
> 人之為言
> 胡得焉

Following the pattern that Mao has established hitherto we could understand the relation between the natural imagery of the first two lines and the subsequent description of human affairs in two ways. The simplest and perhaps most natural reading would be to understand "Cai ling" as narrated by a zealous and virtuous girl who picks the *ling* at the top of the mountain while urging someone (her husband, her friends, her family) not to believe people's evil slander. Such a reading would comply with the connotations of the plant-picking motif (virtue, ritual behavior), using it as a counter-argument to the evil words directed at the narratrix: "you are calling me names but here I am, abiding by the rites, picking the *ling* on the mountain top."

An alternative reading would bank on the model of "Cai ge" (ode 72) and read plant picking as a metaphor for trivial official work, thus transforming the narratrix into a narrator directing himself to his ruler: "Those people slander me, but here I am, zealously performing my humble duties." From the perspective of Mao Heng's hermeneutics, this is a perfectly acceptable reading since the present poem itself talks of slander. By contrast, the "fear of slander" that Mao took as the theme of ode 72 is an extratextual addition made in order to avoid the theme of longing. Indeed, the interpretation that Mao put forward with regard to "Cai ge" would be much more convincing if applied also to this poem, but as we know Mao Heng seldom choses the most convincing and self-evident reading. After the second line of "Cai ling," he introduces an exceptional interpretation in three installments of the xing element: "This is a xing . . . Shou Yang is the name of a mountain. Picking the *ling* plant is minute work. Shou Yang is secluded and remote. Minute work signifies petty behavior. A secluded and remote place signifies falseness [lit. "without evidence" *wu zheng*]" 興也 . . . 首陽, 山名也. 采苓, 細事也. 首陽, 幽辟也. 細事, 喻小行也. 幽辟, 喻無徵也.[87]

As indicated by the double use of the word *yu* 喻, Mao's reading is clearly figurative. The picking of the *ling* plant described in the first line is not to be understood as an act performed in actuality, and, by way of a similar logic, although Shou Yang is the "name of a mountain" we should not take the second line literally, as referring to an actual place. The second step consists of a paraphrase, or a rewriting, of the natural description in order to bring out what Mao conceives of as vital information: to pick the *ling* on the mountain is to *perform minute work in a secluded place*. At this stage, we could certainly still follow the model that Mao has prescribed for ode 72 and understand the narrator as a zealous subject who dutifully performs his small task even at a remote location.

What happens next, in the third step of Mao's text transformation, is an extraordinary and unforeseen twist of meaning in that minute work (that is, plant picking) is made to signify "petty conduct" 小行 and the "secluded and remote" place (the mountain called Shou Yang) to signify "falsity" 無徵. To the reader's great surprise, what was formerly used as an image (metonymical or metaphorical) of zealousness, virtue, and ritual behavior now signifies immoral conduct and lies, as "plant-picker" has become an invective directed against "those people," the slanderers.[88] The narrator does not pronounce the xingish lines to assure the world of his purity; instead, he points his accusing finger, saying "you people are merely picking *ling* on mount Shou Yang—your petty conduct, your slander is groundless." The entire poem must now be understood as a critique against the slanderous people described in the opening lines.

This reading fundamentally contradicts the reader's expectations and the interpretational model that Mao established for the plant-picking motif in odes 72 and 125. Therefore, had Mao simply defined the opening lines as a xing without adding a detailed explanation, the reader would never have been able to arrive at this interpretation; he or she would have understood "Cai ling" as we did prior to Mao's "third step." Finally, Mao's highly rhetorical and complex reading is irreconcilable with the cosmologists' description of Confucian hermeneutics as basically concrete and nonmetaphorical. What I call Mao's third step consists, in fact, of a movement from concretion to abstraction that occurs on the level of language since "minute work" 細事 can signify "petty behavior" 小行 not because there is a concrete similarity between plant picking and slander but because both *expressions* share the common denominator: "smallness." Likewise, "secluded and remote" can signify "falsity" or "groundlessness" not because a remote mountain resembles false speech in any concrete way but because "obscurity" and "remoteness" can be made to signify speech that is "at a distance" from the truth.

Mao's interpretation of the plant-picking motif in "Cai qi" 采芑 (ode 178), deviates, once again, from the previous models:

> [We/I] pick the *qi* plant
> on that new field
> and on this acre but one year under cultivation
> Fang Shu arrived
> his chariots were three thousand
> for use as a host of protectors[89]

> 薄言采芑
> 于彼新田
> 于此菑畝
> 方叔涖之
> 其車三千
> 師干之試

The Fang Shu whom this poem celebrates was, says Mao, a high officer (*qing shi* 卿士) who was appointed a general and, as described by the following stanzas, was highly successful in subduing the tribes that threatened the peace of the state.[90] Nothing in "Cai qi" suggests that the description of plant picking is to be taken figuratively. The poem could instead be read as a eulogy to a brave leader, a worthy, narrated by a chorus of fieldworkers. Naturally, such a reading would still be thoroughly rhetorical since this "peasant-chorus" must be understood as a mere oratorical artifice, organizing the narration of this piece—"simple" peasants in the Zhou Dynasty could hardly have composed such an aristocratic poem. Such a reading would, furthermore, oppose the *stationary* and earth-bound fieldworkers to the agile Fang Shu who rushes around the kingdom to ensure that the peasants can toil in peace. Unsurprisingly, Mao begs to differ, saying (after the third line) that "This is a xing . . . A field that has been cultivated for one year is called *zi*, [a field] cultivated for two years is called 'a new field' . . . King Xuan could renew and beautify the world's knights and, then, use them" 興也 . . . 田一歲曰菑二歲曰新田 . . . 宣王能新美天下之士然後用之.⁹¹

Mao's metaphorization of the opening lines splits the plant-picking motif into two rhetorical figures that overlap and perfect each other. The picking of the plant is analogous to King Xuan's usage of the worthies of this world since he is a "picker" of talented officials such as Fang Shu. On the other hand, Mao makes a subliminal pun on "the *new* field," saying that the king could (in my admittedly clumsy translation) "renew" the knights. Here, Mao casts King Xuan as the tiller, or cultivator, of the field in which talents grow. What first appeared as a literal description of *qi* plant pickers has now turned into a multilayered metaphor that describes the virtuous king simultaneously as a farmer and a reaper of talents and, from another perspective, the "knights of the world" as "plants" that must be nurtured, picked and put to use.

This third permutation of the plant-picking motif concludes my investigation of Mao's pragmatic hermeneutics. One could easily proceed to further examples, such as Mao's complex and "subliminal" interpretation of "Pan shui" 泮水 (ode 299), where the picking of the *qin* plant by the "semi-circular shore" is interpreted, simultaneously, as an analogy for the "picking [i.e., acquisition] of Moral Transformation" and as a literal description of "the waters by the *pan*-temple" 泮宮.⁹² However, I hope to have sufficiently demonstrated how the xing entails both semantic instability and the discontinuity of Mao's interpretational models: for the metonymic-causal model of "Ge tan" was substituted the metaphorical models of "Cai ge," "Cai ling," and "Cai qi." Semantically, "Cai ling" (ode 125) took the description of small and minute work, turned it around 180 degrees and made it into a metaphor for petty behavior, thereby downplaying the earlier connotations of dutifulness and ritual activity. "Cai qi," as concluded just now, banked on a more straightforward interpretation, making the plebeian picking of the *qi* plant an analogy of the virtuous king's selection and usage of worthies.

Chapters 21 and 22 have described Mao's interpretation of the *Shijing* as pragmatic and "arbitrary," yet I shall close my investigation in a positive mood by, once again, pointing out that Mao's Confucian hermeneutics introduces a mode of reading that radically challenges our conception of the poetic text. By asserting that poetry is polysemic, and that it signifies on several rhetorical levels at once, Mao points to the otherness of poetry, or *shi*, and to that which separates it from everyday discourse. Mao's reading, while accurately described as "violent" and disrespectful of the text's integrity, paradoxically generates a poetics that acknowledges the multilayered and polyvalent poetic text.

23

Crisis—Causality

Thus far I have walked along the well-lit, distinct, yet surprisingly lonely path that Zhu Ziqing staked out in the 1940s. I have used Zhu's description of Mao's xing as a trope founded on *piyu* (similitude) as an antidote to the vehement antimetaphoricity of the hyperrealistic program described and discussed in the first part.[1] I have, moreover, categorized this metaphorical trope into "simple," "analogical," and "ironical" variants to show how Mao's concept becomes increasingly complex and, from the analytical point of view I had adopted, unconvincing. The reason I found it unconvincing was not, of course, because the *Commentary* is marred by a lack of logic but because the formalistic, analytical reasoning that I—and so many before me—had employed was inadequate for the task at hand. Through a number of readings I tried to demonstrate the pragmatic character of Mao's xing. But the "simple-ness," the "irony," the "analogy," and the "pragmatics" of the xing notwithstanding, *similitude* was still its major trait. Indeed, if everything else that I have done hitherto will prove to have been in vain, it may be said that it has been proved beyond all reasonable doubt that the majority of Mao's xings are profoundly metaphorical and thereby, in a particular sense, rhetorical. But at this juncture—as a logical result of the lengthy exorcism of Sinological misconceptions hitherto undertaken—the cherished idea of a xing that may be subsumed under the rubric of Similitude must be questioned.

When Zheng Xuan, Kong Yingda, Liu Xie, Zhu Xi, Chen Huan, to name but a few of the worthies in the ancient tradition of *Shijing* exegesis, aimed at a definition of the xing, they did so in the hope of discovering a key principle governing the poetical language of the *Odes*. At the same time, they must have felt part of a strong tradition, emanating from Master

Mao and Confucius, which they wanted to perfect and contribute to. Consequently, their loyalty was directed both at their exegetical forefathers and at the text itself. The *integrity* of the concept was seldom put into question, and with the evolution of an aesthetical and text-oriented hermeneutics, the xing was conceived of as a purely rhetorical device. The fact that Mao's xing had been developed in an environment where at least four schools competed to convince the Confucian world of the excellence of their particular interpretational method had been forgotten. In the preceding chapters I have gathered, I argue, enough evidence to convince the honorable reader of the pragmatic character of the Maoist xing, and I have now reached the point where the ultimate, most painful consequences of my investigation must be confronted.

Indeed, this premise was acknowledged at the very beginning: I would establish a norm of the xing and juxtapose it to deviant examples. That the normal xing stipulates that there obtains a certain similitude between tenor and vehicle is an irrefutable fact, and this is the essential condition from which any alternative definition must deviate. If the horrendous abnormality of a nonmetaphorical xing could be found in the corpus of Mao's *Commentary* it would mean that the xing—the object of more than two thousand years of intense debate—was founded on an all-pervading paradox that would make the heated discussions about the true nature of the concept futile. However, the crisis that we now face does not come as a bolt from a blue sky. In fact, my "discovery" of Mao's metonymic reading of "Ge tan" (ode 2) had always already anticipated it.

"Xing lu" [*or* "Hang lu"] 行露 (ode 17)

"Xing lu" describes how a "forceful and ruthless man" 彊暴之男 tries to compel a girl to marry him. "In the end" (*zhong* 終), the narratrix, apparently initially tempted, refuses his invitations. According to Mao Heng, she "does not discard the ritual principles to follow this forceful and ruthless man" 不棄禮而隨此彊暴之男.[2] The poem opens with three lines that describe her refusal, three lines that Mao defines as a xing:

> Moist is the dew on the road,
> is it not there both morning and evening?
> I say that there is too much dew on the road![3]

厭浥行露
豈不夙夜
謂行多露

Why does Mao label this stanza a xing? Our experience tells us that at the center of a xing there must be a natural object made to carry a metaphorical meaning. But what can "road" (xing 行) or "dew" (lu 露) stand for in this context? It is unlikely that "road"—which Mao redefines as *dao*—could mean "Way" in the sense of Tao, "moral way," since the poem and Mao's comment suggest nothing but literalness. "Dew," on the other hand, may have had awkward connotations for Mao, as there are several odes—seemingly erotic in nature—that begin with descriptions of dew and an abundance thereof.[4] Still, there is nothing whatsoever to suggest that Mao understands either "dew" or "road" metaphorically. Indeed, in the third line the poem's protagonist—the girl herself—states the plain and literal fact that there is an abundance of dew on the road. The third stanza, however, introduces an explicit analogy on which Mao provides an interesting comment:

> Who says that the rat has no teeth?
> By aid of what else could it break through my wall?
> Who says that you have no family?
> By aid of what else could you urge on me a litigation?
> But though you urge on me a litigation
> I still will not follow you.[5]

誰謂鼠無牙
何以穿我墉
誰謂女無家
何以速我訟
雖速我訟
亦不女從

By way of a highly symmetrical parallelism the poem describes the man that Mao calls "forceful and ruthless" as a violent intruder. The subjects, "rat" 鼠 and "you" 女, both occur as the third word in the first and the third lines, respectively. The "aids by which" the intrusion is made—"teeth" and "family" (a synecdoche for wealth)—occur as the fifth words in the first and the fifth lines, respectively, and are furthermore connected by rhyme

(牙 *ya* and 家 *jia*).⁶ But it is not to the analogy between rats and men that Mao directs his attention. Instead, he comments: "By looking at the hole in the wall and drawing one's conclusions from that fact one can say that the rat has teeth" 視牆之穿, 推其類, 可謂鼠有牙.⁷

Again, *lei* 類 ("category") is the pivotal word. A correct understanding of the things and events of the world presupposes that one observes the rules (or "models") of certain phenomena (such as the rites actually described in the *Liji*), and proceeds to apply these rules on other, analogous phenomena.⁸ With reference to "Xing lu," one might assume that the "*lei*-ish," analogical transfer from *this* to *that* phenomena would refer to the rat-man analogy.⁹ But Mao does something entirely different in that he reads the hole in the wall as a sign, a symptom that can and must be interpreted. The analogy between the rat and the "forceful and ruthless" lover in "Xing lu" depends on the relation between two similar objects. By contrast, the hole is the final link in a *causal* chain of events, and from it one may draw conclusions about its provenance and the nature of the beast who made it. Consider here a passage in the *Xunzi* where the philosopher himself expands on how such *lei*-ish inferences are executed: "If there are rules for a particular situation, then one behaves according to those rules; if there are no rules, then one acts as one would in an situation analogous to that at hand. One takes the trunk to infer knowledge about the top, and that which is to the left to infer knowledge about that which is to the right" 有法者以法行. 無法者以類舉. 以其本知末. 以其左知其右.¹⁰

I would immediately propose an alternative translation of the penultimate sentence 以其本知末: "to take the beginning 本 to acquire knowledge about the end 末." To deduce information about the right side of an object by looking at its left side suggests synchronicity and a spatial relationship between two (or more) aspects. On the other hand, to take the root (or the beginning) as a means of understanding the top (or the end) suggests a study of temporal sequences and causality. Although the subject of Xunzi's argument is, as per usual, the rituals, here the focus is more specifically on the method of ritual behavior. And this method not only involves the observation of the relation between two entities or phenomena in terms of similitude but also the observation of cause and effect.

But it is still unclear why Mao defines the first stanza of "Xing lu" as a xing. A passage in the *Commentary* attributed to Mao's predecessor Master Zuo in which the poem is quoted may offer a clue. In the twentieth year of Duke Xi's 僖公 reign (or 640 BCE), the state of Sui 隨 was defeated by the southern state of Chu 楚. In the *Zuozhuan*, a "Superior Man" (*junzi*) comments on this event, saying that "the reason that the state of Sui was defeated was that it did not [correctly] estimate its strength. If one estimates one's strength and acts in accordance with it, one's faults will be few. That one is easily defeated, does it come from oneself or from the other part? An ode says 'Is it not there day and night? I will contend that it is there is too much dew on the road'" 隨之見伐不量力也. 量力而動其過鮮矣. 善敗由自而由人乎哉. 詩曰豈不夙夜, 謂行多露.[11]

This paragraph introduces two versions of rationality. On the one hand, the wise "Superior Man" explains the defeat of Sui in terms of cause and effect in that the generals of that state overestimated their strength and consequently lost the battle. On the other hand, there is the act of estimation itself, which stipulates that one consider all facts and draw one's conclusions in accordance with those considerations, just as the virtuous girl does when she declines the marriage proposal of the "forceful and cruel" man. Thus, by way of this quotation, "Xing lu" was already inscribed in a tradition in which it was understood as speaking of rationality and causality.[12] Returning to the *Commentary* with this in mind, Mao explains that the reason that the girl finally (*zhong* 終) declines the offer is that such a marriage would violate the rites. Therefore, we also know that she has estimated the whole situation, just as she "estimated," or hypothesized, that the rat must have had teeth to make a hole in the wall.

I submit the following hypothesis: Mao's xing tag signals the *fictional* character of the lines describing the abundant road dew. The dew has in itself no significance but is merely a pretext, a polite and ritualized way of declining a marriage proposal that would have violated ritual decorum. The xing element, furthermore, breaks up the temporal sequence of the story narrated by the poem (according to Mao) and begins by presenting the result (the actual refusal) of the deliberation described in the two following stanzas.

My analysis of "Xing lu" must, to some extent, be regarded a failure as I have not been able to fully explain the workings of this xing. This failure notwithstanding, I have at least pointed to something that resembles an aberrant instance of the xing. The realization that Mao's comment focuses on causality instead of similitude well illustrates the subject of this penultimate chapter, namely the instances of xing that do not follow the rules that my model of a metaphorical xing has established. A hole is, strictly speaking, nothing; but this nothingness, this absence of substance, is in this case itself meaningful because it "speaks" of the events that predate it and that caused it.

"Juan er" 卷耳 (ode 3)

Picking and picking the *juan er* plant
[but I] cannot fill the slanting basket

采采卷耳
不盈頃筐

Mao comments that "this is a xing of sorrow. A slanting basket is a tool [for plant-picking] that is easy to fill" 憂之興也. 頃筐易盈之器也. The poem continues:

Oh, I long for the man
[how he] established the ranks of Zhou

嗟我懷人
寘彼周行

Mao comments: "[The speaker is] longing for the [ancient] lord who appointed worthies [*xian ren* 賢人] to offices and established the ranks of Zhou" 思君子官賢人, 置周之列位.[13]

Stanzas two to four run as follows (in Karlgren's translation):

I ascend that craggy height
my horses are all exhausted
meanwhile I pour out a cup from that bronze *lei*-vase
in order not to yearn all the time

I ascend that high ridge
my horses are black and yellow
meanwhile I pour out a cup from that *guang*-vase of rhinoceros
in order not to be pained all the time

I ascend that earth-covered cliff
my horses are all sick
my driver is ill
oh, how grieved I am.[14]

陟彼崔嵬
我馬虺隤

我姑酌彼金罍
維以不永懷
陟彼高岡維
我馬玄黃
我姑酌彼兕觥
以不永傷
陟彼砠矣
我馬瘏矣
我僕痡矣
云何吁矣

Three intertexts must be consulted before Mao's xing label and somewhat enigmatic comments can be understood. The *Zuozhuan* quotes the third and fourth lines of "Juan er" in connection with a discussion about correct statesmanship: "To appoint people to offices is the most urgent task for a state. If the ruler knows how to appoint adequately people for offices, then the populace will have no ambitious hearts. An ode says 'Oh, I think of the lord, establishing the ranks of Zhou'. This refers to the ability to appoint adequately people for offices. That the king and the dukes, the viscounts, the knights, and the great officers of the outer regions all occupied their proper positions—this is what was called 'the ranks of Zhou'" 官人國之疾也. 能官人則民無覦心. 詩云嗟我懷人, 實彼周行. 能官人也. 王及公伯子男甸采衛大夫各居其列. 所謂周行也.[15]

It is in all likelihood to this passage that Mao is referring when he makes his commentary on the first stanza.[16] Indeed, Mao uses Master Zuo's terminology when he says that the speaker of the poem is thinking about how the lord appoints virtuous men to offices (*guan xian ren* 官賢人) and establishes the "ranks of Zhou" (*Zhou hang* 周行). In the wake of the *Zuo Commentary*, most commentators after Mao have interpreted "Juan er" as, in my terminology, an analogical xing that describes the search for virtuous officials in terms of plant picking. The third and fourth lines are thus understood as an instance of "displaying the past to criticize the present" 陳古刺今, with today's ruler in the role of a plant picker thinking of the golden days of the Zhou, when worthies could be easily found, in contrast to the present depressing situation in which one cannot find enough plants (that is, worthies) to fill even a slanting basket. This metaphorizing of the menial work of plant-picking fits nicely with what we have learned about the analogical xing and how descriptions of popular labor are understood as metaphors of ritual behavior and, consequently, of perfect statesmanship.

However, the *Zuozhuan* passage does not tell of the procedures involved in choosing officials; it merely speaks of appointing people and placing them in accordance with an ideal hierarchic system, and only the third and fourth, nonxingish lines of the poem are quoted. Moreover, that interpretation can neither explain Mao's unconventional expression ("this is a xing of sorrow" 憂之興也 instead of the ordinary "this is a xing" 興也), nor make sufficiently clear how the xing figure connects with the obviously important fact that "a slanting basket is a tool that is easy to fill."[17] We must proceed to a second intertext, the *Xunzi*. Just as he was quoting the *Zuozhuan* to explain the lines about "the ranks of Zhou," so Mao seems here to be quoting verbatim from a paragraph from the "Jie bi" 解蔽 chapter of the *Xunzi*. It is not obvious how Xunzi understood "Juan er," but it is clear from the context that Xunzi took it to speak of absentmindedness and lack of concentration: "The ode says 'Picking and picking the *juan er*, but without filling the slanting basket, Oh, I long for the man, [he] established the ranks of Zhou.' A slanting basket is easy to fill and *juan er* are easy to find, but one cannot therefore be confused about the ranks [or path] of Zhou" 詩云采采卷耳, 不盈頃筐, 嗟我懷人, 實彼周行. 傾筐易滿也. 卷耳易得也. 然而不可以貳周行.[18]

Mao leans, in all likelihood, on both the *Zuozhuan* and the *Xunzi* for canonical support. And in light of the above passage from the *Xunzi*, Mao's interpretation of the xing lines undergoes a total transformation. Gone is the analogy between plant picking and the appointment of offices. The empty basket is instead a *symptom* of sorrow since the picker is so full of anxiety and longing for the "ranks of Zhou" that she cannot even concentrate on filling a slanting basket with the ubiquitous *juan er*.[19] As metaphoricity (or analogy) and causality stand in opposition, can my categories be maintained, and "Juan er" understood as an analogical xing? Unfortunately, there is a third intertext that decisively speaks against such an easy solution. Ode 226, "Cai lü," opens with a xing that echoes "Juan er":

All the morning I have been picking the *lü* plant
[but] it does not fill my cupped hands

終朝采綠
不盈一匊

Mao comments: "A xing. *Zhong zhao* 終朝 refers to the time from dusk till breakfast. Two hands [full] is called *ju*" 興也. 自旦及食時為終朝. 兩手曰匊.

My hair is rumpled
I go home to wash it

予髮曲局
薄言歸沐

Mao comments: "When the husband is away the wife does not adorn herself" 婦人夫不在則不容飾.

The whole morning I have gathered the indigo plant
but it does not fill my apron
five days was the appointed time
after six days I (still) do not see (him)[20]

終朝采藍
不盈一襜
五日為期
六日不詹

Like "Juan er," this poem speaks of sorrow and anxiety for someone absent. "Cai lü," however, does not express longing for the lord of yore who established the "ranks of Zhou," as in Mao's comment that made later commentators suppose that Mao understood plant picking as a metaphor for *picking* the right officers. Here, the man longed for is clearly the protagonist's partner whom the second stanza describes as having transgressed the stipulated time. The literalness of Mao's interpretation is confirmed by his explanation of why the woman's hair is rumpled: her husband is away and there is therefore no need for beautification.

Since there is no talk of rulers or of how to govern a state, the xing cannot be an analogy of consummate statesmanship. Nor can it be a simple xing since, according to the *Commentary*, the *lü* plant does not represent anything else beyond itself. Its signatum is identical to its signans. But literalness does not equal lack of significance. In his comment on "Juan er," Mao makes the emptiness of a basket that is easy to fill the hermeneutic center of the poem and calls this a "xing of sorrow." One is justified in understanding the xing element of this poem—the empty hands—in the same way. In both poems, nothingness (just like a hole in the wall) is important precisely as a symptom. This nothingness—this vacuum—appears in the text and begs the question: Why is it there? And according to the

Commentary, the disheveled hair prompts a similar question: Why is it in disorder? Mao answer is that this is a symptom of the husband being away. Rhetorically and formally, the xing trope is identical to that of "Juan er." If the logic of Mao's earlier comment is applied here—a procedure justified because the present poem explicitly speaks of longing and sorrow—there can be no doubt that the xing element is causal since the basket is empty because the narratrix is full of sorrow and cannot concentrate on her task.

Differently put, if the only xingish element of "Juan er" were the alleged analogy between plant picking and appointment of officials (*guan* 官), then the first lines of "Cai lü" could not be labeled a xing since they lack such an analogy (and, indeed, any analogy whatsoever). Returning to the third ode and assembling the evidence given by the three intertexts—the *Xunzi* quotation, the *Zuozhuan* quotation (in which there is no metaphor between picking and governing), and "Cai lü"—I cannot but conclude that this too is a xing built on causality. The empty basket is indeed a symptom or, in Mao's phrasing, a "xing of sorrow."

This is a moment of panic and crisis since a xing founded on causality contradicts the principle that I hitherto have assumed underlies and governs all instances of Mao Heng's xing, in spite of their internal differences—namely the principle of similitude—and it calls for reevaluation and reorientation. Yet one question remains. Why, if the opening lines of "Juan er" and "Cai lü" are to be understood literally, did Mao label them xing? Is there anything that connects this causal, deviant, and utterly frustrating instance of the xing with the norm that I so laboriously tried to establish previously?

In my investigation of the ironic xing and the poetics of "what seems to be but is not" (*si er fei*) I argued that the xing tag functioned as a signal warning the reader not to take the xing image at face value, as a literal description or as a signans with a fixed and conventional signatum. I argued that the *deception* and rhetoric jugglery thus described was, in fact, an appropriate summation of the essence of the xing, since even the imagery of the *jujiu* in "Guanju" is not, says Mao, to be taken as a literal description of calling birds on an islet in the river. Instead, there is an additional, more significant meaning, a metaphorical meaning that does not coincide with the conventional signatum of the linguistic sign (or the graphs) *jujiu*. Similarly, the descriptions of a hole in the wall, of an empty basket or of two empty hands should not be mistaken for carrying the insignificant, literal meaning that a naive and superficial reader would assume—quite to the contrary. Mao, the ideological hermeneut, endows the xing image with *significance* by explaining that it is a symptom, the last link in a causal chain, and that the event that causes this effect, this symptom, is central to our understanding of the poem as a whole.

It is thus with a sense of panic that I realize that, unwittingly, I closed in on "a different order" already in my reading of "Xishuai," when I exhibited Mao's reading of that ode as a prime example of a what xing is not: to wit, literal and nonmetaphoric. Here that other "order"—the logic of causality—is unambiguously defined as a xing.

"Cai shu" (ode 222)

> [I] pick the bean leaves, [I] pick the bean leaves
> [and] put them in square and round baskets

采菽采菽
筐之筥之

Mao comments: "A xing. Bean [leaves] are used to feed the sacrificial animals with which one shall treat the vassals. Sheep are given the *ku* plant [and] hogs the *wei* plant" 興也. 菽, 所以芼大牢而待君子也. 羊則苦豕則薇.[21]

> The vassals come to court
> with what shall we present them?

君子來朝
何賜予之

Mao comments: "*Junzi* refers to the vassals" 君子, 謂諸侯也.[22]

The two opening lines about bean leaf picking pose a problem for Mao. They are—by virtue of their lowly topic—incompatible with the following lines that pertain to the aristocratic sphere by describing vassals coming to court to receive their ritual presents (clothes, horses, and carriages). It is, therefore, Mao's task to reconcile *low* with *high* in order to "save" the poem from anarchic superfluity—or plain incomprehensibility—and to incorporate the first two lines into the aristocratic context of the vassals who abide by the rites. However, he does not do so by virtue of a "simple" xing—there is no metaphoric similarity between the leaves (or baskets) and the poem's personage. And although Mao does transform the description of menial, "lowly" work into a description of something pertaining to the rites, it is decisively not an analogical xing since there occurs no transformation in three instalments of the poem's depiction of concrete work into an extratextual, metaphorical description of the ritual "work" of statecraft. The link between picking and the rites is instead wholly concrete and causal in that the bean leaves are used to feed the *da lao* 大牢, the sacrificial animals (sheep, oxen, and swine), which will subsequently be used to "treat" (*dai* 待) the vassals.

We note that the oblique passage from literal meaning to hermeneutical significance commences with the literal description of the bean leaves being picked and put into baskets. Mao focuses exclusively on the bean leaves (and not the baskets or the act of picking) as carriers of significance and *adds* the extratextual information that the leaves are used to feed the sacrificial beasts. Then, as a final, third step, he connects "bean leaves" to "vassals" (and thus "lowly" meaning to aristocratic, "high" significance) by explaining that the slaughtered animals will be "treats" for the guests. The link between the xing element and the real subject of the poem—the vassals being received by their ruler—is thus causal.

From another point of view, we could also say that Mao's xingish reading here, just as his analysis of "Ge tan" (ode 2), consists of a metonymic chain, showing the continuity between bean leaves and sacrificial beasts and vassals: they are objects that succeed each other in a chronological, as well as causal, order. But if Mao's "trope" is literal, causal and metonymic and therefore not metaphorical, why is this poem labeled a xing? First of all, it may be argued that the reasoning is circular, and the question a consequence of my tentative and not wholly accurate hypothesis about the xing's metaphoricity advanced more than a hundred pages ago. But it has been proved beyond all reasonable doubt that that Mao was as much a pragmatic ideologue as a literary critic and that the xing was primarily an indiscriminately used tool for textual transformation. Second, with the insight of the xing's pragmatic character in mind, the scope of our investigation should perhaps be widened, and a broader definition attempted, one that would cover all instances of Mao's arch trope.

In the earlier examples of the causal xing, the half-empty baskets (and the hole in the wall) were interpreted by Mao as symptoms, that is, as the last links in a chain of events. There, it was the earlier "link," the cause of the symptom, that was important: for instance, the sorrow and the longing for the Superior Man who established the "ranks of Zhou." "Cai shu" reverses the direction of temporality in that the bean leaves instead point forward, toward the usage that they will be put to. It is this *future* role that ensures the texts its wholesomeness, its comprehensibility, and its "aristocratic" significance. The difference in temporal direction notwithstanding, in all cases Mao aspires to rid the text of irrelevant meaning, and the xing is thus a *maker of significance*. In Mao's metaphorical readings, the xing signals a secondary meaning and that the signans does not coincide with its usual, conventional signatum. In Mao's causal readings, the xing signals that the xing element is merely a part of a greater, more important context. Mao's causal xing also presupposes that the text is rhetorically economical and that the poet is saving his breath by just giving one link of the causal chain.

"Dong men zhi yang" (ode 140)

> The poplar of the eastern gate
> its leaves are luxuriant

> 東門之楊
> 其葉牂牂

Mao comments: "A xing. *Zang zang* means luxuriant [in appearance]. It says that man and woman are untimely and will not wait until the time between autumn and winter [that is the proper time for marriage]." 興也. 牂牂然盛貌. 言男女失時不逮秋冬.

The poem continues:

> Dusk was the appointed time
> bright stars are shining[23]

> 昏以為期
> 明星煌煌

Mao's comment on "Dong men zhi fen" (ode 137) defined the eastern gate as a gathering place for lovers.[24] There the opening lines about the elms by the gate and the oaks on the "piled-up hill" were not labeled a xing since Mao took them as a literal description of the trees under which the noble lady of the Zizhong-clan dances. "Dong men zhi yang" is also a love poem. The descriptions of a meeting at dusk, of flourishing trees (a possible metaphor for a young bride, as in "Tao yao") and of bright stars all suggest that the scene is set for romance and sensuality. However, the depiction of the poplar and its luxurious leaves is not understood as a metaphor for a young woman or, indeed, anything else; yet Mao labels it a xing. Why? And what, exactly, is the difference between the nonmetaphoric poplar of this poem and the similarly nonmetaphorical elm and oak of ode 137? The main difference, of course, is that the elm and the oak described in ode 137 unambiguously pertain to a *factual* place where an aristocratic lady carelessly dances. The plain description "The elms of the eastern gate / The oaks on the piled up hill" 東門之枌, 宛丘之栩 leaves little room for a xingish, metaphorical reading, and there are no "luxuriant leaves" that can be understood figuratively. Therefore, Mao has to make that poem a critique of ritual violations without the aid of the xing.

The terse and straightforward sensualism of "Dong men zhi yang" is incompatible with the dictum about the *Odes* as a "storehouse of righteousness" that rules Mao's hermeneutics. We know, therefore, that some measure has to be taken to make the poem ideologically correct. If Mao would read the flourishing trees as a metaphor for the young woman he would only add to the sensualism that he wishes to avoid. The luxuriousness must therefore be explained away; if not, it will remain an irritating and disturbing superfluity that would upset the hermeneutical wholeness that Mao aims for. Mao consequently transforms this obviously amorous poem into its opposite through a reading that understands the arboreal splendor as a temporal indicator, signaling that it is still summer and thus the wrong time for marriage. When the poplar leaves, as symptoms of summer, interact with the description of an amorous meeting, the poem turns into a critique of the violation of rituals and, consequently, no longer speaks of young love under the star-lit firmament.[25]

But how should the relationship between the xing element ("luxuriant poplar leaves") and its new signatum ("summer") be described? Clearly, it depends on a logic quite different from the "normal" order of similitude. First, the semiotic process linking "leaves" to "summer" is wholly automatic, extratextual, and metonymic, since according to the laws of nature and to the eternal flux of yin and yang trees flourish in summer. Thus, independently of any text, luxurious poplar leaves signifies "summer." We have entered, in other words, into a logic of cause-and-effect since summer "causes" trees to flourish. By contrast, there is no natural law that provides a link between *jujiu* and the amorous couple in the poem ("Guanju," ode 1) taken as a model for the metaphorical "simple xing." Just like the hole in the wall, the half-filled basket and the cupped but empty hands, the flourishing leaves are a symptom that leads its interpreter to an important insight. Mao's exclamation that "this is a xing" calls attention to the fact that the opening lines of "Dong men zhi yang" must not be taken as a mere literal description but that they contain information crucial for a correct understanding of the text's message, information not readily available through a "naive" and superficial reading. As we have been able to conclude so many times, Mao's xing tag indicates that rhetoric is at work; it is a sign of warning, saying "there is more to this than meets the eye."

Now we face a causal xing in which "the semiotic play of signans and signatum is extratextual and not the outcome of the interaction between the descriptions of nature and man." I quote myself with bitterness and frustration since my self-quotation signals the end of the present project and, furthermore, the anticipated failure thereof. With "Dong men zhi yang" we have, finally, reached the point where Mao totally and fatally contradicts the xing model established in chapter 18. In that chapter I described—under the heading "First hint of a different order"—how "Xishuai" (ode 114) could not be a xing since it is built on a causal reading that understood the cricket in the hall as a symptom or indicator of autumn. The causal and nonmetaphorical structure of that "counter example" is in fact identical to the causal and nonmetaphorical structure of this xing. The nagging suspicion that first occurred after the encounter with the analogical and the ironical xings has been fully confirmed: Mao's xing is not only pragmatic but also a concept torn apart by contradictions and paradoxes. It is a concept that lacks the whole(some)ness and fundamental coherence presupposed by later scholars in their attempts to find a unique definition that would cover all instances of the xing. Nevertheless, the causal xing is still very much a *trope*, a turn of phrase. From a cursory glance at Mao's reading of ode 140 it may seem as if the cosmologists' theory about cosmological correspondences makes sense since the luxuriousness of the poplar leaves and the season in which they occur and which they signify are after all intimately connected by their mutual dependance on the eternal rotations of yin and yang.

Would it then not be correct to say that a *Shijing* poem—even in Mao's interpretation—is a wholly literal and nonmetaphorical statement about the world and that the so-called metaphors found therein are merely literal representations of text-external correspondences? With reference to the simple, analogical, and ironical xings, I have already sufficiently answered that question. With the causal xing, things are slightly more complicated. Of course, it is true that the causal xing is nonmetaphorical; this is its main characteristic and that by which it may be distinguished as a deviation from my "norm." On the other hand, the causal link between the poplar's foliage and its signatum ("summer") does not differ much from the link between the half-filled basket and its signatum ("sorrow"), in that they both are symptoms. What matters more than the question if they presuppose a reasoning built on the rationality of cause-and-effect, or on the reader's knowledge about the cosmology of yin and yang, is the undeniable fact that they occur in the text precisely as symptoms, referring to something beyond themselves. In Aristotle's simple but effective terminology in the *Rhetoric*, the text uses *this* to say *that*.[26] That "Dong men zhi yang" communicates that it is summer by describing luxurious leaves is thus evidence of a rhetorical strategy on the poet's part: the presence of cosmology and the absence of metaphoricity notwithstanding. Finally, why is this ode and not "Xishuai" labeled a xing? It is a question impossible to answer and a reminder—annoying and frustrating—of the inconsistency of Mao's interpretational undertaking.

"Tao yao" 桃夭 (ode 6)

The youth and vigor of the peach tree
Flourishing [are] its flowers
This bride is on her way to her new home
Appropriate her [new] house and clan

桃之夭夭
灼灼其華
之子于歸
宜其室家

Mao comments: "A xing. When the flowers of the peach tree are flourishing, *yaoyao*-like are their youth and vigor. 'Appropriate' means not to miss the proper time [according to the rites] when going to one's [new] house and clan" 興也. 桃有華之盛者夭夭其少壯也. 宜以有室家無踰時者.[27]

As concluded in the previous lengthy discussion, the xing element of "Tao yao" starts out as a seasonal indicator, signaling that the time is right for marriage and subsequently transforms into a simple metaphor for the young bride. Metaphoricity and causality thus coexist harmoniously without excluding one another. To *accuse* Mao's reading of being paradoxical would not only be a misunderstanding of the pragmatic character of the xing but, moreover, exactly an instance of the anachronistic fallacy that I previously accused so many splendid scholars of, namely the inclination to read the *Commentary* in light of twenty-two hundred years of debate over the nature and origin of the xing.

"Chou mou" 綢繆 (ode 118)

Tied round [is] the bundled firewood
The Three Stars are in the heavens

綢繆束薪
三星在天

Mao comments: "A xing . . . 'In the heavens' means that [The Three Stars] have begun to appear in the east. Man and woman depend on the rites for their [matrimonial] fulfillment just as firewood and hay depend upon man's work to be rolled up in a bundle. When The Three Stars appear in the heavens the time is right for men and women to get married" 興也 . . . 在天, 謂始見東方也. 男女待禮而成, 若薪芻待人事而後束也. 三星在天, 可以嫁娶矣.

As in Mao's comment on "Tao yao," the xing element in "Chou mou" is simultaneously a temporal indicator, as the Three Stars signal that the time is right and an analogical metaphor likening the bundling of firewood to using the rites, as previously argued.

"Wu yi" 無衣 (ode 133)

In Mao's comments on "Tao yao" and "Chou mou," metaphoricity and causality are both integral parts of what Mao calls "xing." I shall round off my illusion-breaking yet hopefully innovative investigation of the causal xing by looking at another of Mao's highly paradoxical, contradictory, and pragmatic readings, ode 133, "Wu yi" 無衣.

The poem begins thus:

Why say "I have no clothes"?
[I] will share my tunic with you

豈曰無衣
與子同袍

Mao comments: "A xing. If he who occupies the highest position shares the same aims as the hundred [recognized] families, the hundred families will gladly go to their deaths [for him]" 興也. 上與百姓同欲則百姓樂致其死.

The poem continues:

The king is raising the army
We prepare our spears and shields
I will share comrades with you

王于興師
脩我戈予
與子同仇

Mao comments: "When the world is properly ordered, rites and music, campaigns and punitory expeditions [all] emerge from the son of heaven" 天下有道則禮樂征伐自天子出.[28]

The reading of "Wu yi" that Mao performs is opaque, complex, and contains elements of both metaphoricity and causality. At first glance this xing seems to be metaphorical: with Mao understanding the text's words about "sharing my tunic" as a metaphor for the king above (*shang* 上), who "shares the aim" of his vassals. Indeed, Mao does perform his usual "subliminal" trick of linking text and commentary by means of identical or near-identical wording, in this case "share . . . with" (*yu . . . tong* 與 . . . 同). This reading necessarily understands the xing element as spoken by the man who "possesses high position" (that is, the king) and the following lines, consequently, as spoken by his loyal vassals who will follow their king on a campaign.

However, the internal structure of the poem contradicts that interpretation. One must instead understand the poem as a dialogue between members of the "hundred families" who are so pleased with their ruler that they will gladly go to war for him, saying to each other: "If you have no clothes I will share mine with you . . . I will share comrades in arms with you." What is it that calls for such a reading? First, we have the parallelism of the second line, where "I will share my tunic with you" 與子同袍 *could* possibly be interpreted as the king's words to his noble subjects. If so, we observe that the king addresses his noblemen as *zi* 子, a polite yet familiar pronoun meaning "you." But nowhere does Mao actually indicate that the narrator of the xing is different from the narrator of the subsequent lines. Moreover, *zi* could possibly be used as a king's address to his subjects but hardly as a *subject's* address to his king, as in "I will share comrades with you" 與子同仇. In other words, there is reason to believe that the whole stanza records the dialogue of noblemen (*bai xing*) willing to share their clothes and go to war for the sake of their king.

If so, the xing must be understood as causal since the willingness of the noble men to sacrifice their comfort (and instead share clothes while going to war) is a *symptom* of the king's benevolence. Thus, "Wu yi" itself only gives the second part of Mao's comment ("the one hundred families will . . .") and Mao has to provide the first link in the causal chain, the poem's *meaning*: he who is in possession of high position shares his aims with the hundred families. The text is rhetorically manipulated not through metaphoricity but by way of an ellipsis that only provides a symptom and forces the reader to trace its cause. Moreover, by asserting that the aristocrats express their love because their king is good (and thus virtuous), Mao has already endowed the poem with Confucian respectability, and it is now a poem that speaks of statecraft well performed.

The argument may be fortified through a reading of ode 122, an intertext that bears the identical name of "Wu yi," where the same opening line occurs. Although the poem is clear enough for my present purposes, it is impossible to know exactly how Mao understood the narration:

Why say "I have no clothes"? They are seven!

豈曰無衣七兮

Mao comments: "The highest of the vassals, according to the rites, get seven enfeoffments, and the ritual caps and garments are [also] seven" 侯伯之禮七命, 冕服七章.

The poem continues:

They are not like your clothes -
comfortable and good

不如子之衣
安且吉兮

Mao comments: "If the vassals do not receive their feoffments from the son of heaven then they cannot become lords" 諸侯不命于天子則不成為君.[29]

This poem contains no xingish metaphoricity or causality. Just like ode 133, it must be understood as a conversation between two vassals and not as a dialogue between a king and a nobleman. Mao explicitly stresses the fact that, according to the rites, the clothes given to vassals as a sign of authority must come in sets of seven. We can thereby infer that the first line refers to the clothes of a vassal. The second and third lines say that "your" (*zi* 子) clothes are better, a statement that elicits Mao's comment about how vassals cannot become lords (*jun* 君) without the edict from the son of heaven. This means that Mao probably understood the person complaining about his "uncomfortable" and "bad" clothes as a vassal who had not been granted the royal edict, as opposed to the vassal with the "comfortable" and "good" clothes. Ode 122 thus strengthens the reading of ode 133 as a dialogue between noblemen taking joy in their king and, by the same token, it also strengthens the causal reading. Furthermore, ode 122 seems to record a moment of tension between two noblemen whereas ode 133 shows their unification and harmony under a good lord, as expressed by Mao's comment about the absolute power that emerges from the son of heaven when the world is in "proper order" and "in possession of the Way."

It has not been my aim to place the xing element appearing in "Wu yi" (ode 133) neatly in a particular category, but indeed to demonstrate the impossibility and pointlessness of such an undertaking. What my reading has established is that the xing is pragmatic, not a coldly analytical tool for literary interpretation where the meaning of the literary text can be reached and fully understood through a formal analysis. As we have seen, there are cases (like "Wu yi") where the Confucian ambition to *find* the "righteousness" of which the *Odes* are a "storehouse" clearly shines through. What Mao does in this case is actually to let the xing represent both the cause and the effect, since it is both understood as a metaphor (the king saying that I will share my tunic with you, meaning that he shares his aim with the noble families) and as the *cause* that makes the hundred families willing to die for him. Simultaneously, and with ode 122 as intertext, we cannot but understand the present poem wholly as words exchanged between members of the hundred families who declare that they will be comrades in the war for the king. Thus, the xing element that was explained as a metaphor only moments ago is now causal, as the happiness and willingness to sacrifice are a *symptom* of the king's sharing the aims of the hundred clans. My conclusion—echoing, ironically enough, Pauline Yu—must be that the xing is here both metaphorical and literal, governed by both similitude and causality and the expression of both a cause (the king's will) and an effect (the noblemen's willingness to fight for their king). The persuasive logic and rationality of Mao's comment on "Guanju" are very distant.

24

Reorientation and Conclusion

Here, at the end of a project that I look back at with both nostalgia and a certain skepticism, I must turn my critical gaze toward myself and ask what I have achieved. What conclusion, as regards Mao Heng's xing, does my investigation arrive at? It could be said that one sentence covers the entire enterprise: Mao's xing is a pragmatic exegetical tool that is predominantly metaphorical. Taken together, these two features—pragmatics and metaphoricity—describe Mao's ideologico-hermeneutic endeavor in a way that goes against both Zhu Ziqing's theory (which I have lauded) and the tenets of the "cosmologists" (toward which I have adopted a more reserved stance). But before I turn to the painful consequences of my investigation, I ask the reader's permission to relate, one last time, my scholarly narrative in its final form.

I set out with the naive intention of establishing a typology of Mao's xing. I thought that I could subject the *Commentary* and its arch trope to a formal and formalist analysis and discern what seemingly mystic and elusive law governed Mao's usage of the xing. Basing myself on Mao's comment on "Guanju" (ode 1), the endeavor paid off very well at first, and I was able to find a clear law-bound pattern that explained why Mao defined some poems as xings, whereas other poems (the so-called counter examples) were not. Just as Zhu Ziqing had explained in his 1945 essay *Shi yan zhi bian*, the xing was based on similitude (*piyu*). I expounded Zhu's theory by claiming that the xing metaphor emerged from the interaction of natural descriptions and descriptions of human activities, whereby the former became metaphors of the latter. Armed with this model of metaphorical stratification and interaction, I argued against Pauline Yu's brilliant and shrewd but lopsided thesis that what may appear as metaphoricity in Confucian readings of the *Shijing* is in fact only nonfigurative and literal representations of extratextual correspondences. In diametrical opposition to Yu's cosmological poetics, I tried to show that the xing did indeed bank on a transfer of meaning that was clearly metaphorical, rhetorical, and textual in nature.

However, with the second chapter, and with the advent of what I called Mao's analogical xing, dark clouds assembled over my positivistically inclined endeavor. What was here labeled a xing banked upon an interpretational model that introduced meaning from outside, *violently* imposing extratextuality on the poem, ridiculing and disregarding the text's integrity. Now Mao's true colors were beginning to shine through. Commenting on "Jian jia" (ode 129), Mao interpreted the opening lines about the frozen dew on the "reeds and rushes" as an analogy about a state's dependence on Confucian rites. Although fundamentally metaphorical, this was a reading that could find no support whatsoever in the text and, therefore, lacked the persuasive force of the simple and intratextual xing. The fact that Mao made a description of plants, dew, and frost into a metaphorical statement about statesmanship fueled my hermeneutics of suspicion, and made Mao look less a text-analyst and more a text-transformer on the noble mission of making the *Odes* "speak Confucianism."

Chapter 20 returned to the first, canonical model of the xing but presented an inverted version thereof. With the ironical xing I came upon a mocking pattern of promise and disappointment to the extent that the poem in question invariably failed to deliver what the xing element had promised. My subsequent reading of "Zheng yue" (ode 192) unraveled the figure of "that which seems to be but is not" (*si er fei*) which I took as emblematic of Mao's ironical xing in that it also presented a description or an "image" that the rest of the poem showed was illusory. Finally, the ironical "Da dong" (ode 203) disclosed a rhetoric so strong, lucid, and all-pervading that I proclaimed it the final nail in the coffin of cosmological poetics. But if the analogical xing had maintained the link-of-similitude between tenor and vehicle, the ironical xing depended more on *comparatio* than on *similitudo*, since it actually marked the difference between vehicle (xing) and tenor (the human action described). In other words, the ironical xing negated the promise of identity and affinity made by the simple xing. At this stage, the crisis was so acute that the project had to be reformulated. I was beginning to suspect that the "rule of the xing" was unreachable through a formal study of the text and that the idea of establishing a typology of Mao's xing was misdirected. In its stead, I put forward another hypothesis: the xing is a tool employed by the pragmatic hermeneut in order to Confucianize the poetic text, just as the analogical xing had led me to suspect. With reference to the passage in the *Zuozhuan* in which the *Odes* are described as a "storehouse of righteousness" I argued that Mao used the xing to *find*, in the secular text, an "aristocratic" meaning suitable for Confucian ears. The aim of Mao's exegesis was to add lofty meaning to the lowly text, not to treat the poetic text as an autonomous and aesthetic artifact: the literary hermeneutics of the *Commentary* was, simultaneously and necessarily, an ideological hermeneutics. This meant, as a consequence, that an understanding of the logical underpinnings of Mao's arch trope could never be reached by way of a formalist analysis.

In the same chapter I claimed that Mao's interpretation of the *Odes* was determined by a rather limited set of topics, and I tried to show how the xing trope enabled Mao to find five versions of the most prominent of those topics—the theme of Confucian hierarchy—in poems that, on the surface, spoke of other matters. At the same time I took pains to show that many motifs could be interpreted according both to the analogical and the "simple" model and that it was the hermeneut's task to step in as a dictatorial arbiter in order to guide the bewildered reader. Although sharing the name of "xing," I argued that the simple and the analogical xing yielded totally different readings.

Intertextual discontinuity and imperfect repetition were the subjects of the chapter 22. I discussed Mao's treatment of five distinguished *Shijing* motifs and the "neurotic" pattern of definition and counter-definition (such as the contradictory reading of the "whirlwind" topos alternately as a metaphor for evil and benevolence) that followed in the wake of a pragmatic hermeneutics. My subsequent analyses of "Ge tan" (ode 2) and "Lü yi" (ode 27), and the motif-clusters employed by these two poems, suggested that Mao's imprecise definition "this is a xing" could comprise all models (simple, analogical, and causal xing). But, I concluded, what appeared to be a radical embrace of ambiguity and of multilayered semiosis was little more than the outcome of Mao's voracious urge to make *every* part of the literary text speak Confucianism. I called this mode of interpretation a "hermeneutic overkill." As an exegetical tool in service of an ideological hermeneutics, the xing aimed both at transformation and whole(some)ness.

Thus, the xing often appeared as a means to hermeneutical economy, trying to incorporate every little scrap of information given by the poem into a greater whole. This *budgetary* tool, I claimed, reallocated meaning in a undemocratic way, making popular meaning serve the aristocratic topics of rituals and statesmanship. In this context, I further referred to the metaphorical nets, complex and far-reaching, that run through the *Odes* and the *Commentary*. The most fundamental of these were, of course, the nature/man dichotomy and its offspring, the commoner/aristocrat dichotomy. Just as the natural element (to wit: the "xing") of a poem had no value of its own but could only be used as metaphor material, the descriptions of menial, popular work could (in Mao's Confucio-ideological readings) only be understood as metaphors for the aristocratic and ritual work of statesmanship. Thus taken to their extreme, "nature" and "populace" were *interchangeable* in that they both represented the antithesis of ritual man. This idea connects directly with the canonized poetics of the *Great Preface*. Because just as nature responds spontaneously and without deliberation to the flux and changes of the yin and the yang, so the *Preface* describes the commoner as an only too *natural* half-beast who responds spontaneously to his emotional whims by foot stomping, hand-waving, and the utterance of "sounds." His behavior is unrestrained by the rites, the very activity that refines the base human raw material.

All these metaphors relate, moreover, to the thesis put forward by Haun Saussy three decades ago—and anticipated by Xunzi and the concept of *wei* 偽—about the arch metaphor with which the whole Confucian program is imprinted. If the Confucian rites polish and perfect man, the metaphorical and xingish reading performed by the Confucian exegete polishes and refines the textual raw material and endows it with significance, and so the Confucian act of reading must *itself* be regarded as ritual work. Yet paradoxically enough, here and there we came upon an ambiguous stance toward nature where it was regarded simultaneously as inferior on a rhetorical level (that is, fit only as metaphor material) *and* as that which establishes the model for human activity.

In the penultimate chapter and with the discovery of the causal xing, the tensions inherent in the narrative as hitherto constructed became too strong, forcing me to abandon the initial hypothesis. No longer could the notion that a similarity—perceived or real—between natural phenomena and human actions was the essential feature of the xing be sustained. No longer could I with Zhu Ziqing *categorically* state that the xing is metaphorical. No longer could "counter examples" be set up to serve as a contrast to the "canonical" version of the xing as found in "Guanju." "Ge tan" (ode 2) and "Juan er" (ode 3) demonstrated how Mao's xingish semiosis built on causality (or metonymy) and not on similitude, and this discovery flatly contradicted the rules adumbrated in the first chapter. From chapter

22 onward, I knew that plant picking—that is, *human action*—could be used as a metaphor for aristocratic activity, and this discovery contradicted the rules of the first chapter. Most conspicuously, it was found that Mao's xingish reading of "Dong fang zhi yang" (ode 140) was built on the same idea as my prime example of a counter example, the nonxingish "Xishuai" (ode 114). This discovery also broke the pattern of the first chapter. The unraveling of this blatantly nonmetaphorical, yet fundamentally rhetorical usage of Mao's trope demonstrated conclusively that the xing, in its first incarnation, was a pragmatic, paradoxical, and even schizophrenic concept—a concept with a *fissure*.

It is thus time to face the consequences of this inquisition into the nature of the *Odes* and Han dynasty hermeneutics. Does my belated insight in the paradoxical nature of Mao's concept render the investigation a failure, the rotten and inedible fruit of endless efforts made in vain? Probably not. Although there is no stable meaning and no universally valid formal law behind the xing, there are certainly *tendencies*: a majority of Mao's xingish readings are metaphorical, in the particular sense used in this study. The project, it seems, has succeeded in refuting the cosmologists and in expounding and refining Zhu Ziqing's thesis: the xing is a pragmatic concept that is fundamentally, but not categorically, metaphorical.

I finally turn to the question that the enthusiastic, naïve and fresh-faced positivist who resides in all of us has been waiting for, irritated and hair-tearingly impatient after several hundred pages of twists and turns: in the final analysis, how can an all-embracing definition of the "xing" as it appears in Mao's *Commentary* be formulated? Including every instance and excluding none it can only be said that Mao's xing is a *marker of otherness*. When Mao defines a xing he indicates that the phrase, image or motif in question refers to something that lies beyond its conventional and commonly accepted signatum, and that there thus is more to the xing phrase than meets the eye. By the same token, it signals that rhetoric is at work since it is a figure of speech in which one thing is said in order to convey another. (And this is a valid description of the simple, analogical, ironical, and causal xing.) Moreover, the "referent" of the xing contains—if understood correctly—the key to the poem, the *clavis* to the message that the text carries. Despite a certain frustration at the arbitrariness and pragmatics of the xing, and despite the presence of causality and my dashed hopes of a typology of Mao's trope, this is perhaps not an unimportant discovery.

The xing, as described above, is a rhetorical figure that overturns the conception of language as a system of fixed signata that underpins the cosmologists' discourse on hermeneutics and poetry making in ancient China. Like the dream divination by the "great man" in ode 190, it is a mode of reading that destabilizes language by implying that meaning is not immediately accessible in the linguistic sign presented to us in speech or writing, and by suggesting that literary meaning is generated and present on several levels at once. If the claim that "all known Han scholars of language and linguistic theory" conceived of words as "immutable cosmological entities . . . [each containing] within itself a kernel of absolute moral and ethical principle" is correct, then Mao Heng's *Commentary* on the *Odes* introduced a language crisis in early Han dynasty China.[1]

The xing is the marker of that crisis; it is the wedge inserted between signifier and signified. It is the xing that rocks the boat of language.

Appendixes

Appendix A

The Xing: Supporting Evidence

1. The Drifting Boat

As opposed to the cluster of motifs treated in chapter 22 and their semantic instability, the image of the floating (or drifting) boat always connotes disorder, despair, and instability in the *Commentary*. It is an interpretation that seems to be warranted by the text itself. For instance, in "Xiao pan" 小弁 (ode 197) the narrator expresses his heart's griefs, describing how his worries keep him from sleeping, and how they cause him distress "like headache" and "like bowel pains."[1] In the fourth stanza, the speaker "compares" his sorrow to "the drifting [straying] of that boat / not knowing its destination" 譬彼舟流, 不知所屆 and immediately goes on to link this imagery to "the sorrows of the heart" 心之憂, saying that "I have no time to steal a moment's sleep" 不遑假寐.[2] Here, the metaphorical connection between the reckless boat and the chaos and distress that the narrator experiences is made perfectly obvious by the text itself: the drifting boat signifies "lack of control" and, as a derivation from this primary meaning, "panic" and "desperation." That similitude is what links the boat-motif to human anxiety is clear from the usage of the copula *pi* 譬, "compare," "resemble."

When the fifth stanza of "Cai shu" (ode 222) says that "drifting, drifting is that poplar boat / but the hemp ropes and bamboo ropes bind it" 汎汎楊舟, 紼纚維之 Mao reads it as metaphor for control and order, commenting that "an enlightened king can restrain and control his vassals" 明王能維持諸侯也.[3] It is thus clear that, for Mao, the motif of the drifting boat suggests potential danger and anarchy, a situation that, in this context, calls for restraint by the firm hand of an "enlightened" ruler.

"Bo zhou" 柏舟 (ode 26) is, just like ode 197, a poem about distress and the "sorrows of the heart." The narrator (or narratrix) complains that all "petty men" are against him and that not even his own relatives can be trusted.[4] The feeling of hopelessness and despair is represented in the first lines by the boat motif: "Drifting is that cypress boat / drifting its floating" 汎彼柏舟, 亦汎其流.[5] Mao comments that "this is a xing" and that cypress wood is suitable material for boat making.[6] The second line, continues Mao, implicates that the boat cannot cross the river.[7] Here, then, is an image connoting sheer frustration; although the boat is made from the appropriate material it cannot perform its duty and reach the other side of the river—it just drifts helplessly with the flow. We can take Mao's xing both as a metaphor for the narrator's state of mind (unstable, floating restlessly) and as a more specified metaphor for a situation that is out of order even though all the right prerequisites are given. A third, equally acceptable, reading would be (in my paraphrase): "Although I am cut from the right material, I am still unable to perform my duties [i.e., cross the river]."

The narratrix (or narrator) of ode 45, also called "Bo zhou" 柏舟, complains that her parents do not believe her when she says that she will have no other spouse.[8] Later commentators, such as the author(s) of the *Minor Prefaces*, understood the poem as narrated by a woman who swears to be faithful to her deceased husband in spite of her parents attempts to have her remarried.[9] The ambiguity of the poem notwithstanding, the sense of despair is represented by yet another boat image that Mao defines as a xing: "Drifting is that cypress boat / in the middle of that river" 汎彼柏舟, 在彼中河.[10]

The drifting boat motif also appears in "Er zi cheng zhou" 二子乘舟 (ode 44), clearly with the same undertones of chaos and desperation. According to Mao's unusually long commentary, ode 44 narrates a well-known story about idealized filial piety and brotherly loyalty. There was a conspiracy in the ducal house of Wei 衛 to kill Ji 伋, one of Duke Xuan's 宣 sons. The duke himself took part in this plot, ordering Ji to travel to another state and then hiring robbers that would lie in ambush and kill his son. However, Ji's younger half-brother Shou 壽 informed his older brother about their father's murderous plans, urging him not to embark on the trip. Ji, as a model Confucian, disregarded this warning, saying that a son must always obey his father's orders. Shou, following the Confucian code of loyalty toward one's elder brothers, then switched places with Ji and was subsequently killed by the hired robbers in a remote mountain pass. When Ji later arrived at the place of Shou's murder, he too was killed.[11]

This is Confucian virtue taken to the extreme, as the elder brother dies in order to obey his father's order, and the younger brother dies to save his elder brother. In the *Commentary*, Mao claims that "Er zi cheng zhou" was composed by the "men of the state" (*guo ren*) who were moved by the story of the two brothers and their gruesome fate. The poem starts with the drifting boat motif and then goes on to express the sadness of its narrators:

Two men board the boat
drifting quickly, it goes far away
Longingly we think of you
in our grieved hearts there is no stability[12]

二子乘舟
汎汎其景
願言思子
中心養養

Mao says that the "two men" of the poem refer to Ji and Shou and that the "men of the state" were "hurt" by their dangerous and ill-fated journey, which was "like riding on a boat and having nowhere to moor" 如乘舟而無所薄, with the boat rushing forward "without restraint [*wu ai* 無礙]."[13]

We observe four things with reference to Mao's interpretation of ode 44. First, it is quite clear that the motif of the drifting boat connotes chaos and danger. Second, by paraphrasing the last line of the first stanza as "grieving, not knowing a stable place" 憂, 不知所定, Mao links the boat motif to the "sorrows of the heart": a heart in despair fidgets and flutters just like an unanchored boat that rushes and speeds without stop—they both suffer from a lack of stability and order.[14] Third, although the poem literally says that the two men traveled by boat, the *Zuozhuan* passage on which Mao builds his reading says nothing about boating. Consequently, Mao reads the first lines as a metaphor in order to make the poem coherent both with the canonical version and the other instances of the drifting boat-motif. Fourth, Mao does not define his explicitly metaphorical reading as a *xing*, a fact that once again shows the irregular and elusive character of the *Commentary*.

2. "Que chao" 鵲巢 (ode 12)

> The magpie has a nest
> the *shijiu*-bird inhabits it
> This lady goes to be married
> a hundred carriages escort her[15]

> 維鵲有巢
> 維鳩居之
> 之子於歸
> 百兩禦之

Mao (after the second line): "A xing . . . The *shijiu*-bird does not build its own nest but inhabits the nest [already] perfected by the magpie" 興也 . . . 鳲鳩不自為巢, 居鵲之成巢.[16]

"Que chao" praises a virtuous bride. The xing is with all certainty a metaphor for the bride who goes to her new home, perfected not by herself but by her husband. Mao makes a subliminal pun on *cheng* ("perfected"), thereby linking the strata together. When the third stanza says that "the hundred carriages perfect her" 百兩成之 Mao comments that this means that the bride "is able to perfect the rites of the hundred carriages" 能成百兩之禮也.[17]

3. "Cao chong" 草蟲 (ode 14)

> *Yao yao* go the insects in the grass
> jumping are the grasshoppers
> When I have not yet seen my lord
> my grieved heart is agitated
> But when I have seen him
> and when I have met him
> my heart calms down[18]

> 喓喓草蟲
> 趯阜螽
> 未見君子
> 憂心忡忡
> 亦既見止
> 亦既覯止
> 我心則降

Mao says (after the second line) that "this is a xing" and that the wives of the ministers act (*xing* 行 lit. "walk") in accordance with the rites and "follow" (*sui cong* 隨從) their husbands.[19] The xing is thus a metaphor for wives following their husbands' "calls" just as the grasshopper responds to the insects' calls by jumping (*yao* 躍), as suggested by Zheng Xuan.[20] Mao's comment clearly suggests that the strata are linked by way of similitude. Furthermore, on a subliminal level, Mao links natural description to human activity (that is, the descriptions of the "acts" of the virtuous wives) through a string of words that all imply motion: *xing* ("walk"), *sui* ("follow"), *cong* ("follow") and *yao* ("jump").

4. "Kai feng" 凱風 (ode 32)

> The joyous wind comes from the south
> it blows on the thorn of the jujube tree

> 凱風自南
> 吹彼棘心

Mao: "A xing. Southern winds are called *kaifeng*. The southern wind nourishes and fosters happily." 興也. 南風謂之凱風. 樂夏之長養者.[21]

> The thorn of the jujube flourishes
> [our] mother toils and suffers [first stanza]
> The joyous wind comes from the south
> it blows on the brushwood of the jujube
> [Our] mother is wise and good
> but we have no good man [second stanza]

> 棘心夭夭
> 母氏劬勞
> 凱風自南
> 吹彼棘薪
> 母氏聖善
> 我無令人

Mao: " 'Brushwood of the jujube': [this is] its achievement" 棘薪, 其成就者.[22]

> Beautiful is appearance of the yellow bird
> it makes fine its song

> There are seven sons
> [but] no one consoles the mother's heart [fourth stanza]²³

> 睍睆黃鳥
> 載好其音
> 有子七人
> 莫慰母心

Here the joyous, southern wind—nourishing and fostering—is a metaphor for the mother who has raised seven sons only to be left alone. Taken as a whole, the poem reads like a symptom of misgovernment; the sons are unable to fulfill their duty of filial piety (*xiao* 孝) and take care of their loving mother. We notice, moreover, that the xing metaphor subtly reflects the passing of time: in the first stanza the wind—the mother—nourishes the small jujube thorn. In the following stanza the wind or mother nourishes something larger, namely the brushwood of the jujube, which Mao argues refers to the mother's "achievement" of having raised seven children.²⁴

5. "Lu e" 蓼莪 (ode 202)

> Tall and big [stands] the *e* plant
> it is not the *e* plant—it is the *hao* plant
> Alas, alas, father and mother
> in bearing me you had great toil [first stanza]

> Father, you begat me
> Mother, you nourished me
> comforted me, cherished me
> brought me up, fostered me
> looked after me, returned to me
> outside and at home carried me in your bosom
> I want to requite this virtue
> but almighty Heaven goes to excess [fourth stanza]²⁵

> 蓼蓼者莪
> 匪莪伊蒿
> 哀哀父母
> 生我劬勞
> 父兮生我

母兮鞠我
拊我畜我
長我育我
顧我複我
出入腹我
欲報之德
昊天罔極

In "Lu e" the speaker laments being unable to take proper care of his or her parents and repay them for raising and nourishing him. Mao says that the first two lines constitute a xing but gives no further guidance as to their meaning, and there are no extant readings by the Three Schools to enlighten us.[26] Yet one may reach a tentative interpretation by comparing ode 202 with other *Shijing* poems with a similar rhetorical arrangement. For example, the xing element in "Lu e" is an instance of the figure of *si er fei* discussed previously in conjunction with the ironical xing; that the *hao* plant at first is mistaken for the *e* plant is an indication that things are not what they seem to be or should be. Compare here the fourth stanza of "Zheng yue" (ode 192), where "firewood and brushwood" were mistaken for a "real" forest.[27] There, the firewood/forest dualism banked on a difference in quality, and the speaker was disappointed because what he had hoped was a "real," dense forest turned out to be "merely" firewood. By contrast, nothing in the *Commentary* indicates that the *hao* is inferior to the *e*. In his comment on "Lu xiao" (ode 173), Mao defines the *xiao* plant 蕭 as identical to the *hao*.[28]

The *xiao* plant, moreover, appears in the second stanza of "Cai ge" (ode 72), and the *Commentary* explains that it is used in rituals, an interpretation verified by the description of sacrifice in the seventh stanza of "Sheng min" (ode 245).[29] Since a plant used for ritual purposes is typically considered valuable, it is hard to ascribe Mao's comment on "Lu e" to the poetics of surprise and disappointment. Instead, we can seize upon Mao's definition of *lu* 蓼 as *chang da* 長大, meaning "tall and big" but also, referring to the growth of a human being, "grown up." This corresponds to this fourth line of the fourth stanza, saying "you [parents] brought me up" 長我.

Furthermore, "Lu e" corresponds to "Kai feng" (ode 32) both thematically and rhetorically as the narrators of both poems lament the fate of their parents and their "toil" (*qu lao* 劬勞). Consequently, since the joyous southern wind in ode 32 functioned as a metaphor for the nurturing mother, the *grown-up* plant described in ode 202 is probably a metaphor for the speaker who, albeit "grown-up," is unable to requite his parents' virtue.[30] In other words, the xing probably imparts that "the little plant"—a metaphor for the son/narrator—has grown up and thinks back on his benevolent parents that nourished him or her as a child.

6. "Bei men" 北門 (ode 40)

> Exiting through the northern gate
> the grieved heart goes *yin yin*
> All worn out and destitute
> no one knows my difficulties[31]

> 出自北門
> 憂心殷殷
> 終窶且貧
> 莫知我艱

Mao comments (after the second line): "A xing. [At] the northern gate, [one] stands with one's back to the light, facing the darkness" 北門, 背明鄉陰.[32] This xing is indeed accomplished through a process that goes from literalness and concretion to figurativeness and abstraction. Mao makes the literal description of "passing through the northern gate" into a metaphor for desperation, as the narrator takes leave of the realm of light and enters into darkness. The trope depends on a pretextual metaphorization of "darkness" and "light," taking the former as referring to evil, gloom, or ignorance and the latter as representing enlightenment.

7. "Bei feng" 北風 (ode 41)

> The northern wind is cold
> the fallen snow is voluminous
> Love me and care for me
> take my hand and walk the road with me
> [. . .] there is urgency[33]

> 北風其涼
> 雨雪其雱
> 惠而好我

攜手同行
既亟隻且

Mao (after the second line): "A xing. The northern wind is cold and chilling" 興也. 北風, 寒涼之風.[34] The northern wind is cold (as opposed to the "joyous" southern wind of ode 32) and functions as a metaphor for the "urgency" described by the poem.

8. "Qiang you ci" 牆有茨 (ode 46)

> On the wall there is the *ci* plant
> it cannot be brushed away
> The words of the inner chamber [?]
> cannot be told
> What can be told
> is the ugliest of words[35]

> 牆有茨
> 不可埽也
> 中冓之言
> 不可道也
> 所可道也
> 言之醜也

Mao (after the second line): "A xing. The function of a wall is to keep extraordinary things at bay ... Wishing to brush it [the *ci* plant] away, one ends up destroying the wall" 興也. 牆所以防非常 ... 欲埽去之反傷牆也.[36] The parallelism of the text itself indicates that the *ci* plant is a metaphor for the shameful secret "of the inner chamber" since it can neither be told nor removed, thus being as adhesive and unremovable as the *ci* plant on the wall. Adding that a wall is used for protection and that the *ci* damages the wall if one attempts to brush it away, Mao introduces a slightly more complex reading, suggesting that an attempt to expose and do away with the sordid business would only increase the damage. Zheng Xuan's annotation succeeds in integrating all parts of the xing into a harmonious interpretation: "The state's ruler uses rituals to protect and control the state, but today there is lewd activities in the inner chambers of the palace, [it is harmful] just like the *ci* plant growing on the wall" 國君以禮防製一國. 今其宮內有淫昏之行者, 猶牆之生蒺藜.[37]

9. "Zhu gan" 竹竿 (ode 59)

> Tapering are the bamboo rods
> with them one can angle in the Qi river[38]

> 籊籊竹竿
> 以釣於淇

Mao: "A xing . . . One angles [with a rod] to catch fish, just as a woman depends on the rituals to make her house and clan accomplished" 興也 . . . 釣以得魚, 如婦人待禮以成為室家.[39] With its typical stress on instrumentality and rites, this is an analogical xing in which the description of the menial work of fish catching is used as an image of ritual mate catching.

10. "Zhong gu you tui" 中谷有蓷 (ode 69)

> In the middle of the valley there are *tui* plants
> withered their fading [sic]
> There is a girl newly separated
> pitiable is her sighing
> Pitiable is her sighing
> having [thus] met with difficulties[40]

> 中谷有蓷
> 暵其乾矣
> 有女仳離
> 嘅其歎矣
> 嘅其歎矣
> 遇人之艱難矣

Mao (after the second line): "A xing . . . when a dryland plant grows in the middle of a valley, it is damaged by the water" 興也 . . . 陸草生於榖中, 傷於水.[41] The xing is a metaphor for the girl who, separated from her family or husband, suffers in a new and unfamiliar situation, just as the dry-land plant is damaged by water when it grows in the middle of the (moist) valley.

11. "Tu yuan" 兔爰 (ode 70)

> There is a hare who moves slowly;
> the pheasant hurries into the net[42]

有兔爰爰
雉離於羅

Mao: "A xing . . . This says that in the government there are slow and urgent matters, and the methods [efforts] are not the same" 興也 . . . 言為政有緩有急, 用心之不均.⁴³ In this rather far-fetched xingish interpretation, the hare represents slowness and the pheasant quickness. Karlgren follows Ma Ruichen and takes Mao's xing as a description of misgovernment in which the petty man, represented by the hare, is allowed to run loose whereas the gentleman (the pheasant) is punished.⁴⁴ However, it is equally probable that Mao's comment is a critique of "uneven methods" (*yong xin bu jun* 用心不均), just as his comment on "Shi jiu" (ode 152) claimed that "if you have a firm grasp of righteousness and constancy, your methods will be steady [i.e., not 'uneven']."⁴⁵

12. "Bi gou" 敝笱 (ode 104)

> The broken fish-traps are by the dam
> the fishes are bream and *guan*
> The lady of Qi goes to her new home
> her entourage is like a cloud⁴⁶

敝笱在梁
其魚魴鰥
齊子歸止
其從如云

Mao (after the second line): "A xing. The *guan* is a big fish" 興也. 鰥, 大魚.⁴⁷ The second stanza of "Bi gou" substitutes the *guan* fish with "tench," also defined by Mao as "a big fish."⁴⁸ The entourage is then described as "resembling rain" (*ru yu* 如雨) which, explains Mao, means "many" (*duo* 多).⁴⁹ The xing (the *big* fish) is thus a metaphor for the *many* people in the entourage. Since "the lady of Qi" is identified as the licentious Wen Jiang 文姜 in Mao's comment on "Nan shan" (ode 101), the big fish in the *broken* fish trap is probably an image of this female intruder in a degenerated ("broken") state.⁵⁰ However, this more comprehensive reading cannot be verified by Mao's comment.

13. "Jiao liao" 椒聊 (ode 117)

> The fruits of the pepper plants
> rich and spreading over a large area they will fill a pint

That gentleman there
very great [without] comparison
Oh the pepper plants
extend so far[51]

椒聊之實
蕃衍盈升
彼其之子
碩大無朋
椒聊且
遠條且

Mao simply comments that the first two lines constitute a xing but gives no further explanation of the trope. At first glance, this xing resembles the causal xings of "Juan er" (ode 3) and "Cai lü" (ode 226). There, the inability to fill a basket was understood as a symptom of grief. Here, the text explicitly says that the pepper plant *does* fill the basket, a description that, against the background of the two intertexts, could be understood as a symptom of happiness, intimating that the narratrix is relaxed and harmonious and therefore able to perform her task to satisfaction. However, when the final lines ("Oh the pepper plants / extend so far" 椒聊且, 遠條且) reappear in the second stanza Mao comments that it means that "[his] reputation can be heard far away" 聲之遠聞.[52] The pepper tree whose plants are "extending so far" is thus a metaphor for the gentleman's far-reaching reputation. Although this xing may seem far-fetched, this interpretation is nonetheless substantiated by the vast number of comments where Mao links the strata together by way of a "subliminal" pun (here, *yuan*: "distant," "far").

14. "Bao yu" 鴇羽 (ode 121)

Flapping are the bustards
they settle on that dense oak
The service to the king must not be defective
I cannot plant my millet
what shall mother and father rely on?[53]

肅肅鴇羽
集於苞栩
王事靡盬

不能蓻稷黍
父母何怙

Mao comments (after the second line): "This is a xing . . . it is not the nature of bustards to settle in trees" 興也 . . . 鴇之性不樹止.⁵⁴ "Bao yu" belongs to a series of poems (such as ode 169, "Di du") that describe the hardships of warfare and how "the service to the king" impedes the tilling of the earth and leaves one's parents unattended. The bustards that, against their nature, settle on the oak are a metaphor for the farmers-cum-soldiers who lead a life that goes against their nature. Alternatively, we can understand the xing element as a general metaphor for a situation that deviates from the norm.

15. "Fuyou" 蜉蝣 (ode 150)

> The wings of the *fuyou*
> are robes, bright and splendid
> Oh! The grief of the heart
> Come home and dwell with me⁵⁵

蜉蝣之羽
衣裳楚楚
心之憂矣
於我歸處

Mao defines the first two lines as a xing and says that the *fuyou* insect "is born in the morning and dies in the evening, it still uses its wings to adorn itself" 朝生夕死, 猶有羽翼以自修飾.⁵⁶ The xing element is a metaphor in its own right, as the wings of the insect are compared to bright clothes. Inverting the normal order of the xing, nature is here described in terms borrowed from the human realm. As for the relationship between the strata, it is most likely that Mao's reading of "Fuyou" belongs to the *carpe diem* theme that appears now and then in the *Odes*. We must then understand the ephemeral insect in its brilliant "clothing" as a metaphor for the human animal (indeed "ephemeral" *sub specie æternitatis*) and its brief youth. Not surprisingly, Zheng Xuan politicizes the xing, making it an image of "petty" officials who carelessly prance about in beautiful clothes not knowing that the country is on the verge of destruction and that they are about to die, just like the ephemeral *fuyou*.⁵⁷

16. "Xia quan" 下泉 (ode 153)

> Cool is that downflowing spring
> it overflows the root of the *lang* plant
> I awake and sign
> thinking of the capital of Zhou[58]

> 洌彼下泉
> 浸彼苞稂
> 愾我寤歎
> 念彼周京

Mao comments (after the second line): "This is a xing . . . When a drought-resistant plant is watered it gets injured" 興也 . . . 非溉草, 得水而病也.[59] Just as in Mao's comment on "Zhong gu you tui" (ode 69), the xing element here banks on an anomaly: the plant is subjected to a treatment that goes against its nature. We may thus understand the xing as a metaphor for the narrator who suffers in a state that does not maintain the high moral standards of the Zhou: he is a "drought-resistant plant" submerged in the "cold waters" of governmental misconduct. Moreover, according to Mao's comment on the fourth line, the narrator is thinking of the "enlightenment of the former kings."[60] A "king" is, naturally, someone who occupies a high position. With this in mind, we may return to the xing and, following Zheng Xuan, understand the *down-flowing* water as a metaphor for the cruel king whose misgovernment only damages the low populace, just like the cold water hurts the *lang* plants.[61] However, this latter reading can neither be completely verified by the *Commentary* nor account for the anomaly (nonaquatic plant submerged in water). The former reading is thus closer to Mao's xing.

17. "Changdi" 常棣 (ode 164)

> The flowers of the *changdi* tree
> open outwardly, ample and brilliant
> Of all today's men
> none are like brothers[62]

> 常棣之華
> 鄂不韡韡

凡今之人
莫如兄弟

Mao (after the second line): "A xing . . . *e* . . . means to open outwardly" 興也 . . . 鄂 . . . 言外發也.⁶³ It is not until the fourth stanza that we understand what Mao is aiming at: "Brothers quarrel inside the house / [but] outside they defend one another from insult" 兄弟鬩於牆, 外禦其務.⁶⁴ As is clear from these lines, the xing describe the brothers who appear brilliant on the outside while keeping their internal quarrels a secret within their house.

18. "He ming" 鶴鳴 (ode 184)

> The crane calls out in the Nine marshes
> its screams can be heard in the wilds (first line)

鶴鳴于九皋
聲聞于野

Mao: "A xing . . . This means that although the body is hidden the reputation is luminous" 興也 . . . 言身隱而名著也.⁶⁵ As stated previously, Mao's comment likely derives from Xunzi's quotation of this poem in the "Ru xiao" chapter: "The Superior Man is hidden yet obvious, faint yet bright, yielding yet conquering" 君子隱而顯, 微而明, 辭讓而勝.⁶⁶ The xing element (the calling crane) is interpreted by Mao as a statement about the ideal ruler (or gentleman) who rules with supreme authority, yet without brutal force. That the xing is founded on similitude between nature and man, and between low and high is clear, and the *tertium comparationis* that unites crane and ruler on the rhetorical level is the notion of being "hidden yet obvious."

19. "Xiao pan" 小弁 (ode 197)

> Happy are those crows
> they fly home in flocks
> Among the populace there is no one who is not happy
> I alone am in misery
> What offense have I committed against Heaven?
> What is my offense?
> The grief of the heart
> what can be done about it?⁶⁷

> 弁彼鸒斯
> 歸飛提提
> 民莫不穀
> 我獨於罹
> 何辜於天
> 我罪伊何
> 心之憂矣
> 云如之何

Mao defines the two first lines as a xing.[68] The image of the (anthropomorphically) "happy" crows who fly home together is, naturally, a metaphor for the similarly "happy" populace. The opening lines thus stand in ironic opposition to the miserable narrator who, by way of this xing, complains about a government that treats the "populace" well while punishing the worthies. Moreover, the conception of birds as carefree and unrestrained is explicit in the fifth stanza of "Bo zhou" (ode 26) where the miserable narrator (or narratrix) complains, in Mao's paraphrase, that "I cannot like a bird rush up and fly away."[69]

20. "Xiang bo" 巷伯 (ode 200)

> [Interlaced] patterns
> form this shell-brocade
> Those slanderers
> are also too excessive[70]

> 萋兮斐兮
> 成是貝錦
> 彼譖人者
> 亦已大甚

The translation above follows Mao's glosses on the first stanza.[71] Mao defines the first two lines as a xing but offers no further explanation.[72] However, the link between the two strata is explicit through the copula *yi* 亦, "also," which makes the interlaced and overelaborated pattern a metaphor for the excessiveness of the slander(ers). I return to this ode, and the metapoetical implications of the comparison between slander and lies and the intricate patterning of the "shell-brocade," in a later work.

21. "Yu liu" 菀柳 (ode 224)

> There is a luxuriant willow tree
> would I not wish to rest under it?
> God on high is very movable
> do not bring yourself too near to him[73]

> 有菀者柳
> 不尚息焉
> 上帝甚蹈
> 無自暱焉

Mao says that the first two lines are a xing.[74] In his comment on "Dang" 蕩 (ode 255) Mao explains that "God on high" (*shangdi* 上帝) refers "obliquely to the king" 以託君王, and I follow this definition here.[75] The description of the luxuriant willow that offers cool shade and protection is a metaphor for the (benevolent) ruler who supports and protects his subjects. The text is strictly parallelistic and the meaning of the xing is carried over to the third and fourth lines, warning against indecorous closeness between a ruler and his minister. The idea of finding comfort and pleasure in the shade of a tree also appears in "Han guang" (ode 9), albeit in a negative mode (you cannot rest under the trees of the south because they offer no shade), and in "Sang rou" (ode 257, see below).[76]

22. "Xi sang" 隰桑 (ode 228)

> The mulberry trees in the swamps are beautiful
> their leaves are ample
> When I have seen my lord
> how great is the joy[77]

> 隰桑有阿
> 其葉有難
> 既見君子
> 其樂如何

Mao defines the first two lines as a xing, saying that the mulberry tree "has that which benefits people" 有以利人.[78] Here the description of a "lord" (or "gentleman," *junzi*) is paired with a xing that speaks of a beautiful flower in the swamps—that is, in a low place. The *Minor Preface* follows the interpretational scheme established by Mao and understands "Xi sang" as a critique against the wicked King You (always an easy target for Han dynasty Confucians) who does not employ the gentleman/worthy but lets him dwell in the wilderness, like the beautiful flower in the swamps.[79] This is, of course, an elaboration on Mao's comment, but it is clear from Mao's focus on the "benefits" of the flower that the xing is a metaphor for the *junzi*, whether he is to be understood as a "worthy" fit for a high governmental position, or as a virtuous husband.

23. "Yu pu" 棫樸 (ode 238)

> Luxuriant are the oaks and the *su* trees
> one makes firewood of them, one piles them
> Stately is our ruler and king
> to the left and right [they] hasten to him[80]

> 芃芃棫樸
> 薪之槱之
> 濟濟辟王
> 左右趣之

Mao (after the second line): "A xing ... The trees on the mountain are flourishing and ample. The populace takes them and uses them for firewood. The worthies are numerous. The state takes them and uses [them] to prosper" 興也 ... 山木茂盛, 萬民得而薪之. 賢人眾多, 國家得用蕃興.[81]

This is an analogical xing concerned with instrumentality and perfect statesmanship. Just as the populace (on the plebeian level) uses the fine trees on the mountain for firewood, so the virtuous king (on the aristocratic level) uses the many worthies to rule the country so that it prospers.

Appendix B

INCONCLUSIVE COMMENTARIES

Due to my resolve to read the *Commentary* in complete isolation and the shortness and sometimes plain hermeticism of Mao's comments, I have been forced to exclude a number of comments that cannot be categorized with the certitude appropriate for my investigation, neither by themselves nor by comparing commentary with primary text—nor with reference to internal (or intertextual) evidence. Furthermore, we saw in Mao's xingish readings of "Ge tan" (ode 2) and "Tao yao" (ode 6) that several interpretational methods (simple, analogical, causal xing) were used simultaneously, and many comments are indeed "uncertain" precisely because Mao's xing label can comprise two or more of these models. In other words, it is precisely the discovery of the ambiguity and arbitrariness inherent in the *Commentary* that makes me unable to categorize some of Mao's comments. I will below give a listing and a short, tentative analysis of these elliptical comments. In no case do I have any reason to believe that these comments fall outside of the categories established in chapters 17–23.

1. "Huang huang zhe hua" 皇皇者華 (ode 163)

I start by once again exemplifying the irregularity of Mao's *Commentary* and the problems that follow in its wake. Ode 163 is not labelled a xing by Mao and yet it is interpreted as an analogy:

> Brilliant are the flowers
> on that high plain and that swamp

> 皇皇者華
> 于彼原隰

Mao comments: "A loyal minister . . . does not get too close [to his lord] nor distance himself [from his lord], just like a flower does not change its color whether found at a high or low altitude" 忠臣 . . . 無遠無近, 如華不以高下易其色.

> Many are the men of rank,
> although having feelings, they [say that they] do not reach [their task][82]

> 駪駪行人
> 每懷靡及

As Zhu Ziqing has noted, although this poem is not labeled a xing, Mao's interpretation of the opening lines are clearly metaphorical, drawing on the familiar high/low dichotomy and, as so often, using it as a metaphor for high and low positions.⁸³ The focus of Mao's figurative reading, however, is the flower that maintains its true colors irrespective of the environment in which it is found just as the loyal minister maintains his ritually prescribed distance, his position (high or low) notwithstanding. The third and fourth lines go on to describe virtuous officers who keep to ritual decorum by modestly expressing that they are inadequate for their tasks.⁸⁴ The metaphorical element in "Huang huang zhe hua" is thus analogical: the static image of the brilliant flower is transformed into dynamic activity by Mao's extratextual claim that the flower does not *change* (*yi* 易) its color whether on a high plain on in the swamps. (The poem itself never mentions the color of the flower.) At the next stage of the analogical process, the description of (non) action in nature—the (lack of) *change* of color—is made into an account of ritual action on a human, aristocratic level: the loyal minister abides by the rites by not changing his behavior. The opening lines that at first spoke of brilliant flowers on the plain and in the swamps have been stripped of all confusing insignificance, and now speak the language of Confucian rituality.

Why is this not labeled xing? It is, of course, a question impossible to answer satisfactorily. Perhaps the text was corrupted and Mao's "this is a xing" disappeared sometime during the twenty-two hundred years of transmission from Mao's hand to our eyes, but this is pure speculation. Instead, we must accept our failure to explain and categorize this "non-xing." I list it here in order to show the incoherence of the *Commentary*, a haphazardness that makes it difficult—not to say impossible—for a reader to find a completely systematic usage of the xing.

2. "Han guang" 漢廣 (ode 9)

> In the south there are tall trees
> [one] cannot rest there
> By the Han river there are girls who go pleasuring
> [one] cannot seek them
> The broad expanse of the Han
> cannot be waded across
> The long course of the Jiang
> cannot be passed by raft [first stanza]
>
> Tall and rising is that mixed firewood
> we cut the leaves of the wild thorn
> This young lady goes to be married
> we feed her horses [second stanza, first four lines]⁸⁵

南有喬木
不可休息
漢有遊女
不可求思
漢之廣矣
不可泳思
江之永矣
不可方思
翹翹錯薪
言刈其楚
之子於歸
言秣其馬

Mao says (after the fourth line): "This is a xing. The trees of the South are beautiful. *Qiao* means 'standing tall'" 興也. 南方之木美. 喬, 上竦也.[86] Mao's comment has puzzled later commentators since the first four lines of the poem contain both a natural element (the high trees) and a human element (the alluring river girls). However, as I have argued all along, Mao was not the poem's author but merely its refiner and thus regarded the text as his raw material, and worked on it as he saw fit. We must, therefore, expect aberrations from the "canonical" structure of "Guanju" (ode 1). Here, the xing is probably a metaphor for the bride who is chaste, pure, and cannot be "rested under" or "sought after," and does therefore not invite to sensuous pleasure. The link between the trees and the bride is suggested by Mao's somewhat catachrestic description of the southern trees as *mei*, "beautiful."

3. "Lü yi" 綠衣 (ode 27)

> Green is the jacket
> a green jacket with yellow lining
> The grief of the heart
> when will it end?[87]

綠兮衣兮
綠衣黃裏
心之憂矣
曷維其亡

Mao (after the second line): "This is a xing. Green is an intermediate color. Yellow is a correct color 興也. 綠, 間色. 黃, 正色."[88] As indicated by Mao's comment, clothes and their colors pertain to a whole semiotic system that is pre- and extratextually determined. Green is an "intermediate" color because it is impure, being a mixture of blue and yellow. By contrast, yellow is a primary color and, therefore, pure and "correct." Mao's xing can thus both be a symptom (that is, a causal xing) or a metaphor, or both. On the one hand, the mixture of clothes of "pure" and "impure" colors may signal that the person (presumably a ruler) who wears them ignores the Confucian dress code: it is a symptom of nonritual behavior.[89] On the other hand, we can understand the mixture of green and yellow simply as a metaphor for disorder and degeneration; today the world (and this ruler) is out of joint, with virtue and wantonness existing side by side just like the unorthodox mixture of green and yellow in a garment. Or we could seize upon the fact that the exterior of the garment is green while the interior (the lining) is yellow, and read the xing as a metaphor for something (a ruler, a situation) that appears to be bad on the outside but whose "true colors" are good and pure. In this manner, Mao's lapidary xing definition allows for a variety of figurative interpretations that understands the poem in completely different ways. However, our initial reading of clothes as a symptom of its owners ritual status is perhaps the most convincing interpretation, not least since "Zi yi" 緇衣 (ode 75) is a eulogy to correct clothing. "How befitting is the black robe!" exclaims the first line, and Mao comments that a black robe is the correct outfit for a *qingshi* official 卿士 when he goes to court.[90] Still, no final conclusions can be drawn from this intertextual reading.

4. "Ye you wan [man] cao" 野有蔓草 (ode 94)

> In the wilderness there is creeping grass
> the falling dew is plentiful
> There is a beautiful person
> the clear forehead how beautiful
> We meet carefree and happy
> and so my desire is satisfied[91]

> 野有蔓草
> 零露溥兮
> 有美一人
> 婉如清揚
> 邂逅相遇
> 與子皆臧

Mao says that the first two lines are a xing but supplies no further evidence.⁹² "Dew" appears in many poems with no fixed meaning. It is possible that Zheng Xuan is right in taking the "plentiful" dew as a temporal marker, indicating that the middle of spring (*zhong chun* 仲春) has come. Mao's lack of interest may simply indicate that the meaning of "Ye you wan cao" had already been fixed in the *Zuo Commentary* as a ritualized way of expressing joy at a meeting ("we meet carefree and happy / and so my desire is satisfied").⁹³

5. "Zhongnan" 終南 (ode 130)

> The Zhongnan mountain, what has it got?
> It has *tiao* trees, it has *mei* trees⁹⁴

> 終南何有
> 有條有梅

Mao comments: "A xing. 'Zhongnan' is the celebrated Mount Zhongnan of Zhou. [This poem] takes the appropriate as a warning against the inappropriate" 興也. 終南, 周之名山中南也 . . . 宜以戒不宜也.

Mao's comment is ambiguous, but Zheng Xuan's interpolation is probably true to the intentions of his forebear. Zheng interprets the xing as saying that it is appropriate for a famed mountain to have luxuriant trees, just as it is appropriate for a ruler to have virtue and splendid clothes.⁹⁵ This ideal situation is thus used as a warning against potential degeneration.

6. "Dong men zhi chi" 東門之池 (ode 139)

> The moat by the eastern gate
> can be used to soak hemp
> The beautiful third lady Ji
> can respond [to you] in song⁹⁶

> 東門之池
> 可以漚麻
> 彼美淑姬
> 可與晤歌

Mao says that the first two lines are a xing but does not go on to further explain the trope.⁹⁷ By way of the parallelism, the text itself suggests a link between "lady Ji" who can sing in unison and the moat that can be used to soak hemp. However, one cannot tell if the relationship between the xing and the third and fourth lines is metaphorical (the girl can sing just as the moat can soak hemp) or causal (the girl soaks hemp in the moat and so demonstrates her zealousness).

7. "Fang you que chao" 防有鵲巢 (ode 142)

> In Fang there are magpies' nests
> on the hill there are sweet peas
> Who has cheated my beautiful one?
> In my heart I am pained⁹⁸

> 防有鵲巢
> 邛有旨苕
> 誰侜予美
> 心焉忉忉

Mao defines the first two lines as a xing but gives no further clues as to their xingish meaning. There are no extant comments from the Three Schools and the post-Mao commentators add nothing to our understanding of Mao's interpretation.

8. "Yue chu" 月出 (143)

> The moon comes forth, brilliant
> That beautiful one
> how easy and beautiful
> My toiled heart is grieved⁹⁹

> 月出皎兮
> 佼人僚兮
> 舒窈糾兮
> 勞心悄兮

Since Mao defines the first line as a xing it is obvious that "moon" is the carrier of figurative, xingish meaning in his interpretation of "Yue chu."¹⁰⁰ It is unclear, however, exactly what the moon signifies. With reference to the investigation of the sun-and-moon dualism above one could interpret the moon as a symbol of the girl since both belong to the yin realm of existence. We could also, with Zheng Xuan, understand the brilliant moon as a metaphor for the beautiful girl or, again, as a temporal marker signifying that the night—the time for love—has fallen.[101] A possible way to politicize "Yue chu" would be to read the moon as a symbol of a "beautiful" (that is, virtuous) subject/minister, thereby returning to the yin/yang dualism (since a ruler is yang and his subject yin).

9. "Ze bi" 澤陂 (ode 145)

> By the slope of that marsh
> there are sedges and lotus plants
> There is a certain beautiful person
> I am pained, not knowing what to do about it
> waking and sleeping, I don't know what to do
> my tears and snivel are flowing[102]
>
> 彼澤之陂
> 有蒲與荷
> 有美一人
> 傷如之何
> 寤寐無為
> 涕泗滂沱

Mao defines the two first lines as a xing but offers no interpretation.[103] When "Shan you fusu" (ode 84) describes lotus flowers in the marsh Mao comments that the small lotus flower befits the *low* swamp just as the bigger *fusu* tree suits the *high* mountain.[104] However, nothing in the *Commentary* indicates that Mao understood this poem as belonging to the same high/low dichotomy. Zheng Xuan's speculations about the erotic undertones of "sedges" and "lotus" are suggestive but do not elucidate Mao's xing.[105]

10. "Xi you chang chu" 隰有萇楚 (ode 148)

> In the swamp there is the *chang* thorn
> soft and pliant its branches
> The strength and beauty of youthfulness—
> I am glad that you have no mate[106]

隰有萇楚
猗儺其枝
夭之沃沃
樂子之無知

Ode 148 resembles "Tao yao" (ode 6), as the peach tree was there described as "youthful and strong [or 'vigorous']" (*yaoyao* 沃沃), and functioned both as a temporal marker and as a metaphor for the young and beautiful bride. In his comment on this poem, Mao defines the first two lines as a xing.[107] Consequently, the third line, "The strength and beauty of youthfulness" (*yao zhi wuwu* 夭之沃沃), pertains to the human realm as a description of the girl who "has no mate." This is remarkable since, in "Tao yao," the word "youthful and strong" (*yao* 沃) referred to the tree that, in its turn, was used as a metaphor for the bride. Our intertextual reading of "Tao yao" thus demonstrates that the girl in ode 148 is described in a language elsewhere reserved for natural descriptions.

As for the imagery employed by the poem, it is likely that Mao understood the "soft" and "pliant" branches as a metaphor for the young bride. An alternative intertext would be "Wanlan" (ode 60), whose description of the *wanlan* plant as "soft and moist" functions as a metaphor for the benevolent and "soft" ruler.[108] Consequently, Mao's xing can comprise at least three different interpretations. First, the "soft and pliant" branches of the *chang* thorn can be read as a metaphor for the young girl described in the fourth line of each stanza. Second, we can understand the branches, the flowers, and the fruits of the *chang* as temporal indicators. (That these two, wholly different, interpretational methods do not exclude each other is clear from Mao's "double" reading of "Tao yao.") Third, with "Wanlan" as intertext, we may understand the xing as an image of the true gentleman who, in Xunzi's words, is "yielding yet conquering" 辭讓而勝.[109]

11. "Lang bo" 狼跋 (160)

> The wolf tramples on his dewlap
> he trips on his tail
> The duke's grandson is great and beautiful
> his red slippers are stud-adorned[110]

狼跋其胡
載疐其尾

公孫碩膚
赤舃幾幾

Mao defines the first two lines as a xing and continues: "The old wolf has a dewlap. When he moves forwards he tramples on his dewlap and when he moves backwards he trips on his tail. Even though he has problems moving forwards and backwards, he maintains his ferociousness" 老狼有胡. 進則躐其胡, 退則跲其尾. 進退有難, 然而不失其猛.[111] It is hard to imagine that Mao's xing could be built on anything but similitude or comparison. Yet it is impossible to say if Mao took the wolf as a metaphor for the "duke's grandson" (King Cheng, according to Mao) or as an image of the duke himself.[112] Zheng Xuan chooses the latter reading, claiming that King Cheng will continue the work of the Duke of Zhou when the latter "moves backwards" (that is, retires).[113] Considering the "subliminal" logic of Confucian *Shijing* exegesis, this reading is quite agreeable since both strata focus on "feet": as a contrast to the old wolf who *trips* and *tramples*, the fourth line introduces the young grandson's stud-adorned red slippers. We may thus understand these extraordinary slippers as a metaphor for the grandson's ability to succeed the great duke. But, of course, we cannot know if this tallies with Mao's initial reading.

12. "Jiang you si" 江有汜 (ode 22), "Quan shui" 泉水 (ode 39), and "Si gan" 斯干 (ode 189)

These odes all link description of rivers and flows to themes of family relations and marriage. The first line of ode 22 is defined by Mao as a xing:

> The Jiang has branches breaking out and reverting
> This young lady went to her new home
> but she would not take us
> She would not take us
> but afterwards she had to repent[114]

> 江有汜
> 之子歸
> 不我與
> 不我與
> 其後也處

Mao says that a *si* 汜 is a stream "breaking out [from a river] and again joining it" 決複入為汜, and that the person described as repenting is the head concubine (*di* 嫡).¹¹⁵ This seems to fortify Zheng Xuan's interpretation of the xing as a metaphor for principle and secondary concubines who should all exist in harmony side by side, just as the small *si* stream runs alongside the bigger, principal river.¹¹⁶ However, both the poem itself and Mao's comment are too obscure to yield any definitive conclusions.

Ode 39 opens up with an image likewise defined as a xing by Mao:

> Bubbling is that spring water
> it flows to the Qi river
> My loving thoughts are in Wei
> there is no day when I am not longing
> Beautiful are those ladies of the Ji clan
> I will take council with them¹¹⁷

> 毖彼泉水
> 亦流於淇
> 有懷於衛
> 靡日不思
> 孌彼諸姬
> 聊與之謀

After declaring the first two lines a xing, Mao says that the "ladies of the Ji-clan" are relatives of the narratrix, thereby introducing the themes of family relations and longing.¹¹⁸ The poem goes on to speak of a young bride's journey to get married and how she goes away from her family. The opening lines of the fourth stanza offer a clue to the meaning of the xing: "I think longingly of the Fei river source / long do I sigh for it" 我思肥泉, 茲之永歎.¹¹⁹ Mao comments that a *fei* 肥 is a river that "emerges from one source but that branches into many different streams" 所出同所歸異, which suggests that the descriptions of rivers, streams, and waters are used as a metaphor for the family tree; family members, just like a *fei*, originate from the same place but are disseminated and estranged from each other through marriage.¹²⁰ As is the case with the kudzu motif, water is simultaneously a metaphor for distance and continuity. We recognize this version of the "family tree" metaphor from our reading of "Mian shui" (ode 183) above. Ode 189, however, is more obscure. The first stanza opens with a description of flowing water:

> Flowing along goes that valley stream
> dark is the south mountain

dense like the bamboo
luxuriant like the pine
Elder brother and younger brothers
may they love each other
and not plot against each other[121]

秩秩斯幹
幽幽南山
如竹苞矣
如鬆茂矣
兄及弟矣
式相好矣
無相猶矣

Mao defines the first two lines as a xing but offers no further explanation.[122] Since the urge to the brothers not to quarrel is paired with a description of a flowing stream, we might speculate that Mao's xing is a metaphor for family relations, but this cannot be substantiated by Mao's brief comment. Both the *Minor Preface* and the school of Lu take "Si gan" as a eulogy to King Xuan and his virtuous behavior in times of havoc.[123] Nothing in the *Commentary*, however, suggests such a reading.

13. "Zhan bi Luo yi" 瞻彼洛矣 (ode 213)

Look at that Luo river
its waters deep and wide
The gentleman comes
felicity and blessings are as piled up on him[124]

瞻彼洛矣
維水泱泱
君子至止
福祿如茨

Here, Mao's xing (the first two lines) is most probably a variant of the "kinship-metaphor," referring to the *length* and *depth* of the blood ties that link the king and the vassals of the same origin.[125] Or, as the *Minor Preface* seems to suggest, it may be a metaphor for the abundant grace conferred upon the vassals by a virtuous king.[126] The abundant water could, alternatively, be interpreted as a seasonal marker (for spring or summer?), referring to the court rituals that took place at that time. Still, Mao's comment is too short to allow any definitive conclusion to be drawn.

14. "Ju xia" 車舝 (ode 218)

I have already discussed, in chapter 16, how "Ju xia" was interpreted by the author, or authors, of the *Minor Preface* and by Zheng Xuan. Mao's indicates that the first two lines constitute a xing, but his reading is abstruse and cannot be sufficiently enlightened by any intertext. Karlgren assumes that the poem describes how a man goes to meet his new bride, but we can also read it as one of the many odes that describe a bride's journey to her new home. If so, the xing element—the inserted linchpins of the carriage—might signify that the bride's carriage is ready for departure.

What follows is then a detailed description of the *bride's* journey, as related by the impatient bridegroom. In the fifth stanza the couple finally meet and the carriage with the inserted linchpins described in the opening line appears before the eyes of the narrator. According to such a reading, the xing, just like the image of the deer in the first stanza of "Ye you si jun," breaks up the temporal sequence by describing the *result* of the event subsequently narrated. In any case, it is hard to see that the image of the inserted linchpin could function as a (simple) metaphor. Most probably, the xing refers to the bride by way of metonymy, the carriage being an "extension" of her.

15. "Shu miao" 黍苗 (ode 227)

> Beautiful is the young millet
> the rain and clouds fattens it
> Long is that southern road
> the prince of Shao worked [built] it[127]

> 芃芃黍苗
> 陰雨膏之
> 悠悠南行
> 召伯勞之

The xing, here the first two lines, clearly parallels the activity described in the human realm: just as the rain "fattens" the plants (*gao zhi* 膏之), making them long and big, so the prince cultivates the state (and thus "fattens" it) by building the southern road (*lao zhi* 勞之).[128] However, since Mao supplies no further information it is impossible to know exactly what this xing refers to. Perhaps, as Zheng Xuan suggests, there is no specific connection between the strata, and perhaps the "fattening" rain is a metaphor for the benevolent king who pours his benevolence over the people.[129]

16. "Bai hua" 白華 (ode 229)

> The white-flowered *jian* plant
> white grass bundles it
> This gentleman goes far away
> he causes me to be alone[130]

> 白華菅兮
> 白茅束兮
> 之子之遠
> 俾我獨兮

Mao's comment, simply indicating a xing after the second line, is too terse to be of any avail.[131] We recognize the white grass used for bundling from "Ye you si jun" (ode 23) where it connoted "virtue" since it was used for ritual purposes.[132] It may or may not have the same function here. "White" (*bai*) typically connotes purity and innocence (like the white egret in ode 298).[133] Karlgren's suggestion that "bundling" is a metaphor for an amorous couple "bundled together" is another option.[134]

17. "Mian" 綿 (ode 237)

> In never-ending rows [grow] the *die* gourds
> When the people [of Zhou] first were born
> they used the soil of Ju and Qi[135]

> 綿綿瓜瓞
> 民之初生
> 自土沮漆

Mao: "A xing. *Mianmian* means 'never-ending'" 興也. 綿綿, 不絕貌.[136] The endlessly growing gourds probably refers to the lineage of the people of Zhou, just as the far-reaching kudzu was understood as a metaphor for ties of blood in odes 2, 71, and 124.

18. "Sang rou" 桑柔 (ode 257)

> Luxuriant is that soft mulberry tree
> beneath it is an even shadow
> If one plucks it, it will become sparse and thin
> Suffering this lower populace
> never-ending is the grief of the heart
> the affliction and distress are long-continued
> Grand is that Great Heaven
> why does it have no pity on us?[137]

菀彼桑柔
其下侯旬
捋采其劉
瘼此下民
不殄心憂
倉兄填兮
倬彼昊天
寧不我矜

Mao does little more than define the first three lines as a xing and provide the glosses on which our translation is built.[138] There is, however, a clear link between the destructive action of plucking (leaving the luxuriant tree stripped) and the "suffering" of the populace. Consequently, Zheng Xuan reads the xing as a metaphor for the benevolent king who bestows his grace on the populace, just like a luxuriant and soft mulberry tree whose "even shadow" provides relief from the hot sun. However, the virtuous king surrounds himself with bad ministers whose wanton behavior damages the state and harms the people: they "pluck" the tree of the state and destroy its comforting shade.[139] Zheng's reading is variant of the high/low dichotomy (the high tree and the lower populace) and, probably, a good approximation of Mao's reading.

Appendix C

Inconclusive Comments about Confucian Hierarchy

The following poems are labelled xing, and they likely develop the theme of Confucian hierarchies as previously outlined, but Mao's *Commentary* is in these instances too brief to allow any definitive conclusions.

1. "Nan you jia yu" 南有嘉魚 (ode 171)

> In the south there are fine fishes
> in great numbers they are taken under baskets
> The lord has wine
> fine guests feast and rejoice [first stanza]
>
> In the south there are trees with down-curving branches
> the sweet gourds cling to them
> the lord has wine
> fine guests feast and comfort him [third stanza]¹⁴⁰

南有嘉魚
烝然罩罩
君子有酒
嘉賓式燕以樂
南有樛木
甘瓠纍之
君子有酒
嘉賓式燕綏之

Mao indicates, anomalously, a xing after the second line of the third stanza, probably reading the "tree with down-curving branches" as a metaphor for the ruler, and the "sweet gourds" that cling to the tree as a metaphor for the subjects who are fed and cultivated by the lord and take him as their "base."¹⁴¹ The metaphor is probably a variant of the xing that occurs in the opening lines of "Jiu mu" 樛木 (ode 4): "In the south there are trees with down-curving branches / the kudzu and the *lei* cling round them" 南有樛木, 葛藟纍之.¹⁴² Mao says that *mu* "designates a down-curving tree" 木下曲曰樛, which suggests that the xing probably banks on the usual metaphorization of "high" and "low."¹⁴³

There are two reasons why Mao does not read the opening lines about the "fine fish" as a xing. First, Mao has already explained the *chang* fish and *sha* fish in his commentary on the preceding poem, "Yu li" 魚麗 (ode 170), as symptoms of a peaceful world where yin and yang are in harmony.¹⁴⁴ The fish imagery in ode 171 might thus be understood likewise. A second reason could be the alleged link between fish and sexuality, a theme much favored by interpreters of the *Shijing* in the first half of the twentieth century.¹⁴⁵ There is indeed support for such a claim since ode 138 ("Heng men" 衡門) builds on an analogy between fish eating and wife taking, and in ode

104 ("Bi gou" 敝笱), the licentious Wen Jiang 文姜 and her entourage are analogously described as fish unrestrainedly slinking in and out of the fish trap.¹⁴⁶ Had Mao defined the lines about the "fine fish" as a xing, he would have claimed that the poem builds on an analogy between "fine fish" (that is, licentious women) and the "fine guests," and—just as in his commentary on ode 23—Mao must avoid a sexualized reading.

2. "Nan shan you tai" 南山有臺 (ode 172)

> On the Southern mountain there are *tai* plants
> on the Northern mountain there are *lai* plants
> Happy be the lord
> he is the foundation of the state.¹⁴⁷

> 南山有台
> 北山有萊
> 樂隻君子
> 邦家之基

Mao simply says, after the second line, that this is a xing but does not provide any further explanation.¹⁴⁸ Zheng Xuan is probably right in taking the mountains as metaphors for ruler(s) and the *tai* and *lai* plants as metaphoric representations of their virtuous subject growing (and thriving) on the mountains.¹⁴⁹ Apart from simple word glosses there are no extant comments from the Three Schools to indicate how this poem was interpreted in Mao's days.¹⁵⁰

3. "Lu xiao" 蓼蕭 (ode 173)

> Tall is that *xiao* plant
> fallen is the dew
> I have seen my lord
> my heart is relieved.¹⁵¹

> 蓼彼蕭斯
> 零露湑兮
> 既見君子
> 我心寫兮

Mao indicates a xing after the second line but with no further indication of its meaning. Zheng Xuan claims that the principle xing element is the dew with which heaven moistens (*run* 潤) an abundance of things just as the ruler the treats the vassals—represented by the *xiao* plant—with his grace and beneficence (*ze* 澤).¹⁵² Zheng is here banking on a "subliminal" pun: *run* means "moisten" as well as "benefit," and *ze* means both "moist" and "beneficence"—both words thus connect to "dew" through their aqueous origin. Another explanation is given by Wang Xianqian who comments that the *xiao* plant was used for ritual purposes, as described in Mao's comment on the second stanza of ode 72, "Cai ge."¹⁵³ If correct, we would have a causal link between the xing and its meaning, as previously described.

4. "Zhan lu" 湛露 (ode 174)

> Soaking is the dew
> without the sun it will not dry
> Peacefully we drink in the night
> without becoming drunk we will not go home.¹⁵⁴

> 湛湛露斯
> 匪陽不晞
> 厭厭夜飲
> 不醉無歸

Mao indicates a xing after the second line, saying that "even though the dew is abundant it will dry when exposed to the sun" 露雖湛湛然, 見陽則乾.¹⁵⁵ This is a curious inversion of the parallelism of the original text where the second line "without the sun it will not dry" 匪陽不晞 is paralleled by the fourth lines "without becoming drunk we will not go home" 匪醉不歸, both referring to the exhaustion of liquids. It would seem, then, that the opening lines are a ritualized and metaphorical exhortation to drinking and not, as could well be imagined in this context, a ruler/subject metaphor. The *Zuozhuan* reports that "Zhan lu" was recited at a banquet given by a king in honor of his vassals, a fact that supports the hypothesis that Mao took "Zhan lu" and, indeed, all the preceding four poems as depictions of happy meetings between a virtuous lord and his virtuous vassals.¹⁵⁶

5. "Shangshang zhe hua" 裳裳者華 (ode 214)

> Magnificent are the flowers
> their leaves are luxuriant
> I have seen this person

> my heart is relieved
> My heart is relieved
> therefore there is joy and tranquility.¹⁵⁷

> 裳裳者華
> 其葉湑兮
> 我覯之子
> 我心寫兮
> 我心寫兮
> 是以有譽處兮

Mao defines the first two lines as a xing but supplies no further information.¹⁵⁸ We could read it as a simple xing, in the vein of "Tao yao"; that is, as a metaphor for a young bride traveling to see her "lord," or as an analogical xing (like the structurally similar ode 176, "Jingjing zhe e") in which a ruler is praised because he can cultivate worthies just like nature can cultivate magnificent flowers. Or we could take the xing element as a temporal indicator, signifying that the time for marriage is right. In this manner, Mao's silence as to the structure and meaning of the xing figure stupefies the reader. Zheng Xuan, not surprisingly, understands the flower, magnificent *above*, as a metaphor for the ruler and the leaves, luxuriant *below*, as a metaphor for his subjects.¹⁵⁹

Afterword and Acknowledgments

This book has a certain history. In the early morning of May 6, 1996, a young man boarded a bus at the intersection of Showers Drive and El Camino Real in Mountain View with the terminus Stanford Quad. Having reached his destination, he disembarked and made his way to the Asian Languages Department and the Computer Room upstairs, and the one computer that was connected to the internet. Exhausted and with trepidation, he sent the manuscript stored in his bulky laptop computer in five installments to the University of Stockholm, where Torbjörn Lodén, professor of Chinese, stoically took on the task of assembling the pieces. If nothing else, that dissertation had the merit of being, in all likelihood, the first manuscript to have traveled from the US West Coast to Scandinavia in cyberspace.

The thesis was defended in Stockholm on June 7 of that year with Zhang Longxi 張隆溪 graciously acting as the discussant. I thank professors Lodén and Zhang for their contributions, and for making that occasion a stimulating experience. I also warmly thank Professor Roland Lysell, who together with Professor Lodén had acted as supervisor, and whose expertise in Western hermeneutics was greatly inspiring. Most of all I thank Haun Saussy for his extraordinary generosity, both intellectually and personally, during the academic year 1995–96. I remember with fondness the many discussions we—or younger versions of ourselves—had in his Stanford office, at restaurants, and occasionally in bars.

The manuscript was accepted for publication in 2015. It was revised, reorganized, and rewritten multiple times, most substantially between 2019 and 2021, taking into the account the many interesting theories on the *Odes* that had emerged in the meantime (and with occasional fits of irritation at the young man who wrote the original manuscript). Some parts have previously been published in the *Journal of the Oriental Society of Australia* (now

404 | Afterword and Acknowledgments

JOSAH: Journal of the Society for Asian Humanities) nos. 30–31 (1998–1999), in the *Bulletin of the Museum of Far Eastern Antiquities* vol. 78 (chapter 2) and vol. 79/80 (chapter 13), and in *Poetics Today* 23:2 (2002) (chapter 20). I am grateful for the permission to reprint these parts here.

I thank Göran Sommardal, Göran Malmqvist (1924–2019), Steven Van Zoeren, Stephen Owen, Lothar von Falkenhausen, Kao Yu-Kung 高友工 (1929–2016), Jao Tsung-I 饒宗頤 (1917–2018), Lee Kar-shui 李家樹, Chou Ying-hsiung 周英雄, Anders Olsson, David Keightley (1932–2017), Pauline Yu, Magnus Fiskesjö, Michael Nylan, Ulrike Middendorf, Roger Greatrex, Sara Danius (1961–2019), David Pankenier, and Michael Schimmelpfennig for stimulating discussions over the years. For the same reason I thank Perry Johansson and Umberto Ansaldo—fellow members of the Triumvirate of Sinological Misfits in Stockholm in the early 1990s—my friends in Taiwan, Ma Ming-hao 馬銘浩, Hu Cheng-chi 胡正之, and Wu Wan-ju 吳婉茹, and my Australian friends Kam Louie, Roderick S Bucknell, and John X Keenan.

During the last stages of preparing the manuscript my colleagues at the University of Gothenburg, Martin Nordeborg and Chloé Avril, kindly helped me through some thorny passages in Japanese and French, and Dinu Luca provided valuable comments on the newly written material.

I thank my editors at SUNY Press, James Peltz, Nancy Ellegate (1959–2015), and Diane Ganeles for all their support, and the two anonymous reviewers for SUNY Press for their thorough readings and constructive criticism of the manuscript. For the shortcomings that remain I am solely responsible.

I am grateful to the Gunvor and Josef Anér Foundation for generously contributing toward the cost of printing this volume, and to Amane Kaneko for designing the handsome cover.

Lastly, tributes are due to my long-suffering but always inspiring research assistant, Juniper Vine. What's more, Letum omnia finit.

Gothenburg, August 3, 2022
MSE

Notes

Introduction

1. The sequential numbering of the *Shijing* poems follows Bernhard Karlgren's *The Book of Odes* (Stockholm: The Museum of Far Eastern Antiquities, 1950). I follow the edition of the *Shijing*, the *Mao Commentary*, the *Minor Prefaces* and Zheng Xuan's 鄭玄 (127–200 CE) *Annotations* given in *Shi sanjia yi ji shu* 詩三家義集疏 (*SSJYJS*), ed. Wang Xianqian 王先謙 (Rpt; Taipei: Mingwen, 1988); I similarly follow the edition of the *Great Preface* and Kong Yingda's 孔穎達 (574–648 CE) *zhengyi* 正義 in Ruan Yuan's 阮元 (1764–1849) *Shisanjing zhushu* 十三經注疏 (*SSJZS*) (Peking: Peking University Press, 1999). For a meticulous translation of the *Shijing*, see Karlgren, *The Book of Odes*. For philological analyses, see Karlgren's *Glosses on the Book of Odes* (Stockholm: The Museum of Far Eastern Antiquities, 1964) and Chen Huan 陳奐 (1786–1863), *Shi Maoshizhuan shu* 詩毛氏傳疏 [Annotations on Mr. Mao's Commentary on the Odes] (Rpt. Taipei: Xuesheng, 1967). For critiques of Karlgren, see Lee Hung-kai, "A Critical Study of Bernhard Karlgren's (1889–1978) Glosses on the *Ya* and the *Song* of the *Shijing*" 高本漢雅頌注釋斠正 (PhD diss., Hong Kong University, 1995), and Paul L.-M. Serruys, "Une Nouvelle Grammaire Du Chinois Litteraire," *Harvard Journal of Asiatic Studies*, vol. 16, no. 1/2 (Jun., 1953): 162–99.

Other recommended translations of the *Odes* are James Legge's *The She King*, vol. 3 of *The Chinese Classics: With a Translation, Critical and Exegetical Notes, Prolegomena, and Copious Indexes* (Rpt. Taipei: SMC Publishing, 1992 [1871]), Arthur Waley's *The Book of Songs: The Ancient Chinese Classic of Poetry* (New York: Grove Weidenfeld, 1987), and Ezra Pound's *Shih-ching: The Classic Anthology Defined by Confucius* (Cambridge, MA: Harvard University Press, 1954).

All translations are mine unless otherwise indicated. I am, of course, greatly indebted to earlier scholars and translators—in the case of the *Odes*, particularly to Karlgren whose unadorned renderings I have often found unsurpassable for the present purpose. In many cases, I have tacitly removed Karlgren's hyphenations ("poplar-boat" thus becoming "poplar boat").

2. The first editions of *Shijing* commentaries may have reached its readers as separate manuscripts, set apart from the *Odes* themselves, as opposed to later versions that have the commentary interspersed with the poems. If so, Mao's tag *xing ye* 興也 ("this is a xing") must have been put after or before the poem as a whole, thereby making it difficult for the reader to know exactly which part of the poem Mao was referring to. This problem, to which few scholars have paid attention, lies beyond the scope of the present work. However, there are three poems—odes 126, 171, and 298—where Mao indicates "xing" after the second and third stanzas, respectively. If the original Mao version of the *Odes* was incorporated with the texts themselves by later editors, Mao must have indicated quite clearly which line(s) and which motifs should be understood as a xing. As I argue below, the anomalies in odes 126, 171, and 298 can be explained by intertextual readings, which lends further credence to the hypothesis that the original Mao version did specify which line(s) should be interpreted as a xing.

3. *SSJYJS*, 655. See stanzas five to seven of the preceding ode ("Si Gan" 斯干, ode 189). Whenever Mao's *Commentary* is discussed, the translation of the *Odes* will, as far as possible, build on Mao's glosses. The *zhao* banner is defined as "tortoise-and-snake" in the *Commentary* on ode 168 (*SSJYJS*, 586) and the *yu* banner as "falcon" in the comment on ode 53 (*SSJYJS*, 245). *Zhenzhen* is glossed as "many" (*SSJYJS*, 655). Karlgren (*Glosses,* entry 510) argues persuasively that *zhong* 眾 in lines two and five means "locust," and that the line 眾維魚矣 thus should be understood as "[there are] locusts, there is fish," with locusts symbolizing fertility and proliferation. While this demonstrates Mao's inclination to distort the *Odes*—here, in order to make *zhong* (in the sense of abundance) the poem's hermeneutic center—it has no bearing on my present argument. For accounts of dream divination in the *Zuozhuan,* see chapter 3 ("The Reading of Signs") in Li Wai-yee's *The Readability of the Past in Early Chinese Historiography* (Cambridge, Mass.: Harvard University Asia Center, 2007).

4. *SSJYJS*, 655.

5. *SSJYJS*, 655. Chinese words or concepts are typically represented by their modern Mandarin pronunciation, but sometimes—particularly when my goal is to identify which words rhyme—by an approximation of how those words were pronounced in Zhou times based on the following works: Bernhard Karlgren, *The Book of Odes*; John Cikoski, *Notes for a Lexicon of Classical Chinese, Volume I: Occasional Jottings on Textual Evidence Possibly Applicable to Some Questions of Palæo-Sinitic Etymology, Arranged in Alphabetic Order by Archaic Chinese Readings* (Saint Mary's, GA: Coprolite Press, 1994–2011; "Version 14, Draft 7, Tweak 171"); Axel Schuessler, *ABC Etymological Dictionary of Old Chinese* (Honolulu: University of Hawai'i Press, 2007); Christoph Harbsmeier 何莫邪 and Jiang Shaoyu 蔣紹愚, Christian Schwermann and Christian Wittern, TLS - Thesaurus Linguae Sericae

漢學文典: An Historical and Comparative Encyclopaedia of Chinese Conceptual Schemes https://hxwd.org; Paul W. Kroll, with the assistance of William G. Boltz, David R. Knechtges, Y. Edmund Lien, Antje Richter, Matthias L. Richter, Ding Xiang Warner, *A Student's Dictionary of Classical and Medieval Chinese* (Leiden: Brill, 2015); William H. Baxter and Laurent Sagart, "Old Chinese reconstruction, version 1.1 (20 September 2014)"; and Baxter and Sagart, *Old Chinese: A New Reconstruction* (Oxford. Oxford University Press, 2014). I have consulted the above works, in their capacity as dictionaries, throughout the study.

6. With the word "fish" 魚 may have been associated the notion of "abundance" 餘, as the two words probably rhymed in Old Chinese (both are of course pronounced *yu* in modern Mandarin).

7. *SSJYJS*, 655.

8. I note (but maintain a respectful scepticism toward) a tendency among some Sinologists to collapse the distinction between a primary and secondary textuality—between text and commentary—claiming, for instance, that "the different manuscript [traditions] that existed in those times were all fixed in their written form in accordance with the individual understanding [of the *Odes*] of a particular Classics' Master or a particular exegetical school." Chan Pak-ka, 陳柏嘉, "Handai 'diwujia *Shi*' shuo xianyi" 漢代「第五家《詩》」說獻疑, *Zhongguo wenhua yanjiusuo xuebao* 中國文化研究所學報 63 (2016): 10. Although I share Chan's assumption that the corpus of odes in circulation before the Han dynasty must have been somewhat malleable, and that the ideological proclivities of the learned men responsible for establishing and maintaining a certain interpretation (or "use") of the *Odes* may explain the differences in wording between the various manuscript traditions to which we have access today, the assertion that "there fundamentally was no uniform, established meaning [of an universally accepted edition of the *Odes*] that could be summarized or expounded by later scholars" seems too categorial and relativizing. As but one example, if there *fundamentally* were no agreed-upon "meaning" of the *Odes*, the two Music Masters at the court of Qi would not have been able to predict the reaction of the two foreign guests to a recitation of "the last stanza of 'Artful Words,'" as described in *Zuozhuan*, Xiang 14 and discussed elsewhere in this chapter. Indeed, the two Music Masters (and also the ruler) would have been uncertain about how "the last stanza" went. Wang Shouqian 王守謙, Jin Shouzhen 金守珍 and Wang Fengchun 王鳳春, eds., *Zuozhuan quanyi* 左傳全譯 (Guizhou: Renmin chubanshe, 1990), 849. Likewise, as I explain in chapter 12, Monica Zikpi's claim that in our understanding of the received *Shijing* there is no "unproblematic 'literal sense' that could be equated with any 'original intention'" builds on premises that, again, may be too generalizing. I believe that enough of an "original," integral meaning or intention survives in, for instance, the Mao version of "Guanju" (ode 1) to make it possible, worthwhile and imperative to contrast Mao's allegorical reading of that poem to what the poem itself communicates, and to explore intertextually the topics, themes and motifs that connect "Guanju" to, for example, odes 9 and

84. I am grateful to Michael Schimmelpfennig (private conversation, December 2022) for making me clarify this point. For an alternative to, or mitigation of, the idea that the Mao *Odes* are overdetermined by their editors and commentators, see Michael Hunter's concept of "reading from the midrange" in *The Poetics of Early Chinese Thought: How the* Shijing *Shaped the Chinese Philosophical Tradition* (New York: Columbia University Press, 2021), 28–32.

9. See for example You Jiazhong 猶家仲, *Shijing di jieshixue yanjiu* 詩經的解釋學研究 (Guangxi shifan daxue chubanche, 2005), 137–40, and Tamara Chin, "Orienting Mimesis: Marriage and the *Book of Songs*," *Representations* 94, no. 1 (2006), 65–72. For a concise and thorough study of Mao Heng and Zheng Xuan and their antecedants, see Wen Xinfu 文幸福 *Shijing Maozhuan Zhengjian bianyi* 詩經毛傳鄭箋辨異 (Taipei: Wen shi zhe chubanche, 1989). Recent years have seen a surge of interest in Zheng Xuan. For an overview of Zheng Xuan's life and work, see Shi Yingyong 史應勇 *Zheng Xuan tongxue ji Zheng-Wang zhi zheng yanjiu* 鄭玄通學及鄭王之爭研究 (Chengdu: Sichuan Publishing Group, Bashu Publishing House, 2007). For an interpretation of how Zheng used the concept of xing, see Lu Hongsheng 魯洪生, "Lun Zheng Xuan *Maoshi Jian* dui xing di renshi" 論鄭玄毛詩箋對興的認識," in *Wenxue yichan* 文學遺產 2006, no. 1, 29–34. For a study of the intellectual *milieu* and antecendents of Zheng Xuan, see Shen Weiwei's 沈薇薇 "Zheng Xuan *Shijing*xue yanjiu" 鄭玄詩經學研究 (PhD diss., Dongbei Shifan Daxue, 2008). On the contradictions between Zheng's analyses of the *Odes* in the *Annotations* and those in commentaries on other classics, see Yang Tianyu's 楊天宇 "Zheng Xuan's *Zhu Jian* zhong *Shi* shuo maodun yuanyin kaozhe" 鄭玄《注》《箋》中《詩》說矛盾原因考析, in Yang's *Jingxue yanyan lu* 經學探研錄 (Shanghai guji, 2004), 23–34, and Lin Yelian's 林葉連 *Zhongguo lidai Shijingxue* 中國歷代詩經學 (Taipei: Xuesheng shuju, 1993), 136–42.

10. See 76–80 of my (uncommonly ill-named) "One Lucky Bastard: On the Hybrid Origins of Chinese 'Literature,'" in *Literature and Literary History in Global Contexts: A Comparative Project. Volume 1: Notions of Literature Across Times and Cultures* (The Hague: Mouton de Gruyter, 2006). For an in-depth study of the history of the *Odes* (and of non-canonized poems in Warring States texts), see Ma Yinqin's 馬銀琴 monumental *Liang Zhou Shi shi* 兩周詩史 (Peking: Shehui kexue wenxian chubanshe, 2006), and the first chapter of Liu Dongying's 劉冬穎 *Shijing bianfeng bianya kaolun* 詩經變風變雅考論 (Peking: Zhongguo shehui kexue chubanshe, 2005). For an analysis of *shi* 詩 in the specific sense of "the *Odes*" and the generic sense of "poetry," and of *Shijing* as a model for what the author calls "secular literature," see Bruce Rusk, *Critics and Commentators: The Book of Poems as Classic and Literature* (Cambridge, Mass.: Harvard University Press, 2012), and Mathias Richter, *The Embodied Text* (Leiden: Brill, 2013). For stimulating and innovative readings of excavated manuscripts relating to the odes, early poetics, and the canonization process that led to the received *Shijing*, see Rens Krijgsman's *Early Chinese Manuscript Collections: Sayings, Memory, Verse, and Knowledge* (Leiden: Brill,

2023), chapter 3. The origins and subsequent redactions of the *Zuozhuan* are, of course, obscure but I consider it at any rate pre-Han and pre-*Maozhuan*. I refer the reader to the masterful translation of and annotations to this work in Stephen Durrant, Wai-yee Li, and David Schaberg, *Zuo Tradition / Zuozhuan: Commentary on the "Spring and Autumn Annals"* (Seattle and London: University of Washington Press, 2016).

11. According to the *Zuozhuan*, after "the final stanza" (*zu chang* 卒章) of "Ye you si jun" was presented by Zipi (a.k.a. Han Hu 罕虎), another person commented that "if we brothers unite for peace we can 'keep the dog from barking'" 吾兄弟 比以安, 尨也可使無吠, where "keep the dog from barking" is a paraphrase of the final line of the received version of ode 23. *Zuozhuan*, Zhao 1; Wang Shouqian et al., *Zuozhuan quanyi*, 1092. See the discussion of ode 23 in chapter 12.

12. "Wu" is quoted in *Zuozhuan*, Xuan 12; Wang et al., *Zuozhuan quanyi*, 550.

13. *Qinghua daxue cang Zhanguo zhujian*, vol. 1 清華大學藏戰國竹簡(壹), ed. Li Xueqin 李學勤 (Shanghai: Zhongxi shuju, 2010), 10–13; 149–56. I concur wholeheartedly with Paul R. Goldin's wish to rid the Sinological lexicon of "fusty" and Eurocentric translations of "aristocratic" titles ("duke," "earl, "baron" etc.) but maintain in the following some conventional designations, such as "Duke of Zhou" for *Zhou gong* 周公; Goldin "Research Note: Etymological Notes on Early Chinese Aristocratic Titles," *T'oung Pao, vol.* 107, issue 3–4 (2021): 475–80. See also Yuri Pines, "Names and Titles in Eastern Zhou Texts," *T'oung Pao*, vol. 106, issue 5–6 (2020): 714–20.

14. *Zuozhuan*, Zhao 16; Wang et al., *Zuozhuan quanyi*, 1265. It is unclear whether "Zheng" 鄭 here refers to the state or the Zheng section of the *Guofeng* (odes 75 to 95) in the Mao recension of the *Odes*.

15. Three odes (80, 120, and 146) in the received *Shijing* are called "Gao xiu" and three odes (68, 92, 116) are called "Yang zhi shui" 揚之水 ("The Perturbed Waters"). There are, furthermore, two odes (131 and 187) titled "Huang niao" 黃鳥 ("Yellow Bird"), two odes (26 and 45) titled "Bo zhou" 柏舟 ("The Cypress Boat"), two odes (122 and 133) called "Wu yi" 無衣 ("No Robes") and two odes (119 and 169) called "Di du" 杕杜 ("The Solitary Pear tree").

16. *Zuozhuan*, Xiang 14; Wang et al., *Zuozhuan quanyi*, 849.

17. For an ostensibly different opinion, cf. Martin Kern, "'Xi shuai' 蟋蟀 ("Cricket") and its Consequences: Issues in Early Chinese Poetry and Textual Studies," *Early China* 42 (2019): 20: "The title 'Xi shuai' [i.e., "The Cricket"] does not signify a single poem; it signifies a multiplicity of poetic expressions or, more precisely, a poetic discourse from which multiple different expressions could be generated." Revealing a striking similarity to C. H. Wang's theory of the *Odes* as oral-formulaic compositions, Kern further writes (31) of "repertoires [of poetic material]" and "sets of topics and phrases that could be compiled in modular ways, yielding ever new poems that were always similar but never the same." I discuss Kern's important article in greater detail in chapter 12.

Cf. here also Michael Puett's statement that "early literary production in China should be understood in terms of an endless process of accretion, in which poetic lines were constantly being utilized in new and surprising ways." In "Text and Commentary: The Early Tradition," *The Oxford Handbook of Classical Chinese Literature*, eds. Wiebke Denecke, Wai-Yee Li, and Xiaofei Tian, 121. Not only would I suggest that we know too little about "early literary production in China" to make such a categorical pronouncement, the claim that "poetic lines" (i.e., formulae already in existence) were *constantly* "utilized in new and surprising ways" is also potentially misleading in that it suggests, on the one hand, that there was little or no consistency in whatever corpus of poems that must have existed at a given time, and, on the other hand, that "literary production" was restricted to the rehashing, however creative, of preexisting formulae. More generally—these are not claims made by Puett—one may add that although the utilization of the *Odes* described in texts such as the *Zuozhuan*, as discussed above, may be called "new," the application of an ode to a new context seems far too conventionalized and coded to have been "surprising" to the person quoting the poem or to his addressee; more importantly, it is doubtful if the quotation and recontextualization of odes can be called a "literary production."

18. See Michael Nylan's "Classics Without Canonization: Learning and Authority in Qin and Han," in *Early Chinese Religion: Part One: Shang through Han (1250 BC–220 AD)* (2 vols.), ed. John Lagerwey and Marc Kalinowski (Leiden: Brill, 2008), Part 1, 721–77. See also Nicolas Zufferey, *To the Origins of Confucianism: The Ru in pre-Qin Times and During the Early Han Dynasty* (Bern: Peter Lang, 2003), and Anne Cheng, "What Did It Mean to Be a *Ru* in Han Times?," *Asia Major* 14, no. 2 (2001): 101–18.

19. See *Lunyu*, "Ji Shi" 季氏 16.13, "Yang Huo" 陽貨 17.9 and 17.10. All quotations from the *Lunyu*—the Confucian *Analects*—follow Wang Xiyuan's 王熙元 *Lunyu tongshi* 論語通釋 (Taipei: Xuesheng shuju, 1981).

20. For Xunzi's use of the *Odes*, see Liu Yunhua 劉耘華 *Quanshixue yu Qian-Qin rujia zhi yiyi shengcheng: Lunyu, Mengzi, Xunzi dui gudai chuantongdi jieshi* 詮釋學與先秦儒家之意義生成——《論語》、《孟子》、《荀子》對古代傳統的解釋 (Shanghai: Shanghai yiwen chubanche, 2002), 132–62. For a comprehensive study of the commentarial tradition surrounding the Confucian classics in the early Han, see Wang Baoxuan 王葆玹, *XiHan jingxue yuanliu* 西漢經學源流 (Taipei: Dongda tushu gongsi, 2008). For genealogies of the different exegetical traditions, see Lin Yelian's *Zhongguo lidai Shijingxue*, chapters 2 and 3. The literature on the excavated texts is vast. For the manuscript promoted by Anhui University, looted and of unknown provenance but by its editors dated to the mid-Warring States period, see Huang Dekuan 黃德寬 and Xu Zaiguo 徐在國, eds., *Anhui daxue cang Zhanguo zhujian* 安徽大學藏戰國竹簡, vol. 1 (Shanghai: Zhongxi shuju, 2019), 1–7; Huang, "Anhui daxue cang Zhanguo zhujian gaishu" 安徽大學藏戰國竹簡概述, *Wenwu* 文物 9 (2017): 54–59; and Xu, "Anhui daxue cang Zhanguo zhujian Shijing shixu yu yiwen" 安

徽大學藏戰國竹簡《詩經》詩序與異文, *Wenwu* 9 (2017): 60–62. For the so-called *Kongzi shilun* 孔子詩論 (Confucian discourses on the *Odes*) and its relationship to other traditions of *Shijing* exegesis during the Han, see Chen Tongsheng 陳桐生, *Kongzi shilun yanjiu* 孔子詩論研究 (Peking: Zhonghua, 2004), especially 240–56 (on 249, Chen curiously attributes an important comment by Zheng Xuan on an equally important passage from the *Great Preface* ["to remonstrate craftily and with an emphasis on form" 主文而譎諫] to Mao Heng). For a critical study of earlier scholarship, and a translation into English of what the author argues is the manuscript slips correctly arranged, see Thies Staack, "Reconstructing the *Kongzi shilun*: From the Arrangement of the Bamboo Slips to a Tentative Translation," *Asiatische Studien / Études Asiatiques* 64 (2010:4), 857–906. For a structural analysis of early Chinese "text production," see Dirk Meyer, "Writing Meaning: Strategies of Meaning-construction in Early Chinese Philosophical Discourse," in *Monumenta Serica* 56 (2008): 55–95, and *Philosophy on Bamboo: Text and the Production of Meaning in Early China* (Leiden & Boston: Brill, 2012), in particular the analysis of the use of the *Odes* in the "Wu xing" manuscript (chapter 3). For the use of the *Odes* in newly found manuscripts, see Martin Kern, "The *Odes* in Excavated Manuscripts," in *Text and Ritual in Early China*, ed. Martin Kern (Seattle: University of Washington Press, 2005), 149–93. For a comparison of Mao and pre-Mao exegesis, see Kern, "Lost in Tradition: The *Classic of Poetry* We Did Not Know," Vol. 5 of Hsiang Lectures on Chinese Poetry (Centre for East Asian Research, McGill University, 2010). For a more general overview of how the excavated texts have remodeled the Sinological landscape, see Edward L. Shaughnessy, *Rewriting Early Chinese Texts* (Albany: State University of New York Press, 2006. For insightful and important discussions on the problems associated with the study of purchased and looted manuscripts, see Paul R. Goldin, "*Heng xian* and the Problem of Studying Looted Artifacts," *Dao* 12 (2013): 153–60; Christopher J. Foster, "Introduction to the Peking University Han Bamboo Slips: On the Authentication and Study of Purchased Manuscripts," *Early China* 40 (2017): 172–81; Martin Kern, "Cricket," 7–11.

21. We note that in the *Zuozhuan*, *yin* 引 is never used to describe recitations of the *Odes*, and that *fu* in the very first entry of the *Zuo* (Yin 1) refers to the "presentation" of a poem that the protagonist has composed himself, rather than to a recitation of a preexisting poem. For a discussion of *fu* and *yin*, see You Jiazhong, *Shijing di jieshixue yanjiu*, 76–118. You Jiazhong's book is an intelligent examination, informed by Western hermeneutics, of the Chinese exegetical tradition surrounding the *Odes*. Chapter 4 of Zhu Jinfa's 朱金發 *Xian-Qin Shijingxue* 先秦詩經學 (Peking: Xueyuan, 2007) provides an overview of the practices of reciting, quoting, and composing *shi* as described in the *Zuozhuan* and *Guoyu* 國語. Luke Waring's "Making Sense of the *Odes*: Speeches as Poetic Commentary in the *Guoyu*," *Journal of the American Oriental Society* 143. 2 (Apr-Jun 2023): 309–29, demonstrates that the *Odes* were not merely quoted in the *Guoyu* but also analyzed and contexualized in a manner that foreshadows Mao's *Commentary* and other similar

exegetical traditions. For a systematizing and deep-probing study of the habit of "referencing" (*yin* 引) ancient exempla, sayings, and texts, see Xu Renfu 徐仁甫, *Gushu yinyu yanjiu* 古書引語研究 (Peking: Zhonghua shuju, 2014). For an overview of *Odes* quotations in pre-Qin texts, see Mark Edward Lewis, *Writing and Authority in Early China* (Albany, N.Y.: State University of New York Press, 1999), 163–72.

22. *Lüshi chunqiu jiaoshi* 呂氏春秋校釋, ed. and annotation Chen Qiyou 陳奇猷 (Taipei: Huazheng shuju, 1988), 1515. *Wei shi* 為詩 unambiguously refers to the exposition of the *Odes* in *Mencius*, "Gaozi 2.23"; *Mengzi yizhu* 孟子譯注, translation and annotation, Yang Bojun 楊伯峻 (Peking: Zhonghua, 2010), 257. "Qian shang" is quoted also in *Zuozhuan*, Zhao 16; Wang et al., *Zuozhuan quanyi*, 1255–56.

23. See Zhao Maolin 趙茂林, *LiangHan san jia Shi yanjiu* 兩漢三家詩研究 (Chengdu: Bashu shushe, 2006); Wen Xinfu, *Shijing Maozhuan Zhengjian bianyi*, 12–110; Lin Yaolin 林耀潾, *XiHan sanjia shixue yanjiu* 西漢三家詩學研究 (Taipei: Wenjin, 1996); Lu Cixing 陸錫興, *Shijing yiwen yanjiu* 詩經異文研究 (Peking: Zhongguo banben tushuguan, 2001); Lin Yelian, *Zhongguo lidai Shijingxue*, chap. 2 and 3; and Shang Jiyu's 尚繼愚 introductions to the "Four Schools" and Zheng Xuan's *Annotations* in Dong Zhian 董治安 and Xia Chuancai 夏傳才, ed., *Shijing yaoji tiyao* 詩經要籍提要 (Peking: Xueyuan chubanshe, 2003), 1–21. For the so-called Fuyang *Odes*, see Chan Pak-ka's "Handai 'diwujia *Shi*' shuo xianyi."

24. The exact meaning of the title *Mao Shi guxunzhuan* 毛詩故訓傳 is unclear. *Guxun* 故訓 is often taken to stand for the homophonic *guxun* 詁訓 ("glosses [on arcane words and phrases]"), but Yu Shujuan 于淑娟—expanding, by and large, on the tripartite structure suggested by Ma Ruichen 馬瑞辰 (1782–1835)—argues that *gu* 故 refers to the historicizing explanations of the *Odes* given in the *Minor Prefaces*, *xun* 訓 to Mao's linguistic glosses and "xingish" analysis of *Shijing* imagery, and *zhuan* 傳 to his elaborations on the moral implications of the poems (to Master Mao's "teachings," in other words). According to Yu, whereas *Maozhuan* simply refers to Mao's *Commentary*, the term *Maoshi* is an abbreviation of *Maoshi gu xun zhuan*, which includes the *Minor Prefaces* (and probably also the *Great Preface*) and should be rendered as *The Mao Recension of The Odes, Incorporating Historical Explanations, Glosses and Literary Analysis, and Didactic Teachings*. Yu Shujuan, "'Maoshi gu xun zhuan' mingyi kaoshi: Jian lun 'Maoshi gu xun zhuan' duzhuan di yuanyin"《毛詩故訓傳》名義考釋—兼論《毛詩故訓傳》獨傳的原因. See also Bernhard Karlgren, "The Early History of the *Chou Li* and *Tso Chuan* Texts" (*BMFEA* 28 [1931]), 14; and Wu Wanzhong 吳萬鐘, *Cong shi dao jing: lun Maoshi jieshi de yuanyuan jiqi tese* 從詩到經：論毛詩解釋的淵源及其特色 (Peking: Zhonghua, 2001), 1–11.

25. For the decline of the "Three Schools," see Zhao Maolin, *LiangHan san jia Shi yanjiu*, 592–643.

26. For a conventional translation, see Siu-Kit Wong, *Early Chinese Literary Criticism* (Hong Kong: Joint Publishing Company, 1983), 1–8. For an interpretation and contextualization, see Stephen Owen, *Readings in Chinese Literary Thought* (Cambridge, MA: Council on East Asian Studies, Harvard University,

1992), 38–56; Paula M. Versano, "Getting There from Here: Locating the Subject in Early Chinese Poetics," *Harvard Journal of Asiatic Studies* 56, no. 2 (December 1996): 375–403; and Lewis, *Writing and Authority*, 173–76. Concisely expressing the Sinological consensus on the *Great Preface*, Versano speaks of the "process of natural, unpremeditated poetic creation first encoded in the 'Great Preface' to the *Shijing*"; *Tracking the Banished Immortal: The Poetry of Li Bo and Its Critical Reception* (Honolulu: University of Hawai'i Press, 2003), 143. In Martin Kern's analysis, the *Preface* describes "original poetic composition" as an "immediate response to historical circumstances" and as "generated by the fundamental participation of the human mind in the workings of the cosmos."; "Early Chinese Literature, Beginnings Through Western Han," in Kang-i Sun Chang and Stephen Owen, eds., *The Cambridge History of Chinese Literature. Vol. 1, To 1375* (Cambridge: Cambridge University Press, 2010), 31. Lewis (174) claims that according to the *Preface*, "the truth of verse is guaranteed by an unreflective spontaneity." I perform a slightly different reading below which has more in common with Qian Zhongshu's analysis of the *Preface* in *Guan zhui bian* 管錐編 (Peking: Zhonghua, 1979), Part 1, 57–58. See also Martin Svensson [Ekström], "A Second Look at the Great Preface on the Way to a New Understanding of Han Dynasty Poetics," *Chinese Literature, Essays, Articles, Reviews* (*CLEAR*) 21 (1999), 6, and Michael Nylan's critique thereof in *The Five "Confucian" Classics* (New Haven, CT: Yale University Press, 2001), 108, despite which I maintain my position (footnotes are not included in Nylan's book but posted at https://yalebooks.yale.edu/sites/default/files/files/Media/978030008185 55/9780300081855_nylan2notes.pdf). See the discussion of *poiein* as referring not only to the "making" of a poem but also to the performance thereof in Alexander Beecroft, *Authorship and Cultural Identity in Early Greece and China: Patterns of Literary Circulation* (Cambridge: Cambridge University Press, 2010), 58–60.

27. See Karlgren, *Glosses, Kuo feng* section, 72. In the following, I refer to Karlgren's glosses by their entry number (1–1206).

28. The identities of these two figures are uncertain. According to Zheng Xuan's lost *Maoshi pu* 毛詩譜, as quoted in the Tang dynasty by Kong Yingda, Meng Zhongzi (or, possibly, "Master Mengzhong") was a disciple of Confucius's grandson Zisi—"serving Zisi together with Meng Ke [Mencius]"—and the author of a book "discussing the *Odes* [*lun shi*]" on which Master Mao based his explanations (*SSJZS, Maoshi zhengyi*, 1284). According to Lu Ji's genealogy of the exegetical and editorial tradition that culminated with the *Maoshi*, Master Meng hailed from the state of Lu ("*Mao Shi" cao mu niao shou chong yu shu* 毛詩草木鳥獸蟲魚疏 as quoted in the *Zongmu* preface to the *Maoshi* in *SSJZS, Maoshi zhengyi*, 1). In *Mencius*, Gong Sun Chou 2 公孫丑下, there appears a figure called Meng Zhongzi, presumably a relative of Mencius's, who may be the person Mao Heng, Zheng Xuan and Lu Ji are referring to (*Mengzi yizhu*, 80). The background of Master Zhongliang is even sketchier. With obvious hesitation, Kong Yingda (*SSJZS, Maoshi zhengyi*, 197) quotes a work, *Zheng zhi* 鄭志, attributed to a descendent of Zheng Xuan's, where

it is stated that Zhongliang was a *shi* 師 ("teacher" or "master") who, like Mao and Meng Zhongzi, came from the state of Lu. Perhaps he is, as Kong seems to suggest, identical or related to the Zhongliang Huai 仲梁懷 mentioned in *Zuozhuan*, Ding 5; *Zuozhuan quanyi*, 1437.

29. The "Old Prefaces" corresponds roughly to the first sentence of each of what is now known as the *Minor Prefaces*. See Liu Zhaijing's 劉兆靜 study "*Maoshi xiaoxu* 'xushou' yu 'xushen zhi pian' guanxi yanjiu" 《毛詩小序》"序首"與"續申之詞" 關系研究 (MA thesis, Liaoning shifan daxue, 2011). The six "lost odes," of which only the titles but not the actual poems remain, have been transmitted with these shorter prefaces but without Mao's *Commentary*, which would seem to indicate that the *Minor Prefaces* indeed consist of an earlier and a later layer, and that the *Old Prefaces* predated the *Commentary*. Despite Wen Xinfu's often persuasive arguments, one cannot conclude that Mao followed the *Old Preface*, hence the necessity to read the *Mao Commentary* in isolation remains. See Steven Van Zoeren, *Poetry and Personality* (Stanford: Stanford University Press, 1991), and Wen Xinfu, *Shijing Maozhuan Zhengjian bianyi*, 207.

Quotations from the *Xunzi* follow (apart from some changes in punctuation) *Xunzi jijie* 荀子集解 (Peking: Zhonghua, 1988), ed. Wang Xianqian 王先謙; here, 511. The quote from the *Kongzi shilun* comes from Ma Chengyuan 馬承源, *Shanghai bowuguancang zhanguo Chu zhushu* 上海博物館藏戰國楚竹書, volume 1 (Shanghai: Shanghai guji, 2001), 140–41. I note that according to the *Shilun* (143), the fourth stanza of "Guanju" "compares [擬?] the joy of the lutes and cithers to the lust in sensuous desire" 以琴瑟之悅擬好色之願, and that "the wisdom [imparted by] 'Han guang' [ode nine] is the knowledge of being unable to attain [a particular goal]" 漢廣之智則知不可得也. Although my translations (and the transcriptions that I follow) are tentative and approximate, they evince a mode of interpretation similar to (1) that of the *Minor Prefaces* in that they ascribe to the ode in question a moralizing intent seemingly at odds with the meaning of the poem when and if read in isolation; (2) Mao Heng's *Commentary* in that the *Shilun*—if my reading is indeed correct—takes an interest in the use of figures of speech such as similes or analogies (*yu* 喻 and *ni* 擬) in the *Odes*; (3) the standard Confucian interpretations of the *Odes* as known from received texts, such as the above quote from the *Xunzi*. For the transcription 擬, see Staack, "Reconstructing the *Kongzi shilun*," 894.

30. The so-called "Wuxingpian" 五行篇, a text found in 1973 in a tomb at Mawangdui, contains short analyses of a handful of *Shijing* poems by way of a concept of 與 (pronounced *yu* in modern Chinese and meaning "give, provide, join," etc.), and whose antonym seems to be *zhi* 直 ("direct" or "forthright" [discourse]). It is generally assumed that the graph *yu* 與 is a variant of *xing* 興. See Ikeda Tomohisa 池田知久, *Mawangdui Hanbo boshu wuxung yanjiu* 馬王堆漢墓帛書五行研究 (Peking: China Social Sciences Press, 2005), 192–94. For a comprehensive introduction to the "Wuxingpian," and a translation of relevant passages, see Jeffrey Riegel, "Eros, Introversion, and The Beginnings of *Shijing* Commentary," *Harvard*

Journal of Asiatic Studies 57, no. 1 (June 1997): 143–77. The "Wuxingpian" predates Mao's *Commentary* and their connection—if any—is unclear. (Like the *Kongzi shilun*, however, the "Wuxingpian" holds that the first ode "explains ritual principles by [describing] sensuous desire," which may suggest an affinity between the two texts.) The coinage of *xing* as a tool for analyzing the imagery of the *Odes* was most likely influenced by Confucius's somewhat enigmatic remark in *Analects* 17.9 *shi ke yi xing* 詩可以興, "the *Odes* can be used to *xing*," where *xing* seems to mean "to arouse the listener" or "impart a subtle message" or "instill joy."

31. For the applicability of the term metaphor to early Chinese "poetry" and "poetics" (two other terms deeply rooted in Western thought), see my "Inscription and Re-reading—Re-reading the Inscribed," *BMFEA* 74 and "Does the Metaphor Translate?," in *Translating China for Western Readers* (Albany: State University of New York, 2014), 45–70.

32. Yu, 46 (quotation marks in the original).

33. Cecile Chu-Chin Sun, *The Poetics of Repetition in English and Chinese Lyric Poetry* (Chicago: University of Chicago Press, 2011), 177.

34. Frederick Mote, "The Cosmological Gulf Between China and the West," in David Buxbaum and Frederick Mote, eds., *Transition and Permanence: Chinese History and Culture* (Hong Kong, 1972), 3–21.

35. Stephen Owen, *Readings in Chinese Literary Thought*, 42.

36. For statistics and tables regarding the xing in Mao's *Commentary* and Zheng's *Annotations*, see 117–97 of Pei Puxian's 裴普賢 indispensable study of the history of the concept of xing in *Shijing yandu zhidao* 詩經研讀指導 (Taipei: Dongda tushu gongsi, 1977), 173–331. For the count of 116, I follow Zhu Ziqing; see *Shijing yandu zhidao*, 190–91.

Chapter 1

1. *Lunyu*, "Yang huo" 陽貨 17.9. In the received *Lunyu*, *xing* appears in the sense of "to rise (from a reclining position)" ("Wei Ling Gong" 衛靈公 15.2); "establish," "invigorate" or "reinvigorate" as opposed to *sang* 喪 ("destroy" or "ruin"; "Zi Lu" 子路 13.13 and "Yao yue" 堯曰 20.1); "prosper" or "flourish" ("Zi Lu" 13.3). In Tai Bo 泰伯 8.2 and 8.8, *xing* seems to have the same meaning as in "Yang huo," that is, "uplift; enthuse; inspire." In the *Odes*, *xing* most often means "to rise (from a reclining position)," but also "raise (an army)" and, probably, in ode 256, "elevate."

2. Zhong Rong, *Shi pin yizhu* 詩品譯注 (Taipei: Guiya wenhua shiye youxiangongsi, 1991), 8; *Wenxin diaolong* 文心雕龍, transl. and annotation Wang Zhibin 王志彬 (Peking: Zhonghua, 2012), 410–14. My rendition of the *Shi pin* passage is perhaps too paraphrastic. A more succinct translation would be "the words have ended yet there is meaning beyond them: this is xing."

3. Cf. also Shirakawa Shizuka 白川靜, *Shijing xue* 詩經學, trans. Tu Cheng-sheng (Taipei: Youshi wenhua shiye gongsi, 1974), 21: "Since it lacks a clear link to the main topic [of the poem], the so-called xing method of expression in the *Shijing* makes it hard to grasp the meaning of a particular poem and, furthermore, easily yields aberrations." The xing, in Shirakawa's mind, evolved from the "singing and chanting that was uttered in order to establish contact with the spirits" (ibid.).

4. For references, see below. For reliable and competent accounts of the history of the concept xing, see Pauline R. Yu "Allegory, Allegoresis and the *Classic of Poetry*," *Harvard Journal of Asiatic Studies* 43, no. 2 (1983), 377–412; the chapter on xing in Huang Zhenmin's *Shijing yanjiu* (Taipei: Zhengzhong shuju, 1982), 121–83; and Peng Feng's 彭鋒 *Shi ke yi xing: Gudai zongjiao, lilun, zhexue yu yishudi meixue chanshi* 詩可以興—古代宗教、倫理、哲學與藝術的美學闡釋 (Hefei: Anhui jiaoyu chubanshe, 2003), 49, 52–105. Pauline Yu's theory of the xing will be discussed in detail later.

5. Cecile Chu-chin Sun, "Mimesis and Xing, Two Modes of Viewing Reality: Comparing English and Chinese Poetry," *Comparative Literature Studies* 43, no. 3 (2006): 326–54.

6. Inoi Makoto 家井眞 *Shikyô no gengiteki kenkyû* 詩經の原意研究 (Tokyo: Kenbun shuppan, 2004); translated by Lu Yue 陸越 as *Shijing yuanyi yanjiu*《詩經》原意研究 (Nanking: Jiangsu renmin chubanshe, 2010), 218.

7. Ye Shuxian 葉舒憲, *Shijing di wenhua chanshi* 詩經的文花闡釋 (Wuhan: Hunan renmin chubanshe, 1994).

8. Peng Feng, *Shi ke yi xing*, 68–105. For xing as a name of a Shang ritual, se Peng, 52–67, 148, and Chow Tse-tsung, *Gu wuyi yu 'liushi' kao: Zhongguo langman wenxue tankao* 古巫醫與《六詩》考: 中國浪漫文學探源 (Taipei: Lianjing shuju, 1986), 217. For the notion (itself derived from Vico and Plato) of a uniquely Chinese "poetic intelligence," see 98. Note that Peng makes a radical and important modification of the earlier analyses of the graph xing by claiming that the four hands lifting an object do not represent an act of actual physical labor but a ritualized enactment with a "strong religious flavour" (61), in which song, dance, and music aim at establishing contact with the spirits (64).

9. See "Illusion, Lie, and Metaphor," *Poetics Today* 23, no. 2 (2002); "Does the Metaphor Translate?"; and my readings of *Lunyu* and the *Mencius* in "The Value of Misreading and the Need for Re-interpretation," *BMFEA* 76: 8–21.

10. For an even more radical formulation, see Zhang Haishan 張海珊: "The Chinese race is a race adept at thinking in images." "Zhonghua minzu shi shanyu xingxiang siwei di minzu: Shiguo aomi zhi yi" 中華民族是善於形象思維的民族——詩國奧祕之一), *Tianjin Shifan daxuebao* 天津師範大學學報 1989, no. 6 (1989): 54–59, quoted with approval in Lin Yelian's *Zhongguo lidai Shijingxue*, 125.

11. Chow Tse-tsung, "The Early History of the Chinese Word *Shih* (Poetry)," in *Wen-lin: Studies in the Chinese Humanities*, ed. Chow Tse-tsung (Madison: University of Wisconsin Press, 1968). Jesper Svenbro, "La parole et le marbre: aux origines de la

poétique grecque" (PhD diss., Lund University, 1976), also available in Italian as *La parola e il marmo: alle origini della poetica greca* (Turin: Boringhieri, 1984). Svenbro explores the different and often conflicting early Greek conceptions of "poetry," of which *poiêsis* was but one. The concept of poetry as an artifact "produced" by a skilled craftsman occurs, Svenbro argues, only with the emergence of the choral poets who were wordsmiths paid to create poetry for special occasions, and Svenbro holds (5, 193) that the concept of *poiêsis* was anachronistically projected upon the Homeric epics already in antiquity.

Rather than a skilled wordsmith, the Homeric bard appears in the *Odyssey* as an inspired mediator of events and narratives that existed both before and beyond himself; we may also exemplify Svenbro's thesis with the famed opening line where the bard calls upon the Muse to relate—through him—the story of Ulysses: "describe to me, Muse (*moi ennepe mousa*), the man of many twists and turns (*andra polutropon*)."

Svenbro's thesis, which like C. H. Wang's analysis of the *Odes* builds on the works of Albert Lord and Milman Parry, is open to criticism but testifies to the need for slow and careful analyses in comparative enterprises. A study, for instance, that intends to bring out the specificity of the early Chinese tradition by comparing it to its Greek counterpart(s) risks reducing the "source" culture to a smooth monolith, in spite of its complexities and internal contradictions. For a stimulating discussion of "La parole et le marbre," see Penelope Murray, "Poetic Inspiration in Early Greece," *Journal of Hellenic Studies* 101 (1981): 98–99.

Chapter 2

1. C. H. Wang, *The Bell and the Drum: "Shih Ching" as Formulaic Poetry in an Oral Tradition* (Berkeley: University of California Press, 1974). This book is almost identical to Wang's PhD thesis, "'Shih Ching': Formulaic Language and Mode of Creation" (University of California at Berkeley, 1971). I will quote the latter whenever the deviations are relevant.

2. Wang, "'Shih Ching': Formulaic Language and Mode of Creation," 160. Note that an "almost" was added before the word "identifiable" when the sentence was reprinted in *The Bell and the Drum*.

3. *The Bell and the Drum*, 107.

4. "*Shih-ching* is conceivably oral, and demonstrably formulaic," *The Bell and the Drum*, "Preface," x.

5. Wang, *The Bell and the Drum*, 43.

6. Wang, *The Bell and the Drum*, 14.

7. Wang, *The Bell and the Drum*, 72.

8. Wang, *The Bell and the Drum*, 70.

9. Wang, *The Bell and the Drum*, 71.

10. *SSJYJS*, 398–400. We note that Kong Yingda interprets the first line as "loosely" 稀疏 woven fiber shoes, which would make better sense in Wang's case; *SSJZS, Maoshi zhengyi*, 362. See Karlgren, *Glosses* 269.

11. Chen Huan, *Shi Maoshizhuan shu*, 265.

12. *Mao Commentary, SSJYJS*, 398.

13. *Zheng Annotation, SSJYJS*, 398.

14. *Zheng Annotation, SSJYJS*, 398.

15. Wang, *The Bell and the Drum*, 3. On page 8, Wang translates Zheng Xuan's annotation on ode 168, and the last sentences are rendered as such: "Cicadas cry in late autumn. This is motivated (*hsing*) right at the time when one perceives [the scene]." But the meaning of Zheng's comment is rather: "When cicadas cry it is late autumn. This [locus or trope] takes that which is seen at this time of year [i.e., late autumn] and uses it as a xing" 草蟲鳴, 晚秋之時也。此以所見而興之. More importantly, Wang claims that the time of year described in the poem is "late winter or early spring," that Zheng's talk about late autumn is erroneous, and that the "inconsistency" of the poem is the result of the vicissitudes of oral composing. However, there are sound reasons for defending Zheng's reading. The usage of "inconsistent" imagery (e.g., descriptions of all four seasons in a single poem) is a method often employed by the *Odes* to suggest the passing of time. There is, furthermore, no real evidence that Zheng sees the cicada as an indication of spring. Zheng's argument is this: When cicadas sing, grasshoppers jump toward them. When the princes heard the news about General Nanzhong they were so happy that they jumped about, just like grasshoppers do when they hear cicadas. Cicadas cry in late autumn, and this poem uses that which one sees at this time of year (namely the grasshoppers jumping toward the cicadas) as a xing. What Zheng emphasizes is the analogy between the cicadas and grasshoppers and the princes, not the time of year.

16. Wang, *The Bell and the Drum*, 6.

17. Wang, *The Bell and the Drum*, 98.

18. Wang, *The Bell and the Drum*, 99. I have simplified Wang's quotations. Here, "plot" is actually called "myth." On page 19, however, Wang himself equates the two terms.

19. For a discussion of the terms "tenor" and "vehicle," their appearance in I. A. Richards's *The Philosophy of Rhetoric* (Oxford: Oxford University Press, 1936), and their relevance for studies of "literary metaphor" today, see chapter 13 and my "Editor's Preface" to *BMFEA* 79/80 (2020), "Sino-methodological Remark on the Metaphor of *Metaphora* and the Limitations of the 'Conceptual Metaphor Theory.'"

20. Wang, *The Bell and the Drum*, 102.

21. Translation Wang's; *The Bell and the Drum*, 103.

22. Wang, *The Bell and the Drum*, 106.

23. Wang, *The Bell and the Drum*, 72n28. One may object that realism is not necessarily the most conspicuous feature of poetry. We also note that in a similar

case, poem 201, also called "Gu feng 谷風," the interplay between imagery and plot is supposed to be perfectly logical.

24. Wang, *The Bell and the Drum*, 105; italics added.

25. Wang, *The Bell and the Drum*, 105.

26. This is further corroborated by Wang's attempt to dismiss the metaphoricity of this ode by claiming that the process took place at an *early* stage. A moment later he refers to what in all probability is a later text (*Dao de jing*) containing the same valley-wife metaphor.

27. Transliteration adapted from William H. Baxter and Laurent Sagart, "Old Chinese reconstruction, version 1.1 (September 20, 2014)," 111.

28. *SSJYJS*, 570–75; trans. Karlgren, *Book of Odes* (Stockholm: Museum of Far Eastern Antiquities, 1950), 108–9.

29. See *The Bell and the Drum*, 106: "The mention of . . . the valley . . . in the composition of the wife's complaint is so conspicuous that the valley motif can be called 'thematic'."

30. Wang, *The Bell and the Drum*, 100.

31. Wang, *The Bell and the Drum*, 19. Wang uses "myth" instead of "plot."

32. Translation Wang's; *The Bell and the Drum*, 66; *SSJYJS*, 647.

33. For the small number of "plant-picking" poems that indeed are labeled xing by Mao (e.g., ode 72) see chapter 22.

34. See 102, "Often a *Shih Ching* theme is heralded by some reference to natural objects which in various evocative forms prepares for the fixed realization of the content." The "reference to natural objects" is of course what constitutes Mao's xing, but we should note the terminological confusion. Wang claims that the oral-formulaic "theme" is "identifiable with the *hsing* [xing] element in the Chinese aesthetics of the short lyric." But on page 102, "theme" is synonymous with the "plot," and thus the opposite of xing.

35. Wang, *The Bell and the Drum*, 108.

36. See chapter 21 of the present work.

37. Lois M. Fusek, review of *The Bell and the Drum*, in *Chinese Literature: Essays, Articles, Reviews* (*CLEAR*) 1 (January 1979): 99–103. See 103: "Throughout Chinese history there has been a continuous overlap between the oral and the written traditions, and it may be suggested that this undoubtedly is true in the *Shih-ching* as well. It would be of special benefit to know, for example, how these traditions interact and with what effect. The attempt to prove that the *Shih-ching* is entirely literate or entirely oral, by whatever means, is almost certainly doomed to failure, for the *Shih-ching* is manifestly a composite of both oral and written features and does not easily conform to the extreme characteristics of either."

38. See here the set of bronze vessels that commemorate King Xuan's 宣 appointment, in ca. 825 BCE, of a man called Song 頌 to the position of manager of the royal warehouses. The inscription on these vessels details an intricate interplay of orality and inscription. See Shirakawa Shizuka, *Kinbun tsûshaku* 金文通釋 (Kobe:

Hakutsuru bijutsukan, 1962–84), 24:153–74; Edward Shaughnessy, "Western Zhou History," in Loewe and Shaughnessy, eds., *The Cambridge History of Ancient China*, 298–99; Martin Kern, "The Performance of Writing in Western Zhou China," in *The Poetics of Grammar and the Metaphysics of Sound and Sign* ed. La Porta and Shulman (Leiden: Brill, 2007), 152–57.

39. See here Constance Cook and Paul Goldin, eds., *A Source Book of Ancient Chinese Bronze Inscriptions*, rev. ed. (Berkeley: Society for the Study of Early China, 2020), with translations by Constance A. Cook, Wolfgang Behr, Robert Eno, Paul R. Goldin, Martin Kern, Maria Khayutina, David W. Pankenier, David Sena, Laura Skosey, and Yan Sun.

Chapter 3

1. "The *Shih Ching*: Its Generic Significance in Chinese Literary History and Poetics" first appeared in the *Bulletin of the Institute of History and Philology, Academia Sinica* XXXIX (1969): 371–413; a version with significant revisions was printed five years later in Cyril Birch, ed., *Studies in Chinese Literary Genres* (Berkeley: University of California Press, 1974). I typically refer to the original version.

2. Chen, "*Shih ching*," 387.

3. Chen, "*Shih ching*," 397, quoted by Chen, with great approval, from Cecil Day Lewis's quotation of H. W. Garrod in Lewis's *The Poetic Image* (New York: Oxford University Press, 1947), 25.

4. Chen, "*Shih ching*," 378.

5. A similar interpretation of the character *xing* is presented by Chow Tse-tsung in *Gu wuyi yu 'liushi' kao*. Chow holds that the earliest instances of the character *xing* depicted four hands holding a tray, *pan* 槃. Chow's theory is that, in ancient times, the *pan*-tray was held by dancers as they rotated around it, that there actually existed a dance by that name, and that ode 296 ("Pan" 槃), refers to this phenomenon. See also Chow's "The Early History of the Chinese Word *Shih* (Poetry)," Ye Shuxian, *Shijing di wenhua chanshi* (Wuhan: Hunan renmin chubanshe, 1994), 402–3, and Sun, *Poetics of Repetition*, 177.

6. Chen, "*Shih ching*," 396; the theory had been elaborated in Chen's "In Search of the Beginnings of Chinese Literary Criticism," in *University of California Publications in Semitic Philology, Semitic and Oriental Studies Presented to William Popper* 11 (1951), 49.

7. Chen, "*Shih ching*," 386.
8. Chen, "*Shih ching*," 387.
9. Chen, "*Shih ching*," 390.
10. Chen, "*Shih ching*," 390.
11. Chen, "*Shih ching*," 402.
12. Chen, "*Shih ching*," 392.

13. Chen, "*Shih ching*," 391.
14. Chen, "*Shih ching*," 406.
15. Chen, "*Shih ching*," 398.
16. Chen, "*Shih ching*," 398.
17. *SSJYJS*, 8. The translation is mine; in the following I adapt the translation of "Guanju" to the context in which it appears.
18. Chen, "*Shih ching*," 399.
19. Chen, "*Shih ching*," 398–99. *Mao Commentary*, *SSJYJS*, 8.
20. Chen, "*Shih ching*," 410.

Chapter 4

1. Zhao Peilin, *Xing di yuanqi - Lishi jidian yu shige yishu* 興的源起——歷史積澱與詩歌藝 (Peking: Zhongguo shehui kexue chubanshe, 1987); Claude Lévi-Strauss, *Le totémisme aujourd'hui* (Paris: Presses Universitaires, 1965 [1962]).
2. Zhao, *Xing di yuanqi*, 19–20.
3. *SSJYJS*, 139.
4. *Mao Commentary*, *SSJYJS*, 139.

Chapter 5

1. *SSJYJS*, 354.
2. *Zuozhuan*, 27; Wang et al., *Zuozhuan quanyi*, 326. The passage in question says that "the *Odes* and the *Book of Documents* [*Shang shu*] are storehouses of righteousness" 詩書, 義之府也.
3. Gu Jiegang, ed., *Gu shi bian* (Rpt. Taipei: Minlun, 1970), vol. 3, 673–77, reprinted in Lin Ch'ing-chang, ed., *Shijing yanjiu lunji* 詩經研究論集 (Taipei: Xuesheng shuju, 1983), vol. 1, 63–67.
4. *SSJYJS*, 8–9. Transliteration of 關關 adapted from Baxter and Sagart, "Old Chinese reconstruction, version 1.1 (20 September 2014)," 31.
5. See Baxter's and Sagart's reconstructions of the "Old Chinese" pronunciation in *Old Chinese: A New Reconstruction*, 105; and Baxter and Sagart, "Old Chinese Reconstruction, Version 1.1 (September 20, 2014)," 140 and 142. For Karlgren's reconstruction, see Karlgren, *Grammata Serica Recensa* (Rpt. Stockholm: MFEA, [1957] 1972), 1086d and 1066k.
6. Gu's hypothesis harks back at least to Zhu Xi 朱熹 (1130–1200): "When, instead of speaking of the subject matter, one uses two lines devoid of meaning relevant to the context to *diaoqi* ["fish something up"; get the reader hooked?], and thence continue on [to the subject matter], this is xing" 本要言其事而虛用兩句釣起, 因而接續去者, 興也. *Zhuzi yulei* 朱子語類, book 80 (Rpt. Peking: Zhonghua,

1994), 2067. For a critique, see Lin Yelian, *Zhongguo lidai Shijingxue*, 130–31. Zhu Xi's theory of xing is, of course, more complex than this single quote suggests.

7. *SSJYJS*, 8–9.

8. See Lin Mingde's essay "Shi lun *Shijing* di diyi shou—Guanju"; *Shijing yanjiu lunji*, 297.

Chapter 6

1. Donald Holzman, "Confucius and Ancient Chinese Literary Criticism"; Adele Austin Rickett, ed., *Chinese Approaches to Literature from Confucius to Liang C'hi-C'hao* (Princeton, NJ: Princeton University Press, 1978), 40–41.

2. Holzman, "Confucius and Ancient Chinese Literary Criticism," 36.

3. *Zuozhuan*, Xiang 27; Wang, *Zuozhuan quanyi*, 998.

4. *SSJYJS*, 369–71. See Karlgren, *Glosses* 341–42.

5. Holzman, "Confucius and Ancient Chinese Literary Criticism," 36. See chapter 43 of Wu Wanzhong's *Cong shi dao jing*, which in a similar way locates the origins of Mao's xing in Confucius's dictum *shi ke yi xing*, and in the quotations of the *Odes* by thinkers like Xunzi.

6. Zhu Ziqing, *Shi yan zhi bian* 詩言志辨 (Taipei: Kaiming Shudian, 1982).

7. Zhu Ziqing, *Shi yan zhi bian*, 53. See also Peng Feng, *Shi ke yi xing*, 82–83.

8. Zhu Ziqing, *Shi yan zhi bian*, 70. See William H. Nienhauser's "Some Preliminary Remarks on the *Shi* in the *Zuo zhuan*," *Oriens Extremus* 50 (2011 [2012]), 75–98, in which Nienhauser draws attention to the inventiveness with which the diplomats adapted the *Odes* to the situation at hand but also to the fact that the messages thus conveyed were sometimes misunderstood.

9. Establishing genealogies of intellectual concepts is a risky enterprise, but it seems that the concept of xing was transformed when the *Odes* were no longer recited but read, that is, during the change from an oral to a textual hermeneutics. Mao's xing was in all likelihood related to Confucius's (i.e., Holzman's *exemplum*), but I would suggest that the former evolved from the latter. If we accept Holzman's thesis, it seems logical that Confucius's xing refers to the act of poetry recital, whereas Mao's xing is a term designed for textual analysis.

Chapter 7

1. Marcel Granet, *Fêtes et chansons anciennes de la Chine*, 2d ed. (Paris: Leroux, [1919] 1929).

2. For an early critique, see Bernhard Karlgren: "Legends and Cults in Ancient China," *BMFEA* 18 (1946): 199–365.

3. Granet might have played a role more important for the structuralist movement than is usually conceived of. See Claude Lévi-Strauss and Didier Eribon,

De près et de loin (Paris: O. Jacob, 1988), 139–40, where Lévi-Strauss accounts for his ardent study of Granet's *Catégories matrimoniales et relations de proximité dans la Chine ancienne* (Paris: Alcan, 1939).

4. Granet, *Fêtes*, 240.
5. Granet, *Fêtes*, 241 and 248.
6. Granet, *Fêtes*, 241.
7. Granet, *Fêtes*, 239.
8. Granet, *Fêtes*, 243.
9. Granet, *Fêtes*, 224.
10. Granet, *Fêtes*, 246, note 1.
11. Granet, *Fêtes*, 247.
12. Granet's definitions are probably inherited from Zhu Xi who regarded the xing as an "intratextual" trope and the *bi* as fundamentally "extratextual."
13. See Granet, *Fêtes*, 52: "Thus, if one chooses natural imagery [*images naturelles*] to express feelings it is not at all due to one's experiencing the beauty of nature but rather because it is moral[ly correct] to conform to nature; where one might at first tend to see artistic intent, there may be a moral intent."
14. Granet is probably referring to ode 49, "Chun zhi benben" 鶉之奔奔. Granet's claim that the phrase *benben* 奔奔 refers to the birds' flying in couples is not corroborated by Mao, nor is the claim (36) that Mao reads the first lines as an indication that the male and female birds take care of their offspring together. Indeed, according to Mao this ode does not contain a xing-element at all (*SSJYJS*, 234).
15. Granet, *Fêtes*, 53 and 39.
16. In *Dadai Liji* 大戴禮記, ed. Wang Pinzhen 王聘珍 (Rpt. Peking: Zhonghua, 1983).
17. Granet, *Fêtes*, 33. *SSJYJS*, 513.
18. Granet, *Fêtes*, 33.
19. *Liji*, "Yueling," *SSJZS*, 471.
20. Granet, *Fêtes*, 55.
21. For a very similar argument, see the "five meteorites, six pheasants" passage of the "Shencha minghao" chapter ascribed to Dong Zhongshu; Su Yu 蘇輿, *Chunqiu fanlu yizheng* 春秋繁露義證 (Peking: Zhonghua shuju, 1992), 266.
22. Granet, *Fêtes*, 56–57.

Chapter 8

1. Pauline Yu, *The Reading of Imagery in the Chinese Poetic Tradition* (Princeton: Princeton University Press, 1987).
2. "[L]e sens figuré ne peut être conçu indépendamment d'une certaine vision du monde," François Jullien, *Le Détour et l'accès : Strategies du sens en Chine, en Grèce* (Paris: Grasset, 1995), 157. See Yu, *The Reading of Imagery*, 13: "Looking at metaphor as a mode of thought and means to knowledge, to be *considered within a*

larger set of cultural and philosophical presuppositions, can go beyond this preoccupation with what are often *superficial linguistic phenomena*." (Italics mine.) Yu is thus not making the claim—certainly an absurd one—that there are no "metaphors" in Chinese, but that a concept like Aristotle's *metaphora* could not be conceived since early Chinese thinking did not separate lived experience from abstract truths (here, the hidden "likeness" which unites the two apparently dissimilar things).

3. *Poetics* 1457b. Yu, *The Reading of Imagery*, 13. The somewhat paraphrasing translation used by Yu is by Ingram Bywater (1840–1914): Aristotle, *Poetics* (rpt; New York: Modern Library, 1954), 255. See my "Inscription and Re-reading" and "Does the Metaphor Translate" for discussions of this passage in Aristotle, and of the notion of *to homoion* in relation to early Chinese theories of figurative language.

4. Yu, *The Reading of Imagery*, 18. Paul Ricoeur, *The Rule of Metaphor: Multi-disciplinary Studies of the Creation of Meaning in Language*, trans. Robert Czerny (London: Routledge, 1978), 22.

5. Yu, *The Reading of Imagery*, 12.

6. Yu, *The Reading of Imagery*, 14 (italics added).

7. Yu, *The Reading of Imagery*, 14.

8. Yu, *The Reading of Imagery*, 54. Yu is here quoting Rosamond Tuve.

9. Jacques Derrida, "White Mythology: Metaphor in the Text of Philosophy," trans. F.C.T. Moore, *New Literary History* 6, no. 1 (1974), 26. "Das Metaphorische gibt es nur innerhalb der Metaphysik." The quote is from the sixth chapter of Heidegger's book.

10. Yu, *The Reading of Imagery*, 54 and 51.

11. Yu, *The Reading of Imagery*, 21.

12. Yu distinguishes Western metaphor from Chinese rhetorical arrangements reminiscent of metaphor, claiming that the former goes from "concretion to abstraction" (54) whereas in the latter the "tenor" and the "vehicle" are both "drawn from the same concrete realm" (54). The above metaphor may be drawn from the same "concrete realm" (that of the human body and of caves and houses) but so are also many text-book metaphors in the Western tradition.

13. We note that Aristotle's words about "observing the likeness" between seemingly different objects or situations, or about the "aptitude," "disposition" or "natural gift" (*euphuia*) that is necessary for such observations, do not indicate that the "metaphorizer" *invents* this likeness or simply conjures it up in his or her phantasy.

14. See here my "The Metaphor of *Metaphora*," 14–26.

15. Yu, *The Reading of Imagery*, 12.

16. Yu, *The Reading of Imagery*, 54.

17. Yu, *The Reading of Imagery*, 54.

18. Yu, *The Reading of Imagery*, 54.

19. Yu, *The Reading of Imagery*, 54. Italics mine.

20. Yu, *The Reading of Imagery*, 60.

21. Christine Brooke-Rose, *A Grammar of Metaphor* (London: Secker and Warburg, 1958), 93; Yu, *The Reading of Imagery*, 12.

22. Yu, *The Reading of Imagery*, 12; *A Grammar of Metaphor*, 92.

23. Ezra Pound, "In a Station of the Metro," in *Imagist Poetry* by Peter Jones (London: Penguin, 1972), 95.

24. See here my discussion of the concept of *pro ommatôn* in "Metapoetic Readings around *Ekphrasis* and *Fu* 賦," *Prism* 17, no. 2 (2020): 353–398.

25. *A Grammar of Metaphor*, 92; italics mine. Brook-Rose continues: "Pound, like Eliot, is justified by sheer elegance and precision, but it is a dangerously lazy method for lesser poets."

26. See also Hugh Kenner, *The Pound Era* (Berkeley: University of California Press, 1971), 184–87.

27. *Mao Commentary*, *SSJYJS*, 8.

28. Following Yu, *The Reading of Imagery*, 50–51. Note that Mao (*SSJYJS*, 8) identifies the female protagonist of "Guanju" as the "queen consort" but not the *junzi* as King Wen. For the date of King Wen's demise (often held to be 1050 BCE), I rely on Pines, "Names and Titles in Eastern Zhou Texts," 717.

29. We note that Mao's interpretation in one crucial respect differs from that of later scholars (see Yu, 50 and Haun Saussy, *The Problem of a Chinese Aesthetic* [Stanford: Stanford University Press, 1993], 97) who interpret the *jujiu* simply as representing the young girl (and not the girl *and* the "lord"). Mao is indeed ambiguous in his comments but there are several reasons for an alternative reading since the latter interpretations diminishes the theme of togetherness that permeates Mao's comment on this ode. The phrase *you bie* 有別 ("in separation") occurs three times in Mao's comment on "Guanju." First, Mao explicitly says that the "ospreys are passionate birds but they [the sexes] live in separation" which condones the male/female dichotomy of my reading. The meaning of the trope is that the birds—and the royal couple—are in full control of their sexual urges and therefore are virtuous. Mao further states that *kroo kroo* are *he sheng* 和聲 which Yu renders as the "cry of birds responding to each other," whereas a more fitting interpretation would be "harmonious calls"—"harmonious" indicating the harmony between the sexes that is a result of restrained sexuality. The second time the phrase *you bie* appears is in a series of descriptions that Yu and Saussy understand as referring to the queen only: "She takes joy in the virtue of her lord and agrees with him on everything. She does not exploit her beauty [to get favors]. She is firmly prudent and deeply reserved just like the ospreys in their separation" (my translation). However, since Mao has already explained that the xing-component refers to the separation of the male and the female, it is more likely that Mao maintains the binary structure, which produces the following interpretation: "She takes joy in the virtue of her lord. There is nothing that is not in harmony and in concord. There is no excess in sensuous matters. There is firm carefulness and deep purity just like the ospreys'

living in separation." Third, Mao asserts that, when the king and queen, through their exemplary behavior, exercise a benevolent influence on the commoners of their state, every man and wife live in separation. The key-phrase about the separation of the sexes appears three times, each time on a different level: in nature, in the royal house and among the people. The Kingly Way 王道 thus commences in nature, is perfected in the palace, and goes on to influence the entire state. It is, therefore, likely that Mao retains the male-female dichotomy in the xing-trope as a whole, thus making the ospreys an image of both the king and the queen. Yu and Saussy follow a prominent tradition whose interpretation in this regard is closer to "Guanju" itself than is Mao's reading.

30. Yu, *The Reading of Imagery,* 56, 65, and 76.

31. Yu, *The Reading of Imagery,* 65.

32. Yu, *The Reading of Imagery,* 65. See Aristotle's "species to species" metaphor, *Poetics,* 1457b.

33. Yu, *The Reading of Imagery,* 65.

34. See 33: "the connections between subject and object . . . are viewed in the Chinese tradition as already pre-established" and the following quote from her 1981 article "Metaphor and Chinese Poetry": "analogies already exist, to be *discovered* by the poet, not manufactured" (*Chinese Literature: Essays, Articles, Reviews* 3:2 [1981], 224). See also Umberto Eco's comment on the relationship between rhetoric and philosophy in Thomas of Aquinas: "[Aquinas] admits that there is only one portion of reality in which things and events themselves acquire metaphorical and allegorical value, inasmuch as they have been created and disposed thus by God himself: sacred history, and for this reason the Bible in itself is literal (it is the things of which it speaks literally that are *figures*)." *Semiotics and the Philosophy of Language* (Bloomington: Indiana University Press, 1985), 104. See also W. J. T. Michell's discussion in *Iconology: Image, Text, Ideology* (Chicago: University of Chicago Press, 1986), 29.

35. See here *Rhetoric* 1412a, where Aristotle develops the similar idea that a successful metaphor should not be immediately understandable, "because he will be more enlightened who has learnt something from grasping that the opposite [of what he expected] is the case, and it is as if the mind (*psuchê*) is saying 'This is indeed true, yet I failed to realize it'" (translation mine).

36. See my "Does the Metaphor Translate?" and "Inscription and Re-reading."

37. Charles Baudelaire, *Oeuvres complètes,* ed. Claude Pichois (Paris: Gallimard, 1975), 1:31–32.

38. Much of what I say about the *Zhouyi* in this chapter draws on Arthur Waley, "The Book of Changes," *BMFEA,* vol. 5 (1933): 121–42; Richard Kunst, "The Original *Yijing*: A Text, Phonetic Transcription, Translation, and Indexes, with Sample Glosses" (PhD diss., University of Berkeley, 1985); and Edward L. Shaughnessy, "The Composition of the *Zhouyi*" (PhD diss., Stanford University, 1983). I have kept the original references but encourage the reader to consult the

2022 reincarnation of the latter work, *The Origin and Early Development of the Zhou Changes* (Leiden: Brill, 2022), which is simultaneously a study of—and an expert introduction to—the "origin," "early development" and meaning of the *Zhouyi* and an overview and analysis of newly excavated manuscripts that bear on the received text. Chapters 6 and 8 explore the relation between the *Odes* and the *Zhouyi*. Commenting on the rhymed couplets that accompany the *Ren* 壬 trigram in a divination text called *Jing jue* 荊決, Shaughnessy writes (168) that "The first and third of these couplets describe a scene in the natural world, while the second and fourth seem to relate that scene to the personal situation of the diviner. This is similar to the *xing* 興 'arousal' or 'evocation' motif so characteristic of poems in the *Shi jing* . . . this *xing* motif is also characteristic of the oracles pronounced within various sorts of divination in ancient China."

39. See Kunst, "The Original *Yijing*," 310–11.

40. See Kunst, "The Original *Yijing*," 240–41.

41. See Kidder Smith, "*Zhouyi* Interpretation from Accounts in the *Zuozhuan*," *Harvard Journal of Asiatic Studies* 49, no. 2 (December 1989): 421–63.

42. Shaughnessy, "The Composition of the *Zhouyi*," 103.

43. For the *Zhouyi* as a diviner's manual, see Zhang Xiaoyu 張曉雨, *Zhouyi shifa jietong* 周易筮法通解 (Jinan: Shandong renmin, 1994).

44. Shaughnessy, "The Composition," 103, 166 and 225–26. See also 99–100 for Shaughnessy's theory—formulated around 1983—of the origins and composition of the *Zhouyi* line statements (and, Shaughnessy suggests, also of a substantial part of the *Shijing*).

45. Shaughnessy, "The Composition," 225–26. See also Shaughnessy, "Western Zhou History," in *The Cambridge History of Ancient China: From the Origins of Civilization to 221 B.C.* (Cambridge, England: Cambridge University Press, 1999), 338–42.

46. We note that the actual use of the *Zhouyi* as a divination "manual" lay in the interpretation of "line statements" such as this to predict the outcome of human actions. The internal relationship between *mingyi* and the man on a potentially dangerous journey was not of primary importance once the *Zhouyi* had been composed and established as a divination manual.

47. Wen Yiduo, "*Zhouyi* yizheng leizuan" 周易義證類纂, in *Wen Yiduo quanji* 聞一多全集 (Wuhan: Hubei renmin chubanshe, 1993), 10:187–252; David W. Pankenier, "Astronomical Dates in Shang and W. Zhou," *Early China* 7 (1981–82): 2–37.

48. According to Shaughnessy's *The Origin and Early Development of the Zhou Changes*, 37, 800 BCE is "a general marker for the time period of the text's creation." For the Dragon constellation, see David Pankenier, *Astrology and Cosmology in Early China: Conforming Earth to Heaven* (Cambridge: Cambridge University Press, 2013), chap. 2; Shaughnessy, "The Composition of 'Qian' and 'Kun' Hexagrams of the *Zhouyi*," in *Before Confucius: Studies in the Creation of the Chinese Classics* (Albany: State University of New York Press, 1997), 200: "While in the

West these stars are split into three constellations, Virgo, Libra, and Scorpius, the Chinese see the composite form of a dragon, marked especially by a long, curling tail and a pair of horns."

49. Kunst, "The Original *Yijing*," 240–41.

50. "The sorrows of the heart / resemble unwashed clothes" 心之憂矣, 如匪 澣衣. *SSJYJS*, 134.

51. Yu, *The Reading of Imagery*, 33.

52. *Poetics*, 1459b.

53. It may again be objected that the two things (the *lu* birds and the humans) are "drawn from the concrete realm" but we note that Zheng Xuan's comment (*SSJYJS*, 1023) clearly involves abstraction; the *lu* bird is white, therefore it may be used to signify the "pure, white virtue" 潔白之德 of the guest, not the guest's complexion or clothing. Similarly, when ode 23 says that "there is a girl like jade" (*SSJYJS*, 111–14), the line in question is not a statement of a cosmological correspondence between an impeccable piece of jade and a girl, but a *description* of the girl. The act of identifying the similarities, by means of the copula *ru* 如, is foremost a linguistic and psychological act.

54. See here volume 72 of the *BMFEA*, dedicated to the discourse on "correlative cosmology."

55. Cf. Ye Shuxian's categorical claim (*Shijing di wenhua chanshi*, 434) that Chinese metaphoricity goes from concretion to concretion whereas the Western counterpart goes from concretion (vehicle) to abstraction (tenor).

56. Yu, *The Reading of Imagery*, 65.

57. Yu, *The Reading of Imagery*, 65.

58. Yu, *The Reading of Imagery*, 65.

59. Yu, *The Reading of Imagery*, 56. Maureen Quilligan, *The Language of Allegory: Defining the Genre* (Ithaca: Cornell University Press, 1979), 281.

60. Quintilian, *Institutio Oratoria*, IIX, 6.44. Translation mine, following the Latin text in the Loeb edition (Cambridge, MA: Harvard University Press, 1996 [1920]), 3:326.

61. See for example Meik Gerhards, "The *Song of Solomon* as an Allegory: Historical Considerations," in Annette Schellenberg and Ludger Schwienhorst-Schönberger, eds., *Interpreting the Song of Songs: Literal or Allegorical?* (Leuven: Peeters, 2016), 51–77. While the allegorical readings of the *Song of Solomon* cannot be refuted on historical grounds—and furthermore add to rather than detract from its literary value—it would be fallacious to deny that it is perfectly "readable" at a literal level, as a love song, or to claim that a reader must choose between a literal and an allegorical interpretation. Indeed, even the most orthodox allegorical reading builds on the assumption that the author(s) could find no better analogy for the love between Christ and the Church, or between God and Israel, than the passion a young couple feel for each other. Similarly, although the allegorical interpretations of "Guanju" in Mao's *Commentary*, the *Kongzi shilun*, and the "Wuxingpian"

obviously testify to a long-standing moralizing reading of this piece, it would be unreasonable to adopt the "everything is interpretation" position, and claim that because we find no non-moralizing readings of this ode in the manuscripts available to us, a non-allegorical reading of "Guanju" (in intertextual dialogue with odes that are thematically similar) as a poem about a man's lust for an unattainable woman should be dismissed as anachronistic and methodologically flawed.

62. Quintilian, *Institutio Oratoria*, IIX, 6.46–47; Loeb, 326–28.
63. Quintilian, *Institutio Oratoria*, IIX, 6.46–47.
64. See Saussy, *The Problem of a Chinese Aesthetic*, 27.

Chapter 9

1. Paul Rouzer, "Review of *Éloge de la Fadeur: À partir de la pensée de l'esthétique de la Chine* by Françocis Jullien," *Harvard Journal of Asiatic Studies* 54, no. 1 (June 1994): 277.

2. Rouzer, "Review of *Éloge de la Fadeur*," 277.

3. François Jullien, *La valeur allusive : Des catégories originales de l'interprétation poétique dans la tradition chinoise (Contribution à une reflexion sur l'altérité interculturelle)* (Paris, École Française d'Extrême-Orient, 1985), 7.

4. ". . . bien plutôt de découvrir d'autres questions, et plus encore, de découvrir que certaines questions qu'il s'est toujours posées—qu'il ne peut pas ne pas se poser—ne sont jamais posées en dehors de son propre context culturel, ne sauraient être posées en dehors de lui." Jullien, *La valeur allusive*, 7.

5. [La notion 'd'auteur'] se fonde sur une conception du sujet qui a été très tôt mise en évidence par nos catégories linguistiques et que s'est appliquée à prendre en charge toute notre histoire de la philosophie. Or rien ne peut nous faire préjuger de ce qu'une telle catégorie ait été aussi déterminante dans la représentation que les Chinois ont élaborée de l'avènement de la littérature : selon la conception 'originale' qui est la leur, l'ordre du littéraire est naturellement référé à l'ordre du Monde dont l'œuvre créée représente à la fois un déploiement et un accomplissement (dont notre 'auteur' apparaît seulement - plutôt - comme le canal)." Jullien, *La valeur allusive*, 6.

6. "Préserver au sein de toute réflexion comparatiste ce qui constitue la perspective originelle de l'une et l'autre culture, le rapport interne qui relie intimement un même champ de représentations, ce geste primitif et unique par lequel est advenue chacune de ces conceptions." Jullien, *La valeur allusive*, 6.

7. Jullien, *La valeur allusive*, 126. See Zhang Longxi's 張隆溪 criticism of Jullien and defense of his former teacher Qian Zhongshu in "Hanxue yu Zhong-Xi wenhua duili—Du Yulian xiangsheng fangtanlu yougan" 漢學與中西文化的對立—讀于連先生訪談錄有感, in *Ershiyi shiji* 二十一世紀 no. 53 (June 1999), 144–48, esp. 146. Zhang's article was prompted by an interview with Jullien that appeared in the previous issue of the journal (pages 17–25), in which, incidentally, Qian Zhongshu

was not mentioned. Jullien then published a rather meek "Reply to Zhang Longxi" (no. 55, October 1999), where he seemingly retracted the critique of Qian's comparative methodology, objecting to Zhang's quotation of a work that at the time was more than fifteen years old, and holding that Qian's "comparatisme de la ressemblance" was simply an alternative "choice," neither more nor less valid than his own method with its focus on the differences between the Chinese and Western traditions. Zhang replied again in no. 57 (February 2000), suggesting provocatively that Jullien had simply not read, or not entirely comprehended, Qian's refined classical prose and that Qian in fact had always been attentive to the differences beneath the superficial intercultural similarities. From the present perspective, the exchange between the two scholars is interestingly frustrating. The opposition of "comparatisme de la ressemblance" and "comparatisme de la différence" is, as Zhang intimates, an oversimplification and dodges the real questions, yet Zhang is not able wholly to refute Jullien's criticism of Qian's methodology.

8. "Le parti pris est donc délibérément ici celui d'une comparaison essentiellement *fictive* mais que valorise sa capacité heuristique puisque aussi bien elle ne saurait demeurer sans effet vis-à-vis des représentations concernées: à partir de ce point de vue extérieur que s'est forgé le comparatiste peuvent être mieux mis en lumière certains 'choix' essentiels, certaines orientations initiales, qui caractérisent telle civilisation particulière mais sont si profondément ancrés en elle que celle-ci ne les perçoit plus d'elle-même, n'y prête plus attention, et ne les véhicule plus que sous forme d'évidence et de banalité." Jullien, *La valeur allusive*, 8.

9. René Wellek and Austin Warren, *Theory of Literature*, 3rd ed. (New York: Harcourt Brace, 1984), 17. For a discussion of the same passage, see Rey Chow, "The Old/New Question of Comparison in Literary Studies: A Post-European Perspective." *English Literary History* 71, no. 2 (Summer 2004): 289–311.

10. "Le sinologue comparatiste n'aura dès lors d'autre ressource que d'opérer de façon stratégique en s'attachant d'abord au *ponctuel* : en œuvrant à partir de représentations individuelles dont il lui paraît qu'elles peuvent être particulièrement représentatives de tout un contexte culturel donné de façon à pouvoir les confronter ensuite au champ culturel *extérieur* de l'autre civilisation." Jullien, *La valeur allusive*, 7.

11. "[Pour le *Maozhuan*], qui lui accorde une importance primordiale, la notion du *xing* sert en général à désigner la façon originale dont dans maints poèmes du *Classique de la poésie* le (ou les) premier(s) vers servent à évoquer un motif naturel et concret avant que ne soit développé le thème humain, à valeur psychologique ou moral." Jullien, *La valeur allusive*, 67.

12. "Dans le cas du second poème, ce rapport est de type plus métonymique que métaphorique"; and "à travers la diversité des examples repérés par le *Maozhuan*, le seul trait constant et régulier du *xing* est le rôle introducteur du motif (en tête de la strophe)." Jullien, *La valeur allusive*, 176.

13. Owen, *Readings in Chinese Literary Thought*, 27.

14. "Son [i.e., le *xing*] originalité tient à la valeur d'*incitation* : suscitée au contact du Monde (l'ordre du *wu* 物), la conscience poétique s'exprime spontanément au travers des éléments naturels qui constituent son paysage et ce motif sert lui-même d'invitation à un développement discursif plus organisé en rapport direct avec la situation affective ou psychologique du sujet." Jullien, *La valeur allusive*, 176.

15. Among many examples, see Li Zehou 李澤厚, *Meixue lunji* 美學論集 (Shanghai: Shanghai wenyi, 1980), 566 and, more recently, Zhu Mengting 朱孟庭, *Shijing di duoyuan chanshi* 詩經的多元闡釋 (Taipei: Weinjin, 2012), 99–105.

Chapter 10

1. For a case in point, see Sun, *Poetics of Repetition*, 48–51.
2. Sun, *Poetics of Repetition*, 104–5.
3. Sun, *Poetics of Repetition*, 104–5.
4. Sun, "Mimesis and Xing," 326.
5. Arthur Rimbaud, *Poésies. Une saison en enfer. Illuminations* (Paris: Gallimard, 1998), 145.
6. Sun, *Poetics of Repetition*, 105.

Chapter 11

1. Aristotle, *Rhetoric* 1405b, *Poetics* 1459a. See chapters 8 and 13 of the present study and my "Inscription and Re-reading" and "Does the Metaphor Translate?" For a discussion of the history of the concept of *metaphora*, see John T. Kirby, "Aristotle on Metaphor," *American Journal of Philology* 118, no. 4 (Winter 1997): 517–54.

2. For two widely different conceptions of catachresis see Umberto Eco, *Semiotics and the Philosophy of Language;* and Paul de Man, "The Epistemology of Metaphor," in *On Metaphor*, ed. Sheldon Sacks (Chicago: University of Chicago Press, 1979). While the former identifies catachresis as the very instance of harmless and practical metaphoric invention—for example, someone naming a previously unnamed part of a chair "the leg"—the latter claims (19) that catachresis can "dismember the texture of reality and reassemble it in the most capricious of ways, pairing man with woman or human being with beast in the most unnatural shapes."

3. Yu, *The Reading of Imagery*, 34–35.
4. Haun Saussy, *The Problem of a Chinese Aesthetic* (Stanford: Stanford University Press, 1993).
5. Saussy, *The Problem of a Chinese Aesthetic*, 48.
6. Saussy, *The Problem of a Chinese Aesthetic*, 48.
7. Saussy, *The Problem of a Chinese Aesthetic*, 116.

8. Note that Saussy reads the Confucian commentators (Mao Heng, Zheng Xuan, Kong Yingda, Zhu Xi) *en bloc*.
9. *Zheng Annotations*, *SSJYJS*, 54.
10. Saussy, *The Problem of a Chinese Aesthetic*, 118.
11. Saussy, *The Problem of a Chinese Aesthetic*, 118.
12. The example is mine. See Xunzi, "Bu gou," *Xunzi jijie*, 41; John Knoblock, "Nothing Indecorous," in *Xunzi: A Translation and Study of the Complete Works*, vol. 1 (Stanford: Stanford University Press, 1988), 175.
13. See Saussy, *The Problem of a Chinese Aesthetic*, 105. I explore the relationship between Xunzi's *wei* and pre-Qin conceptualizations of "metaphorical" language in "Inscription and Re-reading" and in "Does the Metaphor Translate?"
14. Saussy, *The Problem of a Chinese Aesthetic*, 149.
15. *Zuozhuan*, Xi 27; Wang et al., *Zuozhuan quanyi*, 326. For an overview of the relationship between the *Odes* and the *Zuo Commentary*, see Karlgren, "The Early History," 38–41.

Chapter 12

1. *SSJYJS*, 591.
2. According to Mao Heng's reading (*SSJYJS*, 591), which is not my main interest here, ode 170 demonstrates that the abundance of fish and wine is the result of good governance and the "great peace" that follows it, since under such conditions even a simple fish trap ("a widow's fish-basket" 寡婦之笱) overflows with fish.
3. Martin Kern, "'Xi shuai' 蟋蟀 ("Cricket") and its Consequences," 1–36; Monika Zikpi, "On Translation's 'Original' and an Emergent Translation of the *Shijing*," *Journal of Oriental Studies* 49, no. 1 (2016) (Special issue: Experiments in Translating Classical Chinese Poetry), 1–25. See also Edward Shaughnessy, "Unearthed Documents and the Question of the Oral versus Written of the Classic of Poetry," *Harvard Journal of Asiatic Studies* 75, no. 2 (2015): 331–75.
4. Kern, "Cricket," 20.
5. Kern, "Cricket," 15.
6. Kern, "Cricket," 31. Again, Kern's theory of the early history of the odes is strikingly similar to C. H. Wang's.
7. As indicated in footnote 15 in the introduction, there are several odes with identical titles. That the *Zuozhuan* speaks of "'The Lambskin Furcoat' from Zheng" (*Zheng zhi 'Gaoxiu'* 鄭之羔裘) in order to distinguish one piece from another bearing the same title not only suggests that there existed (or was thought to have existed when the *Zuozhuan* was composed) a corpus of "individual" odes; it also indicates—and this partly supports Kern's argument—that the circumstance that several poems would share the same title did not invoke speculations about which piece was the older or the "original."

8. Kern, "Cricket," 28.
9. Kern, "Cricket," 32.
10. Chen Qiyou, *Lüshi chunqiu jiaoshi*, 1527–30.
11. Kern, "Cricket," 34.
12. Kern, "Cricket," 32.

13. Likewise, perhaps the famous passage in the *Mencius* in which the reader of the *Odes* is admonished not to focus on single words (*wen* 文) or sentences (*ci* 辭) in the given poem but instead exhorted to "use his imagination to reach the *zhi* ['author's intent'? 'recorded expression'?]" 以意逆志 was not "exceptional" in early Chinese literary, philosophical, and hermeneutical culture for "emphasizing the persona of the author as well as authorial intent" (Kern, "Cricket," 32n68); instead, it may represent a reasoning so common it was rarely recorded. *Mencius*, "Wan Zhang" I 萬章上; *Mengzi yizhu*, 199. We find the same logic, albeit expressed negatively, in an equally famous statement by Lupu Gui 盧蒲癸 in the *Zuozhuan* (made, interestingly enough, as an analogy with genealogy and the principles of choosing a wife): "When I quote an ode I [disregard the larger context and the poem's origin, and willfully] cut off a stanza [from the poem], taking therefrom what I am seeking [to express in the situation at hand]" 賦詩斷章, 余取所求焉. This statement presupposes a distinction between the meaning carried (or being perceived as carried) originally by a certain poem and the meaning conferred onto a piece of that poem by the person quoting it out of context. *Zuozhuan*, Xiang 28; Wang et al., *Zuozhuan quanyi*, 1013.

14. One example of such (implicit) metapoetics would be to read the passage about Penelope's undoing the tapestry she has been weaving to detract her suitors (Books 2, 19, and 24 of the *Odyssey*) as a self-conscious description by the Homeric bard of his own poetic activity as that of a trickster or deceiver. See Perrine Galand-Hallyn, *Le reflet des fleurs: Description et métalangage poétique d'Homère à la Renaissance* (Geneva: Droz, 1994), 73. For a succinct definition, see Boris Maslov, who defines metapoetics as "the text commenting on its status as an artifact, including self-conscious references to the composer of the text, its performance, or any element of the text's poetics." Maslov, *Pindar and the Emergence of Literature* (Cambridge: Cambridge University Press, 2015), 21.

Other notable metapoetic odes are "Chu ci" 楚茨 (ode 209), which may have been recited or sung by the person(s) performing the rituals that this poem details but in any case proves the intimate connection between *shi* ("poetry") and *li* ("rituals; ritual performance; rituality"); "Jie Nan shan" 節南山 (ode 191; a "song" or "recitation" made by a certain Jiafu 家父 to "expose the king's quarrels / Using it to change your mind" 以究王訩, 式訛爾心); "Xiang Bo" 巷伯 (ode 200, according to whose last stanza "The eunuch Mengzi / Made this poem" 寺人孟子, 作為此詩); and odes 259 ("Song gao" 崧高) and 260 ("Zheng min" 烝民), whose respective last stanza identifies a certain Jifu 吉甫 as the person making or reciting it. Whether the verb *zuo*, or the expression *zuowei* 作為, here means to "to make" (see the Greek *poiein*), "to recite" or to "improvise using a cache of traditional formulae and themes" is debated and debatable; perhaps the difference between the three really was of minor importance in the early history of the *Odes*. However, Kern's hypothesis ("Cricket," 16n28) that the final stanzas of odes 259 and 260, naming Jifu as their reciter or maker, were at some pointed tacked on to the respective poem (since the last stanza differs from the preceding stanzas in rhyme and rhythm) is interesting but impossible either to verify or dismiss. It is possible that the person(s) producing these poems purposefully changed the rhyme and rhythm to mark the end of the poem, as indeed happens in ode 23. Finally, Kern's remark that in the *Odes* "any seemingly self-referential notions of authorship are exceedingly rare" ("Cricket," 16n28) is correct, but I am not persuaded that this in turn indicates "that authorship was not an integral property of such texts." Apart from the complicated question of what constitutes "authorship," that a poem (or text) lacks "self-referential notions of authorship" says little about how that poem came into being and equally little about how that process was viewed by the members of the community in which the poem circulated.

15. Sigmund Freud, *Die Traumdeutung*, in *Gesammelte Werke*, Band II/III (Frankfurt: S. Fischer, 1966 [1900]), 255.

16. Kern, "Cricket," 25.

17. Hung Kuo-liang 洪國樑, "Chongzhang huzu yu *Shi* yi quanshi: jian ping Gu Jiegang 'Chongzhang futa wei yueshi shenshu' shuo"「重障互足」與《詩》義詮釋—兼評顧頡剛「重障複沓為樂師申述」說, in *'Shijing,' xungu yu shixue* 詩經、訓詁與史學 (Taipei: National Library, 2015), 3–50.

18. We find similar notions of narrative progression and "incremental repetition" elsewhere, for instance—ironically enough—in Chen Shih-hsiang's discussion of ode 76; "*Shih-ching*," 39–40 (1974 version).

19. *Zuozhuan*, Zhao 1; Wang et al., *Zuozhuan quanyi*, p. 1092.

20. See my analysis of ode 23 in "One Lucky Bastard," 106–110.

21. *SSJYJS*, 111–12.

22. The reason Mao does not read the motif of the dead deer as a metaphoric description of the young woman is, I suggest, that a xingish interpretation would have led to a sexualizing reading of the sort I previously presented. Both deer and girl are referred to by the pronoun *zhi* in the first stanza, which formally confirms the metaphoric overlap. That Mao does *not* allegorize the poem indirectly confirms what I call his pragmatism (i.e., the lack of a rigorous hermeneutic methodology) and suggests that there existed in Mao's mind a very tangible opposition between the poem and its "literal" meaning and the interpretation thereof.

23. *SSJYJS*, 113.

24. That the "ragged dog" (*mang* 尨) connotes danger is suggested by the quotation of ode 23 in *Zuozhuan*, Zhao 1.

25. See Mao's comment: "during famines one cuts down on rituals [*sha li*], but there are nonetheless ways of maintaining them" 凶荒則殺禮，猶有以將之; *SSJYJS*, 111.

26. In a discussion of "Jiong" 駉 (ode 297) that is both intelligent and erudite, Monika Zikpi claims that "because of the text's multiple origins in oral culture and then manuscript culture, in folk culture and also court culture, there is no unproblematic 'literal sense' that could be equated with any 'original intention.'" "On Translation's 'Original' and an Emergent Translation of the *Shijing*," *Journal of Oriental Studies* 49, no. 1 (2016) (Special issue: Experiments in Translating Classical Chinese Poetry), 8. For several reasons, I would hesitate to apply categorically Zikpi's claim to the *Odes*. It may be argued generally that the notions of "literal sense" and "original intention" (not to mention the notion of equating the two) are never unproblematic; nonetheless, Mao's xingish interpretations—just like the "great man's" interpretation of the shepherd's dream in "Wu yang"—typically bank upon a distinction between the literal (or "non-xingish") and the non-literal (or xingish). And whereas the origin of the ode "Ye you si jun" is unknown, there is enough evidence (as argued above and elsewhere) to postulate not only a "literal" meaning distinct from the Confucian one that Mao confers upon it but also to assume that ode 23—like several odes in the Zhou nan 周南 and Zhao nan 召南 sections—is indeed thematically erotic, and builds on the metaphorical correlation of natural imagery and descriptions of human events that Mao sometimes, but not always, calls xing. Again, while I cannot disprove that this poem was "always already" intended to be read "allegorically," the burden of proof would equally rest upon the person contending there is no literal or original sense. (To the extent that Mao's xingish interpretations are both ideological and text-centred, I agree with Zikpi's assertion [20] that "our best attempt on the 'literal sense' can't but encounter the Mao edition with all its strongly ideological baggage," although one should perhaps add that the "ideological" use of the *Odes* was established well before the Mao edition.)

Chapter 13

1. See my "Does the Metaphor Translate?" and "Sino-methodological Remark," *BMFEA* 79/80.

2. In the past fifteen years, one of the most interesting events in metaphor studies has been the polemic and sometimes curiously heated exchange between Steen and Gibbs over the former's deliberate metaphor theory and Gibbs's simultaneous critique of DMT and defence of CMT—"curious" because Gibbs, at least in the 1992 article that I discuss here, proposes not only that many seemingly incompatible theories of the metaphors are in fact complementary but also (602) that metaphors may sometimes be regarded as "special *products*." Raymond Gibbs, "When Is Metaphor?: The Idea of Understanding in Theories of Metaphor," *Poetics Today*, 13. no. 4 (1992): 575–606.

Gibbs and Elaine Chen wrote in 2017 that "DMT takes us back to a Stone Age time where metaphor was ornamental, deviant, and only employed by special people with highly conscious communicative aims," whereas Steen in his response

(3) modestly emphasized that "conscious metaphorical communication is a very infrequent phenomenon"—which suggests that DMT is simply a modified (but improved) version of CMT. With reference to literary, poetic or psychopathological metaphor, it might be held—pace Steen, Gibbs, and Chen—that sometimes metaphors are precisely "ornamental, deviant, and only employed by special people with highly conscious communicative aims." Raymond W. Gibbs Jr. and Elaine Chen, "Taking Metaphor Studies Back to the Stone Age: A Reply to Xu, Zhang and Wu (2016)," *Intercultural Pragmatics*, vol. 14, no. 1 (2017): 117–24. Gerard Steen, "Deliberate Metaphor Theory: Basic assumptions, Main Tenets, Urgent Issues," *Intercultural Pragmatics*, vol. 14, no. 1 (2017): 1–24.

As I will return to these questions in a later work, I will only adduce one example of how DMT may improve on CMT. In their reading of Pablo Neruda's poem "Love Sonnet XII," Gibbs and Chen (119–20) write that "DMT would argue that [Neruda's line] 'love is a clash of lightnings' conveys metaphoric messages given readers' recognition that the phrase was deliberately produced as a metaphor." As suggested by my argument in this chapter, I have no objection to the claim that Neruda's "expression was *motivated* [emphasis added] by a conceptual metaphor, with all of its constraining cross-domain mappings (cognition)," but I hold that the rhetorical (or aesthetic) *effect* of Neruda's metaphor is not reducible to the conceptual metaphor "love is a force of nature." I also observe that Chen and Gibbs do not explore Neruda's "love is . . . two bodies subdued by one honey" metaphor, presumably because that expression would be harder to reduce to a conceptual metaphor.

3. Christoffer Eckerman, Review of *Pindar and the Emergence of Literature*, *American Journal of Philology* 137, no. 3 (2016): 543. Boris Maslov's book on Pindar was published in 2015 by Cambridge University Press.

4. Eckerman, Review of *Pindar and the Emergence of Literature*, 543–44. Italics mine. Gibbs's article "Psycholinguistic Studies on the Conceptual Basis of Idiomaticity" appeared in *Cognitive Linguistics* 1, no. 4 (1990): 417–52.

5. George Lakoff and Mark Johnson, *Metaphor We Live By* (2nd edition; Chicago: University of Chicago Press, 2003 [1980]), 8.

6. *Poetics* 1459a.

7. Gibbs, "When Is Metaphor?," 596. Gibbs discusses the "time is money" metaphor in the section on the "interaction" theory of metaphor (587).

8. Umberto Eco, "Metafora," in *Enciclopedia* vol. IX: "Mente-Operazioni" (Torino: Einaudi, 1980); translated by Eco and Christopher Paci as "The Scandal of Metaphor: Metaphorology and Semiotics," *Poetics Today* 4, vol. 2 (1983): 217–57; the reference is to Henry's *Métonymie et métaphore* (Paris: Klincksieck, 1971).

9. Gibbs, "When Is Metaphor?," 602.

10. Gibbs, "When Is Metaphor?," 596.

11. I. A. Richards, *The Philosophy of Rhetoric* (Oxford: Oxford University Press, 1936), 94.

12. Richards, *The Philosophy of Rhetoric*, 94; 100, 92.

13. Richards, *The Philosophy of Rhetoric*, 98. For a discussion of *ekphrasis*, the *Progymnasmata* and the genre of *fu*, see my "Metapoetic Readings."

14. Richards, *The Philosophy of Rhetoric*, 96. Richards quotes Samuel Johnson on p. 93.

15. Richards, *The Philosophy of Rhetoric*, 121.

16. Richards, *The Philosophy of Rhetoric*, 122, italics added.

17. Richards, *The Philosophy of Rhetoric*, 122.

18. Gibbs, "When Is Metaphor?," 596.

19. For a comment on Gibbs's reading of Smith's poem, see my "Sino-methodological Remark," 11–14.

20. Richards, *The Philosophy of Rhetoric*, 100.

21. Richards, *The Philosophy of Rhetoric*, 118. See also 127: "the peculiar modification of the tenor which the vehicle brings about is even more the work of their unlikenesses than of their likenesses."

22. Gibbs, "Psycholinguistic Studies," 446.

23. For a discussion of Aristotle's argument that a metaphor is more efficient when it is not immediately understandable, see my "Sino-methodological Remark," 15.

24. Paul Gordon, *The Critical Double: Figurative Meaning in Aesthetic Discourse* (Tuscaloosa: University of Alabama Press, 1995).

25. At this instance in the interpretational process Brooke-Rose must distinguish between poetic forms that allow for a metaphorical reading and those that do not. The parallelism/parataxis distinction depends thus on a subjective (i.e., arbitrary) act of identification ("Can one read this or that as a metaphor of this or that?").

26. *SSJYJS*, 526–31.

27. Wen Yiduo, "Shou yu" 說魚 in *Shenhua yu shi* 神話與詩 (Peking: Gudian, 1956).

28. As was the case with "lamb" as a symbol of Christ, the associative link between "fish" and "genitals" may certainly have originated as a metaphor and then turned into a symbol or even a conventional word.

29. One may add that Wen's reading presupposes a pun on the two meanings (literal and metaphoric/symbolic) of *yu*, that is, the dead metaphor is resuscitated.

30. Julia Kristeva, *Sèméiotikè: Recherches pour une sémanalyse* (Paris: Seuil, 1969), 146.

31. For a comment on and contextualization of Derrida's slogan—equally famous and misunderstood—"il n'y a pas de hors-texte," see "Inscription and Re-Reading," 106.

32. *SSJYJS*, 8–9.

Chapter 14

1. *Hanshu buzhu*, ed. Wang Xianqian (Peking: Zhonghua, 1983), "Yiwen zhi" 藝文志, 870. See also Lin Yelian's 林葉連 *Zhongguo lidai Shijingxue*, 110–42.

2. *Hanshu buzhu*, "Rulin Zhuan" 儒林傳, 1523.

3. *Hanshu buzhu*, "Jing shisan wang zhuan" 景十三王傳, 1117. See Karlgren, "The Early History," 12–13.

4. As quoted by Kong Yingda in *SSJZS*; *Maoshi zhengyi*, 2. The *Zongmu* preface to the *Maoshi* in *SSJZS*, also quoting Zheng Xuan's *Maoshi pu*, records the title as *xunguzhuan* 訓詁傳; *Maoshi zhengyi*, "Mulu" section, 1. Two works called *Maoshi pu* and *Liuyi lun* are attributed to Zheng Xuan in Fan Ye's 范曄 (398–c. 445) *Hou Hanshu* 後漢書, "Zheng Xuan zhuan" 鄭玄傳 (Peking: Zhonghua, 1996), 1212.

5. *SSJZS*; *Maoshi zhengyi*, 2. For the different recensions of *Liuyi lun*, see Zeng Shengyi 曾聖益, "Zheng Xuan 'Liuyi lun' shi zhong jijiao" 鄭玄《六藝論》十種輯斠, *Guoli Zhongyang Tushuguan Taiwan Fenguan guankan* 國立中央圖書館臺灣分館館刊 4, no. 1 (1997): 70–93. For a recent discussion of *Liuyi lun*, see Lu Zhao, *In Pursuit of the Great Peace: Han Dynasty Classicism and the Making of Early Medieval Literati Culture* (Albany: State University of New York Press, 2020), 144–51.

6. Lu Ji, "*Mao Shi*" *cao mu niao shou chong yu shu*, as quoted in the *Zongmu* preface to the *Maoshi*, "Mulu" section, 1. See Karlgren, "The Early History," 12–13.

7. See Karlgren, *Glosses, Kuo feng*, 72; Lee Kar-shui, *Shijing di lishi gongan* (Rpt. Taipei: Daan chubanshe, 1990), 22; Zhu Ziqing, *Shi yan zhi bian*, 57–58. Bernhard Karlgren and Lee Kar-Shui hold that the *Commentary* is the older text, with Lee arguing that Mao Heng would have included comments on the *Minor Preface* (as Zheng Xuan did) had it been at his disposal. Zhu, in *Shi yan zhi bian*, claims that Mao always follows the *Minor Preface* (the reason that the *Commentary* is so short is that Mao always based himself on the *Minor Preface*) and that the two should be read together. Neither argument is conclusive. The *Prefaces* may have been written to clarify what was obscure in the *Commentary*, or (as suggested above) as a complement to the so-called *Old Preface*, or to a similarly historicizing but no longer extant commentary. As regards the authorship of the *Preface*, Lee Kar-Shui points out (23) that neither Ban Gu, Zheng Xuan, nor Kong Yingda says that the two Maos were the authors of the *Preface*. See here Zheng Xuan's intriguing claim that the Masters of Commentary in the early Han Dynasty "changed the sequential order" 移其篇第 of the *Odes*, and Kong Yingda's critique thereof; *SSJZS*, *Maoshi zhengyi*, 552–53 and 718.

8. *SSJYJS*, 94–95. See Lee Kar-shui, *Shijing di lishi gongan*, 21–22.

9. *Mao Commentary*, *SSJYJS*, 95.

10. *Minor Preface*, *SSJYJS*, 95. Alternatively: "Their virtue was as [white as] lambs." See also the Han school annotation on the second line (*SSJYJS*, 74): "*Su* 素 signifies 'purity' [i.e., spotless virtue]." The *Preface* is certainly closer to the Han school reading than to Mao's. For a somewhat different interpretation of the same example (but with the same conclusion), see Lee Kar-shui, *Shijing di lishi gongan*, 20–21.

Chapter 15

1. Li Zehou and Liu Gangji, *Zhongguo meixue shi* 中國美學史 (Peking: Xinhua, 1987), 2:575. This work also includes a good description of the historical background of the piece (575–79). However, I would suggest that Li's and Liu's main argument—that the *Preface* holds that poetry is irrational since it expresses personal feelings—is anachronistic, although the idea of poetry's origin in feelings and spontaneity fits nicely into the antimetaphorical program presented by Chen Shih-Hsiang et al. Furthermore, Li's and Liu's interpretation destroys the congruence of the *Great Preface*. When the *Preface* says that "to proceed from feelings is the nature of the populace [but] to keep within [the boundaries of] the Rites is the grace of kings," it tallies with the distinction already made between *junzi* and *min*. Li and Liu, however, see it as a textual anomaly that contradicts the "democratic" ideals expressed in pre-Qin Confucian theories. A text like the *Great Preface*, founded on the distinction between *hoi polloi* and the "educated" man can, of course, hardly be called "democratic." For a more sympathetic interpretation, see Zhu Ziqing, 20–29. Zhu also distinguishes between intent and feeling but seems to think that they both can be manifested in poetry; that is, he does not stress the distinction between the populace and the poet.

For the distinction between *shi* as a generic concept ("poetry") and as the collective name of the 305 *Odes*, see Bruce Rusk, *Critics and Commentators*, chap. 1. See also Matthias Richter, *The Embodied Text*, chap. 9, for a persuasive argument that "the scribe of *Min zhi fumu [民之父母] probably observed an orthographic distinction between *Odes* as the title of a compilation and the generic sense of the word ode."

2. Owen, *Readings in Chinese Literary Thought*, 42 and Van Zoeren, *Poetry and Personality*, 110.

3. Jullien, *La Valeur allusive*, 63; Versano, "Getting There From Here," 375–403; Beecroft, *Authorship and Cultural Identity*, 29; Kern, "Early Chinese Literature," 31.

4. I follow Li Zehou's and Liu Gangji's reconstructed version in my translation. See Li and Liu, *Zhongguo meixue shi*, 572. For the original text, see Ruan Yuan, *SSJZS*, *Maoshi zhengyi*, 4–21 (1:1.3b–18b).

5. Cf. Owen, *Readings*, 27: "If we translate *shih* as 'poem,' it is merely for the sake of convenience. *Shih* is not a 'poem.' It is not a 'thing made' in the same way one makes a bed or a painting or a shoe." Owen is here commenting on the expression *shi yan zhi* in *Shujing*, which he calls "the primary and most authoritative statement on *shih* throughout the traditional period" (Owen, *Readings*, 27).

The Greek *poiein*, and its related terms *poiêsis* and *poiêtês*, by no means exclusively refer to a "production" of poetry that is conceived as analogous with a craftsman's production of "a bed or a painting or a shoe," that is to say a production that is premeditated, rational, based on skills and rules taught by predecessors, etc.

In Plato's *Ion* (534b), Socrates famously claims that "the poet [*poiêtês*] is a light, winged and sacred thing" who can only create (*poiein*) anything of value when he is "infused with god" (*entheôn*), standing outside common sense (*ekphrôn*), and when his wits (*nous*) are no longer with him; translation based on the Greek text in *Statesman, Philebus, Ion*, Loeb Classical Library 164 (Cambridge, MA: Harvard University Press, 1925), 422.

6. Kern, "Early Chinese Literature, Beginnings Through Western Han," 31.

7. See my "On the *Concept* of Correlative Cosmology," *BMFEA* 72, and Michael Nylan, "Yin-yang, Five Phases, and *qi*," in *China's Early Empires A Re-appraisal*, ed. Michael Nylan and Michael Loewe (Cambridge: University of Cambridge, Oriental Publications, no. 67, 2010), 398–414.

8. Pace Beecroft, *Authorship and Cultural Identity*, 41–42.

9. The question of the author's role—does he or she determine the meaning and argumentative complexity of the text as its author or play a more passive role as its compiler?—is central, as we have seen, to the study of early poetry in general and the *Odes* in particular, as indeed it is to literature and manuscript studies overall. We note a tension between these two poles in recent Sinological scholarship. In his analysis of the "Tang wen" chapter of the *Liezi*, Christian Schwermann speaks of a "schwach ausgeprägtes Autorenbewußtsein," which combined with the prevalence of oral composing in early China, results in the "montage" technique employed by the text. Christian Schwermann, "Collage-Technik als Kompositionsprinzip klassischer chinesischer Prosa: Der Aufbau des Kapitels 'Tang wen' (Die Fragen des Tang) im *Lie zi*," in *Bochumer Jahrbuch zur Ostasienforschung, Bochumer Jahrbuch zur Ostasienforschung* 29, edited by Wolfgang Behr (Bochum: Fakultät f. Ostasienwissenschaften d. Ruhr-Universität Bochum, 2005), 127. By contrast, Dirk Meyer's division between argument-based and nonargument-based texts describes texts of the former kind as carefully and consciously crafted and also offers new ways of understanding the compositional techniques behind early Chinese "philosophical" texts. Dirk Meyer, *Philosophy on Bamboo*. See also William G. Boltz, "The Composite Nature of Early Chinese Texts" in *Text and Ritual in Early China*, ed. Martin Kern (Seattle: University of Washington Press, 2008); and Mary Douglas, *Thinking in Circles: An Essay on Ring Composition* (New Haven, CT: Yale University Press, 2007).

10. For the relationship between "tones" and "music," see *Yue ji*, "What you, sir, are inquiring about is music, but what you actually prefer is tones. Now, music is close to, but not identical with, tones" 今君之所問者樂也，所好者音也。夫樂者與音相近而不同; *Liji zhengyi*, in *Shisanjing zhushu*, 1123.

11. "Chun Guan," "Da shi" 大師; *SSJZS, Zhouli*, 610.

12. See, for instance, Karlgren, *Glosses*, 647.

13. With Zheng Xuan and Kong Yingda, *zhu wen* refers to the correspondence between text (*wen*) and the music to which it is set; *SSJZS, Maoshi zhengyi*, 13–14.

14. *SSJZS, Maoshi zhengyi*, 13–14.

15. *Xunzi jijie*, 366.

16. I argue elsewhere that this congruence is not accidental but that the *Preface*'s theory of linguistic "craftiness" and Xunzi's "phantasmatic" analysis are two related parts of a discourse that underpin what tentatively may be called Xunzian literary thought. See "Illusion, Lie and Metaphor," "Inscription and Re-reading," and "The Phantasmatic Tomb."

17. Stephen Owen, *Readings in Chinese Literary Thought*, 47.

18. I am indebted to the discussion of *min* in Roger Ames and David Hall, *Thinking Through Confucius* (Albany: State University of New York Press, 1987), 140–43. The quote is from *Chunqiu fanlu* 春秋繁露, conventionally attributed to Dong Zhongshu 董仲舒 (179–104 BCE); Su Yu, *Chunqiu fanlu yizheng*, 297. I read 瞑 for 實, in keeping with Su Yu's notes. For my immediate purposes—and certainly as a layman—analyses of oracle bone graphs are intriguing but do not constitute hard evidence in the tracing of a concept's history and development.

19. *Xunzi jijie*, 234.
20. *Xunzi jijie*, 234.
21. *Xunzi jijie*, 234.
22. *Xunzi jijie*, 234.
23. *Lunyu*, "Zi Zhang" 19.10.
24. *Lunyu*, "Wei Zi" 微子 18.8.

25. For a nonironical reading of the expression *min de* 民德, see, for instance, Siufu Tang's valuable discussion of the concept of *de* in the *Xunzi*, "Virtue Through Habituation: Virtue Cultivation in the Xunzi," *Journal of Chinese Philosophy* 48, no. 2 (2021): 158. The passage in question is not unambiguous, but we know the strategy of using a word, so to speak, within quotation marks from Confucius's indignant statement about the "*gu*-vessel that does not [truly function as a] *gu*" 觚不觚 (*Analects* 6.25), and Xunzi's (doubly) ironical use of the word *bao* 寶 is a common trope in Warring States philosophical texts; see my "Inscription and Re-reading," *BMFEA* 74, 114, 118–19, and "Illusion, Lie, and Metaphor," 271.

26. *Xunzi jijie*, 357.

27. See *Liji*, "Li qi" 禮器; *SSJYS*, 751: "When the ancient kings instituted the rites they expressed their meaning precisely by way of the objects [used in the rituals]" 昔先王之制禮也，因其財物而致其義焉爾.

28. *Xunzi jijie*, 357–58. Knoblock (*Xunzi*, 3:62) and Hutton (*Xunzi*, 206) both translate this sentence differently. Knoblock's interpretation—that the Superior Man keeps to the middle way while rejecting abundance and dearth—is attractive thematically but difficult to reconcile with the grammar of the passage.

29. *Xunzi jijie*, 357–58.
30. *Xunzi jijie*, 363.
31. *Xunzi jijie*, 364.
32. Martin Svensson [Ekström], "A Second Look at the *Great Preface*."
33. Notable exceptions are Hermann-Josef Röllicke's *Die Fährte des Herzens*, which (128) speaks of the "two pillars" on which the *Preface* stands, and Gu

Nong's 顧農 "'Fa hu qing, zhi hu li yi': Maoshi Daxu di heli keike" "發乎情, 止乎禮義"—《毛詩大序》的合理內核, *Fujian lunyun* 福建論壇 (June 1983), 100–103. Gu underscores the difference made in the Warring States period between the two concepts (intent and emotion) but supposes that the author of the *Preface* simply held that those of the *Odes* that were emotionally charged responses to a disorderly world still kept within the confines of rites and righteousness.

Chapter 16

1. *Minor Preface, SSJYJS*, 778. Following Kong Yingda's interpretation of the phrase *wudao bingjin* 無道並進; *SSJZS, Maoshi zhengyi*, 871.
2. Or, "Thy virtuous reputation reaches us."
3. *SSJYJS*, 778–81. Trans. modified, Karlgren, *Book of Odes*, 171–72.
4. *Zheng Annotation, SSJYJS*, 778–80.
5. *SSJYJS*, 779.
6. *SSJYJS*, 779.
7. At this point, Zheng is ambiguous. At first he says (*SSJYJS*, 779) that "you" refers to the bride and, one moment later, that it refers to the king. It is clear, however, that the protagonist(s) address(es) the bride directly in the fourth and fifth stanzas, saying, "Happily, we see thee / our hearts are relieved" and "The sight of thee, new bride, sets our hearts at rest" (*SSJYJS*, 780).
8. *SSJYJS*, 780. Zheng unsurprisingly eschews the sensual connotations of the character *xu* 湑: "wet," "dripping with dew," etc. See Karlgren, *Grammata Serica Recensa*, 40, entry 90.e and ode 173, first stanza (*SSJYJS*, 597).
9. *SSJYJS*, 780. We note, with Kong Yingda, that Zheng's analogy is asymmetric since the covering up of the ridge corresponds to the clearing away of the ruler's "brilliance." See Kong Yingda, *SSJZS, Maoshi zhengyi*, 873–74.
10. *SSJYJS*, 780.
11. Or "he sees to it that this is made according to ritual principles."
12. *SSJYJS*, 780.
13. Lu Ji 陸璣 adds a carnivorous flavor to aesthetics in his comment on this piece: "The *jiao* bird [i.e., the pheasant] is tinier than the *di* bird, it calls out while walking, its tail is short and *its meat lovely* 美 [my italics]." From Lu Ji's *Maoshi cao mu niao shou chong yu shu*, quoted in *SSJYJS*, 779.
14. *SSJYJS*, 190.

Chapter 17

1. Saussy, *Problem of a Chinese Aesthetic*, 120.

Chapter 18

1. Zhu Ziqing, *Shi yan zhi bian*, 53–54.
2. Zhu Ziqing, *Shi yan zhi bian*, 54.
3. *Mao Commentary*, *SSJYJS*, 8.
4. *SSJYJS*, 10. See Karlgren, *Glosses* 1. *Junzi* (君子) translates as "lord," "lordling," "gentleman" or "[virtuous] ruler" in the *Commentary*. In the *Xunzi*, *junzi* most often denotes the "gentleman-scholar" or the "worthy" who, rich or poor, in a high or low position, remains his virtuous self. *Jun*, by contrast, refers unambiguously to "ruler." In the following, I distinguish between the two only when referring to Xunzi.
5. *SSJYJS*, 10.
6. For a definition of "the allegorical," see my discussion (76–77) of Pauline Yu and Virgil.
7. In contrast to the similarly oblique fourth stanza of ode 190, "Wu yang," where the transference of signata ("fish" to "harvest") banks on the metonymic principle of shared origin (and, thus, proximity), the xing is here made possible because of certain appearances or characteristics shared by both nature and man: the two strata converge in one single point in the *present*.
8. See the earlier discussion on Pauline Yu.
9. See Ulrike Middendorf's important and original study of the themes of lust and desire in the *Odes*, *Resexualizing the Desexualized: The Language of Desire and Erotic Love in the Classic of Odes* (Pisa: Istituti editoriali e poligrafici internazionali, 2007).
10. *SSJYJS*, 11.
11. Neither Lu Ji nor the *Erya yi* sustain Mao's suggestion that the *xing* plant was used for ritual purposes. While the former dwells on the plant's culinary fields of application, the *Erya yi* says that the *xing* resembles the *chun* plant 蕈 and that it was used by the common people to feed the hogs (hence its vulgar name "hog-chun" 豬蕈) or to fertilize the fields. *SSJYJS*, 12.
12. As for instance in description of the dreaming shepherd in the fourth stanza of ode 190 ("Wu yang").
13. *SSJYJS*, 1023.
14. *SSJYJS*, 1023.
15. For the Lu interpretation, see *SSJYJS*, 1023.
16. *SSJYJS*, 1068; see Karlgren, *Book of Odes*, 254.
17. *SSJYJS*, 1068.
18. *SSJYJS*, 1068.
19. *SSJYJS*, 436 and 593–94. See Zhu Ziqing, 52–53. Zhu contends that Mao deviates from the norm in his comment on odes 298 and 126 simply because he has already defined a similar natural "image" as a xing, but he disregards the

fact that descriptions of horses are never used as xings by Mao. See my treatment of "Ju lin" (ode 126) and "Nan you jia yu" (ode 171) below.

20. Apart from the odes under discussion, the image of the egret appears in the second and third stanzas of ode 136 (*SSJYJS*, 463). In neither place does Mao comment on their whiteness.

21. *Lüshi chunqiu*, "Zhao lei" 召類; Chen Qiyou, *Lüshi chunqiu jiaoshi*, 1360. The passage appears also in the "Zhao tong" chapter, where the concept of *lei* functions as the cornerstone of a "scientific" method of explaining how certain events are not preordained by fate but appear as the consequence of and in conjunction with other events.

22. *SSJYJS*, 551.
23. *SSJYJS*, 551.
24. *SSJYJS*, 551.
25. *SSJYJS*, 551.
26. *SSJYJS*, 464; Karlgren, *Book of Odes*, 87–88.
27. *SSJYJS*, 464. The sentence is ambiguous and we note that Kong Yingda, while also quoting the *Minor Preface*, paraphrases it as "these two trees are found at the intersection between the states, which was where men and women came together" 此二木是國之道路交會, 男女所聚之處也; *SSJZS, Maoshi zhengyi*, 441.
28. *SSJYJS*, 464.
29. *SSJYJS*, 182.
30. *SSJYJS*, 182.
31. See the *Minor Preface*, *SSJYJS*, 181–82.
32. *Ji* 及 can be translated both as "come," "go," and as a particle that maintains the original meaning of "reach."
33. *SSJYJS*, 538. Trans. modified, Karlgren, *Book of Odes*, 102–3.
34. *SSJYJS*, 538.
35. Trans. modified, Karlgren, *Book of Odes*, 102–3.
36. Descriptions of axes and hatchets appear also in the third stanza of "Qi yue" (ode 154).
37. Modified from Karlgren, *Book of Odes*, 103.
38. *SSJYJS*, 541.
39. See my "Inscription and Re-reading," 17.
40. *SSJYJS*, 61.
41. *SSJYJS*, 61–62.
42. I suspect, furthermore, that Mao substitutes *zu* for *zhi* in order to make his gloss, in one reading at least, conform to conventional Confucian language since *zu* may also mean "be sufficient to." The statement 麟信而應禮以足至者也 may thus be read as "this refers to the circumstance that the *lin* is trustworthy and adheres by the Rites, in order to be sufficient to reach perfection."
43. *SSJYJS*, 146–47; Karlgren, *Glosses*, 80.
44. *SSJYJS*, 146–47.

45. *SSJYJS*, 147–48.
46. *SSJYJS*, 274. The opening lines of the fourth stanza of ode 254 are as follows: "Since heaven is now oppressive / do not jest so" 天之方虐, 無然謔謔. See Karlgren, *Book of Odes*, 213.
47. *SSJYJS*, 815. The translation of the first line follows Karlgren, *Glosses*, 619. *Fanfan* 幡幡 is tautologically defined by Mao as "the appearance of gourd leaves" 瓠葉貌.
48. *SSJYJS*, 815.
49. *SSJYJS*, 384. See Karlgren, *Glosses*, 195. In his comment on ode 63, Mao defines *suisui* as 匹行貌 "the appearance of walking in pairs" or, in Karlgren's phrasing, "mating-going fashion." See *Mao Commentary*, *SSJYJS*, 310.
50. *SSJYJS*, 384.
51. *SSJYJS*, 384.
52. *SSJYJS*, 384.
53. *SSJYJS*, 383. Karlgren (*Book of Odes*, 65) mistakes Duke Huan, Wen Jiang's husband, for the licentious Duke Xiang.
54. *SSJYJS*, 310. Karlgren, *Glosses*, 195.
55. *SSJYJS*, 310.
56. *SSJYJS*, 310.
57. *SSJYJS*, 311.
58. See odes 6, 9, 12, 28, and 156.
59. Karlgren, *Book of Odes*, 78.
60. *SSJYJS*, 414.
61. Karlgren, *Book of Odes*, 78.
62. Charles Morris names such temporal markers "descriptors," see *Signs, Language and Behavior* (1946), reprinted in *Writings on the General Theory of Signs* (The Hague: Mouton, 1971), 154. We could also, with Paul de Man's influential reading of a passage in Proust's *A la recherche* in mind, say that the cricket is a synecdoche for autumn. See Paul de Man, *Allegories of Reading* (New Haven, CT: Yale University Press, 1979), 13–19.
63. *SSJYJS*, 41. See Karlgren, *Glosses*, 23.
64. *SSJYJS*, 42. My translation of Mao's rather arcane (or corrupted) comment is tentative. Note that Wang Xianqian (*SSJYJS*, 42) only quotes Mao's central argument "有室家無踰時."
65. See Kong Yingda (*SSJZS*, *Maoshi zhengyi*, 47) who focuses on the last stanza and says that the bride follows the rites by going to her new home in "late autumn" (*qiu dong* 秋冬).
66. *SSJYJS*, 42.
67. The pattern of blossoming flowers as both seasonal markers and a metaphor for a virtuous bride reappears in ode 24, "He bi nong yi" 何彼襛矣. Mao's comment indicates that the first two lines are a xing but is otherwise too short to make any real sense. The Three Schools (according to Wang Xianqian) hold that this

poem describes how the Duke of Qi sends his daughter to be married and that she travels in her mother, Wang Yi's, carriage. According to the *Minor Preface*, this ode celebrates not the bride herself but Wang Yi, whose carriage is not as grand as the queen consort's. Wang Yi, thus, maintains propriety. Since the theme of marriage was well established when Mao wrote his comment, we can safely assume that the xing here functions in a way that resembles the rhetorical structure of "Tao yao." See *SSJYJS*, 114–18. Another variant of this xing trope is found in ode 20, "Biao you mei" 摽有梅, where the plum tree and its falling fruit can be interpreted as a temporal marker, a description of the young girl who waits for the right man to come along, and as a description of the suitors. See *SSJYJS*, 101–3.

68. *SSJYJS*, 43. Ironically, the dualism of "form" (*xing*) and "body" (*ti*) corresponds to the "looks" (*se*) and to the "virtue" (*de*) mentioned previously.

69. Michelle Yeh, "Metaphor and *Bi*: Western and Chinese Poetics," *Comparative Literature* 39 (1987): 237–54.

70. "Metaphor and *Bi*," 250. Yeh's words about *presenting* images indicates that she is referring to the creation rather than interpretation of poetry.

71. "Metaphor and *Bi*," 247.

72. "Metaphor and *Bi*," 251.

73. "Metaphor and *Bi*," 251. In the rhetorical movement between two parts of a "larger context" that Yeh describes there is perhaps an echo of Aristotle's species-to-species metaphor (*Poetics* 1457c-g [Cambridge, MA: Harvard University Press, 1995], 104–5).

74. Since that is precisely the reading that Mao calls a "xing," Yeh's designation *bi* seems superfluous.

75. "Metaphor and *Bi*," 251.

76. *SSJYJS*, 141. 逝不古處 probably means "does not come to the old place" since Mao glosses *shi* 逝 as *dai* 逮 ("reach") and, in the second stanza, as *ji* 及 ("reach"). As both glosses retain the original and concrete sense of the character *shi*, there is no reason to conform to a more abstract reading such as Karlgren's "it has come (the point that) he does not in the old way (place me=) treat me" (*Glosses*, 76). Note that the Lu school contends that "Ri yue" refers to the lore about the two excessively virtuous half-brothers Shou 壽 and Ji 伋 that dictates Mao's reading of "Er zi cheng zhou" (ode 44), *SSJYJS*, 142 and 213–15. See *Zuozhuan*, Huan 16; Wang et al., *Zuozhuan quanyi*, 574–76.

77. Mao Commentary, *SSJYJS*, 141.

78. For the Lu school's account of the palace intrigues that make up the allegorical background of this piece, see *SSJYJS*, 142.

79. *SSJYJS*, 381–82. See Karlgren, *Glosses*, 250–51.

80. *SSJYJS*, 381–82. Also see *Glosses*, 179. I follow Karlgren's pronounciation of 履 as *li*. David W. Pankienier contends that Han dynasty astronomers knew that the moon is illuminated by the sun; see his "Reflections of the Lunar Aspect on Western Chou Chronology," *T'oung Pao*, no. 78 (1992): 33–76.

81. *SSJYJS*, 381.
82. *SSJYJS*, 381.
83. Three stanzas out of eight. *SSJYJS*, 674–76. Karlgren, *Book of Odes*, 138–40, *Glosses*, 550–51.
84. *SSJYJS*, 674 and 677. Zheng Xuan held that this ode in fact "criticizes King Li" 刺厲王 and, as previously noted, that the commentarial masters of the early Han had "changed the order" of the *Odes*.
85. Following Karlgren's reading; *Book of Odes*, 138.
86. The fear of change and deviation seems not to apply to the area of rhetoric. A *tropos*—whether it comes in the form of a xing, a quotation of the *Odes* in the *Zuo Commentary*, or in the *Xunzi*—is never regarded as a "turning away" from a given, "true" path. See Knoblock's insightful discussion of the theme of change, transformation and transmutation in *Xunzi*, 2:168–70.
87. *SSJYJS*, 674.
88. *Mao Commentary*, *SSJYJS*, 676.
89. When these lines are quoted in Xunzi's "Junzi" chapter (*Xunzi jijie*, 452) they do not refer to the usurpation of the ruler's position by his minister but to the degeneration of the state through nepotism.
90. Karlgren, translation modified, *Book of Odes*, 145–46; *Glosses*, 591.
91. *SSJYJS*, 700. How exactly the passage from the *Commentary* should be punctuated is unclear.
92. *SSJYJS*, 700. A similar example appears in the fourth stanza of ode 214, "Shangshang zhe hua" 裳裳者華, where the text says that "to the left he goes, to the left he goes / the gentleman moves with fittingness / to the right he goes, to the right he goes / the gentleman possesses what is needed." Mao comments that "left" is the *yang* path/principle 陽道 and "right" is the *yin* path/principle 陰道. To the former belong the affairs of the court and the sacrifices, to the latter the affairs of mourning and of warfare (*SSJYJS*, 771; see also Appendix C). Consequently, the text *means* that the gentleman has a firm grasp of the affairs of both these realms. We should hereby note two things. First, in the second stanza of ode 127, the same phrase—"go to the left"—refers to shooting, with the concrete and literal meaning "go left and you will hit the target" (*SSJYJS*, 438). Second, Xunzi quotes these lines to exemplify that the *junzi* moves to the left and to the right if necessary, that is, he is *flexible* ("Bu gou," *Xunzi jijie*, 42). Compared to the two intertexts, Mao's reading is oblique, complex and *fuhui*. As so often, Mao depends on the two meanings of *dao*—"path" and "principle." When the text literally says that the *junzi* "goes to the left," Mao understands this as "on the left *path* he goes" and then "to the *yang principles* he goes to attend."
93. *SSJYJS*, 500.
94. *SSJYJS*, 500.
95. *SSJYJS*, 500, following Mao regarding the meaning of the last line.
96. *SSJYJS*, 500. Note what is possibly a graphic pun: 平均如一 "even like the character *yi* 一."

97. Note that Mao's *Commentary* substitutes *yi* 義 ("righteousness") for the text's *yi* 儀 ("deportment").

98. *SSJYJS*, 631. Karlgren, *Glosses*, 86.

99. *SSJYJS*, 631, 634.

100. *SSJYJS*, 772.

101. *Zheng Annotation*, *SSJYJS*, 772.

102. *SSJYJS*, 453 and 695.

103. *Lunyu*, "Tai bo" 泰伯 8.19.

104. *SSJYJS*, 781. *Kai ti* is defined as *leyi* 樂易 "happy and carefree" in Mao's comment on ode 239. See *SSJYJS*, 846.

105. *Zheng Annotation*, *SSJYJS*, 781.

106. Or "the slanderers have no limits"; *SSJYJS*, 782.

107. *SSJYJS*, 819–20.

108. *SSJYJS*, 820.

109. *SSJYJS*, 820.

110. As suggested by the *Minor Preface* and Zheng Xuan; *SSJYJS*, 819.

111. *SSJYJS*, 820. Although it is beside the point in this context, *Luo* 罶 ("the Net") is likely an astronomical term, and the description of the constellation the Three Stars as being in the Net a celestial phenomenon that heralds disaster. See Karlgren's discussion in *Glosses*, 747.

112. Mao's comments on the first two stanzas; *SSJYJS*, 819–20.

113. *SSJYJS*, 820.

114. *SSJYJS*, 645. Karlgren, *Book of Odes*, 129.

115. *SSJYJS*, 645.

116. *SSJYJS*, 645.

117. *SSJYJS*, 645.

118. *SSJYJS*, 412.

119. *SSJYJS*, 412.

120. *SSJYJS*, 412. See Karlgren, *Glosses*, 263.

121. *SSJYJS*, 248.

122. *SSJYJS*, 248–49.

123. For the contemporary pronunciation of the rhyme words, see Baxter and Sagart, *Old Chinese* or Karlgren, *Book of Odes*, 33.

124. See, inter alia, Karlgren, "The Early History," 38–41.

125. *Zuozhuan*, Xiang 27; Wang et al., *Zuozhuan quanyi*, 988.

126. *SSJYJS*, 451. See Karlgren, *Book of Odes*, 84.

127. *SSJYJS*, 814.

128. *SSJYJS*, 527. I tentatively follow Zheng Xuan in understanding *ning* as a marker of the past tense. See Zheng Xuan's comment on ode 29, first stanza, *SSJYJS*, 144: 寧, 猶曾也. We should note Mao's pun: *zhou* 周 ("whole"; "Zhou"). The third line of the ode says "do not destroy my house," inconspicuously altered by Mao to "you cannot destroy my house" 無能毀我室.

129. *SSJYJS*, 528.
130. *SSJYJS*, 528. See Karlgren, *Book of Odes*, 100 and *Glosses*, 379.
131. The story of the benevolent Duke of Zhou, and how he composed a poem called "Chixiao," is told in the "Jin Teng" chapter of the *Shu jing* (*SSJZS, Shangshu zhengyi*, 331–40), and briefly summarized in the *Minor Preface* (*SSJYJS*, 526). Karlgren's translation, *The Book of Documents*, can be found in *BMFEA* 22 (1950), 1–81. See Saussy, *The Problem of a Chinese Aesthetic*, 138–50, where the narratological organization of the "Jin Teng" story is compared to the tropological organization of the xing.
132. *SSJYJS*, 530.
133. The latter clause refers to the third stanza, *SSJYJS*, 529. See Pauline Yu's insightful discussion on this ode, *The Reading of Imagery*, 56.
134. *Mao Commentary*, *SSJYJS*, 529.
135. See *SSJYJS*, 526–27.
136. Han school as quoted in *SSJYJS*, 527.
137. *SSJZS, Shangshu zhengyi*, 331–40.
138. See Shaughnessy, "Western Zhou History," 310–11.
139. Lu school as quoted in *SSJYJS*, 526. See *Shiji*, "Lu Zhougong shijia" 魯周公世家, Zhang Dake 張大可, *Shiji xinzhu* 史記新注 (Peking: Huawen, 2000), 938.
140. *SSJZS, Maoshi zhengyi*, 512–17.
141. Lu school as quoted in *SSJYJS*, 528.
142. *SSJYJS*, 265. Transl., modif., Karlgren, *Book of Odes*, 37.
143. *Minor Preface*, *SSJYJS*, 265.
144. *SSJYJS*, 637. Trans. modified, Karlgren, *Book of Odes*, 126–27.
145. *SSJYJS*, 637. See Karlgren, *Glosses*, 482. As Karlgren indicates, Zheng Xuan elaborates on Mao's comment by claiming that "the xing-element—rivers flowing toward, and joining, the sea—is an instance of a smaller entity approaching a larger one, intimating that the vassals paying court to the Son of Heaven is also like this. When the vassals meet the Son of Heaven in spring, it is called *chao*; in the summer, *zong*" 興者, 水流而入海, 小就大也. 喻諸侯朝天子亦猶是也. 諸侯春見天子曰朝, 夏見曰宗.
146. *SSJYJS*, 637.
147. *SSJYJS*, 637.
148. *SSJYJS*, 637.
149. *SSJYJS*, 637.
150. *SSJYJS*, 638.
151. *SSJYJS*, 638.
152. *SSJYJS*, 638.
153. *SSJYJS*, 638.
154. *SSJYJS*, 638. Trans. modified, Karlgren, *Book of Odes*, 126–27.
155. In several passages in the *Zuo Commentary*, among them the story of the six fishhawks that appeared to fly backward over the state of Song (*Zuozhuan*,

Xi 16; Wang et al., *Zuozhuan quanyi*, 264), ying and yang are described as natural forces that certainly affect the human realm but are not part of any greater or more complex cosmological system, wherefore their workings do not foretell future events: the birds were simply blown backward over Song by unusually strong winds and did not portend a future disaster. See also Xunzi, "Tian lun," 天論 where the philosopher argues that Heaven's "movements are constant" and that man creates his own fortune or misfortune (*Xunzi jijie*, 306–7), and that sacrifices provide a cultural pattern (*wen*) to human existence but are without effect (316).

156. See Michelle Yeh, "Metaphor and *Bi*," 251. Yeh claims that Chinese *bi* "metaphors" differ from Western metaphors because there is no "assimilation" between nature and man. Such an assimilation is, of course, exactly what we have here.

Chapter 19

1. *SSJYJS*, 542. Trans. modified, Karlgren, *Book of Odes*, 104.
2. *SSJYJS*, 541.
3. Comparing this A B (C D) structure to a metaphor *in extenso* such as Aristotle's metaphor for old age as "the evening of life," we see that the relationship between what is textually given and what is added from the outside is quite different. In the latter example evening (A) is to day (B) as old age (C) is to life (D). The A (B C) D structure signals, of course, that the expression is itself metaphoric, without metatextual additions.
4. *SSJZS, Maoshi zhengyi*, 533.
5. *SSJYJS*, 542.
6. *SSJYJS*, 403. My translation follows Wang Xianqian's extrapolation: 園有桃則食其實. 國有民則得其力 (*SSJYJS*, 403).
7. *SSJYJS*, 403. Karlgren, *Book of Odes*, 70. I follow Karlgren's translation of the last line.
8. *Zheng Annotation, SSJYJS*, 404. The *Minor Preface* interprets "Yuan you tao" as a criticism of the king of Wei made by the "great officials" of that state. Mao, as so often, does not supply enough information.
9. *SSJYJS*, 422–23. Trans. modified, Karlgren, *Book of Odes*, 76. Karlgren is probably right to translate the first lines as firewood "bundled together" (thus emphasizing the firewood rather than the act of bundling) rather than as "[I am] arranging firewood into round bundles," since *shu xin* clearly means "bundle of firewood," not "bundling firewood" in ode 68.
10. As explained in Mao's comment on the third stanza, *SSJYJS*, 424.
11. *SSJYJS*, 424.
12. *SSJYJS*, 370.
13. Zheng Xuan and the *Minor Preface* obviously follow Mao's earlier gloss (*SSJYJS*, 422–23). Both the *Preface* and Zheng go against Mao in their interpretation

of this ode as a critique (*ci*) of the chaotic state of Jin 晉. "The state is in chaos and, therefore, the marriages do not occur on time," the *Preface* states. Zheng understands the xing element as the Three Stars, which signal that the proper time of marriage has not yet come. The firewood, Zheng claims, is not a metaphor but an object picked in the wilds by the narrator who looks up in the sky, sees the Three Stars, and concludes that the time for coupling has not yet arrived. See also Karlgren's discussion on *xiehou* in *Glosses*, 242. Karlgren—following Chen Huan—argues forcefully that Mao's comment on "Ye you wan cao" does not refer to *xiehou* but to the verb *yu* 遇, which indeed means "to meet by accident" (*SSJYJS*, 370–71). Yet Han Ying's gloss (*SSJYJS*, 423) on *xiehou* is *bu gu* 不固, "without proper conduct," which is quite close to the idea of extra-ritual behavior. Furthermore, *xiehou* is a compound word that is already inscribed in a context—"Ye you wan cao"—that talk of amorous extra-ritual meetings in the wilderness (*ye* 野).

14. *SSJYJS*, 605. See Karlgren, *Book of Odes*, 119–20. *Junzi* generally means Superior Man (or possibly "gentleman") in the *Xunzi*. Here, "ruler" (normally called *jun*) is better.

15. Karlgren, *Book of Odes*, 119–20.

16. The phrase appears in full in odes 10, 168, and 217 and in part in odes 90, 116, 126, 173, and 228.

17. *SSJYJS*, 774–75. Trans. modified from Karlgren, *Book of Odes*, 169.

18. See Baxter and Sargant, "Old Chinese reconstruction," 5 and 7.

19. Ma Ruichen, *Shijing Maoshi zhuan jian tong shi* 毛詩傳箋通釋, quoted in *SSJYJS*, 775. As indicated by the title of his book—*A Comprehensive Explanation of the* Commentary *and [Zheng Xuan's]* Annotations *to the* Maoshi—Ma sets out to explain Mao's (and Zheng's) comments as well as the *Odes* themselves.

20. *SSJYJS*, 328–29.

21. *SSJYJS*, 448–50. Trans. modified from Karlgren, *Book of Odes*, 83–84, *Glosses*, 290. I put the translation of *wan* 宛 within brackets since Mao does not gloss the word in his comment. *Wan* is defined, however, in the comments on ode 115 (as "dead-like"), ode 107 ("pliantly") and ode 196 ("smallish"); *SSJYJS*, 419, 400, 692.

22. See my "Does the Metaphor Translate?"

23. These themes are first treated by Mao in his comment on ode 34, "Pao you ku ye."

24. See Karlgren, *Glosses*, 718.

25. Trans. modified from Karlgren, *Book of Odes*, 177.

26. *SSJYJS*, 162.

27. *SSJYJS*, 162.

28. *SSJYJS*, 163.

29. *SSJYJS*, 162.

30. *SSJYJS*, 453.

31. Trans. modified from Karlgren, *Book of Odes*, 66–67.

32. Transl. modified from Karlgren, *Book of Odes*, 66–67.
33. *SSJYJS*, 387.

Chapter 20

1. While the ironical xing stands in opposition to the "simple" xing, since it negates the latter's positiveness, the analogical xing may be simultaneously ironical since it is already to a large degree extratextual.

2. *SSJYJS*, 302.

3. *SSJYJS*, 302. See Karlgren, *Book of Odes*, 42.

4. *SSJYJS*, 302. The last line of the second stanza (*SSJYJS*, 303–4) must thus be understood as "you cannot [say] 'I don't care'" 能不我甲. It is tempting to assume that "gentleman" (*junzi* 君子) differs from "ruler" (*jun* 人君), and that the xing actually refers to the speaker (and not to the young ruler), who fancies himself a "gentleman." However, that interpretation is feasible only if we follow Karlgren's translation of the fourth lines as "can he [the ruler] fail to know me [the gentlemanly speaker]?," a rendering that, as Karlgren himself acknowledges, contradicts Mao's comment.

5. The "young lord" is identified by all four schools as Duke Hui 惠. Note Mi Wenkai's and Pei Puxian's amusing reading of "Wanlan" as a satirical folk song about a henpecked husband, *Shijing xinshang yu yanjiu*, 1:312–14. Xunzi's inconspicuous quotation of "Wanlan" contradicts Mao's reading. In Xunzi's interpretation, the poem is saying that a true *junzi* "is easy to know but difficult to be intimate with" 君子易知而難狎; *Xunzi jijie*, 37.

6. *SSJYJS*, 354. See the "minor" (or "lower") preface: "What is held up as beautiful is in fact not beautiful" 所美非美然.

7. Note that Zheng Xuan (*SSJYJS*, 354) reads the xing as ironic in itself. Admittedly, the *Commentary* does say that the *fusu* is a "smallish" tree, but the big/small dualism still holds and is, moreover, repeated in the second stanza that opposes the "high pine tree" to the small *long* plant.

8. See Constance Cook's survey of onomatopoeic binomes in sixth-century Zhou bronze inscriptions; Cook and Goldin, *A Source Book of Ancient Chinese Bronze Inscriptions*, 259–60.

9. *SSJYJS*, 150–60. See Karlgren, *Book of Odes*, 20.

10. *SSJYJS*, 455. Trans. modified from Karlgren, *Book of Odes*, 85.

11. For other instances of the *aprosdoketon* and the poetics of surprise, see ode 202: "Full-grown are the *e* plants / They are not *e* plants, they are *hao* plants" (*SSJYJS*, 724), and ode 159: "The fish in the fine-meshed net / [are] rudd and bream" (Mao: "The fine-meshed net is a net for small fish. Rudd and bream are big fish"; *SSJYJS*, 542).

12. *SSJYJS*, 169. Trans. modified from Karlgren, *Book of Odes*, 22, *Glosses*, 90.

13. *SSJYJS*, 174. Mao glosses *xie* 屑 as *jie* 絜 (alt. reading: *xie*), which here could mean "tie together." It is more probable, *pace* Karlgren and Schuessler, that Mao's *jie* was a loan character for *jie* 潔 meaning "clear" or "pure," an assumption fortified by Mao's comment that the white egret described in the first stanza of ode 298 (and in 278) refers to the "white" and "pure" 絜 official (*SSJYJS*, 1068). This reading tallies better with the opening metaphor of the third stanza: "The Jing-river becomes muddy through the Wei-river" (modified from Karlgren, *Book of Odes*, 22). We have seen how family relations are often described in terms of rivers and river branches (i.e., as an early Chinese variant of the "family tree" metaphor). Our line here should thus mean, with Mao, that the narratrix accuses her estranged husband of regarding her as a "muddy river" that would "pollute" his family. See Wang Xianqian's comment, *SSJYJS*, 174.

14. *SSJYJS*, 721–22. See Karlgren, *Book of Odes*, 152. *Tui* 頹 and *fen lun* 焚輪 have puzzled many post-Maoist commentators. It is clear, however, from the context that Mao here refers to two weak winds that become strong by uniting their forces. See Wang Xianqian's thorough summary of linguistic glosses on this word (*SSJYJS*, 722).

15. *SSJYJS*, 776.

16. Karlgren, *Glosses* 197.

17. Trans. Karlgren, *Book of Odes*, 170. Mao comments: "The mistletoe is a parasite . . . This says [by way of a simile] that the dukes have no gravitas of their own but [like a parasite] rely upon the king's gravitas" 蔦, 寄生也 . . . 喻諸公非自有尊, 託王之尊 (*SSJYJS*, 776). Kong Yingda supposes that Mao's "xing" refers to a perceived analogy—which also constitutes a "simple xing"—between the headgear and the ruler; *SSJZS*, *Maoshi zhengyi*, 868.

18. For Zheng's commentaries on the "Three Books of Rites," see Yang Tianyu's 楊天宇 *Zheng Xuan Sanli zhu yanjiu* 鄭玄三禮注研究 (Tianjin: Tianjin renmin chubanshe, 2007) and Liang Xifeng's 梁錫鋒 "Zheng Xuan yi li jian *Shi* yanjiu" 鄭玄以禮箋《詩》研究 (PhD-diss., Zhengzhou university, 2004).

19. *SSJYJS*, 776.

20. See *Liji*, "Yu zao" 玉藻; *SSJZS*, *Liji zhengyi*, 876.

21. *SSJYJS*, 776.

22. *SSJYJS*, 692. See Karlgren, *Book of Odes*, 144.

23. See here my "One Lucky Bastard" and "Inscription and Re-reading."

24. *SSJYJS*, 727.

25. Trans. modified from Karlgren, *Book of Odes*, 154–55.

26. *SSJYJS*, 730. Karlgren, *Book of Odes*, 154–55. *Glosses*, 630. *Si ren* is defined as "domestic servants" 家臣 in Mao's comment on ode 259; *SSJYJS*, 963.

27. *SSJYJS*, 730. For 舟 ("boat") Zheng Xuan reads 周 ("Zhou").

28. *SSJYJS*, 734. See Karlgren, *Book of Odes*, 155.

29. The relation between Mao's rhetorical interpretations of the *Odes* by way of the xing and the philosophical discourse on the correctness and falsity of "names"

is a huge topic, far beyond the scope of the present project. It is certain, however, that the questions of the xing-trope and of xingish irony must be seen in the light of the fervent discussion about the "rectification of names" (*zheng ming* 正名) in the works of Confucius and Xunzi. While Confucius and Xunzi—linguistic paranoiacs—sought to rectify the ancient order of a *signans* coupled with the proper *signatum*, Mao's xing introduces a new order where the xing-image, *as a "name,"* does not possess its conventional "proper" *signatum* but one that exists only on a rhetorical, and thus illusionary, level. Yet this appropriation, this metaphorical usage of the conventional signatum is made in the name of Truth: Mao, as a ritual "worker," appropriates the natural image and gives it another a higher, more aristocratic and therefore *truer* meaning. I return to this topic in a forthcoming work.

30. *SSJYJS*, 329.

31. As noted previously, in his comment on "Bi gong" (ode 300, see *SSJYJS*, 1077) Mao refers to an earlier (oral or written) commentary by Meng Zhongzi 孟仲子, traditionally described as Mao's predecessor as the transmitter of Confucius's version of the *Shi*. Likewise, Mao refers to a Master Zhongliang 仲梁子 in his reading of ode 50.

32. *SSJYJS*, 665.

33. *SSJYJS*, 665.

34. *SSJYJS*, 665. For frost in the *zheng*-month as an anomaly, see the quotation of "Zheng yue" in *Hanshu*, "Chu Yuan wang zhuan" 楚元王傳, and the accompanying comment: "[this refers to] frost falling out of bounds and out of time" 霜降失節, 不以其時; *Hanshu buzhu*, 956. See also Mi Wenkai and Pei Puxian, *Shijing xinshang yu yanjiu*, 2:928, and *SSJYJS*, 665.

35. *SSJYJS*, 666.

36. *SSJYJS*, 666; Karlgren, *Book of Odes*, 136 and *Glosses*, 533. Karlgren's logical and persuasive discussion of these lines reminds us that he sought the "true" meaning of the *Odes*, not the true meaning of Mao's ideologico-literary *hermeneutica*.

37. *SSJYJS*, 669.

38. *Mao Commentary* and *Zheng Annotation*, *SSJYJS*, 669. Following our hermeneutics of suspicion, we can assume that, in another context, the image of flourishing grain on the slope would be interpreted as an image of a *good* ruler, who—much like the slope—is able to make grain (i.e., talented ministers) flourish.

39. *SSJYJS*, 672.

40. *SSJYJS*, 639–40.

41. *SSJYJS*, 667. Trans. modified from Karlgren, *Book of Odes*, 135.

Chapter 21

1. Derrida, "White Mythology," 30.
2. *Zuozhuan*, Xi 27; Wang et al., *Zuozhuan quanyi*, 326.

3. Xunzi, "Wangba" 王霸; *Xunzi jijie*, 136.
4. See, for instance, Xunzi's "Jundao"; *Xunzi jijie*, 237–38.
5. Mao uses *jun* and *junzi* more freely than Xunzi. With Mao, *jun* can refer to the vassals (*zhuhou*) and *junzi* to a (virtuous) ruler, as in "Guanju" or in Mao's comment on stanza five of ode 192: "on the throne is no gentleman-ruler [*junzi*] but a petty man" (*SSJYJS*, 667). See also Mao's comment on ode 115, "Shan you shu," where "ruler" (*guojun*) is clearly synonymous with *junzi* (*SSJYJS*, 417–18), and "Junzi yang yang" (ode 67), where Mao defines *junzi* as "lord of the state" (*guojun*), that is, as "ruler" (*SSJYJS*, 319).
6. "Fuguo" 富國; *Xunzi jijie*, 177.
7. The first and fourth chapters of John Henderson's *Scripture, Canon and Commentary: A Comparison of Confucian and Western Exegesis* (Princeton, NJ: Princeton University Press, 1991) correctly describe the "commentarial assumptions" of the Confucian tradition as holding the canons, that is, the classics, to be consistent, comprehensive, coherent, profound, and without internal paradoxes. The *xing* proved to be an excellent tool for making the *Odes* fit those assumptions, hence the success of the Mao version.
8. Xunzi, "Wangzhi" 王制; *Xunzi jijie*, 152–53.
9. Xunzi, "Jundao"; *Xunzi jijie*, 234.
10. *Xunzi jijie*, 234.
11. *Zuozhuan*, Zhao 32; Wang et al., *Zuozhuan quanyi*, 1408. Trans. modified from Burton Watson, *The Tso Chuan: Selections from China's Oldest Narrative History* (New York: Columbia University Press, 1989), 192. Trans. of ode 193, from Karlgren, *Book of Odes*, 138–40.
12. *SSJYJS*, 676.
13. *SSJYJS*, 354–55. Trans. modified from Karlgren, *Book of Odes*, 56–57.
14. See *Mao Commentary*, *SSJYJS*, 355.
15. Mi and Pei, *Shijing xinshang yu yanjiu*, 1:404.
16. *SSJYJS*, 354–55.
17. *SSJYJS*, 356.
18. *SSJYJS*, 356.
19. *SSJYJS*, 356.
20. See Wang Xianqian's discussion, *SSJYJS*, 357.
21. See *Zheng Annotation*, *SSJYJS*, 356.
22. Note that the *Minor Preface* acknowledges the paradox: "The ruler is weak and the ministers strong. There is no initiation and joining in" 君弱臣強, 不倡而和也; *SSJYJS*, 356.
23. *SSJYJS*, 381–82. Karlgren, *Glosses*, 250–51.
24. *SSJYJS*, 381–82.
25. *SSJYJS*, 605. See Karlgren, *Book of Odes*, 119–20.
26. *SSJYJS*, 605.

27. *SSJYJS*, 570–71. With reference to the fourth line, Mao defines *qian* 遷 as *xi* 徙 ("move") in his comment on stanza two of ode 58; *SSJYJS*, 294.

28. *SSJYJS*, 570.

29. *SSJYJS*, 471. Trans. modified from Karlgren, *Book of Odes*, 89. Mao defines *fu* 夫 as *fuxiang* 傅相, "aide to the minister."

30. *SSJYJS*, 472.

31. *SSJYJS*, 471.

32. *SSJYJS*, 639–40. Trans. modified from Karlgren, *Book of Odes*, 127.

33. See chapter 12.

34. See Lu Ji's 陸璣 deadpan (and decidedly non-metaphorical) annotation: "when the crane cries it can be heard at a distance of eight to nine *li*" (*SSJYJS*, 639).

35. *SSJYJS*, 639. Mao here defines *tuo* 蘀, which typically means "withered leaves," as *luo* 落 ("fallen [leaves or fruit]"). The phrase "using what has been discarded" 用滯 in his comment on lines 5–7 (*SSJYJS*, 640) probably refers metaphorically to the fruits that lie unused and uneaten under the tree, as *zhi* 滯 has this meaning ("leftover [eatables]") in the third stanza of ode 212 (*SSJYJS*, 766). I follow Zheng Xuan and Kong Yingda (*SSJZS*, *Maoshi zhengyi*, 669) in taking *zhi* 之 to mean "go to."

36. *SSJYJS*, 639.

37. *Xunzi jijie*, 128. See Knoblock's translation in *Xunzi*, 2:74. See also Saussy, *The Problem of a Chinese Aesthetic*, 143.

38. *SSJYJS*, 639.

39. *SSJYJS*, 640.

40. As I argue in chapter 12, perhaps we can see in the poem's refusal to follow the xing with a description of human action a similar resistance to interpretation: let *other* texts serve as Confucian allegories.

41. Zhu Xi, *Shi ji zhuan* 詩集傳 and *Shi xu bian shuo* 詩序辨說 (comments on ode 115), as quoted in Hao Zhida 郝志達, ed. *Guofeng shizhi cuan jie* 國風詩旨篹解 (Tianjin: Nankai daxue chubanshe, 1990), 422–23.

42. *SSJYJS*, 416–18. Trans. modified from Karlgren, *Book of Odes*, 74–75. See *Glosses*, 289–91. I read *wan* 宛 as "limpid," "lifeless" rather than as "wither."

43. *SSJYJS*, 417.

44. *SSJYJS*, 605. The extant text has *cai* 材 not *cai* 財, but the two words are certainly cognate.

45. *SSJYJS*, 435–37. Trans. modified from Karlgren, *Book of Odes*, 81. See *Glosses*, 308–9.

46. He Jie 何楷 (1594–1645) argues that the people described sitting side by side are court musicians; *Shijing shiben guyi* 詩經世本古義, as quoted in Hao Zhida, *Guofeng shizhi cuan jie*, 463.

47. *SSJYJS*, 436.

48. See Zhu Ziqing, 52–53.

Chapter 22

1. *SSJYJS*, 905. Trans. modified from Karlgren, *Book of Odes*, 209.
2. *SSJYJS*, 909.
3. In light of this argument, Karlgren's translation of the last two lines as "*I* have composed a few verses, in order to have them sung" (my italics) must be discarded unless the "lord" (*junzi*) whom the entire poem is praising suddenly begins to speak himself. See Karlgren, *Book of Odes*, 209.
4. *SSJYJS*, 905. See Karlgren, *Book of Odes*, 210 and *Glosses*, 496.
5. *Mao Commentary*, *SSJYJS*, 136.
6. See the *Preface* and Zheng Xuan's exhaustive annotation, *SSJYJS*, 905.
7. Karlgren, *Book of Odes*, 209–10. For a very different rendering of this interestingly problematic ode, cf. Mi Wenkai and Pei Puxian (*Shijing yandu zhidao* 3:1346) who understand *junzi* as referring to the king, and the whole poem as a eulogy composed by a vassal.
8. *Mao Commentary*, *SSJYJS*, 907.
9. Transl., modif., Karlgren, *Book of Odes*, 210.
10. *SSJYJS*, 908. With Mao, the birds and the trees function as symptoms of a harmonious government. There is thus no cause for Zheng Xuan's and Wang Xianqian's (*SSJYJS*, 908) claims that this stanza describes, metaphorically, the harmony between the king's ministers ("subjects") and the populace.
11. *SSJYJS*, 909. Trans. modified from Karlgren, *Book of Odes*, 210.
12. *SSJYJS*, 909.
13. *SSJYJS*, 905.
14. At first glance, it would seem plausible to understand the metaphor as describing how the evil men are dispersed by the "virtuous transformation," just as the slope stalls (and disperses) the (evil) whirlwind. Yet such a reading must ignore the active/passive dichotomy that organizes Mao's analogical *xing*, namely the contention that the virtuous transformation *disperses* the evil men just as the forceful whirlwind *enters* the slope. "Virtuous transformation" and "whirlwind" are both agents, whereas the evil men and the slope are the objects of actions. Furthermore, to *enter* and to *disperse* both share a connotation of violence and strength. Lastly, Zheng Xuan agrees with this reading, albeit with a different twist, claiming that the whirlwind from the south is a benevolent wind that enters the slope and nurtures it, just as the worthies will come and "nurture" the enlightened king (*SSJYJS*, 905).
15. *SSJYJS*, 490. Karlgren (*Book of Odes*, 94), following Zheng Xuan (*SSJYJS*, 490), translates *gu* as "turn one's head," but there is no reason to believe that Mao understood *qiaozhan* as anything else but a compound meaning "to look at."
16. *SSJYJS*, 491.
17. *SSJYJS*, 491. *Fafa* 發發 is glossed as *ji* 疾 "rush" in Mao's comment on ode 202, stanza 5, *SSJYJS*, 726.

18. *SSJYJS*, 491.

19. *SSJYJS*, 491. Despite Mao's silence, the state in question is likely *Kuai* 檜, which has given its name to the part of the *Guofeng* in which "Fei feng" appears.

20. The fact that "Fei feng" is not defined as a xing proves the irregular character of the *Commentary* and the difficulties in finding an all-comprising description of Mao's usage of the concept of xing.

21. *SSJYJS*, 712. See Karlgren, *Book of Odes*, 149.

22. *SSJYJS*, 712.

23. *SSJYJS*, 726. Trans. modified by Karlgren, *Book of Odes*, 153. See *Glosses*, 627.

24. *SSJYJS*, 736.

25. See Appendix A.

26. *SSJYJS*, 381–82 and 142–46.

27. *SSJYJS*, 381–82.

28. *SSJYJS*, 363. See Karlgren, *Book of Odes*, 59 and *Glosses*, 41.

29. *Mao Commentary, SSJYJS*, 18.

30. *SSJYJS*, 363.

31. *Minor Preface, SSJYJS*, 363. *Zheng Annotation* (*SSJYJS*, 363), and Kong Yingda, *SSJZS, Maoshi zhengyi*, 313.

32. *SSJYJS*, 375.

33. *SSJYJS*, 376. For translations that bring out the love theme, see Karlgren, *Book of Odes*, 62–63 and Mi and Pei, *Shijing xinshang yu yanjiu*, 1:445–548.

34. *SSJYJS*, 375. See Karlgren *Glosses*, 247.

35. As quoted by Wang Xianqian in *SSJYJS*, 375.

36. *SSJYJS*, 424–26. Trans. modified from Karlgren, *Book of Odes*, 76–77; *Glosses*, 298–99.

37. *SSJYJS*, 424–25.

38. See Karlgren, *Glosses*, 298.

39. Karlgren, *Glosses*, 298; *Mao Commentary, SSJYJS*, 770. Karlgren's claim that Mao's comment on this ode has been corrupted is widely accepted; see Yu, *The Reading of Imagery*, 75.

40. *SSJYJS*, 429–30. See Karlgren, *Book of Odes*, 79 and *Glosses* 303 and 76.

41. *SSJYJS*, 429.

42. We should, however, observe how Mao echoes "Han guang" (ode 9) and its sensuous imagery: "In the south there are high trees / you cannot rest [休息] under them / On the Han river there are playing [游] girls / you cannot reach them." Mao's comment on ode 123 might provide an intertextual clue to ode 9, condoning the passion by saying that the narratrix is indeed a "tree" under which it is appropriate (*yi*) to "rest." *SSJYJS*, 51–55.

43. *SSJYJS*, 588–90. Trans. modified from Karlgren, *Book of Odes*, 114. See *Glosses*, 439–41.

44. See "Bao yu" (ode 121) and "Si mu" (ode 162).

45. See Mao's comment on "Ge tan" (ode 2), *SSJYJS*, 17 and my analysis of this ode in this chapter.

46. *SSJYJS*, 588–90. Trans. modified from Karlgren, *Book of Odes*, 114.

47. *SSJYJS*, 589.

48. One might object that *xuxu* means "scattered," and that a strictly analogical reading would have to disregard the metaphorical relationship between the sparse tree and the separation of family members, but Mao's gloss is *de facto* already an arbitrary choice. Furthermore, an analogical reading would depend on the description of flourishing leaves in the second stanza.

49. *SSJYJS*, 322. See Karlgren, *Book of Odes*, 46.

50. *Mao Commentary*, *SSJYJS*, 322.

51. The "perturbed waters" imagery has naturally elicited an abundance of comments from later scholars. Zheng Xuan (*SSJYJS*, 322) reads it as an image of the inability of King Ping to pass on "grace and beneficence" to the populace whereas Kong Yingda (*SSJZS*, *Maoshi zhengyi*, 259) understands Mao's xing as a rhetorical question (which may suggest that ode 68 was somehow mistaken for ode 92) but largely with the same meaning as Zheng. Karlgren (*Book of Odes*, 46) takes the firewood as a metaphor for an affectionate couple that is so well "bundled" together that they, or it, cannot be washed away or dissolved by the stirred water.

52. *SSJYJS*, 366. See Karlgren, *Book of Odes*, 60.

53. *SSJYJS*, 366.

54. *SSJZS*, *Maoshi zhengyi*, 259.

55. *SSJYJS*, 419–20. See Karlgren, *Book of Odes*, 75 and *Glosses*, 292.

56. *SSJYJS*, 420.

57. *Mao Commentary*, *SSJYJS*, 421. Karlgren, *Glosses*, 294.

58. *SSJYJS*, 420.

59. *SSJYJS*, 431–32. Trans. modified, Karlgren, *Book of Odes*, 79–80.

60. *SSJYJS*, 431.

61. *Mao Commentary*, *SSJYJS*, 431.

62. *SSJYJS*, 17. Only the first three lines of the first stanza are quoted.

63. Lu school, as quoted by Wang Xianqian, *SSJYJS*, 16.

64. *Mao Commentary*, *SSJYJS*, 17.

65. *SSJYJS*, 19. See Karlgren, *Book of Odes*, 3.

66. *SSJYJS*, 19.

67. *Mao Commentary*, *SSJYJS*, 19–20.

68. *SSJYJS*, 328.

69. *SSJYJS*, 21–22. See Karlgren, *Book of Odes*, 2–3 and *Glosses* 10–11.

70. *Mao Commentary*, *SSJYJS*, 21. This instruction took place in the "ancestral temple if the shrine dedicated to the high ancestor had not yet been removed" 祖廟未毀, 教於公宮 or, if so, "in the clan hall" 於宗室 (*SSJYJS*, 21). Mao is here apparently quoting the "Hun yi" 昏義 chapter of the *Liji* (*SSJZS*, *Liji*, 1622).

71. *SSJYJS*, 327. Trans. modified from Karlgren, *Book of Odes*, 48–49.

72. *SSJYJS*, 327.

73. *SSJYJS*, 327.

74. Mao's far-fetched and unconvincing analogical reading of ode 214 is in fact wholly governed by the third stanza's nostalgic description of the bedding and of the lamenting of lonely mornings. It obviously connotes sensualism, and if Mao had used the simple model that takes the length of the kudzu as an image of the simultaneous distance and continuity between family members in separation, he would have presented a reading that *formally* would have been more convincing but that would have underlined the theme of longing. By way of the analogical xing, Mao is able, in a single stroke, to make the third stanza speak of rites and the first stanza speak of perfection. That is why he takes the third line and what he considers as a description of ritual behavior as the hermeneutic center.

75. William Empson, *Seven Types of Ambiguity* (London: Chatto and Windus, 1947 [1930]). For early theories of literary ambiguity in the West, see Peter Szondi, *Introduction to Literary Hermeneutics* (Cambridge: Cambridge University Press, 1995), 25–26.

76. Ode 37, *SSJYJS*, 181–85 and ode 4, *SSJYJS*, 32. See also my analyses of these odes in the first and fourth chapters.

77. *SSJYJS*, 12. For the interpretation of *cenci* 參差, see Karlgren, *Glosses*, 70.

78. See Baxter and Sargant, "Old Chinese reconstruction," 143 and 140.

79. *SSJYJS*, 12.

80. *SSJYJS*, 70. I follow Zheng Xuan (*SSJYJS*, 70) in translating *yu yi* 于以 as "going to" (*wang yi* 往以). *You shi* (有事 lit. "having affairs") was a stock phrase in the *Yijing* and the oracle bones inscriptions, referring to offerings (*ji* 祭). See Mi and Pei, *Shijing xinshang yu yanjiu*, 50.

81. *SSJYJS*, 70.

82. *SSJYJS*, 78–83. *Mao Commentary*, *SSJYJS*, 81. See Karlgren, *Book of Odes*, 9–10.

83. *SSJYJS*, 328–29.

84. *SSJYJS*, 328–29.

85. *Jun* 君 unambiguously refers to a "ruler" and not to a plant-picking girl's husband (*junzi*).

86. *SSJYJS*, 432–33. See Karlgren, *Book of Odes*, 80–81.

87. *SSJYJS*, 432. *Wu zheng* 無徵 can also mean "without appointment [from a ruler]." If thus interpreted the second line could indeed refer to a virtuous "gentleman" living unemployed in obscurity, just as our intertext (ode 72) suggests. However, since the "*ling*-picker" of the first line must be identical to this unrecognized gentleman (the whole metaphor being "to pick *ling* at Shou Yang equals minute work in a remote place"), and since "plant-picking," that "minute work," is described as "petty conduct," the first and second lines are incompatible: the conduct of a virtuous man cannot be described as "petty." See Kong Yingda who says that the xing here "criticizes that the ruler employs slanderers" 刺君用讒, an

interpretation that indeed reads "*ling*-picking" as a metaphor for "petty conduct"; *SSJZS*, *Maoshi zhengyi*, 402.

88. Nothing in Mao's comment refers to the famous story about the two brothers Bo Yi 伯夷 and Shu Qi 叔齊 who refused to serve King Wu and, instead, chose to live of plants on a mountain called Shou Yang where they subsequently starved to death. For a reading that follows this tradition, see Wang Zhi 王質, *Shi zong wen* 詩總聞 (comment on ode 125), as quoted in Hao Zhida, *Guofeng shizhi cuan jie*, 458.

89. *SSJYJS*, 614–15. Trans. modified from Karlgren, *Book of Odes*, 122. See *Glosses*, 11 and 460.

90. *Mao Commentary*, *SSJYJS*, 615.

91. *Mao Commentary*, *SSJYJS*, 614–15.

92. *Mao Commentary*, *SSJYJS*, 1069. See Karlgren, *Glosses*, 853–54.

Chapter 23

1. See Zhu Ziqing, 59. Zhu here makes the distinction, not uncommon in the Chinese tradition, between "implicit" (*yinyu*) and "explicit" (*xianyu*) simile. Despite the fact that Zhu makes the third ode an example of a *yinyu*, he does not understand it as a xing based on a symptomatic relationship between *signans* and *signatum* but as a synecdoche. In other words, the poem mentions the plant picking as one of the queen-consort's "arduous tasks" in order to signify implicitly the more specific "arduous task" that concerns the consort, namely the "promotion of virtuous officials."

2. *Mao Commentary*, *SSJYJS*, 93.

3. *SSJYJS*, 91. Trans. modified from Karlgren, *Book of Odes*, 10.

4. See "Ye you wan cao" (ode 94), "Jian jia" (ode 129) and "Lu xiao" (ode 173). "Ye you wan cao," in particular, is interesting with regard to or present ode since it too suggests an extra-ritual meeting between man and woman. The word *lu* 露 "dew" occurs in seven poems in all.

5. Trans. Karlgren, *Book of Odes*, 10. Note that the second stanza contains an ambiguity that has puzzled many commentators after Mao. The first line says: "Who says that the sparrow has no beak? / By aid of what else could it break through into my house?" 誰謂雀無角, 何以穿我屋 (Karlgren, *Book of Odes*, 10). The word translated as "beak" is *jue* 角, literally meaning "horn." Zheng Xuan, consequently, paraphrases the first four lines as saying that the sparrow has no *jue* and that the man has no right to force the narratrix to marry him: "Everyone says that since the sparrow can break into the house it seems to have horns, and that since the forceful and ruthless man can bring me to court he seems to have treated me in a manner proper to the affair of marriage" 人皆謂雀之穿屋似有角, 彊暴之男召我而獄, 似有室家之道於我也 (*SSJYJS*, 92). Both renderings move within what we may call

a hermeneutical circle. Karlgren (and, among others, Mi Wenkai and Pei Puxian) interpret *jue* as "beak" because it fits the lines about the rat in the third stanza. Zheng, on the other hand, must understand the third stanza as saying that the rat in fact has no teeth and that things are not what they seem (*si er fei*), that is, the man might seem virtuous on the surface whereas in reality he is not.

6. See Baxter and Sargant, "Old Chinese reconstruction," 8 and 7.

7. *SSJYJS*, 93.

8. As far as the meaning of *lei* is concerned, Mao's comment on "Xing lu" is an exception. In all other odes, *lei* is defined either as *shan* 善 ("good"), or as the name of a particular ritual. For the former meaning, see odes 241 (stanza 4), 247 (st. 5), 255 (st. 3), 257 (st. 13), 264 (st. 5); for the latter, see odes 2 (st. 17) and 241 (st. 8).

9. The idea of an analogy between phenomena that are essentially identical is, of course, the central notion of Pauline Yu's and Michelle Yeh's descriptions of Mao's xing. See Yu, 65.

10. Xunzi, "Da lüe"; *Xunzi jijie*, 329.

11. *Zuozhuan*, Xi 20; Wang et al., *Zuozhuan quanyi*, 276.

12. For the argument that the *Zuozhuan* was known by Mao, see Karlgren, "The Early History," 38–41. The same lines are quoted again in Xiang 7; *Zuozhuan quanyi*, 783.

13. I have translated Mao's commentary in the past tense following the *Lu* commentary: "Thinking about the lords of yore" 思古君子; *SSJYJS*, 23.

14. *SSJYJS*, 23–32. See Karlgren, *Book of Odes*, 3–4 and *Glosses*, 12.

15. *Zuozhuan*, Xiang 15; Wang et al., *Zuozhuan quanyi*, 861. *Zhou hang* 周行 "the ranks of Zhou" can also mean "the road of Zhou," hence Karlgren's final translation: "I place it [the basket] here on the road of Chou [=Zhou]"; *Book of Odes*, 3.

16. See Karlgren, "The Early History," 38.

17. It is grammatically and logically possible (but contextually unlikely) that 憂之興也 means "this is [an account of] sorrow rising in the mind of the narrator."

18. *Xunzi jijie*, 398.

19. This reading has been suggested by, among others, Zheng Xuan (*SSJYJS*, 23–32). It is evidence of Zhu Ziqing's great genius that he pointed out the anomaly of this xing, adequately calling it a trope that "cites one [thing] to exemplify the rest" 舉一例餘. However, Zhu did not take the full consequences of his insight about this synecdochic xing but classified it as a *piyu*. Zhu Ziqing, *Shi yan zhi bian*, 59.

20. *SSJYJS*, 804. Trans. modification, Karlgren, *Book of Odes*, 179.

21. In his comment on ode 196, "Xiao yuan," Mao defines *shu* as *huo* 藿, "leaves," an interpretation that Zheng Xuan follows in his annotation on our present ode; *SSJYJS*, 693.

22. *SSJYJS*, 790. See Karlgren, *Book of Odes*, 175–76. Note that Zheng Xuan says (*SSJYJS*, 792–93) that it is the first lines of stanza four that contain the xing element: "The branches of the oak / abundant are their leaves / happy be the lords

/ they pacify the state" 維柞之枝，其葉蓬蓬，樂隻君子，殿天子之邦. Zheng annotates: "This is the xing. The trunk [of the oak] is like the fore-fathers. The branches are like their descendants. Its abundance signifies wisdom and competence" 此興也。柞之幹，猶先祖也。枝，猶子孫也。其葉蓬蓬，喻賢才也. However, nothing in Mao's comment on these lines suggests that he took it as the xing. Second, Zheng's xingish reading differs significantly from Mao's xing in that he performs, as he so often does, an interpretational overkill: *every* part of the xing—the trunk, the leaves, and their abundance—must be incorporated into the hermeneutic whole. As a contrast to Zheng's overwhelming hermeneutics, Mao's more subdued mode of reading would probably have understood the tree as a metaphor for the ruler and the branches as a metaphor for his ministers. Moreover, Zheng's reading probably derives from a passage in the *Zuozhuan* describing how a certain Duke Mu quotes (*fu*) "Jingjing zhe e" (ode 176) in response to a previous quotation of "Cai shu." After this ritual exchange, a third nobleman, Duke Zhao, comments: "If you do not possess that with which you rule a state, could it [the state] persist for long?" 不有以國其能久乎; *Zuozhuan*, Zhao 17; Wang et al. *Zuozhuan quanyi*, 1268. Zheng must have understood the topic here—"that with which you rule a state"—as referring to the wise vassals, described in the fourth stanza, who could "pacify the state."

23. *SSJYJS*, 470. See Karlgren, *Book of Odes*, 89. In the *Odes*, *hun* 昏 can mean both "dim-witted" (ode 196, stanza two) and "wife" (as a loan character for *hun* 婚, as in ode 35, stanza two) and probably "dusk." Even if the penultimate line of this stanza is translated as "marriage had been agreed on" it would not affect our analysis of Mao's xing. See also Kong Yingda's assertion (*SSJZS, Maoshi zhengyi*, 446) that Mao claims that "late autumn" is the proper time for marriages.

24. *SSJYJS*, 464.

25. Mao comments on the third and fourth lines, saying that "the appointment was made but he [or she] did not come" 期而不至也. Here a curious turning occurs: Mao makes the poem speak of *virtue* by claiming that someone—the man or the woman we do not know—does not appear for the scheduled, extra-ritual meeting. Mao opposes "dusk" to the "bright stars," suggesting that the time agreed on (dusk) has passed and turned into deep night, as represented by the bright stars (or, with Karlgren, "the morning star").

26. *Rhetoric*, 1410b, 3.10.2. 394, following the Greek text in J. H. Freese, trans., *Art of Rhetoric* (Cambridge, MA: Harvard University Press, 1964 [1926]). Aristotle is here commenting that an *eikôn* (a "simile"), in contrast to a *metaphora*, "does not say that 'this' is 'that'" (*ou legei hôs touto ekeino*).

27. *SSJYJS*, 41–42. See Karlgren, *Glosses*, 23.

28. *SSJYJS*, 456–58. See Karlgren, *Book of Odes*, 86. We can observe how Zheng Xuan's reading (*SSJYJS*, 456–58) totally contradicts Mao's. Zheng understands "Wu yi," not as an aristocratic eulogy to a good king but as a critique against a war-loving ruler voiced by the *populace* (*min* 民). Furthermore, *bai xing* 百姓 cannot be synonymous with *min*, which is proven by Mao's comment on the fifth stanza

of ode 166 where he defines *bai xing* as an ellipsis of 百官族姓 "the families of the one hundred officials," that is, the ruling elite (*SSJYJS*, 579).

29. *SSJYJS*, 428–29.

Chapter 24

1. Roy Andrew Miller, "Shih ming," *Early Chinese Texts, A Bibliographical Guide*, ed. Michael Loewe (Berkeley: The Institute of East Asian Studies, 1993), 425. Note that Miller refers to the late Han Dynasty work *Shi ming* 釋名 and not to the literary hermeneutics that is our subject here.

Appendix

1. *SSJYJS*, 699.
2. *SSJYJS*, 701. The last line is Karlgren's, *Book of Odes*, 146.
3. *SSJYJS*, 793.
4. *SSJYJS*, 126–34. See Karlgren, *Book of Odes*, 15–16.
5. *SSJYJS*, 127. For suggestive speculations about the difference in connotations between poplar and cypress boats, see C. H. Wang, *The Bell and the Drum*, 110–14.
6. *SSJYJS*, 127.
7. *SSJYJS*, 127.
8. *SSJYJS*, 217–18.
9. *Great Preface* (ode 45), *SSJYJS*, 216.
10. *SSJYJS*, 217.
11. *SSJYJS*, 214. Mao's account probably derives from *Zuozhuan*, Huan 16; Wang et al., *Zuozhuan quanyi*, 104.
12. *SSJYJS*, 214. See Karlgren, *Book of Odes*, 29 and *Glosses*, 125–27.
13. *SSJYJS*, 214, reading *bo* 薄 as synonymous with *bo* 泊; see also Saussy's reading of this ode, *The Problem of a Chinese Aesthetic*, 126–29.
14. *SSJYJS*, 214. I follow Kong Yingda's paraphrase (*SSJZS*, "Maoshi zhengyi," 179): 思此二子則中心為之憂養養然, 不知所定.
15. *SSJYJS*, 65–67. See Karlgren, *Book of Odes*, 7.
16. *SSJYJS*, 65.
17. *SSJYJS*, 69.
18. *SSJYJS*, 75–76. See Karlgren, *Book of Odes*, 9.
19. *SSJYJS*, 75–76.
20. *SSJYJS*, 75.
21. *SSJYJS*, 156. See Karlgren, *Book of Odes*, 20. In my somewhat tentative translation of what is likely a corrupt, truncated passage, I follow Wang Xianqian's recension, and Kong Yingda's paraphrase of *lexia* 樂夏 as *kaile* 凱樂; *SSJZS*, *Maoshi*

zhengyi, 133n2 and *SSJYJS*, 156. "Taking delight in the nourishing and fostering qualities of summer" is perhaps a more reasonable interpretation of 樂夏之長養者. Axel Schuessler suggests that 豈 *kai* "joyous" and *kai* 凱 "southern wind" are cognate; *A Dictionary of Early Zhou Chinese* (Honolulu: University of Hawaii Press, 1987), 345.

22. *SSJYJS*, 157. See Kong Yingda's explanation of Mao's enigmatic comment: *SSJZS, Maoshi zhengyi*, 134.

23. *SSJYJS*, 158.

24. Zhu Xi is perhaps the commentator that best expounds this particular comment in Mao's *Commentary*, see *Shi ji zhuan* as quoted in Hao Zhida, *Guofeng shizhi cuan jie*, 121–22. Note also Wang Zhi's hyperliteral and antimetaphorical interpretation of the jujube thorn as food picked by the impoverished mother; *Shi zongwen* as quoted in *Guofeng shizhi cuan jie*, 121.

25. *SSJYJS*, 724–26. Trans. modified from Karlgren, *Book of Odes*, 152–53.

26. *SSJYJS*, 724.

27. *SSJYJS*, 667.

28. *SSJYJS*, 597. The same gloss is given in Mao's comment on "Xia quan" (ode 153), *SSJYJS*, 506.

29. *SSJYJS*, 328 and *SSJYJS*, 882–83.

30. The xing element in "Lu e" has elicited numerous speculations. Zheng Xuan (*SSJYJS*, 724) reads it as a symptom of distress: that the speaker mistakes *e* for *hao* signals that she worries so much about not being able to support her parents that she cannot concentrate on her task. Wang Xianqian (*SSJYJS*, 724), banking on Lu Ji's botanical glosses, claims that the *e* plant is, in fact, identical to the *hao* plant. This plant is called *e* when young and edible whereas the grown-up, *inedible* plant is called *hao*. Wang thus subscribes to the poetics of disappointment: the speaker thinks he has found food but, alas, the *e* has already turned into the *hao*.

31. *SSJYJS*, 198.

32. *SSJYJS*, 198.

33. *SSJYJS*, 201–2. See Karlgren, *Book of Odes*, 27.

34. *SSJYJS*, 201.

35. *SSJYJS*, 220. Trans. modified from Karlgren, *Book of Odes*, 30. For a discussion of Mao's rather obscure comments, see *Glosses*, 130.

36. *SSJYJS*, 220.

37. *SSJYJS*, 220.

38. *SSJYJS*, 299. Trans. modified from Karlgren, *Book of Odes*, 41.

39. *SSJYJS*, 299.

40. *SSJYJS*, 323–33. See Karlgren, *Book of Odes*, 47 and *Glosses*, 202.

41. *SSJYJS*, 323. Trans. Karlgren, *Glosses, Kuo feng*, 167.

42. *SSJYJS*, 325.

43. *SSJYJS*, 325.

44. Ma Ruichen, *Maoshi zhuan jian tongshi*, as quoted in *SSJYJS*, 325. Karlgren, *Glosses*, 207.
45. *SSJYJS*, 500.
46. *SSJYJS*, 389–90. Trans. modified from Karlgren, *Book of Odes*, 67.
47. *SSJYJS*, 389.
48. *SSJYJS*, 390.
49. *SSJYJS*, 390.
50. *Mao Commentary* (ode 101), *SSJYJS*, 384.
51. *SSJYJS*, 421–22. Trans. modif. from Karlgren, *Book of Odes*, 76.
52. *SSJYJS*, 322.
53. *SSJYJS*, 427. Trans. modified from Karlgren, *Book of Odes*, 78.
54. *SSJYJS*, 427.
55. *SSJYJS*, 494–95. Trans. modified from Karlgren, *Book of Odes*, 94 and Legge, *The She King*, 220.
56. *SSJYJS*, 494.
57. *SSJYJS*, 494.
58. *SSJYJS*, 504–6. Trans. modified from Karlgren, *Book of Odes*, 96.
59. *SSJYJS*, 504–5.
60. *SSJYJS*, 506.
61. *SSJYJS*, 505.
62. *SSJYJS*, 563–64. See Karlgren, *Glosses*, 410.
63. *SSJYJS*, 563.
64. *SSJYJS*, 563. Trans. modified from Karlgren, *Book of Odes*, 107.
65. *SSJYJS*, 639.
66. *Xunzi jijie*, 128. See Knoblock's translation in *Xunzi*, 2:74. See also Saussy, *The Problem of a Chinese Aesthetic*, 143.
67. *SSJYJS*, 698. Trans. modified from Karlgren, *Book of Odes*, 145.
68. *SSJYJS*, 698.
69. *SSJYJS*, 134. See Karlgren, *Book of Odes*, 16.
70. *SSJYJS*, 716. Trans. modified Karlgren, *Book of Odes*, 151 and *Glosses*, 616.
71. *SSJYJS*, 716.
72. *SSJYJS*, 716.
73. Ode 224, first four lines; *SSJYJS*, 798. Trans. modified from Karlgren, *Book of Odes*, 178. I have followed Zheng Xuan's (and Karlgren's) translation of *bu shang* 不尚 as "would [I] not," although the exact function of *shang* is not clear. Since "Han guang" (ode 9) refers to "beautiful" trees by saying "one cannot rest there" 不可休息, the second line of ode 224 could perhaps be likewise interpreted. However, such a reading cannot be substantiated by Mao's comment, and it is therefore safer to follow the post-Mao tradition.
74. *SSJYJS*, 799.
75. *Mao Commentary* (ode 255), *SSJYJS*, 922.
76. Ode 9, *SSJYJS*, 51.

77. *SSJYJS*, 809. Trans. modified from Karlgren, *Book of Odes*, 181.
78. *SSJYJS*, 809.
79. *Great Preface*, *SSJYJS*, 809.
80. *SSJYJS*, 843. Trans. modified from Karlgren, *Book of Odes*, 191.
81. *SSJYJS*, 843.
82. *SSJYJS*, 559–60. Trans. modified from Karlgren, *Book of Odes*, 106. See Karlgren, *Glosses*, 405.
83. Zhu Ziqing, *Shi yan zhi bian*, 61.
84. This is made quite clear by Mao's comment on the fifth stanza; *SSJYJS*, 562. See Karlgren, *Glosses*, 405.
85. *SSJYJS*, 51–55. Trans. modified from Karlgren, *Book of Odes*, 6.
86. *SSJYJS*, 51.
87. *SSJYJS*, 134–36. Trans. modified from Karlgren, *Book of Odes*, 16.
88. *SSJYJS*, 134.
89. See the Qi-school reading as quoted in *SSJYJS*, 134.
90. *SSJYJS*, 335.
91. *SSJYJS*, 370. Trans. modified from Karlgren, *Book of Odes*, 61.
92. *SSJYJS*, 370.
93. See, inter alia, *Zuozhuan*, Xiang 27.
94. *SSJYJS*, 450–53. Karlgren, *Book of Odes*, 84.
95. *SSJYJS*, 450.
96. *SSJYJS*, 468–69. See Karlgren, *Book of Odes*, 89 and James Legge, *The She King*, 208.
97. *SSJYJS*, 468.
98. *SSJYJS*, 473–74. Trans. modified from Karlgren, *Book of Odes*, 90. See *Glosses*, 343.
99. *SSJYJS*, 475–76. Trans. modified from Karlgren, *Book of Odes*, 90.
100. *SSJYJS*, 475.
101. See *SSJYJS*, 475.
102. *SSJYJS*, 479–80. Trans. modified from Karlgren, *Book of Odes*, 92.
103. *SSJYJS*, 479.
104. *SSJYJS*, 354.
105. *SSJYJS*, 479.
106. *SSJYJS*, 489. Trans. modified from Karlgren, *Book of Odes*, 93 and *Glosses*, 355–56.
107. *SSJYJS*, 489.
108. *SSJYJS*, 302.
109. *Xunzi jijie*, 128.
110. *SSJYJS*, 545. Trans. modified from Karlgren, *Book of Odes*, 104.
111. *SSJYJS*, 545.
112. *SSJYJS*, 546.
113. *SSJYJS*, 546.

114. *SSJYJS*, 108. Trans. modified from Karlgren, *Book of Odes*, 13.
115. *SSJYJS*, 108. Trans. modified from Karlgren, *Glosses*, 56.
116. *SSJYJS*, 108.
117. *SSJYJS*, 141–42. Trans. modified from Karlgren, *Book of Odes*, 25.
118. *SSJYJS*, 192.
119. *SSJYJS*, 196. Trans. modified from Karlgren, *Book of Odes*, 25.
120. *SSJYJS*, 196.
121. *SSJYJS*, 649. Trans. modified from Karlgren, *Book of Odes*, 130 and *Glosses*, 317.
122. *SSJYJS*, 649.
123. *Great Preface* and Lu-school, *SSJYJS*, 648.
124. *SSJYJS*, 768. Trans. modified from Karlgren, *Book of Odes*, 167.
125. *SSJYJS*, 768.
126. *Great Preface*, *SSJYJS*, 768.
127. *SSJYJS*, 806. Karlgren's translation (*Book of Odes*, 179–80) "the prince of Shao has awarded *us*" is curious, especially since *zhi* in the second line of the fourth stanza ("the prince of Shao planned it [*ying zhi* 營之]") refers to the *work* carried out by the prince and not to the workers ("us") allegedly awarded. See also Mao's interpretation of the third stanza of ode 153 (*SSJYJS*, 507): "Beautiful is the young millet / The rain and clouds fattens it / The [vassals of the] four states has the kingly business [i.e., court rituals]/ Bo of Xun leads them [*lao zhi* 勞之]."
128. *SSJYJS*, 806.
129. *SSJYJS*, 806.
130. *SSJYJS*, 810. Trans. modified from Karlgren, *Book of Odes*, 182.
131. *SSJYJS*, 810.
132. See Mao's and Zheng's comments on ode 23, *SSJYJS*, 111.
133. See *SSJYJS*, 1068.
134. Karlgren, *Book of Odes*, 182. We note that Karlgren's reading would make this xing ironical since the rest of the poem describes the separation between man and woman.
135. *SSJYJS*, 834–35. See Karlgren, *Glosses*, 300.
136. *SSJYJS*, 835.
137. *SSJYJS*, 941–42. Trans. modified from Karlgren, *Book of Odes*, 220.
138. *SSJYJS*, 942.
139. *SSJYJS*, 942.
140. *SSJYJS*, 593–94. Trans. modified from Karlgren, *Book of Odes*, 115. See *Glosses*, 443.
141. *SSJYJS*, 594.
142. *SSJYJS*, 32. Trans. modified from Karlgren, *Book of Odes*, 4.
143. *SSJYJS*, 32.
144. *SSJYJS*, 591.

145. See Wen Yiduo's "Shuo yu." The fish-sexuality link also occupies an important place in Zhao Peilin's *Xing di yuanqi*, 24–36. See Zhu Ziqing, 52–53. Zhu does not dwell on the sensuous connotations of "fish" but claims that the only reason for Mao's deviation is the fact that he has already defined a similar image as a xing.

146. *SSJYJS*, 468 and 390. See also "Yu zao" (ode 221).

147. *SSJYJS*, 595. Karlgren, *Book of Odes*, 116.

148. *SSJYJS*, 593.

149. *SSJYJS*, 593.

150. In his comment on the second stanza of ode 225, Mao informs us that the *tai* plant was used to make hats that shelter from rain (*SSJYJS*, 802).

151. *SSJYJS*, 597. Trans. modified from Karlgren, *Book of Odes*, 116–17.

152. *SSJYJS*, 597.

153. *SSJYJS*, 597 and *SSJYJS*, 328.

154. *SSJYJS*, 601. Trans. modified from Karlgren, *Book of Odes*, 118.

155. *SSJYJS*, 601.

156. *Zuozhuan*, Wen 4; Wang et al., *Zuozhuan quanyi*, 398.

157. *SSJYJS*, 770. Trans. modified from Karlgren, *Book of Odes*, 168.

158. *SSJYJS*, 770.

159. *SSJYJS*, 770.

Bibliography

Included here are only works referred to or tacitly consulted.

Works in Western Languages

Ames, Roger, and David Hall. *Thinking through Confucius*. Albany: State University of New York Press, 1987.

Aristotle. *Poetics*. Translated by T. S. Dorsch. London: Penguin, 1989.

Aristotle. *Art of Rhetoric*. Translated by J. H. Freese. Cambridge, MA: Harvard University Press, 1964 [1926].

Bataille, George. *Erotism: Death and Sensuality*. Translated by Mary Dalwood. San Francisco: City Lights Books, 1986 [1962].

Baxter, William H., and Laurent Sagart. "Old Chinese reconstruction, version 1.1 (September 20, 2014)." https://ocbaxtersagart.lsait.lsa.umich.edu/BaxterSagartOCbyGSR2014-09-20.pdf.

Baxter, William H., and Laurent Sagart. *Old Chinese: A New Reconstruction*. Oxford. Oxford University Press, 2014.

Baudelaire, Charles. *Oeuvres complètes*. 2 vols. Edited by Claude Pichois. Paris: Gallimard, 1975.

Beecroft, Alexander. *Authorship and Cultural Identity in Early Greece and China: Patterns of Literary Circulation*. Cambridge: Cambridge University Press, 2010.

Boltz, William G. "The Composite Nature of Early Chinese Texts." In *Text and Ritual in Early China*, edited by Martin Kern, 50–78. Seattle: University of Washington Press, 2008.

Brooke-Rose, Christine. *A Grammar of Metaphor*. London: Secker and Warburg, 1958.

Chen Shih-hsiang 陳世驤. "In Search of the Beginnings of Chinese Literary Criticism." *University of California Publications in Semitic Philology, Semitic and Oriental Studies Presented to William Popper* 11 (1951): 45–64.

Chen Shih-hsiang."The *Shih Ching*: Its Generic Significance in Chinese Literary History and Poetics." In the *Bulletin of the Institute of History and Philology,*

Academia Sinica XXXIX (1969): 371–413. Revised and reprinted in Cyril Birch, ed., *Studies in Chinese Literary Genres*. Berkeley: University of California Press, 1974, 8–41.

Cheng, Anne. "What Did It Mean to Be a *Ru* in Han Times?" *Asia Major* 14, no. 2 (2001): 101–18.

Chin, Tamara. "Orienting Mimesis: Marriage and the *Book of Songs*." *Representations* 94, no. 1 (2006): 65–72.

Chou Ying-hsiung 周英雄. "The Linguistic and Mythical Structure of *Hsing* as a Combinational Model." In *Chinese and Western Comparative Literature Theory and Strategy*, edited by John J. Deeney, 151–209. Hong Kong: Chinese University Press, 1980.

Chow, Rey 周蕾. "The Old/New Question of Comparison in Literary Studies: A Post-European Perspective." *English Literary History* 71, no. 2 (Summer 2004): 289–311.

Chow Tse-tsung 周策縱. "The Early History of the Chinese Word *Shih* (Poetry)." In *Wen-lin: Studies in the Chinese Humanities*, edited by Chow Tse-tsung. Madison: University of Wisconsin Press, 1968.

Cikoski, John. *Notes for a Lexicon of Classical Chinese, Volume I: Occasional Jottings on Textual Evidence Possibly Applicable to Some Questions of Palæo-Sinitic Etymology, Arranged in Alphabetic Order by Archaic Chinese Readings*. Saint Mary's, GA: The Coprolite Press, 1994–2011 ("Version 14, Draft 7, Tweak 171").

Cook, Constance A., and Paul R. Goldin, eds. *A Source Book of Ancient Chinese Bronze Inscriptions*. Rev. ed. Berkeley: Society for the Study of Early China, 2020.

de Man, Paul. *Allegories of Reading*. New Haven, CT: Yale University Press, 1979.

de Man, Paul. "The Epistemology of Metaphor." In *On Metaphor*, edited by Sheldon Sachs. Chicago: Chicago University Press, 1979.

Derrida, Jacques. "White Mythology: Metaphor in the Text of Philosophy." Translated by F. C. T. Moore. *New Literary History* 6, no. 1 (1974): 5–74. Reprinted in *Margins of Philosophy*. Chicago: University of Chicago Press, 1982.

Dobson, W. A. C. H. *The Language of the "Book of Songs."* Toronto: University of Toronto Press, 1968.

Douglas, Mary. *Thinking in Circles: An Essay on Ring Composition*. New Haven, CT: Yale University Press, 2007.

Durrant, Stephen, Wai-yee Li, and David Schaberg. Translated by *Zuo Tradition / Zuozhuan: Commentary on the "Spring and Autumn Annals."* Seattle and London: University of Washington Press, 2016.

Eco, Umberto. "The Scandal of Metaphor: Metaphorology and Semiotics." *Poetics Today* 4, vol. 2 (1983): 217–57.

Eco, Umberto. *Semiotics and the Philosophy of Language*. Bloomington: Indiana University Press, 1985.

Eckerman, Christoffer. Review of *Pindar and the Emergence of Literature*. *American Journal of Philology* 137, no. 3 (2016): 541–45.

Empson, William. *Seven Types of Ambiguity*. London: Chatto and Windus, 1947 [1930].
Foster, Christopher J. "Introduction to the Peking University Han Bamboo Slips: On the Authentication and Study of Purchased Manuscripts." *Early China* 40 (2017): 172–81.
Foucault, Michel. "What Is an Author." In *Language, Counter-Memory, Practice*. Ithaca, NY: Cornell University Press, 1977.
Frankel, Hans. *The Flowering Plum and the Palace Lady. Interpretations of Chinese Poetry*. New Haven and London, CT: Yale University Press, 1976.
Freud, Sigmund. *Die Traumdeutung*. In *Gesammelte Werke*, Band II/III. Frankfurt: S. Fischer, 1966 [1900].
Galand-Hallyn, Perrine. *Le reflet des fleurs : Description et métalangage poétique d'Homère à la Renaissance*. Geneva: Droz, 1994.
Gerhards, Meik. "The *Song of Solomon* as an Allegory: Historical Considerations." In *Interpreting the Song of Songs: Literal or Allegorical?*, edited by Annette Schellenberg and Ludger Schwienhorst-Schönberger, 51–77. Leuven: Peeters, 2016.
Gibbs, Raymond W. Jr. "When Is Metaphor?: The Idea of Understanding in Theories of Metaphor." *Poetics Today* 13, no. 4 (1992): 575–606.
Gibbs, Raymond W. Jr., and Elaine Chen. "Taking Metaphor Studies Back to the Stone Age: A Reply to Xu, Zhang, and Wu (2016)." *Intercultural Pragmatics*, vol. 14, no. 1 (2017): 117–24.
Goldin, Paul R. "*Heng xian* and the Problem of Studying Looted Artifacts." *Dao* 12 (2013): 153–60.
Goldin, Paul R. "Research Note: Etymological Notes on Early Chinese Aristocratic Titles." *T'oung Pao* 107, no. 3–4 (2021): 475–80.
Gordon, Paul. *The Critical Double: Figurative Meaning in Aesthetic Discourse*. Tuscaloosa: University of Alabama Press, 1995.
Granet, Marcel. *Catégories matrimoniales et relations de proximité dans la Chine ancienne*. Paris: Alcan, 1939.
Granet, Marcel. *Fêtes et chansons anciennes de la Chine*. 2d ed. Paris: Leroux, 1929 [1919].
Harbsmeier, Christoph, Jiang Shaoyu 蔣紹愚, Christian Schwermann and Christian Wittern. *TLS - Thesaurus Linguae Sericae* 漢學文典: *An Historical and Comparative Encyclopaedia of Chinese Conceptual Schemes*. https://hxwd.org.
Heidegger, Martin. *Sein und Zeit*. Tübingen: Max Niemeyer Verlag, 1967.
Henderson, John. *Scripture, Canon and Commentary: A Comparison of Confucian and Western Exegesis*. Princeton, NJ: Princeton University Press, 1991.
Hightower, James Robert, trans. *Han Shih Wai Chuan: Han Ying's Illustrations of the Didactic Application of the "Classic of Songs."* Harvard-Yenching Institute Monograph Series, vol. 2. Cambridge, MA: Harvard University Press, 1952.
Holzman, Donald. "Confucius and Ancient Chinese Literary Criticism." In *Chinese Approaches to Literature from Confucius to Liang Ch'i-Ch'ao*, edited by Adele Austin Rickett, 21–42. Princeton, NJ: Princeton University Press, 1978.

Hucker, Charles. O. *A Dictionary of Official Titles in Imperial China*. Stanford: Stanford University Press, 1985.
Hunter, Michael. *The Poetics of Early Chinese Thought: How the* Shijing *Shaped the Chinese Philosophical Tradition*. New York: Columbia University Press, 2021.
Hutton, Eric L., trans. *Xunzi: The Complete Text*. Princeton, NJ: Princeton University Press, 2014.
Jakobson, Roman. "Closing Statement: Linguistics and Poetics." In *Style in Language*, edited by Thomas A. Sebok, 350–77. Cambridge, MA: MIT Press, 1960.
Jones, Peter, ed. *Imagist Poetry*. London: Penguin, 1972.
Jullien, François. *La valeur allusive : Des catégories originales de l'interprétation poétique dans la tradition chinoise (Contribution à une réflexion sur l'altérité interculturelle)*. Paris: École française d'extrême-orient, 1985.
Jullien, François. *Le Détour et l'accès : Strategies du sens en Chine, en Grèce*. Paris: Grasset, 1995.
Karlgren, Bernhard. *The Book of Odes: Chinese Text, Transcription and Translation*. Stockholm: Museum of Far Eastern Antiquities, 1950.
Karlgren, Bernhard. "The Early History of the *Chou Li* and *Tso Chuan* Texts." *BMFEA* 28 (1931): 1–58.
Karlgren, Bernhard. *Glosses on the Book of Odes*. Stockholm: Museum of Far Eastern Antiquities, 1964.
Karlgren, Bernhard. *Grammata Serica Recensa*. Stockholm: Museum of Far Eastern Antiquities, 1972.
Karlgren, Bernhard. "Legends and Cults in Ancient China." *BMFEA* 18 (1946): 199–365.
Kenner, Hugh. *The Pound Era*. Berkeley: University of California Press, 1971.
Kern, Martin. "Early Chinese Literature, Beginnings Through Western Han." In *The Cambridge History of Chinese Literature. Vol. 1, To 1375*, edited by Kang-i Sun Chang and Stephen Owen. Cambridge: Cambridge University Press, 2010.
Kern, Martin, ed. *Text and Ritual in Early China*. Seattle: University of Washington Press, 2008.
Kern, Martin. "The *Odes* in Excavated Manuscripts." In *Text and Ritual in Early China*, edited by Martin Kern, 149–93. Seattle: University of Washington Press, 2005.
Kern, Martin. "Early Chinese Literature, Beginnings Through Western Han." In Kang-i Sun Chang and Stephen Owen, eds. *The Cambridge History of Chinese Literature. Vol. 1, To 1375*. Cambridge: Cambridge University Press, 2010.
Kern, Martin. "Lost in Tradition: The *Classic of Poetry* We Did Not Know." In *Hsiang Lectures on Chinese Poetry*. Vol. 5. Montréal: Centre for East Asian Research, McGill University, 2010.
Kern, Martin. "The Performance of Writing in Western Zhou China." In *The Poetics of Grammar and the Metaphysics of Sound and Sign*, edited by La Porta and Shulman, 152–57. Jerusalem Studies in Religion and Culture. Leiden: Brill, 2007.

Kern, Martin. "'Xi shuai' 蟋蟀 ("Cricket") and its Consequences: Issues in Early Chinese Poetry and Textual Studies." *Early China* 42 (2019): 1–36.
Kirby, John T. "Aristotle on Metaphor." *The American Journal of Philology* 118, no. 4 (Winter, 1997): 517–54.
Knoblock, John, trans. *Xunzi: A Translation and Study of the Complete Works*. 3 vols. Stanford: Stanford University Press, 1988–1994.
Kristeva, Julia. *Sèméiotikè. Recherches pour une sémanalyse*. Paris: Seuil, 1969.
Krijgsman, Rens. *Early Chinese Manuscript Collections: Sayings, Memory, Verse, and Knowledge*. Leiden: Brill, 2023.
Kroll, Paul W. (with the assistance of William G. Boltz, David R. Knechtges, Y. Edmund Lien, Antje Richter, Matthias L. Richter, and Ding Xiang Warner.) *A Student's Dictionary of Classical and Medieval Chinese*. Leiden: Brill, 2015.
Kunst, Richard. "The Original *Yijing*: A Text, Phonetic Transcription, Translation, and Indexes, with Sample Glosses." PhD diss., University of Berkeley, 1985.
Lakoff, George, and Mark Johnson. *The Metaphors We Live By*. 2nd ed. Chicago: University of Chicago Press, 2003 [1980].
Legge, James, trans. *The Chinese Classics*. 5 vols. Hong Kong: University of Hong Kong Press, 1960.
Legge, James. *The Ch'un Ts'ew, with the Tso Chuen*. 2 vols. Hong Kong: London Missionary Society's Printing Office, 1939.
Legge, James. *The She King*. See *The Chinese Classics*.
Lévi-Strauss, Claude, and Didier Eribon. *De près et de loin*. Paris: O. Jacob, 1988.
Lévi-Strauss, Claude. *Le totémisme aujourd'hui*. Paris: Presses Universitaires, 1965.
Lewis, C. Day. *The Poetic Image*. New York: Oxford University Press, 1947.
Lewis, Mark Edward. *Writing and Authority in Early China*. Albany: State University of New York Press, 1999.
Li Wai-yee. *The Readability of the Past in Early Chinese* Historiography. Cambridge, MA: Harvard University Asia Center, 2007.
Loewe, Michael. "Shih Ching." In *Early Chinese Texts: A Bibliographical Guide*, edited by Michael Loewe, 415–23. Berkeley: Society for the Study of Early China and Institute of East Asian Studies, 1993.
Lu Zhao. *In Pursuit of the Great Peace: Han Dynasty Classicism and the Making of Early Medieval Literati Culture*. Albany: State University of New York Press, 2020.
Maslov, Boris. *Pindar and the Emergence of Literature*. Cambridge: Cambridge University Press, 2015.
Meyer, Dirk. *Philosophy on Bamboo*. Leiden: Brill, 2012.
Meyer, Dirk. "Writing Meaning: Strategies of Meaning-Construction in Early Chinese Philosophical Discourse." *Monumenta Serica* 56 (2008): 55–95.
Middendorf, Ulrike. *Resexualizing the Desexualized: The Language of Desire and Erotic Love in the Classic of Odes*. Pisa: Istituti editoriali e poligrafici internazionali, 2007.
Miller, Roy Andrew. "Shih ming." In *Early Chinese Texts: A Bibliographical Guide*, edited by Michael Loewe, 424–28. Berkeley: The Society for the Study of Early China and Institute of East Asian Studies, 1993.

Mittag, Achim. "Notes on the Genesis and Early Reception of Chu Hsi's *Shih Chi-Chuan:* Some Facets for Reevaluation of Sung Classical Learning." In *Papers on Society and Culture of Early Modern China*. Taipei: Academica Sinica, 1992.

Morris, Charles. *Writings on the General Theory of Signs*. The Hague: Mouton, 1971.

Mote, Frederick. "The Cosmological Gulf between China and the West." In *Transition and Permanence: Chinese History and Culture*, edited by David Buxbaum and Frederick Mote, 3–21 (Hong Kong, 1972).

Murray, Penelope. "Poetic Inspiration in Early Greece." *The Journal of Hellenic Studies* 101 (1981): 87–100.

Nienhauser, William H. "Some Preliminary Remarks on the *Shi* in the *Zuo zhuan*." *Oriens Extremus* 50 (2011 [2012]): 75–98.

Nylan, Michael. *The Five "Confucian" Classics* (New Haven, CT: Yale University Press, 2001). https://yalebooks.yale.edu/sites/default/files/files/Media/9780300081855/9780300081855_nylan2notes.pdf.

Nylan, Michael. "Classics Without Canonization: Learning and Authority in Qin and Han." In *Early Chinese Religion: Part One: Shang through Han (1250 BC–220 AD)* 2 vols. Edited by John Lagerwey and Marc Kalinowski. Leiden: Brill, 2008.

Nylan, Michael. "Yin-yang, Five Phases, and *qi*." In *China's Early Empires A: Reappraisal*, edited by Michael Nylan and Michael Loewe, 398–414. Cambridge: University of Cambridge, Oriental Publications, no. 67, 2010.

Owen, Stephen. *Readings in Chinese Literary Thought*. Cambridge, MA: Harvard University Press, 1992.

Oxford Companion to English Literature. 6th ed. Edited by Margaret Drabble. Oxford: Oxford University Press, 2000.

Quilligan, Maureen. *The Language of Allegory: Defining the Genre*. Ithaca, NY: Cornell University Press, 1979.

Quintilianus, M. F. *Institutio Oratoria*. Loeb edition with translation by H. E. Butler. Cambridge, MA: Harvard University Press, 1996 [1920].

Pankienier, David W. *Astrology and Cosmology in Early China: Conforming Earth to Heaven*. Cambridge: Cambridge University Press, 2013.

Pankienier, David W. "Reflections of the Lunar Aspect on Western Chou Chronology." *T'oung Pao, vol.* 78, no. 1 (1992): 33–76.

Pines, Yuri. "Names and Titles in Eastern Zhou Texts." *T'oung Pao* 106, no. 56 (2020): 714–20.

Plato. *Statesman, Philebus, Ion. Statesman, Philebus, Ion.* Translated by Harold North Fowler and W. R. M. Lamb. Loeb Classical Library 164. Cambridge, MA: Harvard University Press, 1925.

Pound, Ezra. *Shih-ching: The Classic Anthology Defined by Confucius*. Cambridge, MA: Harvard University Press, 1954.

Richter, Matthias. *The Embodied Text*. Leiden: Brill, 2013.

Richards, I. A. *The Philosophy of Rhetoric*. Oxford: Oxford University Press, 1936.

Ricoeur, Paul. "The Metaphorical Process." In *On Metaphor*, edited by Sheldon Sachs. Chicago: Chicago University Press, 1979.

Ricoeur, Paul. *The Rule of Metaphor: Multi-disciplinary Studies of the Creation of Meaning in Language*. Translated by Robert Czerny. London: Routledge, 1978.

Riegel, Jeffrey. "Eros, Introversion, and The Beginnings of *Shijing* Commentary." *Harvard Journal of Asiatic Studies* 57, no. 1 (June 1997): 143–77.

Riffaterre, Michael. *Semiotics of Poetry*. Bloomington: Indiana University Press, 1978.

Rimbaud, Arthur. *Poésies. Une saison en enfer. Illuminations*. Paris: Gallimard, 1998.

Rouzer, Paul. "Review of *Éloge de la Fadeur: À partir de la pensée de l'esthétique de la Chine* by Françocis Jullien." *Harvard Journal of Asiatic Studies* 54, no. 1 (June 1994): 277–80.

Röllicke, Hermann-Josef. *Die Färthe des Herzens: Die Lehre vom Herzensbe-streben (zhi) im grossen Vorword zum Shijing*. Berlin: Dietrich Reimer, 1992.

Saussure, Ferdinand de. *Course in General Linguistics*. Translated by Wade Baskin. New York: McGraw-Hill, 1969.

Saussy, Haun. *The Problem of a Chinese Aesthetic*. Stanford: Stanford University Press, 1993.

Schuessler, Axel. *A Dictionary of Early Zhou Chinese*. Honolulu: University of Hawaii Press, 1987.

Schuessler, Axel. *ABC Etymological Dictionary of Old Chinese*. Honolulu: University of Hawai'i Press, 2007.

Schwermann, Christian. "Collage-Technik als Kompositionsprinzip klassischer chinesischer Prosa: Der Aufbau des Kapitels 'Tang wen' (Die Fragen des Tang) im *Lie zi*." In *Bochumer Jahrbuch zur Ostasienforschung* 29, edited by Wolfgang Behr, 125–57. Bochum: Fakultät f. Ostasienwissenschaften d. Ruhr-Universität Bochum, 2005.

Serruys, Paul L.-M. "Une Nouvelle Grammaire Du Chinois Litteraire." *Harvard Journal of Asiatic Studies* 16, no. 1/2 (June 1953): 162–99.

Shaughnessy, Edward L. *Before Confucius: Studies in the Creation of the Chinese Classics*. Albany: State University of New York Press, 1997.

Shaughnessy, Edward L. "The Composition of the *Zhouyi*." PhD diss., Stanford University, 1983.

Shaughnessy, Edward L. *Rewriting Early Chinese Texts*. Albany: State University of New York Press, 2006.

Shaughnessy, Edward L. "Unearthed Documents and the Question of the Oral versus Written of the Classic of Poetry." *Harvard Journal of Asiatic Studies* 75, no. 2 (2015): 331–75.

Shaughnessy, Edward L. "Western Zhou History." In *The Cambridge History of Ancient China*, edited by Loewe and Shaughnessy. Cambridge, Cambridge University Press, 2008.

Shaughnessy, Edward L. The *Origin and Early Development of the* Zhou Changes. Leiden: Brill, 2022.

Smith, Kidder. "*Zhouyi* Interpretation from Accounts in the *Zuozhuan*." *Harvard Journal of Asiatic Studies* 49, no. 2 (December 1989): 421–63.

Sobolev, Dennis. "Metaphor Revisited." *New Literary History* 39, no. 4 (Autumn 2008): 915–16.

Staack, Thies. "Reconstructing the *Kongzi shilun*: From the Arrangement of the Bamboo Slips to a Tentative Translation." *Asiatische Studien / Études Asiatiques* 64, no. 4 (2010): 857–906.

Steen, Gerard. "Deliberate Metaphor Theory: Basic assumptions, Main Tenets, Urgent Issues," *Intercultural Pragmatics*, vol. 14, no. 1 (2017): 1–24.

Sun, Cecile Chu-chin. *The Poetics of Repetition in English and Chinese Lyric Poetry*. Chicago: University of Chicago Press, 2011.

Svenbro, Jesper. "La parole et le marbre : aux origines de la poétique grecque." PhD diss., Lund University, 1976.

Svensson [Ekström], Martin. "A Second Look at the *Great Preface* on the Way to a New Understanding of Han Dynasty Poetics." *Chinese Literature, Essays, Articles, Reviews (CLEAR)* 21 (1999): 95–128.

Svensson Ekström, Martin. "Does the Metaphor Translate?" In *Translating China for Western Readers*, edited by Mingdong Gu and Rainer Schulte. Albany: State University of New York Press, 2014.

Svensson Ekström, Martin. "Inscription and Re-reading, Re-reading the Inscribed (A Figure in the Chinese Philosophical Text)." *BMFEA* 74.

Svensson Ekström, Martin. "Metapoetic Readings around *Ekphrasis* and *Fu* 賦." *Prism* 17, no. 2 (2020): 353–98.

Svensson Ekström, Martin. "Illusion, Lie, and Metaphor." *Poetics Today* 23, no. 2 (2002): 251–89.

Svensson Ekström, Martin. "On the *Concept* of Correlative Cosmology." *BMFEA* 72: 7–12.

Svensson Ekström, Martin. "One Lucky Bastard: On the Hybrid Origins of Chinese 'Literature'." *Literature and Literary History in Global Contexts: A Comparative Project. Volume 1: Notions of Literature Across Times and Cultures*. The Hague: Mouton de Gruyter, 2006.

Svensson Ekström, Martin. "Sino-methodological Remark on the Metaphor of *Metaphora* and the Limitations of the 'Conceptual Metaphor Theory'." *BMFEA* 79/80: 5–30.

Svensson Ekström, Martin. "The Value of Misreading and the Need for Reinterpretation." *BMFEA* 76: 8–21.

Szondi, Peter. *Introduction to Literary Hermeneutics*. Translated by Martha Woodmansee. Cambridge: Cambridge University Press, 1995.

Siufu Tang. "Virtue Through Habituation: Virtue Cultivation in the Xunzi." *Journal of Chinese Philosophy* 48, no. 2 (2021): 157–69.

Van Zoeren, Steven. *Poetry and Personality: Reading, Exegesis and Hermeneutics in Ancient China*. Stanford: Stanford University Press, 1991.

Waley, Arthur, trans. *The Book of Songs*. Boston and New York: Houghton Mifflin, 1937.

Waley, Arthur. "The *Book of Changes*." *BMFEA* 5 (1931): 121–42.

Waring, Luke. "Making Sense of the *Odes*: Speeches as Poetic Commentary in the *Guoyu*." *Journal of the American Oriental Society* 143, no. 2 (Apr–Jun 2023): 309–29.
Wellek, René and Austin Warren. *Theory of Literature*. 3rd ed. New York: Harcourt Brace, 1984.
Versano, Paula M. *Tracking the Banished Immortal: The Poetry of Li Bo and Its Critical Reception*. Honolulu: University of Hawai'i Press, 2003.
Versano, Paula M. "Getting There from Here: Locating the Subject in Early Chinese Poetics." *Harvard Journal of Asiatic Studies* 56, no. 2 (December 1996): 375–403.
Wang, C. H. 王靖獻. *The Bell and the Drum: "Shih Ching" as Formulaic Poetry in an Oral Tradition*. Berkeley: University of California Press, 1974.
Wang, C. H. "'Shih Ching': Formulaic Language and Mode of Creation." PhD diss., University of California at Berkeley, 1971.
Watson, Burton. *The Tso Chuan: Selections from China's Oldest Narrative History*. New York: Columbia University Press, 1989.
Wong Siu-kit 黃兆傑 and Lee Kar-shui 李家樹. "Ideology With a Vengeance: The *Gushibian* Interpretation of the *Shijing*." *Journal of Oriental Studies* 31, no. 1 (1993): 28–37.
Wong Siu-Kit. *Early Chinese Literary Criticism*. Hong Kong: Joint Publishing Company, 1983.
Yeh, Michelle 奚密. "Metaphor and *Bi*: Western and Chinese Poetics." *Comparative Literature* 39 (1987): 237–54.
Yu, Pauline R 余寶琳. "Metaphor and Chinese Poetry." *Chinese Literature: Essays, Articles, Reviews* 3, no. 2 (1981): 205–24.
Yu, Pauline R. "Allegory, Allegoresis and the *Classic of Poetry*." *Harvard Journal of Asian Studies* 43, no. 2 (1983): 377–412.
Yu, Pauline R. *The Reading of Imagery in the Chinese Poetic Tradition*. Princeton, NJ: Princeton University Press, 1987.
Zhang Longxi 張隆溪. "The Letter or the Spirit: The *Song of Songs*, Allegoresis, and the *Book of Poetry*." *Comparative Literature* 39 (1987): 193–217.
Zhang Longxi. *The Tao and the Logos*. Durham, NC: Duke University Press, 1992.
Zikpi, Monica. "On Translation's 'Original' and an Emergent Translation of the *Shijing*." Experiments in Translating Classical Chinese Poetry. *Journal of Oriental Studies* 49, no. 1 (2016): 1–25.
Zufferey, Nicolas. *To the Origins of Confucianism: The Ru in pre-Qin Times and During the Early Han Dynasty*. Bern: Peter Lang, 2003.

Works in Chinese and Japanese

Ban gu 班固. *Hanshu buzhu* 漢書補注. Ed. Wang Xianqian 王先謙. Peking: Zhonghua, 1983.

Cai Yingjun 蔡英俊. *Bixing wuse yu qingjingjiaorong* 比興物色與情景交融. Taipei: Daan, 1986.
Chan Pak-ka 陳柏嘉. "Handai 'diwujia *Shi*' shuo xianyi" 漢代「第五家《詩》」說獻疑. *Zhongguo wenhua yanjiusuo xuebao* 中國文化研究所學報 63 (2016): 1–32.
Chen Huan 陳奐, ed. *Shi Maoshi zhuan shu* 詩毛氏傳疏. Taipei: Xuesheng, 1986 [1847].
Chen Qiyou 陳奇猷, ed. *Lüshi chunqiu jiaoshi* 呂氏春秋校釋. Taipei: Huazheng shuju, 1988.
Chen Tongsheng 陳桐生. *Kongzi shilun yanjiu* 孔子詩論研究. Peking: Zhonghua, 2004.
Chow Tse-tsung 周策縱. *Gu wuyi yu 'liushi' kao: Zhongguo langman wenxue tankao* 古巫醫與《六詩》考：中國浪漫文學探源. Taipei: Lianjing, 1986.
Da xu 大序 (The *Great Preface*). In Ruan Yuan 阮元. Ed. *Shisan jing zhushu* (*SSJZS*) 十三經注疏. Peking University Press, 1999. (詩經 1:1.3b–18b).
Dong Zhongshu 董仲舒, see Su Yu.
Dong Zhian 董治安 and Xia Chuancai 夏傳才, eds. *Shijing yaoji tiyao* 詩經要籍提要. Peking: Xueyuan chubanshe, 2003.
Fan Ye 范曄. *Hou Hanshu* 後漢書. Peking: Zhonghua, 1996.
Fang Yurun 方玉潤. *Shijing yuanshi* 詩經原始. Peking: Zhonghua, 1986.
Gao Baoguang 高葆光. *Shijing xin pingjia* 詩經新評價. Taizhong: Sili Donghai Daxue, 1965.
Gao Heng 高亨. *Shijing jin zhu* 詩經今注. Shanghai: Guji, 1980.
Gu Jiegang 顧頡剛, Luo Genze 羅根澤, and Lü Simian 呂思勉, eds. *Gu shi bian* 古史辨. 7 vols., 1926–41. Hong Kong: Taiping, 1962.
Gu Jiegang 顧頡剛. "Qi xing" 起興. In *Shijing yanjiu lunji*, edited by Lin Ch'ing-chang, 63–68.
Gu Nong 顧農. "'Fa Hu Qing, Zhi Hu Li Yi': Maoshi Daxu di heli keike" "發乎情，止乎禮"—《毛詩大序》的合理內核. *Fujian lunyun* 福建論壇 (June 1983): 100–103.
Guo Shaoyu 郭紹虞. *Zhongguo wenxue piping shi* 中國文學批評史. Hong Kong: Hongzhi, 1978.
Han Ying 韓嬰. *Han Shi wai zhuan* 韓詩外傳. In *Sibu congkan* 四部叢刊. Shanghai: Shangwu, 1929.
Hao Zhida 郝志達, ed. *Guofeng shizhi cuan jie* 國風詩旨纂解. Tianjin: Nankai daxue chubanshe, 1990.
He Kai 何楷. *Shijing shiben guyi* 詩經世本古義. See Hao Zhida 郝志達, ed. *Guofeng shizhi cuan jie* 國風詩旨纂解. Tianjin: Nankai daxue chubanshe, 1990.
Hu Pengsheng 胡平生 and Han Ziqiang 韓自強. *Fuyang Hanjian "Shijing" yanjiu* 阜陽漢簡詩經研究. Shanghai: Guji, 1988.
Huang Dekuan 黃德寬 and Xu Zaiguo 徐在國, eds. *Anhui daxue cang Zhanguo zhujian* 安徽大學藏戰國竹簡. Vol. 1 (*Shijing*). Shanghai: Zhongxi shuju, 2019.
Huang Dekuan. "Anhui daxue cang Zhanguo zhujian gaishu" 安徽大學藏戰國竹簡概述. *Wenwu* 文物 9 (2017): 54–59.

Huang Zhenmin 黃振民. *Shijing yanjiu* 詩經研究. Taipei: Zhengzhong shuju, 1982.
Hung Kuo-liang 洪國樑. "Chongzhang huzu yu *Shi* yi quanshi: jian ping Gu Jiegang 'Chongzhang futa wei yueshi shenshu' shuo"「重障互足」與《詩》義詮釋─兼評顧頡剛「重障複沓為樂師申述」說. In '*Shijing*', *xungu yu shixue* 詩經、訓詁與史學, 3-50. Taipei: National Library Publishing House, 2015.
Ikeda Tomohisa 池田知久. *Mawangdui Hanbo boshu wuxung yanjiu* 馬王堆漢墓帛書五行研究 Translated by Wang Qifa 王啟發. Peking: China Social Sciences Press, 2005.
Inoi Makoto 家井眞 *Shikyô no gengiteki kenkyû* 詩經の原意研究. Tokyo: Kenbun shuppan, 2004.
Inoi Makoto. *Shijing yuanyi yanjiu*《詩經》原意研究. Translated by Lu Yue 陸越. Nanking: Jiangsu renmin chubanshe, 2010.
Kong Yingda 孔穎達. *Maoshi zhengyi* 毛詩正義. In Ruan Yuan. *SSJZS*.
Lee Kar-shui 李家樹. *Chuantong yiwai di Shijing xue* 傳統以外詩經學. Hong Kong: University of Hong Kong Press, 1994.
Lee Kar-shui 李家樹. *Shijing di lishi gongan* 詩經的歷史公案. Reprinted-Taipei: Daan, 1990.
Li Guangdi 李光地. *Shi suo* 詩所. See Hao Zhida 郝志達, ed. *Guofeng shizhi cuan jie* 國風詩旨纂解. Tianjin: Nankai daxue chubanshe, 1990.
Liji. 禮記. In Ruan Yuan. *SSJZS*.
Li Xiang 李湘. "Xingfa fenlei kao" 興法分類考. *Zhongzhou xuebao* 1983, 5:83–98.
Li Xueqin 李學勤. Ed. *Qinghua daxue cang Zhanguo zhujian*, vol. I 清華大學藏戰國竹簡（壹）. Shanghai: Zhongxi, 2010.
Li Zehou 李澤厚 and Liu Gangji 劉綱紀. *Zhongguo meixue shi* 中國美學史. 2 vols. Peking: Xinhua, 1984–87.
Liang Xifeng 梁錫鋒. "Zheng Xuan yi li jian *Shi* yanjiu" 鄭玄以禮箋《詩》研究. PhD diss., Zhengzhou university, 2004.
Lin Ch'ing-chang 林慶彰, ed. *Shijing yanjiu lunji* 詩經研究論集. 2 vols. Taipei: Xuesheng, 1983.
Lin Mingde 林明德. "Shi lun *Shijing* de di yi shou - *Guanju*" 試論詩經的弟一首關雎. In Lin Ch'ing-chang, ed. *Shijing yanjiu lunji*, 285–306.
Lin Yaolin 林耀潾. *XiHan sanjia shixue yanjiu* 西漢三家詩學研究. Taipei: Wenjin, 1996.
Lin Yelian 林葉連. *Zhongguo lidai Shijingxue* 中國歷代詩經學. Taipei: Xuesheng shuju, 1993.
Liu Dongying 劉冬穎 *Shijing bianfeng bianya kaolun* 詩經變風變雅考論. Peking: Zhongguo shehui kexue chubanshe, 2005.
Liu Yunhua 劉耘華. *Quanshixue yu Qian-Qin rujia zhi yiyi shengcheng: Lunyu, Mengzi, Xunzi dui gudai chuantongdi jieshi* 詮釋學與先秦儒家之意義生成 ─《論語》、《孟子》、《荀子》對古代傳統的解釋. Shanghai: Shanghai yiwen chubanche, 2002.
Liu Xiang 劉向. *Lie nü zhuan* 列女傳. In *Sibu congkan*. Shanghai: Shangwu, 1929.
Liu Xie 劉勰. *Wenxin diaolong* 文心雕龍. Transl. and annotation Wang Zhibin 王志彬. Peking: Zhonghua, 2012.

Liu Zhaijing 劉兆靜. "*Maoshi xiaoxu* 'xushou' yu 'xushen zhi pian' guanxi yanjiu" 《毛詩小序》" 序首" 與" 續申之詞" 關係研究. MA thesis, Liaoning shifan daxue, 2011.

Lu Hongsheng 魯洪生. "Lun Zheng Xuan *Maoshi Jian* dui xing di renshi" 論鄭玄《毛詩箋》對興的認識." *Wenxue yichan* 文學遺產 (2006:1): 29–34.

Lu Ji 陸璣. "*Mao Shi*" cao mu niao shou chong yu shu 毛詩草木鳥獸蟲魚疏. Peking: Zhonghua shuju, 1985.

Lu Cixing 陸錫興 *Shijing yiwen yanjiu* 詩經異文研究. Peking: Zhongguo banben tushuguan, 2001.

Lunyu tongshi 論語通釋. See Wang Xiyuan 王熙元.

Lushi gu 魯詩故 (Lu school of *Shijing* exegesis). In Wang Xianqian 王先謙, ed. *Shi sanjia yi jishu* (*SSJYJS*) 詩三家義集疏. 2 vols. Taipei: Mingwen, 1988.

Ma Ruichen 馬瑞辰. *Maoshi zhuan jian tong shi* 毛詩傳箋通釋. Peking: Zhonghua, 1989.

Ma Yinqin 馬銀琴. *Liang Zhou Shi shi* 兩周詩史. Peking: Shehui kexue wenxian chubanshe, 2006.

Maoshi yinde 毛詩引得. Harvard-Yenching Sinological Index Series, vol. 9. Peking: Harvard-Yenching Institute, 1934.

Maozhuan 毛傳. In Wang Xianqian 王先謙, ed. *Shi sanjia yi jishu* (*SSJYJS*) 詩三家義集疏. 2 vols. Taipei: Mingwen, 1988.

Mengzi yizhu 孟子譯注. Translated and annotated by Yang Bojun 楊伯峻. Peking: Zhonghua, 2010.

Mi Wenkai 糜文開 and Pei Puxian 裴普賢. *Shijing xinshang yu yanjiu* 詩經欣賞與研究. 4 vols. Taipei: Sanmin, 1987.

Ouyang Xiu 歐陽修. *Maoshi benyi* 毛詩本義. See Hao Zhida 郝志達, edited by *Guofeng shizhi cuan jie* 國風詩旨纂解. Tianjin: Nankai daxue chubanshe, 1990.

Peng Feng 彭鋒. *Shi ke yi xing: Gudai zongjiao, lilun, zhexue yu yishudi meixue chanshi* 詩可以興—古代宗教、倫理、哲學與藝術的美學闡釋. Hefei: Anhui jiaoyu chubanshe, 2003.

Qishi zhuan 齊詩傳 (Qi school of *Shijing* exegesis). In Wang Xianqian 王先謙, ed. *Shi sanjia yi jishu* (*SSJYJS*) 詩三家義集疏. 2 vols. Taipei: Mingwen, 1988.

Qian Zhongshu 錢鍾書. *Guan zhui bian* 管錐編. Peking: Zhonghua, 1979.

Ruan Yuan 阮元, ed. *Shisan jing zhushu* (*SSJZS*) 十三經注疏. Peking University Press, 1999.

Shen Weiwei 沈薇薇. "Zheng Xuan *Shijing*xue yanjiu" 鄭玄詩經學研究. PhD diss., Dongbei Shifan Daxue, 2008.

Shi Yingyong 史應勇. *Zheng Xuan tongxue ji Zheng-Wang zhi zheng yanjiu* 鄭玄通學及鄭王之爭研究. Chengdu: Sichuan publishing group, Bashu publishing house, 2007.

Shirakawa Shizuka 白川靜. *Shijing xue* 詩經學. Transl. Tu Cheng-sheng. Taipei: Youshi wenhua shiye gongsi, 1974.

Shirakawa Shizuka 白川靜. *Shiyô: Chûgoku no kodai kayô* 詩經: 中國の古代歌謠. Tokyo: Chûô kôronsha, 1970.

Shirakawa Shizuka 白川靜. *Kinbun tsûshaku* 金文通釋. Kobe: Hakutsuru bijutsukan, 1962–1984.

Sima Qian 司馬遷. *Shiji* 史記. In *Shiji xinzhu* 史記新注. Edited by and annotation by Zhang Dake 張大可. Peking: Huawen, 2000.

Su Yu 蘇輿. *Chunqiu fanlu yizheng* 春秋繁露義證. Peking: Zhonghua shuju, 1992.

Wang Baoxuan 王葆玹. *XiHan jingxue yuanliu* 西漢經學源流. Taipei: Dongda tushu gongsi, 2008.

Wang Fuzhi 王夫之. *Shi guang zhuan* 詩廣傳. Shanghai: Zhonghua shuju, 1965.

Wang Shouqian 王守謙, Jin Shouzhen 金守珍, and Wang Fengchun 王鳳春, eds. *Zuozhuan quanyi* 左傳全譯. Guizhou: Renmin, 1990.

Wang Zhi 王質. *Shi zong wen* 詩總聞. See Hao Zhida 郝志達, ed. *Guofeng shizhi cuan jie* 國風詩旨纂解. Tianjin: Nankai daxue chubanshe, 1990.

Wang Xiyuan 王熙元. *Lunyu tongshi* 論語通釋. Taipei: Xuesheng shuju, 1981.

Wang Xianqian 王先謙, ed. *Shi sanjia yi jishu* (*SSJYJS*) 詩三家義集疏. 2 vols. Taipei: Mingwen, 1988.

Wen Xinfu 文幸福. *Shijing Maozhuan Zhengjian bianyi* 詩經毛傳鄭箋辨異. Taipei: Wen shi zhe chubanche, 1989.

Wen Yiduo 聞一多. *Shenhua yu shi* 神話與詩. Shanghai: Guji, 1956.

Wen Yiduo. *Wen Yiduo quanji* 聞一多全集. Wuhan: Hubei renmin chubanshe, 1993.

Wu Wanzhong 吳萬鐘. *Cong shi dao jing: lun Maoshi jieshi di yuanyuan yiqi tese* 從詩到經: 論毛詩解釋的淵源及其特色. Peking: Zhonghua, 2001.

Xia Chuancai 夏傳才. *Shijing yanjiushi gaiyao* 詩經研究史概要. Taipei: Zhongyang tushuguan, 1993.

Xiao xu 小序 (*Minor Preface*). In Wang Xianqian 王先謙, ed. *Shi sanjia yi jishu* (*SSJYJS*) 詩三家義集疏. 2 vols. Taipei: Mingwen, 1988.

Xu Fuguan 徐復觀. "Shi shi de bixing - chongxin dianding Zhongguo shi di xinshang jichu" 釋詩的比興重新奠定中國詩的欣賞基礎. In Lin Ch'ing-chang, edited by *Shijing yanjiu lunji*, 69–89.

Xu Renfu 徐仁甫. *Gushu yinyu yanjiu* 古書引語研究. Peking: Zhonghua shuju, 2014.

Xu Zaiguo. "Anhui daxue cang Zhanguo zhujian Shijing shixu yu yiwen" 安徽大學藏戰國竹簡《詩經》詩序與異文. *Wenwu* 文物 9 (2017): 60–62.

Xunzi jijie 荀子集解. Ed. Wang, Xianqian 王先謙. Taipei: Huazheng, 1988.

Yang Tianyu 楊天宇. "Zheng Xuan *Zhu Jian* zhong *Shi* shuo maodun yuanyin kaozhe" 鄭玄《注》《箋》中《詩》說矛盾原因考析. In Yang Tianyu, *Jingxue yanyan lu* 經學探研錄. Shanghai guji, 2004.

Yang Tianyu 楊天宇. *Zheng Xuan Sanli zhu yanjiu* 鄭玄三禮注研究. Tianjin: Tianjin renmin chubanshe, 2007.

Yijing (*Book of Changes*) 易經. In Ruan Yuan 阮元. Ed. *Shisan jing zhushu* (*SSJZS*) 十三經注疏. Peking University Press, 1999.

Yi li. 禮儀. In Ruan Yuan 阮元, edited by *Shisan jing zhushu (SSJZS)* 十三經注疏. Peking University Press, 1999.

Yu Shujuan 于淑娟. "'Maoshi gu xun zhuan' mingyi kaoshi: Jian lun 'Maoshi gu xun zhuan' duzhuan di yuanyin"《毛詩故訓傳》名義考釋—兼論《毛詩故訓傳》獨傳的原因.

Ye Shuxian 葉舒憲. *Shijing di wenhua chanshi* 詩經的文化闡釋. Wuhan: Hunan renmin chubanshe, 1994.

You Jiazhong 猶家仲. *Shijing di jieshixue yanjiu* 詩經的解釋學研究. Guangxi shifan daxue chubanche, 2005.

Zeng Shengyi 曾聖益. "Zheng Xuan 'Liuyi lun' shi zhong jijiao" 鄭玄《六藝論》十種輯斠. *Guoli Zhongyang Tushuguan Taiwan Fenguan guankan* 國立中央圖書館臺灣分館館刊 4, no. 1 (1997): 70–93.

Zhang Haishan 張海珊. "Zhonghua minzu shi shanyu xingxiang siwei di minzu: shiguo aomi zhi yi" 中華民族是善於形象思維的民族——詩國奧祕之一. *Tianjin Shifan daxuebao* 天津師範大學學報1989, no. 6 (1989): 54–59.

Zhang Longxi 張隆溪. "Hanxue yu Zhong-Xi wenhua duili—Du Yulian xiangsheng fangtanlu yougan" 漢學與中西文化的對立—讀于連先生訪談錄有感. *Ershiyi shiji* 二十一世紀 no. 53 (June 1999): 144–48.

Zhang Xiaoyu 張曉雨. *Zhouyi shifa jietong* 周易筮法通解. Jinan: Shandong renmin, 1994.

Zhao Maolin 趙茂林. *LiangHan san jia Shi yanjiu* 兩漢三家詩研究. Chengdu: Bashu shushe, 2006.

Zhao Peilin 趙沛霖. *Xing di yuanqi: lishi jidian yu shige yishu* 興的源起：歷史積澱與詩歌藝術. Introduction by Li Zehou. Peking: Zhongguo shehui kexue chubanshe, 1980.

Zhao Zhiyang 趙制陽. *Shijing mingzhu pingjie* 詩經名著評介. Taipei: Xuesheng, 1983.

Zheng Qiao 鄭樵. *Shi bian wang* 詩辨妄. See Hao Zhida 郝志達, edited by *Guofeng shizhi cuan jie* 國風詩旨纂解. Tianjin: Nankai daxue chubanshe, 1990.

Zheng Xuan 鄭玄. *Maoshi Zhengjian* 毛詩鄭箋. In Wang Xianqian 王先謙, ed. *Shi sanjia yi jishu (SSJYJS)* 詩三家義集疏. 2 vols. Taipei: Mingwen, 1988.

Zhong Rong 鐘嶸. *Shi pin* 詩品, trans. Zhao Zhongyi in *Shi pin yizhu* 詩品譯注. Taipei: Guiya wenhua shiye youxiangongsi, 1991.

Zhou li 周禮. In Ruan Yuan 阮元. Ed. *Shisan jing zhushu (SSJZS)* 十三經注疏. Peking University Press, 1999.

Zhu Jinfa 朱金發. *Xian-Qin Shijingxue* 先秦詩經學. Peking: Xueyuan, 2007.

Zhu Mengting 朱孟庭. *Shijing di duoyuan chanshi* 詩經的多元闡釋. Taipei: Weinjin, 2012.

Zhu Xi 朱熹. *Shi ji zhuan* 詩集傳. Taipei: Zhenghua, 1975.

Zhu Xi 朱熹. *Shi xu bianshuo* 詩序辨說. In *Siku quanshu* 四庫全疏, 69: 3–42.

Zhu Xi 朱熹. *Zhuzi yulei* 朱子語類. 8 vols. Peking: Zhonghua, 1986.

Zhu Ziqing 朱自清. *Shi yan zhi bian* 詩言志辨. Reprinted-Taipei: Kaiming, 1982 [1947].

Index I

Index of odes quoted and analyzed. In the main, the transcriptions of the titles follow Karlgren, *Book of Odes* (1950), as does the numbering of the poems.

1. 關雎 "Guanju": 9, 40, 41, 47–49, 64–77, 86, 89, 93, 116, 155–62, 165, 167, 192, 194, 219, 221, 227, 241–42, 246, 267, 269–71, 330–31, 350, 354, 360–61, 364, 387, 407n8, 414n29, 425n28–29, 428n61, 455n5
2. 葛覃 "Ge tan": 310, 325–30, 333–34, 338, 342, 352, 363–64, 385, 459n45
3. 卷耳 "Juan er": 346–50, 364, 378
4. 樛木 "Jiu mu": 330, 399
6. 桃夭 "Tao yao": 181, 183–85, 281, 313, 353, 356–57, 385, 392, 402, 446
9. 漢廣 "Han guang": 89–90, 383, 386, 414n29, 458n42, 466n73
11. 麟之趾 "Lin zhi zhi": 174–75
12. 鵲巢 "Que chao": 379
13. 采蘩 "Cai fan": 331
14. 草蟲 "Cao chong": 370–71
15. 采蘋 "Cai pin": 331–32
17. 行露 "Xing lu": 342–45, 462n8
18. 羔羊 "Gao yang": 120–21
20. 摽有梅 "Biao you mei": 446
22. 江有汜 "Jiang you si": 393–94
23. 野有死麇 "Ye you si jun": 5–6, 100, 104, 167, 396–97, 409n11, 435n26
24. 何彼襛矣 "He bi nong yi": 445n67
26. 柏舟 "Bo zhou": 368, 382
27. 綠衣 "Lü yi": 299, 363, 387–88
28. 燕燕 "Yanyan": 43–44, 256
29. 日月 "Ri yue": 185, 308, 446n7630.
終風 "Zhong feng": 175–76
32. 凱風 "Kai feng": 371–73
33. 雄雉 "Xiong zhi": 245–47
34. 匏有苦葉 "Pao You ku ye": 235–37, 246, 451n23
35. 谷風 "Gu feng": 28–30, 33, 248–50
37. 旄丘 "Mao qiu": 170–71, 330
39. 泉水 "Quan shui": 150, 394
40. 北門 "Bei men": 374
41. 北風 "Bei feng": 374–75
44. 二子乘舟 "Er zi cheng zhou": 9, 368–69, 446n76
45. 柏舟 "Bo zhou": 368
46. 牆有茨 "Qiang you ci": 375
49. 鶉之奔奔 "Chun zhi ben ben": 423n14
50. 定之方中 "Ding zhi fang zhong": 454n31

52. 相鼠 "Xiang shu": 202–204
55. 淇奥 "Qi yu": 210, 444*n*36
59. 竹竿 "Zhu gan": 376
60. 芄蘭 "Wanlan": 242–44, 252–53, 392, 452*n*5
63. 有狐 "You hu": 177–79
68. 揚之水 "Yang zhi shui," 319–20
69. 中谷有蓷 "Zhong gu you tui": 376, 380
70. 兔爰 "Tu yuan": 376–77
71. 葛藟 "Ge lei": 328–29
72. 采葛 "Cai ge": 228–30, 326, 332–38, 373, 401
73. 大車 "Da ju": 261
75. 緇衣 "Zi yi": 388
80. 羔裘 "Gao qiu": 6, 432*n*7
82. 女曰雞鳴 "Nü yue ji ming": 309
84. 山有扶蘇 "Shan you fusu": 45–46, 244–45, 273–76, 282, 286, 292–95, 297, 391
85. 蘀兮 "Tuo xi": 276–78, 282
87. 褰裳 "Qian shang" ("Qian chang"): 7–8, 166, 412*n*22
90. 風雨 "Feng yu": 309–11
92. 揚之水 "Yang zhi shui": 320–21
94. 野有蔓草 "Ye you wan cao": 51–52, 58, 61, 224, 388–89, 451*n*13, 461*n*14
96. 雞鳴 "Ji ming": 309–311
99. 東方之日 "Dong fang zhi ri": 186–88, 191, 278–80
101. 南山 "Nan shan": 176–78, 195, 263, 387
102. 甫田 "Fu tian": 237–39
104. 敝笱 "Bi gou": 377, 400
105. 載驅 "Zai qu": 143
107. 葛屨 "Ge ju": 25–27
109. 園有桃 "Yuan you tao": 219–22, 251, 260, 287, 450*n*6, 450*n*8
113. 碩鼠 "Shi shu": ("Shuo shu") 201–202, 204, 206–207, 209
114. 蟋蟀 "Xishuai": ("Xi shuai") 6, 96, 98, 104, 179–80, 289–90, 294, 309, 351, 355–56, 365, 409*n*17
115. 山有樞 "Shan you ou": ("Shan you shu") 289–96, 307, 451*n*21, 455*n*5
116. 揚之水 "Yang zhi shui": 321–22
117. 椒聊 "Jiao liao": 377–78
118. 綢繆 "Chou mou": 222–24, 357
119. 杕杜 "Di du": 312–19
121. 鴇羽 "Bao yu": 378–79, 458*n*54
122. 無衣 "Wu yi": 359–60
123. 有杕之杜 "You di zhi du": 314–16
124. 葛生 "Ge sheng": 323–25, 327–29
125. 采苓 "Cai ling": 335–27, 338
126. 車鄰 "Ju lin": 293–95
131. 黃鳥 "Huang niao": 149, 196, 204–205, 237
133. 無衣 "Wu yi": 357–69, 463*n*28
137. 東門之枌 "Dong men zhi fen": 169–70, 353–54
138. 衡門 "Heng men": 399–400
139. 東門之池 "Dong men zhi chi": 389–90
140. 東門之楊 "Dong men zhi yang": 353–56
141. 墓門 "Mu men": 284–85
142. 防有鵲巢 "Fang you que chao": 390
143. 月出 "Yue chu": 390–91
145. 澤陂 "Ze pi": 391
148. 隰有萇楚 "Xi you chang chu": 391–92
149. 匪風 "Fei feng": 302–304, 458*n*19–20
150. 蜉蝣 "Fuyou": 379
152. 鳲鳩 "Shijiu": 99, 193–94
153. 下泉 "Xia quan": 380
154. 七月 "Qi yue": 59
155. 鴟鴞 "Chixiao": 116–17, 205–209, 449*n*131

157. 破斧 "Po Fu": 171–72, 229
158. 伐柯 "Fa ke": 172–73
159. 九罭 "Jiu yu": 216–19, 452n11
160. 狼跋 "Lang bo": 392–93
161. 鹿鳴 "Lu ming": 167–69
163. 皇皇者華 "Huang Huang zhe hua": 385–86
164. 常棣 "Changdi": 380–81
165. 伐木 "Fa mu": 30–32, 282–85, 288
169. 杕杜 "Di du": 316–19
170. 魚麗 "Yu li": 93–95, 99–100, 399
171. 南有嘉魚 "Nan you jia yu": 117, 165, 399–400
172. 南山有臺 "Nan shan you tai": 400
173. 蓼蕭 "Lu Xiao": 400–401
174. 湛露 "Zhan lu": 401
176. 菁菁者莪 "Jingjing zhe e": 224–26, 268, 280–81, 292, 402, 463n22
178. 采芑 "Cai qi": 337–38
181. 鴻雁 "Hong yan": 194
183. 沔水 "Mian shui": 210–14, 237, 394
184. 鶴鳴 "He ming": 103–104, 259, 285–88, 296, 381
187. 黃鳥 "Huang niao": 200, 204
188. 我行其野 "Wo xing qi ye": 33–34
189. 斯干 "Si Gan": 12, 394–95, 406n3
190. 無羊 "Wu yang": 1–4, 8, 71, 94, 98, 149, 193, 198, 366, 435n26, 443n7
191. 節南山 "Jie Nan shan": 194–95, 433n14
192. 正月 "Zheng yue": 69, 136, 255, 260–65, 286–87, 362, 373, 454n34
193. 十月之交 "Shi yue zhi jiao": 188–92
196. 小宛 "Xiao yuan": 196, 254–55, 462n21
197. 小弁 "Xiao pan": 9, 192–93, 367, 381–82
198. 巧言 "Qiao yan": 6
199. 何人斯 "He ren si": 303–305
200. 巷伯 "Xiang bo": 382, 433n14
201. 谷風 "Gu feng": 250–51, 418n23
202. 蓼莪 "Lu e": 304, 373–74, 452n11
203. 大東 "Da dong": 25, 255–60, 286
204. 四月 "Si yue": 304
209. 楚茨 "Chu ci": 433n14
211. 甫田 "Fu tian": 237–39
213. 瞻彼洛矣 "Zhan bi Luo yi": 395–96
214. 裳裳者華 "Shangshang zhe hua": 401–402, 447n92
215. 桑扈 "Sang hu": 195–96
216. 鴛鴦 "Yuanyang": 216–28, 260
217. 頍弁 "Kui bian": 251–53
218. 車舝 "Ju xia": 144–49, 396
219. 青蠅 "Qing ying": 196–97
222. 采菽 "Cai shu": 332, 351–53, 367, 462n22
223. 角弓 "Jue gong": 234–35
224. 菀柳 "Yu liu": 383
226. 采綠 "Cai lü": 348–51, 378
227. 黍苗 "Shu miao": 396–97
228. 隰桑 "Xi sang": 383–84
229. 白華 "Bai hua": 397
230. 綿蠻 "Mian man": 205
231. 瓠葉 "Hu ye": 176
233. 苕之華 "Tiao zhi hua": 197–99
238. 棫樸 "Yu pu": 384
252. 卷阿 "Quan e": 298–308
254. 板 "Ban": 176
255. 蕩 "Dang": 383
257. 桑柔 "Sang rou": 398
259. 崧高 "Song gao": 443n14
260. 烝民 "Zheng min": 443n14

278. 振鷺 "Zhen lu": 70, 73–75, 162
285. 武 "Wu": 6
297. 駉 "Jiong": 235n26
298. 有駜 "You bi": 164–68, 196
299. 泮水 "Pan shui": 338
300. 閟宮 "Bi gong": 454n31

Index II

allegoresis: 11, 61, 76–77, 158; "Guanju" and the *Song of Songs* and, 428*n*61

allegory: 12–13, 63, 65–69; allegory vs. spontaneous production of *shi*, 12; Quintilian and, 76–77; allegory *sine translatione*, 76–77

analogical xing, 221–22; instrumentality and, 216–19; focus on action and, 225–26, nature and rituals in, 219; vs. "simple" xing; ritualization of the poetic text, 291

analogy: "cosmological" poetics (Pauline Yu) and, 166

aprosdoketon ("the unexpected"): 255–60, 285–88, 452*n*11; misnaming and, 69; "Da dong" (ode 203) vs. "cosmological" poetics, 69

Aristotle: metaphor and, 356, 424*n*13; analogy, 450*n*3

author, "author function," and authorial intent: 80–81, 95–98, 103–105, 249–50, 407*n*8, 433*n*13 (Mencius); 435*n*26, 440*n*9; scribes and author function, 97. *See also* textual integrity

Baudelaire, Charles, 69

bi 比: 184; 450*n*156 (Michelle Yeh)

Brooke-Rose, Christine, 66, 268

Cao Pi, 51

carpe diem: topos of, 179, 251–52, 289–92, 294–95, 379

Chen Huan, 25, 90, 203, 450*n*13

Chen Shih-hsiang: 10–11, 37–41, 65, 68, 85, 123; shared origins of *shi* ("poetry") and xing, 11, 18, 37–38; analysis of the graph *xing*, 18, 37–38

catachresis, 87, 431*n*2

Chow Tse-tsung: definition of xing, 416*n*8, 420*n*5; definition of *shi*, 416*n*11

comparative literature: methodology of, 20–21. *See also* Jullien, François

conceptual metaphor theory (CMT): 109–11, 197–98; poetic metaphor and, 435*n*2; limitations of, 114–15, 435*n*2

Confucius: 119, 136, 196, 253, 415, 422*n*5; the *Odes* and, 7, 17, 51–52, 119. See also *zheng ming*

correlative cosmology: 72–74, 166; as blanket term for *lei*, yin and yang, five phases (*wu xing*), stimulus and correlative cosmology *(continued)* response *(gan ying)*, 74, 125; rituals and, 133. *See also lei*

deliberate metaphor theory (DMT), 115, 435*n*2
Dong Zhongshu, 423*n*21
Doubters of Antiquity *(yigu xuepai)* 疑古學派, 27

Eco, Umberto, 111
emotions, *see* Great Preface, *li*, *shi*, Xunzi
euphuia ("aptness, natural ability"); metaphor and, 68, 424*n*13. *See also homoion*

feng 風 ("air," "song"; first section of the *Odes*): 129–30; "changed airs," 130–32, 190
fu 賦 ("presentation" or "quotation" of odes), 5–8, 100, 149–50, 203, 269, 347, 407*n*8, 411*n*21, 433*n*14. *See also* Holzman, Donald
fuhui 附會 ("adding meaning [to an ode]," "far-fetched interpretation"), 172, 447*n*92; and Confucian exegesis, 88
Fenollosa, Ernest, 59
Fusek, Lois, 419*n*37

Gibbs, Raymond W.: 109–10; metatheory of the metaphor, 111–12; critique of DMT, 435*n*2
Gordon, Paul, 115
Granet, Marcel: 55–60; *Odes* as products of pre-Confucian society, 56–57; on Confucian commentators, 57; "natural" syntax of poetry, 59
Great Preface *(Maoshi daxu)*: theory of *shi* ("poetry") in, 123–41; on "changed airs and *ya*," 130–32, 141; *qing* ("raw emotion") and *min* ("populace") vs. *li* ("rituality") in, 133; narrative organization of, 126, 128, 140; *Yueji* and, 125; *Zhou li* and, 129. *See also* Xunzi
gu 故: as (pseudo-)conjunction, 127–28
Gu Jiegang, 46–49, 59, 65, 71–72, 84

Heidegger, Martin, 62–63: "the metaphorical" and metaphysics and, 63
hermeneutics: 19–20; divination and, 1–4; Mencius and, 433*n*13; Lupu Gui *(Zuozhuan)* and, 433*n*13; inherent limitations of, 19–20, 44, 271, 281
Holzman, Donald, 17–18, 166; xing as metaphorizing recitation of odes, 51–53
homoion ("likeness"): 68; ontological status of, 166, 424*n*12–13; 426*n*34; compared to *lei* ("similarity," "correlative category"), 68–69

incremental repetition, 41
Inoi Makoto 家井眞, 18
instrumentality, 116–19, 173. *See also* analogical xing
intratextuality, 116–17
intertextuality, 117
ironical xing, see *"xing"*
irony, 441*n*25. *See also* aprosdoketon

jue jian 譎諫 ("remonstrate craftily"): 130–32, 134, 147, 259
Jullien, François: 10, 61, 63, 79–84, 85; metatheory of figurality, 61, 64, 69; comparative methodology, 82–84; debate with Zhang Longxi, 429*n*7

Karlgren, Bernhard: on *Maozhuan* and *Zuozhuan*, 203; methodology, 314; translations of and glosses on *Odes*, 405*n*1 and *passim*
Kern, Martin, 96, 98–99, 102, 413*n*26, 432*n*6–7, 433*n*13
Kong Yingda, 131–32, 208, 216–17, 228, 252, 310, 321, 341, 413*n*28, 418*n*10, 438*n*4, 438*n*7, 440*n*13, 442*n*1, 442*n*9, 444*n*27, 445*n*65, 452*n*17, 456*n*35, 459*n*51, 460*n*87, 463*n*23, 464*n*14, 464*n*21, 465*n*22
Kongzi shilun, 9, 125, 414*n*29–30

Lakoff, George and Mark Johnson, 109–11, 197–98. *See also* conceptual metaphor theory, deliberate metaphor theory
Levi-Strauss, Claude, 422*n*3
lei 類 ("correlative category"): 344; *locus classicus* of (*Lüshi chunqiu*), 166, 462*n*8. See also *homoion*
li 禮 ("ritual, rituality, ritual principles"): 9, 11, 132–34, 148, 160–63, 187, 203, 218, 223–24, 230, 235–37, 253, 269–70, 302–302, 326, 329, 344–45, 347; work as metaphor for, 90–91, 171–74, 352, 364, 375–76; 359, 386; rituals as "falsification" of human nature, 91; vs. emotion (*qing*), 133; vs. spontaneity and raw emotions, 134; *shi* ("poetry") as, 140, 146–47; instrumentality and, 216–17, 249; the *Odes* as expressions of, 13, 35, 95, 124; plant-picking as expression for, 330–39
Liu, James, 80–81
Liu Xie, 17
Lu Ji 陸璣, 120, 413*n*28, 442*n*13, 443*n*11, 456*n*34, 465*n*30
Lüshi chunqiu (Master Lü's Annals), 17–18, 96–98, 69, 166, 173

Master Zhongliang 仲梁子, 9, 413*n*28
Mao Commentary (*Maozhuan*) 毛傳: origins of, 119–20; organization of, 406*n*2; relation to other "schools" of *Odes* exegesis, 8–9; relation to the *Great Preface* and *Minor Prefaces*, 119–21, 438*n*7; keywords in, 269; name of, 412*n*24; "Wuxingpian" and, 414*n*30; *Zuozhuan* and, 203, 348, 462*n*12; *Xunzi* and, 348
Mao Heng 毛亨, 1, 8, 17, 34, 52, 88, 119–20
Mao shi 毛詩 (Mao recension of the *Odes*): 9, 119
Mencius 孟子: 7, 413*n*28; hermeneutic methodology of, 433*n*13
Meng Zhongzi 孟仲子: 9, 413*n*28, 454*n*31
metapoetics: 433*n*14; "Crane Calls" and, 103–104; in the *Odes*, 433*n*14; *see also* primary metapoetics
metaphor: concretion vs. abstraction and, 69; vs. "evocative image"; embellishment and, 114; as ormamental and "highly conscious," 435*n*2; delayed understanding of, 64, 426*n*35; and parataxis; vs. simile (*eikôn*), 463*n*26; Aristotle and, 356, 463*n*26; exemplification of metaphor vs. xing in *Maozhuan*, 268 See also *homoion*
metonymy, 1, 3–34, 295, 322, 329, 332–33, 364, 396; and synecdoche, 18, 179–80, 295, 326, 343, 445, 461
mimesis: 1, 62, 87; and xing (Cecile Sun), 18, 85; and metaphor, 166
min ("populace, *vulgus*," "mankind"): 195, 206, 212, 219, 261–62, 270, 272, 384, 439; 436*n*28; connotations of, 218; as the xing's "vehicle," 226, 364; equal to

min (continued)
"nature," 226, 364; *guo ren* ("men of the state") and, 143–44, 149, 369; *junzi* ("Superior Man") and, 270; *bai xing* and, 463*n*28; meaning in the *Xunzi*, 135–40; meaning in the *Great Preface*, 132–41

Minor Prefaces (*Maoshi xiaoxu*): 9, 53, 119–21, 143–51, 168, 177, 190, 200, 210; 227–28, 252, 260–61, 310, 368, 384, 395–96, 412*n*24, 414*n*29, 438*n*7, 444*n*27, 445*n*67, 449*n*131, 450*n*8, 450*n*13, 455*n*22, extratextuality and 9, 53; the *Great Preface* and; the "Old Preface" and; the *Kongzi shilun* and, 414*n*29, 438*n*7

misnaming: 265; *gu*-goblet and, 253, 441*n*25. See also *si er fei*, *aprosdoketon*

Mote, Frederick: "cosmological gulf," 11

music, 40: tones and, 440*n*10

oral-formulaic poetry, *see* Wang, C. H.

parataxis, 66, 184, 214, 437*n*25
performance culture: in pre-Qin China, 95–98
piyu 譬喻 ("simile"), 18, 52, 132, 155, 168, 179, 182, 219, 242, 267, 341, 361, 462*n*19
primary vs. secondary meaning, 407*n*8. See also authorial intent
primary metapoetics, 102–105. See also authorial intent, metapoetics
pro ommatôn (putting "before the eyes"), 112
poiêsis: meaning of in early Greece, 416*n*11. See also *xing*
Pound, Ezra: 59; "In a Station of the Metro," 66, 75

Puett, Michael: on "early literary production in China," 409*n*17

"Qi ye" 耆夜 manuscript, 6, 96, 98, 104
Quintilian, 76–77, 112, 268

repetition: thematic development and, 99–102; intertextuality and, 288–96. See also incremental repetition
Richards, Ivor Armstrong, 109, 112–14. See also tenor and vehicle

Saussy, Haun, 87–91, 151, 161, 364
Shaughnessy, Edward: 71–72; *Zhouyi* and origins of xing, 426*n*38
shi 詩 ("poetry, odes"): *poiêsis* and, 20, 439*n*5; authorial intent and; emotions and spontaneity and, 12, 35, 38–40, 65–66, 86, 88, 124–26; as consciously created artifact, 69, 123–24, 134, 140–41; 143–50; 255–65; Mencius and, 412*n*22, 433*n*13, distinction between *Shi* ("canonized odes") and *shi* (odes or "poetry" generically), 407*n*8, 439*n*1. See also *Great Preface*, *Minor Prefaces*, oral-formulaic poetry, irony
si er fei 似而非 ("seems to be but is not"), 258, 264–65, 311, 350, 362, 373. See also *aprosdoketon*, misnaming
sign, the: 152–53; signans and signatum and, 152–53
Shijing 詩經 (The *Odes*, The *Book of Odes*): quotations of, 7–8; origins of 433*n*14 (Kern); early history of, 409*n*17; early editions of, 409*n*11, 413*n*28, 438*n*7; changed sequential order of, 438*n*7, 447*n*84; Mencius and, 412*n*22, 433*n*13
Shi pin 詩品, *see* Zhong Rong

Steen, Gerard, 109–10, 112, 115, 435*n*2
Su Zhe 蘇轍, 65
Sun, Cecile Chu-Chin, 10–11, 18, 37, 79, 85–86
Svenbro, Jesper, 20, 35, 416*n*11
Swedenborg, Emanuel: cosmological correspondences and, 69–70
Szondi, Peter, 460*n*75

tenor and vehicle: 109–16; as concepts alien to early Chinese tradition, 85, 184; disjunction between, 113–14. See also Richards, Ivor Armstrong
text: concept of the, 96–98
textual integrity: 93–98, 103–105; vs. "all is interpretation," 428*n*61. See also allegoresis

Virgil, 76–77

Wang, C. H.: 10–11, 16, 18, 23–35, 37, 57, 86, 93, 95, 99, 104, 117, 157, 162; 268; 296, 307, 409*n*17, 416*n*11, 464*n*5; definition of "xing," 34; definition of "theme," 28; relation between "theme" and "plot," 29–30; repetition of theme in different poems, 25–26; imagery in oral-formulaic poetry as "wild, excessive," 24, 28–29, 39, 57, 95, 99, 102, 256, 268
wei 偽 ("falsification, refining"): 11, 132, 432*n*13; and *xing* 性 ("human nature") 11, 91, 132; and Confucian exegesis, 90–91
wu xing 五行 ("five phases"), *see* correlative cosmology
"Wuxingpian" 五行篇: 414*n*30; "forthright" (*zhi*) discourse vs. *yu* [xing?], 414*n*30

xing 興: tentative definition of "xing" as used in *Maozhuan*, 9–10, 365–66; proposed original meaning of, 416*n*8; mimesis and, 18, 85; "simple" ("canonical") xing, 39, 162–66; analogical xing, 215–19; ironical xing, 242–44; causal xing, 327, 350–51, 341–60; as undetermined and in need of further elaborations, 209, 293, 297–98, 323, 338, 385; pragmatisism and, 13, 160, 168, 202, 209, 222, 226, 255, 267–69, 434*n*22; vs. conventional metaphors in the *Odes*, 268; *Zhouyi* and, 70–72, 426*n*38; meaning of in *Lunyu*, 415*n*1. See also analogical xing, aprosdoketon, *Zhouyi*, Chen Shih-hsiang, Chow Tse-tsung
Xunzi 荀子: 7, 9, 11, 90–91, 132, 134–40, 191, 232–33, 269–70, 272, 287–88, 344–45, 348, 350, 364, 381, 392, 443*n*14, 452*n*5; *wen* ("pattern, form, culture") vs. *qing* ("raw emotion") in rituals, 137–39; "rectification of names" and, 435*n*29; "Xunzian literary thought," 441*n*16; Xunzian "rationality," 449*n*155. See also *min*, *wei*

yan 言 ("bespeak, impart"), 191–92
Yili 儀禮, 25, 252
yin and yang 陰陽: as organizing principles of early Chinese society and thinking (Granet), 56–57; as "proto-science" 444*n*21, 449*n*155
Yu, Pauline: 10, 61–77, 85–88, 157–58, 166, 180–81, 191, 241, 246, 249, 269, 360–62; Western metaphor vs. Chinese "discovery" of analogies, 166; metaphor vs. theory of the metaphor, 423*n*2

Zhao Peilin, 18, 43–44

zheng ming 正名 ("rectification of names"): and xing, 453*n*29

Zheng Xuan 鄭玄: 5, 26–29, 35, 37, 89–90, 119, 132, 147–48, 216, 252, 375, 119, 408*n*9, 413*n*28, 428*n*53, 438*n*4, 438*n*7, 440*n*13, 450*n*13, 452*n*7; vs. the *Mao Commentary*, 463*n*28

Zhong Rong 鍾嶸: definition of "xing," 415*n*2

Zhouyi 周易: imagistic structure of and xing in the *Odes*, 70–72, 427*n*46; dating of, 427*n*48

Zhu Ziqing 朱自清: 52–53, 83; 168–69, 179–80, 182, 215, 219, 241, 247, 259, 341, 361, 354–65; definition of xing, 155–56

Zhu Xi: definition of xing, 421*n*6

Zikpi, Monica, 407*n*8, 435*n*26

zuo 作 ("make, fabricate"): 6–7, 96, 144, 149–50; performace of poetry and, 6. *See also* authorial intent

Zuozhuan 左傳 (Master Zuo's Commentary): 5–7, 100, 119, 203; the *Odes* as "storehouse of righteousness," 46, 269, 272, 277, 344–45, 347–50, 363, 369, 401, 406*n*3, 409*n*11–12, 411*n*21, 432*n*7, 433*n*13, 449*n*155; and *Zhouyi*, 71; and *Maozhuan* 203

www.ingramcontent.com/pod-product-compliance
Lightning Source LLC
Chambersburg PA
CBHW031701230426
43668CB00006B/62